The Editor

DEIDRE SHAUNA LYNCH is Chancellor Jackman Professor and Associate Professor of English at the University of Toronto. She is the author of *The Economy of Character*, which was awarded the MLA's Prize for a First Book, and editor of *Janeites: Austen's Disciples and Devotees* and, with William B. Warner, *Cultural Institutions of the Novel*. She is also an editor of *The Norton Anthology of English Literature*. She is the recipient of fellowships from the National Humanities Center and the John Simon Guggenheim Memorial Foundation, of the State University of New York Chancellor's Award for Excellence in Teaching, and of the Northeast Association of Graduate Schools' Graduate Faculty Teaching Award.

W. W. NORTON & COMPANY, INC.
Also Publishes

ENGLISH RENAISSANCE DRAMA: A NORTON ANTHOLOGY
edited by David Bevington et al.

THE NORTON ANTHOLOGY OF AFRICAN AMERICAN LITERATURE
edited by Henry Louis Gates Jr. and Nellie Y. McKay et al.

THE NORTON ANTHOLOGY OF AMERICAN LITERATURE
edited by Nina Baym et al.

THE NORTON ANTHOLOGY OF CHILDREN'S LITERATURE
edited by Jack Zipes et al.

THE NORTON ANTHOLOGY OF ENGLISH LITERATURE
edited by M. H. Abrams and Stephen Greenblatt et al.

THE NORTON ANTHOLOGY OF LITERATURE BY WOMEN
edited by Sandra M. Gilbert and Susan Gubar

THE NORTON ANTHOLOGY OF MODERN AND CONTEMPORARY POETRY
edited by Jahan Ramazani, Richard Ellmann, and Robert O'Clair

THE NORTON ANTHOLOGY OF POETRY
edited by Margaret Ferguson, Mary Jo Salter, and Jon Stallworthy

THE NORTON ANTHOLOGY OF SHORT FICTION
edited by R. V. Cassill and Richard Bausch

THE NORTON ANTHOLOGY OF THEORY AND CRITICISM
edited by Vincent B. Leitch et al.

THE NORTON ANTHOLOGY OF WORLD LITERATURE
edited by Sarah Lawall et al.

THE NORTON FACSIMILE OF THE FIRST FOLIO OF SHAKESPEARE
prepared by Charlton Hinman

THE NORTON INTRODUCTION TO LITERATURE
edited by Alison Booth, J. Paul Hunter, and Kelly J. Mays

THE NORTON INTRODUCTION TO THE SHORT NOVEL
edited by Jerome Beaty

THE NORTON READER
edited by Linda H. Peterson and John C. Brereton

THE NORTON SAMPLER
edited by Thomas Cooley

THE NORTON SHAKESPEARE, BASED ON THE OXFORD EDITION
edited by Stephen Greenblatt et al.

For a complete list of Norton Critical Editions, visit
wwnorton.com/college/English/nce_home.htm

A NORTON CRITICAL EDITION

Mary Wollstonecraft

A VINDICATION OF THE RIGHTS OF WOMAN

AN AUTHORITATIVE TEXT
BACKGROUNDS AND CONTEXTS
CRITICISM

THIRD EDITION

Edited by

DEIDRE SHAUNA LYNCH

UNIVERSITY OF TORONTO

W. W. NORTON & COMPANY

New York • London

W. W. Norton & Company has been independent since its founding in 1923, when William Warder Norton and Mary D. Herter Norton first published lectures delivered at the People's Institute, the adult education division of New York City's Cooper Union. The firm soon expanded its program beyond the Institute, publishing books by celebrated academics from America and abroad. By mid-century, the two major pillars of Norton's publishing program—trade books and college texts—were firmly established. In the 1950s, the Norton family transferred control of the company to its employees, and today—with a staff of four hundred and a comparable number of trade, college, and professional titles published each year—W. W. Norton & Company stands as the largest and oldest publishing house owned wholly by its employees.

Composition by TexTech, Inc.
Manufacturing by the Courier Companies—Westford division.
Book design by Antonina Krass.
Production manager: Eric Pier-Hocking.

Library of Congress Cataloging-in-Publication Data

Wollstonecraft, Mary, 1759–1797.
A vindication of the rights of woman : an authoritative text backgrounds and contexts criticism / Mary Wollstonecraft ; edited by Deidre Shauna Lynch. — 3rd ed.
    p.   cm. — (A Norton critical edition)
Includes bibliographical references.

ISBN 978-0-393-92974-4 (pbk.)

1. Women's rights—Great Britain.   2. Women—Education—Great Britain.
I. Lynch, Deidre.   II. Title.
HQ1596.W6 2009
305.420941—dc22   2008053411

W. W. Norton & Company, Inc., 500 Fifth Avenue,
New York, N.Y. 10110
www.wwnorton.com

W. W. Norton & Company Ltd., Castle House,
75/76 Wells Street, London W1T 3QT

2 3 4 5 6 7 8 9 0

Contents

Preface to the Third Edition   vii
Note on the Text   x

The Text of *A Vindication of the Rights of Woman, with Strictures on Political and Moral Subjects*   1

Backgrounds and Contexts   205

LEGACIES OF ENGLISH RADICALISM   207
John Milton • *From* Paradise Lost   208
John Locke • *From* Second Treatise of Civil Government   211
Mary Astell • *From* Reflections upon Marriage   214

EDUCATION   221
John Locke • *From* Some Thoughts Concerning
    Education   222
Mary Astell • *From* A Serious Proposal to the Ladies   225
Jean-Jacques Rousseau • *From* Emilius and Sophia;
    or, A New System of Education   229
John Gregory • *From* A Father's Legacy to His Daughters   236
Catharine Macaulay • *From* Letters on Education   239
Hannah More • *From* Strictures on the Modern
    System of Female Education   244

WOLLSTONECRAFT'S REVOLUTIONARY MOMENT   248
Richard Price • *From* A Discourse on the Love of
    Our Country   249
Edmund Burke • *From* Reflections on the Revolution
    in France   253
Mary Wollstonecraft • *From* A Vindication of the
    Rights of Men   258
Mary Wollstonecraft • *From* An Historical and
    Moral View of the Origin and Progress of the
    French Revolution   265

THE WOLLSTONECRAFT CONTROVERSY   271
   Anonymous • *From* Review of *A Vindication of the
     Rights of Woman*   272
   William Enfield • *From* Review of *A Vindication of the
     Rights of Woman*   275
   Anna Laetitia Barbauld • The Rights of Woman   277
   Thomas Taylor • *From* A Vindication of the Rights
     of Brutes   278
   Mary Hays • *From* Letters and Essays, Moral and
     Miscellaneous   281
   William Godwin • *From* Memoirs of the Author of
     A Vindication of the Rights of Woman   282
   Richard Polwhele • *From* The Unsex'd Females   288
   Mary Hays • *From* Memoirs of Mary Wollstonecraft   291
   Maria Edgeworth • *From* Belinda   294
   Benjamin Silliman • *From* The Letters of Shahcoolen   297
   William Thompson • *From* Appeal of One Half the
     Human Race, Women, against the Pretensions of
     the Other Half, Men   300

Criticism   307

   Elissa S. Guralnick • Radical Politics in Mary
     Wollstonecraft's *A Vindication of the Rights of Woman* 309
   Mitzi Myers • Reform or Ruin: "A Revolution in
     Female Manners"   319
   Cora Kaplan • *From* Wild Nights: Pleasure/Sexuality/
     Feminism   335
   Mary Poovey • [*A Vindication of the Rights of Woman*
     and Female Sexuality]   349
   Claudia L. Johnson • *From* The Distinction of the Sexes 363
   Barbara Taylor • The Religious Foundations of Mary
     Wollstonecraft's Feminism   375

   Mary Wollstonecraft • A Chronology   396
   Selected Bibliography   400

Preface to the Third Edition

In the wonderfully exuberant letter that she wrote to her sister Everina in November 1787, shortly after arriving in London to make her
fortune, Mary Wollstonecraft declared herself "the first of a new
genus": a female intellectual living by her pen. "You know I am not
born to tread in the beaten track—the peculiar bent of my nature
pushes me on." Even at the distance of more than two centuries,
there remains something breathtaking about the determination and
bravery of the plan for economic and mental independence that this
letter announces. When in 1975 she prepared the first Norton Critical Edition of Wollstonecraft's *Vindication of the Rights of Woman*,
Carol Poston also became the first of a new genus—a courageous
pioneer of a new kind of feminist editing. To survey the excellent
scholarship on Wollstonecraft and her age that has appeared over
the last three and a half decades is to notice time and again how
transformative and invigorating Poston's influence has been. After
1975 it became in new ways both possible and urgent to see Wollstonecraft as a participant in eighteenth-century culture's debates
and to give her feminism and our feminism a history.

The resulting discussions of Wollstonecraft's writings—and the
many undergraduate and graduate classes on (for instance) the literature of the 1790s, on women's writing, on revolution and romanticism, on the history and theory of feminism, and on the history and
theory of human rights, that have both tapped those scholarly discussions and energized them in turn—have also created a need that
this new critical edition of Wollstonecraft's most famous work aims
to fulfill. *The Rights of Woman* used to be assessed mainly as a work
on education, and the lineage of second-wave feminism was thus
traced to its call for women's educational equality. Nowadays we are
better equipped to trace Wollstonecraft's dialogues with and challenges to a whole crowd of Enlightenment thinkers: not just contemporary advocates of educational reform but also political
theorists meditating on authority and tyranny in the body politic,
sentimental novelists and moral philosophers pitting the virtues of
love against the dangers of the passions, theologians coming to grips
with the democracy of God's grace, the practitioners of conjectural

history—we would now call them anthropologists—who correlated the status of women with the advance of civilization. For better and for worse, our own historical context has obliged twenty-first-century readers of Wollstonecraft to be more sensitive to the conflicts *within* feminism and readier to recognize that there were in 1792, as now, competing programs for "a revolution in female manners."

The changes I have made for this third Norton Critical Edition of the *Rights of Woman* are intended to register those new discussions at the same time that they also aim to provide a text that will be useful and clear to a new generation of students. The annotations to the text have been expanded, in part to document more fully than previous editors have the truly tremendous range of Wollstonecraft's reading. The "Criticism" section has been updated, which means, to my regret, that some valuable essays from the 1970s have had to be excluded (they do continue to be pointed out in the updated bibliography).

The most substantial change involves the "Backgrounds" section that appeared in the two previous editions. Expanded significantly, it has become a section, in four parts, that is devoted to "Backgrounds and Contexts" and that is framed to give student readers a close-up view of the debates in which Wollstonecraft was enrolled and which she herself occasioned. The first of those parts offers a view of the legacies, and the unfinished business, that Wollstonecraft inherited from the seventeenth century and specifically from three writers— John Milton, John Locke, and Mary Astell—who made sense of that era's political crises. The second part gathers materials that should assist readers in situating Wollstonecraft's thoughts about women's right to mental improvement within a broad spectrum of plans for pedagogic reform and accounts of the capacities of the female mind. The third, dedicated to the Revolution Controversy that obsessed Britain in the last years of Wollstonecraft's life and giving pride of place to Wollstonecraft's own responses to the fall of the French monarchy, aims in its selection of materials to clarify the relation between her vision of a revolution in female manners and contemporary projects of political renovation. The fourth preserves many of the episodes in the reception history of the *Vindication of the Rights of Woman* that Carol Poston documented in her 1988 edition and also borrows her title, "The Wollstonecraft Controversy." However, this particular sampling of that reception history zeroes in on the fervent and highly conflicted responses of Wollstonecraft's contemporaries, presenting a more representative sampling of their interpretations of her writing and life.

Wollstonecraft's text has been edited several times since 1975, and it is a pleasure to acknowledge my debt, in many of this edition's annotations, to the editors who followed in Poston's footsteps: in particular Janet Todd, Ulrich Hardt, D. L. Macdonald, and Kathleen Scherf. Many friends and scholars of Wollstonecraft were generous with their counsel and learning while I prepared the annotations and, before that, while I pondered this edition's table of contents. To Donna Andrew, Lynn Festa, Susan Gubar, Sonia Hofkosh, Vivien Jones, Cora Kaplan, Mary Nyquist, Daniel O' Quinn, Adela Pinch, Cynthia Richards, Barbara Taylor, Orrin Wang, and Nicholas Williams, thank you all. Carol Bemis's encouragement and patience have been much appreciated. While working on this edition, I also benefited from the philanthropy of the John Simon Guggenheim Memorial Foundation, the research support of the University of Toronto, and the efficient research assistance given me by Laura Stenberg. As always, I was sustained by Tom Keirstead's affection, talents for domestic life, and willingness to revise domestic life's gendered scripts.

This edition is dedicated to Barbara Lynch, with love and gratitude for her feminist thoughts on the education of daughters.

Note on the Text

Despite the fact that most of the changes Wollstonecraft made for the second edition are probably not of great consequence, she deleted one long passage that is worth noting. In the letter to Talleyrand in the first edition, Wollstonecraft had addressed the French politician with a mixture of deference and apology. After "to induce you to," the passage originally read:

> read it with attention; and because I think that you will understand me, which I do not suppose many pert witlings will, who may ridicule the arguments they are unable to answer. But, Sir, I carry my respect for your understanding still farther; so far, that I am confident you will not throw my work aside, and hastily conclude that I am in the wrong, because you did not view the subject in the same light yourself.—And, pardon my frankness, but I must observe, that you treated it in too cursory a manner, continued to consider it as it had been considered formerly, when the rights of man, not to advert to woman, were trampled on as chimerical—I call upon you, therefore, now to

The first edition then ends the sentence in the same manner as the second: "weigh what I have advanced respecting the rights of woman, and national education." By the time of the second edition, perhaps buoyed by her success, Wollstonecraft was less deferential and, by revising the whole passage, was showing a firmer grip on her own prose style. Interested students will no doubt want to look at the first 1792 edition, which is now available in a modern reprint series.

The text that follows reproduces faithfully the second edition save for the following instances:

   p. 34: The sentence that begins "But if" (;) > (,) for sense.
   p. 37: "condered" > "considered"
   p. 52: "vicegerents" > "viceregents"
   p. 58: note 7: restore "to" in the last line of the Barbauld poem
   p. 60: "you sport" > "your sport"
   p. 87: "it it" > "it is"
   p. 88: provide close quote after "obedience"

p. 93: remove end quote after "error"
p. 108: add begin quote to "They are free"
p. 131: note 1: "conserved" > "conversed"
p. 139: "become" > "becomes"
p. 184: "participate the" > "participate in the"

Finally, nonsubstantive changes in styling have been made to bring the eighteenth-century text into conformity with modern printing practices.

The Text of
A VINDICATION OF THE RIGHTS OF WOMAN
with Strictures on Political
and Moral Subjects

Contents

[TO M. TALLEYRAND-PÉRIGORD   5]
[ADVERTISEMENT   9]
[INTRODUCTION   9]

CHAP. I
The rights and involved duties of mankind considered   14

CHAP. II
The prevailing opinion of a sexual character discussed   21

CHAP. III
The same subject continued   41

CHAP. IV
Observations on the state of degradation to which
woman is reduced by various causes   56

CHAP. V
Animadversions on some of the writers who have rendered
women objects of pity, bordering on contempt   83

CHAP. VI
The effect which an early association of ideas has
upon the character   122

CHAP. VII
Modesty.—Comprehensively considered, and not
as a sexual virtue   128

CHAP. VIII
Morality undermined by sexual notions of the
importance of a good reputation   139

CHAP. IX
Of the pernicious effects which arise from the
unnatural distinctions established in society   148

CHAP. X
    Parental affection   159

CHAP. XI
    Duty to parents   161

CHAP. XII
    On national education   166

CHAP. XIII
    Some instances of the folly which the ignorance of
        women generates; with concluding reflections on
        the moral improvement that a revolution in female
        manners might naturally be expected to produce   188

To
M. Talleyrand-Périgord,[1]

Late Bishop of Autun

SIR,

Having read with great pleasure a pamphlet which you have lately published,[2] I dedicate this volume to you; to induce you to reconsider the subject, and maturely weigh what I have advanced respecting the rights of woman and national education: and I call with the firm tone of humanity; for my arguments, Sir, are dictated by a disinterested spirit—I plead for my sex—not for myself. Independence I have long considered as the grand blessing of life, the basis of every virtue—and independence I will ever secure by contracting my wants, though I were to live on a barren heath.

It is then an affection for the whole human race that makes my pen dart rapidly along to support what I believe to be the cause of virtue: and the same motive leads me earnestly to wish to see woman placed in a station in which she would advance, instead of retarding, the progress of those glorious principles that give a substance to morality. My opinion, indeed, respecting the rights and duties of woman, seems to flow so naturally from these simple principles, that I think it scarcely possible, but that some of the enlarged minds who formed your admirable constitution, will coincide with me.[3]

In France there is undoubtedly a more general diffusion of knowledge than in any part of the European world, and I attribute it, in a great measure, to the social intercourse which has long subsisted between the sexes.[4] It is true, I utter my sentiments with freedom, that in France the very essence of sensuality has been extracted to

---

1. Charles Maurice de Talleyrand-Périgord (1754–1838), famous French diplomat who managed, by means of a brilliant mind and conniving personality, to make himself useful during some of the most tumultuous history in French politics.
2. Talleyrand's report on public education to the Constituent Assembly, *Rapport sur L'Instruction Publique, fait au nom du Comité de Constitution* (Paris, 1791). France's present system of compulsory free education owes a great deal to the model recommended over two hundred years ago by Talleyrand.
3. Parts of the French Constitution of 1791 had been ratified as early as 1789. It had been commissioned as a result of the Tennis Court Oath of June 20, 1789, when the National Assembly vowed not to dissolve until the country had a new constitution.
4. Whereas men and women in polite society in Britain tended to lead segregated social lives, with, for instance, women withdrawing after dinner and leaving their male companions together at the table, observers through the eighteenth century noted that the French ordered civil life differently. Wollstonecraft may refer here to France's celebrated salons, evening parties presided over by women where the sexes mingled in literary and political discussion and where ideas that became central to the Revolution received their first airing.

regale the voluptuary, and a kind of sentimental lust has prevailed, which, together with the system of duplicity that the whole tenour of their political and civil government taught, have given a sinister sort of sagacity to the French character, properly termed finesse; from which naturally flow a polish of manners that injures the substance, by hunting sincerity out of society.—And, modesty, the fairest garb of virtue! has been more grossly insulted in France than even in England, till their women have treated as *prudish* that attention to decency, which brutes instinctively observe.

Manners[5] and morals are so nearly allied that they have often been confounded; but, though the former should only be the natural reflection of the latter, yet, when various causes have produced factitious and corrupt manners, which are very early caught, morality becomes an empty name. The personal reserve, and sacred respect for cleanliness and delicacy in domestic life, which French women almost despise, are the graceful pillars of modesty; but, far from despising them, if the pure flame of patriotism have reached their bosoms, they should labour to improve the morals of their fellow-citizens, by teaching men, not only to respect modesty in women, but to acquire it themselves, as the only way to merit their esteem.

Contending for the rights of woman, my main argument is built on this simple principle, that if she be not prepared by education to become the companion of man, she will stop the progress of knowledge and virtue; for truth must be common to all, or it will be inefficacious with respect to its influence on general practice. And how can woman be expected to co-operate unless she know why she ought to be virtuous? unless freedom strengthen her reason till she comprehend her duty, and see in what manner it is connected with her real good? If children are to be educated to understand the true principle of patriotism, their mother must be a patriot; and the love of mankind, from which an orderly train of virtues spring, can only be produced by considering the moral and civil interest of mankind; but the education and situation of woman, at present, shuts her out from such investigations.

In this work I have produced many arguments, which to me were conclusive, to prove that the prevailing notion respecting a sexual[6] character was subversive of morality, and I have contended, that to render the human body and mind more perfect, chastity must more universally prevail, and that chastity will never be respected in the

5. Throughout Wollstonecraft uses *manners* not simply as a synonym for "etiquette" but, more comprehensively, to designate society's customs.
6. Here as elsewhere in the *Vindication*, the word *sexual* is equivalent to the modern term "gender-specific."

male world till the person of a woman is not, as it were, idolized,
when little virtue or sense embellish it with the grand traces of mental beauty, or the interesting simplicity of affection.

Consider, Sir, dispassionately, these observations—for a glimpse
of this truth seemed to open before you when you observed, 'that to
see one half of the human race excluded by the other from all participation of government, was a political phænomenon that, according
to abstract principles, it was impossible to explain.'[7] If so, on what
does your constitution rest?[8] If the abstract rights of man will bear
discussion and explanation, those of woman, by a parity of reasoning, will not shrink from the same test: though a different opinion
prevails in this country, built on the very arguments which you use
to justify the oppression of woman—prescription.[9]

Consider, I address you as a legislator, whether, when men contend for their freedom, and to be allowed to judge for themselves
respecting their own happiness, it be not inconsistent and unjust to
subjugate women, even though you firmly believe that you are acting
in the manner best calculated to promote their happiness? Who
made man the exclusive judge, if woman partake with him the gift
of reason?

In this style, argue tyrants of every denomination, from the weak
king to the weak father of a family; they are all eager to crush reason;
yet always assert that they usurp its throne only to be useful. Do you
not act a similar part, when you *force* all women, by denying them
civil and political rights, to remain immured in their families groping
in the dark? for surely, Sir, you will not assert, that a duty can be
binding which is not founded on reason? If indeed this be their destination, arguments may be drawn from reason: and thus augustly
supported, the more understanding women acquire, the more they
will be attached to their duty—comprehending it—for unless they
comprehend it, unless their morals be fixed on the same immutable
principle as those of man, no authority can make them discharge it
in a virtuous manner. They may be convenient slaves, but slavery
will have its constant effect, degrading the master and the abject
dependent.

---

7. Possibly a liberal translation from Talleyrand's *Rapport, op. cit.*, p. 9: "*sur quel principe l'un des deux pourroit-il en être déshérité par la Societé protectrice des droits de tous?*"
8. In France's Constitution of 1791 only males over twenty-five were citizens. Women were not to get the vote until 1944.
9. Samuel Johnson's *Dictionary of the English Language* of 1755 (the later eighteenth cen-
tury's authoritative guide to usage) defines *prescription* as "rules produced and authorised
by long custom: custom continued till it has the force of law." In her first *Vindication*
Wollstonecraft noted how the doctrine of prescription motivated Edmund Burke's antagonism toward the dismantling of inherited privileges in revolutionary France and, accordingly, identified his *Reflections on the Revolution* as championing the rich, who invoke
"prescription," she asserted, as "an immortal boundary against innovation" (*A Vindication
of the Rights of Men* [London, 1790], p. 11; see p. 258 herein).

But, if women are to be excluded, without having a voice, from a participation of the natural rights of mankind, prove first, to ward off the charge of injustice and inconsistency, that they want reason— else this flaw in your NEW CONSTITUTION will ever shew that man must, in some shape, act like a tyrant, and tyranny, in whatever part of society it rears its brazen front, will ever undermine morality.

I have repeatedly asserted, and produced what appeared to me irrefragable arguments drawn from matters of fact, to prove my assertion, that women cannot, by force, be confined to domestic concerns; for they will, however ignorant, intermeddle with more weighty affairs, neglecting private duties only to disturb, by cunning tricks, the orderly plans of reason which rise above their comprehension.

Besides, whilst they are only made to acquire personal accomplishments, men will seek for pleasure in variety, and faithless husbands will make faithless wives; such ignorant beings, indeed, will be very excusable when, not taught to respect public good, nor allowed any civil rights, they attempt to do themselves justice by retaliation.

The box of mischief thus opened in society,[1] what is to preserve private virtue, the only security of public freedom and universal happiness?

Let there be then no coercion *established* in society, and the common law of gravity prevailing, the sexes will fall into their proper places. And, now that more equitable laws are forming your citizens, marriage may become more sacred: your young men may choose wives from motives of affection, and your maidens allow love to root out vanity.

The father of a family will not then weaken his constitution and debase his sentiments, by visiting the harlot, nor forget, in obeying the call of appetite, the purpose for which it was implanted. And, the mother will not neglect her children to practise the arts of coquetry, when sense and modesty secure her the friendship of her husband.

But, till men become attentive to the duty of a father, it is vain to expect women to spend that time in their nursery which they, 'wise in their generation,'[2] choose to spend at their glass; for this exertion of cunning is only an instinct of nature to enable them to obtain indirectly a little of that power of which they are unjustly denied a share: for if women are not permitted to enjoy legitimate rights, they will render both men and themselves vicious, to obtain illicit privileges.

1. Refers to the story of Pandora, who in Greek mythology was the first woman, and to her opening of the box that Zeus, king of the gods, had sent down to earth with her. That action released evil into the world.
2. Luke 16:8: "For the children of this world are in their generation wiser than the children of light."

I wish, Sir, to set some investigations of this kind afloat in France; and should they lead to a confirmation of my principles, when your constitution is revised the Rights of Woman may be respected, if it be fully proved that reason calls for this respect, and loudly demands JUSTICE for one half of the human race.

I am, SIR,
Your's respectfully,
M. W.

Advertisement

When I began to write this work, I divided it into three parts, supposing that one volume would contain a full discussion of the arguments which seemed to me to rise naturally from a few simple principles; but fresh illustrations occurring as I advanced, I now present only the first part to the public.

Many subjects, however, which I have cursorily alluded to, call for particular investigation, especially the laws relative to women, and the consideration of their peculiar duties. These will furnish ample matter for a second volume, which in due time will be published, to elucidate some of the sentiments, and complete many of the sketches begun in the first.[3]

Introduction

After considering the historic page, and viewing the living world with anxious solicitude, the most melancholy emotions of sorrowful indignation have depressed my spirits, and I have sighed when obliged to confess, that either nature has made a great difference between man and man, or that the civilization which has hitherto taken place in the world has been very partial. I have turned over various books written on the subject of education, and patiently observed the conduct of parents and the management of schools; but what has been the result?—a profound conviction that the neglected education of my fellow-creatures is the grand source of the misery I deplore; and that women, in particular, are rendered weak and wretched by a variety of concurring causes, originating from one hasty conclusion. The conduct and manners of women, in

---

3. Only one volume was ever published, and so far as is known from Wollstonecraft's papers, she never began the other volume.

, evidently prove that their minds are not in a healthy state; for, like the flowers which are planted in too rich a soil, strength and usefulness are sacrificed to beauty; and the flaunting leaves, after having pleased a fastidious eye, fade, disregarded on the stalk, long before the season when they ought to have arrived at maturity.— One cause of this barren blooming[4] I attribute to a false system of education, gathered from the books written on this subject by men who, considering females rather as women than human creatures, have been more anxious to make them alluring mistresses than affectionate wives and rational mothers; and the understanding of the sex has been so bubbled[5] by this specious homage, that the civilized women of the present century, with a few exceptions, are only anxious to inspire love, when they ought to cherish a nobler ambition, and by their abilities and virtues exact respect.

In a treatise, therefore, on female rights and manners, the works which have been particularly written for their improvement must not be overlooked; especially when it is asserted, in direct terms, that the minds of women are enfeebled by false refinement; that the books of instruction, written by men of genius, have had the same tendency as more frivolous productions; and that, in the true style of Mahometanism, they are treated as a kind of subordinate beings,[6] and not as a part of the human species, when improveable reason is allowed to be the dignified distinction which raises men above the brute creation, and puts a natural sceptre in a feeble hand.

Yet, because I am a woman, I would not lead my readers to suppose that I mean violently to agitate the contested question respecting the equality or inferiority of the sex; but as the subject lies in my way, and I cannot pass it over without subjecting the main tendency of my reasoning to misconstruction, I shall stop a moment to deliver, in a few words, my opinion.—In the government of the physical world it is observable that the female in point of strength is, in general, inferior to the male. This is the law of nature; and it does not appear to be suspended or abrogated in favour of woman. A degree of physical superiority cannot, therefore, be denied—and it is a noble prerogative![7] But not content with this natural pre-eminence,

---

4. Wollstonecraft compares women to "luxuriants," botanical science's technical term for those plants that late-eighteenth-century gardeners, drawing on the latest techniques, cultivated for their showy blooms and at the expense of their seeds.
5. Deluded, cheated (archaic).
6. It was a common but mistaken opinion among Europeans that in the Koran, the sacred text of Islam, the Prophet Mohammed taught that women have no souls and would not be permitted an afterlife.
7. The first edition reads ". . . the female, in general, is inferior to the male. The male pursues, the female yields—this is the law of nature; and it does not appear to be suspended or abrogated in favour of woman. This physical superiority cannot be denied—and it is a noble prerogative!"

men endeavour to sink us still lower, merely to render us alluring objects for a moment, and women, intoxicated by the adoration which men, under the influence of their senses, pay them, do not seek to obtain a durable interest in their hearts, or to become the friends of the fellow creatures who find amusement in their society.

I am aware of an obvious inference:—from every quarter have I heard exclamations against masculine women; but where are they to be found? If by this appellation men mean to inveigh against their ardour in hunting, shooting, and gaming, I shall most cordially join in the cry; but if it be against the imitation of manly virtues, or, more properly speaking, the attainment of those talents and virtues, the exercise of which ennobles the human character, and which raise females in the scale of animal being, when they are comprehensively termed mankind;—all those who view them with a philosophic eye must, I should think, wish with me, that they may every day grow more and more masculine.

This discussion naturally divides the subject. I shall first consider women in the grand light of human creatures, who, in common with men, are placed on this earth to unfold their faculties; and afterwards I shall more particularly point out their peculiar designation.

I wish also to steer clear of an error which many respectable writers have fallen into; for the instruction which has hitherto been addressed to women, has rather been applicable to *ladies*, if the little indirect advice, that is scattered through Sandford and Merton,[8] be excepted; but, addressing my sex in a firmer tone, I pay particular attention to those in the middle class, because they appear to be in the most natural state.[9] Perhaps the seeds of false-refinement, immorality, and vanity, have ever been shed by the great. Weak, artificial beings, raised above the common wants and affections of their race, in a premature unnatural manner, undermine the very foundation of virtue, and spread corruption through the whole mass of society. As a class of mankind they have the strongest claim to pity; the education of the rich tends to render them vain and helpless, and the unfolding mind is not strengthened by the practice of those duties which dignify the human character.—They only live to amuse themselves, and by the same law which in nature invariably produces certain effects, they soon only afford barren amusement.

---

8. *Sandford and Merton*, a children's book by Thomas Day (London, published in three volumes, 1786–89), is the story of Tommy Merton, a spoiled wealthy child, who is befriended by Harry Sandford, a poor but principled lad. Their instruction by the tutor Mr. Barlow often includes moral tales, one of which is mentioned approvingly by Wollstonecraft in Chapter III.

9. Wollstonecraft considers the middle classes to be more "natural" and also more educable than the aristocracy—"the great"—because they are as yet uncorrupted by the artificiality of leisure-class life.

But as I purpose taking a separate view of the different ranks of society, and of the moral character of women, in each, this hint is, for the present, sufficient; and I have only alluded to the subject, because it appears to me to be the very essence of an introduction to give a cursory account of the contents of the work it introduces.

My own sex, I hope, will excuse me, if I treat them like rational creatures, instead of flattering their *fascinating* graces, and viewing them as if they were in a state of perpetual childhood, unable to stand alone. I earnestly wish to point out in what true dignity and human happiness consists—I wish to persuade women to endeavour to acquire strength, both of mind and body, and to convince them that the soft phrases, susceptibility of heart, delicacy of sentiment, and refinement of taste, are almost synonymous with epithets of weakness, and that those beings who are only the objects of pity and that kind of love, which has been termed its sister, will soon become objects of contempt.

Dismissing then those pretty feminine phrases, which the men condescendingly use to soften our slavish dependence, and despising that weak elegancy of mind, exquisite sensibility, and sweet docility of manners, supposed to be the sexual characteristics of the weaker vessel, I wish to shew that elegance is inferior to virtue, that the first object of laudable ambition is to obtain a character as a human being, regardless of the distinction of sex; and that secondary views should be brought to this simple touchstone.

This is a rough sketch of my plan; and should I express my conviction with the energetic emotions that I feel whenever I think of the subject, the dictates of experience and reflection will be felt by some of my readers. Animated by this important object, I shall disdain to cull my phrases or polish my style;—I aim at being useful, and sincerity will render me unaffected; for, wishing rather to persuade by the force of my arguments, than dazzle by the elegance of my language, I shall not waste my time in rounding periods,[1] or in fabricating the turgid bombast of artificial feelings, which, coming from the head, never reach the heart.—I shall be employed about things, not words!—and, anxious to render my sex more respectable members of society, I shall try to avoid that flowery diction which has slided from essays into novels, and from novels into familiar letters and conversation.

These pretty superlatives, dropping glibly from the tongue, vitiate the taste, and create a kind of sickly delicacy that turns away from simple unadorned truth; and a deluge of false sentiments and over-stretched feelings, stifling the natural emotions of the heart, render

---

1. Formulating balanced sentences.

the domestic pleasures insipid, that ought to sweeten the exercise of those severe duties, which educate a rational and immortal being for a nobler field of action.

The education of women has, of late, been more attended to than formerly; yet they are still reckoned a frivolous sex, and ridiculed or pitied by the writers who endeavour by satire or instruction to improve them. It is acknowledged that they spend many of the first years of their lives in acquiring a smattering of accomplishments;[2] meanwhile strength of body and mind are sacrificed to libertine notions of beauty, to the desire of establishing themselves,—the only way women can rise in the world,—by marriage. And this desire making mere animals of them, when they marry they act as such children may be expected to act:—they dress; they paint, and nick-name God's creatures.[3]—Surely these weak beings are only fit for a seraglio![4]—Can they be expected to govern a family with judgment, or take care of the poor babes whom they bring into the world?

If then it can be fairly deduced from the present conduct of the sex, from the prevalent fondness for pleasure which takes place of ambition and those nobler passions that open and enlarge the soul; that the instruction which women have hitherto received has only tended, with the constitution of civil society, to render them insignificant objects of desire—mere propagators of fools!—if it can be proved that in aiming to accomplish them, without cultivating their understandings, they are taken out of their sphere of duties, and made ridiculous and useless when the short-lived bloom of beauty is over,[5] I presume that *rational* men will excuse me for endeavouring to persuade them to become more masculine and respectable.

Indeed the word masculine is only a bugbear; there is little reason to fear that women will acquire too much courage or fortitude; for their apparent inferiority with respect to bodily strength, must render them, in some degree, dependent on men in the various relations of life; but why should it be increased by prejudices that give a sex to virtue, and confound simple truths with sensual reveries?

---

2. I.e., the lessons in music, dancing, art, and needlework that were central elements in the education provided for genteel young women and that were supposed to enhance their value on the marriage market.
3. Shakespeare's Hamlet, charging Ophelia with the faults characteristic of women, says, "you jig, you amble, and you lisp and nickname God's creatures" (*Hamlet* III.i.143–44). Cf. Wollstonecraft's recollection of this phrase in her *Vindication of the Rights of Men*, p. 262 herein.
4. Harem, the women's quarters in a Muslim household.
5. "A lively writer, I cannot recollect his name, asks what business women turned of forty have to do in the world?" [Wollstonecraft's note]. Perhaps Wollstonecraft is referring to a passage in Frances Burney's popular novel *Evelina* spoken by the licentious Lord Merton: "I don't know what the devil a woman lives for after thirty: she is only in other folks' way" (*Evelina* [London and New York, 1958], p. 253).

Women are, in fact, so much degraded by mistaken notions of female excellence, that I do not mean to add a paradox when I assert, that this artificial weakness produces a propensity to tyrannize, and gives birth to cunning, the natural opponent of strength, which leads them to play off those contemptible infantine airs that undermine esteem even whilst they excite desire. Let men become more chaste and modest, and if women do not grow wiser in the same ratio, it will be clear that they have weaker understandings. It seems scarcely necessary to say, that I now speak of the sex in general. Many individuals have more sense than their male relatives; and, as nothing preponderates where there is a constant struggle for an equilibrium, without it has[6] naturally more gravity, some women govern their husbands without degrading themselves, because intellect will always govern.

Chap. I

The Rights and Involved Duties of Mankind Considered

In the present state of society it appears necessary to go back to first principles in search of the most simple truths, and to dispute with some prevailing prejudice every inch of ground. To clear my way, I must be allowed to ask some plain questions, and the answers will probably appear as unequivocal as the axioms on which reasoning is built; though, when entangled with various motives of action, they are formally contradicted, either by the words or conduct of men.

In what does man's pre-eminence over the brute creation consist? The answer is as clear as that a half is less than the whole; in Reason.

What acquirement exalts one being above another? Virtue, we spontaneously reply.

For what purpose were the passions implanted? That man by struggling with them might attain a degree of knowledge denied to the brutes; whispers Experience.

Consequently the perfection of our nature and capability of happiness, must be estimated by the degree of reason, virtue, and knowledge, that distinguish the individual, and direct the laws which bind society: and that from the exercise of reason, knowledge and virtue naturally flow, is equally undeniable, if mankind be viewed collectively.

The rights and duties of man thus simplified, it seems almost impertinent to attempt to illustrate truths that appear so incontrovertible; yet such deeply rooted prejudices have clouded reason, and such spurious qualities have assumed the name of virtues, that it is necessary to pursue the course of reason as it has been perplexed and involved in

6. We would probably say, "without its having."

error, by various adventitious circumstances, comparing the simple axiom with casual deviations.

Men, in general, seem to employ their reason to justify prejudices, which they have imbibed, they can scarcely trace how, rather than to root them out. The mind must be strong that resolutely forms its own principles; for a kind of intellectual cowardice prevails which makes many men shrink from the task, or only do it by halves. Yet the imperfect conclusions thus drawn, are frequently very plausible, because they are built on partial experience, on just, though narrow, views.

Going back to first principles, vice skulks, with all its native deformity, from close investigation; but a set of shallow reasoners are always exclaiming that these arguments[7] prove too much, and that a measure rotten at the core may be expedient. Thus expediency is continually contrasted with simple principles, till truth is lost in a mist of words, virtue, in forms, and knowledge rendered a sounding nothing, by the specious prejudices that assume its name.

That the society is formed in the wisest manner, whose constitution is founded on the nature of man, strikes, in the abstract, every thinking being so forcibly, that it looks like presumption to endeavour to bring forward proofs; though proof must be brought, or the strong hold of prescription will never be forced by reason; yet to urge prescription as an argument to justify the depriving men (or women) of their natural rights, is one of the absurd sophisms which daily insult common sense.

The civilization of the bulk of the people of Europe is very partial; nay, it may be made a question, whether they have acquired any virtues in exchange for innocence, equivalent to the misery produced by the vices that have been plastered over unsightly ignorance, and the freedom which has been bartered for splendid slavery. The desire of dazzling by riches, the most certain pre-eminence that man can obtain, the pleasure of commanding flattering sycophants, and many other complicated low calculations of doting self-love, have all contributed to overwhelm the mass of mankind, and make liberty a convenient handle for mock patriotism. For whilst rank and titles are held of the utmost importance, before which Genius "must hide its diminished head,"[8] it is, with a few exceptions, very unfortunate for a nation when a man of abilities, without rank or property, pushes himself forward to notice.—Alas! what unheard of misery have thousands suffered to purchase a cardinal's hat for an intriguing obscure adventurer, who longed to be ranked with princes, or lord it over them by seizing the triple crown![9]

7. Those based on principled reason.
8. Milton, *Paradise Lost* IV. 34–35: "At whose sight all the stars / Hide their diminish'd heads."
9. Perhaps a reference to Cardinal Dubois (1656–1723), chief adviser to Louis XV. "Triple crown": the traditional tiara worn by popes, suggesting Dubois's papal ambitions. See p. 18, n. 3.

Such, indeed, has been the wretchedness that has flowed from hereditary honours, riches, and monarchy, that men of lively sensibility have almost uttered blasphemy in order to justify the dispensations of providence. Man has been held out as independent of his power who made him, or as a lawless planet darting from its orbit to steal the celestial fire of reason; and the vengeance of heaven, lurking in the subtile flame, like Pandora's pent up mischiefs,[1] sufficiently punished his temerity, by introducing evil into the world.

Impressed by this view of the misery and disorder which pervaded society, and fatigued with jostling against artificial fools, Rousseau became enamoured of solitude, and, being at the same time an optimist, he labours with uncommon eloquence to prove that man was naturally a solitary animal.[2] Misled by his respect for the goodness of God, who certainly—for what man of sense and feeling can doubt it!—gave life only to communicate happiness, he considers evil as positive,[3] and the work of man; not aware that he was exalting one attribute at the expence of another, equally necessary to divine perfection.[4]

Reared on a false hypothesis his arguments in favour of a state of nature are plausible, but unsound. I say unsound; for to assert that a state of nature is preferable to civilization, in all its possible perfection, is, in other words, to arraign supreme wisdom; and the paradoxical exclamation, that God has made all things right, and that error has been introduced by the creature, whom he formed, knowing what he formed, is as unphilosophical as impious.[5]

When that wise Being who created us and placed us here, saw the fair idea, he willed, by allowing it to be so, that the passions should unfold our reason, because he could see that present evil would produce future good. Could the helpless creature whom he called from nothing break loose from his providence, and boldly learn to know good by practising evil, without his permission? No.—How could that energetic advocate for immortality[6] argue so inconsistently? Had mankind remained for ever in the brutal state of nature,

1. In Greek myth Prometheus stole fire to give to man, even though Zeus had forbidden it. Zeus' revenge was to give man Pandora (see p. 8, n. 1).
2. In his 1755 *Discourse on the Origin and Foundations of Inequality among Men*, the French philosopher Jean-Jacques Rousseau (1712–1778) theorized that humans had, when in the state of nature, been solitary beings and that their increasing need for social connection had led, over time, to their increasing wickedness.
3. In this context, the opposite of *natural* or *inherent*. Johnson defines positive as "settled by arbitrary appointment" (*Dictionary*).
4. For Rousseau God is consummate goodness, so evil has to be man-made, a product of human society.
5. *Émile*, the mix of educational treatise and novel Rousseau published in 1762, begins, "All things are good as their Creator made them, but every thing degenerates in the hands of man" (translated as *Emilius and Sophia: Or. A New System of Education* [London, 1762–63], I, i, p. i; all references are to this edition).
6. I. e., Rousseau. His religious beliefs are found in "The Creed of a Savoyard Priest," *Émile* iv.

which even his magic pen cannot paint as a state in which a single virtue took root, it would have been clear, though not to the sensitive unreflecting wanderer, that man was born to run the circle of life and death, and adorn God's garden for some purpose which could not easily be reconciled with his attributes.

But if, to crown the whole, there were to be rational creatures produced, allowed to rise in excellence by the exercise of powers implanted for that purpose; if benignity itself thought fit to call into existence a creature above the brutes,[7] who could think and improve himself, why should that inestimable gift, for a gift it was, if man was so created as to have a capacity to rise above the state in which sensation produced brutal ease, be called, in direct terms, a curse? A curse it might be reckoned, if the whole of our existence were bounded by our continuance in this world; for why should the gracious fountain of life give us passions, and the power of reflecting, only to imbitter our days and inspire us with mistaken notions of dignity? Why should he lead us from love of ourselves to the sublime emotions which the discovery of his wisdom and goodness excites, if these feelings were not set in motion to improve our nature, of which they make a part,[8] and render us capable of enjoying a more godlike portion of happiness? Firmly persuaded that no evil exists in the world that God did not design to take place, I build my belief on the perfection of God.

Rousseau exerts himself to prove that all *was* right originally: a crowd of authors that all *is* now right: and I, that all will be right.

But, true to his first position, next to a state of nature, Rousseau celebrates barbarism, and apostrophizing the shade of Fabricius,[9] he

---

7. "Contrary to the opinion of anatomists, who argue by analogy from the formation of the teeth, stomach, and intestines, Rousseau will not allow a man to be a carnivorous animal. And, carried away from nature by a love of system, he disputes whether man be a gregarious animal, though the long and helpless state of infancy seems to point him out as particularly impelled to pair, the first step towards herding" [Wollstonecraft's note]. *Emilius* I, i, p. 53 and I, ii, p. 285.

8. "What would you say to a mechanic whom you had desired to make a watch to point out the hour of the day, if, to show his ingenuity, he added wheels to make it a repeater, &c. that perplexed the simple mechanism; should he urge, to excuse himself—had you not touched a certain spring, you would have known nothing of the matter, and that he should have amused himself by making *an experiment* without doing you any harm: would you not retort fairly upon him, by insisting that if he had not added those needless wheels and springs, the accident could not have happened?" [Wollstonecraft's note]. It would be unthinkable that God would give human beings the ability to reason to his power and beauty if they were, at the end, to be mortal. God's perfect plan includes humankind's discovery and use of reason to reach for—though never attain—godlike happiness.

9. In the essay now known as *Discourse on the Sciences and the Arts* (1750), in which he argues that the progress of knowledge has contributed nothing to human happiness, Rousseau imagines how, brought back from the dead, the statesman and military commander Gaius Fabricius (third century B.C.E.) might have reacted to Rome's transformation since his lifetime: "what destructive splendor is this that has succeeded our *Roman* simplicity? . . . You that were masters of the world have reduced yourselves to become slaves to those idle and frivolous people whom you conquered" (from the first English translation, *The Discourse Which Carried the Praemium at the Academy of Dijon* [London, 1751], p. 28).

forgets that, in conquering the world, the Romans never dreamed of establishing their own liberty on a firm basis, or of extending the reign of virtue. Eager to support his system, he stigmatizes, as vicious, every effort of genius; and, uttering the apotheosis of savage virtues, he exalts those to demi-gods, who were scarcely human— the brutal Spartans, who, in defiance of justice and gratitude, sacrificed, in cold blood, the slaves who had shewn themselves heroes to rescue their oppressors.[1]

Disgusted with artificial manners and virtues, the citizen of Geneva,[2] instead of properly sifting the subject, threw away the wheat with the chaff, without waiting to inquire whether the evils which his ardent soul turned from indignantly, were the consequence of civilization or the vestiges of barbarism. He saw vice tramping on virtue, and the semblance of goodness taking place of the reality; he saw talents bent by power to sinister purposes, and never thought of tracing the gigantic mischief up to arbitrary power, up to the hereditary distinctions that clash with the mental superiority that naturally raises a man above his fellows. He did not perceive that regal power, in a few generations, introduces idiotism into the noble stem, and holds out baits to render thousands idle and vicious.

Nothing can set the regal character in a more contemptible point of view, than the various crimes that have elevated men to the supreme dignity.—Vile intrigues, unnatural crimes, and every vice that degrades our nature, have been the steps to this distinguished eminence; yet millions of men have supinely allowed the nerveless limbs of the posterity of such rapacious prowlers to rest quietly on their ensanguined thrones.[3]

What but a pestilential vapour can hover over society when its chief director is only instructed in the invention of crimes, or the

---

1. While Rousseau lauds Sparta for banishing the arts and so preserving its simplicity, Wollstonecraft counters this praise by referring to an incident from Sparta's history: having promised freedom to those of their slaves who distinguished themselves battling the forces of Athens, the Spartans killed them all after the battle, on the grounds that they were precisely the slaves most likely to rebel (Thucydides, *History of the Peloponnesian War*, IV, lxxx, pp. 3–4).
2. I.e., Rousseau. He was born in Geneva (Switzerland) but left at age sixteen. He often identified himself as "citizen of Geneva" on the title pages of his books, calling attention to his origin in an independent republic.
3. "Could there be a greater insult offered to the rights of man than the beds of justice in France, when an infant was made the organ of the detestable Dubois!" [Wollstonecraft's note]. "Beds of justice": The *lits de justice*, the solemn meeting of king and Parliament in France to determine common policy. Wollstonecraft is likely referring to how Philippe, Duc d'Orléans, during the infancy of Louis XV, ruled over France with the assistance of Cardinal Dubois, the Duke's former tutor (see p. 15, n. 9). Wollstonecraft had reviewed *Vie Privée du Cardinal Dubois* in August 1789, and had said of the cardinal's influence on the future regent: "so little alive was he to the restriction of conscience, so dead to the voice of honour, that he indulged the Duke in his favourite vice, an unbridled passion for women" (*Works*, ed. Janet Todd and Marilyn Butler, VII, p. 138; all references are to this edition).

stupid routine of childish ceremonies? Will men never be wise?—will they never cease to expect corn from tares, and figs from thistles?[4]

It is impossible for any man, when the most favourable circumstances concur, to acquire sufficient knowledge and strength of mind to discharge the duties of a king, entrusted with uncontrouled power; how then must they be violated when his very elevation is an insuperable bar to the attainment of either wisdom or virtue; when all the feelings of a man are stifled by flattery, and reflection shut out by pleasure! Surely it is madness to make the fate of thousands depend on the caprice of a weak fellow creature, whose very station sinks him *necessarily* below the meanest of his subjects! But one power should not be thrown down to exalt another—for all power inebriates weak man; and its abuse proves that the more equality there is established among men, the more virtue and happiness will reign in society. But this and any similar maxim deduced from simple reason, raises an outcry—the church or the state is in danger, if faith in the wisdom of antiquity is not implicit; and they who, roused by the sight of human calamity, dare to attack human authority, are reviled as despisers of God, and enemies of man. These are bitter calumnies, yet they reached one of the best of men,[5] whose ashes still preach peace, and whose memory demands a respectful pause, when subjects are discussed that lay so near his heart.—

After attacking the sacred majesty of Kings, I shall scarcely excite surprise by adding my firm persuasion that every profession, in which great subordination of rank constitutes its power, is highly injurious to morality.

A standing army, for instance, is incompatible with freedom; because subordination and rigour are the very sinews of military discipline; and despotism is necessary to give vigour to enterprizes that one will directs.[6] A spirit inspired by romantic notions of honour, a kind of morality founded on the fashion of the age, can only be felt by a few officers, whilst the main body must be moved by command, like the waves of the sea; for the strong wind of authority pushes the

---

4. Matthew 7:16. "Ye shall know them by their fruits. Do men gather grapes of thorns, or figs of thistles?" and Luke 6:44: "For every tree is known by his own fruit. For of thorns men do not gather figs, nor of a bramble bush gather they grapes." "Tares": Weeds.
5. "Dr Price" [Wollstonecraft's note]. Richard Price (1723–1791) was a radical political philosopher and a clergyman whose chapel Wollstonecraft attended during 1786. His 1789 *A Discourse on the Love of Our Country* (see p. 249 herein), which celebrated the Revolution in France as the legitimate continuation of both the American Revolution and England's Glorious Revolution of 1688, made Price a target for Edmund Burke, who attacked him vehemently in *Reflections*. (see p. 253 herein).
6. The notion that liberty was endangered in nations that maintained professional armies and in which soldiering had become a distinct profession was a key premise of radical political thought. Authors such as John Millar in *The Origin of the Distinction of Ranks* (1771) and James Burgh in *Political Disquisitions* (1774–75) advocated for citizen militias and predicted corruption and a loss of virility for the citizenry that provided for its defense by employing others.

crowd of subalterns forward, they scarcely know or care why, with headlong fury.

Besides, nothing can be so prejudicial to the morals of the inhabitants of country towns as the occasional residence of a set of idle superficial young men, whose only occupation is gallantry, and whose polished manners render vice more dangerous, by concealing its deformity under gay ornamental drapery. An air of fashion, which is but a badge of slavery, and proves that the soul has not a strong individual character, awes simple country people into an imitation of the vices, when they cannot catch the slippery graces, of politeness. Every corps is a chain of despots, who, submitting and tyrannizing without exercising their reason, become dead weights of vice and folly on the community. A man of rank or fortune, sure of rising by interest, has nothing to do but to pursue some extravagant freak; whilst the needy *gentleman*, who is to rise, as the phrase turns, by his merit, becomes a servile parasite or vile pander.

Sailors, the naval gentlemen, come under the same description, only their vices assume a different and a grosser cast. They are more positively indolent, when not discharging the ceremonials of their station; whilst the insignificant fluttering of soldiers may be termed active idleness. More confined to the society of men, the former acquire a fondness for humour and mischievous tricks; whilst the latter, mixing frequently with well-bred women, catch a sentimental cant.—But mind is equally out of the question, whether they indulge the horse-laugh, or polite simper.

May I be allowed to extend the comparison to a profession where more mind is certainly to be found; for the clergy have superior opportunities of improvement, though subordination almost equally cramps their faculties? The blind submission imposed at college to forms of belief serves as a novitiate to the curate, who must obsequiously respect the opinion of his rector or patron, if he mean to rise in his profession. Perhaps there cannot be a more forcible contrast than between the servile dependent gait of a poor curate and the courtly mien of a bishop. And the respect and contempt they inspire render the discharge of their separate functions equally useless.

It is of great importance to observe that the character of every man is, in some degree, formed by his profession. A man of sense may only have a cast of countenance that wears off as you trace his individuality, whilst the weak, common man has scarcely ever any character, but what belongs to the body; at least, all his opinions have been so steeped in the vat consecrated by authority, that the faint spirit which the grape of his own vine yields cannot be distinguished.

Society, therefore, as it becomes more enlightened, should be very careful not to establish bodies of men who must necessarily be made foolish or vicious by the very constitution of their profession.

In this time of enlightenment, don't let the same mistakes happen.

In the infancy of society, when men were just emerging out of barbarism, chiefs and priests, touching the most powerful springs of savage conduct, hope and fear, must have had unbounded sway. An aristocracy, of course, is naturally the first form of government. But, clashing interests soon losing their equipoise, a monarchy and hierarchy break out of the confusion of ambitious struggles, and the foundation of both is secured by feudal tenures. This appears to be the origin of monarchical and priestly power, and the dawn of civilization. But such combustible materials cannot long be pent up; and, getting vent in foreign wars and intestine insurrections,[7] the people acquire some power in tumult, which obliges their rulers to gloss over their oppression with a shew of right. Thus, as wars, agriculture, commerce, and literature, expand the mind, despots are compelled, to make covert corruption hold fast the power which was formerly snatched by open force.[8] And this baneful lurking gangrene is most quickly spread by luxury and superstition, the sure dregs of ambition. The indolent puppet of a court first becomes a luxurious monster, or fastidious sensualist, and then makes the contagion which his unnatural state spread, the instrument of tyranny.

It is the pestiferous purple[9] which renders the progress of civilization a curse, and warps the understanding, till men of sensibility doubt whether the expansion of intellect produces a greater portion of happiness or misery. But the nature of the poison points out the antidote; and had Rousseau mounted one step higher in his investigation, or could his eye have pierced through the foggy atmosphere, which he almost disdained to breathe, his active mind would have darted forward to contemplate the perfection of man in the establishment of true civilization, instead of taking his ferocious flight back to the night of sensual ignorance.

Chap. II

The Prevailing Opinion of a Sexual Character Discussed

To account for, and excuse the tyranny of man, many ingenious arguments have been brought forward to prove, that the two sexes, in the acquirement of virtue, ought to aim at attaining a very different character: or, to speak explicitly, women are not allowed to have sufficient strength of mind to acquire what really deserves the name of virtue. Yet it should seem, allowing them to have souls, that there

---

7. Internal strife.
8. "Men of abilities scatter seeds that grow up and have a great influence on the forming opinion; and when once the public opinion preponderates, through the exertion of reason, the overthrow of arbitrary power is not very distant" [Wollstonecraft's note].
9. The color of royalty or high rank.

is but one way appointed by Providence to lead *mankind* to either virtue or happiness.

If then women are not a swarm of ephemeron triflers, why should they be kept in ignorance under the specious name of innocence? Men complain, and with reason, of the follies and caprices of our sex, when they do not keenly satirize our headstrong passions and groveling vices.—Behold, I should answer, the natural effect of ignorance! The mind will ever be unstable that has only prejudices to rest on, and the current will run with destructive fury when there are no barriers to break its force. Women are told from their infancy, and taught by the example of their mothers, that a little knowledge of human weakness, justly termed cunning, softness of temper, *outward* obedience, and a scrupulous attention to a puerile kind of propriety, will obtain for them the protection of man; and should they be beautiful, every thing else is needless, for, at least, twenty years of their lives.

Thus Milton describes our first frail mother; though when he tells us that women are formed for softness and sweet attractive grace,[1] I cannot comprehend his meaning, unless, in the true Mahometan strain, he meant to deprive us of souls,[2] and insinuate that we were beings only designed by sweet attractive grace, and docile blind obedience, to gratify the senses of man when he can no longer soar on the wing of contemplation.

How grossly do they insult us who thus advise us only to render ourselves gentle, domestic brutes! For instance, the winning softness so warmly, and frequently, recommended, that governs by obeying. What childish expressions, and how insignificant is the being— can it be an immortal one? who will condescend to govern by such sinister methods! 'Certainly,' says Lord Bacon, 'man is of kin to the beasts by his body; and if he be not of kin to God by his spirit, he is a base and ignoble creature!'[3] Men, indeed, appear to me to act in a very unphilosophical manner when they try to secure the good conduct of women by attempting to keep them always in a state of childhood. Rousseau was more consistent when he wished to stop the progress of reason in both sexes, for if men eat of the tree of knowledge, women will come in for a taste; but, from the imperfect cultivation which their understandings now receive, they only attain a knowledge of evil.[4]

---

1. *Paradise Lost* IV. 297–99: "For contemplation he and valor formed, / For softness she and sweet attractive grace; / He for God only, she for God in him."
2. See p. 10, n. 6.
3. Francis Bacon, Essay XVI, "Of Atheism."
4. Both Adam and Eve ate the fruit from the tree of knowledge of good and evil in the garden of Eden. In the fallen state both men and women need to work at virtue, but according to Wollstonecraft, women have been denied the education, and thus the means, to attain it.

Children, I grant, should be innocent; but when the epithet is applied to men, or women, it is but a civil term for weakness. For if it be allowed that women were destined by Providence to acquire human virtues, and by the exercise of their understandings, that stability of character which is the firmest ground to rest our future hopes upon, they must be permitted to turn to the fountain of light, and not forced to shape their course by the twinkling of a mere satellite. Milton, I grant, was of a very different opinion; for he only bends to the indefeasible right of beauty, though it would be difficult to render two passages which I now mean to contrast, consistent. But into similar inconsistencies are great men often led by their senses.

'To whom thus Eve with *perfect beauty* adorn'd.
'My Author and Disposer, what thou bidst
'*Unargued* I obey; So God ordains;
'God is *thy law, thou mine:* to know no more
'Is Woman's *happiest* knowledge and her *praise.*'[5]

These are exactly the arguments that I have used to children; but I have added, your reason is now gaining strength, and, till it arrives at some degree of maturity, you must look up to me for advice—then you ought to *think*, and only rely on God.

Yet in the following lines Milton seems to coincide with me; when he makes Adam thus expostulate with his Maker.

'Hast thou not made me here thy substitute,
'And these inferior far beneath me set?
'Among *unequals* what society
'Can sort, what harmony or true delight?
'Which must be mutual, in proportion due
'Giv'n and receiv'd; but in *disparity*
'The one intense, the other still remiss
'Cannot well suit with either, but soon prove
'Tedious alike: of *fellowship* I speak
'Such as I seek, fit to participate
'All rational delight[6]—

In treating, therefore, of the manners of women, let us, disregarding sensual arguments, trace what we should endeavour to make them in order to co-operate, if the expression be not too bold, with the supreme Being.

By individual education, I mean, for the sense of the word is not precisely defined, such an attention to a child as will slowly sharpen the senses, form the temper,[7] regulate the passions as they begin to

5. *Paradise Lost* IV.634–38. The italics are Wollstonecraft's.
6. *Paradise Lost* VIII. 381–92. The italics are Wollstonecraft's.
7. Temperament, character.

ferment, and set the understanding to work before the body arrives at maturity; so that the man may only have to proceed, not to begin, the important task of learning to think and reason.

To prevent any misconstruction, I must add, that I do not believe that a private education can work the wonders which some sanguine writers have attributed to it. Men and women must be educated, in a great degree, by the opinions and manners of the society they live in. In every age there has been a stream of popular opinion that has carried all before it, and given a family character, as it were, to the century. It may then fairly be inferred, that, till society be differently constituted, much cannot be expected from education. It is, however, sufficient for my present purpose to assert, that, whatever effect circumstances have on the abilities, every being may become virtuous by the exercise of its own reason; for if but one being was created with vicious inclinations, that is positively bad, what can save us from atheism? or if we worship a God, is not that God a devil?

Consequently, the most perfect education, in my opinion, is such an exercise of the understanding as is best calculated to strengthen the body and form the heart. Or, in other words, to enable the individual to attain such habits of virtue as will render it independent. In fact, it is a farce to call any being virtuous whose virtues do not result from the exercise of its own reason. This was Rousseau's opinion respecting men: I extend it to women, and confidently assert that they have been drawn out of their sphere by false refinement, and not by an endeavour to acquire masculine qualities. Still the regal homage which they receive is so intoxicating, that till the manners of the times are changed, and formed on more reasonable principles, it may be impossible to convince them that the illegitimate power, which they obtain, by degrading themselves, is a curse, and that they must return to nature and equality if they wish to secure the placid satisfaction that unsophisticated affections impart. But for this epoch we must wait—wait, perhaps, till kings and nobles, enlightened by reason, and, preferring the real dignity of man to childish state, throw off their gaudy hereditary trappings: and if then women do not resign the arbitrary power of beauty—they will prove that they have *less* mind than man.

I may be accused of arrogance; still I must declare what I firmly believe, that all the writers who have written on the subject of female education and manners from Rousseau to Dr. Gregory,[8] have contributed to render women more artificial, weak characters, than

8. John Gregory (1724–1773), Scottish physician, philosopher, and professor at the University of Edinburgh. In her edited anthology *The Female Reader* (1789) Wollstonecraft had quoted extensively from Gregory's widely read advice book, *A Father's Legacy to His Daughters* (1774; see p. 236 herein). Here she returns to that work in a more critical spirit.

Beauty is such a superficial form of power + if women are ok with it and use it, they have highly weak minds. Women should want to overcome it and have intellectual beauty

they would otherwise have been; and, consequently, more useless members of society. I might have expressed this conviction in a lower key; but I am afraid it would have been the whine of affectation, and not the faithful expression of my feelings, of the clear result, which experience and reflection have led me to draw. When I come to that division of the subject, I shall advert to the passages that I more particularly disapprove of, in the works of the authors I have just alluded to; but it is first necessary to observe, that my objection extends to the whole purport of those books, which tend, in my opinion, to degrade one half of the human species, and render women pleasing at the expense of every solid virtue.

Though, to reason on Rousseau's ground, if man did attain a degree of perfection of mind when his body arrived at maturity, it might be proper, in order to make a man and his wife *one*, that she should rely entirely on his understanding; and the graceful ivy, clasping the oak that supported it, would form a whole in which strength and beauty would be equally conspicuous. But, alas! husbands, as well as their helpmates, are often only overgrown children; nay, thanks to early debauchery, scarcely men in their outward form—and if the blind lead the blind, one need not come from heaven to tell us the consequence.[9] all tea, all shade

Many are the causes that, in the present corrupt state of society, contribute to enslave women by cramping their understandings and sharpening their senses. One, perhaps, that silently does more mischief than all the rest, is their disregard of order.

To do every thing in an orderly manner, is a most important precept, which women, who, generally speaking, receive only a disorderly kind of education, seldom attend to with that degree of exactness that men, who from their infancy are broken into method, observe. This negligent kind of guess-work, for what other epithet can be used to point out the random exertions of a sort of instinctive common sense, never brought to the test of reason? prevents their generalizing matters of fact—so they do to-day, what they did yesterday, merely because they did it yesterday.

This contempt of the understanding in early life has more baneful consequences than is commonly supposed; for the little knowledge which women of strong minds attain, is, from various circumstances, of a more desultory kind than the knowledge of men, and it is acquired more by sheer observations on real life, than from comparing what has been individually observed with the results of experience generalized by speculation. Led by their dependent situation and domestic employments more into society, what they learn is

9. Matthew 15:14: "And if the blind lead the blind, both shall fall into the ditch." "One . . . from heaven": Jesus.

rather by snatches; and as learning is with them, in general, only a secondary thing, they do not pursue any one branch with that persevering ardour necessary to give vigour to the faculties, and clearness to the judgment. In the present state of society, a little learning is required to support the character of a gentleman; and boys are obliged to submit to a few years of discipline. But in the education of women, the cultivation of the understanding is always subordinate to the acquirement of some corporeal accomplishment; even while enervated by confinement and false notions of modesty, the body is prevented from attaining that grace and beauty which relaxed half-formed limbs never exhibit. Besides, in youth their faculties are not brought forward by emulation; and having no serious scientific study, if they have natural sagacity it is turned too soon on life and manners. They dwell on effects, and modifications, without tracing them back to causes; and complicated rules to adjust behaviour are a weak substitute for simple principles.

As a proof that education gives this appearance of weakness to females, we may instance the example of military men, who are, like them, sent into the world before their minds have been stored with knowledge or fortified by principles. The consequences are similar; soldiers acquire a little superficial knowledge, snatched from the muddy current of conversation, and, from continually mixing with society, they gain, what is termed a knowledge of the world; and this acquaintance with manners and customs has frequently been confounded with a knowledge of the human heart. But can the crude fruit of casual observation, never brought to the test of judgment, formed by comparing speculation and experience, deserve such a distinction? Soldiers, as well as women, practice the minor virtues with punctilious politeness. Where is then the sexual difference, when the education has been the same? All the difference that I can discern, arises from the superior advantage of liberty, which enables the former to see more of life.

It is wandering from my present subject, perhaps, to make a political remark; but, as it was produced naturally by the train of my reflections, I shall not pass it silently over.

Standing armies can never consist of resolute, robust men; they may be well disciplined machines, but they will seldom contain men under the influence of strong passions, or with very vigorous faculties. And as for any depth of understanding, I will venture to affirm, that it is as rarely to be found in the army as amongst women; and the cause, I maintain, is the same. It may be further observed, that officers are also particularly attentive to their persons, fond of dancing, crowded rooms, adventures, and ridicule.[1] Like the *fair*

1. "Why should women be censured with petulant acrimony, because they seem to have a passion for a scarlet coat? Has not education placed them more on a level with soldiers than any other class of men?" [Wollstonecraft's note].

sex,[2] the business of their lives is gallantry. —They were taught to please, and they only live to please. Yet they do not lose their rank in the distinction of sexes, for they are still reckoned superior to women, though in what their superiority consists, beyond what I have just mentioned, it is difficult to discover.

The great misfortune is this, that they both acquire manners before morals, and a knowledge of life before they have, from reflection, any acquaintance with the grand ideal outline of human nature. The consequence is natural; satisfied with common nature, they become a prey to prejudices, and taking all their opinions on credit, they blindly submit to authority. So that, if they have any sense, it is a kind of instinctive glance, that catches proportions, and decides with respect to manners; but fails when arguments are to be pursued below the surface, or opinions analyzed.

May not the same remark be applied to women? Nay, the argument may be carried still further, for they are both thrown out of a useful station by the unnatural distinctions established in civilized life. Riches and hereditary honours have made cyphers of women to give consequence to the numerical figure;[3] and idleness has produced a mixture of gallantry and despotism into society, which leads the very men who are the slaves of their mistresses to tyrannize over their sisters, wives, and daughters. This is only keeping them in rank and file, it is true. Strengthen the female mind by enlarging it, and there will be an end to blind obedience; but, as blind obedience is ever sought for by power, tyrants and sensualists are in the right when they endeavour to keep women in the dark, because the former only want slaves, and the latter a play-thing. The sensualist, indeed, has been the most dangerous of tyrants, and women have been duped by their lovers, as princes by their ministers, whilst dreaming that they reigned over them.

I now principally allude to Rousseau, for his character of Sophia[4] is, undoubtedly, a captivating one, though it appears to me grossly unnatural; however it is not the superstructure, but the foundation of her character, the principles on which her education was built, that I mean to attack; nay, warmly as I admire the genius of that able writer, whose opinions I shall often have occasion to cite,

2. Women.
3. As a zero added to a number multiplies its value by a factor of ten, in a hierarchical society women magnify the status of the men with whom they are allied. The heroine of Samuel Richardson's tragic novel *Clarissa* (discussed by Wollstonecraft in Chapter IV) uses the same metaphor to describe her relationship with her sadistic suitor: "I am but a cypher, to give him significance and myself pain" ([London, 1747–48], v. 4, p. 2).
4. "*Sophie ou la Femme*" is the title of Book v of *Émile* (translatable either as "Sophie, or, The Wife" or "Sophie, or, The Woman"). Having tracked the development of Émile, his imaginary pupil, up to age twenty, Rousseau invents the character of Sophie (Sophia in the 1762 English translation) to supply his hero with a wife and to address, belatedly, the topic of female education (see p. 229 herein).

indignation always takes place of admiration, and the rigid frown of insulted virtue effaces the smile of complacency, which his eloquent periods are wont to raise, when I read his voluptuous reveries. Is this the man, who, in his ardour for virtue, would banish all the soft arts of peace, and almost carry us back to Spartan discipline? Is this the man who delights to paint the useful struggles of passion, the triumphs of good dispositions, and the heroic flights which carry the glowing soul out of itself?—How are these mighty sentiments lowered when he describes the pretty foot and enticing airs of his little favourite! But, for the present, I wave[5] the subject, and, instead of severely reprehending the transient effusions of overweening sensibility, I shall only observe, that whoever has cast a benevolent eye on society, must often have been gratified by the sight of a humble mutual love, not dignified by sentiment, or strengthened by a union in intellectual pursuits. The domestic trifles of the day have afforded matters for cheerful converse, and innocent caresses have softened toils which did not require great exercise of mind or stretch of thought: yet, has not the sight of this moderate felicity excited more tenderness than respect? An emotion similar to what we feel when children are playing, or animals sporting,[6] whilst the contemplation of the noble struggles of suffering merit has raised admiration, and carried our thoughts to that world where sensation will give place to reason.

Women are, therefore, to be considered either as moral beings, or so weak that they must be entirely subjected to the superior faculties of men.

Let us examine this question. Rousseau declares that a woman should never, for a moment, feel herself independent, that she should be governed by fear to exercise her natural cunning, and made a coquetish slave in order to render her a more alluring object of desire, a *sweeter* companion to man, whenever he chooses to relax himself. He carries the arguments, which he pretends to draw from the indications of nature, still further, and insinuates that truth and fortitude, the corner stones of all human virtue, should be cultivated with certain restrictions, because, with respect to the female

5. A common spelling for "waive" in the eighteenth century.
6. "Similar feelings has Milton's pleasing picture of paradisiacal happiness ever raised in my mind; yet, instead of envying the lovely pair, I have, with conscious dignity, or Satanic pride, turned to hell for sublimer objects. In the same style, when viewing some noble monument of human art, I have traced the emanation of the Deity in the order I admired, till, descending from that giddy height, I have caught myself contemplating the grandest of all human sights;—for fancy quickly placed, in some solitary recess, an outcast of fortune, rising superior to passion and discontent" [Wollstonecraft's note]. Wollstonecraft is referring to the portrait of Adam and Eve in Book IV of Milton's *Paradise Lost* and stating what has since become critical commonplace, that Milton's Eden, for all its bliss, is not as compelling as his suffering Satan.

character, obedience is the grand lesson which ought to be impressed with unrelenting rigour.[7]

What nonsense! when will a great man arise with sufficient strength of mind to puff away the fumes which pride and sensuality have thus spread over the subject! If women are by nature inferior to men, their virtues must be the same in quality, if not in degree, or virtue is a relative idea; consequently, their conduct should be founded on the same principles, and have the same aim.

[margin note: If men were so great their? overcame societal norms.]

Connected with man as daughters, wives, and mothers, their moral character may be estimated by their manner of fulfilling those simple duties; but the end, the grand end of their exertions should be to unfold their own faculties and acquire the dignity of conscious virtue. They may try to render their road pleasant; but ought never to forget, in common with man, that life yields not the felicity which can satisfy an immortal soul. I do not mean to insinuate, that either sex should be so lost in abstract reflections or distant views, as to forget the affections and duties that lie before them, and are, in truth, the means appointed to produce the fruit of life; on the contrary, I would warmly recommend them, even while I assert, that they afford most satisfaction when they are considered in their true, sober light.

Probably the prevailing opinion, that woman was created for man, may have taken its rise from Moses's poetical story;[8] yet, as very few, it is presumed, who have bestowed any serious thought on the subject, ever supposed that Eve was, literally speaking, one of Adam's ribs, the deduction must be allowed to fall to the ground; or, only be so far admitted as it proves that man, from the remotest antiquity, found it convenient to exert his strength to subjugate his companion, and his invention to shew that she ought to have her neck bent under the yoke, because the whole creation was only created for his convenience or pleasure.

Let it not be concluded that I wish to invert the order of things; I have already granted, that, from the constitution of their bodies, men seem to be designed by Providence to attain a greater degree of virtue. I speak collectively of the whole sex; but I see not the shadow of a reason to conclude that their virtues should differ in respect to their nature. In fact, how can they, if virtue has only one eternal standard? I must therefore, if I reason consequentially, as

---

7. *Emilius,* IV, v, 32: "The first and most important qualification in a woman is good nature or sweetness of temper: formed to obey a being so imperfect as man, often full of vices, and always full of faults, she ought to learn betimes even to suffer injustice, and to bear the insults of a husband without complaint: it is not for his sake, but her own, that she should be of a mild disposition."

8. See Genesis 2:21–23 for one account of the creation of woman. Moses was thought to be the author of the first five books of the Old Testament (the Pentateuch).

[handwritten note at bottom: If men cant see women as equals, or at least more than just a pretty face, how can it be said that they have morals & are virtuous?]

strenuously maintain that they have the same simple direction, as that there is a God.

It follows then that cunning should not be opposed to wisdom, little cares to great exertions, or insipid softness, varnished over with the name of gentleness, to that fortitude which grand views alone can inspire.

I shall be told that woman would then lose many of her peculiar graces, and the opinion of a well known poet might be quoted to refute my unqualified assertion. For Pope has said, in the name of the whole male sex,

> 'Yet ne'er so sure our passion to create,
> 'As when she touch'd the brink of all we hate.'[9]

In what light this sally places men and women, I shall leave to the judicious to determine; meanwhile I shall content myself with observing, that I cannot discover why, unless they are mortal, females should always be degraded by being made subservient to love or lust.

To speak disrespectfully of love is, I know, high treason against sentiment and fine feelings; but I wish to speak the simple language of truth, and rather to address the head than the heart. To endeavour to reason love out of the world, would be to out Quixote Cervantes,[1] and equally offend against common sense; but an endeavour to restrain this tumultuous passion, and to prove that it should not be allowed to dethrone superior powers, or to usurp the sceptre which the understanding should ever coolly wield, appears less wild.

Youth is the season for love in both sexes; but in those days of thoughtless enjoyment provision should be made for the more important years of life, when reflection takes place of sensation. But Rousseau, and most of the male writers who have followed his steps, have warmly inculcated that the whole tendency of female education ought to be directed to one point:—to render them pleasing.

Let me reason with the supporters of this opinion who have any knowledge of human nature, do they imagine that marriage can eradicate the habitude of life? The woman who has only been taught to please will soon find that her charms are oblique sunbeams, and that they cannot have much effect on her husband's heart when they are seen every day, when the summer is passed and gone. Will she then have sufficient native energy to look into herself for comfort, and cultivate her dormant faculties? or, is it not more rational to expect that she will try to please other men; and, in the emotions

9. Alexander Pope, "Of the Characters of Women," Epistle 2, lines 51–52, of his *Moral Essays* (1735).
1. I.e., to outdo the idealistic but ineffectual hero of Miguel de Cervantes's *Don Quixote* (1605) in trying to accomplish the impossible.

raised by the expectation of new conquests, endeavour to forget the mortification her love or pride has received? When the husband ceases to be a lover—and the time will inevitably come, her desire of pleasing will then grow languid, or become a spring of bitterness; and love, perhaps, the most evanescent of all passions, gives place to jealousy or vanity.

I now speak of women who are restrained by principle or prejudice; such women, though they would shrink from an intrigue with real abhorrence, yet, nevertheless, wish to be convinced by the homage of gallantry that they are cruelly neglected by their husbands; or, days and weeks are spent in dreaming of the happiness enjoyed by congenial souls till their health is undermined and their spirits broken by discontent. How then can the great art of pleasing be such a necessary study? it is only useful to a mistress; the chaste wife, and serious mother, should only consider her power to please as the polish of her virtues, and the affection of her husband as one of the comforts that render her task less difficult and her life happier.— But, whether she be loved or neglected, her first wish should be to make herself respectable, and not to rely for all her happiness on a being subject to like infirmities with herself.

The worthy Dr. Gregory fell into a similar error. I respect his heart; but entirely disapprove of his celebrated Legacy to his Daughters.

He advises them to cultivate a fondness for dress, because a fondness for dress, he asserts, is natural to them.[2] I am unable to comprehend what either he or Rousseau mean, when they frequently use this indefinite term.[3] If they told us that in a pre-existent state the soul was fond of dress, and brought this inclination with it into a new body, I should listen to them with a half smile, as I often do when I hear a rant about innate elegance.—But if he only meant to say that the exercise of the faculties will produce this fondness— I deny it.—It is not natural; but arises, like false ambition in men, from a love of power.

Dr. Gregory goes much further; he actually recommends dissimulation, and advises an innocent girl to give the lie to her feelings, and not dance with spirit, when gaiety of heart would make her feel eloquent without making her gestures immodest. In the name of truth and common sense, why should not one woman acknowledge that she can take more exercise than another? or, in other words, that she has a sound constitution; and why, to damp innocent vivacity, is she darkly to be told that men will draw conclusions which she little

2. "The love of dress is natural to you, and therefore it is proper and reasonable." John Gregory, *A Father's Legacy to His Daughters*, 2nd ed. [London, 1775], p. 55; all references are to this edition.
3. I.e., "natural."

thinks of?[4]—Let the libertine draw what inference he pleases; but, I hope, that no sensible mother will restrain the natural frankness of youth by instilling such indecent cautions. Out of the abundance of the heart the mouth speaketh;[5] and a wiser than Solomon hath said, that the heart should be made clean,[6] and not trivial ceremonies observed, which it is not very difficult to fulfill with scrupulous exactness when vice reigns in the heart.

Women ought to endeavour to purify their heart; but can they do so when their uncultivated understandings make them entirely dependent on their senses for employment and amusement, when no noble pursuit sets them above the little vanities of the day, or enables them to curb the wild emotions that agitate a reed over which every passing breeze has power? To gain the affections of a virtuous man is affectation necessary? Nature has given woman a weaker frame than man; but, to ensure her husband's affections, must a wife, who by the exercise of her mind and body whilst she was discharging the duties of a daughter, wife, and mother, has allowed her constitution to retain its natural strength, and her nerves a healthy tone, is she, I say, to condescend to use art and feign a sickly delicacy in order to secure her husband's affection? Weakness may excite tenderness, and gratify the arrogant pride of man; but the lordly caresses of a protector will not gratify a noble mind that pants for, and deserves to be respected. Fondness is a poor substitute for friendship!

In a seraglio, I grant, that all these arts are necessary; the epicure must have his palate tickled, or he will sink into apathy; but have women so little ambition as to be satisfied with such a condition? Can they supinely dream life away in the lap of pleasure, or the languor of weariness, rather than assert their claim to pursue reasonable pleasures and render themselves conspicuous by practising the virtues which dignify mankind? Surely she has not an immortal soul who can loiter life away merely employed to adorn her person, that she may amuse the languid hours, and soften the cares of a fellow-creature who is willing to be enlivened by her smiles and tricks, when the serious business of life is over.

4. For this and the previous sentence see Gregory, pp. 57–58: "I would have you to dance with spirit; but never allow yourselves to be so far transported with mirth, as to forget the delicacy of your sex.—Many a girl dancing in the gaiety and innocence of her heart, is thought to discover a spirit she little dreams of."
5. Matthew 12:34.
6. "Wiser than Solomon": Jesus (who describes himself in comparable terms in Luke 11:31). In Luke 11:39–44 and Matthew 23:25–28, Jesus speaks of purifying the inner self and denounces the Pharisees' self-righteous observance of the letter of the law. Cf. Wollstonecraft's characterization of her heroine Mary: "She saw that religion does not consist in ceremonies; and that many prayers fall from the lips without purifying the heart" (*Mary: A Fiction* [London, 1788], p. 34).

if she establishes herself it won't be reading to please her husband

Besides, the woman who strengthens her body and exercises her mind will, by managing her family and practising various virtues, become the friend, and not the humble dependent of her husband; and if she, by possessing such substantial qualities, merit his regard, she will not find it necessary to conceal her affection, nor to pretend to an unnatural coldness of constitution to excite her husband's passions. In fact, if we revert to history, we shall find that the women who have distinguished themselves have neither been the most beautiful nor the most gentle of their sex.

Nature, or, to speak with strict propriety, God, has made all things right; but man has sought him out many inventions to mar the work. I now allude to that part of Dr. Gregory's treatise, where he advises a wife never to let her husband know the extent of her sensibility or affection.[7] Voluptuous precaution, and as ineffectual as absurd.— Love, from its very nature, must be transitory. To seek for a secret that would render it constant, would be as wild a search as for the philosopher's stone, or the grand panacea:[8] and the discovery would be equally useless, or rather pernicious to mankind. The most holy band of society is friendship. It has been well said, by a shrewd satirist, "that rare as true love is, true friendship is still rarer."[9]

This is an obvious truth, and the cause not lying deep, will not elude a slight glance of inquiry.

Love, the common passion, in which chance and sensation take place of choice and reason, is, in some degree, felt by the mass of mankind; for it is not necessary to speak, at present, of the emotions that rise above or sink below love. This passion, naturally increased by suspense and difficulties, draws the mind out of its accustomed state, and exalts the affections; but the security of marriage, allowing the fever of love to subside, a healthy temperature is thought insipid, only by those who have not sufficient intellect to substitute the calm tenderness of friendship, the confidence of respect, instead of blind admiration, and the sensual emotions of fondness.

This is, must be, the course of nature.—Friendship or indifference inevitably succeeds love.—And this constitution seems perfectly to harmonize with the system of government which prevails in the moral world. Passions are spurs to action, and open the mind; but they sink into mere appetites, become a personal and momentary gratification, when the object is gained, and the satisfied mind rests in enjoyment. The man who had some virtue whilst he was

---

7. Gregory, pp. 86–87: "If you love him, let me advise you never to discover to him the full extent of your love, no, not although you marry him."
8. A medicine reputed to cure all diseases. "Philosopher's stone": sought by alchemists because it was supposed to have the power to transmute base metals into gold.
9. La Rochefoucauld (1613–1680, French noble), *Les Maximes*, No. 473: "*Quelque rare que soit que la véritable amour, il l'est encore moins que la véritable amitié.*"

struggling for a crown, often becomes a voluptuous tyrant when it graces his brow; and, when the lover is not lost in the husband, the dotard, a prey to childish caprices, and fond jealousies, neglects the serious duties of life, and the caresses which should excite confidence in his children are lavished on the overgrown child, his wife.

In order to fulfil the duties of life, and to be able to pursue with vigour the various employments which form the moral character, a master and mistress of a family ought not to continue to love each other with passion. I mean to say, that they ought not to indulge those emotions which disturb the order of society, and engross the thoughts that should be otherwise employed. The mind that has never been engrossed by one object wants vigour—if it can long be so, it is weak.

A mistaken education, a narrow, uncultivated mind, and many sexual prejudices, tend to make women more constant than men; but, for the present, I shall not touch on this branch of the subject. I will go still further, and advance, without dreaming of a paradox, that an unhappy marriage is often very advantageous to a family, and that the neglected wife is, in general, the best mother.[1] And this would almost always be the consequence if the female mind were more enlarged: for, it seems to be the common dispensation of Providence, that what we gain in present enjoyment should be deducted from the treasure of life, experience; and that when we are gathering the flowers of the day and revelling in pleasure, the solid fruit of toil and wisdom should not be caught at the same time. The way lies before us, we must turn to the right or left; and he who will pass life away in bounding from one pleasure to another, must not complain if he acquire neither wisdom nor respectability of character.

Supposing, for a moment, that the soul is not immortal, and that man was only created for the present scene,—I think we should have reason to complain that love, infantine fondness, ever grew insipid and palled upon the sense. Let us eat, drink, and love, for to-morrow we die, would be, in fact, the language of reason, the morality of life; and who but a fool would part with a reality for a fleeting shadow? But, if awed by observing the improbable[2] powers of the mind, we disdain to confine our wishes or thoughts to such a comparatively mean field of action, that only appears grand and important, as it is connected with a boundless prospect and sublime hopes, what necessity is there for falsehood in conduct, and why must the sacred majesty of truth be violated to detain a deceitful good that saps the very foundation of virtue? Why must the female

---

1. Wollstonecraft's point is that a woman who is not preoccupied with her husband (and his attentions to her) has more time and energy for her children.
2. The first edition reads "improvable" here, which makes more sense in context.

friendship is above in relationships

mind be tainted by coquetish arts to gratify the sensualist, and prevent love from subsiding into friendship, or compassionate tenderness, when there are not qualities on which friendship can be built? Let the honest heart shew itself, and *reason* teach passion to submit to necessity; or, let the dignified pursuit of virtue and knowledge raise the mind above those emotions which rather imbitter than sweeten the cup of life, when they are not restrained within due bounds.

I do not mean to allude to the romantic passion, which is the concomitant of genius.—Who can clip its wing? But that grand passion not proportioned to the puny enjoyments of life, is only true to the sentiment, and feeds on itself. The passions which have been celebrated for their durability have always been unfortunate. They have acquired strength by absence and constitutional melancholy.—The fancy has hovered round a form of beauty dimly seen[3]—but familiarity might have turned admiration into disgust; or, at least, into indifference, and allowed the imagination leisure to start fresh game. With perfect propriety, according to this view of things, does Rousseau make the mistress of his soul, Eloisa, love St. Preux, when life was fading before her;[4] but this is no proof of the immortality of the passion.

Of the same complexion is Dr. Gregory's advice respecting delicacy of sentiment, which he advises a woman not to acquire, if she have determined to marry.[5] This determination, however, perfectly consistent with his former advice, he calls *indelicate*, and earnestly persuades his daughters to conceal it, though it may govern their conduct;—as if it were indelicate to have the common appetites of human nature.

Noble morality! and consistent with the cautious prudence of a little soul that cannot extend its views beyond the present minute division of existence. If all the faculties of woman's mind are only to be cultivated as they respect her dependence on man; if, when a husband be obtained, she have arrived at her goal, and meanly proud rests satisfied with such a paltry crown, let her grovel contentedly, scarcely raised by her employments above the animal kingdom;

3. Mary Hays applies these sentences about the passions that accompany genius to Wollstonecraft herself in the course of her cautious account of the latter's unhappy love life: "Memoir of Mary Wollstonecraft," *The Annual Necrology for 1797–8* (London, 1800), p. 424. "Fancy": Imagination.
4. In Rousseau's *Julie; ou la Nouvelle Héloïse* (1761), the heroine, Julie, reveals her long-held passionate love for St. Preux as she is dying, even though she has been a faithful wife to Wolmar throughout the novel.
5. Gregory, pp. 116–18: "But if you find that marriage is absolutely essential to your happiness . . . shun . . . reading and conversation that warms the imagination, which engages and softens the heart, and raises the taste above the level of common life . . . [otherwise] you may be tired with insipidity and dullness; shocked with indelicacy, or mortified by indifference."

but, if, struggling for the prize of her high calling,[6] she look beyond the present scene, let her cultivate her understanding without stopping to consider what character the husband may have whom she is destined to marry. Let her only determine, without being too anxious about present happiness, to acquire the qualities that ennoble a rational being, and a rough inelegant husband may shock her taste without destroying her peace of mind. She will not model her soul to suit the frailties of her companion, but to bear with them: his character may be a trial, but not an impediment to virtue.

If Dr. Gregory confined his remark to romantic expectations of constant love and congenial feelings, he should have recollected that experience will banish what advice can never make us cease to wish for, when the imagination is kept alive at the expence of reason.

I own it frequently happens that women who have fostered a romantic unnatural delicacy of feeling, waste their[7] lives in *imagining* how happy they should have been with a husband who could love them with a fervid increasing affection every day, and all day. But they might as well pine married as single—and would not be a jot more unhappy with a bad husband than longing for a good one. That a proper education; or, to speak with more precision, a well stored mind, would enable a woman to support a single life with dignity, I grant; but that she should avoid cultivating her taste, lest her husband should occasionally shock it, is quitting a substance for a shadow. To say the truth, I do not know of what use is an improved taste, if the individual be not rendered more independent of the casualties of life; if new sources of enjoyment, only dependent on the solitary operations of the mind, are not opened. People of taste, married or single, without distinction, will ever be disgusted by various things that touch not less observing minds. On this conclusion the argument must not be allowed to hinge; but in the whole sum of enjoyment is taste to be denominated a blessing?

The question is, whether it procures most pain or pleasure? The answer will decide the propriety of Dr. Gregory's advice, and shew how absurd and tyrannic it is thus to lay down a system of slavery; or to attempt to educate moral beings by any other rules than those deduced from pure reason, which apply to the whole species.

Gentleness of manners, forbearance and long-suffering, are such amiable Godlike qualities, that in sublime poetic strains the Deity has been invested with them; and, perhaps, no representation of his goodness so strongly fastens on the human affections as those that

---

6. An echo of Philippians 3:14, where Saint Paul writes, "I press toward the mark for the prize of the high calling of God in Christ Jesus."
7. "For example, the herd of Novelists" [Wollstonecraft's note].

represent him abundant in mercy and willing to pardon.[8] Gentleness, considered in this point of view, bears on its front all the characteristics of grandeur, combined with the winning graces of condescension; but what a different aspect it assumes when it is the submissive demeanour of dependence, the support of weakness that loves, because it wants protection; and is forbearing, because it must silently endure injuries; smiling under the lash at which it dare not snarl. Abject as this picture appears, it is the portrait of an accomplished woman, according to the received opinion of female excellence, separated by specious reasoners from human excellence. Or, they[9] kindly restore the rib, and make one moral being of a man and woman; not forgetting to give her all the 'submissive charms.'[1]

How women are to exist in that state where there is to be neither marrying nor giving in marriage, we are not told.[2] For though moralists have agreed that the tenor of life seems to prove that *man* is prepared by various circumstances for a future state, they constantly concur in advising *woman* only to provide for the present. Gentleness, docility, and a spaniel-like affection are, on this ground, consistently recommended as the cardinal virtues of the sex; and, disregarding the arbitrary economy of nature, one writer has declared that it is masculine for a woman to be melancholy.[3] She was created to be the toy of man, his rattle, and it must jingle in his ears whenever, dismissing reason, he chooses to be amused.

To recommend gentleness, indeed, on a broad basis is strictly philosophical. A frail being should labour to be gentle. But when forbearance confounds right and wrong, it ceases to be a virtue; and, however convenient it may be found in a companion—that companion will ever be considered as an inferior, and only inspire a vapid tenderness, which easily degenerates into contempt. Still, if advice could really make a being gentle, whose natural disposition admitted not of such a fine polish, something towards the advancement of order would be attained; but if, as might quickly be demonstrated, only affectation be produced by this indiscriminate counsel, which

8. Isaiah 55:7: "And he will have mercy upon him; and to our God, for he will abundantly pardon."
9. "Vide Rousseau, and Swedenborg" [Wollstonecraft's note]. For Rousseau's denial of independent moral agency to women, see the passage from Book v of *Émile* that Wollstonecraft cites on p. 95 herein. The Swedish mystic Emmanuel Swedenborg (1688–1772) believed that in the afterlife each married couple would form a single angel, with the wife contributing her capacity for love and the husband his wisdom.
1. *Paradise Lost* IV. 497–99: "he in delight / Both of her Beauty and submissive charms / Smil'd with superior love."
2. An echo of Jesus' account of the resurrection in Matthew 22:30.
3. Perhaps a recollection of Edmund Burke's *Philosophical Enquiry into the Origins of Our Ideas of the Sublime and the Beautiful* (1757). In attempting to distinguish the aesthetic category of "the beautiful" from the aesthetic category of "the sublime," Burke resorts frequently to analogy and so devotes many pages to outlining his notions of the distinctions that separate femininity from masculinity.

throws a stumbling-block in the way of gradual improvement, and true melioration of temper, the sex is not much benefited by sacrificing solid virtues to the attainment of superficial graces, though for a few years they may procure the individuals regal sway.

As a philosopher, I read with indignation the plausible epithets which men use to soften their insults; and, as a moralist, I ask what is meant by such heterogeneous associations, as fair defects, amiable weaknesses, &c.?[4] If there be but one criterion of morals, but one archetype for man, women appear to be suspended by destiny, according to the vulgar tale of Mahomet's coffin;[5] they have neither the unerring instinct of brutes, nor are allowed to fix the eye of reason on a perfect model. They were made to be loved, and must not aim at respect, lest they should be hunted out of society as masculine.

But to view the subject in another point of view. Do passive indolent women make the best wives? Confining our discussion to the present moment of existence, let us see how such weak creatures perform their part? Do the women who, by the attainment of a few superficial accomplishments, have strengthened the prevailing prejudice, merely contribute to the happiness of their husbands? Do they display their charms merely to amuse them? And have women, who have early imbibed notions of passive obedience, sufficient character to manage a family or educate children? So far from it, that, after surveying the history of woman, I cannot help, agreeing with the severest satirist, considering the sex as the weakest as well as the most oppressed half of the species. What does history disclose but marks of inferiority, and how few women have emancipated themselves from the galling yoke of sovereign man?—So few, that the exceptions remind me of an ingenious conjecture respecting Newton: that he was probably a being of a superior order, accidentally caged in a human body.[6] Following the same train of thinking, I have been led to imagine that the few extraordinary women who have rushed in eccentrical directions out of the orbit prescribed to their sex, were *male* spirits, confined by mistake in female frames. But if it be not philosophical to think of sex when the soul is mentioned, the inferiority must depend on the organs; or the heavenly fire, which is to ferment the clay, is not given in equal portions.

4. *Paradise Lost* X.891–92: "This fair defect / Of nature"; and Pope, "Of the Characters of Women," line 44: "Fine by defect, and delicately weak."
5. Wollstonecraft refers to a discredited European legend maintaining that at Mohammed's tomb in Medina giant magnets were used to suspend his coffin in midair.
6. Possibly a reference to Pope's 1733–34 *Essay on Man*, Epistle II, lines 31–34: "Superior beings, when of late they saw / A mortal Man unfold all Nature's law, / Admir'd such wisdom in an earthly shape, / And shew'd a NEWTON as we shew an Ape." Isaac Newton (1643–1727) was revered across Europe for his foundational work of physics, the *Principia* (1687), in which he formulated the laws of gravitation and motion. See also James Thomson's 1727 "A Poem Sacred to the Memory of Sir Isaac Newton," lines 161–65.

Allow women to be people and see where they really see where the sex stands

But avoiding, as I have hitherto done, any direct comparison of the two sexes collectively, or frankly acknowledging the inferiority of woman, according to the present appearance of things, I shall only insist that men have increased that inferiority till women are almost sunk below the standard of rational creatures. Let their faculties have room to unfold, and their virtues to gain strength, and then determine where the whole sex must stand in the intellectual scale. Yet let it be remembered, that for a small number of distinguished women I do not ask a place.

It is difficult for us purblind mortals to say to what height human discoveries and improvements may arrive when the gloom of despotism subsides, which makes us stumble at every step; but, when morality shall be settled on a more solid basis, then, without being gifted with a prophetic spirit, I will venture to predict that woman will be either the friend or slave of man. We shall not, as at present, doubt whether she is a moral agent, or the link which unites man with brutes. But, should it then appear, that like the brutes they were principally created for the use of man, he will let them patiently bite the bridle, and not mock them with empty praise; or, should their rationality be proved, he will not impede their improvement merely to gratify his sensual appetites. He will not, with all the graces of rhetoric, advise them to submit implicitly their understanding to the guidance of man. He will not, when he treats of the education of women, assert that they ought never to have the free use of reason, nor would he recommend cunning and dissimulation to beings who are acquiring, in like manner as himself, the virtues of humanity.

Surely there can be but one rule of right, if morality has an eternal foundation, and whoever sacrifices virtue, strictly so called, to present convenience, or whose *duty* it is to act in such a manner, lives only for the passing day, and cannot be an accountable creature.

The poet then should have dropped his sneer when he says,

> "If weak women go astray,
> "The stars are more in fault than they."[7]

For that they are bound by the adamantine chain of destiny is most certain, if it be proved that they are never to exercise their own reason, never to be independent, never to rise above opinion, or to feel the dignity of a rational will that only bows to God, and often forgets that the universe contains any being but itself and the model of perfection to which its ardent gaze is turned, to adore attributes that, softened into virtues, may be imitated in kind, though the degree overwhelms the enraptured mind.

---

7. Matthew Prior, "Hans Carvel" (1700), lines 11–12.

If, I say, for I would not impress by declamation when Reason offers her sober light, if they be really capable of acting like rational creatures, let them not be treated like slaves; or, like the brutes who are dependent on the reason of man, when they associate with him; but cultivate their minds, give them the salutary, sublime curb of principle, and let them attain conscious dignity by feeling themselves only dependent on God. Teach them, in common with man, to submit to necessity, instead of giving, to render them more pleasing, a sex to morals.

Let it be proven that Women really are at the level of men

Further, should experience prove that they cannot attain the same degree of strength of mind, perseverance, and fortitude, let their virtues be the same in kind, though they may vainly struggle for the same degree; and the superiority of man will be equally clear, if not clearer; and truth, as it is a simple principle, which admits of no modification, would be common to both. Nay, the order of society as it is at present regulated would not be inverted, for woman would then only have the rank that reason assigned her, and arts could not be practised to bring the balance even, much less to turn it.

men shouldn't fear Women being Superior

These may be termed Utopian dreams.—Thanks to that Being who impressed them on my soul, and gave me sufficient strength of mind to dare to exert my own reason, till, becoming dependent only on him for the support of my virtue, I view, with indignation, the mistaken notions that enslave my sex.

I love man as my fellow; but his scepter, real, or usurped, extends not to me, unless the reason of an individual demands my homage; and even then the submission is to reason, and not to man. In fact, the conduct of an accountable being must be regulated by the operations of its own reason; or on what foundation rests the throne of God?

It appears to me necessary to dwell on these obvious truths, because females have been insulated, as it were; and, while they have been stripped of the virtues that should clothe humanity, they have been decked with artificial graces that enable them to exercise a short-lived tyranny. Love, in their bosoms, taking place of every nobler passion, their sole ambition is to be fair, to raise emotion instead of inspiring respect; and this ignoble desire, like the servility in absolute monarchies, destroys all strength of character. Liberty is the mother of virtue, and if women be, by their very constitution, slaves, and not allowed to breathe the sharp invigorating air of freedom, they must ever languish like exotics,[8] and be reckoned beautiful flaws in nature.

8. Hothouse plants, which do not thrive in the English climate. Wollstonecraft also echoes here the language of the *Mansfield Judgment* of 1772, the legal decision that prohibited slavery within England by declaring "the air of England . . . too pure for slaves to breathe in."

As to the argument respecting the subjection in which the sex has ever been held, it retorts on man. The many have always been enthralled by the few; and monsters, who scarcely have shewn any discernment of human excellence, have tyrannized over thousands of their fellow-creatures. Why have men of superiour endowments submitted to such degradation? For, is it not universally acknowledged that kings, viewed collectively, have ever been inferior, in abilities and virtue, to the same number of men taken from the common mass of mankind—yet, have they not, and are they not still treated with a degree of reverence that is an insult to reason? China is not the only country where a living man has been made a God.[9] *Men* have submitted to superior strength to enjoy with impunity the pleasure of the moment—*women* have only done the same, and therefore till it is proved that the courtier, who servilely resigns the birthright of a man, is not a moral agent, it cannot be demonstrated that woman is essentially inferior to man because she has always been subjugated.

Brutal force has hitherto governed the world, and that the science of politics is in its infancy, is evident from philosophers scrupling to give the knowledge most useful to man that determinate distinction.

I shall not pursue this argument any further than to establish an obvious inference, that as sound politics diffuse liberty, mankind, including woman, will become more wise and virtuous.

Chap. III

The Same Subject Continued

Bodily strength from being the distinction of heroes is now sunk into such unmerited contempt that men, as well as women, seem to think it unnecessary: the latter, as it takes from their feminine graces, and from that lovely weakness the source of their undue power; and the former, because it appears inimical to the character of a gentleman.

That they have both by departing from one extreme run into another, may easily be proved; but first it may be proper to observe, that a vulgar error has obtained a degree of credit, which has given force to a false conclusion, in which an effect has been mistaken for a cause.

People of genius have, very frequently, impaired their constitutions by study or careless inattention to their health, and the

---

9. The emperors of China were known as the "sons of heaven."

violence of their passions bearing a proportion to the vigour of their intellects, the sword's destroying the scabbard has become almost proverbial,[1] and superficial observers have inferred from thence, that men of genius have commonly weak, or, to use a more fashionable phrase, delicate constitutions. Yet the contrary, I believe, will appear to be the fact; for, on diligent inquiry, I find that strength of mind has, in most cases, been accompanied by superior strength of body,—natural soundness of constitution,—not that robust tone of nerves and vigour of muscles, which arise from bodily labour, when the mind is quiescent, or only directs the hands.

Dr. Priestley has remarked, in the preface to his biographical chart,[2] that the majority of great men have lived beyond forty-five. And, considering the thoughtless manner in which they have lavished their strength, when investigating a favourite science they have wasted the lamp of life, forgetful of the midnight hour; or, when, lost in poetic dreams, fancy has peopled the scene, and the soul has been disturbed, till it shook the constitution, by the passions that meditation had raised; whose objects, the baseless fabric of a vision,[3] faded before the exhausted eye, they must have had iron frames. Shakspeare never grasped the airy dagger with a nerveless[4] hand, nor did Milton tremble when he led Satan far from the confines of his dreary prison.—These were not the ravings of imbecility, the sickly effusions of distempered brains; but the exuberance of fancy, that 'in a fine phrenzy'[5] wandering, was not continually reminded of its material shackles.

I am aware that this argument would carry me further than it may be supposed I wish to go; but I follow truth, and, still adhering to my first position, I will allow that bodily strength seems to give man a natural superiority over woman; and this is the only solid basis on which the superiority of the sex can be built. But I still insist, that not only the virtue, but the *knowledge* of the two sexes should be the same in nature, if not in degree, and that women, considered not only as moral, but rational creatures, ought to endeavour to acquire human virtues (or perfections) by the *same* means as men, instead of

where did men gain intell. superiority as well

---

1. "The sword wears out the scabbard. . . . That is my story. My passions have made me live, and my passions have killed me" (Rousseau, *The Confessions*, trans. Christopher Kelly, vol. 5 of *Collected Writings of Rousseau* [Hanover, N.H., 1995], p. 183).
2. Joseph Priestley's *Description of a Chart of Biography* (London, 1765) represented the lives of historical figures by means of lines arrayed against a scale of 2,950 years. It was, in fact, one of the earliest time lines and popularized this now-familiar mode of encoding information.
3. *The Tempest* IV.i.151: "Like the baseless fabric of this vision."
4. I.e., without strength (Johnson's *Dictionary*). "Airy dagger": *Macbeth* III.iv.62–63: "This is the air-drawn dagger which, you said, led you to Duncan."
5. A *Midsummer Night's Dream* V.i.12: "The poet's eye, in a fine frenzy rolling."

being educated like a fanciful kind of *half* being—one of Rousseau's wild chimeras.[6]

But, if strength of body be, with some shew of reason, the boast of men, why are women so infatuated as to be proud of a defect? Rousseau has furnished them with a plausible excuse, which could only have occurred to a man, whose imagination had been allowed to run wild, and refine on the impressions made by exquisite senses;— that they might, forsooth, have a pretext for yielding to a natural appetite without violating a romantic species of modesty, which gratifies the pride and libertinism of man.

Women, deluded by these sentiments, sometimes boast of their weakness, cunningly obtaining power by playing on the *weakness* of men; and they may well glory in their illicit sway, for, like Turkish bashaws,[7] they have more real power than their masters: but virtue is sacrificed to temporary gratifications, and the respectability of life to the triumph of an hour.

Women, as well as despots, have now, perhaps, more power than they would have if the world, divided and subdivided into kingdoms

6. "'Researches into abstract and speculative truths, the principles and axioms of sciences, in short, every thing which tends to generalize our ideas, is not the proper province of women; their studies should be relative to points of practice; it belongs to them to apply those principles which men have discovered; and it is their part to make observations, which direct men to the establishment of general principles. All the ideas of women, which have not the immediate tendency to points of duty, should be directed to the study of men, and to the attainment of those agreeable accomplishments which have taste for their object; for as to works of genius, they are beyond their capacity; neither have they sufficient precision or power of attention to succeed in sciences which require accuracy: and as to physical knowledge, it belongs to those only who are most active, most inquisitive; who comprehend the greatest variety of objects: in short, it belongs to those who have the strongest powers, and who exercise them most, to judge of the relations between sensible beings and the laws of nature. A woman who is naturally weak, and does not carry her ideas to any great extent, knows how to judge and make a proper estimate of those movements which she sets to work, in order to aid her weakness; and these movements are the passions of men. The mechanism she employs is much more powerful than ours; for all her levers move the human heart. She must have the skill to incline us to do every thing which her sex will not enable her to do herself, and which is necessary or agreeable to her; therefore she ought to study the mind of man thoroughly, not the mind of man in general, abstractedly, but the dispositions of those men to whom she is subject, either by the laws of her country or by the force of opinion. She should learn to penetrate into their real sentiments from their conversation, their actions, their looks, and gestures. She should also have the art, by her own conversation, actions, looks, and gestures, to communicate those sentiments which are agreeable to them, without seeming to intend it. Men will argue more philosophically about the human heart; but women will read the heart of man better than they. It belongs to women, if I may be allowed the expression, to form an experimental morality, and to reduce the study of man to a system. Women have most wit, men have most genius; women observe, men reason: from the concurrence of both we derive the clearest light and the most perfect knowledge, which the human mind is, of itself, capable of attaining. In one word, from hence we acquire the most intimate acquaintance, both with ourselves and others, of which our nature is capable; and it is thus that art has a constant tendency to perfect those endowments which nature has bestowed,—The world is the book of women.' Rousseau's Emilius. I hope my readers still remember the comparison, which I have brought forward, between women and officers" [Wollstonecraft's note]. The quotation is from *Emilius* IV, v, pp. 74–75.
7. An older term for *pashas*: Turkish officers of high rank, notorious in Wollstonecraft's era for their tyranny.

and families, were governed by laws deduced from the exercise of reason; but in obtaining it, to carry on the comparison, their character is degraded, and licentiousness spread through the whole aggregate of society. The many become pedestal to the few. I, therefore, will venture to assert, that till women are more rationally educated, the progress of human virtue and improvement in knowledge must receive continual checks. And if it be granted that woman was not created merely to gratify the appetite of man, or to be the upper servant, who provides his meals and takes care of his linen, it must follow, that the first care of those mothers or fathers, who really attend to the education of females, should be, if not to strengthen the body, at least, not to destroy the constitution by mistaken notions of beauty and female excellence; nor should girls ever be allowed to imbibe the pernicious notion that a defect can, by any chemical process of reasoning, become an excellence. In this respect, I am happy to find, that the author of one of the most instructive books, that our country has produced for children, coincides with me in opinion; I shall quote his pertinent remarks to give the force of his respectable authority to reason.[8]

But should it be proved that woman is naturally weaker than man, whence does it follow that it is natural for her to labour to become still weaker than nature intended her to be? Arguments of this cast are an insult to common sense, and savour of passion. The *divine*

---

8. "A respectable old man gives the following sensible account of the method he pursued when educating his daughter. 'I endeavoured to give both to her mind and body a degree of vigour, which is seldom found in the female sex. As soon as she was sufficiently advanced in strength to be capable of the lighter labours of husbandry and gardening, I employed her as my constant companion. Selene, for that was her name, soon acquired a dexterity in all these rustic employments, which I considered with equal pleasure and admiration. If women are in general feeble both in body and mind, it arises less from nature than from education. We encourage a vicious indolence and inactivity, which we falsely call delicacy; instead of hardening their minds by the severer principles of reason and philosophy, we breed them to useless arts, which terminate in vanity and sensuality. In most of the countries which I had visited, they are taught nothing of an higher nature than a few modulations of the voice, or useless postures of the body; their time is consumed in sloth or trifles, and trifles become the only pursuits capable of interesting them. We seem to forget, that it is upon the qualities of the female sex that our own domestic comforts and the education of our children must depend. And what are the comforts or the education which a race of beings, corrupted from their infancy, and unacquainted with all the duties of life, are fitted to bestow? To touch a musical instrument with useless skill, to exhibit their natural or affected graces to the eyes of indolent and debauched young men, to dissipate their husband's patrimony in riotous and unnecessary expences, these are the only arts cultivated by women in most of the polished nations I had seen. And the consequences are uniformly such as may be expected to proceed from such polluted sources, private misery and public servitude.

"'But Selene's education was regulated by different views, and conducted upon severer principles; if that can be called severity which opens the mind to a sense of moral and religious duties, and most effectually arms it against the inevitable evils of life.' Mr. Day's *Sandford and Merton*, Vol. III" [Wollstonecraft's note].

The quoted selection is from "The Conclusion of the Story of Sophron and Tigranes." One of several didactic narratives in Day's work, this one is about a wise old man, Chares, who, after a life of adventure, settles down to domesticity. He explains how his only child, a daughter, is to be raised.

right of husbands, like the divine right of kings,[9] may, it is to be hoped, in this enlightened age, be contested without danger, and, though conviction may not silence many boisterous disputants, yet, when any prevailing prejudice is attacked, the wise will consider, and leave the narrow-minded to rail with thoughtless vehemence at innovation.

The mother, who wishes to give true dignity of character to her daughter, must, regardless of the sneers of ignorance, proceed on a plan diametrically opposite to that which Rousseau has recommended with all the deluding charms of eloquence and philosophical sophistry: for his eloquence renders absurdities plausible, and his dogmatic conclusions puzzle, without convincing, those who have not ability to refute them.

Throughout the whole animal kingdom every young creature requires almost continual exercise, and the infancy of children, conformable to this intimation, should be passed in harmless gambols, that exercise the feet and hands, without requiring very minute direction from the head, or the constant attention of a nurse. In fact, the care necessary for self-preservation is the first natural exercise of the understanding, as little inventions to amuse the present moment unfold the imagination. But these wise designs of nature are counteracted by mistaken fondness or blind zeal. The child is not left a moment to its own direction, particularly a girl, and thus rendered dependent—dependence is called natural.

To preserve personal beauty, woman's glory! the limbs and faculties are cramped with worse than Chinese bands,[1] and the sedentary life which they are condemned to live, whilst boys frolic in the open air, weakens the muscles and relaxes the nerves.—As for Rousseau's remarks, which have since been echoed by several writers, that they have naturally, that is from their birth, independent of education, a fondness for dolls, dressing, and talking[2]—they are so puerile as not to merit a serious refutation. That a girl, condemned to sit for hours together listening to the idle chat of weak nurses, or to attend at her mother's toilet, will endeavour to join the conversation, is, indeed, very natural; and that she will imitate her mother or aunts, and amuse herself by adorning her lifeless doll, as they do in dressing

---

9. The belief that monarchs were not answerable to the people but derived their authority from God alone and, by extension, that the disputing of the will of a monarch was tantamount to a blasphemous disputing of the will of God. The belief was the cornerstone of royalist political thought in seventeenth-century England.

1. Up to the early twentieth century in China elite families would bind their daughters' feet to keep them small and dainty.

2. "The doll is the peculiar amusement of the females" (*Emilius,* IV, v, p. 25). "Girls are from their earliest infancy fond of dress. Not content with being pretty, they are desirous of being thought so; we see, by all their little airs, that this thought engages their attention" (IV, v, p. 21). "[G]irls . . . early acquire an agreeable mode of prattle . . . they are emphatic in their discourse, even before they well know what they say" (IV, v, p. 45).

her, poor innocent babe! is undoubtedly a most natural conse-quence. For men of the greatest abilities have seldom had sufficient strength to rise above the surrounding atmosphere; and, if the page of genius have always been blurred by the prejudices of the age, some allowance should be made for a sex, who, like kings, always see things through a false medium.

Pursuing these reflections, the fondness for dress, conspicuous in women, may be easily accounted for, without supposing it the result of a desire to please the sex on which they are dependent. The absurdity, in short, of supposing that a girl is naturally a coquette, and that a desire connected with the impulse of nature to propagate the species,[3] should appear even before an improper education has, by heating the imagination, called it forth prematurely, is so unphilosophical, that such a sagacious observer as Rousseau would not have adopted it, if he had not been accustomed to make reason give way to his desire of singularity, and truth to a favourite paradox.

Yet thus to give a sex to mind was not very consistent with the principles of a man who argued so warmly, and so well, for the immortality of the soul.[4]—But what a weak barrier is truth when it stands in the way of an hypothesis! Rousseau respected—almost adored virtue—and yet he allowed himself to love with sensual fond-ness. His imagination constantly prepared inflammable fewel[5] for his inflammable senses; but, in order to reconcile his respect for self-denial, fortitude, and those heroic virtues, which a mind like his could not coolly admire, he labours to invert the law of nature, and broaches a doctrine pregnant with mischief and derogatory to the character of supreme wisdom.[6]

His ridiculous stories, which tend to prove that girls are *naturally* attentive to their persons,[7] without laying any stress on daily ex-ample, are below contempt.—And that a little miss should have such a correct taste as to neglect the pleasing amusement of making O's, merely because she perceived that it was an ungraceful attitude, should be selected with the anecdotes of the learned pig.[8]

3. "Woman is by her situation a coquette, but her coquetry changes its form and object according to her views: let us regulate these views, therefore, by those of nature, and women will be properly educated" (*Emilius*, IV, v, p. 21).
4. In Book iv of *Emile*, "The Creed of a Savoyard Priest" summarizes Rousseau's argument for the immortality of the soul.
5. A common eighteenth-century variant for *fuel*.
6. Wollstonecraft's charge here seems to be that Rousseau, because he himself had passions that he found hard to discipline, needed to think that women were natural coquettes to justify his own selfish, sensual use of them.
7. I.e., their physical appearance.
8. "'I once knew a young person who learned to write before she learned to read, and began to write with her needle before she could use a pen. At first, indeed, she took it into her head to make no other letter than the O: this letter she was constantly making of all sizes, and always the wrong way. Unluckily, one day, as she was intent on this employment, she happened to see herself in the looking-glass; when, taking a dislike to the constrained

I have, probably, had an opportunity of observing more girls in their infancy than J. J. Rousseau—I can recollect my own feelings, and I have looked steadily around me; yet, so far from coinciding with him in opinion respecting the first dawn of the female character, I will venture to affirm, that a girl, whose spirits have not been damped by inactivity, or innocence tainted by false shame, will always be a romp, and the doll will never excite attention unless confinement allows her no alternative. Girls and boys, in short, would play harmlessly together, if the distinction of sex was not inculcated long before nature makes any difference.—I will go further, and affirm, as an indisputable fact, that most of the women, in the circle of my observation, who have acted like rational creatures, or shewn any vigour of intellect, have accidentally been allowed to run wild—as some of the elegant formers of the fair sex would insinuate.

The baneful consequences which flow from inattention to health during infancy, and youth, extend further than is supposed—dependence of body naturally produces dependence of mind; and how can she be a good wife or mother, the greater part of whose time is employed to guard against or endure sickness? Nor can it be expected that a woman will resolutely endeavour to strengthen her constitution and abstain from enervating indulgencies, if artificial notions of beauty, and false descriptions of sensibility,[9] have been early entangled with her motives of action. Most men are sometimes obliged to bear with bodily inconveniencies, and to endure, occasionally, the inclemency of the elements; but genteel women are, literally speaking, slaves to their bodies, and glory in their subjection.

I once knew a weak woman of fashion, who was more than commonly proud of her delicacy and sensibility. She thought a distinguishing taste and puny appetite the height of all human perfection, and acted accordingly.—I have seen this weak sophisticated being neglect all the duties of life, yet recline with self-complacency on

attitude in which she sat while writing, she threw away her pen, like another Pallas, and determined against making the O any more. Her brother was also equally adverse to writing: it was the confinement, however, and not the constrained attitude, that most disgusted him.' *Rousseau's Emilius*" [Wollstonecraft's note]. The quotation is from *Emilius* IV, v, p. 29.

The learned pig was exhibited across England during the 1780s. Chapter IX of Sarah Trimmer's *Fabulous Histories* (1784) describes how the animal appeared to pick out letters of the alphabet so as to spell words and to tell time by nosing the numbers on a large clock.

9. Often celebrated in literature and probed in scientific discussions of the human nervous system, "sensibility" was a much debated concept during Wollstonecraft's lifetime: the mania "of the day," she declares in the first *Vindication* ([London, 1790], p. 5). Beginning in the mid-eighteenth century the term had come to designate certain individuals' special capacity for refined feeling and readiness to be moved emotionally. This emotional responsiveness was often identified with compassion for suffering and so assessed favorably as a source of social stability, but the relationship between sensibility and the exercise of reason, as between sensibility and sincerity, worries Wollstonecraft throughout both her *Vindications*.

a sofa, and boast of her want of appetite as a proof of delicacy that extended to, or, perhaps, arose from, her exquisite sensibility: for it is difficult to render intelligible such ridiculous jargon.—Yet, at the moment, I have seen her insult a worthy old gentlewoman, whom unexpected misfortunes had made dependent on her ostentatious bounty, and who, in better days, had claims on her gratitude. Is it possible that a human creature could have become such a weak and depraved being, if, like the Sybarites,[1] dissolved in luxury, every thing like virtue had not been worn away, or never impressed by precept, a poor substitute, it is true, for cultivation of mind, though it serves as a fence against vice?

Such a woman is not a more irrational monster than some of the Roman emperors, who were depraved by lawless power. Yet, since kings have been more under the restraint of law, and the curb, however weak, of honour, the records of history are not filled with such unnatural instances of folly and cruelty, nor does the despotism that kills virtue and genius in the bud, hover over Europe with that destructive blast which desolates Turkey,[2] and renders the men, as well as the soil, unfruitful.

Women are every where in this deplorable state; for, in order to preserve their innocence, as ignorance is courteously termed, truth is hidden from them, and they are made to assume an artificial character before their faculties have acquired any strength. Taught from their infancy that beauty is woman's sceptre, the mind shapes itself to the body, and, roaming round its gilt cage, only seeks to adorn its prison. Men have various employments and pursuits which engage their attention, and give a character to the opening mind; but women, confined to one, and having their thoughts constantly directed to the most insignificant part of themselves, seldom extend their views beyond the triumph of the hour. But were their understanding once emancipated from the slavery to which the pride and sensuality of man and their short-sighted desire, like that of dominion in tyrants, of present sway, has subjected them, we should probably read of their weaknesses with surprise. I must be allowed to pursue the argument a little farther.

Perhaps, if the existence of an evil being were allowed, who, in the allegorical language of scripture, went about seeking whom he should devour,[3] he could not more effectually degrade the human character than by giving a man absolute power.

1. Inhabitants of Sybaris, an ancient Greek city located in southern Italy, famed for its life of ease and voluptuousness.
2. The hot south wind, known as the simoom or simoon and believed especially unhealthy, here is a symbol of the debilitating effects that despotic rule produced within the Ottoman Empire.
3. 1 Peter 5:8: "Be sober, be vigilant; because your adversary the devil, as a roaring lion, walketh about, seeking whom he may devour."

This argument branches into various ramifications.—Birth, riches, and every extrinsic advantage that exalt a man above his fellows, without any mental exertion, sink him in reality below them. In proportion to his weakness, he is played upon by designing men, till the bloated monster has lost all traces of humanity. And that tribes of men, like flocks of sheep, should quietly follow such a leader, is a solecism that only a desire of present enjoyment and narrowness of understanding can solve. Educated in slavish dependence, and enervated by luxury and sloth, where shall we find men who will stand forth to assert the rights of man;—or claim the privilege of moral beings, who should have but one road to excellence? Slavery to monarchs and ministers, which the world will be long in freeing itself from, and whose deadly grasp stops the progress of the human mind, is not yet abolished.

Let not men then in the pride of power, use the same arguments that tyrannic kings and venal ministers have used, and fallaciously assert that woman ought to be subjected because she has always been so.—But, when man, governed by reasonable laws, enjoys his natural freedom, let him despise woman, if she do not share it with him; and, till that glorious period arrives, in descanting on the folly of the sex, let him not overlook his own.

Women, it is true, obtaining power by unjust means, by practising or fostering vice, evidently lose the rank which reason would assign them, and they become either abject slaves or capricious tyrants. They lose all simplicity, all dignity of mind, in acquiring power, and act as men are observed to act when they have been exalted by the same means.

It is time to effect a revolution in female manners—time to restore to them their lost dignity—and make them, as a part of the human species, labour by reforming themselves to reform the world. It is time to separate unchangeable morals from local manners.—If men be demi-gods—why let us serve them! And if the dignity of the female soul be as disputable as that of animals—if their reason does not afford sufficient light to direct their conduct whilst unerring instinct is denied—they are surely of all creatures the most miserable! and, bent beneath the iron hand of destiny, must submit to be a *fair defect* in creation. But to justify the ways of Providence respecting them,[4] by pointing out some irrefragable reason for thus making such a large portion of mankind accountable and not accountable, would puzzle the subtilest casuist.

The only solid foundation for morality appears to be the character of the supreme Being; the harmony of which arises from a balance

---

4. *Paradise Lost* I.25–26: "I may assert Eternal Providence, / And justify the ways of God to men."

of attributes;—and, to speak with reverence, one attribute seems to imply the *necessity* of another. He must be just, because he is wise, he must be good, because he is omnipotent. For to exalt one attribute at the expence of another equally noble and necessary, bears the stamp of the warped reason of man—the homage of passion. Man, accustomed to bow down to power in his savage state, can seldom divest himself of this barbarous prejudice, even when civilization determines how much superior mental is to bodily strength; and his reason is clouded by these crude opinions, even when he thinks of the Deity.—His omnipotence is made to swallow up, or preside over his other attributes, and those mortals are supposed to limit his power irreverently, who think that it must be regulated by his wisdom.

I disclaim that specious humility which, after investigating nature, stops at the author.—The High and Lofty One, who inhabiteth eternity, doubtless possesses many attributes of which we can form no conception; but reason tells me that they cannot clash with those I adore—and I am compelled to listen to her voice.

It seems natural for man to search for excellence, and either to trace it in the object that he worships, or blindly to invest it with perfection, as a garment. But what good effect can the latter mode of worship have on the moral conduct of a rational being? He bends to power; he adores a dark cloud, which may open a bright prospect to him, or burst in angry, lawless fury, on his devoted head—he knows not why. And, supposing that the Deity acts from the vague impulse of an undirected will, man must also follow his own, or act according to rules, deduced from principles which he disclaims as irreverent. Into this dilemma have both enthusiasts and cooler thinkers fallen, when they laboured to free men from the wholesome restraints which a just conception of the character of God imposes.

It is not impious thus to scan the attributes of the Almighty: in fact, who can avoid it that exercises his faculties? For to love God as the fountain of wisdom, goodness, and power, appears to be the only worship useful to a being who wishes to acquire either virtue or knowledge. A blind unsettled affection may, like human passions, occupy the mind and warm the heart, whilst, to do justice, love mercy, and walk humbly with our God, is forgotten.[5] I shall pursue this subject still further, when I consider religion in a light opposite to that recommended by Dr. Gregory, who treats it as a matter of sentiment or taste.[6]

To return from this apparent digression. It were to be wished that women would cherish an affection for their husbands, founded on

5. Micah 6:8: "What doth the Lord require of thee, but to do justly, and to love mercy, and to walk humbly with thy God?"
6. "Religion is rather a matter of sentiment than reasoning" (Gregory, p. 13).

the same principle that devotion ought to rest upon. No other firm
base is there under heaven—for let them beware of the fallacious
light of sentiment; too often used as a softer phrase for sensuality. It
follows then, I think, that from their infancy women should either
be shut up like eastern princes, or educated in such a manner as to
be able to think and act for themselves.

Why do men halt between two opinions, and expect impossibil-
ities? Why do they expect virtue from a slave, from a being whom the
constitution of civil society has rendered weak, if not vicious?

Still I know that it will require a considerable length of time to
eradicate the firmly rooted prejudices which sensualists have planted;
it will also require some time to convince women that they act contrary to their real interest on an enlarged scale, when they cherish or
affect weakness under the name of delicacy, and to convince the
world that the poisoned source of female vices and follies, if it be
necessary, in compliance with custom, to use synonymous terms in
a lax sense, has been the sensual homage paid to beauty:—to beauty
of features; for it has been shrewdly observed by a German writer,
that a pretty woman, as an object of desire, is generally allowed to be
so by men of all descriptions; whilst a fine woman, who inspires
more sublime emotions by displaying intellectual beauty, may be
overlooked or observed with indifference, by those men who find
their happiness in the gratification of their appetites.[7] I foresee an
obvious retort—whilst man remains such an imperfect being as he
appears hitherto to have been, he will, more or less, be the slave of
his appetites; and those women obtaining most power who gratify a
predominant one, the sex is degraded by a physical, if not by a moral
necessity.

This objection has, I grant, some force; but while such a sublime
precept exists, as, 'be pure as your heavenly Father is pure;'[8] it would
seem that the virtues of man are not limited by the Being who alone
could limit them; and that he may press forward without considering
whether he steps out of his sphere by indulging such a noble ambition. To the wild billows it has been said, 'thus far shalt thou go, and
no further; and here shall thy proud waves be stayed.'[9] Vainly then
do they beat and foam, restrained by the power that confines the
struggling planets in their orbits, matter yields to the great governing
Spirit.—But an immortal soul, not restrained by mechanical laws[1]
and struggling to free itself from the shackles of matter, contributes

7. Immanuel Kant's 1764 *Observations on the Feeling on the Beautiful and Sublime* (trans.
   John T. Goldthwait [Berkeley, 1960], pp. 89–90).
8. Matthew 5:48: "Be ye therefore perfect, even as your Father which is in heaven is
   perfect."
9. Job 38:11.
1. The laws pertaining to physical conditions.

to, instead of disturbing, the order of creation, when, co-operating with the Father of spirits, it tries to govern itself by the invariable rule that, in a degree, before which our imagination faints, regulates the universe.

Besides, if women be educated for dependence; that is, to act according to the will of another fallible being, and submit, right or wrong, to power, where are we to stop? Are they to be considered as viceregents allowed to reign over a small domain, and answerable for their conduct to a higher tribunal, liable to error?

It will not be difficult to prove that such delegates will act like men subjected by fear, and make their children and servants endure their tyrannical oppression. As they submit without reason, they will, having no fixed rules to square their conduct by, be kind, or cruel, just as the whim of the moment directs; and we ought not to wonder if sometimes, galled by their heavy yoke, they take a malignant pleasure in resting it on weaker shoulders.

But, supposing a woman, trained up to obedience, be married to a sensible man, who directs her judgment without making her feel the servility of her subjection, to act with as much propriety by this reflected light as can be expected when reason is taken at second hand, yet she cannot ensure the life of her protector; he may die and leave her with a large family.

A double duty devolves on her; to educate them in the character of both father and mother; to form their principles and secure their property. But, alas! she has never thought, much less acted for herself. She has only learned to please[2] men, to depend gracefully on them; yet, encumbered with children, how is she to obtain another protector—a husband to supply the place of reason? A rational man,

2. "'In the union of the sexes, both pursue one common object, but not in the same manner. From their diversity in this particular, arises the first determinate difference between the moral relations of each. The one should be active and strong, the other passive and weak: it is necessary the one should have both the power and the will, and that the other should make little resistance.

    "'This principle being established, it follows that woman is expressly formed to please the man: if the obligation be reciprocal also, and the man ought to please in his turn, it is not so immediately necessary: his great merit is in his power, and he pleases merely because he is strong. This, I must confess, is not one of the refined maxims of love; it is, however, one of the laws of nature, prior to love itself.

    "'If woman be formed to please and be subjected to man, it is her place, doubtless, to render herself agreeable to him, instead of challenging his passion. The violence of his desires depends on her charms; it is by means of these she should urge him to the exertion of those powers which nature hath given him. The most successful method of exciting them, is, to render such exertion necessary by resistance; as, in that case, self-love is added to desire, and the one triumphs in the victory which the other obliged to acquire. Hence arise the various modes of attack and defence between the sexes; the boldness of one sex and the timidity of the other; and, in a word, that bashfulness and modesty with which nature hath armed the weak, in order to subdue the strong.' *Rousseau's Emilius.* I shall make no other comment on this ingenious passage, than just to observe, that it is the philosophy of lasciviousness" [Wollstonecraft's note]. The quotation is from *Emilius* IV, v, p. 4.

for we are not treading on romantic ground, though he may think her a pleasing docile creature, will not choose to marry a *family* for love, when the world contains many more pretty creatures. What is then to become of her? She either falls an easy prey to some mean fortune-hunter, who defrauds her children of their paternal inheritance, and renders her miserable; or becomes the victim of discontent and blind indulgence. Unable to educate her sons, or impress them with respect; for it is not a play on words to assert, that people are never respected, though filling an important station, who are not respectable; she pines under the anguish of unavailing impotent regret. The serpent's tooth[3] enters into her very soul, and the vices of licentious youth bring her with sorrow, if not with poverty also, to the grave.

This is not an overcharged[4] picture; on the contrary, it is a very possible case, and something similar must have fallen under every attentive eye.

I have, however, taken it for granted, that she was well-disposed, though experience shews, that the blind may as easily be led into a ditch as along the beaten road. But supposing, no very improbable conjecture, that a being only taught to please must still find her happiness in pleasing;—what an example of folly, not to say vice, will she be to her innocent daughters! The mother will be lost in the coquette, and, instead of making friends of her daughters, view them with eyes askance, for they are rivals—rivals more cruel than any other, because they invite a comparison, and drive her from the throne of beauty, who has never thought of a seat on the bench of reason.

It does not require a lively pencil, or the discriminating outline of a caricature, to sketch the domestic miseries and petty vices which such a mistress of a family diffuses. Still she only acts as a woman ought to act, brought up according to Rousseau's system. She can never be reproached for being masculine, or turning out of her sphere; nay, she may observe another of his grand rules, and, cautiously preserving her reputation free from spot, be reckoned a good kind of woman. Yet in what respect can she be termed good? She abstains, it is true, without any great struggle, from committing gross crimes; but how does she fulfil her duties? Duties!—in truth she has enough to think of to adorn her body and nurse a weak constitution.

With respect to religion, she never presumed to judge for herself; but conformed, as a dependent creature should, to the ceremonies

3. *King Lear* I.iv.310–11: "How sharper than a serpent's tooth it is / To have a thankless child!"
4. Exaggerated.

of the church which she was brought up in, piously believing that wiser heads than her own have settled that business:—and not to doubt is her point of perfection.[5] She therefore pays her tythe of mint and cummin[6]—and thanks her God that she is not as other women are. These are the blessed effects of a good education! These the virtues of man's help-mate![7]

I must relieve myself by drawing a different picture.

Let fancy now present a woman with a tolerable understanding, for I do not wish to leave the line of mediocrity, whose constitution, strengthened by exercise, has allowed her body to acquire its full vigour; her mind, at the same time, gradually expanding itself to comprehend the moral duties of life, and in what human virtue and dignity consist.

Formed thus by the discharge of the relative duties of her station, she marries from affection, without losing sight of prudence, and looking beyond matrimonial felicity, she secures her husband's respect before it is necessary to exert mean arts[8] to please him and feed a dying flame, which nature doomed to expire when the object became familiar, when friendship and forbearance take place of a more ardent affection.—This is the natural death of love, and domestic peace is not destroyed by struggles to prevent its extinction. I also suppose the husband to be virtuous; or she is still more in want of independent principles.

Fate, however, breaks this tie.—She is left a widow, perhaps, without a sufficient provision; but she is not desolate! The pang of nature is felt; but after time has softened sorrow into melancholy resignation, her heart turns to her children with redoubled fondness, and anxious to provide for them, affection gives a sacred heroic cast to her maternal duties. She thinks that not only the eye sees her virtuous efforts from whom all her comfort now must flow, and whose approbation is life; but her imagination, a little abstracted and exalted by grief, dwells on the fond hope that the eyes which her trembling hand closed, may still see how she subdues every wayward passion to fulfil the double duty of being the father as well as the mother of her children. Raised to heroism by misfortunes, she represses the first faint dawning of a natural inclination, before

5. Sophie is taught to defer to her husband in religious matters (*Emilius* IV, v, pp. 48 ff.).
6. Matthew 23:23: "Woe unto you, scribes and Pharisees, hypocrites! for ye pay tithe of mint and anise and cummin, and have omitted the weightier matters of the law, judgment, mercy, and faith."
7. "'O how lovely,' exclaims Rousseau, speaking of Sophia, 'is her ignorance! Happy is he who is destined to instruct her! She will never pretend to be the tutor of her husband, but will be content to be his pupil. Far from attempting to subject him to her taste, she will accommodate herself to his. She will be more estimable to him, than if she was learned: he will have a pleasure in instructing her.' *Rousseau's Emilius.* I shall content myself with simply asking, how friendship can subsist, when love expires, between the master and his pupil?" [Wollstonecraft's note]. The quotation is from *Emilius*, IV, v, p. 128.
8. Vulgar trickery.

it ripens into love, and in the bloom of life forgets her sex—forgets the pleasure of an awakening passion, which might again have been inspired and returned. She no longer thinks of pleasing, and conscious dignity prevents her from priding herself on account of the praise which her conduct demands. Her children have her love, and her brightest hopes are beyond the grave, where her imagination often strays.

I think I see her surrounded by her children, reaping the reward of her care. The intelligent eye meets hers, whilst health and innocence smile on their chubby cheeks, and as they grow up the cares of life are lessened by their grateful attention. She lives to see the virtues which she endeavoured to plant on principles, fixed into habits, to see her children attain a strength of character sufficient to enable them to endure adversity without forgetting their mother's example.

The task of life thus fulfilled, she calmly waits for the sleep of death, and rising from the grave, may say—Behold, thou gavest me a talent—and here are five talents.[9]

I wish to sum up what I have said in a few words, for I here throw down my gauntlet, and deny the existence of sexual virtues, not excepting modesty. For man and woman, truth, if I understand the meaning of the word, must be the same; yet the fanciful female character, so prettily drawn by poets and novelists, demanding the sacrifice of truth and sincerity, virtue becomes a relative idea, having no other foundation than utility, and of that utility men pretend arbitrarily to judge, shaping it to their own convenience.

Women, I allow, may have different duties to fulfil; but they are *human* duties, and the principles that should regulate the discharge of them, I sturdily maintain, must be the same.

To become respectable, the exercise of their understanding is necessary, there is no other foundation for independence of character; I mean explicitly to say that they must only bow to the authority of reason, instead of being the *modest* slaves of opinion.

In the superior ranks of life how seldom do we meet with a man of superior abilities, or even common acquirements? The reason appears to me clear, the state they are born in was an unnatural one. The human character has ever been formed by the employments the individual, or class, pursues; and if the faculties are not sharpened by necessity, they must remain obtuse. The argument may fairly be extended to women; for, seldom occupied by serious business, the

9. In the parable of the talents (Matthew 25:15–28), a master distributes talents to his servants, to each according to his ability. The servant who receives the most—five talents—invests them wisely and doubles their value, while the servant given one talent foolishly buries it. The parable illustrates the wise use of God's gifts.

pursuit of pleasure gives that insignificancy to their character which renders the society of the *great* so insipid. The same want of firmness, produced by a similar cause, forces them both to fly from themselves to noisy pleasures, and artificial passions, till vanity takes place of every social affection, and the characteristics of humanity can scarcely be discerned. Such are the blessings of civil governments, as they are at present organized, that wealth and female softness equally tend to debase mankind, and are produced by the same cause; but allowing women to be rational creatures, they should be incited to acquire virtues which they may call their own, for how can a rational being be ennobled by any thing that is not obtained by its own exertions?

Chap. IV

Observations on the State of Degradation to Which Woman Is Reduced by Various Causes

That woman is naturally weak, or degraded by a concurrence of circumstances, is, I think, clear. But this position I shall simply contrast with a conclusion, which I have frequently heard fall from sensible men in favour of an aristocracy: that the mass of mankind cannot be anything, or the obsequious slaves, who patiently allow themselves to be driven forward, would feel their own consequence, and spurn their chains. Men, they further observe, submit every where to oppression, when they have only to lift up their heads to throw off the yoke; yet, instead of asserting their birthright, they quietly lick the dust, and say, let us eat and drink, for to-morrow we die. Women, I argue from analogy, are degraded by the same propensity to enjoy the present moment; and, at last, despise the freedom which they have not sufficient virtue to struggle to attain. But I must be more explicit.

With respect to the culture of the heart, it is unanimously allowed that sex is out of the question; but the line of subordination in the mental powers is never to be passed over.[1] Only 'absolute in loveliness,'[2] the portion of rationality granted to woman, is, indeed, very

---

1. "Into what inconsistencies do men fall when they argue without the compass of principles. Women, weak women, are compared with angels; yet, a superiour order of beings should be supposed to possess more intellect than man; or, in what does their superiority consist? In the same strain, to drop the sneer, they are allowed to possess more goodness of heart, piety, and benevolence.—I doubt the fact, though it be courteously brought forward, unless ignorance be allowed to be the mother of devotion; for I am firmly persuaded that, on an average, the proportion between virtue and knowledge, is more upon a par than is commonly granted" [Wollstonecraft's note].
2. *Paradise Lost* VIII.547–48. "So absolute she seems / And in herself complete" (Adam's words about Eve).

scanty; for, denying her genius and judgment, it is scarcely possible
to divine what remains to characterize intellect.

The stamen[3] of immortality, if I may be allowed the phrase, is the
perfectibility of human reason; for, were man created perfect, or did
a flood of knowledge break in upon him, when he arrived at maturity, that precluded error, I should doubt whether his existence
would be continued after the dissolution of the body. But, in the
present state of things, every difficulty in morals that escapes from
human discussion, and equally baffles the investigation of profound
thinking, and the lightning glance of genius, is an argument on
which I build my belief of the immortality of the soul. Reason is,
consequentially, the simple power of improvement; or, more properly speaking, of discerning truth. Every individual is in this respect
a world in itself. More or less may be conspicuous in one being than
another; but the nature of reason must be the same in all, if it be an
emanation of divinity, the tie that connects the creature with the
Creator; for, can that soul be stamped with the heavenly image, that
is not perfected by the exercise of its own reason?[4] Yet outwardly
ornamented with elaborate care, and so adorned to delight man,
'that with honour he may love,'[5] the soul of woman is not allowed to
have this distinction, and man, ever placed between her and reason,
she is always represented as only created to see through a gross
medium, and to take things on trust. But dismissing these fanciful
theories, and considering woman as a whole, let it be what it will,
instead of a part of man, the inquiry is whether she have reason or
not. If she have, which, for a moment, I will take for granted, she
was not created merely to be the solace of man, and the sexual
should not destroy the human character.

Into this error men have, probably, been led by viewing education
in a false light; not considering it as the first step to form a being
advancing gradually towards perfection;[6] but only as a preparation
for life. On this sensual error, for I must call it so, has the false system of female manners been reared, which robs the whole sex of its
dignity, and classes the brown and fair with the smiling flowers that
only adorn the land. This has ever been the language of men, and
the fear of departing from a supposed sexual character, has made

3. Essence or fundamental element.
4. "'The brutes,' says Lord Monboddo, 'remain in the state in which nature has placed them,
   except in so far as their natural instinct is improved by the culture *we* bestow upon
   them.'" [Wollstonecraft's note]. The quotation is from James Burnett, Lord Monboddo,
   Of the Origin and Progress of Language (Edinburgh, 1774), p. 137. The italics are
   Wollstonecraft's.
5. "Vide Milton" [Wollstonecraft's note]. *Paradise Lost* VIII.57–58: "O when meet now /
   Such pairs, in love and mutual honour join'd?"
6. "This word is not strictly just, but I cannot find a better" [Wollstonecraft's note].

even women of superiour sense adopt the same sentiments.[7] Thus understanding, strictly speaking, has been denied to woman; and instinct, sublimated into wit and cunning, for the purposes of life, has been substituted in its stead.

The power of generalizing ideas, of drawing comprehensive conclusions from individual observations, is the only acquirement, for an immortal being, that really deserves the name of knowledge. Merely to observe, without endeavouring to account for any thing, may (in a very incomplete manner) serve as the common sense of life; but where is the store laid up that is to clothe the soul when it leaves the body?

This power has not only been denied to women; but writers have insisted that it is inconsistent, with a few exceptions, with their sexual character. Let men prove this, and I shall grant that woman only exists for man. I must, however, previously remark, that the power of generalizing ideas, to any great extent, is not very common amongst men or women. But this exercise is the true cultivation of the understanding; and every thing conspires to render the cultivation of the understanding more difficult in the female than the male world.

I am naturally led by this assertion to the main subject of the present chapter, and shall now attempt to point out some of the causes that degrade the sex, and prevent women from generalizing their observations.

---

7. "'Pleasure's the portion of th' *inferior* kind; / But glory, virtue, Heaven for *man* design'd.' After writing these lines, how could Mrs. Barbauld write the following ignoble comparison?

> '*To a Lady, with some painted flowers.*
> Flowers to the fair: to you these flowers I bring,
> And strive to greet you with an earlier spring.
> *Flowers* SWEET, *and gay, and* DELICATE LIKE YOU;
> *Emblems of innocence, and beauty too.*
> With flowers the Graces bind their yellow hair,
> And flowery wreaths consenting lovers wear.
> *Flowers, the sole luxury which nature knew,*
> In Eden's pure and guiltless garden grew.
> *To loftier forms are rougher tasks assign'd;*
> *The sheltering oak resists the stormy wind,*
> *The tougher yew repels invading foes,*
> *And the tall pine for future navies grows;*
> *But this soft family, to cares unknown,*
> *Were born for pleasure and delight* ALONE.
> Gay without toil, and lovely without art,
> *They spring to* CHEER *the sense, and* GLAD *the heart.*
> Nor blush, my fair, to own you copy these;
> *Your* BEST, *your* SWEETEST *empire is*—TO PLEASE.'

So the men tell us; but virtue, says reason, must be acquired by *rough* toils, and useful struggles with worldly *cares*" [Wollstonecraft's note]. Both quotations are from *Poems* by Anna Laetitia Aikin (later Barbauld) (London, 1773). The first couplet is from "To Mrs. P[riestley]," with some Drawings of Birds and Insects." The word *man* in these lines includes "woman." "The inferior kind": birds and insects. The second poem is quoted in its entirety. For a sense of how Barbauld (1743–1825) reacted to her appearance in this note, see p. 277 herein.

I shall not go back to the remote annals of antiquity to trace the history of woman; it is sufficient to allow that she has always been either a slave, or a despot, and to remark, that each of these situations equally retards the progress of reason. The grand source of female folly and vice has ever appeared to me to arise from narrowness of mind; and the very constitution of civil governments has put almost insuperable obstacles in the way to prevent the cultivation of the female understanding:—yet virtue can be built on no other foundation! The same obstacles are thrown in the way of the rich, and the same consequences ensue.

Necessity has been proverbially termed the mother of invention—the aphorism may be extended to virtue. It is an acquirement, and an acquirement to which pleasure must be sacrificed—and who sacrifices pleasure when it is within the grasp, whose mind has not been opened and strengthened by adversity, or the pursuit of knowledge goaded on by necessity?—Happy is it when people have the cares of life to struggle with; for these struggles prevent their becoming a prey to enervating vices, merely from idleness! But, if from their birth men and women be placed in a torrid zone,[8] with the meridian sun of pleasure darting directly upon them, how can they sufficiently brace their minds to discharge the duties of life, or even to relish the affections that carry them out of themselves?

Pleasure is the business of woman's life, according to the present modification of society, and while it continues to be so, little can be expected from such weak beings. Inheriting, in a lineal descent from the first fair defect in nature,[9] the sovereignty of beauty, they have, to maintain their power, resigned the natural rights, which the exercise of reason might have procured them, and chosen rather to be short-lived queens than labour to obtain the sober pleasures that arise from equality. Exalted by their inferiority (this sounds like a contradiction), they constantly demand homage as women, though experience should teach them that the men who pride themselves upon paying this arbitrary insolent respect to the sex, with the most scrupulous exactness, are most inclined to tyrannize over, and despise, the very weakness they cherish. Often do they repeat Mr. Hume's sentiments; when, comparing the French and Athenian character, he alludes to women. 'But what is more singular in this whimsical nation, say I to the Athenians, is, that a frolick of yours during the Saturnalia,[1] when the slaves are served by their masters,

---

8. Tropical region. Eighteenth-century geographers believed the heat of the tropical sun robbed the inhabitants of their initiative and moral fiber.
9. After the fall, Adam denounces Eve as "this fair defect / Of nature" (*Paradise Lost* X.891–92).
1. In classic antiquity a midwinter festival dedicated to the god Saturn, in which distinctions of rank were temporarily suspended.

is seriously continued by them through the whole year, and through the whole course of their lives; accompanied too with some circumstances, which still further augment the absurdity and ridicule. Your sport only elevates for a few days those whom fortune has thrown down, and whom she too, in sport, may really elevate for ever above you. But this nation gravely exalts those, whom nature has subjected to them, and whose inferiority and infirmities are absolutely incurable. The women, though without virtue, are their masters and sovereigns.'[2]

Ah! why do women, I write with affectionate solicitude, condescend to receive a degree of attention and respect from strangers, different from that reciprocation of civility which the dictates of humanity and the politeness of civilization authorise between man and man? And, why do they not discover, when 'in the noon of beauty's power,'[3] that they are treated like queens only to be deluded by hollow respect, till they are led to resign, or not assume, their natural prerogatives? Confined then in cages like the feathered race, they have nothing to do but to plume themselves, and stalk with mock majesty from perch to perch. It is true they are provided with food and raiment, for which they neither toil nor spin;[4] but health, liberty, and virtue, are given in exchange. But, where, amongst mankind, has been found sufficient strength of mind to enable a being to resign these adventitious prerogatives; one who, rising with the calm dignity of reason above opinion, dared to be proud of the privileges inherent in man? And it is vain to expect it whilst hereditary power chokes the affections and nips reason in the bud.

The passions of men have thus placed women on thrones, and, till mankind become more reasonable, it is to be feared that women will avail themselves of the power which they attain with the least exertion, and which is the most indisputable. They will smile,—yes, they will smile, though told that—

'In beauty's empire is no mean,
'And woman, either slave or queen,
'Is quickly scorn'd when not ador'd.'[5]

But the adoration comes first, and the scorn is not anticipated.

2. "A Dialogue," appendix to David Hume's posthumously published *Essays and Treatises on several subjects* (London, 1777), II, p. 386. Hume (1711–1776) was a Scottish philosopher, historian, and religious skeptic.
3. In the *Analytical Review* in 1788 Wollstonecraft used the same phrase in reviewing a translation from the German of Christoph Martin Wieland's novel *Henrietta of Gerstenfeld*, apparently recalling the statement there that "the beauty of Henrietta obscures that of her mother as much as the meridian splendours of the sun outshine the light of the moon" (Wollstonecraft, *Works*, VII, p. 20; *Henrietta of Gerstenfeld* [London, 1787–88], v. 2, p. 24).
4. Matthew 6:28; Luke 12:27
5. Anna Laetitia Barbauld, "Song V," lines 16–18, in her *Poems* (London, 1773), p. 78.

Lewis the XIVth, in particular, spread factitious manners, and caught, in a specious way, the whole nation in his toils; for, establishing an artful chain of despotism, he made it the interest of the people at large, individually to respect his station and support his power.[6] And women, whom he flattered by a puerile attention to the whole sex, obtained in his reign that prince-like distinction so fatal to reason and virtue.

A king is always a king—and a woman always a woman:[7] his authority and her sex, ever stand between them and rational converse. With a lover, I grant, she should be so, and her sensibility will naturally lead her to endeavour to excite emotion, not to gratify her vanity, but her heart. This I do not allow to be coquetry, it is the artless impulse of nature, I only exclaim against the sexual desire of conquest when the heart is out of the question.

This desire is not confined to women; 'I have endeavoured,' says Lord Chesterfield, 'to gain the hearts of twenty women, whose persons I would not have given a fig for.'[8] The libertine, who, in a gust of passion, takes advantage of unsuspecting tenderness, is a saint when compared with this cold-hearted rascal; for I like to use significant words. Yet only taught to please, women are always on the watch to please, and with true heroic ardour endeavour to gain hearts merely to resign or spurn them, when the victory is decided, and conspicuous.

I must descend to the minutiae of the subject.

I lament that women are systematically degraded by receiving the trivial attentions, which men think it manly to pay to the sex, when, in fact, they are insultingly supporting their own superiority. It is not condescension to bow to an inferior. So ludicrous, in fact, do these ceremonies appear to me, that I scarcely am able to govern my muscles, when I see a man start with eager, and serious solicitude, to lift a handkerchief, or shut a door, when the *lady* could have done it herself, had she only moved a pace or two.

---

6. During his seventy-two year reign, Louis XIV (1638–1715) consolidated the power of the monarchy and put his court at the center of French culture. To participate in the court ceremonies of Versailles came, for many of his subjects, to represent the pinnacle of their ambition, so that the "Sun King" (as Louis was called) was able to render even powerful aristocrats his dependent satellites.
7. "And a wit, always a wit, might be added; for the vain fooleries of wits and beauties to obtain attention, and make conquests, are much upon a par" [Wollstonecraft's note].
8. Wollstonecraft is misquoting Chesterfield's *Letters to His Son*, Letter CCXCIV (November 16, 1752): "And, moreover, I will own to you, under the secrecy of confession, that my vanity has very often made me take pains to make a woman in love with me, if I could, for whose person I would not have given a pinch of snuff."
   The letters of advice that diplomat and man of fashion Philip Dormer Stanhope, fourth Earl of Chesterfield (1694–1773), wrote to his illegitimate son (who died in 1768) were published after the earl's death as, their preface stated, a "complete system of education." Their publication (by the son's impoverished widow) struck many as scandalous: Wollstonecraft was not alone in believing that the polish and urbanity of Chesterfield's letters were offset by the immorality of the code of conduct they promoted.

A wild wish has just flown from my heart to my head, and I will not stifle it though it may excite a horse-laugh.—I do earnestly wish to see the distinction of sex confounded in society, unless where love animates the behaviour. For this distinction is, I am firmly persuaded, the foundation of the weakness of character ascribed to woman; is the cause why the understanding is neglected, whilst accomplishments are acquired with sedulous care: and the same cause accounts for their preferring the graceful before the heroic virtues.

Mankind, including every description, wish to be loved and respected by *something*; and the common herd will always take the nearest road to the completion of their wishes. The respect paid to wealth and beauty is the most certain, and unequivocal; and, of course, will always attract the vulgar eye of common minds. Abilities and virtues are absolutely necessary to raise men from the middle rank of life into notice; and the natural consequence is notorious, the middle rank contains most virtue and abilities. Men have thus, in one station, at least an opportunity of exerting themselves with dignity, and of rising by the exertions which really improve a rational creature; but the whole female sex are, till their character is formed, in the same condition as the rich: for they are born, I now speak of a state of civilization, with certain sexual privileges, and whilst they are gratuitously granted them, few will ever think of works of supererogation, to obtain the esteem of a small number of superiour people.

When do we hear of women who, starting out of obscurity, boldly claim respect on account of their great abilities or daring virtues? Where are they to be found? 'To be observed, to be attended to, to be taken notice of with sympathy, complacency, and approbation, are all the advantages which they seek.'[9]—True! my male readers will probably exclaim; but let them, before they draw any conclusion, recollect that this was not written originally as descriptive of women, but of the rich. In Dr. Smith's Theory of Moral Sentiments, I have found a general character of people of rank and fortune, that, in my opinion, might with the greatest propriety be applied to the female sex. I refer the sagacious reader to the whole comparison; but must be allowed to quote a passage to enforce an argument that I mean to insist on, as the one most conclusive against a sexual character. For if, excepting warriors, no great men, of any denomination,

---

9. Adam Smith, *The Theory of Moral Sentiments* (Oxford, 1976), p. 50. All subsequent references are to this edition. The chapter Wollstonecraft cites (I, iii) is titled "Of the Origin of Ambition, and of the Distinction of Ranks." Smith (1723–1790), Scottish philosopher and political economist, is most famous for his *Wealth of Nations* (1776). He published *The Theory of Moral Sentiments* in 1759 and revised it extensively for the sixth edition of 1790.

have ever appeared amongst the nobility, may it not be fairly inferred that their local situation swallowed up the man, and produced a character similar to that of women, who are *localized*, if I may be allowed the word, by the rank they are placed in, by *courtesy*? Women, commonly called Ladies, are not to be contradicted in company, are not allowed to exert any manual strength; and from them the negative virtues only are expected, when any virtues are expected, patience, docility, good-humour, and flexibility; virtues incompatible with any vigorous exertion of intellect. Besides, by living more with each other, and being seldom absolutely alone, they are more under the influence of sentiments than passions. ~~Solitude and reflection are necessary to give to wishes the force of passions, and to enable the imagination to enlarge the object, and make it the most desirable. The same may be said of the rich; they do not sufficiently deal in general ideas, collected by impassioned thinking, or calm investigation, to acquire that strength of character on which great resolves are built.~~ But hear what an acute observer says of the great.

'Do the great seem insensible of the easy price at which they may acquire the publick admiration; or do they seem to imagine that to them, as to other men, it must be the purchase either of sweat or of blood? By what important accomplishments is the young nobleman instructed to support the dignity of his rank, and to render himself worthy of that superiority over his fellow-citizens, to which the virtue of his ancestors had raised them? Is it by knowledge, by industry, by patience, by self-denial, or by virtue of any kind? As all his words, as all his motions are attended to, he learns an habitual regard to every circumstance of ordinary behaviour, and studies to perform all those small duties with the most exact propriety. As he is conscious how much he is observed, and how much mankind are disposed to favour all his inclinations, he acts, upon the most indifferent occasions, with that freedom and elevation which the thought of this naturally inspires. His air, his manner, his deportment, all mark that elegant and graceful sense of his own superiority, which those who are born to inferior station can hardly ever arrive at. These are the arts by which he proposes to make mankind more easily submit to his authority, and to govern their inclinations according to his own pleasure: and in this he is seldom disappointed. These arts, supported by rank and pre-eminence, are, upon ordinary occasions, sufficient to govern the world. Lewis XIV during the greater part of his reign, was regarded, not only in France, but over all Europe, as the most perfect model of a great prince. But what were the talents and virtues by which he acquired this great reputation? Was it by the scrupulous and inflexible justice of all his undertakings, by the immense dangers and difficulties with which they were attended, or by the unwearied and unrelenting application with which he pursued them? Was it by his extensive knowledge, by his exquisite judgment, or by his heroic valour? It was by none of these qualities. But he was, first of all, the most powerful prince in Europe, and consequently held the highest rank among kings; and then, says his historian, "he surpassed all his courtiers in the gracefulness of his shape, and the majestic beauty of his features. The sound of his voice, noble and affecting, gained those hearts which his presence intimidated. He had a step and a deportment which could suit only him and his rank, and which would have been ridiculous in any other person. The embarrassment which he occasioned to those who spoke to him, flattered that secret satisfaction with which he felt his own superiority." These frivolous accomplishments, supported by his rank, and, no doubt too, by a degree of other talents and virtues, which seems, however, not to have been much above mediocrity, established this prince in the esteem of his own age, and have drawn, even from posterity, a good deal of respect for his memory. Compared with these, in his own times, and in his own presence, no other virtue, it seems, appeared to have any merit. Knowledge, industry, valour, and beneficence, trembled, were abashed, and lost all dignity before them.'[1]

Woman also thus 'in herself complete,'[2] by possessing all these *frivolous* accomplishments, so changes the nature of things

> ————'That what she wills to do or say
> 'Seems wisest, virtuousest, discreetest, best;
> 'All higher knowledge in her *presence* falls
> 'Degraded. Wisdom in discourse with her
> 'Loses discountenanc'd, and, like Folly, shows;
> 'Authority and Reason on her wait.'[3]

And all this is built on her loveliness!

In the middle rank of life, to continue the comparison, men, in their youth, are prepared for professions, and marriage is not considered as the grand feature in their lives; whilst women, on the contrary, have no other scheme to sharpen their faculties. It is not business, extensive plans, or any of the excursive flights of ambition, that engross their attention; no, their thoughts are not employed in rearing such noble structures. To rise in the world, and have the liberty of running from pleasure to pleasure, they must marry advantageously, and to this object their time is sacrificed, and their persons often legally prostituted. A man when he enters any profession has

---

1. Smith, *Theory of Moral Sentiments*, I, iii, pp. 53–54. Lewis XIV's "historian" is Voltaire; Smith quotes Chapter 25 of Voltaire's history *Le Siècle de Louis XIV* (1751).
2. Adam's characterization of Eve in *Paradise Lost* VIII.548.
3. *Paradise Lost* VIII.549–54. The italics are Wollstonecraft's.

his eye steadily fixed on some future advantage (and the mind gains great strength by having all its efforts directed to one point), and, full of his business, pleasure is considered as mere relaxation; whilst women seek for pleasure as the main purpose of existence. In fact, from the education, which they receive from society, the love of pleasure may be said to govern them all; but does this prove that there is a sex in souls? It would be just as rational to declare that the courtiers in France, when a destructive system of despotism had formed their character, were not men, because liberty, virtue, and humanity, were sacrificed to pleasure and vanity.—Fatal passions, which have ever domineered over the *whole* race!

The same love of pleasure, fostered by the whole tendency of their education, gives a trifling turn to the conduct of women in most circumstances: for instance, they are ever anxious about secondary things; and on the watch for adventures, instead of being occupied by duties.

A man, when he undertakes a journey, has, in general, the end in view; a woman thinks more of the incidental occurrences, the strange things that may possibly occur on the road; the impression that she may make on her fellow-travellers; and, above all, she is anxiously intent on the care of the finery that she carries with her, which is more than ever a part of herself, when going to figure on a new scene; when, to use an apt French turn of expression, she is going to produce a sensation.—Can dignity of mind exist with such trivial cares?

In short, women, in general, as well as the rich of both sexes, have acquired all the follies and vices of civilization, and missed the useful fruit. It is not necessary for me always to premise, that I speak of the condition of the whole sex, leaving exceptions out of the question. Their senses are inflamed, and their understandings neglected, consequently they become the prey of their senses, delicately termed sensibility, and are blown about by every momentary gust of feeling. Civilized women are, therefore, so weakened by false refinement, that, respecting morals, their condition is much below what it would be were they left in a state nearer to nature. Ever restless and anxious, their over exercised sensibility not only renders them uncomfortable themselves, but troublesome, to use a soft phrase, to others. All their thoughts turn on things calculated to excite emotion; and feeling, when they should reason, their conduct is unstable, and their opinions are wavering—not the wavering produced by deliberation or progressive views, but by contradictory emotions. By fits and starts they are warm in many pursuits; yet this warmth, never concentrated into perseverance, soon exhausts itself; exhaled by its own heat, or meeting with some other fleeting passion, to which reason has never given any specific gravity, neutrality ensues. Miserable, indeed, must be that being whose cultivation of mind has only tended to inflame its passions! A distinction should be made between inflaming and strengthening them. The passions thus pampered, whilst the judgment is left unformed, what can be expected to ensue?—Undoubtedly, a mixture of madness and folly!

This observation should not be confined to the *fair* sex; however, at present, I only mean to apply it to them.

Novels, music, poetry, and gallantry, all tend to make women the creatures of sensation, and their character is thus formed in the mould of folly during the time they are acquiring accomplishments, the only improvement they are excited, by their station in society, to acquire. This overstretched sensibility naturally relaxes the other powers of the mind, and prevents intellect from attaining that sovereignty which it ought to attain to render a rational creature useful to others, and content with its own station: for the exercise of the understanding, as life advances, is the only method pointed out by nature to calm the passions.

Satiety has a very different effect, and I have often been forcibly struck by an emphatical description of damnation:—when the spirit is represented as continually hovering with abortive eagerness round the defiled body, unable to enjoy any thing without the organs of sense. Yet, to their senses, are women made slaves, because it is by their sensibility that they obtain present power.

And will moralists pretend to assert, that this is the condition in which one half of the human race should be encouraged to remain with listless inactivity and stupid acquiescence? Kind instructors! what were we created for? To remain, it may be said, innocent; they mean in a state of childhood.—We might as well never have been born, unless it were necessary that we should be created to enable man to acquire the noble privilege of reason, the power of discerning good from evil, whilst we lie down in the dust from whence we were taken, never to rise again.—

It would be an endless task to trace the variety of meannesses, cares, and sorrows, into which women are plunged by the prevailing opinion, that they were created rather to feel than reason, and that all the power they obtain, must be obtained by their charms and weakness:

'Fine by defect, and amiably weak!'[4]

And, made by this amiable weakness entirely dependent, excepting what they gain by illicit sway, on man, not only for protection, but advice, is it surprising that, neglecting the duties that reason alone points out, and shrinking from trials calculated to strengthen their minds, they only exert themselves to give their defects a graceful

4. A misquotation of Pope, "Of the Characters of Women," line 44: "Fine by defect, and delicately weak."

covering, which may serve to heighten their charms in the eye of the voluptuary, though it sink them below the scale of moral excellence?

Fragile in every sense of the word, they are obliged to look up to man for every comfort. In the most trifling dangers they cling to their support, with parasitical tenacity, piteously demanding succour; and their *natural* protector extends his arm, or lifts up his voice, to guard the lovely trembler—from what? Perhaps the frown of an old cow, or the jump of a mouse; a rat, would be a serious danger. In the name of reason, and even common sense, what can save such beings from contempt; even though they be soft and fair?

These fears, when not affected, may produce some pretty attitudes; but they shew a degree of imbecility which degrades a rational creature in a way women are not aware of—for love and esteem are very distinct things.

I am fully persuaded that we should hear of none of these infantine airs, if girls were allowed to take sufficient exercise, and not confined in close rooms till their muscles are relaxed, and their powers of digestion destroyed. To carry the remark still further, if fear in girls, instead of being cherished, perhaps, created, were treated in the same manner as cowardice in boys, we should quickly see women with more dignified aspects. It is true, they could not then with equal propriety be termed the sweet flowers that smile in the walk of man; but they would be more respectable members of society, and discharge the important duties of life by the light of their own reason. 'Educate women like men,' says Rousseau, 'and the more they resemble our sex the less power will they have over us.'[5] This is the very point I aim at. I do not wish them to have power over men; but over themselves.

In the same strain have I heard men argue against instructing the poor; for many are the forms that aristocracy assumes. 'Teach them to read and write,' say they, 'and you take them out of the station assigned them by nature.' An eloquent Frenchman has answered them, I will borrow his sentiments. But they know not, when they make man a brute, that they may expect every instant to see him transformed into a ferocious beast.[6] Without knowledge there can be no morality!

Ignorance is a frail base for virtue! Yet, that it is the condition for which woman was organized, has been insisted upon by the writers who have most vehemently argued in favour of the superiority of

5. The passage continues: "and when once they become like ourselves, we shall then be truly their masters" (*Emilius*, IV, v, p. 17).
6. Wollstonecraft might be remembering a remark made in 1790 by the statesman Mirabeau, responding to the aggressive tone of the debates in revolutionary France's new Constituent Assembly and reflecting, more generally, on the power the common people had come to exercise in the nation's political arguments: "you have loosed the bull: do you expect he will not use his horns?"

man; a superiority not in degree, but essence; though, to soften the argument, they have laboured to prove, with chivalrous generosity, that the sexes ought not to be compared; man was made to reason, woman to feel: and that together, flesh and spirit, they make the most perfect whole, by blending happily reason and sensibility into one character.

And what is sensibility? 'Quickness of sensation; quickness of perception; delicacy.' Thus is it defined by Dr. Johnson;[7] and the definition gives me no other idea than of the most exquisitely polished instinct. I discern not a trace of the image of God in either sensation or matter. Refined seventy times seven,[8] they are still material; intellect dwells not there; nor will fire ever make lead gold!

I come round to my old argument; if woman be allowed to have an immortal soul, she must have, as the employment of life, an understanding to improve. And when, to render the present state more complete, though every thing proves it to be but a fraction of a mighty sum, she is incited by present gratification to forget her grand destination, nature is counteracted, or she was born only to procreate and rot. Or, granting brutes, of every description, a soul, though not a reasonable one, the exercise of instinct and sensibility may be the step, which they are to take, in this life, towards the attainment of reason in the next; so that through all eternity they will lag behind man, who, why we cannot tell, had the power given him of attaining reason in his first mode of existence.

When I treat of the peculiar duties of women, as I should treat of the peculiar duties of a citizen or father, it will be found that I do not mean to insinuate that they should be taken out of their families, speaking of the majority. 'He that hath wife and children,' says Lord Bacon, 'hath given hostages to fortune; for they are impediments to great enterprises, either of virtue or mischief. Certainly the best works, and of greatest merit for the public, have proceeded from the unmarried or childless men.'[9] I say the same of women. But, the welfare of society is not built on extraordinary exertions; and were it more reasonably organized, there would be still less need of great abilities, or heroic virtues.

In the regulation of a family, in the education of children, understanding, in an unsophisticated sense, is particularly required: strength both of body and mind; yet the men who, by their writings, have most earnestly laboured to domesticate women, have endeavoured, by arguments dictated by a gross appetite, which satiety had

---

7. Wollstonecraft cites the emended definition Johnson included in the fourth (1773) edition of his *Dictionary*.
8. Matthew 18:22: "Jesus saith unto him, I say not unto thee, Until seven times: but, Until seventy times seven."
9. Francis Bacon, Essay VIII, "Of Marriage and the Single Life."

rendered fastidious, to weaken their bodies and cramp their minds. But, if even by these sinister methods they really *persuaded* women, by working on their feelings, to stay at home, and fulfil the duties of a mother and mistress of a family, I should cautiously oppose opinions that led women to right conduct, by prevailing on them to make the discharge of such important duties the main business of life, though reason were insulted. Yet, and I appeal to experience, if by neglecting the understanding they be as much, nay, more detached from these domestic employments, than they could be by the most serious intellectual pursuit, though it may be observed, that the mass of mankind will never vigorously pursue an intellectual object,[1] I may be allowed to infer that reason is absolutely necessary to enable a woman to perform any duty properly, and I must again repeat, that sensibility is not reason.

The comparison with the rich still occurs to me; for, when men neglect the duties of humanity, women will follow their example; a common stream hurries them both along with thoughtless celerity. Riches and honours prevent a man from enlarging his understanding, and enervate all his powers by reversing the order of nature, which has ever made true pleasure the reward of labour. Pleasure—enervating pleasure is, likewise, within women's reach without earning it. But, till hereditary possessions are spread abroad, how can we expect men to be proud of virtue? And, till they are, women will govern them by the most direct means, neglecting their dull domestic duties to catch the pleasure that sits lightly on the wing of time.

'The power of the woman,' says some author, 'is her sensibility;'[2] and men, not aware of the consequence, do all they can to make this power swallow up every other. Those who constantly employ their sensibility will have most: for example; poets, painters, and composers.[3] Yet, when the sensibility is thus increased at the expence of reason, and even the imagination, why do philosophical men complain of their fickleness? The sexual attention of man particularly acts on female sensibility, and this sympathy has been exercised from their youth up. A husband cannot long pay those attentions with the passion necessary to excite lively emotions, and the heart, accustomed to lively emotions, turns to a new lover, or pines in secret, the prey of virtue or prudence. I mean when the heart has really been rendered susceptible, and the taste formed; for I am apt

1. "The mass of mankind are rather the slaves of their appetites than of their passions" [Wollstonecraft's note].
2. Possibly a recollection of *A Father's Legacy to His Daughters*, in which Gregory, discussing women's blushing, asserts "That extreme sensibility which it indicates, may be a weakness and incumbrance in our sex . . . but in yours it is peculiarly engaging" (p. 27).
3. "Men of these descriptions pour it into their compositions, to amalgamate the gross materials; and, moulding them with passion, give to the inert body a soul; but, in woman's imagination, love alone concentrates these ethereal beams" [Wollstonecraft's note].

conclude, from what I have seen in fashionable life, that vanity is oftener fostered than sensibility by the mode of education, and the intercourse between the sexes, which I have reprobated; and that coquetry more frequently proceeds from vanity than from that inconstancy, which overstrained sensibility naturally produces.

Another argument that has had great weight with me, must, I think, have some force with every considerate benevolent heart. Girls who have been thus weakly educated, are often cruelly left by their parents without any provision; and, of course, are dependent on, not only the reason, but the bounty of their brothers. These brothers are, to view the fairest side of the question, good sort of men, and give as a favour, what children of the same parents had an equal right to. In this equivocal humiliating situation, a docile female may remain some time, with a tolerable degree of comfort. But, when the brother marries, a probable circumstance, from being considered as the mistress of the family, she is viewed with averted looks as an intruder, an unnecessary burden on the benevolence of the master of the house, and his new partner.

Who can recount the misery, which many unfortunate beings, whose minds and bodies are equally weak, suffer in such situations—unable to work, and ashamed to beg? The wife, a cold-hearted, narrow-minded, woman, and this is not an unfair supposition; for the present mode of education does not tend to enlarge the heart any more than the understanding, is jealous of the little kindness which her husband shews to his relations; and her sensibility not rising to humanity, she is displeased at seeing the property of *her* children lavished on an helpless sister.

These are matters of fact, which have come under my eye again and again. The consequence is obvious, the wife has recourse to cunning to undermine the habitual affection, which she is afraid openly to oppose; and neither tears nor caresses are spared till the spy is worked out of her home, and thrown on the world, unprepared for its difficulties; or sent, as a great effort of generosity, or from some regard to propriety, with a small stipend, and an uncultivated mind, into joyless solitude.

These two women may be much upon a par, with respect to reason and humanity; and changing situations, might have acted just the same selfish part; but had they been differently educated, the case would also have been very different. The wife would not have had that sensibility, of which self is the centre, and reason might have taught her not to expect, and not even to be flattered by, the affection of her husband, if it led him to violate prior duties. She would wish not to love him merely because he loved her, but on account of his virtues; and the sister might have been able to struggle for herself instead of eating the bitter bread of dependence.

I am, indeed, persuaded that the heart, as well as the understanding, is opened by cultivation; and by, which may not appear so clear,
strengthening the organs; I am not now talking of momentary
flashes of sensibility, but of affections. And, perhaps, in the education of both sexes, the most difficult task is so to adjust instruction
as not to narrow the understanding, whilst the heart is warmed by
the generous juices of spring, just raised by the electric fermentation
of the season; nor to dry up the feelings by employing the mind in
investigations remote from life.

With respect to women, when they receive a careful education,
they are either made fine ladies, brimful of sensibility, and teeming
with capricious fancies; or mere notable women.[4] The latter are
often friendly, honest creatures, and have a shrewd kind of good
sense joined with worldly prudence, that often render them more
useful members of society than the fine sentimental lady, though
they possess neither greatness of mind nor taste. The intellectual
world is shut against them; take them out of their family or neighbourhood, and they stand still; the mind finding no employment, for
literature affords a fund of amusement which they have never
sought to relish, but frequently to despise. The sentiments and taste
of more cultivated minds appear ridiculous, even in those whom
chance and family connections have led them to love; but in mere
acquaintance they think it all affectation.

A man of sense can only love such a woman on account of her sex,
and respect her, because she is a trusty servant. He lets her, to preserve his own peace, scold the servants, and go to church in clothes
made of the very best materials. A man of her own size of understanding would, probably, not agree so well with her; for he might
wish to encroach on her prerogative, and manage some domestic
concerns himself. Yet women, whose minds are not enlarged by cultivation, or the natural selfishness of sensibility expanded by reflection, are very unfit to manage a family; for, by an undue stretch of
power, they are always tyrannizing to support a superiority that only
rests on the arbitrary distinction of fortune. The evil is sometimes
more serious, and domestics are deprived of innocent indulgences,
and made to work beyond their strength, in order to enable the
notable woman to keep a better table, and outshine her neighbours
in finery and parade. If she attend to her children, it is, in general, to
dress them in a costly manner—and, whether this attention arise
from vanity or fondness, it is equally pernicious.

Besides, how many women of this description pass their days; or,
at least, their evenings, discontentedly. Their husbands acknowledge
that they are good managers, and chaste wives; but leave home to

4. I.e., industrious and energetic housewives.

seek for more agreeable, may I be allowed to use a significant French word, *piquant* society; and the patient drudge, who fulfils her task, like a blind horse in a mill, is defrauded of her just reward; for the wages due to her are the caresses of her husband; and women who have so few resources in themselves, do not very patiently bear this privation of a natural right.

A fine lady, on the contrary, has been taught to look down with contempt on the vulgar employments of life; though she has only been incited to acquire accomplishments that rise a degree above sense; for even corporeal accomplishments cannot be acquired with any degree of precision unless the understanding has been strengthened by exercise. Without a foundation of principles taste is superficial, grace must arise from something deeper than imitation. The imagination, however, is heated, and the feelings rendered fastidious, if not sophisticated; or, a counterpoise of judgment is not acquired, when the heart still remains artless, though it becomes too tender.

These women are often amiable; and their hearts are really more sensible to general benevolence, more alive to the sentiments that civilize life, than the square-elbowed family drudge; but, wanting a due proportion of reflection and self-government, they only inspire love; and are the mistresses of their husbands, whilst they have any hold on their affections; and the platonic friends of his male acquaintance. These are the fair defects in nature; the women who appear to be created not to enjoy the fellowship of man, but to save him from sinking into absolute brutality, by rubbing off the rough angles of his character; and by playful dalliance to give some dignity to the appetite that draws him to them.—Gracious Creator of the whole human race! hast thou created such a being as woman, who can trace thy wisdom in thy works, and feel that thou alone art by thy nature exalted above her,—for no better purpose?—Can she believe that she was only made to submit to man, her equal, a being, who, like her, was sent into the world to acquire virtue?—Can she consent to be occupied merely to please him; merely to adorn the earth, when her soul is capable of rising to thee?—And can she rest supinely dependent on man for reason, when she ought to mount with him the arduous steeps of knowledge?—

Yet, if love be the supreme good, let women be only educated to inspire it, and let every charm be polished to intoxicate the senses; but, if they be moral beings, let them have a chance to become intelligent; and let love to man be only a part of that glowing flame of universal love, which, after encircling humanity, mounts in grateful incense to God.

To fulfil domestic duties much resolution is necessary, and a serious kind of perseverance that requires a more firm support than emotions, however lively and true to nature. To give an example of order, the soul of virtue, some austerity of behaviour must be adopted, scarcely to be expected from a being who, from its infancy, has been made the weathercock of its own sensations. Whoever rationally means to be useful must have a plan of conduct; and, in the discharge of the simplest duty, we are often obliged to act contrary to the present impulse of tenderness or compassion. Severity is frequently the most certain, as well as the most sublime proof of affection; and the want of this power over the feelings, and of that lofty, dignified affection, which makes a person prefer the future good of the beloved object to a present gratification, is the reason why so many fond mothers spoil their children, and has made it questionable whether negligence or indulgence be most hurtful, but I am inclined to think, that the latter has done most harm.

Mankind seem to agree that children should be left under the management of women during their childhood. Now, from all the observation that I have been able to make, women of sensibility are the most unfit for this task, because they will infallibly, carried away by their feelings, spoil a child's temper. The management of the temper, the first, and most important branch of education, requires the sober steady eye of reason; a plan of conduct equally distant from tyranny and indulgence: yet these are the extremes that people of sensibility alternately fall into; always shooting beyond the mark. I have followed this train of reasoning much further, till I have concluded, that a person of genius is the most improper person to be employed in education, public or private. Minds of this rare species see things too much in masses, and seldom, if ever, have a good temper. That habitual cheerfulness, termed good-humour, is, perhaps, as seldom united with great mental powers, as with strong feelings. And those people who follow, with interest and admiration, the flights of genius; or, with cooler approbation suck in the instruction which has been elaborately prepared for them by the profound thinker, ought not to be disgusted, if they find the former choleric, and the latter morose; because liveliness of fancy, and a tenacious comprehension of mind, are scarcely compatible with that pliant urbanity which leads a man, at least, to bend to the opinions and prejudices of others, instead of roughly confronting them.

But, treating of education or manners, minds of a superior class are not to be considered, they may be left to chance; it is the multitude, with moderate abilities, who call for instruction, and catch the colour of the atmosphere they breathe. This respectable concourse, I contend, men and women, should not have their sensations heightened in the hot-bed of luxurious indolence, at the expence of their understanding; for, unless there be a ballast of understanding, they will never become either virtuous or free: an aristocracy, founded on property, or sterling talents, will ever sweep before it, the alternately timid, and ferocious, slaves of feeling.

Numberless are the arguments, to take another view of the subject, brought forward with a shew of reason, because supposed to be deduced from nature, that men have used morally and physically, to degrade the sex. I must notice a few.

The female understanding has often been spoken of with contempt, as arriving sooner at maturity than the male. I shall not answer this argument by alluding to the early proofs of reason, as well as genius, in Cowley, Milton, and Pope,[5] but only appeal to experience to decide whether young men, who are early introduced into company (and examples now abound), do not acquire the same precocity. So notorious is this fact, that the bare mentioning of it must bring before people, who at all mix in the world, the idea of a number of swaggering apes of men, whose understandings are narrowed by being brought into the society of men when they ought to have been spinning a top or twirling a hoop.

It has also been asserted, by some naturalists, that men do not attain their full growth and strength till thirty; but that women arrive at maturity by twenty.[6] I apprehend that they reason on false ground, led astray by the male prejudice, which deems beauty the perfection of woman—mere beauty of features and complexion, the vulgar acceptation of the word, whilst male beauty is allowed to have some connection with the mind. Strength of body, and that character of countenance, which the French term a *physionomie*,[7] women do not acquire before thirty, any more than men. The little artless tricks of children, it is true, are particularly pleasing and attractive; yet, when the pretty freshness of youth is worn off, these artless graces become studied airs, and disgust every person of taste. In the countenance of girls we only look for vivacity and bashful modesty; but, the springtide of life over, we look for soberer sense in the face, and for traces of passion, instead of the dimples of animal spirits; expecting to see individuality of character, the only fastener of the affections.[8] We then wish to converse, not to fondle; to give scope to our imaginations as well as to the sensations of our hearts.

At twenty the beauty of both sexes is equal; but the libertinism of man leads him to make the distinction, and superannuated coquettes are commonly of the same opinion; for, when they can no longer

---

5. "Many other names might be added" [Wollstonecraft's note]. Abraham Cowley (1618–1667) claimed to have written one of the poems in his first published collection at age ten. The juvenile writing of John Milton (1608–1674) included verse in Latin as well as in English. At fourteen Alexander Pope (1688–1744) wrote an epic poem, "Alexander," which he later destroyed.
6. George-Louis Leclerc, Comte de Buffon (1707–1784), drew this conclusion in his *Natural History*: "A woman at twenty years is as perfectly formed as a man at thirty" (trans. William Smellie [Edinburgh, 1780], II, p. 436).
7. Cast of the features that reveal one's special character.
8. "The strength of an affection is, generally, in the same proportion as the character of the species in the object beloved, is lost in that of the individual" [Wollstonecraft's note].

inspire love, they pay for the vigour and vivacity of youth. The French, who admit more of mind into their notions of beauty, give the preference to women of thirty. I mean to say that they allow women to be in their most perfect state, when vivacity gives place to reason, and to that majestic seriousness of character, which marks maturity;—or, the resting point. In youth, till twenty, the body shoots out, till thirty the solids are attaining a degree of density; and the flexible muscles, growing daily more rigid, give character to the countenance; that is, they trace the operations of the mind with the iron pen of fate, and tell us not only what powers are within, but how they have been employed.

It is proper to observe, that animals who arrive slowly at maturity, are the longest lived, and of the noblest species. Men cannot, however, claim any natural superiority from the grandeur of longevity; for in this respect nature has not distinguished the male.

Polygamy is another physical degradation; and a plausible argument for a custom, that blasts every domestic virtue, is drawn from the well-attested fact, that in the countries where it is established, more females are born than males. This appears to be an indication of nature, and to nature, apparently reasonable speculations must yield. A further conclusion obviously presented itself; if polygamy be necessary, woman must be inferior to man, and made for him.

With respect to the formation of the fetus in the womb, we are very ignorant; but it appears to me probable, that an accidental physical cause may account for this phenomenon, and prove it not to be a law of nature. I have met with some pertinent observations on the subject in Forster's Account of the Isles of the South-Sea, that will explain my meaning. After observing that of the two sexes amongst animals, the most vigorous and hottest constitution always prevails, and produces its kind;[9] he adds,—'If this be applied to the inhabitants of Africa, it is evident that the men there, accustomed to polygamy, are enervated by the use of so many women, and therefore less vigorous; the women, on the contrary, are of a hotter constitution, not only on account of their more irritable nerves, more sensible organization, and more lively fancy; but likewise because they are deprived in their matrimony of that share of physical love which, in a monogamous condition, would all be theirs; and thus, for the above reasons, the generality of children are born females.

'In the greater part of Europe it has been proved by the most accurate lists of mortality, that the proportion of men to women is nearly

9. Wollstonecraft is referring to whether the fetus will be male or female. We know now that the "accidental physical cause" is a matter of X and Y chromosomes. Johann Reinhold Forster's argument here, on the contrary, is that the child will be of the same sex as the dominant parent, so that, as he explains, the foals born of a worn-out stallion's copulation with a vigorous mare will tend to be female more often than male.

equal, or, if any difference takes place, the males born are more numerous, in the proportion of 105 to 100.'[1]

The necessity of polygamy, therefore, does not appear; yet when a man seduces a woman, it should, I think, be termed a *left-handed*[2] marriage, and the man should be *legally* obliged to maintain the woman and her children, unless adultery, a natural divorcement, abrogated the law. And this law should remain in force as long as the weakness of women caused the word seduction to be used as an excuse for their frailty and want of principle; nay, while they depend on man for a subsistence, instead of earning it by the exertion of their own hands or heads. But these women should not, in the full meaning of the relationship, be termed wives, or the very purpose of marriage would be subverted, and all those endearing charities that flow from personal fidelity, and give a sanctity to the tie, when neither love nor friendship unites the hearts, would melt into selfishness. The woman who is faithful to the father of her children demands respect, and should not be treated like a prostitute; though I readily grant that if it be necessary for a man and woman to live together in order to bring up their offspring, nature never intended that a man should have more than one wife.

Still, highly as I respect marriage, as the foundation of almost every social virtue, I cannot avoid feeling the most lively compassion for those unfortunate females who are broken off from society, and by one error torn from all those affections and relationships that improve the heart and mind. It does not frequently even deserve the name of error; for many innocent girls become the dupes of a sincere, affectionate heart, and still more are, as it may emphatically be termed, *ruined* before they know the difference between virtue and vice:—and thus prepared by their education for infamy, they become infamous. Asylums and Magdalenes[3] are not the proper

---

1. Wollstonecraft quotes *Observations Made during a Voyage Round the World* (1778) by the scientist Johann Reinhold Forster, who accompanied Captain Cook on his second great voyage of exploration in 1772–75. As travelers encountered marital arrangements deviating from European norms, polygamy became a much debated topic for eighteenth-century British moral philosophy and even mooted as a solution to problems in gender relations within Britain. Wollstonecraft enters the debate so as to argue against those who held that marriages involving a plurality of wives might be natural or might be a solution to the social problems created when women outnumbered men. She suggests, on the contrary, that this arrangement would be a cause of those problems: drawing on Forster's observations on sex ratios in South Seas populations, she proposes that such polygynous marriages would actually exacerbate the disproportion between male and female births. This is because children born of men who are, in Forster's words, "enervated by the use of so many women" will themselves tend to be female.
2. Illegal, or "morganatic," marriage in which the groom gives his left hand instead of right. Offspring of such marriages would have no legal rights, since the marriage was usually undertaken by a man in an exalted rank and a woman in a lower station with the provision that the children be supported but not be permitted to claim the rank or possessions of the titled father.
3. Institutions for the reformation of prostitutes.

remedies for these abuses. It is justice, not charity, that is wanting in the world!

A woman who has lost her honour, imagines that she cannot fall lower, and as for recovering her former station, it is impossible; no exertion can wash this stain away. Losing thus every spur, and having no other means of support, prostitution becomes her only refuge, and the character is quickly depraved by circumstances over which the poor wretch has little power, unless she possesses an uncommon portion of sense and loftiness of spirit. Necessity never makes prostitution the business of men's lives; though numberless are the women who are thus rendered systematically vicious. This, however, arises, in a great degree, from the state of idleness in which women are educated, who are always taught to look up to man for a maintenance, and to consider their persons as the proper return for his exertions to support them. Meretricious airs, and the whole science of wantonness, have then a more powerful stimulus than either appetite or vanity; and this remark gives force to the prevailing opinion, that with chastity all is lost that is respectable in woman. Her character depends on the observance of one virtue, though the only passion fostered in her heart—is love. Nay, the honour of a woman is not made even to depend on her will.

When Richardson[4] makes Clarissa tell Lovelace that he had robbed her of her honour, he must have had strange notions of honour and virtue. For, miserable beyond all names of misery is the condition of a being, who could be degraded without its own consent! This excess of strictness I have heard vindicated as a salutary error. I shall answer in the words of Leibnitz—'Errors are often useful; but it is commonly to remedy other errors.'[5]

Most of the evils of life arise from a desire of present enjoyment that outruns itself. The obedience required of women in the marriage state comes under this description; the mind, naturally weakened by depending on authority, never exerts its own powers, and the obedient wife is thus rendered a weak indolent mother. Or, supposing that this is not always the consequence, a future state of existence is scarcely taken into the reckoning when only negative virtues

4. "Dr. Young supports the same opinion, in his plays, when he talks of the misfortune that shunned the light of day" [Wollstonecraft's note]. Wollstonecraft recalls, in the text, words that Clarissa, heroine of Samuel Richardson's novel, uses when she confronts Lovelace after he has raped her (*Clarissa* [London: 1797–98]), v, p. 250. In Act I, scene 1 of Edward Young's 1719 tragedy *Busiris, King of Egypt,* the character Mandane unfolds a "black story" that "well might shun the day," and that involves Busiris' killing of the rightful king. The woman who persuades Busiris to the deed and beds him afterward was the sister of the victim.
5. From the preface to the German philosopher's famous religious work, *Theodicy* (G. W. Leibniz, *Theodicy*, ed. Austin Farrer, trans. E. M. Huggard [New Haven, Conn., 1952], p. 56). Leibniz (1646–1716) is probably most famous for his doctrine of the "pre-established harmony" of the universe.

are cultivated. For, in treating of morals, particularly when women are alluded to, writers have too often considered virtue in a very limited sense, and made the foundation of it *solely* worldly utility; nay, a still more fragile base has been given to this stupendous fabric, and the wayward fluctuating feelings of men have been made the standard of virtue. Yes, virtue as well as religion, has been subjected to the decisions of taste.

It would almost provoke a smile of contempt, if the vain absurdities of man did not strike us on all sides, to observe, how eager men are to degrade the sex from whom they pretend to receive the chief pleasure of life; and I have frequently with full conviction retorted Pope's sarcasm on them;[6] or, to speak explicitly, it has appeared to me applicable to the whole human race. A love of pleasure or sway seems to divide mankind, and the husband who lords it in his little haram thinks only of his pleasure or his convenience. To such lengths, indeed, does an intemperate love of pleasure carry some prudent men, or worn out libertines, who marry to have a safe bedfellow, that they seduce their own wives.—Hymen[7] banishes modesty, and chaste love takes its flight.

Love, considered as an animal appetite, cannot long feed on itself without expiring. And this extinction in its own flame, may be termed the violent death of love. But the wife who has thus been rendered licentious, will probably endeavour to fill the void left by the loss of her husband's attentions; for she cannot contentedly become merely an upper servant after having been treated like a goddess. She is still handsome, and, instead of transferring her fondness to her children, she only dreams of enjoying the sunshine of life. Besides, there are many husbands so devoid of sense and parental affection, that during the first effervescence of voluptuous fondness they refuse to let their wives suckle their children. They are only to dress and live to please them: and love—even innocent love, soon sinks into lasciviousness when the exercise of a duty is sacrificed to its indulgence.

Personal attachment is a very happy foundation for friendship; yet, when even two virtuous young people marry, it would, perhaps, be happy if some circumstances checked their passion; if the recollection of some prior attachment, or disappointed affection, made it on one side, at least, rather a match founded on esteem. In that case they would look beyond the present moment, and try to render the whole of life respectable, by forming a plan to regulate a friendship which only death ought to dissolve.

6. Alexander Pope, "Of the Characters of Women," lines 207–10: "In Men we various Ruling Passions find, / In Women, two almost divide the Kind, / Those only fix'd, they first or last obey; / The Love of Pleasure, and the Love of Sway."
7. Greek god of marriage.

Friendship is a serious affection; the most sublime of all affections, because it is founded on principle, and cemented by time. The very reverse may be said of love. In a great degree, love and friendship cannot subsist in the same bosom; even when inspired by different objects they weaken or destroy each other, and for the same object can only be felt in succession. The vain fears and fond jealousies, the winds which fan the flame of love, when judiciously or artfully tempered, are both incompatible with the tender confidence and sincere respect of friendship.

Love, such as the glowing pen of genius has traced, exists not on earth, or only resides in those exalted, fervid imaginations that have sketched such dangerous pictures. Dangerous, because they not only afford a plausible excuse, to the voluptuary who disguises sheer sensuality under a sentimental veil; but as they spread affectation, and take from the dignity of virtue. Virtue, as the very word imports, should have an appearance of seriousness, if not of austerity; and to endeavour to trick her out in the garb of pleasure, because the epithet has been used as another name for beauty, is to exalt her on a quicksand; a most insidious attempt to hasten her fall by apparent respect. Virtue and pleasure are not, in fact, so nearly allied in this life as some eloquent writers have laboured to prove. Pleasure prepares the fading wreath, and mixes the intoxicating cup; but the fruit which virtue gives, is the recompence of toil: and, gradually seen as it ripens, only affords calm satisfaction; nay, appearing to be the result of the natural tendency of things, it is scarcely observed. Bread, the common food of life, seldom thought of as a blessing, supports the constitution and preserves health; still feasts delight the heart of man, though disease and even death lurk in the cup or dainty that elevates the spirits or tickles the palate. The lively heated imagination likewise, to apply the comparison, draws the picture of love, as it draws every other picture, with those glowing colours, which the daring hand will steal from the rainbow that is directed by a mind, condemned in a world like this, to prove its noble origin by panting after unattainable perfection; ever pursuing what it acknowledges to be a fleeting dream. An imagination of this vigorous cast can give existence to insubstantial forms, and stability to the shadowy reveries which the mind naturally falls into when realities are found vapid. It can then depict love with celestial charms, and dote on the grand ideal object—it can imagine a degree of mutual affection that shall refine the soul, and not expire when it has served as a 'scale to heavenly;'[8] and, like devotion, make it absorb every

---

8. An echo of *Paradise Lost*. Having listened critically to Adam's account of his passion for Eve, the archangel Raphael describes how "true love" "refines / The thoughts, and heart enlarges, hath his seat / In reason, and is judicious, is the scale / By which to heav'nly love thou may'st ascend" (VIII.589–94).

meaner affection and desire. In each others arms, as in a temple, with its summit lost in the clouds, the world is to be shut out, and every thought and wish, that do not nurture pure affection and permanent virtue.—Permanent virtue! alas! Rousseau, respectable visionary! thy paradise would soon be violated by the entrance of some unexpected guest. Like Milton's it would only contain angels, or men sunk below the dignity of rational creatures. Happiness is not material, it cannot be seen or felt! Yet the eager pursuit of the good which every one shapes to his own fancy, proclaims man the lord of this lower world, and to be an intelligential creature, who is not to receive, but acquire happiness. They, therefore, who complain of the delusions of passion, do not recollect that they are exclaiming against a strong proof of the immortality of the soul.

But leaving superior minds to correct themselves, and pay dearly for their experience, it is necessary to observe, that it is not against strong, persevering passions; but romantic wavering feelings that I wish to guard the female heart by exercising the understanding: for these paradisiacal reveries are oftener the effect of idleness than of a lively fancy.

Women have seldom sufficient serious employment to silence their feelings; a round of little cares, or vain pursuits frittering away all strength of mind and organs, they become naturally only objects of sense.—In short, the whole tenour of female education (the education of society) tends to render the best disposed romantic and inconstant; and the remainder vain and mean. In the present state of society this evil can scarcely be remedied, I am afraid, in the slightest degree; should a more laudable ambition ever gain ground they may be brought nearer to nature and reason, and become more virtuous and useful as they grow more respectable.

But, I will venture to assert that their reason will never acquire sufficient strength to enable it to regulate their conduct, whilst the making an appearance in the world is the first wish of the majority of mankind. To this weak wish the natural affections, and the most useful virtues are sacrificed. Girls marry merely to *better themselves*, to borrow a significant vulgar phrase, and have such perfect power over their hearts as not to permit themselves to *fall in love* till a man with a superiour fortune offers. On this subject I mean to enlarge in a future chapter; it is only necessary to drop a hint at present, because women are so often degraded by suffering the selfish prudence of age to chill the ardour of youth.

From the same source[9] flows an opinion that young girls ought to dedicate great part of their time to needle-work; yet, this employment contracts their faculties more than any other that could have

9. I.e., society's idea of female education.

been chosen for them, by confining their thoughts to their persons. Men order their clothes to be made, and have done with the subject; women make their own clothes, necessary or ornamental, and are continually talking about them; and their thoughts follow their hands. It is not indeed the making of necessaries that weakens the mind; but the frippery of dress. For when a woman in the lower rank of life makes her husband's and children's clothes, she does her duty, this is her part of the family business; but when women work only to dress better than they could otherwise afford, it is worse than sheer loss of time. To render the poor virtuous they must be employed, and women in the middle rank of life, did they not ape the fashions of the nobility, without catching their ease, might employ them, whilst they themselves managed their families, instructed their children, and exercised their own minds. Gardening, experimental philosophy,[1] and literature, would afford them subjects to think of and matter for conversation, that in some degree would exercise their understandings. The conversation of French women, who are not so rigidly nailed to their chairs to twist lappets, and knot ribands,[2] is frequently superficial; but, I contend, that it is not half so insipid as that of those English women whose time is spent in making caps, bonnets, and the whole mischief of trimmings, not to mention shopping, bargain-hunting, &c. &c.: and it is the decent, prudent women, who are most degraded by these practices; for their motive is simply vanity. The wanton who exercises her taste to render her passion alluring, has something more in view.

These observations all branch out of a general one, which I have before made, and which cannot be too often insisted upon, for, speaking of men, women, or professions, it will be found that the employment of the thoughts shapes the character both generally and individually. The thoughts of women ever hover round their persons, and is it surprising that their persons are reckoned most valuable? Yet some degree of liberty of mind is necessary even to form the person; and this may be one reason why some gentle wives have so few attractions beside that of sex. Add to this, sedentary employments render the majority of women sickly—and false notions of female excellence make them proud of this delicacy, though it be another fetter, that by calling the attention continually to the body, cramps the activity of the mind.

Women of quality seldom do any of the manual part of their dress, consequently only their taste is exercised, and they acquire, by thinking less of the finery, when the business of their toilet is over, that ease, which seldom appears in the deportment of women, who

1. I.e., natural science.
2. I.e., ribbons. "Lappets": streamers attached to a woman's bonnet.

dress merely for the sake of dressing. In fact, the observation with respect to the middle rank, the one in which talents thrive best, extends not to women; for those of the superior class, by catching, at least, a smattering of literature, and conversing more with men, on general topics, acquire more knowledge than the women who ape their fashions and faults without sharing their advantages. With respect to virtue, to use the word in a comprehensive sense, I have seen most in low life. Many poor women maintain their children by the sweat of their brow, and keep together families that the vices of the fathers would have scattered abroad; but gentlewomen are too indolent to be actively virtuous, and are softened rather than refined by civilization. Indeed, the good sense which I have met with, among the poor women who have had few advantages of education, and yet have acted heroically, strongly confirmed me in the opinion that trifling employments have rendered woman a trifler. Man, taking her[3] body, the mind is left to rust; so that while physical love enervates man, as being his favourite recreation, he will endeavour to enslave woman:—and, who can tell, how many generations may be necessary to give vigour to the virtue and talents of the freed posterity of abject slaves?[4]

In tracing the causes that, in my opinion, have degraded woman, I have confined my observations to such as universally act upon the morals and manners of the whole sex, and to me it appears clear that they all spring from want of understanding. Whether this arise from a physical or accidental weakness of faculties, time alone can determine; for I shall not lay any great stress on the example of a few women[5] who, from having received a masculine education, have acquired courage and resolution; I only contend that the men who have been placed in similar situations, have acquired a similar character—I speak of bodies of men, and that men of genius and talents have started out of a class, in which women have never yet been placed.

3. "'I take her body,' says Ranger" [Wollstonecraft's note]. Ranger, the dissolute rake in Benjamin Hoadly's play, *The Suspicious Husband* comes into his chambers from a night of carousing and reads from one of William Congreve's *Poems on Several Occasions* titled simply, "Song": "You think she's false. I'm sure she's kind, / I take her body, you her mind; / Which has the better bargain?"
4. "'Supposing that women are voluntary slaves—slavery of any kind is unfavourable to human happiness and improvement.' *Knox's Essays*" [Wollstonecraft's note]. Wollstonecraft quotes Vicesimus Knox, "On the Fear of Appearing Singular," Essay No. 5 in *Essays Moral and Literary* (new ed., London, 1782). In the original, Knox does not, in fact, refer to women but instead identifies as "voluntary slaves" all those who conform to the fashions in "thinking and living" established by "self-erected tyrants." As examples of those tyrants he mentions "some rich, gross, unphilosophical man, or some titled frivolous lady, distinguished for boldness, but not for excellence" (p. 21).
5. "Sappho, Eloisa, Mrs. Macaulay, the Empress of Russia, Madame d'Eon, &c. These, and many more, may be reckoned exceptions; and, are not all heroes, as well as heroines,

Chap. V

Animadversions on Some of the Writers Who Have Rendered Women Objects of Pity, Bordering on Contempt

The opinions speciously supported, in some modern publications on the female character and education, which have given the tone to most of the observations made, in a more cursory manner, on the sex, remain now to be examined. Rousseau, man...

SECT. I

yikes.

I shall begin with Rousseau, and give a sketch of his character of woman, in his own words, interspersing comments and reflections. My comments, it is true, will all spring from a few simple principles, and might have been deduced from what I have already said; but the artificial structure has been raised with so much ingenuity, that it seems necessary to attack it in a more circumstantial manner, and make the application myself.

Sophia, says Rousseau, should be as perfect a woman as Emilius is a man, and to render her so, it is necessary to examine the character which nature has given to the sex.[6]

He then proceeds to prove that woman ought to be weak and passive, because she has less bodily strength than man; and hence infers, that she was formed to please and to be subject to him; and that it is her duty to render herself *agreeable* to her master—this being the grand end of her existence.[7] Still, however, to give a little mock dignity to lust, he insists that man should not exert his strength, but depend on the will of the woman, when he seeks for pleasure with her.

---

exceptions to general rules? I wish to see women neither heroines not brutes; but reasonable creatures" [Wollstonecraft's note]. Sappho was an eminent poet in classical Greece, c. 600 B.C.E. The French noblewoman Héloïse (c. 1101–1164) secretly wedded the philosopher Peter Abelard and was herself a scholar; the love-letters chronicling their unhappy liaison inspired Rousseau's *Julie*. Catharine Macaulay (1731–1791), sometimes known, after her second marriage in 1778, as Catharine Macaulay Graham, was, like Wollstonecraft, a defender of the Revolution in France and author of a critical response to Edmund Burke, *Observations on the Reflections of the Right Honourable Edmund Burke on the Revolution in France* (1790). Her monumental *History of England,* which she focused on the checkered fortunes of English liberty, was published in eight volumes between 1763 and 1783. Catherine II (1729–1796) was, after the coup in which she deposed her husband, empress of Russia and a patron of Enlightenment philosophy. The Chevalier d'Eon (1728–1810), an eminent French soldier, spy, and author, alternated between male and female dress during much of his diplomatic career; in 1775 his pension from the king was made contingent on his dressing in a mode appropriate to his sex, and he by and large stuck to female dress thereafter, while tacitly encouraging rumors that "she" had as a child been forced by "her" parents to dress as a member of the opposite sex. In 1810 the examination of d'Eon's corpse proved him male, but Wollstonecraft was likely never aware of his true sex.

6. *Emilius* IV, v, p. 2.
7. "I have already Inserted the passage, page 99" [Wollstonecraft's note]. See p. 43 herein.

'Hence we deduce a third consequence from the different constitutions of the sexes; which is, that the strongest should be master in appearance, and be dependent in fact on the weakest; and that not from any frivolous practice of gallantry or vanity of protectorship, but from an invariable law of nature, which, furnishing woman with a greater facility to excite desires than she has given man to satisfy them, makes the latter dependent on the good pleasure of the former, and compels him to endeavour to please in his turn, *in order to obtain her consent that he should be strongest.*[8] On these occasions, the most delightful circumstance a man finds in his victory is, to doubt whether it was the woman's weakness that yielded to his superior strength, or whether her inclinations spoke in his favour: the females are also generally artful enough to leave this matter in doubt. The understanding of women answers in this respect perfectly to their constitution: so far from being ashamed of their weakness, they glory in it; their tender muscles make no resistance; they affect to be incapable of lifting the smallest burthens, and would blush to be thought robust and strong. To what purpose is all this? Not merely for the sake of appearing delicate, but through an artful precaution: it is thus they provide an excuse beforehand, and a right to be feeble when they think it expedient.'[9]

I have quoted this passage, lest my readers should suspect that I warped the author's reasoning to support my own arguments. I have already asserted that in educating women these fundamental principles lead to a system of cunning and lasciviousness.

Supposing woman to have been formed only to please, and be subject to man, the conclusion is just, she ought to sacrifice every other consideration to render herself agreeable to him: and let this brutal desire of self-preservation be the grand spring of all her actions, when it is proved to be the iron bed of fate,[1] to fit which her character should be stretched or contracted, regardless of all moral or physical distinctions. But, if, as I think, may be demonstrated, the purposes, of even this life, viewing the whole, be subverted by practical rules built upon this ignoble base, I may be allowed to doubt whether woman was created for man: and, though the cry of irreligion, or even atheism, be raised against me, I will simply declare, that were an angel from heaven to tell me that Moses's beautiful, poetical cosmogony, and the account of the fall of man,[2] were literally true, I could not believe what my reason told me was derogatory

8. "What nonsense!" [Wollstonecraft's note].
9. *Emilius* IV, v, p. 8.
1. A reference to Procrustes, the figure from ancient Greek legend who fit passers-by to his bed, stretching them on the rack if they were too short for it, hacking off their limbs if they were too tall.
2. It was assumed in the eighteenth century that Moses had written Genesis.

to the character of the Supreme Being: and, having no fear of the devil before mine eyes, I venture to call this a suggestion of reason, instead of resting my weakness on the broad shoulders of the first seducer of my frail sex.

'It being once demonstrated,' continues Rousseau, 'that man and woman are not, nor ought to be, constituted alike in temperament and character, it follows of course that they should not be educated in the same manner. In pursuing the directions of nature, they ought indeed to act in concert, but they should not be engaged in the same employments: the end of their pursuits should be the same, but the means they should take to accomplish them, and of consequence their tastes and inclinations, should be different.'[3]

*

'Whether I consider the peculiar destination of the sex, observe their inclinations, or remark their duties, all things equally concur to point out the peculiar method of education best adapted to them. Woman and man were made for each other; but their mutual dependence is not the same. The men depend on the women only on account of their desires; the women on the men both on account of their desires and their necessities: we could subsist better without them than they without us.'

*

'For this reason, the education of the women should be always relative to the men. To please, to be useful to us, to make us love and esteem them, to educate us when young, and take care of us when grown up, to advise, to console us, to render our lives easy and agreeable: these are the duties of women at all times, and what they should be taught in their infancy. So long as we fail to recur to this principle, we run wide of the mark, and all the precepts which are given them contribute neither to their happiness nor our own.'[4]

*

'Girls are from their earliest infancy fond of dress. Not content with being pretty, they are desirous of being thought so; we see, by all their little airs, that this thought engages their attention; and they are hardly capable of understanding what is said to them, before they are to be governed by talking to them of what people will think of their behaviour. The same motive, however, indiscreetly made use of with boys, has not the same effect: provided they are let pursue their amusements at pleasure, they care very little what people think of them. Time and pains are necessary to subject boys to this motive.

---

3. *Emilius* IV, v, p. 15.
4. The foregoing two selections are from *Emilius*, IV, v, pp. 18–19, 19–20.

'Whencesoever girls derive this first lesson, it is a very good one. As the body is born, in a manner, before the soul, our first concern should be to cultivate the former; this order is common to both sexes, but the object of that cultivation is different. In the one sex it is the development of corporeal powers; in the other, that of personal charms: not that either the quality of strength or beauty ought to be confined exclusively to one sex; but only that the order of the cultivation of both is in that respect reversed. Women certainly require as much strength as to enable them to move and act gracefully, and men as much address as to qualify them to act with ease.'[5]

*

'Children of both sexes have a great many amusements in common; and so they ought; have they not also many such when they are grown up? Each sex has also its peculiar taste to distinguish in this particular. Boys love sports of noise and activity; to beat the drum, to whip the top, and to drag about their little carts: girls, on the other hand, are fonder of things of show and ornament; such as mirrours, trinkets, and dolls: the doll is the peculiar amusement of the females; from whence we see their taste plainly adapted to their destination. The physical part of the art of pleasing lies in dress; and this is all which children are capacitated to cultivate of that art.'[6]

*

'Here then we see a primary propensity firmly established, which you need only to pursue and regulate. The little creature will doubtless be very desirous to know how to dress up her doll, to make its sleeve-knots, its flounces, its head-dress, &c. she is obliged to have so much recourse to the people about her, for their assistance in these articles, that it would be much more agreeable to her to owe them all to her own industry. Hence we have a good reason for the first lessons that are usually taught these young females: in which we do not appear to be setting them a task, but obliging them, by instructing them in what is immediately useful to themselves. And, in fact, almost all of them learn with reluctance to read and write; but very readily apply themselves to the use of their needles. They imagine themselves already grown up, and think with pleasure that such qualifications will enable them to decorate themselves.'[7]

This is certainly only an education of the body; but Rousseau is not the only man who has indirectly said that merely the person of a *young* woman, without any mind, unless animal spirits come under that description, is very pleasing. To render it weak, and what some may call beautiful, the understanding is neglected, and girls forced

---

5. *Emilius* IV, v, pp. 21–22.
6. *Emilius* IV, v, p. 25.
7. *Emilius* IV, v, pp. 26–27.

to sit still, play with dolls and listen to foolish conversations;—the effect of habit is insisted upon as an undoubted indication of nature. I know it was Rousseau's opinion that the first years of youth should be employed to form the body, though in educating Emilius he deviates from this plan; yet, the difference between strengthening the body, on which strength of mind in a great measure depends, and only giving it an easy motion, is very wide.

Rousseau's observations, it is proper to remark, were made in a country where the art of pleasing was refined only to extract the grossness of vice.[8] He did not go back to nature, or his ruling appetite disturbed the operations of reason, else he would not have drawn these crude inferences.

In France boys and girls, particularly the latter, are only educated to please, to manage their persons, and regulate their exterior behaviour; and their minds are corrupted, at a very early age, by the wordly and pious cautions they receive to guard them against immodesty. I speak of past times. The very confessions which mere children were obliged to make, and the questions asked by the holy men,[9] I assert these facts on good authority, were sufficient to impress a sexual character; and the education of society was a school of coquetry and art. At the age of ten or eleven; nay, often much sooner, girls began to coquet, and talked, unreproved, of establishing themselves in the world by marriage.

In short, they were treated like women, almost from their very birth, and compliments were listened to instead of instruction. These, weakening the mind, Nature was supposed to have acted like a step-mother, when she formed this after-thought of creation.

Not allowing them understanding, however, it was but consistent to subject them to authority independent of reason; and to prepare them for this subjection, he gives the following advice:

'Girls ought to be active and diligent; nor is that all; they should also be early subjected to restraint. This misfortune, if it really be one, is inseparable from their sex; nor do they ever throw it off but to suffer more cruel evils. They must be subject, all their lives, to the most constant and severe restraint, which is that of decorum: it is, therefore, necessary to accustom them early to such confinement, that it may not afterwards cost them too dear; and to the suppression of their caprices, that they may the more readily submit to the will of others. If, indeed, they be fond of being always at work, they should be sometimes compelled to lay it aside. Dissipation, levity,

8. I.e., in France.
9. Wollstonecraft's mistrust of the Catholic practice of confession and suspicion that there was a sexual dimension to the questions priests posed to their confessants are typical of English Protestants during her lifetime. She speaks of "past times" because the social influence priests exercised was reduced radically as the Revolution unfolded in France.

and inconstancy, are faults that readily spring up from their first propensities, when corrupted or perverted by too much indulgence. To prevent this abuse, we should teach them, above all things, to lay a due restraint on themselves. The life of a modest woman is reduced, by our absurd institutions, to a perpetual conflict with herself: not but it is just that this sex should partake of the sufferings which arise from those evils it hath caused us.'[1]

And why is the life of a modest woman a perpetual conflict? I should answer, that this very system of education makes it so. Modesty, temperance, and self-denial, are the sober offspring of reason; but when sensibility is nurtured at the expence of the understanding, such weak beings must be restrained by arbitrary means, and be subjected to continual conflicts; but give their activity of mind a wider range, and nobler passions and motives will govern their appetites and sentiments.

'The common attachment and regard of a mother, nay, mere habit, will make her beloved by her children, if she do nothing to incur their hate. Even the constraint she lays them under, if well directed, will increase their affection, instead of lessening it; because a state of dependence being natural to the sex, they perceive themselves formed for obedience.'[2]

This is begging the question; for servitude not only debases the individual, but its effects seem to be transmitted to posterity. Considering the length of time that women have been dependent, is it surprising that some of them hug their chains, and fawn like the spaniel? 'These dogs,' observes a naturalist, 'at first kept their ears erect; but custom has superseded nature, and a token of fear is become a beauty.'[3]

'For the same reason,' adds Rousseau, 'women have, or ought to have, but little liberty; they are apt to indulge themselves excessively in what is allowed them. Addicted in every thing to extremes, they are even more transported at their diversions than boys.'[4]

The answer to this is very simple. Slaves and mobs have always indulged themselves in the same excesses, when once they broke loose from authority.—The bent bow recoils with violence, when the hand is suddenly relaxed that forcibly held it; and sensibility, the play-thing of outward circumstances, must be subjected to authority, or moderated by reason.

1. *Emilius* IV, v, p. 30.
2. *Emilius* IV, v, p. 31.
3. Possibly recalling the naturalist William Smellie's account of the alterations that domestication produces in animals. For Smellie (1740–1795), the droopy ears of most dogs represented "marks of domestic servitude and fear," which he contrasted with the erect ears universal among wild dogs (*The Philosophy of Natural History* [Edinburgh, 1790], p. 462). Wollstonecraft reviewed this work for the *Analytical Review* (*Works*, VII, pp. 293–300).
4. *Emilius* IV, v, p. 31.

'There results,' he continues, 'from this habitual restraint a tractableness which women have occasion for during their whole lives, as they constantly remain either under subjection to the men, or to the opinions of mankind; and are never permitted to set themselves above those opinions. The first and most important qualification in a woman is good-nature or sweetness of temper: formed to obey a being so imperfect as man, often full of vices, and always full of faults, she ought to learn betimes even to suffer injustice, and to bear the insults of a husband without complaint; it is not for his sake, but her own, that she should be of a mild disposition. The perverseness and ill-nature of the women only serve to aggravate their own misfortunes, and the misconduct of their husbands; they might plainly perceive that such are not the arms by which they gain the superiority.'[5]

Formed to live with such an imperfect being as man, they ought to learn from the exercise of their faculties the necessity of forbearance; but all the sacred rights of humanity are violated by insisting on blind obedience; or, the most sacred rights belong *only* to man.

The being who patiently endures injustice, and silently bears insults, will soon become unjust, or unable to discern right from wrong. Besides, I deny the fact, this is not the true way to form or meliorate the temper; for, as a sex, men have better tempers than women, because they are occupied by pursuits that interest the head as well as the heart; and the steadiness of the head gives a healthy temperature to the heart. People of sensibility have seldom good tempers. The formation of the temper is the cool work of reason, when, as life advances, she mixes with happy art, jarring elements. I never knew a weak or ignorant person who had a good temper, though that constitutional good humour, and that docility, which fear stamps on the behaviour, often obtains the name. I say behaviour, for genuine meekness never reached the heart or mind, unless as the effect of reflection; and that simple restraint produces a number of peccant humours in domestic life, many sensible men will allow, who find some of these gentle irritable creatures, very troublesome companions.

'Each sex,' he further argues, 'should preserve its peculiar tone and manner; a meek husband may make a wife impertinent; but mildness of disposition on the woman's side will always bring a man back to reason, at least if he be not absolutely a brute, and will sooner or later triumph over him.'[6] Perhaps the mildness of reason might sometimes have this effect; but abject fear always inspires

5. *Emilius* IV, v, pp. 32–33.
6. *Emilius* IV, v, p. 33.

contempt; and tears are only eloquent when they flow down fair cheeks.

Of what materials can that heart be composed, which can melt when insulted, and instead of revolting at injustice, kiss the rod? Is it unfair to infer that her virtue is built on narrow views and selfishness, who can caress a man, with true feminine softness, the very moment when he treats her tyrannically? Nature never dictated such insincerity;—and, though prudence of this sort be termed a virtue, morality becomes vague when any part is supposed to rest on falsehood. These are mere expedients, and expedients are only useful for the moment.

Let the husband beware of trusting too implicitly to this servile obedience; for if his wife can with winning sweetness caress him when angry, and when she ought to be angry, unless contempt had stifled a natural effervescence, she may do the same after parting with a lover. These are all preparations for adultery; or, should the fear of the world, or of hell, restrain her desire of pleasing other men, when she can no longer please her husband, what substitute can be found by a being who was only formed, by nature and art, to please man? what can make her amends for this privation, or where is she to seek for a fresh employment? where find sufficient strength of mind to determine to begin the search, when her habits are fixed, and vanity has long ruled her chaotic mind?

But this partial moralist recommends cunning systematically and plausibly.

'Daughters should be always submissive; their mothers, however, should not be inexorable. To make a young person tractable, she ought not to be made unhappy, to make her modest she ought not to be rendered stupid. On the contrary, I should not be displeased at her being permitted to use some art, not to elude punishment in case of disobedience, but to exempt herself from the necessity of obeying. It is not necessary to make her dependence burdensome, but only to let her feel it. Subtilty is a talent natural to the sex; and, as I am persuaded, all our natural inclinations are right and good in themselves, I am of opinion this should be cultivated as well as the others: it is requisite for us only to prevent its abuse.'[7]

'Whatever is, is right,'[8] he then proceeds triumphantly to infer. Granted;—yet, perhaps, no aphorism ever contained a more paradoxical assertion. It is a solemn truth with respect to God. He, reverentially I speak, sees the whole at once, and saw its just proportions in the womb of time; but man, who can only inspect disjointed parts, finds many things wrong; and it is a part of the system, and therefore

7. *Emilius* IV, v, p. 33.
8. *Emilius* IV, v, p. 35. Rousseau's translator here quotes Pope's *An Essay on Man*, I, l. 294: "One truth is clear, whatever IS, is RIGHT."

right, that he should endeavour to alter what appears to him to be so, even while he bows to the Wisdom of his Creator, and respects the darkness he labours to disperse.

The inference that follows is just, supposing the principle to be sound. 'The superiority of address,[9] peculiar to the female sex, is a very equitable indemnification for their inferiority in point of strength: without this, woman would not be the companion of man; but his slave: it is by her superiour art and ingenuity that she preserves her equality, and governs him while she affects to obey. Woman has every thing against her, as well our faults, as her own timidity and weakness; she has nothing in her favour, but her subtilty and her beauty. Is it not very reasonable, therefore, she should cultivate both?'[1] Greatness of mind can never dwell with cunning, or address; for I shall not boggle about words, when their direct signification is insincerity and falsehood, but content myelf with observing, that if any class of mankind be so created that it must necessarily be educated by rules not strictly deducible from truth, virtue is an affair of convention. How could Rousseau dare to assert, after giving this advice, that in the grand end of existence the object of both sexes should be the same, when he well knew that the mind, formed by its pursuits, is expanded by great views swallowing up little ones, or that it becomes itself little?

Men have superiour strength of body; but were it not for mistaken notions of beauty, women would acquire sufficient to enable them to earn their own subsistence, the true definition of independence; and to bear those bodily inconveniencies and exertions that are requisite to strengthen the mind.

Let us then, by being allowed to take the same exercise as boys, not only during infancy, but youth, arrive at perfection of body, that we may know how far the natural superiority of man extends. For what reason or virtue can be expected from a creature when the seed-time of life is neglected? None—did not the winds of heaven casually scatter many useful seeds in the fallow ground.

'Beauty cannot be acquired by dress, and coquetry is an art not so early and speedily attained. While girls are yet young, however, they are in a capacity to study agreeable gesture, a pleasing modulation of voice, an easy carriage and behaviour; as well as to take the advantage of gracefully adapting their looks and attitudes to time, place, and occasion. Their application, therefore, should not be solely confined to the arts of industry and the needle, when they come to display other talents, whose utility is already apparent.'[2]

9. Persuasive skill.
1. *Emilius* IV, v, p. 35–36.
2. *Emilius* IV, v, p. 40.

'For my part, I would have a young Englishwoman cultivate her agreeable talents, in order to please her future husband, with as much care and assiduity as a young Circassian cultivates her's, to fit her for the Haram of an Eastern bashaw.'[3]

To render women completely insignificant, he adds—'The tongues of women are very voluble; they speak earlier, more readily, and more agreeably, than the men; they are accused also of speaking much more: but so it ought to be, and I should be very ready to convert this reproach into a compliment; their lips and eyes have the same activity, and for the same reason. A man speaks of what he knows, a woman of what pleases her; the one requires knowledge, the other taste; the principal object of a man's discourse should be what is useful, that of a woman's what is agreeable. There ought to be nothing in common between their different conversation but truth.

'We ought not, therefore, to restrain the prattle of girls, in the same manner as we should that of boys, with that severe question; *To what purpose are you talking?* but by another, which is no less difficult to answer, *How will your discourse be received?* In infancy, while they are as yet incapable to discern good from evil, they ought to observe it, as a law, never to say any thing disagreeable to those whom they are speaking to: what will render the practice of this rule also the more difficult, is, that it must ever be subordinate to the former, of never speaking falsely or telling an untruth.'[4] To govern the tongue in this manner must require great address indeed; and it is too much practised both by men and women.—Out of the abundance of the heart how few speak![5] So few, that I, who love simplicity, would gladly give up politeness for a quarter of the virtue that has been sacrificed to an equivocal quality which at best should only be the polish of virtue.

But, to complete the sketch. 'It is easy to be conceived, that if male children be not in a capacity to form any true notions of religion, those ideas must be greatly above the conception of the females: it is for this very reason, I would begin to speak to them the earlier on this subject; for if we were to wait till they were in a capacity to discuss methodically such profound questions, we should run a risk of never speaking to them on this subject as long as they lived. Reason in women is a practical reason, capacitating them artfully to discover the means of attaining a known end, but which would never enable them to discover that end itself. The social relations of the

3. *Emilius* IV, v, p. 42. The women of Circassia, a region in the Caucasus Mountains, were famed for their beauty and often sold for concubines in the slave markets of the Ottoman Empire.
4. *Emilius* IV, v, pp. 4–6.
5. Matthew 12:34: "for out of the abundance of the heart the mouth speaketh."

sexes are indeed truly admirable: from their union there results a moral person, of which woman may be termed the eyes, and man the hand, with this dependence on each other, that it is from the man that the woman is to learn what she is to see, and it is of the woman that man is to learn what he ought to do. If woman could recur to the first principles of things as well as man, and man was capacitated to enter into their *minutiæ* as well as woman, always independent of each other, they would live in perpetual discord, and their union could not subsist. But in the present harmony which naturally subsists between them, their different faculties tend to one common end; it is difficult to say which of them conduces the most to it: each follows the impulse of the other; each is obedient, and both are masters.

'As the conduct of a woman is subservient to the public opinion, her faith in matters of religion should, for that very reason, be subject to authority. *Every daughter ought to be of the same religion as her mother, and every wife to be of the same religion as her husband: for, though such religion should be false, that docility which induces the mother and daughter to submit to the order of nature, takes away, in the sight of God, the criminality of their error.*[6] As they are not in a capacity to judge for themselves, they ought to abide by the decision of their fathers and husbands as confidently as by that of the church.

'As authority ought to regulate the religion of the women, it is not so needful to explain to them the reasons for their belief, as to lay down precisely the tenets they are to believe: for the creed, which presents only obscure ideas to the mind, is the source of fanaticism; and that which presents absurdities, leads to infidelity.'[7]

Absolute, uncontroverted authority, it seems, must subsist somewhere: but is not this a direct and exclusive appropriation of reason? The *rights* of humanity have been thus confined to the male line from Adam downwards. Rousseau would carry his male aristocracy still further, for he insinuates, that he should not blame those, who contend for leaving woman in a state of the most profound ignorance, if it were not necessary in order to preserve her chastity and justify the man's choice, in the eyes of the world, to give her a little knowledge of men, and the customs produced by human passions; else she might propagate at home without being rendered less voluptuous and innocent by the exercise of her understanding: excepting,

6. "What is to be the consequence, if the mother's and husband's opinion should *chance* not to agree? An ignorant person cannot be reasoned out of an error—and when *persuaded* to give up one prejudice for another the mind is unsettled. Indeed, the husband may not have any religion to teach her, though in such a situation she will be in great want of a support to her virtue, independent of worldly considerations" [Wollstonecraft's note]. The quotation is from *Emilius* IV, v, pp. 48–49. The italics are Wollstonecraft's.
7. *Emilius* IV, v, p. 50.

indeed, during the first year of marriage, when she might employ it to dress like Sophia. 'Her dress is extremely modest in appearance, and yet very coquettish in fact: she does not make a display of her charms, she conceals them; but in concealing them, she knows how to affect your imagination. Every one who sees her will say, There is a modest and discreet girl; but while you are near her, your eyes and affections wander all over her person, so that you cannot withdraw them; and you would conclude, that every part of her dress, simple as it seems, was only put in its proper order to be taken to pieces by the imagination.'[8] Is this modesty? Is this a preparation for immortality? Again.—What opinion are we to form of a system of education, when the author says of his heroine, 'that with her, doing things well, is but a *secondary* concern; her principal concern is to do them *neatly.*'[9]

Secondary, in fact, are all her virtues and qualities, for, respecting religion, he makes her parents thus address her, accustomed to submission—'Your husband will instruct you in *good time.*'[1]

After thus cramping a woman's mind, if, in order to keep it fair, he have not made it quite a blank, he advises her to reflect, that a reflecting man may not yawn in her company, when he is tired of caressing her.[2]—What has she to reflect about who must obey? and would it not be a refinement on cruelty only to open her mind to make the darkness and misery of her fate *visible?*[3] Yet, these are his sensible remarks; how consistent with what I have already been obliged to quote, to give a fair view of the subject, the reader may determine.

'They who pass their whole lives in working for their daily bread, have no ideas beyond their business or their interest, and all their understanding seems to lie in their fingers' ends. This ignorance is neither prejudicial to their integrity nor their morals; it is often of service to them. Sometimes, by means of reflection, we are led to compound with our duty, and we conclude by substituting a jargon of words, in the room of things. Our own conscience is the most enlightened philosopher. There is no need to be acquainted with Tully's[4] offices, to make a man of probity: and perhaps the most virtuous woman in the world, is the least acquainted with the definition of virtue. But it is no less true, that an improved understanding only can render society agreeable; and it is a melancholy thing for a father of a family, who is fond of home, to be obliged to be

8. *Emilius* IV, v, p. 91.
9. *Emilius* IV, v, p. 94. The italics are Wollstonecraft's.
1. *Emilius* IV, v, p. 97. The italics are Wollstonecraft's.
2. Perhaps *Emilius* IV, v, p. 124.
3. *Paradise Lost* I.63: "No light, but rather darkness visible."
4. Marcus Tullius Cicero (106–43 B.C.E.), whose treatise *De Officiis* had since the Renaissance been deemed an essential text in the education of young gentlemen.

always wrapped up in himself, and to have nobody about him to whom he can impart his sentiments.

'Besides, how should a woman void of reflection be capable of educating her children? How should she discern what is proper for them? How should she incline them to those virtues she is unacquainted with, or to that merit of which she has no idea? She can only sooth or chide them; render them insolent or timid; she will make them formal coxcombs, or ignorant blockheads; but will never make them sensible or amiable.'⁵ How indeed should she, when her husband is not always at hand to lend her his reason?—when they both together make but one moral being. A blind will, 'eyes without hands,'⁶ would go a very little way; and perchance his abstract reason, that should concentrate the scattered beams of her practical reason, may be employed in judging of the flavour of wine, descanting on the sauces most proper for turtle; or, more profoundly intent at a card-table, he may be generalizing his ideas as he bets away his fortune, leaving all the *minutiæ* of education to his helpmate, or to chance.

But, granting that woman ought to be beautiful, innocent, and silly, to render her a more alluring and indulgent companion;—what is her understanding sacrificed for? And why is all this preparation necessary only, according to Rousseau's own account, to make her the mistress of her husband, a very short time? For no man ever insisted more on the transient nature of love. Thus speaks the philosopher. 'Sensual pleasures are transient. The habitual state of the affections always loses by their gratification. The imagination, which decks the object of our desires, is lost in fruition. Excepting the Supreme Being, who is self-existent, there is nothing beautiful but what is ideal.'⁷

But he returns to his unintelligible paradoxes again, when he thus addresses Sophia. 'Emilius, in becoming your husband, is become your master; and claims your obedience. Such is the order of nature. When a man is married, however, to such a wife as Sophia, it is proper he should be directed by her: this is also agreeable to the order of nature: it is, therefore, to give you as much authority over his heart as his sex gives him over your person, that I have made you the arbiter of his pleasures. It may cost you, perhaps, some disagreeable self-denial; but you will be certain of maintaining your empire over him, if you can preserve it over yourself—what I have already observed, also, shows me, that this difficult attempt does not surpass your courage.

5. *Emilius* IV, v, pp. 124–25.
6. A reference to the quotation from Rousseau on p. 93 herein: "from their union there results a moral person, of which woman may be termed the eyes, and man the hand."
7. *Emilius* IV, v, p. 214.

'Would you have your husband constantly at your feet? keep him at some distance from your person. You will long maintain the authority in love, if you know but how to render your favours rare and valuable. It is thus you may employ even the arts of coquetry in the service of virtue, and those of love in that of reason.'[8]

I shall close my extracts with a just description of a comfortable couple. 'And yet you must not imagine, that even such management will always suffice. Whatever precaution be taken, enjoyment will, by degrees, take off the edge of passion. But when love hath lasted as long as possible, a pleasing habitude supplies its place, and the attachment of a mutual confidence succeeds to the transports of passion. Children often form a more agreeable and permanent connection between married people than even love itself. When you cease to be the mistress of Emilius, you will continue to be his wife and friend, you will be the mother of his children.'[9]

Children, he truly observes, form a much more permanent connexion between married people than love. Beauty, he declares, will not be valued, or even seen after a couple have lived six months together; artificial graces and coquetry will likewise pall on the senses: why then does he say that a girl should be educated for her husband with the same care as for an eastern haram?

I now appeal from the reveries of fancy and refined licentiousness to the good sense of mankind, whether, if the object of education be to prepare women to become chaste wives and sensible mothers, the method so plausibly recommended in the foregoing sketch, be the one best calculated to produce those ends? Will it be allowed that the surest way to make a wife chaste, is to teach her to practise the wanton arts of a mistress, termed virtuous coquetry, by the sensualist who can no longer relish the artless charms of sincerity, or taste the pleasure arising from a tender intimacy, when confidence is unchecked by suspicion, and rendered interesting by sense?

The man who can be contented to live with a pretty, useful companion, without a mind, has lost in voluptuous gratifications a taste for more refined enjoyments; he has never felt the calm satisfaction, that refreshes the parched heart, like the silent dew of heaven,—of being beloved by one who could understand him.—In the society of his wife he is still alone, unless when the man is sunk in the brute. 'The charm of life,' says a grave philosophical reasoner, is 'sympathy; nothing pleases us more than to observe in other men a fellow-feeling with all the emotions of our own breast.'[1]

---

8. *Emilius* IV, v, pp. 288–89.
9. "Rousseau's Emilius" [Wollstonecraft's note]. The quotation is from IV, v, pp. 289–90.
1. Smith, *The Theory of Moral Sentiments:* "But whatever may be the cause of sympathy, or however it may be excited, nothing pleases us more than to observe in other men a fellow-feeling with all the emotions of our own breast" (p. 13).

But, according to the tenour of reasoning, by which women are kept from the tree of knowledge, the important years of youth, the usefulness of age, and the rational hopes of futurity, are all to be sacrificed to render women an object of desire for a *short* time. Besides, how could Rousseau expect them to be virtuous and constant when reason is neither allowed to be the foundation of their virtue, nor truth the object of their inquiries?

But all Rousseau's errors in reasoning arose from sensibility, and sensibility to their charms women are very ready to forgive! When he should have reasoned he became impassioned, and reflection inflamed his imagination instead of enlightening his understanding. Even his virtues also led him farther astray; for, born with a warm constitution and lively fancy, nature carried him toward the other sex with such eager fondness, that he soon became lascivious. Had he given way to these desires, the fire would have extinguished itself in a natural manner; but virtue, and a romantic kind of delicacy, made him practise self-denial; yet, when fear, delicacy, or virtue, restrained him, he debauched his imagination, and reflecting on the sensations to which fancy gave force, he traced them in the most glowing colours, and sunk them deep into his soul.

He then sought for solitude, not sleep[2] with the man of nature; or calmly investigate the causes of things under the shade where Sir Isaac Newton indulged contemplation,[3] but merely to indulge his feelings. And so warmly has he painted, what he forcibly felt, that, interesting the heart and inflaming the imagination of his readers; in proportion to the strength of their fancy, they imagine that their understanding is convinced when they only sympathize with a poetic writer, who skilfully exhibits the objects of sense, most voluptuously shadowed or gracefully veiled—And thus making us feel whilst dreaming that we reason, erroneous conclusions are left in the mind.

Why was Rousseau's life divided between ecstasy and misery? Can any other answer be given than this, that the effervescence of his imagination produced both; but, had his fancy been allowed to cool, it is possible that he might have acquired more strength of mind. Still, if the purpose of life be to educate the intellectual part of man, all with respect to him was right; yet, had not death led to a nobler scene of action, it is probable that he would have enjoyed more equal happiness on earth, and have felt the calm sensations of the man of nature instead of being prepared for another stage of existence by nourishing the passions which agitate the civilized man.

2. The first edition reads "not to sleep," which makes more sense.
3. Tradition has it that as Newton sat under a shade tree in a garden in 1665 and saw an apple fall, he was set to thinking about his theory of gravity.

But peace to his manes![4] I war not with his ashes, but his opinions. I war only with the sensibility that led him to degrade woman by making her the slave of love.

> ————'Curs'd vassalage,
> 'First idoliz'd till love's hot fire be o'er,
> 'Then slaves to those who courted us before.'
>
> *Dryden*.[5]

The pernicious tendency of those books, in which the writers insidiously degrade the sex whilst they are prostrate before their personal charms, cannot be too often or too severely exposed.

Let us, my dear contemporaries, arise above such narrow prejudices! If wisdom be desirable on its own account, if virtue, to deserve the name, must be founded on knowledge; let us endeavour to strengthen our minds by reflection, till our heads become a balance for our hearts; let us not confine all our thoughts to the petty occurrences of the day, or our knowledge to an acquaintance with our lovers' or husbands' hearts; but let the practice of every duty be subordinate to the grand one of improving our minds, and preparing our affections for a more exalted state!

Beware then, my friends, of suffering the heart to be moved by every trivial incident: the reed is shaken by a breeze, and annually dies, but the oak stands firm, and for ages braves the storm!

Were we, indeed, only created to flutter our hour out and die—why let us then indulge sensibility, and laugh at the severity of reason.— Yet, alas! even then we should want strength of body and mind, and life would be lost in feverish pleasures or wearisome languor.

But the system of education, which I earnestly wish to see exploded, seems to presuppose what ought never to be taken for granted, that virtue shields us from the casualties of life; and that fortune, slipping off her bandage, will smile on a well-educated female, and bring in her hand an Emilius or a Telemachus.[6] Whilst, on the contrary, the reward which virtue promises to her votaries is confined, it seems clear, to their own bosoms; and often must they contend with the most vexatious worldly cares, and bear with the vices and humours of relations for whom they can never feel a friendship.

---

4. Spirit or "shade" of a departed person.
5. From John Dryden's opera adapting *Paradise Lost*, *The State of Innocence: and Fall of Man* V. i. 58–60. The first line, spoken by Eve, should read "Curs'd vassalage of all my future kind."
6. Book v of *Émile* imagines a scenario in which Sophie, Rousseau's heroine, languishes after her reading of *The Adventures of Telemachus, the Son of Ulysses*, a didactic epic in prose by Bishop François de Salignac de la Mothe-Fénelon (published 1699). Smitten with its hero, she is primed for her introduction to Émile—ready to consider him Telemachus come to life (see *Emilius* IV, v, pp. 115ff.). "Bandage": blindfold.

There have been many women in the world who, instead of being supported by the reason and virtue of their fathers and brothers, have strengthened their own minds by struggling with their vices and follies; yet have never met with a hero, in the shape of a husband; who, paying the debt that mankind owed them, might chance to bring back their reason to its natural dependent state, and restore the usurped prerogative, of rising above opinion, to man.

SECT. II

Dr. Fordyce's sermons have long made a part of a young woman's library; nay, girls at school are allowed to read them; but I should instantly dismiss them from my pupil's, if I wished to strengthen her understanding, by leading her to form sound principles on a broad basis; or, were I only anxious to cultivate her taste; though they must be allowed to contain many sensible observations.[7]

Dr. Fordyce may have had a very laudable end in view; but these discourses are written in such an affected style, that were it only on that account, and had I nothing to object against his *mellifluous* precepts, I should not allow girls to peruse them, unless I designed to hunt every spark of nature out of their composition, melting every human quality into female meekness and artificial grace. I say artificial, for true grace arises from some kind of independence of mind.

Children, careless of pleasing, and only anxious to amuse themselves, are often very graceful; and the nobility who have mostly lived with inferiours, and always had the command of money, acquire a graceful ease of deportment, which should rather be termed habitual grace of body, than that superiour gracefulness which is truly the expression of the mind. This mental grace, not noticed by vulgar eyes, often flashes across a rough countenance, and irradiating every feature, shows simplicity and independence of mind.—It is then we read characters of immortality in the eye, and see the soul in every gesture, though when at rest, neither the face nor limbs may have much beauty to recommend them; or the behaviour, any thing peculiar to attract universal attention. The mass of mankind, however, look for more *tangible* beauty; yet simplicity is, in general, admired, when people do not consider what they admire; and can there be simplicity without sincerity? But, to have done with remarks that are in some measure desultory, though naturally excited by the subject—

---

7. James Fordyce (1720–1796), a Presbyterian minister much admired in the mid-eighteenth century for the sentimental style of his preaching, published *Sermons to Young Women* in 1765. It was frequently reprinted and translated into several European languages.

In declamatory periods[8] Dr. Fordyce spins out Rousseau's eloquence; and in most sentimental rant, details his opinions respecting the female character, and the behaviour which woman ought to assume to render her lovely.

He shall speak for himself, for thus he makes Nature address man. 'Behold these smiling innocents, whom I have graced with my fairest gifts, and committed to your protection; behold them with love and respect; treat them with tenderness and honour. They are timid and want to be defended. They are frail; O do not take advantage of their weakness! Let their fears and blushes endear them. Let their confidence in you never be abused.—But is it possible, that any of you can be such barbarians, so supremely wicked, as to abuse it? Can you find in your hearts[9] to despoil the gentle, trusting creatures of their treasure, or do any thing to strip them of their native robe of virtue? Curst be the impious hand that would dare to violate the unblemished form of Chastity! Thou wretch! thou ruffian! forbear; nor venture to provoke heaven's fiercest vengeance.'[1] I know not any comment that can be made seriously on this curious passage, and I could produce many similar ones; and some, so very sentimental, that I have heard rational men use the word indecent, when they mentioned them with disgust.

Throughout there is a display of cold artificial feelings, and that parade of sensibility which boys and girls should be taught to despise as the sure mark of a little vain mind. Florid appeals are made to heaven, and to the *beauteous innocents*, the fairest images of heaven here below, whilst sober sense is left far behind.—This is not the language of the heart, nor will it ever reach it, though the ear may be tickled.

I shall be told, perhaps, that the public have been pleased with these volumes.—True—and Hervey's Meditations[2] are still read, though he equally sinned against sense and taste.

I particularly object to the lover-like phrases of pumped up passion, which are every where interspersed. If women be ever allowed to walk without leading-strings,[3] why must they be cajoled into virtue by artful flattery and sexual compliments?—Speak to them the language of truth and soberness, and away with the lullaby strains of condescending endearment! Let them be taught to respect

---

8. In a fervid, studied style.
9. "Can you?—Can you? would be the most emphatical comment, were it drawled out in a whining voice" [Wollstonecraft's note].
1. Fordyce, *Sermons to Young Women* (London, 1766), I, p. 51. All references are to this edition.
2. James Hervey (1714–1758) was a devotional writer whose *Meditations and Contemplations*, a highly popular piece of inspirational writing, had reached a twenty-fifth edition by 1791.
3. Straps used to hold up children learning to walk.

themselves as rational creatures, and not led to have a passion for their own insipid persons. It moves my gall to hear a preacher descanting on dress and needle-work; and still more, to hear him address the *British fair, the fairest of the fair,* as if they had only feelings.

Even recommending piety he uses the following argument. 'Never, perhaps, does a fine woman strike more deeply, than when, composed into pious recollection, and possessed with the noblest considerations, she assumes, without knowing it, superiour dignity and new graces; so that the beauties of holiness seem to radiate about her, and the by-standers are almost induced to fancy her already worshipping amongst her kindred angels!'[4] Why are women to be thus bred up with a desire of conquest? the very word, used in this sense, gives me a sickly qualm! Do religion and virtue offer no stronger motives, no brighter reward? Must they always be debased by being made to consider the sex of their companions? Must they be taught always to be pleasing? And when levelling their small artillery at the heart of man, is it necessary to tell them that a little sense is sufficient to render their attention *incredibly soothing?* 'As a small degree of knowledge entertains in a woman, so from a woman, though for a different reason, a small expression of kindness delights, particularly if she have beauty!'[5] I should have supposed for the same reason.

Why are girls to be told that they resemble angels; but to sink them below women? Or, that a gentle innocent female is an object that comes nearer to the idea which we have formed of angels than any other. Yet they are told, at the same time, that they are only like angels when they are young and beautiful; consequently, it is their persons, not their virtues, that procure them this homage.

Idle empty words! What can such delusive flattery lead to, but vanity and folly? The lover, it is true, has a poetic licence to exalt his mistress; his reason is the bubble[6] of his passion, and he does not utter a falsehood when he borrows the language of adoration. His imagination may raise the idol of his heart, unblamed, above humanity; and happy would it be for women, if they were only flattered by the men who loved them; I mean, who love the individual, not the sex; but should a grave preacher interlard his discourses with such fooleries?

In sermons or novels, however, voluptuousness is always true to its text. Men are allowed by moralists to cultivate, as Nature directs, different qualities, and assume the different characters, that the

<hr />

4. Fordyce, *Sermons*, II, p. 224. Fordyce here instructs women on appropriate behavior in church.
5. Fordyce, *Sermons*, II, p. 245.
6. Dupe.

same passions, modified almost to infinity, give to each individual. A virtuous man may have a choleric or a sanguine constitution, be gay or grave, unreproved; be firm till he is almost over-bearing, or, weakly submissive, have no will or opinion of his own; but all women are to be levelled, by meekness and docility, into one character of yielding softness and gentle compliance.

I will use the preacher's own words. 'Let it be observed, that in your sex manly exercises are never graceful; that in them a tone and figure, as well as an air and deportment, of the masculine kind, are always forbidding; and that men of sensibility desire in every woman soft features, and a flowing voice, a form, not robust, and demeanour delicate and gentle.'[7]

Is not the following portrait—the portrait of a house slave? 'I am astonished at the folly of many women, who are still reproaching their husbands for leaving them alone, for preferring this or that company to theirs, for treating them with this and the other mark of disregard or indifference; when, to speak the truth, they have themselves in a great measure to blame. Not that I would justify the men in any thing wrong on their part. But had you behaved to them with more *respectful observance*, and a more *equal tenderness; studying their humours, overlooking their mistakes, submitting to their opinions* in matters indifferent, passing by little instances of unevenness, caprice, or passion, giving *soft* answers to hasty words, complaining as seldom as possible, and making it your daily care to relieve their anxieties and prevent their wishes, to enliven the hour of dulness, and call up the ideas of felicity: had you pursued this conduct, I doubt not but you would have maintained and even increased their esteem, so far as to have secured every degree of influence that could conduce to their virtue, or your mutal satisfaction; and your house might at this day have been the abode of domestic bliss.'[8] Such a woman ought to be an angel—or she is an ass—for I discern not a trace of the human character, neither reason nor passion in this domestic drudge, whose being is absorbed in that of a tyrant's.

Still Dr. Fordyce must have very little acquaintance with the human heart, if he really supposed that such conduct would bring back wandering love, instead of exciting contempt. No, beauty, gentleness, &c. &c. may gain a heart; but esteem, the only lasting affection, can alone be obtained by virtue supported by reason. It is respect for the understanding that keeps alive tenderness for the person.

As these volumes are so frequently put into the hands of young people, I have taken more notice of them than, strictly speaking,

---

7. Fordyce, *Sermons*, II, p. 245.
8. Fordyce, *Sermons*, II, p. 299. The italics are Wollstonecraft's.

they deserve; but as they have contributed to vitiate the taste, and enervate the understanding of many of my fellow-creatures, I could not pass them silently over.

Such paternal solicitude pervades Dr. Gregory's Legacy to his Daughters, that I enter on the task of criticism with affectionate respect;[9] but as this little volume has many attractions to recommend it to the notice of the most respectable part of my sex, I cannot silently pass over arguments that so speciously support opinions which, I think, have had the most baneful effect on the morals and manners of the female world.

His easy familiar style is particularly suited to the tenor of his advice, and the melancholy tenderness which his respect for the memory of a beloved wife, diffuses through the whole work, renders it very interesting; yet there is a degree of concise elegance conspicuous in many passages that disturbs this sympathy; and we pop on[1] the author, when we only expected to meet the—father.

Besides, having two objects in view, he seldom adhered steadily to either; for wishing to make his daughters amiable, and fearing lest unhappiness should only be the consequence, of instilling sentiments that might draw them out of the track of common life without enabling them to act with consonant independence and dignity, he checks the natural flow of his thoughts, and neither advises one thing nor the other.

In the preface he tells them a mournful truth, 'that they will hear, at least once in their lives, the genuine sentiments of a man who has no interest in deceiving them.'[2]

Hapless woman! what can be expected from thee when the beings on whom thou art said naturally to depend for reason and support, have all an interest in deceiving thee! This is the root of the evil that has shed a corroding mildew on all thy virtues; and blighting in the bud thy opening faculties, has rendered thee the weak thing thou art! It is this separate interest—this insidious state of warfare, that undermines morality, and divides mankind!

If love have made some women wretched—how many more has the cold unmeaning intercourse of gallantry rendered vain and useless! yet this heartless attention to the sex is reckoned so manly, so polite that, till society is very differently organized, I fear, this vestige

---

9. Gregory wrote *A Father's Legacy to His Daughters* while in failing health, and it was published the year after his death, in 1774. His avowed purpose is to instruct his motherless daughters while he can. See p. 236 herein.
1. Come upon suddenly.
2. Gregory, p. 6.

of gothic[3] manners will not be done away by a more reasonable and affectionate mode of conduct. Besides, to strip it of its imaginary dignity, I must observe, that in the most uncivilized European states this lip-service prevails in a very great degree, accompanied with extreme dissoluteness of morals. In Portugal, the country that I particularly allude to, it takes place of the most serious moral obligations; for a man is seldom assassinated when in the company of a woman. The savage hand of rapine is unnerved by this chivalrous spirit; and, if the stroke of vengeance cannot be stayed—the lady is entreated to pardon the rudeness and depart in peace, though sprinkled, perhaps, with her husband's or brother's blood.[4]

I shall pass over his strictures on religion, because I mean to discuss that subject in a separate chapter.

The remarks relative to behaviour, though many of them very sensible, I entirely disapprove of, because it appears to me to be beginning, as it were, at the wrong end. A cultivated understanding, and an affectionate heart, will never want starched rules of decorum—something more substantial than seemliness will be the result; and, without understanding the behaviour here recommended, would be rank affection. Decorum, indeed, is the one thing needful!—decorum is to supplant nature, and banish all simplicity and variety of character out of the female world. Yet what good end can all this superficial counsel produce? It is, however, much easier to point out this or that mode of behaviour, than to set the reason to work; but, when the mind has been stored with useful knowledge, and strengthened by being employed, the regulation of the behaviour may safely be left to its guidance.

Why, for instance, should the following caution be given when art of every kind must contaminate the mind; and why entangle the grand motives of action, which reason and religion equally combine to enforce, with pitiful worldly shifts and slight of hand tricks to gain the applause of gaping tasteless fools? 'Be even cautious in displaying your good sense.[5] It will be thought you assume a superiority over the rest of the company—But if you happen to have any learning, keep it a profound secret, especially from the men who generally

3. Barbarous or uncouth.
4. Wollstonecraft may be remembering *Sketches of Society and Manners in Portugal* (London, 1787), by Arthur William Costigan (pseudonym used by James Ferriar), which she reviewed for the *Analytical Review* in August 1788. It tells the story of the feuding between two Portuguese cousins, rivals in love. One, an infantry officer, shoots the other when he encounters him traveling with his sister, "this being done, he asked a thousand pardons of the lady, for having so incommoded her, and begged to know whither she wished to be conducted" (p. 403). Wollstonecraft recommends the book to readers "who wish to observe the effect a religion the most absurd, and a government the most arbitrary, would have in modifying the human passions" (*Works*, VII, p. 29).
5. "Let women once acquire good sense—and if it deserve the name, it will teach them; or, of what use will it be? how to employ it" [Wollstonecraft's note].

look with a jealous and malignant eye on a woman of great parts, and a cultivated understanding.'[6] If men of real merit, as he afterwards observes, be superior to this meanness, where is the necessity that the behaviour of the whole sex should be modulated to please fools, or men, who having little claim to respect as individuals, choose to keep close in their phalanx. Men, indeed, who insist on their common superiority, having only this sexual superiority, are certainly very excusable.

There would be no end to rules for behaviour, if it be proper always to adopt the tone of the company; for thus, for ever varying the key, a *flat* would often pass for a *natural* note.

Surely it would have been wiser to have advised women to improve themselves till they rose above the fumes of vanity; and then to let the public opinion come round—for where are rules of accommodation to stop? The narrow path of truth and virtue inclines neither to the right nor left—it is a straightforward business, and they who are earnestly pursuing their road, may bound over many decorous prejudices, without leaving modesty behind. Make the heart clean, and give the head employment, and I will venture to predict that there will be nothing offensive in the behaviour.

The air of fashion, which many young people are so eager to attain, always strikes me like the studied attitudes of some modern pictures, copied with tasteless servility after the antiques;—the soul is left out, and none of the parts are tied together by what may properly be termed character. This varnish of fashion, which seldom sticks very close to sense, may dazzle the weak; but leave nature to itself, and it will seldom disgust the wise. Besides, when a woman has sufficient sense not to pretend to any thing which she does not understand in some degree, there is no need of determining to hide her talents under a bushel.[7] Let things take their natural course, and all will be well.

It is this system of dissimulation, throughout the volume, that I despise. Women are always to *seem* to be this and that—yet virtue might apostrophize them, in the words of Hamlet—Seems! I know not seems!—Have that within that passeth show![8]—

Still the same tone occurs; for in another place, after recommending, without sufficiently discriminating delicacy, he adds, 'The men will complain of your reserve. They will assure you that a franker behaviour would make you more amiable. But, trust me, they are not

6. Gregory, pp. 31–32.
7. Wollstonecraft combines the New Testament parable of the candle under the bushel (Matthew 5:15; Mark 4:21; Luke 11:33) with the parable of the talents (Matthew 25: 14–30).
8. *Hamlet* I.ii.76 and 85: "Seems, Madam! nay it is; I know not 'seems' . . . / But I have that within which passeth show."

sincere when they tell you so.—I acknowledge that on some occasions it might render you more agreeable as companions, but it would make you less amiable as women: an important distinction, which many of your sex are not aware of.'[9]—

This desire of being always women, is the very consciousness that degrades the sex. Excepting with a lover, I must repeat with emphasis, a former observation,—it would be well if they were only agreeable or rational companions.—But in this respect his advice is even inconsistent with a passage which I mean to quote with the most marked approbation.

'The sentiment, that a woman may allow all innocent freedoms, provided her virtue is secure, is both grossly indelicate and dangerous, and has proved fatal to many of your sex.'[1] With this opinion I perfectly coincide. A man, or a woman, of any feeling, must always wish to convince a beloved object that it is the caresses of the individual, not the sex, that are received and returned with pleasure; and, that the heart, rather than the senses, is moved. Without this natural delicacy, love becomes a selfish personal gratification that soon degrades the character.

I carry this sentiment still further. Affection, when love is out of the question, authorises many personal endearments, that naturally flowing from an innocent heart, give life to the behaviour; but the personal intercourse of appetite, gallantry, or vanity, is despicable. When a man squeezes the hand of a pretty woman, handing her to a carriage, whom he has never seen before, she will consider such an impertinent freedom in the light of an insult, if she have any true delicacy, instead of being flattered by this unmeaning homage to beauty. These are the privileges of friendship, or the momentary homage which the heart pays to virtue, when it flashes suddenly on the notice—mere animal spirits have no claim to the kindnesses of affection!

Wishing to feed the affections with what is now the food of vanity, I would fain persuade my sex to act from simpler principles. Let them merit love, and they will obtain it, though they may never be told that—'The power of a fine woman over the hearts of men, of men of the finest parts, is even beyond what she conceives.'[2]

I have already noticed the narrow cautions with respect to duplicity, female softness, delicacy of constitution; for these are the changes which he rings round without ceasing—in a more decorous manner, it is true, than Rousseau; but it all comes home to the same point, and whoever is at the trouble to analyze these sentiments, will find the first principles not quite so delicate as the superstructure.

9. Gregory, pp. 36–37.
1. Gregory, p. 44.
2. Gregory, p. 42.

The subject of amusements is treated in too cursory a manner; but with the same spirit.

When I treat of friendship, love, and marriage, it will be found that we materially differ in opinion; I shall not then forestall what I have to observe on these important subjects; but confine my remarks to the general tenor of them, to that cautious family prudence, to those confined views of partial unenlightened affection, which exclude pleasure and improvement, by vainly wishing to ward off sorrow and error—and by thus guarding the heart and mind, destroy also all their energy.—It is far better to be often deceived than never to trust; to be disappointed in love than never to love; to lose a husband's fondness than forfeit his esteem.

Happy would it be for the world, and for individuals, of course, if all this unavailing solicitude to attain worldly happiness, on a confined plan, were turned into an anxious desire to improve the understanding.—'Wisdom is the principal thing: *therefore* get wisdom; and with all thy gettings get understanding.'[3]—'How long, ye simple ones, will ye love simplicity, and hate knowledge?'[4] Saith Wisdom to the daughters of men!—

SECT. IV

I do not mean to allude to all the writers who have written on the subject of female manners—it would, in fact, be only beating over the old ground, for they have, in general, written in the same strain; but attacking the boasted prerogative of man—the prerogative that may emphatically be called the iron sceptre of tyranny, the original sin of tyrants, I declare against all power built on prejudices, however hoary.

If the submission demanded be founded on justice—there is no appealing to a higher power—for God is Justice itself. Let us then, as children of the same parent, if not bastardized by being the younger born, reason together, and learn to submit to the authority of reason—when her voice is distinctly heard. But, if it be proved, that this throne of prerogative only rests on a chaotic mass of prejudices, that have no inherent principle of order to keep them together, or on an elephant, tortoise, or even the mighty shoulders of a son of the earth,[5] they may escape, who dare to brave the consequence, without any breach of duty, without sinning against the order of things.

---

3. Proverbs 4:7.
4. Proverbs 1:22: "How long, ye simple ones, will ye love simplicity? and the scorners delight in their scorning, and fools hate knowledge?"
5. The Titan god Atlas who supported the earth on his shoulders. In ancient Indian cosmogony, the earth was a huge tray supported by three elephants who themselves stood on the back of a giant tortoise.

Whilst reason raises man above the brutal herd, and death is big with promises, they alone are subject to blind authority who have no reliance on their own strength. 'They are free—who will be free!'[6]—

The being who can govern itself has nothing to fear in life; but if any thing be dearer than its own respect, the price must be paid to the last farthing. Virtue, like every thing valuable, must be loved for herself alone; or she will not take up her abode with us. She will not impart that peace, 'which passeth understanding,'[7] when she is merely made the stilts of reputation; and respected, with pharisaical exactness, because 'honesty is the best policy.'

That the plan of life which enables us to carry some knowledge and virtue into another world, is the one best calculated to ensure content in this, cannot be denied; yet few people act according to this principle, though it be universally allowed that it admits not of dispute. Present pleasure, or present power, carry before it these sober convictions; and it is for the day, not for life, that man bargains with happiness. How few!—how very few! have sufficient foresight, or resolution, to endure a small evil at the moment, to avoid a greater hereafter.

Woman in particular, whose virtue[8] is built on mutable prejudices, seldom attains to this greatness of mind; so that, becoming the slave of her own feelings, she is easily subjugated by those of others. Thus degraded, her reason, her misty reason! is employed rather to burnish than to snap her chains.

Indignantly have I heard women argue in the same track as men, and adopt the sentiments that brutalize them, with all the pertinacity of ignorance.

I must illustrate my assertion by a few examples. Mrs. Piozzi,[9] who often repeated by rote, what she did not understand, comes forward with Johnsonian periods.

'Seek not for happiness in singularity; and dread a refinement of wisdom as a deviation into folly.' Thus she dogmatically addresses a new married man; and to elucidate this pompous exordium, she adds, 'I said that the person of your lady would not grow more pleasing to you, but pray let her never suspect that it grows less so: that a woman will pardon an affront to her understanding much sooner

6. "He is the free man, whom the *truth* makes free!'" [Wollstonecraft's note]. From William Cowper's poem *The Task* (1785), "The Winter Morning Walk," line 733. Cowper is recalling John 8:32.
7. Philippians 4:7: "And the peace of God, which passeth all understanding, shall keep your hearts and minds through Christ Jesus."
8. "I mean to use a word that comprehends more than chastity the sexual virtue" [Wollstonecraft's note].
9. Hester Lynch Thrale Piozzi (1741–1821), woman of letters famous for her friendship with Samuel Johnson, whose biography she published in 1786. The imitability of Johnson's distinctive prose style—of his "periods"—irked many observers of the late-eighteenth-century literary scene.

than one to her person, is well known; nor will any of us contradict
the assertion. All our attainments, all our arts, are employed to gain
and keep the heart of man; and what mortification can exceed the
disappointment, if the end be not obtained? There is no reproof
however pointed, no punishment however severe, that a woman of
spirit will not prefer to neglect; and if she can endure it without
complaint, it only proves that she means to make herself amends by
the attention of others for the slights of her husband!'

These are truly masculine sentiments.—'All our *arts* are employed
to gain and keep the heart of man:'[1]—and what is the inference?—if
her person, and was there ever a person, though formed with
Medicean[2] symmetry, that was not slighted? be neglected, she will
make herself amends by endeavouring to please other men. Noble
morality! But thus is the understanding of the whole sex affronted,
and their virtue deprived of the common basis of virtue. A woman
must know, that her person cannot be as pleasing to her husband
as it was to her lover, and if she be offended with him for being a
human creature, she may as well whine about the loss of his heart
as about any other foolish thing.—And this very want of discernment or unreasonable anger, proves that he could not change his
fondness for her person into affection for her virtues or respect for
her understanding.

Whilst women avow, and act up to such opinions, their understandings, at least, deserve the contempt and obloquy that men, *who
never* insult their persons, have pointedly levelled at the female
mind. And it is the sentiments of these polite men, who do not wish
to be encumbered with mind, that vain women thoughtlessly adopt.
Yet they should know, that insulted reason alone can spread that
sacred reserve about the person, which renders human affections,
for human affections have always some base alloy, as permanent as
is consistent with the grand end of existence—the attainment of
virtue.

The Baroness de Stael[3] speaks the same language as the lady just
cited, with more enthusiasm. Her eulogium on Rousseau was accidentally put into my hands, and her sentiments, the sentiments of
too many of my sex, may serve as the text for a few comments.
'Though Rousseau,' she observes, 'has endeavoured to prevent
women from interfering in public affairs, and acting a brilliant part

1. From "Letter to a Gentleman Newly Married," incorporated into Piozzi's *Letters to and
   from the Late Samuel Johnson* (London, 1788), Letter 72, pp. 98, 100.
2. The reference is to the ancient marble statue in Florence known as the Venus de Medici.
   It was celebrated by eighteenth-century English connoisseurs as the classic example of
   perfect female proportions. "Person": Body.
3. Madame de Staël (1766–1817), born Anne Louise Germaine Necker, daughter of the
   finance minister of France, was an essayist and novelist.

in the theatre of politics; yet in speaking of them, how much has he done it to their satisfaction! If he wished to deprive them of some rights foreign to their sex, how has he for ever restored to them all those to which it has a claim! And in attempting to diminish their influence over the deliberations of men, how sacredly has he established the empire they have over their happiness! In aiding them to descend from an usurped throne, he has firmly seated them upon that to which they were destined by nature; and though he be full of indignation against them when they endeavour to resemble men, yet when they come before him with all the *charms, weaknesses, virtues* and *errors,* of their sex, his respect for their *persons* amounts almost to adoration.'[4] True!—For never was there a sensualist who paid more fervent adoration at the shrine of beauty. So devout, indeed, was his respect for the person, that excepting the virtue of chastity, for obvious reasons, he only wished to see it embellished by charms, weaknesses, and errors. He was afraid lest the austerity of reason should disturb the soft playfulness of love. The master wished to have a meretricious slave to fondle, entirely dependent on his reason and bounty; he did not want a companion, whom he should be compelled to esteem, or a friend to whom he could confide the care of his children's education, should death deprive them of their father, before he had fulfilled the sacred task. He denies woman reason, shuts her out from knowledge, and turns her aside from truth; yet his pardon is granted, because 'he admits the passion of love.' It would require some ingenuity to shew why women were to be under such an obligation to him for thus admitting love; when it is clear that he admits it only for the relaxation of men, and to perpetuate the species; but he talked with passion, and that powerful spell worked on the sensibility of a young encomiast. 'What signifies it,' pursues this rhapsodist, 'to women, that his reason disputes with them the empire, when his heart is devotedly theirs.'[5] It is not empire,—but equality, that they should contend for. Yet, if they only wished to lengthen out their sway, they should not entirely trust to their persons, for though beauty may gain a heart, it cannot keep it, even while the beauty is in full bloom, unless the mind lend, at least, some graces.

When women are once sufficiently enlightened to discover their real interest, on a grand scale, they will, I am persuaded, be very ready to resign all the prerogatives of love, that are not mutual, speaking of them as lasting prerogatives, for the calm satisfaction of friendship, and the tender confidence of habitual esteem. Before

4. De Staël, *Letters on the Works and Character of J. J. Rousseau* (London, 1789), pp. 15–16 The italics are Wollstonecraft's.
5. De Staël, *Letters,* p.16.

marriage they will not assume any insolent airs, or afterwards abjectly submit; but endeavouring to act like reasonable creatures, in both situations, they will not be tumbled from a throne to a stool.

Madame Genlis has written several entertaining books for children; and her Letters on Education afford many useful hints, that sensible parents will certainly avail themselves of; but her views are narrow, and her prejudices as unreasonable as strong.[6]

I shall pass over her vehement argument in favour of the eternity of future punishments,[7] because I blush to think that a human being should ever argue vehemently in such a cause, and only make a few remarks on her absurd manner of making the parental authority supplant reason. For every where does she inculcate not only *blind* submission to parents; but to the opinion of the world.[8]

She tells a story of a young man engaged by his father's express desire to a girl of fortune. Before the marriage could take place, she is deprived of her fortune, and thrown friendless on the world. The father practises the most infamous arts to separate his son from her, and when the son detects his villany, and following the dictates of honour marries the girl, nothing but misery ensues, because forsooth he married *without* his father's consent.[9] On what ground can religion or morality rest when justice is thus sct as defiance? With the same view she represents an accomplished young woman, as ready to marry any body that her *mama* pleased to recommend; and, as actually marrying the young man of her own choice, without feeling any emotions of passion, because that a well educated girl had not time to be in love. Is it possible to have much respect for a system of education that thus insults reason and nature?

Many similar opinions occur in her writings, mixed with sentiments that do honour to her head and heart. Yet so much superstition is mixed with her religion, and so much worldly wisdom with her morality, that I should not let a young person read her works,

6. Stéphanie-Félicité Ducrest de Saint-Albin, Comtesse de Genlis (1746–1830), French author of *Adelaide and Theodore, or Letters on Education,* a mixture of novel and educational treatise that was widely read in Britain after its translation in 1783.
7. The argument is made in *Adelaide and Theodore* through the story of Cecilia, who is forced by her father to enter a convent and, although in love with Chevalier de Murville, takes her vows. So unhappy is she that she wishes to destroy herself. Her father finally realizes his error and near the end of her short life, understands that he is "perhaps the cause of her eternal condemnation" (I, p. 183), for "Heaven punishes with such severity" (I, p. 225).
8. "A person is not to act in this or that way, though convinced they are right in so doing, because some equivocal circumstances may lead the world to *suspect* that they acted from different motives.—This is sacrificing the substance for a shadow. Let people but watch their own hearts, and act rightly, as far as they can judge, and they may patiently wait till the opinion of the world comes round. It is best to be directed by a simple motive—for justice has too often been sacrificed to propriety;—another word for convenience" [Wollstonecraft's note].
9. "Theophilus and Olympia, or, the Errors of Youth and Age," in Genlis's book of stories for young people, *Tales of the Castle* (trans. Thomas Holcroft, London, 1785), Vol. 3.

unless I could afterwards converse on the subjects, and point out the contradictions.

Mrs. Chapone's Letters[1] are written with such good sense, and unaffected humility, and contain so many useful observations, that I only mention them to pay the worthy writer this tribute of respect. I cannot, it is true, always coincide in opinion with her; but I always respect her.

The very word respect brings Mrs. Macaulay[2] to my remembrance. The woman of the greatest abilities, undoubtedly, that this country has ever produced.—And yet this woman has been suffered to die without sufficient respect being paid to her memory.

Posterity, however, will be more just; and remember that Catharine Macaulay was an example of intellectual acquirements supposed to be incompatible with the weakness of her sex. In her style of writing, indeed, no sex appears, for it is like the sense it conveys, strong and clear.

I will not call hers a masculine understanding, because I admit not of such an arrogant assumption of reason; but I contend that it was a sound one, and that her judgment, the matured fruit of profound thinking, was a proof that a woman can acquire judgment, in the full extent of the word. Possessing more penetration than sagacity, more understanding than fancy, she writes with sober energy and argumentative closeness; yet sympathy and benevolence give an interest to her sentiments, and that vital heat to arguments, which forces the reader to weigh them.[3]

When I first thought of writing these strictures I anticipated Mrs. Macaulay's approbation, with a little of that sanguine ardour, which it has been the business of my life to depress; but soon heard with the sickly qualm of disappointed hope; and the still seriousness of regret—that she was no more![4]

SECT. V

Taking a view of the different works which have been written on education, Lord Chesterfield's Letters must not be silently passed over. Not that I mean to analyze his unmanly, immoral system, or even to cull any of the useful, shrewd remarks which occur in his

1. Hester Mulso Chapone (1727–1801) was a prominent member of the circle of intellectual women known as the bluestockings. Queen Charlotte modeled the education of her eldest daughter on Chapone's Letters on the Improvement of the Mind (1773), and Wollstonecraft included an excerpt from it in The Female Reader (1789).
2. Macaulay published her Letters on Education, to which Wollstonecraft refers here, in 1790. See also p. 82, n. 5 and p. 239 herein.
3. "Coinciding in opinion with Mrs. Macaulay relative to many branches of education, I refer to her valuable work, instead of quoting her sentiments to support my own" [Wollstonecraft's note].
4. Macaulay died June 22, 1791.

epistles[5]—No, I only mean to make a few reflections on the avowed tendency of them—the art of acquiring an early knowledge of the world. An art, I will venture to assert, that preys secretly, like the worm in the bud, on the expanding powers, and turns to poison the generous juices which should mount with vigour in the youthful frame, inspiring warm affections and great resolves.[6]

For every thing, saith the wise man, there is a season;[7]—and who would look for the fruits of autumn during the genial months of spring? But this is mere declamation, and I mean to reason with those worldly-wise instructors, who, instead of cultivating the judgment, instill prejudices, and render hard the heart that gradual experience would only have cooled. An early acquaintance with human infirmities; or, what is termed knowledge of the world, is the surest way, in my opinion, to contract the heart and damp the natural youthful ardour which produces not only great talents, but great virtues. For the vain attempt to bring forth the fruit of experience, before the sapling has thrown out its leaves, only exhausts its strength, and prevents its assuming a natural form; just as the form and strength of subsiding metals are injured when the attraction of cohesion is disturbed.

Tell me, ye who have studied the human mind, is it not a strange way to fix principles by showing young people that they are seldom stable? And how can they be fortified by habits when they are proved to be fallacious by example? Why is the ardour of youth thus to be damped, and the luxuriancy of fancy cut to the quick? This dry caution may, it is true, guard a character from worldly mischances; but will infallibly preclude excellence in either virtue or knowledge.[8] The stumbling-block thrown across every path by suspicion, will prevent any vigorous exertions of genius or benevolence, and life will be stripped of its most alluring charm long before its calm evening, when man should retire to contemplation for comfort and support.

A young man who has been bred up with domestic friends, and led to store his mind with as much speculative knowledge as can be acquired by reading and the natural reflections which youthful ebullitions of animal spirits and instinctive feelings inspire, will enter the

5. The first edition reads "frivolous correspondence" for "epistles" and perhaps reflects more honestly Wollstonecraft's attitude toward Lord Chesterfield's *Letters to His Son*.
6. "That children ought to be constantly guarded against the vices and follies of the world, appears, to me, a very mistaken opinion; for in the course of my experience, and my eyes have looked abroad, I never knew a youth educated in this manner, who had early imbibed these chilling suspicions, and repeated by rote the hesitating *if* of age, that did not prove a selfish character" [Wollstonecraft's note].
7. Ecclesiastes 3:1: "To every thing there is a season, and a time to every purpose under the heaven."
8. "I have already observed that an early knowledge of the world, obtained in a natural way, by mixing in the world, has the same effect: instancing officers and women" [Wollstonecraft's note].

world with warm and erroneous expectations. But this appears to be the course of nature; and in morals, as well as in works of taste, we should be observant of her sacred indications, and not presume to lead when we ought obsequiously to follow.

In the world few people act from principle; present feelings, and early habits, are the grand springs: but how would the former be deadened, and the latter rendered iron corroding fetters, if the world were shewn to young people just as it is; when no knowledge of mankind or their own hearts, slowly obtained by experience, rendered them forbearing? Their fellow creatures would not then be viewed as frail beings; like themselves, condemned to struggle with human infirmities, and sometimes displaying the light, and sometimes the dark side of their character; extorting alternate feelings of love and disgust; but guarded against as beasts of prey, till every enlarged social feeling, in a word,—humanity, was eradicated.

In life, on the contrary, as we gradually discover the imperfections of our nature, we discover virtues, and various circumstances attach us to our fellow creatures, when we mix with them, and view the same objects, that are never thought of in acquiring a hasty unnatural knowledge of the world. We see a folly swell into a vice, by almost imperceptible degrees, and pity while we blame; but, if the hideous monster burst suddenly on our sight, fear and disgust rendering us more severe than man ought to be, might lead us with blind zeal to usurp the character of omnipotence, and denounce damnation on our fellow mortals, forgetting that we cannot read the heart, and that we have seeds of the same vices lurking in our own.

I have already remarked that we expect more from instruction, than mere instruction can produce: for, instead of preparing young people to encounter the evils of life with dignity, and to acquire wisdom and virtue by the exercise of their own faculties, precepts are heaped upon precepts, and blind obedience required, when conviction should be brought home to reason.

Suppose, for instance, that a young person in the first ardour of friendship deifies the beloved object—what harm can arise from this mistaken enthusiastic attachment? Perhaps it is necessary for virtue first to appear in a human form to impress youthful hearts; the ideal model, which a more matured and exalted mind looks up to, and shapes for itself, would elude their sight. He who loves not his brother whom he hath seen, how can he love God? asked the wisest of men.[9]

It is natural for youth to adorn the first object of its affection with every good quality, and the emulation produced by ignorance, or, to

9. 1 John 4:20: "If a man say, I love God, and hateth his brother, he is a liar: for he that loveth not his brother whom he hath seen, how can he love God whom he hath not seen?"

speak with more propriety, by inexperience, brings forward the mind capable of forming such an affection, and when, in the lapse of time, perfection is found not to be within the reach of mortals, virtue, abstractedly, is thought beautiful, and wisdom sublime. Admiration then gives place to friendship, properly so called, because it is cemented by esteem; and the being walks alone only dependent on heaven for that emulous panting after perfection which ever glows in a noble mind. But this knowledge a man must gain by the exertion of his own faculties; and this is surely the blessed fruit of disappointed hope! for He who delighteth to diffuse happiness and shew mercy to the weak creatures, who are learning to know him, never implanted a good propensity to be a tormenting ignis fatuus.[1]

Our trees are now allowed to spread with wild luxuriance, nor do we expect by force to combine the majestic marks of time with youthful graces; but wait patiently till they have struck deep their root, and braved many a storm.—Is the mind then, which, in proportion to its dignity, advances more slowly towards perfection, to be treated with less respect? To argue from analogy, every thing around us is in a progressive state; and when an unwelcome knowledge of life produces almost a satiety of life, and we discover by the natural course of things that all that is done under the sun is vanity,[2] we are drawing near the awful close of the drama. The days of activity and hope are over, and the opportunities which the first stage of existence has afforded of advancing in the scale of intelligence, must soon be summed up.—A knowledge at this period of the futility of life, or earlier, if obtained by experience, is very useful, because it is natural; but when a frail being is shewn the follies and vices of man, that he may be taught prudently to guard against the common casualties of life by sacrificing his heart—surely it is not speaking harshly to call it the wisdom of this world, contrasted with the nobler fruit of piety and experience.

I will venture a paradox, and deliver my opinion without reserve; if men were only born to form a circle of life and death, it would be wise to take every step that foresight could suggest to render life happy. Moderation in every pursuit would then be supreme wisdom; and the prudent voluptuary might enjoy a degree of content, though he neither cultivated his understanding nor kept his heart pure. Prudence, supposing we were mortal, would be true wisdom, or, to be more explicit, would procure the greatest portion of happiness, considering the whole of life, but knowledge beyond the conveniences of life would be a curse.

1. Foolish fire (Latin); a designation for the ghostly phosphorescent lights that are sometimes seen hovering at night over marshes and that lead travelers astray, hence a symbol of what is misleading.
2. Ecclesiastes 1:2 and 1:9: "all is vanity . . . and there is no new thing under the sun."

Why should we injure our health by close study? The exalted pleasure which intellectual pursuits afford would scarcely be equivalent
to the hours of languor that follow; especially, if it be necessary to
take into the reckoning the doubts and disappointments that cloud
our researches. Vanity and vexation close every inquiry: for the cause
which we particularly wished to discover flies like the horizon before
us as we advance. The ignorant, on the contrary, resemble children,
and suppose, that if they could walk straight forward they should at
last arrive where the earth and clouds meet. Yet, disappointed as we
are in our researches, the mind gains strength by the exercise, sufficient, perhaps, to comprehend the answers which, in another step of
existence, it may receive to the anxious questions it asked, when the
understanding with feeble wing was fluttering round the visible
effects to dive into the hidden cause.

The passions also, the winds of life, would be useless, if not injurious, did the substance which composes our thinking being, after we
have thought in vain, only become the support of vegetable life, and
invigorate a cabbage, or blush in a rose. The appetites would answer
every earthly purpose, and produce more moderate and permanent
happiness. But the powers of the soul that are of little use here, and,
probably, disturb our animal enjoyments, even while conscious dignity makes us glory in possessing them, prove that life is merely an
education, a state of infancy, to which the only hopes worth cherishing should not be sacrificed. I mean, therefore, to infer, that we
ought to have a precise idea of what we wish to attain by education,
for the immortality of the soul is contradicted by the actions of many
people who firmly profess the belief.

If you mean to secure ease and prosperity on earth as the first
consideration, and leave futurity to provide for itself; you act prudently in giving your child an early insight into the weaknesses of his
nature. You may not, it is true, make an Inkle[3] of him; but do not
imagine that he will stick to more than the letter of the law, who has
very early imbibed a mean opinion of human nature; nor will he
think it necessary to rise much above the common standard. He may
avoid gross vices, because honesty is the best policy; but he will
never aim at attaining great virtues. The example of writers and
artists will illustrate this remark.

I must therefore venture to doubt whether what has been thought
an axiom in morals may not have been a dogmatical assertion made

3. Richard Steele's story of Inkle and Yarico, published in the periodical *The Spectator* in
1711, was much anthologized through the eighteenth century. Wollstonecraft included it
in *The Female Reader*. The story concerns an Englishman who, en route to the West Indies
where he means to make his fortune, is attacked by hostile Indians but is saved from cap-
ture by a beautiful Indian maiden, who falls in love with him. A "prudent and frugal young
man," Thomas Inkle repays Yarico's kindness by selling her off as a slave when he finally
reaches his destination. See *The Spectator*, ed. Donald F. Bond (Oxford, 1965), 1, p. 51.

by men who have coolly seen mankind through the medium of books, and say, in direct contradiction to them, that the regulation of the passions is not, always, wisdom.—On the contrary, it should seem, that one reason why men have superiour judgment, and more fortitude than women, is undoubtedly this, that they give a freer scope to the grand passions, and by more frequently going astray enlarge their minds. If then by the exercise of their own[4] reason they fix on some stable principle, they have probably to thank the force of their passions, nourished by *false* views of life, and permitted to overleap the boundary that secures content. But if, in the dawn of life, we could soberly survey the scenes before as in perspective, and see every thing in its true colours, how could the passions gain sufficient strength to unfold the faculties?

Let me now as from an eminence survey the world stripped of all its false delusive charms. The clear atmosphere enables me to see each object in its true point of view, while my heart is still. I am calm as the prospect in a morning when the mists, slowly dispersing, silently unveil the beauties of nature, refreshed by rest.

In what light will the world now appear?—I rub my eyes and think, perchance, that I am just awaking from a lively dream.

I see the sons and daughters of men pursuing shadows, and anxiously wasting their powers to feed passions which have no adequate object—if the very excess of these blind impulses, pampered by that lying, yet constantly trusted guide, the imagination, did not, by preparing them for some other state, render short-sighted mortals wiser without their own concurrence; or, what comes to the same thing, when they were pursuing some imaginary present good.

After viewing objects in this light, it would not be very fanciful to imagine that this world was a stage on which a pantomime is daily performed for the amusement of superior beings. How would they be diverted to see the ambitious man consuming himself by running after a phantom, and, 'pursuing the bubble fame in the cannon's mouth'[5] that was to blow him to nothing: for when consciousness is lost, it matters not whether we mount in a whirlwind or descend in rain. And should they compassionately invigorate his sight and shew him the thorny path which led to eminence, that like a quicksand sinks as he ascends, disappointing his hopes when almost within his grasp, would he not leave to others the honour of amusing them, and labour to secure the present moment, though from the constitution of his nature he would not find it very easy to catch the flying stream? Such slaves are we to hope and fear!

4. "'I find that all is but lip-wisdom which wants experience,' says Sidney" [Wollstonecraft's note]. Sir Philip Sidney, *Arcadia*, ed. Albert Feuillerat (Cambridge, 1965), I, p. 113: "I find indeed, that all is but lip-wisdome, which wants experience."

5. *As You Like It* II.vii.152–53: "Seeking the bubble reputation / Even in the cannon's mouth."

But, vain as the ambitious man's pursuits would be, he is often striving for something more substantial than fame—that indeed would be the veriest meteor, the wildest fire that could lure a man to ruin.—What! renounce the most trifling gratification to be applauded when he should be no more! Wherefore this struggle, whether man be mortal or immortal, if that noble passion did not really raise the being above his fellows?—

And love! What diverting scenes would it produce—Pantaloon's[6] tricks must yield to more egregious folly. To see a mortal adorn an object with imaginary charms, and then fall down and worship the idol which he had himself set up—how ridiculous! But what serious consequences ensue to rob man of that portion of happiness, which the Deity by calling him into existence has (or, on what can his attributes rest?) indubitably promised: would not all the purposes of life have been much better fulfilled if he had only felt what had been termed physical love? And, would not the sight of the object, not seen through the medium of the imagination, soon reduce the passion to an appetite, if reflection, the noble distinction of man, did not give it force, and make it an instrument to raise him above this earthy dross, by teaching him to love the centre of all perfection; whose wisdom appears clearer and clearer in the works of nature, in proportion as reason is illuminated and exalted by contemplation, and by acquiring that love of order which the struggles of passion produce?

The habit of reflection, and the knowledge attained by fostering any passion, might be shewn to be equally useful, though the object be proved equally fallacious; for they would all appear in the same light, if they were not magnified by the governing passion implanted in us by the Author of all good, to call forth and strengthen the faculties of each individual, and enable it to attain all the experience that an infant can obtain, who does certain things, it cannot tell why.

I descend from my height, and mixing with my fellow-creatures, feel myself hurried along the common stream; ambition, love, hope, and fear, exert their wonted power, though we be convinced by reason that their present and most attractive promises are only lying dreams; but had the cold hand of circumspection damped each generous feeling before it had left any permanent character, or fixed some habit, what could be expected, but selfish prudence and reason just rising above instinct? Who that has read Dean Swift's disgusting description of the Yahoos, and insipid one of Houyhnhnm[7]

---

6. A stock comic character in the pantomimes of eighteenth-century England, as in the Italian commedia dell'arte on which they were based.
7. The world that Jonathan Swift imagines in the fourth book of *Gulliver's Travels* (1726) has two populations: the brutish Yahoos, who are filthy, apelike humans, and the intelligent Houyhnhnms, the horses who rule this world. The Houyhnhnms' thorough-going commitment to rationality leaves their society without space for the emotions.

with a philosophical eye, can avoid seeing the futility of degrading the passions, or making man rest in contentment?

The youth should *act*; for had he the experience of a grey head he would be fitter for death than life, though his virtues, rather residing in his head than his heart, could produce nothing great, and his understanding, prepared for this world, would not, by its noble flights, prove that it had a title to a better.

Besides, it is not possible to give a young person a just view of life; he must have struggled with his own passions before he can estimate the force of the temptation which betrayed his brother into vice. Those who are entering life, and those who are departing, see the world from such very different points of view, that they can seldom think alike, unless the unfledged reason of the former never attempted a solitary flight.

When we hear of some daring crime—it comes full on us in the deepest shade of turpitude, and raises indignation; but the eye that gradually saw the darkness thicken, must observe it with more compassionate forbearance. The world cannot be seen by an unmoved spectator, we must mix in the throng, and feel as men feel before we can judge of their feelings. If we mean, in short, to live in the world to grow wiser and better, and not merely to enjoy the good things of life, we must attain a knowledge of others at the same time that we become acquainted with ourselves—knowledge acquired any other way only hardens the heart and perplexes the understanding.

I may be told, that the knowledge thus acquired, is sometimes purchased at too dear a rate. I can only answer that I very much doubt whether any knowledge can be attained without labour and sorrow; and those who wish to spare their children both, should not complain, if they are neither wise nor virtuous. They only aimed at making them prudent; and prudence, early in life, is but the cautious craft of ignorant self-love.

I have observed that young people, to whose education particular attention has been paid, have, in general, been very superficial and conceited, and far from pleasing in any respect, because they had neither the unsuspecting warmth of youth, nor the cool depth of age. I cannot help imputing this unnatural appearance principally to that hasty premature instruction, which leads them presumptuously to repeat all the crude notions they have taken upon trust, so that the careful education which they received, makes them all their lives the slaves of prejudices.

Mental as well as bodily exertion is, at first, irksome; so much so, that the many would fain let others both work and think for them. An observation which I have often made will illustrate my meaning. When in a circle of strangers, or acquaintances, a person of moderate abilities asserts an opinion with heat, I will venture to affirm, for

I have traced this fact home, very often, that it is a prejudice. These echoes have a high respect for the understanding of some relation or friend, and without fully comprehending the opinions, which they are so eager to retail, they maintain them with a degree of obstinacy, that would surprise even the person who concocted them.

I know that a kind of fashion now prevails of respecting prejudices; and when any one dares to face them, though actuated by humanity and armed by reason, he is superciliously asked whether his ancestors were fools. No, I should reply; opinions, at first, of every description, were all, probably, considered, and therefore were founded on some reason; yet not unfrequently, of course, it was rather a local expedient than a fundamental principle, that would be reasonable at all times. But, moss-covered opinions assume the disproportioned form of prejudices, when they are indolently adopted only because age has given them a venerable aspect, though the reason on which they were built ceases to be a reason, or cannot be traced. Why are we to love prejudices, merely because they are prejudices?[8] A prejudice is a fond obstinate persuasion for which we can give no reason; for the moment a reason can be given for an opinion, it ceases to be a prejudice, though it may be an error in judgment: and are we then advised to cherish opinions only to set reason at defiance? This mode of arguing, if arguing it may be called, reminds me of what is vulgarly termed a woman's reason. For women sometimes declare that they love, or believe, certain things, *because* they love, or believe them.

It is impossible to converse with people to any purpose, who only use affirmatives and negatives. Before you can bring them to a point, to start fairly from, you must go back to the simple principles that were antecedent to the prejudices broached by power; and it is ten to one but you are stopped by the philosophical assertion, that certain principles are as practically false as they are abstractly true.[9] Nay, it may be inferred, that reason has whispered some doubts, for it generally happens that people assert their opinions with the greatest heat when they begin to waver; striving to drive out their own doubts by convincing their opponent, they grow angry when those gnawing doubts are thrown back to prey on themselves.

---

8. "Vide Mr. Burke" [Wollstonecraft's note]. In *Reflections on the Revolution in France* (1790), Burke decries the political theorizing that fuels the Revolution and praises, instead, the "untaught feelings" of the British. The British way, he states, is not to cast "away all our old prejudices" but instead to "cherish them because they are prejudices," because prejudice crystallizes all the wisdom and experience of the past (*The French Revolution*, Vol. V of *The Writings and Speeches of Edmund Burke*, ed. L. G. Mitchell [Oxford, 1990], p. 87).
9. "'Convince a man against his will, / He's of the same opinion still'" [Wollstonecraft's note]. Samuel Butler, *Hudibras, Third Part*, Canto III, lines 547–48: "He that complies against his will, / Is of his own opinion still."

The fact is, that men expect from education, what education cannot give. A sagacious parent or tutor may strengthen the body and sharpen the instruments by which the child is to gather knowledge; but the honey must be the reward of the individual's own industry. It is almost as absurd to attempt to make a youth wise by the experience of another, as to expect the body to grow strong by the exercise which is only talked of, or seen.[1] Many of those children whose conduct has been most narrowly watched, become the weakest men, because their instructors only instill certain notions into their minds, that have no other foundation than their authority; and if they be loved or respected, the mind is cramped in its exertions and wavering in its advances. The business of education in this case, is only to conduct the shooting tendrils to a proper pole; yet after laying precept upon precept, without allowing a child to acquire judgment itself, parents expect them to act in the same manner by this borrowed fallacious light, as if they had illuminated it themselves; and be, when they enter life, what their parents are at the close. They do not consider that the tree, and even the human body, does not strengthen its fibres till it has reached its full growth.

There appears to be something analogous in the mind. The senses and the imagination give a form to the character, during childhood and youth; and the understanding, as life advances, gives firmness to the first fair purposes of sensibility—till virtue, arising rather from the clear conviction of reason than the impulse of the heart, morality is made to rest on a rock against which the storms of passion vainly beat.

I hope I shall not be misunderstood when I say, that religion will not have this condensing energy, unless it be founded on reason. If it be merely the refuge of weakness or wild fanaticism, and not a governing principle of conduct, drawn from self-knowledge, and a rational opinion respecting the attributes of God, what can it be expected to produce? The religion which consists in warming the affections, and exalting the imagination, is only the poetical part, and may afford the individual pleasure without rendering it a more moral being. It may be a substitute for worldly pursuits; yet narrow, instead of enlarging the heart: but virtue must be loved as in itself sublime and excellent, and not for the advantages it procures or the evils it averts, if any great degree of excellence be expected. Men will not become moral when they only build airy castles in a future world

1. "'One sees nothing when one is content to contemplate only; it is necessary to act oneself to be able to see how others act.' *Rousseau*" [Wollstonecraft's note]. Perhaps recollecting a passage in Rousseau's novel *Julie*. The novel's 1761 English translator rendered it thus: "We can have the opportunity of seeing others act, in proportion only as we act with them; in the school of the world, as well as in that of love, we must begin by practicing whatever we desire to learn" (*Eloisa: or, a Series of Original Letters Collected and Published by J. J. Rousseau*, 2d ed. [London, 1761], II, p. 50).

to compensate for the disappointments which they meet with in this; if they turn their thoughts from relative duties to religious reveries.

Most prospects in life are marred by the shuffling worldly wisdom of men, who, forgetting that they cannot serve God and mammon, endeavour to blend contradictory things.—If you wish to make your son rich, pursue one course—if you are only anxious to make him virtuous, you must take another; but do not imagine that you can bound from one road to the other without losing your way.[2]

Chap. VI

The Effect Which an Early Association of Ideas Has upon the Character

Educated in the enervating style recommended by the writers on whom I have been animadverting; and not having a chance, from their subordinate state in society, to recover their lost ground, is it surprising that women every where appear a defect in nature?[3] Is it surprising, when we consider what a determinate effect an early association of ideas has on the character, that they neglect their understandings, and turn all their attention to their persons?

The great advantages which naturally result from storing the mind with knowledge, are obvious from the following considerations. The association of our ideas is either habitual or instantaneous; and the latter mode seems rather to depend on the original temperature[4] of the mind than on the will. When the ideas, and matters of fact, are once taken in, they lie by for use, till some fortuitous circumstance makes the information dart into the mind with illustrative force, that has been received at very different periods of our lives.[5] Like the lightning's flash are many recollections; one idea assimilating and explaining another, with astonishing rapidity. I do not now allude to that quick perception of truth, which is so intuitive that it baffles

2. "See an excellent essay on this subject by Mrs. Barbauld, in *Miscellaneous Pieces in Prose*" [Wollstonecraft's note]. Barbauld's essay, published in 1773, is titled "Against Inconsistency in our Expectations."
3. Another echo of *Paradise Lost* X.891–92.
4. Constitution.
5. Wollstonecraft is discussing associationism, the theory of the workings of the mind that was developed out of John Locke's *Essay Concerning Human Understanding* (1690) and David Hume's *Treatise of Human Nature* (1739–40). The most influential exposition of the theory was David Hartley's 1749 *Observations on Man*. Associationists emphasized the role of habit in mental life and the way that certain ideas, though first aligned by accident, come over time to be linked automatically. Locke calls attention to this process in order that "those who have Children, or the charge of their Education, would think it worth their while diligently to watch, and carefully to prevent the undue Connexion of Ideas in the mind of young People. This is the time most susceptible of lasting Impressions" (*Essay*, ed. Peter H. Nidditch [Oxford, 1975], II, xxxiii, p. 397).

research, and makes us at a loss to determine whether it is reminis-
cence or ratiocination, lost sight of in its celerity, that opens the dark
cloud. Over those instantaneous associations we have little power;
for when the mind is once enlarged by excursive flights, or profound
reflection, the raw materials will, in some degree, arrange themselves. The understanding, it is true, may keep us from going out of
drawing[6] when we group our thoughts, or transcribe from the imagination the warm sketches of fancy; but the animal spirits, the individual character, give the colouring. Over this subtile electric fluid,[7]
how little power do we possess, and over it how little power can reason obtain! These fine intractable spirits appear to be the essence of
genius, and beaming in its eagle eye, produce in the most eminent
degree the happy energy of associating thoughts that surprise,
delight, and instruct. These are the glowing minds that concentrate
pictures for their fellow-creatures; forcing them to view with interest the objects reflected from the impassioned imagination, which
they passed over in nature.

I must be allowed to explain myself. The generality of people cannot see or feel poetically, they want fancy, and therefore fly from solitude in search of sensible objects;[8] but when an author lends them
his eyes they can see as he saw, and be amused by images they could
not select, though lying before them.

Education thus only supplies the man of genius with knowledge
to give variety and contrast to his associations; but there is an habitual association of ideas, that grows 'with our growth,'[9] which has a
great effect on the moral character of mankind; and by which a turn
is given to the mind that commonly remains throughout life. So ductile is the understanding, and yet so stubborn, that the associations
which depend on adventitious circumstances, during the period that
the body takes to arrive at maturity, can seldom be disentangled by
reason. One idea calls up another, its old associate, and memory,

---

6. I.e., losing perspective.
7. "I have sometimes, when inclined to laugh at materalists, asked whether, as the most
   powerful effects in nature are apparently produced by fluids, the magnetic, &c. the passions might not be fine volatile fluids that embraced humanity, keeping the more refrac-
   tory elementary parts together—or whether they were simply a liquid fire that pervaded
   the more sluggish materials, giving them life and heat?" [Wollstonecraft's note]. Material-
   ists believed, to the alarm of the religiously minded, that phenomena ordinarily attributed
   to the soul were actually the results of physical processes. In *Observations on Man* David
   Hartley thus used Newtonian physics to explain, in terms anticipating modern neuro-
   science, the workings of consciousness, suggesting that all feeling and thinking in the
   individual arose from the vibrations imparted and transmitted by a subtle fluid running
   through the nerves of the body. Hartley founded his conception of that fluid on Newton's
   speculations about the ether that, Newton conjectured, pervaded and connected the
   entire universe.
8. The objects that appeal to the physical senses and are sought by those who lack imagination ("want fancy").
9. Pope, *An Essay on Man* (1733–34), II.136: "Grows with his growth, and strengthens with
   his strength."

faithful to the first impressions, particularly when the intellectual powers are not employed to cool our sensations, retraces them with mechanical exactness.

This habitual slavery, to first impressions, has a more baneful effect on the female than the male character, because business and other dry employments of the understanding, tend to deaden the feelings and break associations that do violence to reason. But females, who are made women of when they are mere children, and brought back to childhood when they ought to leave the go-cart[1] forever, have not sufficient strength of mind to efface the superinductions of art that have smothered nature.

Every thing that they see or hear serves to fix impressions, call forth emotions, and associate ideas, that give a sexual character to the mind. False notions of beauty and delicacy stop the growth of their limbs and produce a sickly soreness, rather than delicacy of organs; and thus weakened by being employed in unfolding instead of examining the first associations, forced on them by every surrounding object, how can they attain the vigour necessary to enable them to throw off their factitious character?—where find strength to recur to reason and rise superiour to a system of oppression, that blasts the fair promises of spring? This cruel association of ideas, which every thing conspires to twist into all their habits of thinking, or, to speak with more precision, of feeling, receives new force when they begin to act a little for themselves; for they then perceive that it is only through their address to excite emotions in men, that pleasure and power are to be obtained. Besides, the books professedly written for their instruction, which make the first impression on their minds, all inculcate the same opinions. Educated then in worse than Egyptian bondage,[2] it is unreasonable, as well as cruel, to upbraid them with faults that can scarcely be avoided, unless a degree of native vigour be supposed, that falls to the lot of very few amongst mankind.

For instance, the severest sarcasms have been levelled against the sex, and they have been ridiculed for repeating 'a set of phrases learnt by rote,'[3] when nothing could be more natural, considering the education they receive, and that their 'highest praise is to obey, unargued'[4]—the will of man. If they be not allowed to have reason sufficient to govern their own conduct—why, all they learn—must be learned by rote! And when all their ingenuity is called forth to

1. A wheeled walker in which an infant could learn to walk without risk of falling.
2. Refers to the years of slavery endured by the Jewish people in Egypt before their delivery by Moses.
3. Jonathan Swift, "The Furniture of a Woman's Mind" (1727), line 1.
4. Eve thus addresses Adam in *Paradise Lost* IV.636–38: "Unargued I obey; so God ordains, / God is thy law, thou mine: to know no more / Is woman's happiest knowledge and her praise."

adjust their dress, 'a passion for a scarlet coat,'[5] is so natural, that it never surprised me; and, allowing Pope's summary of their character to be just, 'that every woman is at heart a rake,'[6] why should they be bitterly censured for seeking a congenial mind, and preferring a rake to a man of sense?

Rakes know how to work on their sensibility, whilst the modest merit of reasonable men has, of course, less effect on their feelings, and they cannot reach the heart by the way of the understanding, because they have few sentiments in common.

It seems a little absurd to expect women to be more reasonable than men in their *likings*, and still to deny them the uncontrouled use of reason. When do men *fall-in-love* with sense? When do they, with their superior powers and advantages, turn from the person to the mind? And how can they then expect women, who are only taught to observe behaviour, and acquire manners rather than morals, to despise what they have been all their lives labouring to attain? Where are they suddenly to find judgment enough to weigh patiently the sense of an awkward virtuous man, when his manners, of which they are made critical judges, are rebuffing, and his conversation cold and dull, because it does not consist of pretty repartees, or well turned compliments? In order to admire or esteem any thing for a continuance, we must, at least, have our curiosity excited by knowing, in some degree, what we admire; for we are unable to estimate the value of qualities and virtues above our comprehension. Such a respect, when it is felt, may be very sublime; and the confused consciousness of humility may render the dependent creature an interesting object, in some points of view; but human love must have grosser ingredients; and the person very naturally will come in for its share—and, an ample share it mostly has!

Love is, in a great degree, an arbitrary passion, and will reign, like some other stalking mischiefs, by its own authority, without deigning to reason; and it may also be easily distinguished from esteem, the foundation of friendship, because it is often excited by evanescent beauties and graces, though, to give an energy to the sentiment, something more solid must deepen their impression and set the imagination to work, to make the most fair—the first good.

Common passions are excited by common qualities.—Men look for beauty and the simper of good-humoured docility: women are captivated by easy manners; a gentleman-like man seldom fails to please them, and their thirsty ears eagerly drink the insinuating nothings of politeness, whilst they turn from the unintelligible sounds of

5. Swift, "The Furniture of a Woman's Mind," line 2.
6. Pope, "Of the Characters of Women," lines 215–16: "Men, some to Bus'ness, some to Pleasure take; / But ev'ry Woman is at heart a Rake."

the charmer—reason, charm he never so wisely. With respect to
superficial accomplishments, the rake certainly has the advantage;
and of these females can form an opinion, for it is their own ground.
Rendered gay and giddy by the whole tenor of their lives, the very
aspect of wisdom, or the severe graces of virtue, must have a lugubri-
ous appearance to them; and produce a kind of restraint from which
they and love, sportive child, naturally revolt. Without taste, excepting of the lighter kind, for taste is the offspring of judgment, how can
they discover that true beauty and grace must arise from the play of
the mind? and how can they be expected to relish in a lover what they
do not, or very imperfectly, possess themselves? The sympathy that
unites hearts, and invites to confidence, in them is so very faint, that
it cannot take fire, and thus mount to passion. No, I repeat it, the
love cherished by such minds, must have grosser fewel!

The inference is obvious; till women are led to exercise their
understandings, they should not be satirized for their attachment
to rakes; or even for being rakes at heart, when it appears to be
the inevitable consequence of their education. They who live to
please—must find their enjoyments, their happiness, in pleasure! It
is a trite, yet true remark, that we never do any thing well, unless we
love it for its own sake.

Supposing, however, for a moment, that women were, in some
future revolution of time, to become, what I sincerely wish them to
be, even love would acquire more serious dignity, and be purified in
its own fires; and virtue giving true delicacy to their affections, they
would turn with disgust from a rake. Reasoning then, as well as feeling, the only province of woman, at present, they might easily guard
against exteriour graces, and quickly learn to despise the sensibility
that had been excited and hackneyed in the ways of women, whose
trade was vice; and allurements, wanton airs. They would recollect
that the flame, one must use appropriated expressions, which they
wished to light up, had been exhausted by lust, and that the sated
appetite, losing all relish for pure and simple pleasures, could only
be roused by licentious arts or variety. What satisfaction could a
woman of delicacy promise herself in a union with such a man,
when the very artlessness of her affection might appear insipid?
Thus does Dryden describe the situation,

————'Where love is duty, on the female side,
'On theirs mere sensual gust, and sought with surly pride.'[7]

But one grand truth women have yet to learn, though much it
imports them to act accordingly. In the choice of a husband, they
should not be led astray by the qualities of a lover—for a lover the

7. John Dryden, *Palamon and Arcite* (1700), III.231–32. "Gust": satisfaction of an appetite.

husband, even supposing him to be wise and virtuous, cannot long remain.

Were women more rationally educated, could they take a more comprehensive view of things, they would be contented to love but once in their lives; and after marriage calmly let passion subside into friendship—into that tender intimacy, which is the best refuge from care; yet is built on such pure, still affections, that idle jealousies would not be allowed to disturb the discharge of the sober duties of life, or to engross the thoughts that ought to be otherwise employed. This is a state in which many men live; but few, very few women. And the difference may easily be accounted for, without recurring to a sexual character. Men, for whom we are told women were made, have too much occupied the thoughts of women; and this association has so entangled love with all their motives of action; and, to harp a little on an old string, having been solely employed either to prepare themselves to excite love, or actually putting their lessons in practice, they cannot live without love. But, when a sense of duty, or fear of shame, obliges them to restrain this pampered desire of pleasing beyond certain lengths, too far for delicacy, it is true, though far from criminality, they obstinately determine to love, I speak of the passion, their husbands to the end of the chapter—and then acting the part which they foolishly exacted from their lovers, they become abject woers, and fond slaves.

Men of wit and fancy are often rakes; and fancy is the food of love. Such men will inspire passion. Half the sex, in its present infantine state, would pine for a Lovelace;[8] a man so witty, so graceful, and so valiant: and can they *deserve* blame for acting according to principles so constantly inculcated? They want a lover, and protector; and behold him kneeling before them—bravery prostrate to beauty! The virtues of a husband are thus thrown by love into the background, and gay hopes, or lively emotions, banish reflection till the day of reckoning comes; and come it surely will, to turn the sprightly lover into a surly suspicious tyrant, who contemptuously insults the very weakness he fostered. Or, supposing the rake reformed, he cannot quickly get rid of old habits.[9] When a man of abilities is first carried away by his passions, it is necessary that sentiment and taste varnish the enormities of vice, and give a zest to brutal indulgences; but when the gloss of novelty is worn off, and pleasure palls upon the sense, lasciviousness becomes barefaced, and enjoyment only the desperate effort of weakness flying from reflection as from a

8. The libertine Lovelace is first the suitor, then the rapist, of Clarissa, heroine of Samuel Richardson's 1747–48 novel.
9. In a preface Richardson declares that *Clarissa* is intended to warn young women against "that dangerous, but too commonly received Notion, that a Reformed Rake makes the best Husband" (I, p. viii).

legion of devils. Oh! virtue, thou art not an empty name! All that life can give—thou givest!

If much comfort cannot be expected from the friendship of a reformed rake of superiour abilities, what is the consequence when he lacketh sense, as well as principles? Verily misery, in its most hideous shape. When the habits of weak people are consolidated by time, a reformation is barely possible; and actually makes the beings miserable who have not sufficient mind to be amused by innocent pleasure; like the tradesman who retires from the hurry of business, nature presents to them only a universal blank; and the restless thoughts prey on the damped spirits.[1] Their reformation, as well as his retirement, actually makes them wretched because it deprives them of all employment, by quenching the hopes and fears that set in motion their sluggish minds.

If such be the force of habit; if such be the bondage of folly, how carefully ought we to guard the mind from storing up vicious associations; and equally careful should we be to cultivate the understanding, to save the poor wight[2] from the weak dependent state of even harmless ignorance. For it is the right use of reason alone which makes us independent of every thing—excepting the unclouded Reason—'Whose service is perfect freedom.'[3]

Chap. VII

Modesty.—Comprehensively Considered, and Not as a Sexual Virtue

Modesty! Sacred offspring of sensibility and reason!—true delicacy of mind!—may I unblamed presume to investigate thy nature, and trace to its covert the mild charm, that mellowing each harsh feature of a character, renders what would otherwise only inspire cold admiration—lovely!—Thou that smoothest the wrinkles of wisdom, and softenest the tone of the sublimest virtues till they all melt into humanity;—thou that spreadest the ethereal cloud that, surrounding love, heightens every beauty, it half shades, breathing

---

1. "I have frequently seen this exemplified in women whose beauty could no longer be repaired. They have retired from the noisy scenes of dissipation; but, unless they became methodists, the solitude of the select society of their family connections or acquaintance, has presented only a fearful void; consequently, nervous complaints, and all the vapourish train of idleness, rendered them quite as useless, and far more unhappy, than when they joined the giddy throng" [Wollstonecraft's note].
2. Creature.
3. Wollstonecraft echoes the Morning Prayer, Second Collect, for Peace, from the Anglican Church's *Book of Common Prayer*, in which, however, it is God "whose service is perfect freedom." She might also be remembering Macaulay's *Letters on Education:* "'In my service there is perfect freedom,' says the Messiah; and the reason is plain; for the empire of religious sentiment, and the empire of reason, is the same" (III, Letter vii, pp. 422–23).

those coy sweets that steal into the heart, and charm the senses—modulate for me the language of persuasive reason, till I rouse my sex from the flowery bed, on which they supinely sleep life away!

In speaking of the association of our ideas, I have noticed two distinct modes;[4] and in defining modesty, it appears to me equally proper to discriminate that purity of mind, which is the effect of chastity, from a simplicity of character that leads us to form a just opinion of ourselves, equally distant from vanity or presumption, though by no means incompatible with a lofty consciousness of our own dignity. Modesty, in the latter signification of the term, is, that soberness of mind which teaches a man not to think more highly of himself than he ought to think, and should be distinguished from humility, because humility is a kind of self-abasement.

A modest man often conceives a great plan, and tenaciously adheres to it, conscious of his own strength, till success gives it a sanction that determines its character. Milton was not arrogant when he suffered a suggestion of judgment to escape him that proved a prophesy;[5] nor was General Washington when he accepted of the command of the American forces. The latter has always been characterized as a modest man; but had he been merely humble, he would probably have shrunk back irresolute, afraid of trusting to himself the direction of an enterprise, on which so much depended.

A modest man is steady, an humble man timid, and a vain one presumptuous:—this is the judgment, which the observation of many characters, has led me to form. Jesus Christ was modest, Moses was humble, and Peter vain.

Thus, discriminating modesty from humility in one case, I do not mean to confound it with bashfulness in the other. Bashfulness, in fact, is so distinct from modesty, that the most bashful lass, or raw country lout, often become the most impudent; for their bashfulness being merely the instinctive timidity of ignorance, custom soon changes it into assurance.[6]

The shameless behaviour of the prostitutes, who infest the streets of this metropolis, raising alternate emotions of pity and disgust, may

4. It "is either habitual or instantaneous," p. 122.
5. For instance, the prophecy of his future greatness Milton incorporated into the Latin poem he addressed to his father, "Ad Patrem," written some thirty years before the publication of *Paradise Lost*.
6.   " 'Such is the country-maiden's fright,
      When first a red-coat is in sight;
      Behind the door she hides her face;
      Next time at distance eyes the lace:
      She now can all his terrors stand,
      Nor from his squeeze withdraws her hand.
      She plays familiar in his arms,
      And ev'ry soldier hath his charms;
      From tent to tent she spreads her flame;
      For custom conquers fear and shame'
      Gay" [Wollstonecraft's note]. The quotation is from John Gay, "The Tame Stag," lines 27–36 (*Fables* [1727]), no. XIII.

serve to illustrate this remark. They trample on virgin bashfulness with a sort of bravado, and glorying in their shame, become more audaciously lewd than men, however depraved, to whom this sexual quality has not been gratuitously granted, ever appear to be. But these poor ignorant wretches never had any modesty to lose, when they consigned themselves to infamy; for modesty is a virtue, not a quality. No, they were only bashful, shame-faced innocents; and losing their innocence, their shame-facedness was rudely brushed off; a virtue would have left some vestiges in the mind, had it been sacrificed to passion, to make us respect the grand ruin.

Purity of mind, or that genuine delicacy, which is the only virtuous support of chastity, is near akin to that refinement of humanity, which never resides in any but cultivated minds. It is something nobler than innocence, it is the delicacy of reflections, and not the coyness of ignorance. The reserve of reason, which, like habitual cleanliness, is seldom seen in any great degree, unless the soul is active, may easily be distinguished from rustic shyness or wanton skittishness; and, so far from being incompatible with knowledge, it is its fairest fruit. What a gross idea of modesty had the writer of the following remark! 'The lady who asked the question whether women may be instructed in the modern system of botany, consistently with female delicacy?—was accused of ridiculous prudery: nevertheless, if she had proposed the question to me, I should certainly have answered—They cannot.'[7] Thus is the fair book of knowledge[8] to be shut with an everlasting seal! On reading similar passages I have reverentially lifted up my eyes and heart to Him who liveth for ever and ever, and said, O my Father, hast Thou by the very constitution of her nature forbid Thy child to seek Thee in the fair forms of truth? And, can her soul be sullied by the knowledge that awfully calls her to Thee?

I have then philosophically pursued these reflections till I inferred that those women who have most improved their reason must have the most modesty—though a dignified sedateness of deportment may have succeeded the playful, bewitching bashfulness of youth.[9]

And thus have I argued. To render chastity the virtue from which unsophisticated modesty will naturally flow, the attention should be called away from employments which only exercise the sensibility;

7. John Berkenhout, A Volume of Letters to His Son at the University (Cambridge, 1790), p. 307. Berkenhout reacts here to the system of botanical classification introduced by Swedish naturalist Carl Linnaeus's 1753 Species Plantarum. In the Linnaean system the work of assigning plants to particular botanical species involved close attention to those plants' sexual parts—their stamens and pistils.
8. In Paradise Lost III.47–49 Milton uses this phrase while describing the consequence of the losses brought by his blindness: "for the book of knowledge fair / Presented with a universal blank / Of nature's works to me expunged and razed."
9. "Modesty, is the graceful calm virtue of maturity; bashfulness, the charm of vivacious youth" [Wollstonecraft's note].

and the heart made to beat time to humanity, rather than to throb with love. The woman who has dedicated a considerable portion of her time to pursuits purely intellectual, and whose affections have been exercised by humane plans of usefulness, must have more purity of mind, as a natural consequence, than the ignorant beings whose time and thoughts have been occupied by gay pleasures or schemes to conquer hearts.[1] The regulation of the behaviour is not modesty, though those who study rules of decorum are, in general, termed modest women. Make the heart clean, let it expand and feel for all that is human, instead of being narrowed by selfish passions; and let the mind frequently contemplate subjects that exercise the understanding, without heating the imagination, and artless modesty will give the finishing touches to the picture.

She who can discern the dawn of immortality, in the streaks that shoot athwart the misty night of ignorance, promising a clearer day, will respect, as a sacred temple, the body that enshrines such an improvable soul. True love, likewise, spreads this kind of mysterious sanctity round the beloved object, making the lover most modest when in her presence.[2] So reserved is affection that, receiving or returning personal endearments, it wishes, not only to shun the human eye, as a kind of profanation; but to diffuse an encircling cloudy obscurity to shut out even the saucy sparkling sunbeams. Yet, that affection does not deserve the epithet of chaste, which does not receive a sublime gloom of tender melancholy, that allows the mind for a moment to stand still and enjoy the present satisfaction, when a consciousness of the Divine presence is felt—for this must ever be the food of joy!

As I have always been fond of tracing to its source in nature any prevailing custom, I have frequently thought that it was a sentiment of affection for whatever had touched the person of an absent or lost friend, which gave birth to that respect for relicks, so much abused by selfish priests. Devotion, or love, may be allowed to hallow the garments as well as the person; for the lover must want fancy who has not a sort of sacred respect for the glove or slipper of his mistress. He could not confound them with vulgar things of the same

---

1. "I have conversed, as man with man, with medical men, on anatomical subjects; and compared the proportions of the human body with artists—yet such modesty did I meet with, that I was never reminded by word or look of my sex, of the absurd rules which make modesty a pharisaical cloak of weakness. And I am persuaded that in the pursuit of knowledge women would never be insulted by sensible men, and rarely by men of any description, if they did not by mock modesty remind them that they were women: actuated by the same spirit as the Portugueze ladies, who would think their charms insulted, if, when left alone with a man, he did not, at least, attempt to be grossly familiar with their persons. Men are not always men in the company of women, nor would women always remember that they are women, if they were allowed to acquire more understanding" [Wollstonecraft's note].
2. "Male or female; for the world contains many modest men" [Wollstonecraft's note].

kind. This fine sentiment, perhaps, would not bear to be analyzed by the experimental philosopher[3]—but of such stuff is human rapture made up!—A shadowy phantom glides before us, obscuring every other object; yet when the soft cloud is grasped, the form melts into common air, leaving a solitary void, or sweet perfume, stolen from the violet, that memory long holds dear. But, I have tripped unawares on fairy ground, feeling the balmy gale of spring stealing on me, though november frowns.

As a sex, women are more chaste than men, and as modesty is the effect of chastity, they may deserve to have this virtue ascribed to them in rather an appropriated sense;[4] yet, I must be allowed to add an hesitating if:—for I doubt whether chastity will produce modesty, though it may propriety of conduct, when it is merely a respect for the opinion of the world,[5] and when coquetry and the lovelorn tales of novelists employ the thoughts. Nay, from experience, and reason, I should be led to expect to meet with more modesty amongst men than women, simply because men exercise their understandings more than women.

But, with respect to propriety of behaviour, excepting one class of females, women have evidently the advantage. What can be more disgusting than that impudent dross of gallantry, thought so manly, which makes many men stare insultingly at every female they meet? Can it be termed respect for the sex? No, this loose behaviour shews such habitual depravity, such weakness of mind, that it is vain to expect much public or private virtue, till both men and women grow more modest—till men, curbing a sensual fondness for the sex, or an affectation of manly assurance, more properly speaking, impudence, treat each other with respect—unless appetite or passion give the tone, peculiar to it, to their behaviour. I mean even personal respect—the modest respect of humanity, and fellow-feeling—not the libidinous mockery of gallantry, nor the insolent condescension of protectorship.

To carry the observation still further, modesty must heartily disclaim, and refuse to dwell with that debauchery of mind, which leads a man coolly to bring forward, without a blush, indecent allusions, or obscene witticisms, in the presence of a fellow creature; women are now out of the question, for then it is brutality. Respect for man, as man, is the foundation of every noble sentiment. How much more modest is the libertine who obeys the call of appetite or fancy, than the lewd joker who sets the table in a roar!

3. Scientist.
4. A limited sense.
5. "The immodest behaviour of many married women, who are nevertheless faithful to their husbands' beds, will illustrate this remark" [Wollstonecraft's note].

This is one of the many instances in which the sexual distinction[6] respecting modesty has proved fatal to virtue and happiness. It is, however, carried still further, and woman, weak woman! made by her education the slave of sensibility, is required, on the most trying occasions, to resist that sensibility. 'Can any thing,' says Knox, 'be more absurd than keeping women in a state of ignorance, and yet so vehemently to insist on their resisting temptation?'[7]—Thus when virtue or honour make it proper to check a passion, the burden is thrown on the weaker shoulders, contrary to reason and true modesty, which, at least, should render the self-denial mutual, to say nothing of the generosity of bravery, supposed to be a manly virtue.

In the same strain runs Rousseau's and Dr. Gregory's advice respecting modesty, strangely miscalled! for they both desire a wife to leave it in doubt whether sensibility or weakness led her to her husband's arms.—The woman is immodest who can let the shadow of such a doubt remain in her husband's mind a moment.[8]

But to state the subject in a different light.—The want of modesty, which I principally deplore as subversive of morality, arises from the state of warfare so strenuously supported by voluptuous men as the very essence of modesty, though, in fact, its bane; because it is a refinement on lust, that men fall into who have not sufficient virtue to relish the innocent pleasures of love. A man of delicacy carries his notions of modesty still further, for neither weakness nor sensibility will gratify him—he looks for affection.

Again; men boast of their triumphs over women, what do they boast of? Truly the creature of sensibility was surprised by her sensibility into folly—into vice;[9] and the dreadful reckoning falls heavily on her own weak head, when reason wakes. For where art thou to find comfort, forlorn and disconsolate one? He who ought to have directed thy reason, and supported thy weakness, has betrayed thee! In a dream of passion thou consented to wander through flowery lawns, and heedlessly stepping over the precipice to which thy guide, instead of guarding, lured thee, thou startest from thy dream only to face a sneering, frowning world, and to find thyself alone in a waste, for he that triumphed in thy weakness is now pursuing new conquests; but for thee—there is no redemption on this side the grave!—And what resource hast thou in an enervated mind to raise a sinking heart?

---

6. Gender difference.
7. This may paraphrase the argument of Vicesimus Knox's "On the Necessity and Method of Encouraging in the Community the Prevalence of Virtuous Love," essay 34 in his *Essays Moral and Literary*, I, pp. 150–55.
8. See *Emilius*, p. 229 herein.
9. "The poor moth fluttering round a candle, burns its wings" [Wollstonecraft's note].

But, if the sexes be really to live in a state of warfare, if nature have pointed it out, let them act nobly, or let pride whisper to them, that the victory is mean when they merely vanquish sensibility. The real conquest is that over affection not taken by surprise—when, like Heloisa,[1] a woman gives up all the world, deliberately, for love. I do not now consider the wisdom or virtue of such a sacrifice, I only contend that it was a sacrifice to affection, and not merely to sensibility, though she had her share.—And I must be allowed to call her a modest woman, before I dismiss this part of the subject, by saying, that till men are more chaste women will be immodest. Where, indeed, could modest women find husbands from whom they would not continually turn with disgust? Modesty must be equally cultivated by both sexes, or it will ever remain a sickly hot-house plant, whilst the affectation of it, the fig leaf borrowed by wantonness, may give a zest to voluptuous enjoyments.

Men will probably still insist that woman ought to have more modesty than man; but it is not dispassionate reasoners who will most earnestly oppose my opinion. No, they are the men of fancy, the favourites of the sex, who outwardly respect and inwardly despise the weak creatures whom they thus sport with. They cannot submit to resign the highest sensual gratification, nor even to relish the epicurism of virtue—self-denial.

To take another view of the subject, confining my remarks to women.

The ridiculous falsities[2] which are told to children, from mistaken notions of modesty, tend very early to inflame their imaginations and set their little minds to work, respecting subjects, which nature never intended they should think of till the body arrived at some degree of maturity; then the passions naturally begin to take place of the senses, as instruments to unfold the understanding, and form the moral character.

1. Probably referring to Rousseau's heroine Julie, who resolves to act on her desire for her tutor Saint-Preux; knowing all the while that the consequences of their sexual liaison will be unhappy. *Julie, ou la Nouvelle Héloïse* was originally translated into English as *Eloisa* by a translator who throughout substituted the latter name wherever Rousseau had written "Julie."
2. "Children very early see cats with their kittens, birds with their young ones, &c. Why then are they not to be told that their mothers carry and nourish them in the same way? As there would then be no appearance of mystery they would never think of the subject more. Truth may always be told to children, if it be told gravely; but it is the immodesty of affected modesty, that does all the mischief; and this smoke heats the imagination by vainly endeavouring to obscure certain objects. If, indeed, children could be kept entirely from improper company, we should never allude to any such subjects; but as this is impossible, it is best to tell them the truth, especially as such information, not interesting them, will make no impression on their imagination" [Wollstonecraft's note]. Introducing her translation of Christian Gotthilf Salzmann's *Elements of Morality, for the Use of Children* (London, 1790), Wollstonecraft had recommended, even more explicitly, that we "speak to children of the organs of generation as freely as we speak of the other parts of the body, and explain to them the noble use which they were designed for, and how they may be injured" (I, p. xii).

In nurseries, and boarding-schools, I fear, girls are first spoiled; particularly in the latter. A number of girls sleep in the same room, and wash together. And, though I should be sorry to contaminate an innocent creature's mind by instilling false delicacy, or those indecent prudish notions, which early cautions respecting the other sex naturally engender, I should be very anxious to prevent their acquiring nasty, or immodest habits; and as many girls have learned very nasty tricks, from ignorant servants, the mixing them thus indiscriminately together, is very improper.[3]

To say the truth women are, in general, too familiar with each other, which leads to that gross degree of familiarity that so frequently renders the marriage state unhappy. Why in the name of decency are sisters, female intimates, or ladies and their waiting-women, to be so grossly familiar as to forget the respect which one human creature owes to another? That squeamish delicacy which shrinks from the most disgusting offices when affection[4] or humanity lead us to watch at a sick pillow, is despicable. But, why women in health should be more familiar with each other than men are, when they boast of their superiour delicacy, is a solecism in manners which I could never solve.

In order to preserve health and beauty, I should earnestly recommend frequent ablutions, to dignify my advice that it may not offend the fastidious ear; and, by example, girls ought to be taught to wash and dress alone, without any distinction of rank;[5] and if custom should make them require some little assistance, let them not require it till that part of the business is over which ought never to be done before a fellow-creature; because it is an insult to the majesty of human nature. Not on the score of modesty, but decency; for the care which some modest women take, making at the same time a display of that care, not to let their legs be seen, is as childish as immodest.[6]

I could proceed still further, till I animadverted on some still more nasty customs, which men never fall into. Secrets are told—where silence ought to reign; and that regard to cleanliness, which some religious sects have, perhaps, carried too far, especially the Essenes,[7]

3. In *Thoughts on the Education of Daughters* (London, 1787) Wollstonecraft, like many eighteenth-century writers on education, deplores the consequences that ensue when parents abandon child care to their servants: "the first notions [the children] imbibe are mean and vulgar. They are taught cunning, the wisdom of that class of people" (p. 113).
4. "Affection would rather make one choose to perform these offices, to spare the delicacy of a friend, by still keeping a veil over them, for the personal helplessness, produced by sickness, is of an humbling nature" [Wollstonecraft's note].
5. In the upper ranks of British society at this time, even adult women expected to call on the aid of maidservants when they got dressed.
6. "I remember to have met with a sentence, in a book of education, that made me smile. 'It would be needless to caution you against putting your hand, by chance, under your neck-handkerchief; for a modest woman never did so!'" [Wollstonecraft's note].
7. A Jewish communal sect that lived in Palestine from about the second century B.C.E. to the end of the first century C.E. It stressed meticulous adherence to laws of purity and practiced ritual washings.

amongst the Jews, by making that an insult to God which is only an insult to humanity, is violated in a beastly manner. How can *delicate* women obtrude on notice that part of the animal oeconomy, which is so very disgusting?[8] And is it not very rational to conclude, that the women who have not been taught to respect the human nature of their own sex, in these particulars, will not long respect the mere difference of sex in their husbands? After their maidenish bashfulness is once lost, I, in fact, have generally observed, that women fall into old habits; and treat their husbands as they did their sisters or female acquaintance.

Besides, women from necessity, because their minds are not cultivated, have recourse very often to what I familiarly term bodily wit; and their intimacies are of the same kind. In short, with respect to both mind and body, there are too intimate. That decent personal reserve which is the foundation of dignity of character, must be kept up between woman and woman, or their minds will never gain strength or modesty.

On this account also, I object to many females being shut up together in nurseries, schools, or convents. I cannot recollect without indignation, the jokes and hoiden tricks, which knots of young women indulge themselves in, when in my youth accident threw me, an awkward rustic, in their way. They were almost on a par with the double meanings, which shake the convivial table when the glass has circulated freely. But, it is vain to attempt to keep the heart pure, unless the head is furnished with ideas, and set to work to compare them, in order to acquire judgment, by generalizing simple ones; and modesty, by making the understanding damp the sensibility.

It may be thought that I lay too great a stress on personal reserve; but it is ever the handmaid of modesty. So that were I to name the graces that ought to adorn beauty, I should instantly exclaim, cleanliness, neatness, and personal reserve. It is obvious, I suppose, that the reserve I mean, has nothing sexual in it, and that I think it *equally* necessary in both sexes. So necessary, indeed, is that reserve and cleanliness which indolent women too often neglect, that I will venture to affirm that when two or three women live in the same house, the one will be most respected by the male part of the family, who reside with them, leaving love entirely out of the question, who pays this kind of habitual respect to her person.

When domestic friends meet in a morning, there will naturally prevail an affectionate seriousness, especially, if each look forward to the discharge of daily duties; and it may be reckoned fanciful, but this sentiment has frequently risen spontaneously in my mind,

---

8. Wollstonecraft selects decorous terms to criticize women who defecate or urinate (undertake "part of the animal oeconomy") in front of others. "Obtrude": thrust forward.

I have been pleased after breathing the sweet-bracing morning air, to see the same kind of freshness in the countenances I particularly loved; I was glad to see them braced, as it were, for the day, and ready to run their course with the sun. The greetings of affection in the morning are by these means more respectful than the familiar tenderness which frequently prolongs the evening talk. Nay, I have often felt hurt, not to say disgusted, when a friend has appeared, whom I parted with full dressed the evening before, with her clothes huddled on, because she chose to indulge herself in bed till the last moment.

Domestic affection can only be kept alive by these neglected attentions; yet if men and women took half as much pains to dress habitually neat, as they do to ornament, or rather to disfigure, their persons, much would be done towards the attainment of purity of mind. But women only dress to gratify men of gallantry; for the lover is always best pleased with the simple garb that fits close to the shape. There is an impertinence in ornaments that rebuffs affection; because love always clings round the idea of home.

As a sex, women are habitually indolent; and every thing tends to make them so. I do not forget the spurts of activity which sensibility produces; but as these flights of feelings only increase the evil, they are not to be confounded with the slow, orderly walk of reason. So great in reality is their mental and bodily indolence, that till their body be strengthened and their understanding enlarged by active exertions, there is little reason to expect that modesty will take place of bashfulness. They may find it prudent to assume its semblance; but the fair veil will only be worn on gala days.

Perhaps, there is not a virtue that mixes so kindly with every other as modesty.—It is the pale moon-beam that renders more interesting every virtue it softens, giving mild grandeur to the contracted horizon. Nothing can be more beautiful than the poetical fiction, which makes Diana[9] with her silver crescent, the goddess of chastity. I have sometimes thought, that wandering with sedate step in some lonely recess, a modest dame of antiquity must have felt a glow of conscious dignity when, after contemplating the soft shadowy landscape, she has invited with placid fervour the mild reflection of her sister's beams to turn to her chaste bosom.

A Christian has still nobler motives to incite her to preserve her chastity and acquire modesty, for her body has been called the Temple of the living God;[1] of that God who requires more than modesty of mien. His eye searcheth the heart; and let her remember, that

9. Roman goddess of the moon, a virgin, huntress, and patron of women in childbirth.
1. I Corinthians 3:16: "Know ye not that ye are the temple of God, and that the Spirit of God dwelleth in you?"

if she hope to find favour in the sight of purity itself, her chastity must be founded on modesty, and not on worldly prudence; or verily a good reputation will be her only reward; for that awful intercourse, that sacred communication, which virtue establishes between man and his Maker, must give rise to the wish of being pure as he is pure![2]

After the foregoing remarks, it is almost superfluous to add, that I consider all those feminine airs of maturity, which succeed bashfulness, to which truth is sacrificed, to secure the heart of a husband, or rather to force him to be still a lover when nature would, had she not been interrupted in her operations, have made love give place to friendship, as immodest. The tenderness which a man will feel for the mother of his children is an excellent substitute for the ardour of unsatisfied passion; but to prolong that ardour it is indelicate, not to say immodest, for women to feign an unnatural coldness of constitution. Women as well as men ought to have the common appetites and passions of their nature, they are only brutal when unchecked by reason: but the obligation to check them is the duty of mankind, not a sexual duty. Nature, in these respects, may safely be left to herself; let women only acquire knowledge and humanity, and love will teach them modesty.[3] There is no need of falsehoods, disgusting as futile, for studied rules of behaviour only impose on shallow observers; a man of sense soon sees through, and despises the affectation.

The behaviour of young people, to each other, as men and women, is the last thing that should be thought of in education. In fact, behaviour in most circumstances is now so much thought of, that simplicity of character is rarely to be seen: yet, if men were only anxious to cultivate each virtue, and let it take root firmly in the mind, the grace resulting from it, its natural exteriour mark, would soon strip affectation of its flaunting plumes; because, fallacious as unstable, is the conduct that is not founded upon truth!

Would ye, O my sisters, really possess modesty, ye must remember that the possession of virtue, of any denomination, is incompatible with ignorance and vanity! ye must acquire that soberness of mind, which the exercise of duties, and the pursuit of knowledge, alone inspire, or ye will still remain in a doubtful dependent situation, and only be loved whilst ye are fair! The downcast eye, the rosy blush, the retiring grace, are all proper in their season; but modesty, being the child of reason, cannot long exist with the sensibility that is not tempered by reflection. Besides, when love, even innocent love, is

2. Matthew 5:48: "Be ye therefore perfect, even as your Father which is in heaven is perfect."
3. "The behaviour of many newly married women has often disgusted me. They seem anxious never to let their husbands forget the privilege of marriage; and to find no pleasure in his society unless he is acting the lover. Short, indeed, must be the reign of love, when the flame is thus constantly blown up, without its receiving any solid fewel!" [Wollstonecraft's note].

the whole employ of your lives, your hearts will be too soft to afford modesty that tranquil retreat, where she delights to dwell, in close union with humanity.

Chap. VIII

Morality Undermined by Sexual Notions of the Importance of a Good Reputation

It has long since occurred to me that advice respecting behaviour, and all the various modes of preserving a good reputation, which have been so strenuously inculcated on the female world, were specious poisons, that incrusting morality eat away the substance. And, that this measuring of shadows produced a false calculation, because their length depends so much on the height of the sun, and other adventitious circumstances.

Whence arises the easy fallacious behaviour of a courtier? From his situation, undoubtedly: for standing in need of dependents, he is obliged to learn the art of denying without giving offence, and, of evasively feeding hope with the chameleon's food:[4] thus does politeness sport with truth, and eating away the sincerity and humanity natural to man, produce the fine gentleman.

Women likewise acquire, from a supposed necessity, an equally artificial mode of behaviour. Yet truth is not with impunity to be sported with, for the practised dissembler, at last, becomes the dupe of his own arts, loses that sagacity, which has been justly termed common sense; namely, a quick perception of common truths: which are constantly received as such by the unsophisticated mind, though it might not have had sufficient energy to discover them itself, when obscured by local prejudices. The greater number of people take their opinions on trust to avoid the trouble of exercising their own minds, and these indolent beings naturally adhere to the letter, rather than the spirit of a law, divine or human. 'Women,' says some author, I cannot recollect who, 'mind not what only heaven sees.' Why, indeed, should they? it is the eye of man that they have been taught to dread—and if they can lull their Argus[5] to sleep, they seldom think of heaven or themselves, because their reputation is safe; and it is reputation, not chastity and all its fair train, that they are employed to keep free from spot, not as a virtue, but to preserve their station in the world.

---

4. Legend held that chameleons could subsist on air.
5. In Greek myth a hundred-eyed monster, assigned by the goddess Hera to keep watch over Io and so prevent Zeus, Hera's lecherous husband, from committing adultery with that human maiden. Zeus's messenger, Hermes, contrived to lull Argus to sleep and kill him.

To prove the truth of this remark, I need only advert to the intrigues of married women, particularly in high life, and in countries where women are suitably married, according to their respective ranks, by their parents. If an innocent girl become a prey to love, she is degraded for ever, though her mind was not polluted by the arts which married women, under the convenient cloke of marriage, practise; nor has she violated any duty—but the duty of respecting herself. The married woman, on the contrary, breaks a most sacred engagement, and becomes a cruel mother when she is a false and faithless wife. If her husband have still an affection for her, the arts which she must practise to deceive him, will render her the most contemptible of human beings; and, at any rate, the contrivances necessary to preserve appearances, will keep her mind in that childish, or vicious, tumult, which destroys all its energy. Besides, in time, like those people who habitually take cordials to raise their spirits, she will want an intrigue to give life to her thoughts, having lost all relish for pleasures that are not highly seasoned by hope or fear.

Sometimes married women act still more audaciously; I will mention an instance.

A woman of quality, notorious for her gallantries, though as she still lived with her husband, nobody chose to place her in the class where she ought to have been placed, made a point of treating with the most insulting contempt a poor timid creature, abashed by a sense of her former weakness, whom a neighbouring gentleman had seduced and afterwards married. This woman had actually confounded virtue with reputation; and, I do believe, valued herself on the propriety of her behaviour before marriage, though when once settled to the satisfaction of her family, she and her lord were equally faithless,—so that the half alive heir to an immense estate came from heaven knows where!

To view this subject in another light.

I have known a number of women who, if they did not love their husbands, loved nobody else, give themselves entirely up to vanity and dissipation, neglecting every domestic duty; nay, even squandering away all the money which should have been saved for their helpless younger children, yet have plumed themselves on their unsullied reputation, as if the whole compass of their duty as wives and mothers was only to preserve it. Whilst other indolent women, neglecting every personal duty, have thought that they deserved their husbands' affection, because, forsooth, they acted in this respect with propriety.

Weak minds are always fond of resting in the ceremonials of duty, but morality offers much simpler motives; and it were to be wished that superficial moralists had said less respecting behaviour, and outward observances, for unless virtue, of any kind, be built on knowledge, it will only produce a kind of insipid decency. Respect for the opinion of the world, has, however, been termed the principal duty of woman in the most express words, for Rousseau declares, 'that reputation is no less indispensable than chastity.' 'A man,' adds he, 'secure in his own good conduct, depends only on himself, and may brave the public opinion: but a woman, in behaving well, performs but half her duty; as what is thought of her, is as important to her as what she really is. It follows hence, that the system of a woman's education should, in this respect, be directly contrary to that of ours. Opinion is the grave of virtue among the men; but its throne among women.'[6] It is strictly logical to infer that the virtue that rests on opinion is merely worldly, and that it is the virtue of a being to whom reason has been denied. But, even with respect to the opinion of the world, I am convinced that this class of reasoners are mistaken.

This regard for reputation, independent of its being one of the natural rewards of virtue, however, took its rise from a cause that I have already deplored as the grand source of female depravity, the impossibility of regaining respectability by a return to virtue, though men preserve theirs during the indulgence of vice. It was natural for women then to endeavour to preserve what once lost—was lost for ever, till this care swallowing up every other care, reputation for chastity, became the one thing needful to the sex. But vain is the scrupulosity of ignorance, for neither religion nor virtue, when they reside in the heart, require such a puerile attention to mere ceremonies, because the behaviour must, upon the whole, be proper, when the motive is pure.

To support my opinion I can produce very respectable authority; and the authority of a cool reasoner ought to have weight to enforce consideration, though not to establish a sentiment. Speaking of the general laws of morality, Dr. Smith observes,—'That by some very extraordinary and unlucky circumstance, a good man may come to be suspected of a crime of which he was altogether incapable, and upon that account be most unjustly exposed for the remaining part of his life to the horror and aversion of mankind. By an accident of this kind he may be said to lose his all, notwithstanding his integrity and justice, in the same manner as a cautious man, notwithstanding his utmost circumspection, may be ruined by an earthquake or an inundation. Accidents of the first kind, however, are perhaps still more rare, and still more contrary to the common course of things than those of the second; and it still remains true, that the practice of truth, justice, and humanity, is a certain and almost infallible

6. *Emilius* IV, v, p. 19.

method of acquiring what those virtues chiefly aim at, the confidence and love of those we live with. A person may be easily misrepresented with regard to a particular action; but it is scarce possible that he should be so with regard to the general tenor of his conduct. An innocent man may be believed to have done wrong: this, however, will rarely happen. On the contrary, the established opinion of the innocence of his manners will often lead us to absolve him where he has really been in the fault, notwithstanding very strong presumptions.'[7]

I perfectly coincide in opinion with this writer, for I verily believe that few of either sex were ever despised for certain vices without deserving to be despised. I speak not of the calumny of the moment, which hovers over a character, like one of the dense morning fogs of November, over this metropolis,[8] till it gradually subsides before the common light of day, I only contend that the daily conduct of the majority prevails to stamp their character with the impression of truth. Quietly does the clear light, shining day after day, refute the ignorant surmise, or malicious tale, which has thrown dirt on a pure character. A false light distorted, for a short time, its shadow—reputation; but it seldom fails to become just when the cloud is dispersed that produced the mistake in vision.

Many people, undoubtedly, in several respects obtain a better reputation than, strictly speaking, they deserve; for unremitting industry will mostly reach its goal in all races. They who only strive for this paltry prize, like the Pharisees, who prayed at the corners of streets, to be seen of men,[9] verily obtain the reward they seek; for the heart of man cannot be read by man! Still the fair fame that is naturally reflected by good actions, when the man is only employed to direct his steps aright, regardless of the lookers-on, is, in general, not only more true, but more sure.

There are, it is true, trials when the good man must appeal to God from the injustice of man; and amidst the whining candour or hissings of envy, erect a pavilion in his own mind to retire to till the rumour be overpast; nay, the darts of undeserved censure may pierce an innocent tender bosom through with many sorrows; but these are all exceptions to general rules. And it is according to common laws that human behaviour ought to be regulated. The eccentric orbit of the comet never influences astronomical calculations respecting the invariable order established in the motion of the principal bodies of the solar system.

7. Smith, *Theory of Moral Sentiments*, III, v, p. 167.
8. I.e., London.
9. Matthew 6:5: "And when thou prayest, thou shalt not be as the hypocrites are: for they love to pray standing in the synagogues and in the corners of the streets, that they may be seen of men." Pharisees lived by the letter, not the spirit, of the law.

I will then venture to affirm, that after a man is arrived at maturity, the general outline of his character in the world is just, allowing for the before-mentioned exceptions to the rule. I do not say that a prudent, worldly-wise man, with only negative virtues and qualities, may not sometimes obtain a smoother reputation than a wiser or a better man. So far from it, that I am apt to conclude from experience, that where the virtue of two people is nearly equal, the most negative character will be liked best by the world at large, whilst the other may have more friends in private life. But the hills and dales, clouds and sunshine, conspicuous in the virtues of great men, set off each other; and though they afford envious weakness a fairer mark to shoot at, the real character will still work its way to light, though bespattered by weak affection, or ingenious malice.[1]

With respect to that anxiety to preserve a reputation hardly earned, which leads sagacious people to analyze it, I shall not make the obvious comment; but I am afraid that morality is very insidiously undermined, in the female world, by the attention being turned to the shew instead of the substance. A simple thing is thus made strangely complicated; nay, sometimes virtue and its shadow are set at variance. We should never, perhaps, have heard of Lucretia,[2] had she died to preserve her chastity instead of her reputation. If we really deserve our own good opinion we shall commonly be respected in the world; but if we pant after higher improvement and higher attainments, it is not sufficient to view ourselves as we suppose that we are viewed by others, though this has been ingeniously argued, as the foundation of our moral sentiments.[3] Because each by-stander may have his own prejudices, beside the prejudices of his age or country. We should rather endeavour to view ourselves as we suppose that Being views us who seeth each thought ripen into action, and whose judgment never swerves from the eternal rule of right. Righteous are all his judgments—just as merciful!

The humble mind that seeketh to find favour in His sight, and calmly examines its conduct when only His presence is felt, will

1. "I allude to various biographical writings, but particularly to Boswell's Life of Johnson" [Wollstonecraft's note]. When it appeared in 1791, many readers remarked on the tension within the *Life of Samuel Johnson* between James Boswell's heroicizing of Johnson and his attention to Johnson's foibles and to the humble details of his private life.
2. Sextus Tarquinius, a Roman prince, forced Lucretia, a matron celebrated for her chastity, to submit to his sexual advances by telling her that if she resisted he would not only murder her but also place her corpse next to that of a naked slave so as to suggest that her death had occurred during an act of dishonorable adultery. After her rape, Lucretia called on her husband and father to avenge her and then stabbed herself. Her suicide impelled her kinsmen to overthrow the Tarquins and their tyrannical rule in 509 B.C.E. and to establish Rome as a republic (Livy, *History of Rome*, I, p. i).
3. "Smith" [Wollstonecraft's note]. In *Theory of Moral Sentiments* Smith proposes that society alone provides individuals with the mirror in which they may judge themselves. See, e.g., III, i, p. 110: "We can never survey our own sentiments and motives, we can never form any judgment concerning them, unless we . . . [endeavour] to view them with the eyes of other people, or as other people are likely to view them."

seldom form a very erroneous opinion of its own virtues. During the still hour of self-collection the angry brow of offended justice will be fearfully deprecated, or the tie which draws man to the Deity will be recognized in the pure sentiment of reverential adoration, that swells the heart without exciting any tumultuous emotions. In these solemn moments man discovers the germ of those vices, which like the Java tree[4] shed a pestiferous vapour around—death is in the shade! and he perceives them without abhorrence, because he feels himself drawn by some cord of love to all his fellow-creatures, for whose follies he is anxious to find every extenuation in their nature—in himself. If I, he may thus argue, who exercise my own mind, and have been refined by tribulation, find the serpent's egg[5] in some fold of my heart, and crush it with difficulty, shall not I pity those who have stamped with less vigour, or who have heedlessly nurtured the insidious reptile till it poisoned the vital stream it sucked? Can I, conscious of my secret sins, throw off my fellow-creatures, and calmly see them drop into the chasm of perdition, that yawns to receive them.—No! no! The agonized heart will cry with suffocating impatience—I too am a man! and have vices, hid, perhaps, from human eye, that bend me to the dust before God, and loudly tell me, when all is mute, that we are formed of the same earth, and breathe the same element. Humanity thus rises naturally out of humility, and twists the cords of love that in various convolutions entangle the heart.

This sympathy extends still further, till a man well pleased observes force in arguments that do not carry conviction to his own bosom, and he gladly places in the fairest light, to himself, the shews of reason that have led others astray, rejoiced to find some reason in all the errors of man; though before convinced that he who rules the day makes his sun to shine on all. Yet, shaking hands thus as it were with corruption, one foot on earth, the other with bold stride mounts to heaven, and claims kindred with superiour natures. Virtues, unobserved by man, drop their balmy fragrance at this cool hour, and the thirsty land, refreshed by the pure streams of comfort that suddenly gush out, is crowned with smiling verdure; this is the living green on which that eye may look with complacency that is too pure to behold iniquity!

But my spirits flag; and I must silently indulge the reverie these reflections lead to, unable to describe the sentiments, that have calmed my soul, when watching the rising sun, a soft shower drizzling through the leaves of neighbouring trees, seemed to fall on my lan-

---

4. European travelers reported, erroneously, that the upas tree of Java emitted vapors so poisonous that they killed all living things they touched.
5. *Julius Caesar* II.i.32–33: "Therefore think him as a serpent's egg / Which, hatch'd, would, as his kind, grow mischievous."

guid, yet tranquil spirits, to cool the heart that had been heated by the passions which reason laboured to tame.

The leading principles which run through all my disquisitions, would render it unnecessary to enlarge on this subject, if a constant attention to keep the varnish of the character fresh, and in good condition, were not often inculcated as the sum total of female duty; if rules to regulate the behaviour, and to preserve the reputation, did not too frequently supersede moral obligations. But, with respect to reputation, the attention is confined to a single virtue—chastity. If the honour of a woman, as it is absurdly called, be safe, she may neglect every social duty; nay, ruin her family by gaming and extravagance; yet still present a shameless front—for truly she is an honourable woman!

Mrs. Macaulay has justly observed, that 'there is but one fault which a woman of honour may not commit with impunity.'[6] She then justly and humanely adds—'This has given rise to the trite and foolish observation, that the first fault against chastity in woman has a radical power to deprave the character. But no such frail beings come out of the hands of nature. The human mind is built of nobler materials than to be easily corrupted; and with all their disadvantages of situation and education, women seldom become entirely abandoned till they are thrown into a state of desperation, by the venomous rancour of their own sex.'[7]

But, in proportion as this regard for the reputation of chastity is prized by women, it is despised by men: and the two extremes are equally destructive to morality.

Men are certainly more under the influence of their appetites than women; and their appetites are more depraved by unbridled indulgence and the fastidious contrivances of satiety. Luxury has introduced a refinement in eating, that destroys the constitution; and, a degree of gluttony which is so beastly, that a perception of seemliness of behaviour must be worn out before one being could eat immoderately in the presence of another, and afterwards complain of the oppression that his intemperance naturally produced. Some women, particularly French women, have also lost a sense of decency in this respect; for they will talk very calmly of an indigestion. It were to be wished that idleness was not allowed to generate, on the rank soil of wealth, those swarms of summer insects that feed on putrefaction, we should not then be disgusted by the sight of such brutal excesses.

---

6. Macaulay elaborates on the "one fault" as follows: "let her only take care that she is not caught in a love intrigue, and she may lie, she may deceive, she may defame, she may ruin her family with gaming, and the peace of twenty others with her coquettry, and yet preserve both her reputation and her peace" (*Letters on Education*, p. 210).
7. Macaulay, p. 212.

There is one rule relative to behaviour that, I think, ought to regulate every other; and it is simply to cherish such an habitual respect for mankind as may prevent us from disgusting a fellow-creature for the sake of a present indulgence. The shameful indolence of many married women, and others a little advanced in life, frequently leads them to sin against delicacy. For, though convinced that the person is the band of union between the sexes, yet, how often do they from sheer indolence, or, to enjoy some trifling indulgence, disgust?

The depravity of the appetite which brings the sexes together, has had a still more fatal effect. Nature must ever be the standard of taste, the gauge of appetite—yet how grossly is nature insulted by the voluptuary. Leaving the refinements of love out of the question; nature, by making the gratification of an appetite, in this respect, as well as every other, a natural and imperious law to preserve the species, exalts the appetite, and mixes a little mind and affection with a sensual gust. The feelings of a parent mingling with an instinct merely animal, give it dignity; and the man and woman often meeting on account of the child, a mutual interest and affection is excited by the exercise of a common sympathy. Women then having necessarily some duty to fulfil, more noble than to adorn their persons, would not contentedly be the slaves of casual lust; which is now the situation of a very considerable number who are, literally speaking, standing dishes to which every glutton may have access.

I may be told that great as this enormity is, it only affects a devoted[8] part of the sex—devoted for the salvation of the rest. But, false as every assertion might easily be proved, that recommends the sanctioning a small evil to produce a greater good; the mischief does not stop here, for the moral character, and peace of mind, of the chaster part of the sex, is undermined by the conduct of the very women to whom they allow no refuge from guilt: whom they inexorably consign to the exercise of arts that lure their husbands from them, debauch their sons, and force them, let not modest women start, to assume, in some degree, the same character themselves. For I will venture to assert, that all the causes of female weakness, as well as depravity, which I have already enlarged on, branch out of one grand cause—want of chastity in men.

This intemperance, so prevalent, depraves the appetite to such a degree, that a wanton stimulus is necessary to rouse it; but the parental design of nature is forgotten, and the mere person, and that

8. Here, sacrificed. Eighteenth-century writers who wished to see prostitution legalized or at least tolerated sometimes argued that prostitutes saved the remainder of the female population—the so-called modest women Wollstonecraft addresses next—from men's libertinism. Wollstonecraft contests this argument again in her 1792 review for the *Analytical Review* of the anonymously authored *The Evils of Adultery and Prostitution* (*Works*, VII, pp. 457–59).

for a moment, alone engrosses the thoughts. So voluptuous, indeed, often grows the lustful prowler, that he refines on female softness. Something more soft than woman is then sought for; till, in Italy and Portugal, men attend the levees of equivocal beings,[9] to sigh for more than female languor.

To satisfy this genus of men, women are made systematically voluptuous, and though they may not all carry their libertinism to the same height, yet this heartless intercourse with the sex, which they allow themselves, depraves both sexes, because the taste of men is vitiated; and women, of all classes, naturally square their behaviour to gratify the taste by which they obtain pleasure and power. Women becoming, consequently, weaker, in mind and body, than they ought to be, were one of the grand ends of their being taken into the account, that of bearing and nursing children, have not sufficient strength to discharge the first duty of a mother; and sacrificing to lasciviousness the parental affection, that ennobles instinct, either destroy the embryo in the womb, or cast it off when born.[1] Nature in every thing demands respect, and those who violate her laws seldom violate them with impunity. The weak enervated women who particularly catch the attention of libertines, are unfit to be mothers, though they may conceive; so that the rich sensualist, who has rioted among women, spreading depravity and misery, when he wishes to perpetuate his name, receives from his wife only an half-formed being that inherits both its father's and mother's weakness.

Contrasting the humanity of the present age with the barbarism of antiquity, great stress has been laid on the savage custom of exposing the children[2] whom their parents could not maintain; whilst the man of sensibility, who thus, perhaps, complains, by his promiscuous amours produces a most destructive barrenness and contagious flagitiousness[3] of manners. Surely nature never intended that women, by satisfying an appetite, should frustrate the very purpose for which it was implanted?

I have before observed, that men ought to maintain the women whom they have seduced; this would be one means of reforming female manners, and stopping an abuse that has an equally fatal effect on population and morals. Another, no less obvious, would be to turn the attention of woman to the real virtue of chastity; for to little respect has that woman a claim, on the score of modesty,

9. Probably homosexuals. "Levees": miscellaneous receptions of visitors.
1. The lecherous husband spreads syphilis to his wife, who for her part is so unhealthy that she either miscarries or bears a deformed child whom she abandons.
2. To expose to the elements, and allow to die, those infants who had deformities or who were for other reasons unwanted was common in ancient Greece.
3. Corruption.

though her reputation may be white as the driven snow, who smiles on the libertine whilst she spurns the victims of his lawless appetites and their own folly.

Besides, she has a taint of the same folly, pure as she esteems herself, when she studiously adorns her person only to be seen by men, to excite respectful sighs, and all the idle homage of what is called innocent gallantry. Did women really respect virtue for its own sake, they would not seek for a compensation in vanity, for the self-denial which they are obliged to practise to preserve their reputation, nor would they associate with men who set reputation at defiance.

The two sexes mutually corrupt and improve each other. This I believe to be an indisputable truth, extending it to every virtue. Chastity, modesty, public spirit, and all the noble train of virtues, on which social virtue and happiness are built, should be understood and cultivated by all mankind, or they will be cultivated to little effect. And, instead of furnishing the vicious or idle with a pretext for violating some sacred duty, by terming it a sexual one, it would be wiser to shew that nature has not made any difference, for that the unchaste man doubly defeats the purpose of nature, by rendering women barren, and destroying his own constitution, though he avoids the shame that pursues the crime in the other sex. These are the physical consequences, the moral are still more alarming; for virtue is only a nominal distinction when the duties of citizens, husbands, wives, fathers, mothers, and directors of families, become merely the selfish ties of convenience.

Why then do philosophers look for public spirit? Public spirit must be nurtured by private virtue, or it will resemble the factitious sentiment which makes women careful to preserve their reputation, and men their honour. A sentiment that often exists unsupported by virtue, unsupported by that sublime morality which makes the habitual breach of one duty a breach of the whole moral law.

Chap. IX

Of the Pernicious Effects Which Arise from the Unnatural Distinctions Established in Society

From the respect paid to property flow, as from a poisoned fountain, most of the evils and vices which render this world such a dreary scene to the contemplative mind. For it is in the most polished society that noisome reptiles and venomous serpents lurk under the rank herbage; and there is voluptuousness pampered by the still sultry air, which relaxes every good disposition before it ripens into virtue.

One class presses on another; for all are aiming to procure respect on account of their property: and property, once gained, will procure the respect due only to talents and virtue. Men neglect the duties incumbent on man, yet are treated like demi-gods; religion is also separated from morality by a ceremonial veil, yet men wonder that the world is almost, literally speaking, a den of sharpers or oppressors.

There is a homely proverb, which speaks a shrewd truth, that whoever the devil finds idle he will employ. And what but habitual idleness can hereditary wealth and titles produce? For man is so constituted that he can only attain a proper use of his faculties by exercising them, and will not exercise them unless necessity, of some kind, first set the wheels in motion. Virtue likewise can only be acquired by the discharge of relative duties; but the importance of these sacred duties will scarcely be felt by the being who is cajoled out of his humanity by the flattery of sycophants. There must be more equality established in society, or morality will never gain ground, and this virtuous equality will not rest firmly even when founded on a rock, if one half of mankind be chained to its bottom by fate, for they will be continually undermining it through ignorance or pride.

It is vain to expect virtue from women till they are, in some degree, independent of men; nay, it is vain to expect that strength of natural affection, which would make them good wives and mothers. Whilst they are absolutely dependent on their husbands they will be cunning, mean, and selfish, and the men who can be gratified by the fawning fondness of spaniel-like affection, have not much delicacy, for love is not to be bought, in any sense of the words, its silken wings are instantly shrivelled up when any thing beside a return in kind is sought. Yet whilst wealth enervates men; and women live, as it were, by their personal charms, how can we expect them to discharge those ennobling duties which equally require exertion and self-denial. Hereditary property sophisticates the mind, and the unfortunate victims to it, if I may so express myself, swathed from their birth, seldom exert the locomotive faculty of body or mind;[4] and, thus viewing every thing through one medium, and that a false one, they are unable to discern in what true merit and happiness consist. False, indeed, must be the light when the drapery of situation hides the man, and makes him stalk in masquerade, dragging from one scene of dissipation to another the nerveless limbs that hang with stupid listlessness, and rolling round the vacant eye which plainly tells us that there is no mind at home.

4. Wollstonecraft's metaphor aligns hereditary property with the swaddling clothes in which newborn infants were wrapped ("swathed") to prevent them from moving their limbs. Condemned by physicians and educational theorists such as Locke and Rousseau, swaddling had fallen into disuse by her day. "Sophisticates": corrupts.

I mean, therefore, to infer that the society is not properly organized which does not compel men and women to discharge their
respective duties, by making it the only way to acquire that countenance from their fellow-creatures, which every human being wishes
some way to attain. The respect, consequently, which is paid to
wealth and mere personal charms, is a true north-east blast, that
blights the tender blossoms of affection and virtue. Nature has
wisely attached affections to duties, to sweeten toil, and to give that
vigour to the exertions of reason which only the heart can give. But,
the affection which is put on merely because it is the appropriated
insignia of a certain character, when its duties are not fulfilled, is
one of the empty compliments which vice and folly are obliged to
pay to virtue and the real nature of things.

To illustrate my opinion, I need only observe, that when a woman
is admired for her beauty, and suffers herself to be so far intoxicated
by the admiration she receives, as to neglect to discharge the indispensable duty of a mother, she sins against herself by neglecting to
cultivate an affection that would equally tend to make her useful
and happy. True happiness, I mean all the contentment, and virtuous satisfaction, that can be snatched in this imperfect state, must
arise from well regulated affections; and an affection includes a
duty. Men are not aware of the misery they cause, and the vicious
weakness they cherish, by only inciting women to render themselves
pleasing; they do not consider that they thus make natural and artificial duties clash, by sacrificing the comfort and respectability of a
woman's life to voluptuous notions of beauty, when in nature they all
harmonize.

Cold would be the heart of a husband, were he not rendered
unnatural by early debauchery, who did not feel more delight at seeing his child suckled by its mother, than the most artful wanton
tricks could ever raise; yet this natural way of cementing the matrimonial tie, and twisting esteem with fonder recollections, wealth
leads women to spurn.[5] To preserve their beauty, and wear the flowery crown of the day, which gives them a kind of right to reign for a
short time over the sex, they neglect to stamp impressions on their
husbands' hearts, that would be remembered with more tenderness
when the snow on the head began to chill the bosom, than even
their virgin charms. The maternal solicitude of a reasonable affectionate woman is very interesting, and the chastened dignity with
which a mother returns the caresses that she and her child receive
from a father who has been fulfilling the serious duties of his station,
is not only a respectable, but a beautiful sight. So singular, indeed,

5. Despite campaigning by eighteenth-century physicians, it remained the case that babies
born to wealthy families were not always breast-fed by their mothers but often, instead,
by poor women hired as wet nurses.

are my feelings, and I have endeavoured not to catch factitious ones, that after having been fatigued with the sight of insipid grandeur and the slavish ceremonies that with cumberous pomp supplied the place of domestic affections, I have turned to some other scene to relieve my eye by resting it on the refreshing green every where scattered by nature. I have then viewed with pleasure a woman nursing her children, and discharging the duties of her station with, perhaps, merely a servant maid to take off her hands the servile part of the household business. I have seen her prepare herself and children, with only the luxury of cleanliness, to receive her husband, who returning weary home in the evening found smiling babes and a clean hearth. My heart has loitered in the midst of the group, and has even throbbed with sympathetic emotion, when the scraping of the well known foot has raised a pleasing tumult.

Whilst my benevolence has been gratified by contemplating this artless picture, I have thought that a couple of this description, equally necessary and independent of each other, because each fulfilled the respective duties of their station, possessed all that life could give.—Raised sufficiently above abject poverty not to be obliged to weigh the consequence of every farthing they spend, and having sufficient to prevent their attending to a frigid system of œconomy, which narrows both heart and mind. I declare, so vulgar are my conceptions, that I know not what is wanted to render this the happiest as well as the most respectable situation in the world, but a taste for literature, to throw a little variety and interest into social converse, and some superfluous money to give to the needy and to buy books. For it is not pleasant when the heart is opened by compassion and the head active in arranging plans of usefulness, to have a prim urchin continually twitching back the elbow to prevent the hand from drawing out an almost empty purse, whispering at the same time some prudential maxim about the priority of justice.

[Destructive, however, as riches and inherited honours are to the human character, women are more debased and cramped, if possible, by them, than men, because men may still, in some degree, unfold their faculties[6] by becoming soldiers and statesmen.]

As soldiers, I grant, they can now only gather, for the most part, vain glorious laurels, whilst they adjust to a hair the European balance, taking especial care that no bleak northern nook or sound incline the beam.[7] But the days of true heroism are over, when a

6. Develop their minds.
7. The wars Britain waged through the eighteenth century to prevent France from becoming the predominant global power and to preserve equilibrium ("balance") in international relations could unfold at the farthest reaches of the empire. Wollstonecraft likely puns here on Nootka Sound ("northern nook"), a bay on the northwest coast of North America, where Spain, then a French ally, had seized four British ships in 1790. War between Britain and France was averted then but finally broke out in 1793.

citizen fought for his country like a Fabricius[8] or a Washington, and then returned to his farm to let his virtuous fervour run in a more placid, but not a less salutary, stream. No, our British heroes are oftener sent from the gaming table than from the plow;[9] and their passions have been rather inflamed by hanging with dumb suspense on the turn of a die, than sublimated by panting after the adventurous march of virtue in the historic page.

The statesman, it is true, might with more propriety quit the Faro Bank,[1] or card-table, to guide the helm, for he has still but to shuffle and trick. The whole system of British politics, if system it may courteously be called, consisting in multiplying dependents and contriving taxes which grind the poor to pamper the rich; thus a war, or any wild goose chace, is, as the vulgar use the phrase, a lucky turn-up of patronage for the minister, whose chief merit is the art of keeping himself in place. It is not necessary then that he should have bowels[2] for the poor, so he can secure for his family the odd trick. Or should some shew of respect, for what is termed with ignorant ostentation an Englishman's birth-right, be expedient to bubble the gruff mastiff that he has to lead by the nose, he can make an empty shew, very safely, by giving his single voice, and suffering his light squadron to file off to the other side. And when a question of humanity is agitated he may dip a sop in the milk of human kindness, to silence Cerberus,[3] and talk of the interest which his heart takes in an attempt to make the earth no longer cry for vengeance as it sucks in its children's blood, though his cold hand may at the very moment rivet their chains, by sanctioning the abominable traffick.[4] A minister is no longer a minister, than while he can carry a point, which he is determined to carry.—Yet it is not necessary that a minister should feel like a man, when a bold push might shake his seat.

But, to have done with these episodical observations, let me return to the more specious slavery which chains the very soul of woman, keeping her for ever under the bondage of ignorance.

8. Statesman and military commander who exemplified the moral incorruptibility and simple lifestyle distinguishing the republican era in the history of Rome (see also p. 17, n. 9).
9. General Washington returned to rural life after his victory over the British army. His determination to remain in public life no longer than necessary was, for some contemporaries, reminiscent of the high moral standards of the Roman republic; those contemporaries called Washington the "American Cincinnatus" because, like the Roman commander, he had been called out of rural retirement and away from his plow to serve the republic in its hour of need.
1. Gaming house where the card game "faro," popular with fashionable society in the 1790s, was played and where vast sums were rumored to change hands.
2. Compassion.
3. The three-headed dog that guarded the entrance to the underworld. The Greeks and Romans are said to have put cakes into the hands of the dead to be used as a bribe so the beast would allow their spirits to pass freely.
4. I.e., the trade in slaves, which was legal in the British Empire when Wollstonecraft wrote despite a decade of antislavery agitation. It would be abolished in 1807, with full emancipation postponed until 1833.

The preposterous distinctions of rank, which render civilization a curse, by dividing the world between voluptuous tyrants, and cunning envious dependents, corrupt, almost equally, every class of people, because respectability is not attached to the discharge of the relative duties of life, but to the station, and when the duties are not fulfilled the affections cannot gain sufficient strength to fortify the virtue of which they are the natural reward. Still there are some loop-holes out of which a man may creep, and dare to think and act for himself; but for a woman it is an herculean task, because she has difficulties peculiar to her sex to overcome, which require almost superhuman powers.

A truly benevolent legislator always endeavours to make it the interest of each individual to be virtuous; and thus private virtue becoming the cement of public happiness, an orderly whole is consolidated by the tendency of all the parts towards a common centre. But, the private or public virtue of woman is very problematical; for Rousseau, and a numerous list of male writers, insist that she should all her life be subjected to a severe restraint, that of propriety. Why subject her to propriety—blind propriety, if she be capable of acting from a nobler spring, if she be an heir of immortality? Is sugar always to be produced by vital blood? Is one half of the human species, like the poor African slaves, to be subject to prejudices that brutalize them, when principles would be a surer guard, only to sweeten the cup of man?[5] Is not this indirectly to deny woman reason? for a gift is a mockery, if it be unfit for use.

Women are, in common with men, rendered weak and luxurious by the relaxing pleasures which wealth procures; but added to this they are made slaves to their persons, and must render them alluring that man may lend them his reason to guide their tottering steps aright. Or should they be ambitious, they must govern their tyrants by sinister tricks, for without rights there cannot be any incumbent duties. The laws respecting woman, which I mean to discuss in a future part, make an absurd unit of a man and his wife;[6] and then, by the easy transition of only considering him as responsible, she is reduced to a mere cypher.

The being who discharges the duties of its station is independent; and, speaking of women at large, their first duty is to themselves as

---

5. Throughout 1791–92 campaigners for the abolition of the slave trade called for a consumer boycott of the cane sugar Britons used to sweeten their tea and publicized the violence involved in its production in the plantations of Britain's colonies in the West Indies.
6. The legal doctrine of coverture, as laid out by Sir William Blackstone in the period's most influential law book, his *Commentaries on the Laws of England* ([Oxford, 1765] I, xv, p. 430), stated: "By marriage, the husband and wife are one person in law: that is, the very being or legal existence of the woman is suspended during the marriage, or at least is incorporated and consolidated into that of the husband: under whose wing, protection, and *cover*, she performs everything."

rational creatures, and the next, in point of importance, as citizens, is that, which includes so many, of a mother. The rank in life which dispenses with their fulfilling this duty, necessarily degrades them by making them mere dolls. Or, should they turn to something more important than merely fitting drapery upon a smooth block, their minds are only occupied by some soft platonic attachment; or, the actual management of an intrigue may keep their thoughts in motion; for when they neglect domestic duties, they have it not in their power to take the field and march and countermarch like soldiers, or wrangle in the senate to keep their faculties from rusting.

I know that, as a proof of the inferiority of the sex, Rousseau has exultingly exclaimed, How can they leave the nursery for the camp![7]—And the camp has by some moralists been termed the school of the most heroic virtues; though, I think, it would puzzle a keen casuist to prove the reasonableness of the greater number of wars that have dubbed heroes. I do not mean to consider this question critically; because, having frequently viewed these freaks of ambition as the first natural mode of civilization, when the ground must be torn up, and the woods cleared by fire and sword, I do not choose to call them pests; but surely the present system of war has little connection with virtue of any denomination, being rather the school of *finesse* and effeminacy, than of fortitude.

Yet, if defensive war, the only justifiable war, in the present advanced state of society, where virtue can shew its face and ripen amidst the rigours which purify the air on the mountain's top, were alone to be adopted as just and glorious, the true heroism of antiquity might again animate female bosoms.—But fair and softly, gentle reader, male or female, do not alarm thyself, for though I have compared the character of a modern soldier with that of a civilized woman, I am not going to advise them to turn their distaff into a musket, though I sincerely wish to see the bayonet converted into a pruning-hook.[8] I only recreated an imagination, fatigued by contemplating the vices and follies which all proceed from a feculent stream of wealth that has muddied the pure rills of natural affection, by supposing that society will some time or other be so constituted, that man must necessarily fulfil the duties of a citizen, or be despised, and that while he was employed in any of the departments of civil life, his wife, also an active citizen, should be equally intent to manage her family, educate her children, and assist her neighbours.

But, to render her really virtuous and useful, she must not, if she discharge her civil duties, want,[9] individually, the protection of civil

---

7. *Emilius* IV, v, p. 13: "Can a woman be one day a nurse and the next a soldier?"
8. Isaiah 2:4: "and they shall beat their swords into plowshares, and their spears into pruninghooks."
9. Lack.

laws; she must not be dependent on her husband's bounty for her subsistence during his life, or support after his death—for how can a being be generous who has nothing of its own? or, virtuous, who is not free? The wife, in the present state of things, who is faithful to her husband, and neither suckles nor educates her children, scarcely deserves the name of a wife, and has no right to that of a citizen. But take away natural rights, and duties become null.

Women then must be considered as only the wanton solace of men, when they become so weak in mind and body, that they cannot exert themselves, unless to pursue some frothy pleasure, or to invent some frivolous fashion. What can be a more melancholy sight to a thinking mind, than to look into the numerous carriages that drive helter-skelter about this metropolis in a morning full of pale-faced creatures who are flying from themselves. I have often wished, with Dr. Johnson, to place some of them in a little shop with half a dozen children looking up to their languid countenances for support.[1] I am much mistaken, if some latent vigour would not soon give health and spirit to their eyes, and some lines drawn by the exercise of reason on the blank cheeks, which before were only undulated by dimples, might restore lost dignity to the character, or rather enable it to attain the true dignity of its nature. Virtue is not to be acquired even by speculation, much less by the negative supineness that wealth naturally generates.

Besides, when poverty is more disgraceful than even vice, is not morality cut to the quick? Still to avoid misconstruction, though I consider that women in the common walks of life are called to fulfil the duties of wives and mothers, by religion and reason, I cannot help lamenting that women of a superior cast have not a road open by which they can pursue more extensive plans of usefulness and independence. I may excite laughter, by dropping an hint, which I mean to pursue, some future time, for I really think that women ought to have representatives, instead of being arbitrarily governed without having any direct share allowed them in the deliberations of government.

But, as the whole system of representation is now, in this country, only a convenient handle for despotism, they need not complain, for they are as well represented as a numerous class of hard working mechanics,[2] who pay for the support of royalty when they can scarcely stop their children's mouths with bread. How are they represented whose very sweat supports the splendid stud of an heir apparent, or varnishes the chariot of some female favourite who looks down on shame? Taxes on the very necessaries of life, enable an endless tribe of idle princes and princesses to pass with stupid

1. Wollstonecraft may be referring to the *Rambler* Essay No. 85 (January 8, 1751), "The Mischiefs of Total Idleness."
2. Men having a manual occupation or working at a trade.

pomp before a gaping crowd, who almost worship the very parade which costs them so dear. This is mere gothic grandeur, something like the barbarous useless parade of having sentinels on horseback at Whitehall,[3] which I could never view without a mixture of contempt and indignation.

How strangely must the mind be sophisticated when this sort of state impresses it! But, till these monuments of folly are levelled by virtue, similar follies will leaven the whole mass. For the same character, in some degree, will prevail in the aggregate of society: and the refinements of luxury, or the vicious rcpinings of envious poverty, will equally banish virtue from society, considered as the characteristic of that society, or only allow it to appear as one of the stripes of the harlequin coat, worn by the civilized man.

In the superiour ranks of life, every duty is done by deputies, as if duties could ever be waved, and the vain pleasures which consequent idleness forces the rich to pursue, appear so enticing to the next rank, that the numerous scramblers for wealth sacrifice every thing to tread on their heels. The most sacred trusts are then considered as sinecures, because they were procured by interest, and only sought to enable a man to keep *good company*. Women, in particular, all want to be ladies. Which is simply to have nothing to do, but listlessly to go they scarcely care where, for they cannot tell what.

But what have women to do in society? I may be asked, but to loiter with easy grace; surely you would not condemn them all to suckle fools and chronicle small beer![4] No. Women might certainly study the art of healing, and be physicians as well as nurses. And midwifery, decency seems to allot to them, though I am afraid the word midwife, in our dictionaries, will soon give place to *accoucheur*,[5] and one proof of the former delicacy of the sex be effaced from the language.

They might, also, study politics, and settle their benevolence on the broadest basis; for the reading of history will scarcely be more useful than the perusal of romances, if read as mere biography; if the character of the times, the political improvements, arts, &c. be not observed. In short, if it be not considered as the history of man; and not of particular men, who filled a niche in the temple of fame, and dropped into the black rolling stream of time, that silently sweeps all before it, into the shapeless void called—eternity.—For shape, can it be called, 'that shape hath none?'[6]

---

3. The famous Horse Guards who daily post guard on Whitehall, the hub of the British government.
4. Iago's account of what the ideal woman is good for (*Othello* II.i.162).
5. The name that in the eighteenth century began to be used for a man who assisted women in childbirth (from the French).
6. *Paradise Lost* II.666–67.

Business of various kinds, they might likewise pursue, if they were educated in a more orderly manner, which might save many from common and legal prostitution. Women would not then marry for a support, as men accept of places under government, and neglect the implied duties; nor would an attempt to earn their own subsistence, a most laudable one! sink them almost to the level of those poor abandoned creatures who live by prostitution. For are not milliners and mantua-makers[7] reckoned the next class? The few employments open to women, so far from being liberal, are menial; and when a superiour education enables them to take charge of the education of children as governesses, they are not treated like the tutors of sons, though even clerical tutors are not always treated in a manner calculated to render them respectable in the eyes of their pupils, to say nothing of the private comfort of the individual. But as women educated like gentlewomen, are never designed for the humiliating situation which necessity sometimes forces them to fill; these situations are considered in the light of a degradation; and they know little of the human heart, who need to be told, that nothing so painfully sharpens sensibility as such a fall in life.[8]

Some of these women might be restrained from marrying by a proper spirit or delicacy, and others may not have had it in their power to escape in this pitiful way from servitude; is not that government then very defective, and very unmindful of the happiness of one half of its members, that does not provide for honest, independent women, by encouraging them to fill respectable stations? But in order to render their private virtue a public benefit, they must have a civil existence in the state, married or single; else we shall continually see some worthy woman, whose sensibility has been rendered painfully acute by undeserved contempt, droop like 'the lily broken down by a plow-share.'[9]

It is a melancholy truth; yet such is the blessed effect of civilization! the most respectable women are the most oppressed; and, unless they have understandings far superiour to the common run of understandings, taking in both sexes, they must, from being treated like contemptible beings, become contemptible. How many women thus waste life away the prey of discontent, who might have practised as physicians, regulated a farm, managed a shop, and stood

---

7. Dressmakers.
8. Wollstonecraft had spent one year as governess to the older daughters of the Viscount Kingsborough, County Cork, Ireland.
9. Perhaps quoting Fénelon's *The Adventures of Telemachus:* when the Cretan king Idomeneus kills his son to fulfill a vow rashly made to the god Neptune, the youth dies "As a beautiful Lilly in the midst of the Field, cut up from the Root by the Plowshare, lies down and languishes on the Ground" (trans. [London, 1699–1700], I, p. 52).

erect, supported by their own industry, instead of hanging their heads surcharged with the dew of sensibility, that consumes the beauty to which it at first gave lustre; nay, I doubt whether pity and love are so near akin as poets feign, for I have seldom seen much compassion excited by the helplessness of females, unless they were fair; then, perhaps, pity was the soft handmaid of love, or the harbinger of lust.

How much more respectable is the woman who earns her own bread by fulfilling any duty, than the most accomplished beauty!—beauty did I say?—so sensible am I of the beauty of moral loveliness, or the harmonious propriety that attunes the passions of a well-regulated mind, that I blush at making the comparison; yet I sigh to think how few women aim at attaining this respectability by withdrawing from the giddy whirl of pleasure, or the indolent calm that stupifies the good sort of women it sucks in.

Proud of their weakness, however, they must always be protected, guarded from care, and all the rough toils that dignify the mind.—If this be the fiat of fate, if they will make themselves insignificant and contemptible, sweetly to waste 'life away,' let them not expect to be valued when their beauty fades, for it is the fate of the fairest flowers to be admired and pulled to pieces by the careless hand that plucked them. In how many ways do I wish, from the purest benevolence, to impress this truth on my sex; yet I fear that they will not listen to a truth that dear bought experience has brought home to many an agitated bosom, nor willingly resign the privileges of rank and sex for the privileges of humanity, to which those have no claim who do not discharge its duties.

Those writers are particularly useful, in my opinion, who make man feel for man, independent of the station he fills, or the drapery of factitious sentiments. I then would fain convince reasonable men of the importance of some of my remarks, and prevail on them to weigh dispassionately the whole tenor of my observations.—I appeal to their understandings; and, as a fellow-creature, claim, in the name of my sex, some interest in their hearts. I entreat them to assist to emancipate their companion, to make her a *help meet* for them!

Would men but generously snap our chains, and be content with rational fellowship instead of slavish obedience, they would find us more observant daughters, more affectionate sisters, more faithful wives, more reasonable mothers—in a word, better citizens. We should then love them with true affection, because we should learn to respect ourselves; and the peace of mind of a worthy man would not be interrupted by the idle vanity of his wife, nor the babes sent to nestle in a strange bosom, having never found a home in their mother's.

Chap. X

Parental Affection

Parental affection is, perhaps, the blindest modification of perverse self-love; for we have not, like the French,[9] two terms to distinguish the pursuit of a natural and reasonable desire, from the ignorant calculations of weakness. Parents often love their children in the most brutal manner, and sacrifice every relative duty to promote their advancement in the world.—To promote, such is the perversity of unprincipled prejudices, the future welfare of the very beings whose present existence they imbitter by the most despotic stretch of power. Power, in fact, is ever true to its vital principle, for in every shape it would reign without controul or inquiry. Its throne is built across a dark abyss, which no eye must dare to explore, lest the baseless fabric should totter under investigation. Obedience, unconditional obedience, is the catch-word of tyrants of every description, and to render 'assurance doubly sure,'[1] one kind of despotism supports another. Tyrants would have cause to tremble if reason were to become the rule of duty in any of the relations of life, for the light might spread till perfect day appeared. And when it did appear, how would men smile at the sight of the bugbears at which they started during the night of ignorance, or the twilight of timid inquiry.

Parental affection, indeed, in many minds, is but a pretext to tyrannize where it can be done with impunity, for only good and wise men are content with the respect that will bear discussion. Convinced that they have a right to what they insist on, they do not fear reason, or dread the sifting of subjects that recur to natural justice: because they firmly believe that the more enlightened the human mind becomes the deeper root will just and simple principles take. They do not rest in expedients, or grant that what is metaphysically true can be practically false;[2] but disdaining the shifts of the moment they calmly wait till time, sanctioning innovation, silences the hiss of selfishness or envy.

If the power of reflecting on the past, and darting the keen eye of contemplation into futurity, be the grand privilege of man, it must be

---

9. *L'amour propre. L'amour de soi même* [sic]" [Wollstonecraft's note]. The distinction was set out in La Rochefoucauld's *Maximes* (in the suppressed maxim, No. 563) and in Rousseau's *Discourse on the Origin of Inequality.* "Amour de soi": The instinct for self-preservation. "Amour-propre": Something more egotistical, arising from the competitive comparisons one draws between oneself and others.
1. *Macbeth* IV.i.83.
2. Wollstonecraft here echoes, to ironic effect, the language of Burke's *Reflections on the Revolution in France.* Burke denounced the "rights" asserted by the revolutionaries on the grounds that while they were "metaphysically true," they were nonetheless "morally and politically false" (*The French Revolution,* Vol. V of *The Writings and Speeches of Edmund Burke,* ed L. G. Mitchell [Oxford, 1990], p. 62).

granted that some people enjoy this prerogative in a very limited degree. Every thing new appears to them wrong; and not able to distinguish the possible from the monstrous, they fear where no fear should find a place, running from the light of reason, as if it were a firebrand; yet the limits of the possible have never been defined to stop the sturdy innovator's hand.

Woman, however, a slave in every situation to prejudice, seldom exerts enlightened maternal affection; for she either neglects her children, or spoils them by improper indulgence. Besides, the affection of some women for their children is, as I have before termed it, frequently very brutish: for it eradicates every spark of humanity. Justice, truth, every thing is sacrificed by these Rebekah's,[3] and for the sake of their *own* children they violate the most sacred duties, forgetting the common relationship that binds the whole family on earth together. Yet, reason seems to say, that they who suffer one duty, or affection, to swallow up the rest, have not sufficient heart or mind to fulfil that one conscientiously. It then loses the venerable aspect of a duty, and assumes the fantastic form of a whim.

As the care of children in their infancy is one of the grand duties annexed to the female character by nature, this duty would afford many forcible arguments for strengthening the female understanding, if it were properly considered.

The formation of the mind must be begun very early, and the temper, in particular, requires the most judicious attention—an attention which women cannot pay who only love their children because they are their children, and seek no further for the foundation of their duty, than in the feelings of the moment. It is this want of reason in their affections which makes women so often run into extremes, and either be the most fond or most careless and unnatural mothers.

To be a good mother—a woman must have sense, and that independence of mind which few women possess who are taught to depend entirely on their husbands. Meek wives are, in general, foolish mothers; wanting their children to love them best, and take their part, in secret, against the father, who is held up as a scarecrow. When chastisement is necessary, though they have offended the mother, the father must inflict the punishment; he must be the judge in all disputes: but I shall more fully discuss this subject when I treat of private education,[4] I now only mean to insist, that unless the understanding of woman be enlarged, and her character rendered more firm, by being allowed to govern her own conduct, she will

---

3. In Genesis 27, Rebekah, wife of Isaac and mother of the twins Jacob and Esau, attempts to gain the blind father's blessing for her favorite son, Jacob, thus earning her reputation as an ambitious and designing mother.
4. Education at home.

never have sufficient sense or command of temper to manage children properly) Her parental affection, indeed, scarcely deserves the name, when it does not lead her to suckle her children, because the discharge of this duty is equally calculated to inspire maternal and filial affection: and it is the indispensable duty of men and women to fulfil the duties which give birth to affections that are the surest preservatives against vice. Natural affection, as it is termed, I believe to be a very faint tie, affections must grow out of the habitual exercise of a mutual sympathy; and what sympathy does a mother exercise who sends her babe to a nurse, and only takes it from a nurse to send it to a school?

In the exercise of their maternal feelings providence has furnished women with a natural substitute for love, when the lover becomes only a friend, and mutual confidence takes place of overstrained admiration—a child then gently twists the relaxing cord, and a mutual care produces a new mutual sympathy.—But a child, though a pledge of affection, will not enliven it, if both father and mother be content to transfer the charge to hirelings; for they who do their duty by proxy should not murmur if they miss the reward of duty—parental affection produces filial duty.

Chap. XI

Duty to Parents

There seems to be an indolent propensity in man to make prescription always take place of reason, and to place every duty on an arbitrary foundation. The rights of kings are deduced in a direct line from the King of kings; and that of parents from our first parent.

Why do we thus go back for principles that should always rest on the same base, and have the same weight to-day that they had a thousand years ago—and not a jot more? If parents discharge their duty they have a strong hold and sacred claim on the gratitude of their children; but few parents are willing to receive the respectful affection of their offspring on such terms. They demand blind obedience, because they do not merit a reasonable service: and to render these demands of weakness and ignorance more binding, a mysterious sanctity is spread round the most arbitrary principle; for what other name can be given to the blind duty of obeying vicious or weak beings merely because they obeyed a powerful instinct?

The simple definition of the reciprocal duty, which naturally subsists between parent and child, may be given in a few words: The parent who pays proper attention to helpless infancy has a right to require the same attention when the feebleness of age comes upon him. But to subjugate a rational being to the mere will of another, after he is of age to answer to society for his own conduct, is a most cruel and undue stretch of power; and, perhaps, as injurious to morality as those religious systems which do not allow right and wrong to have any existence, but in the Divine will.

I never knew a parent who had paid more than common attention to his children, disregarded;[5] on the contrary, the early habit of relying almost implicitly on the opinion of a respected parent is not easily shook, even when matured reason convinces the child that his father is not the wisest man in the world. This weakness, for a weakness it is, though the epithet amiable may be tacked to it, a reasonable man must steel himself against; for the absurd duty, too often inculcated, of obeying a parent only on account of his being a parent, shackles the mind, and prepares it for a slavish submission to any power but reason.

I distinguish between the natural and accidental duty due to parents.

The parent who sedulously endeavours to form the heart and enlarge the understanding of his child, has given that dignity to the discharge of a duty, common to the whole animal world, that only reason can give. This is the parental affection of humanity, and leaves instinctive natural affection far behind. Such a parent acquires all the rights of the most sacred friendship, and his advice, even when his child is advanced in life, demands serious consideration.

With respect to marriage, though after one and twenty a parent seems to have no right to withhold his consent on any account; yet twenty years of solicitude call for a return, and the son ought, at least, to promise not to marry for two or three years, should the object of his choice not entirely meet with the approbation of his first friend.

But, respect for parents is, generally speaking, a much more debasing principle; it is only a selfish respect for property. The father who is blindly obeyed, is obeyed from sheer weakness, or from motives that degrade the human character.

A great proportion of the misery that wanders, in hideous forms, around the world, is allowed to rise from the negligence of parents; and still these are the people who are most tenacious of what they term a natural right, though it be subversive of the birth-right of man, the right of acting according to the direction of his own reason.

I have already very frequently had occasion to observe, that vicious or indolent people are always eager to profit by enforcing arbitrary privileges; and, generally, in the same proportion as they

5. "Dr. Johnson makes the same observation" [Wollstonecraft's note]. See Johnson's *Rambler*, Essay No. 148 (August 17, 1751), "On the Tyranny of Parents."

neglect the discharge of the duties which alone render the privileges reasonable. This is at the bottom a dictate of common sense, or the instinct of self-defence, peculiar to ignorant weakness; resembling that instinct, which makes a fish muddy the water it swims in to elude its enemy, instead of boldly facing it in the clear stream.

From the clear stream of argument, indeed, the supporters of prescription, of every denomination, fly; and, taking refuge in the darkness, which, in the language of sublime poetry, has been supposed to surround the throne of Omnipotence, they dare to demand that implicit respect which is only due to His unsearchable ways. But, let me not be thought presumptuous, the darkness which hides our God from us, only respects speculative truths—it never obscures moral ones, they shine clearly, for God is light,[6] and never, by the constitution of our nature, requires the discharge of a duty, the reasonableness of which does not beam on us when we open our eyes.

The indolent parent of high rank may, it is true, extort a shew of respect from his child, and females on the continent[7] are particularly subject to the views of their families, who never think of consulting their inclination, or providing for the comfort of the poor victims of their pride. The consequence is notorious; these dutiful daughters become adulteresses, and neglect the education of their children, from whom they, in their turn, exact the same kind of obedience.

Females, it is true, in all countries, are too much under the dominion of their parents; and few parents think of addressing their children in the following manner, though it is in this reasonable way that Heaven seems to command the whole human race. It is your interest to obey me till you can judge for yourself; and the Almighty Father of all has implanted an affection in me to serve as a guard to you whilst your reason is unfolding; but when your mind arrives at maturity, you must only obey me, or rather respect my opinions, so far as they coincide with the light that is breaking in on your own mind.

A slavish bondage to parents cramps every faculty of the mind; and Mr. Locke very judiciously observes, that 'if the mind be curbed and humbled too much in children; if their spirits be abased and broken much by too strict an hand over them; they lose all their vigour and industry.'[8] This strict hand may in some degree account for the weakness of women; for girls, from various causes, are more kept down by their parents, in every sense of the word, than boys. The duty expected from them is, like all the duties arbitrarily

6. 1 John 1:5.
7. I.e., in Europe.
8. Locke, *Some Thoughts Concerning Education* (1693), article 46.2. For Locke's thinking about the authority of parents, see p. 222 herein.

imposed on women, more from a sense of propriety, more out of respect for decorum, than reason; and thus taught slavishly to submit to their parents, they are prepared for the slavery of marriage. I may be told that a number of women are not slaves in the marriage state. True, but they then become tyrants; for it is not rational freedom, but a lawless kind of power resembling the authority exercised by the favourites of absolute monarchs, which they obtain by debasing means. I do not, likewise, dream of insinuating that either boys or girls are always slaves, I only insist that when they are obliged to submit to authority blindly, their faculties are weakened, and their tempers rendered imperious or abject. I also lament that parents, indolently availing themselves of a supposed privilege, damp the first faint glimmering of reason, rendering at the same time the duty, which they are so anxious to enforce, an empty name; because they will not let it rest on the only basis on which a duty can rest securely: for unless it be founded on knowledge, it cannot gain sufficient strength to resist the squalls of passion, or the silent sapping of self-love. But it is not the parents who have given the surest proof of their affection for their children, or, to speak more properly, who by fulfilling their duty, have allowed a natural parental affection to take root in their hearts, the child of exercised sympathy and reason, and not the over-weening offspring of selfish pride, who most vehemently insist on their children submitting to their will merely because it is their will. On the contrary, the parent, who sets a good example, patiently lets that example work; and it seldom fails to produce its natural effect—filial reverence.

Children cannot be taught too early to submit to reason, the true definition of that necessity, which Rousseau insisted on, without defining it; for to submit to reason is to submit to the nature of things, and to that God, who formed them so, to promote our real interest.

Why should the minds of children be warped as they just begin to expand, only to favour the indolence of parents, who insist on a privilege without being willing to pay the price fixed by nature? I have before had occasion to observe, that a right always includes a duty, and I think it may, likewise, fairly be inferred, that they forfeit the right, who do not fulfil the duty.

It is easier, I grant, to command than reason; but it does not follow from hence that children cannot comprehend the reason why they are made to do certain things habitually: for, from a steady adherence to a few simple principles of conduct flows that salutary power which a judicious parent gradually gains over a child's mind. And this power becomes strong indeed, if tempered by an even display of affection brought home to the child's heart. For, I believe, as a general rule, it must be allowed that the affection which we inspire always resembles that we cultivate; so that natural affections, which have been supposed almost distinct from reason, may be found more nearly connected with judgment than is commonly allowed. Nay, as another proof of the necessity of cultivating the female understanding, it is but just to observe, that the affections seem to have a kind of animal capriciousness when they merely reside in the heart.

It is the irregular exercise of parental authority that first injures the mind, and to these irregularities girls are more subject than boys. The will of those who never allow their will to be disputed, unless they happen to be in a good humour, when they relax proportionally, is almost always unreasonable. To elude this arbitrary authority girls very early learn the lessons which they afterwards practise on their husbands; for I have frequently seen a little sharp-faced miss rule a whole family, excepting that now and then mamma's angry will burst out of some accidental cloud;—either her hair was ill dressed,[9] or she had lost more money at cards, the night before, than she was willing to own to her husband; or some such moral cause of anger.

After observing sallies of this kind, I have been led into a melancholy train of reflection respecting females, concluding that when their first affection must lead them astray, or make their duties clash till they rest on mere whims and customs, little can be expected from them as they advance in life. How indeed can an instructor remedy this evil? for to teach them virtue on any solid principle is to teach them to despise their parents. Children cannot, ought not, to be taught to make allowance for the faults of their parents, because every such allowance weakens the force of reason in their minds, and makes them still more indulgent to their own. It is one of the most sublime virtues of maturity that leads us to be severe with respect to ourselves, and forbearing to others; but children should only be taught the simple virtues, for if they begin too early to make allowance for human passions and manners, they wear off the fine edge of the criterion by which they should regulate their own, and become unjust in the same proportion as they grow indulgent.

The affections of children, and weak people, are always selfish; they love their relatives, because they are beloved by them, and not on account of their virtues. Yet, till esteem and love are blended together in the first affection, and reason made the foundation of the first duty, morality will stumble at the threshold. But, till society is very differently constituted, parents, I fear, will still insist on being obeyed, because they will be obeyed, and constantly endeavour to settle that power on a Divine right which will not bear the investigation of reason.

9. "I myself heard a little girl once say to a servant, 'My mama has been scolding me finely this morning, because her hair was not dressed to please her.' Though this remark was pert, it was just. And what respect could a girl acquire for such a parent without doing violence to reason?" [Wollstonecraft's note].

Chap. XII

On National Education[1]

The good effects resulting from attention to private education will ever be very confined, and the parent who really puts his own hand to the plow, will always, in some degree, be disappointed, till education becomes a grand national concern. A man cannot retire into a desert with his child, and if he did he could not bring himself back to childhood, and become the proper friend and play-fellow of an infant or youth. And when children are confined to the society of men and women, they very soon acquire that kind of premature manhood which stops the growth of every vigorous power of mind or body. In order to open their faculties they should be excited to think for themselves; and this can only be done by mixing a number of children together, and making them jointly pursue the same objects.

A child very soon contracts a benumbing indolence of mind, which he has seldom sufficient vigour afterwards to shake off, when he only asks a question instead of seeking for information, and then relies implicitly on the answer he receives. With his equals in age this could never be the case, and the subjects of inquiry, though they might be influenced, would not be entirely under the direction of men, who frequently damp, if not destroy, abilities, by bringing them forward too hastily: and too hastily they will infallibly be brought forward, if the child could be confined to the society of a man, however sagacious that man may be.

Besides, in youth the seeds of every affection should be sown, and the respectful regard, which is felt for a parent, is very different from the social affections that are to constitute the happiness of life as it advances. Of these equality is the basis, and an intercourse of sentiments unclogged by that observant seriousness which prevents disputation, though it may not inforce submission. Let a child have ever such an affection for his parent, he will always languish to play and prattle with children; and the very respect he feels, for filial esteem always has a dash of fear mixed with it, will, if it do not teach him cunning, at least prevent him from pouring out the little secrets which first open the heart to friendship and confidence, gradually leading to more expansive benevolence. Added to this, he will never acquire that frank ingenuousness of behaviour, which young people can only attain by being frequently in society where they dare to speak what they think; neither afraid of being reproved for their presumption, nor laughed at for their folly.

1. The title of the pamphlet outlining Talleyrand's proposal, to which Wollstonecraft refers in her dedication.

Forcibly impressed by the reflections which the sight of schools, as they are at present conducted, naturally suggested, I have formerly delivered my opinion rather warmly in favour of a private education;[2] but further experience has led me to view the subject in a different light. I still, however, think schools, as they are now regulated, the hot-beds of vice and folly, and the knowledge of human nature, supposed to be attained there, merely cunning selfishness.

At school boys become gluttons and slovens, and, instead of cultivating domestic affections, very early rush into the libertinism which destroys the constitution before it is formed; hardening the heart as it weakens the understanding.

I should, in fact, be averse to boarding-schools, if it were for no other reason than the unsettled state of mind which the expectation of the vacations produce. On these the children's thoughts are fixed with eager anticipating hopes, for, at least, to speak with moderation, half of the time, and when they arrive they are spent in total dissipation and beastly indulgence.

But, on the contrary, when they are brought up at home, though they may pursue a plan of study in a more orderly manner than can be adopted when near a fourth part of the year is actually spent in idleness, and as much more in regret and anticipation; yet they there acquire too high an opinion of their own importance, from being allowed to tyrannize over servants, and from the anxiety expressed by most mothers, on the score of manners, who, eager to teach the accomplishments of a gentleman, stifle, in their birth, the virtues of a man. Thus brought into company when they ought to be seriously employed, and treated like men when they are still boys, they become vain and effeminate.

The only way to avoid two extremes equally injurious to morality, would be to contrive some way of combining a public and private education. Thus to make men citizens two natural steps might be taken, which seem directly to lead to the desired point; for the domestic affections, that first open the heart to the various modifications of humanity, would be cultivated, whilst the children were nevertheless allowed to spend great part of their time, on terms of equality, with other children.

I still recollect, with pleasure, the country day school; where a boy trudged in the morning, wet or dry, carrying his books, and his dinner, if it were at a considerable distance; a servant did not then lead master by the hand, for, when he had once put on coat and breeches, he was allowed to shift for himself, and return alone in the evening to recount the feats of the day close at the parental knee.

2. In 1790, in reviewing Macaulay's *Letters on Education* for the *Analytical Review* (*Works*, VII, p. 311).

His father's house was his home, and was ever after fondly remembered; nay, I appeal to many superiour men, who were educated in this manner, whether the recollection of some shady lane where they conned[3] their lesson; or, of some stile, where they sat making a kite, or mending a bat, has not endeared their country to them?

But, what boy ever recollected with pleasure the years he spent in close confinement, at an academy near London? unless, indeed, he should, by chance, remember the poor scare-crow of an usher,[4] whom he tormented; or, the tartman, from whom he caught a cake, to devour it with a cattish appetite of selfishness. At boarding-schools of every description, the relaxation of the junior boys is mischief; and of the senior, vice. Besides, in great schools,[5] what can be more prejudicial to the moral character than the system of tyranny and abject slavery which is established amongst the boys, to say nothing of the slavery to forms, which makes religion worse than a farce? For what good can be expected from the youth who receives the sacrament of the Lord's supper, to avoid forfeiting half a guinea, which he probably afterwards spends in some sensual manner? Half the employment of the youths is to elude the necessity of attending public worship; and well they may, for such a constant repetition of the same thing must be a very irksome restraint on their natural vivacity. As these ceremonies have the most fatal effect on their morals, and as a ritual performed by the lips, when the heart and mind are far away, is not now stored up by our church as a bank to draw on for the fees of the poor souls in purgatory, why should they not be abolished?

But the fear of innovation, in this country, extends to every thing.—This is only a covert fear, the apprehensive timidity of indolent slugs, who guard, by sliming it over, the snug place, which they consider in the light of an hereditary estate; and eat, drink, and enjoy themselves, instead of fulfilling the duties, excepting a few empty forms, for which it was endowed. These are the people who most strenuously insist on the will of the founder being observed, crying out against all reformation, as if it were a violation of justice. I am now alluding particularly to the relicks of popery retained in our colleges, when the protestant members seem to be such sticklers for the established church; but their zeal never makes them lose sight of the spoil of ignorance, which rapacious priests of superstitious memory have scraped together. No, wise in their generation,[6]

3. Studied or learned; usually used as a past participle, as in "well conned."
4. An assistant to a schoolmaster or headmaster.
5. In 1786 Wollstonecraft had visited Eton College, likely one of the "great schools" to which she here refers; her acquaintance Mr. Prior, a schoolmaster there, helped secure Wollstonecraft her position as governess in the household of Lady Kingsborough.
6. Luke 16:8: "the children of this world are in their generation wiser than the children of light."

they venerate the prescriptive right of possession, as a strong hold, and still let the sluggish bell tinkle to prayers, as during the days when the elevation of the host was supposed to atone for the sins of the people, lest one reformation should lead to another, and the spirit kill the letter. These Romish customs[7] have the most baneful effect on the morals of our clergy; for the idle vermin who two or three times a day perform in the most slovenly manner a service which they think useless, but call their duty, soon lose a sense of duty. At college, forced to attend or evade public worship, they acquire an habitual contempt for the very service, the performance of which is to enable them to live in idleness. It is mumbled over as an affair of business, as a stupid boy repeats his task, and frequently the college cant escapes from the preacher the moment after he has left the pulpit, and even whilst he is eating the dinner which he earned in such a dishonest manner.

Nothing, indeed, can be more irreverent than the cathedral service as it is now performed in this country, neither does it contain a set of weaker men than those who are the slaves of this childish routine. A disgusting skeleton of the former state is still exhibited; but all the solemnity that interested the imagination, if it did not purify the heart, is stripped off. The performance of high mass on the continent must impress every mind, where a spark of fancy glows, with that awful melancholy, that sublime tenderness, so near akin to devotion. I do not say that these devotional feelings are of more use, in a moral sense, than any other emotion of taste; but I contend that the theatrical pomp which gratifies our senses, is to be preferred to the cold parade that insults the understanding without reaching the heart.

Amongst remarks on national education, such observations cannot be misplaced, especially as the supporters of these establishments, degenerated into puerilities, affect to be the champions of religion.—Religion, pure source of comfort in this vale of tears! how has thy clear stream been muddied by the dabblers, who have presumptuously endeavoured to confine in one narrow channel, the living waters that ever flow towards God—the sublime ocean of existence! What would life be without that peace which the love of God, when built on humanity, alone can impart? Every earthly affection turns back, at intervals, to prey upon the heart that feeds it; and the purest effusions of benevolence, often rudely damped by man, must mount as a free-will offering to Him who gave them birth, whose bright image they faintly reflect.

7. Pertaining to the Roman Catholic Church and the "relicks of popery" cited earlier in this paragraph. Although Wollstonecraft never formally left the Anglican fold, she echoes in this chapter many of the Dissenters' criticisms of the established church's commitment to public ceremony rather than individuals' private judgment.

In public schools, however, religion, confounded with irksome ceremonies and unreasonable restraints, assumes the most ungracious aspect: not the sober austere one that commands respect whilst it inspires fear; but a ludicrous cast, that serves to point a pun. For, in fact, most of the good stories and smart things which enliven the spirits that have been concentrated at whist, are manufactured out of the incidents to which the very men labour to give a droll turn who countenance the abuse to live on the spoil.

There is not, perhaps, in the kingdom, a more dogmatical, or luxurious set of men, than the pedantic tyrants who reside in colleges and preside at public schools. The vacations are equally injurious to the morals of the masters and pupils, and the intercourse, which the former keep up with the nobility, introduces the same vanity and extravagance into their families, which banish domestic duties and comforts from the lordly mansion, whose state is awkwardly aped. The boys, who live at a great expence with the masters and assistants, are never domesticated, though placed there for that purpose; for, after a silent dinner, they swallow a hasty glass of wine, and retire to plan some mischievous trick, or to ridicule the person or manners of the very people they have just been cringing to, and whom they ought to consider as the representatives of their parents.

Can it then be a matter of surprise that boys become selfish and vicious who are thus shut out from social converse? or that a mitre often graces the brow of one of these diligent pastors?[8]

The desire of living in the same style, as the rank just above them, infects each individual and every class of people, and meanness is the concomitant of this ignoble ambition; but those professions are most debasing whose ladder is patronage; yet, out of one of these professions the tutors of youth are, in general, chosen. But, can they be expected to inspire independent sentiments, whose conduct must be regulated by the cautious prudence that is ever on the watch for preferment?

So far, however, from thinking of the morals of boys, I have heard several masters of schools argue, that they only undertook to teach Latin and Greek; and that they had fulfilled their duty, by sending some good scholars to college.

A few good scholars, I grant, may have been formed by emulation and discipline; but, to bring forward these clever boys, the health and morals of a number have been sacrificed. The sons of our gentry and wealthy commoners are mostly educated at these

---

8. Wollstonecraft asserts that the pastors who curry favor with the local nobility are often promoted in the church. "Mitre": a bishop's hat.

seminaries, and will any one pretend to assert that the majority, making every allowance, come under the description of tolerable scholars?

It is not for the benefit of society that a few brilliant men should be brought forward at the expence of the multitude. It is true, that great men seem to start up, as great revolutions occur, at proper intervals, to restore order, and to blow aside the clouds that thicken over the face of truth; but let more reason and virtue prevail in society, and these strong winds would not be necessary. Public education, of every denomination, should be directed to form citizens; but if you wish to make good citizens, you must first exercise the affections of a son and a brother. This is the only way to expand the heart; for public affections, as well as public virtues, must ever grow out of the private character, or they are merely meteors that shoot athwart a dark sky, and disappear as they are gazed at and admired.

Few, I believe, have had much affection for mankind, who did not first love their parents, their brothers, sisters, and even the domestic brutes, whom they first played with. The exercise of youthful sympathies forms the moral temperature; and it is the recollection of these first affections and pursuits that gives life to those that are afterwards more under the direction of reason. In youth, the fondest friendships are formed, the genial juices mounting at the same time, kindly mix; or, rather the heart, tempered for the reception of friendship, is accustomed to seek for pleasure in something more noble than the churlish gratification of appetite.

In order then to inspire a love of home and domestic pleasures, children ought to be educated at home, for riotous holidays only make them fond of home for their own sakes. Yet, the vacations, which do not foster domestic affections, continually disturb the course of study, and render any plan of improvement abortive which includes temperance; still, were they abolished, children would be entirely separated from their parents, and I question whether they would become better citizens by sacrificing the preparatory affections, by destroying the force of relationships that render the marriage state as necessary as respectable. But, if a private education produce self-importance, or insulate a man in his family, the evil is only shifted, not remedied.

This train of reasoning brings me back to a subject, on which I mean to dwell, the necessity of establishing proper day-schools.

But, these should be national establishments, for whilst schoolmasters are dependent on the caprice of parents, little exertion can be expected from them, more than is necessary to please ignorant people. Indeed, the necessity of a master's giving the parents some sample of the boys abilities, which during the vacation is shewn to

A VINDICATION OF THE RIGHTS OF WOMAN

every visitor,[9] is productive of more mischief than would at first be supposed. For it is seldom done entirely, to speak with moderation, by the child itself; thus the master countenances falsehood, or winds the poor machine up to some extraordinary exertion, that injures the wheels, and stops the progress of gradual improvement. The memory is loaded with unintelligible words, to make a shew of, without the understanding's acquiring any distinct ideas; but only that education deserves emphatically to be termed cultivation of mind, which teaches young people how to begin to think. The imagination should not be allowed to debauch the understanding before it gained strength, or vanity will become the foreunner of vice: for every way of exhibiting the acquirements of a child is injurious to its moral character.

How much time is lost in teaching them to recite what they do not understand? whilst, seated on benches, all in their best array, the mammas listen with astonishment to the parrot-like prattle, uttered in solemn cadences, with all the pomp of ignorance and folly. Such exhibitions only serve to strike the spreading fibres of vanity through the whole mind; for they neither teach children to speak fluently, nor behave gracefully. So far from it, that these frivolous pursuits might comprehensively be termed the study of affectation; for we now rarely see a simple, bashful boy, though few people of taste were ever disgusted by that awkward sheepishness so natural to the age, which schools and an early introduction into society, have changed into impudence and apish grimace.

Yet, how can these things be remedied whilst school-masters depend entirely on parents for a subsistence; and, when so many rival schools hang out their lures, to catch the attention of vain fathers and mothers, whose parental affection only leads them to wish that their children should outshine those of their neighbours?

Without great good luck, a sensible, conscientious man, would starve before he could raise a school, if he disdained to bubble weak parents by practising the secret tricks of the craft.

In the best regulated schools, however, where swarms are not crammed together, many bad habits must be acquired; but, at common schools, the body, heart, and understanding, are equally stunted, for parents are often only in quest of the cheapest school, and the master could not live, if he did not take a much greater number than he could manage himself; nor will the scanty pittance, allowed for each child, permit him to hire ushers sufficient to assist in the discharge of the mechanical part of the business. Besides, whatever appearance the house and garden may make, the children do not

9. "I now particularly allude to the numerous academies in and about London, and to the behaviour of the trading part of this great city" [Wollstonecraft's note].

enjoy the comfort of either, for they are continually reminded by irksome restrictions that they are not at home, and the state-rooms, garden, &c. must be kept in order for the recreation of the parents; who, of a Sunday, visit the school, and are impressed by the very parade that renders the situation of their children uncomfortable.

With what disgust have I heard sensible women, for girls are more restrained and cowed than boys, speak of the wearisome confinement, which they endured at school. Not allowed, perhaps, to step out of one broad walk in a superb garden, and obliged to pace with steady deportment stupidly backwards and forwards, holding up their heads and turning out their toes, with shoulders braced back, instead of bounding, as nature directs to complete her own design, in the various attitudes so conducive to health.[1] The pure animal spirits, which make both mind and body shoot out, and unfold the tender blossoms of hope, are turned sour, and vented in vain wishes or pert repinings, that contract the faculties and spoil the temper; else they mount to the brain, and sharpening the understanding before it gains proportionable strength, produce that pitiful cunning which disgracefully characterizes the female mind—and I fear will ever characterize it whilst women remain the slaves of power!

The little respect paid to chastity in the male world is, I am persuaded, the grand source of many of the physical and moral evils that torment mankind, as well as of the vices and follies that degrade and destroy women; yet at school, boys infallibly lose that decent bashfulness, which might have ripened into modesty, at home.

And what nasty indecent tricks do they not also learn from each other, when a number of them pig together in the same bedchamber, not to speak of the vices, which render the body weak, whilst they effectually prevent the acquisition of any delicacy of mind.[2] The little attention paid to the cultivation of modesty, amongst men, produces great depravity in all the relationships of society; for, not

1. "I remember a circumstance that once came under my own observation, and raised my indignation. I went to visit a little boy at a school where young children were prepared for a larger one. The master took me into the school-room, &c. but whilst I walked down a broad gravel walk, I could not help observing that the grass grew very luxuriantly on each side of me. I immediately asked the child some questions, and found that the poor boys were not allowed to stir off the walk, and that the master sometimes permitted sheep to be turned in to crop the untrodden grass. The tyrant of this domain used to sit by a window that overlooked the prison yard, and one nook turning from it, where the unfortunate babes could sport freely, he enclosed, and planted it with potatoes. The wife likewise was equally anxious to keep the children in order, lest they should dirty or tear their clothes" [Wollstonecraft's note].
2. Probably a reference to masturbation, subject of numerous alarmist treatises in the eighteenth century. Rousseau, for instance, cautions the prospective educator that should a young man "once acquire the knowledge of this destructive supplement, he would be utterly undone. His body and mind would from that time become enervated, carrying to the grave the deplorable effects of a most pernicious habit" (*Emilius* IV, iii, p. 211).

only love—love that ought to purify the heart, and first call forth all the youthful powers, to prepare the man to discharge the benevolent duties of life, is sacrificed to premature lust; but, all the social affections are deadened by the selfish gratifications, which very early pollute the mind, and dry up the generous juices of the heart. In what an unnatural manner is innocence often violated; and what serious consequences ensue to render private vices a public pest. Besides, an habit of personal order, which has more effect on the moral character, than is, in general, supposed, can only be acquired at home, where that respectable reserve is kept up which checks the familiarity, that sinking into beastliness, undermines the affection it insults.

I have already animadverted on the bad habits which females acquire when they are shut up together; and, I think, that the observation may fairly be extended to the other sex, till the natural inference is drawn which I have had in view throughout—that to improve both sexes they ought, not only in private families, but in public schools, to be educated together. If marriage be the cement of society, mankind should all be educated after the same model, or the intercourse of the sexes will never deserve the name of fellowship, nor will women ever fulfil the peculiar duties of their sex, till they become enlightened citizens, till they become free by being enabled to earn their own subsistence, independent of men; in the same manner, I mean, to prevent misconstruction, as one man is independent of another. Nay, marriage will never be held sacred till women, by being brought up with men, are prepared to be their companions rather than their mistresses; for the mean doublings of cunning will ever render them contemptible, whilst oppression renders them timid. So convinced am I of this truth, that I will venture to predict that virtue will never prevail in society till the virtues of both sexes are founded on reason; and, till the affections common to both are allowed to gain their due strength by the discharge of mutual duties.

Were boys and girls permitted to pursue the same studies together, those graceful decencies might early be inculcated which produce modesty without those sexual distinctions that taint the mind. Lessons of politeness, and that formulary of decorum, which treads on the heels of falsehood, would be rendered useless by habitual propriety of behaviour. Not, indeed, put on for visitors like the courtly robe of politeness, but the sober effect of cleanliness of mind. Would not this simple elegance of sincerity be a chaste homage paid to domestic affections, far surpassing the meretricious compliments that shine with false lustre in the heartless intercourse of fashionable life? But, till more understanding preponderates in society, there will ever be a want of heart and taste, and the harlot's *rouge* will supply the place of that celestial suffusion which only virtuous affections can give to the face. Gallantry, and what is called love, may subsist without simplicity of character; but the main pillars of friendship, are respect and confidence—esteem is never founded on it cannot tell what!

A taste for the fine arts requires great cultivation; but not more than a taste for the virtuous affections; and both suppose that enlargement of mind which opens so many sources of mental pleasure. Why do people hurry to noisy scenes, and crowded circles? I should answer, because they want activity of mind, because they have not cherished the virtues of the heart. They only, therefore, see and feel in the gross, and continually pine after variety, finding every thing that is simple insipid.

This argument may be carried further than philosophers are aware of, for if nature destined woman, in particular, for the discharge of domestic duties, she made her susceptible of the attached affections in a great degree. Now women are notoriously fond of pleasure; and, naturally must be so according to my definition, because they cannot enter into the minutiae of domestic taste; lacking judgment, the foundation of all taste. For the understanding, in spite of sensual cavillers, reserves to itself the privilege of conveying pure joy to the heart.

With what a languid yawn have I seen an admirable poem thrown down, that a man of true taste returns to, again and again with rapture; and, whilst melody has almost suspended respiration, a lady has asked me where I bought my gown. I have seen also an eye glanced coldly over a most exquisite picture, rest, sparkling with pleasure, on a caricature rudely sketched; and whilst some terrific feature in nature has spread a sublime stillness through my soul, I have been desired to observe the pretty tricks of a lap-dog, that my perverse fate forced me to travel with. Is it surprising that such a tasteless being should rather caress this dog than her children? Or, that she should prefer the rant of flattery to the simple accents of sincerity?

To illustrate this remark I must be allowed to observe, that men of the first genius, and most cultivated minds, have appeared to have the highest relish for the simple beauties of nature; and they must have forcibly felt, what they have so well described, the charm which natural affections, and unsophisticated feelings spread round the human character. It is this power of looking into the heart, and responsively vibrating with each emotion, that enables the poet to personify each passion, and the painter to sketch with a pencil of fire.

True taste is ever the work of the understanding employed in observing natural effects; and till women have more understanding, it is vain to expect them to possess domestic taste. Their lively senses will ever be at work to harden their hearts, and the emotions struck out of them will continue to be vivid and transitory, unless a proper education store their mind with knowledge.

It is the want of domestic taste, and not the acquirement of knowledge, that takes women out of their families, and tears the smiling babe from the breast that ought to afford it nourishment. Women have been allowed to remain in ignorance, and slavish dependence, many, very many years, and still we hear of nothing but their fondness of pleasure and sway, their preference of rakes and soldiers, their childish attachment to toys, and the vanity that makes them value accomplishments more than virtues.

History brings forward a fearful catalogue of the crimes which their cunning has produced, when the weak slaves have had sufficient address to over-reach their masters. In France, and in how many other countries, have men been the luxurious[3] despots, and women the crafty ministers?—Does this prove that ignorance and dependence domesticate them? Is not their folly the by-word of the libertines, who relax in their society; and do not men of sense continually lament that an immoderate fondness for dress and dissipation carries the mother of a family for ever from home? Their hearts have not been debauched by knowledge, or their minds led astray by scientific pursuits; yet, they do not fulfil the peculiar duties which as women they are called upon by nature to fulfil. On the contrary, the state of warfare which subsists between the sexes, makes them employ those wiles, that often frustrate the more open designs of force.

When, therefore, I call women slaves, I mean in a political and civil sense; for, indirectly they obtain too much power, and are debased by their exertions to obtain illicit sway.

Let an enlightened nation[4] then try what effect reason would have to bring them back to nature, and their duty; and allowing them to share the advantages of education and government with man, see whether they will become better, as they grow wiser and become free. They cannot be injured by the experiment; for it is not in the power of man to render them more insignificant than they are at present.

To render this practicable, day schools, for particular ages, should be established by government, in which boys and girls might be educated together. The school for the younger children, from five to nine years of age, ought to be absolutely free and open to all classes.[5] A sufficient number of masters should also be chosen by a select

---

3. One definition in Johnson's *Dictionary* is "voluptuous, enslaved to pleasure."
4. "France" [Wollstonecraft's note].
5. "Treating this part of the subject, I have borrowed some hints from a very sensible pamphlet, written by the late bishop of Autun on Public Education" [Wollstonecraft's note]. The reference is to Talleyrand's *Rapport sur L'Instruction Publique* (Paris, 1791).

committee, in each parish, to whom any complaint of negligence, &c. might be made, if signed by six of the children's parents.

Ushers would then be unnecessary; for I believe experience will ever prove that this kind of subordinate authority is particularly injurious to the morals of youth. What, indeed, can tend to deprave the character more than outward submission and inward contempt? Yet how can boys be expected to treat an usher with respect, when the master seems to consider him in the light of a servant, and almost to countenance the ridicule which becomes the chief amusement of the boys during the play hours?

But nothing of this kind could occur in an elementary day-school, where boys and girls, the rich and poor, should meet together. And to prevent any of the distinctions of vanity, they should be dressed alike, and all obliged to submit to the same discipline, or leave the school. The school-room ought to be surrounded by a large piece of ground, in which the children might be usefully exercised, for at this age they should not be confined to any sedentary employment for more than an hour at a time. But these relaxations might all be rendered a part of elementary education, for many things improve and amuse the senses, when introduced as a kind of show, to the principles of which, dryly laid down, children would turn a deaf ear. For instance, botany, mechanics, and astronomy. Reading, writing, arithmetic, natural history, and some simple experiments in natural philosophy, might fill up the day; but these pursuits should never encroach on gymnastic plays in the open air. The elements of religion, history, the history of man, and politics, might also be taught by conversations, in the socratic form.

After the age of nine, girls and boys, intended for domestic employments, or mechanical trades, ought to be removed to other schools, and receive instruction, in some measure appropriated to the destination of each individual, the two sexes being still together in the morning; but in the afternoon, the girls should attend a school, where plain-work, mantua-making, millinery, &c. would be their employment.

The young people of superior abilities, or fortune, might now be taught, in another school, the dead and living languages, the elements of science, and continue the study of history and politics, on a more extensive scale, which would not exclude polite literature.

Girls and boys still together? I hear some readers ask: yes. And I should not fear any other consequence than that some early attachment might take place; which, whilst it had the best effect on the moral character of the young people, might not perfectly agree with the views of the parents, for it will be a long time, I fear, before the world will be so far enlightened that parents, only anxious to render their children virtuous, shall allow them to choose companions for life themselves.

Besides, this would be a sure way to promote early marriages, and from early marriages the most salutary physical and moral effects naturally flow. What a different character does a married citizen assume from the selfish coxcomb, who lives, but for himself, and who is often afraid to marry lest he should not be able to live in a certain style. Great emergencies excepted, which would rarely occur in a society of which equality was the basis, a man can only be prepared to discharge the duties of public life, by the habitual practice of those inferiour ones which form the man.

In this plan of education the constitution of boys would not be ruined by the early debaucheries, which now make men so selfish, or girls rendered weak and vain, by indolence, and frivolous pursuits. But, I presuppose, that such a degree of equality should be established between the sexes as would shut out gallantry and coquetry, yet allow friendship and love to temper the heart for the discharge of higher duties.

These would be schools of morality—and the happiness of man, allowed to flow from the pure springs of duty and affection, what advances might not the human mind make? Society can only be happy and free in proportion as it is virtuous; but the present distinctions, established in society, corrode all private, and blast all public virtue.

I have already inveighed against the custom of confining girls to their needle, and shutting them out from all political and civil employments; for by thus narrowing their minds they are rendered unfit to fulfil the peculiar duties which nature has assigned them.

Only employed about the little incidents of the day, they necessarily grow up cunning. My very soul has often sickened at observing the sly tricks practised by women to gain some foolish thing on which their silly hearts were set. Not allowed to dispose of money, or call any thing their own, they learn to turn the market penny;[6] or, should a husband offend, by staying from home, or give rise to some emotions of jealousy—a new gown, or any pretty bawble, smooths Juno's[7] angry brow.

But these *littlenesses* would not degrade their character, if women were led to respect themselves, if political and moral subjects were opened to them; and, I will venture to affirm, that this is the only way to make them properly attentive to their domestic duties.— An active mind embraces the whole circle of its duties, and finds time enough for all. It is not, I assert, a bold attempt to emulate

6. To keep the change left over when they have bought something on another's behalf.
7. I.e., wife of Jupiter (or Zeus) and the prototypical demanding, nagging wife in mythology.

masculine virtues; it is not the enchantment of literary pursuits, or the steady investigation of scientific subjects, that leads women astray from duty. No, it is indolence and vanity—the love of pleasure and the love of sway,[8] that will reign paramount in an empty mind. I say empty emphatically, because the education which women now receive scarcely deserves the name. For the little knowledge that they are led to acquire, during the important years of youth, is merely relative to accomplishments; and accomplishments without a bottom, for unless the understanding be cultivated, superficial and monotonous is every grace. Like the charms of a made up face, they only strike the senses in a crowd; but at home, wanting mind, they want variety. The consequence is obvious; in gay scenes of dissipation we meet the artificial mind and face, for those who fly from solitude dread, next to solitude, the domestic circle; not having it in their power to amuse or interest, they feel their own insignificance, or find nothing to amuse or interest themselves.

Besides, what can be more indelicate than a girl's *coming out*[9] in the fashionable world? Which, in other words, is to bring to market a marriageable miss, whose person is taken from one public place to another, richly caparisoned. Yet, mixing in the giddy circle under restraint, these butterflies long to flutter at large, for the first affection of their souls is their own persons, to which their attention has been called with the most sedulous care whilst they were preparing for the period that decides their fate for life. Instead of pursuing this idle routine, sighing for tasteless shew, and heartless state, with what dignity would the youths of both sexes form attachments in the schools that I have cursorily pointed out; in which, as life advanced, dancing, music, and drawing, might be admitted as relaxations, for at these schools young people of fortune ought to remain, more or less, till they were of age. Those, who were designed for particular professions, might attend, three or four mornings in the week, the schools appropriated for their immediate instruction.

I only drop these observations at present, as hints; rather, indeed, as an outline of the plan I mean, than a digested one; but I must add, that I highly approve of one regulation mentioned in the pamphlet[1] already alluded to, that of making the children and youths independent of the masters respecting punishments. They should be tried by their peers, which would be an admirable method of fixing sound principles of justice in the mind, and might have the happiest effect on the temper, which is very early soured or irritated by tyranny, till it becomes peevishly cunning, or ferociously overbearing.

8. Another echo of Pope's "Of the Characters of Women," line 210.
9. A young lady's social debut.
1. "The Bishop of Autun's" [Wollstonecraft's note]. I.e., Talleyrand's *Rapport sur L' Instruction Publique*.

My imagination darts forward with benevolent fervour to greet these amiable and respectable groups, in spite of the sneering of cold hearts, who are at liberty to utter, with frigid self-importance, the damning epithet—romantic; the force of which I shall endeavour to blunt by repeating the words of an eloquent moralist.— 'I know not whether the allusions of a truly humane heart, whose zeal renders every thing easy, be not preferable to that rough and repulsing reason, which always finds in indifference for the public good, the first obstacle to whatever would promote it.'

I know that libertines will also exclaim, that woman would be unsexed by acquiring strength of body and mind, and that beauty, soft bewitching beauty! would no longer adorn the daughters of men. I am of a very different opinion, for I think that, on the contrary, we should then see dignified beauty, and true grace; to produce which, many powerful physical and moral causes would concur.— Not relaxed beauty, it is true, or the graces of helplessness; but such as appears to make us respect the human body as a majestic pile fit to receive a noble inhabitant, in the relics of antiquity.

I do not forget the popular opinion that the Grecian statues were not modelled after nature. I mean, not according to the proportions of a particular man; but that beautiful limbs and features were selected from various bodies to form an harmonious whole. This might, in some degree, be true. The fine ideal picture of an exalted imagination might be superiour to the materials which the statuary found in nature, and thus it might with propriety be termed rather the model of mankind than of a man. It was not, however, the mechanical selection of limbs and features; but the ebullition of an heated fancy that burst forth, and the fine senses and enlarged understanding of the artist selected the solid matter, which he drew into this glowing focus.

I observed that it was not mechanical, because a whole was produced—a model of that grand simplicity, of those concurring energies, which arrest our attention and command our reverence. For only insipid lifeless beauty is produced by a servile copy of even beautiful nature. Yet, independent of these observations, I believe that the human form must have been far more beautiful than it is at present, because extreme indolence, barbarous ligatures, and many causes, which forcibly act on it, in our luxurious state of society, did not retard its expansion, or render it deformed. Exercise and cleanliness appear to be not only the surest means of preserving health, but of promoting beauty, the physical causes only considered; yet, this is not sufficient, moral ones must concur, or beauty will be merely of that rustic kind which blooms on the innocent, wholesome, countenances of some country people, whose minds have not been exercised. To render the person perfect, physical and moral beauty ought to be attained at the same time; each lending and receiving force by the combination. Judgment must reside on the brow, affection and fancy beam in the eye, and humanity curve the cheek, or vain is the sparkling of the finest eye or the elegantly turned finish of the fairest features: whilst in every motion that displays the active limbs and well-knit joints, grace and modesty should appear. But this fair assemblage is not to be brought together by chance; it is the reward of exertions calculated to support each other; for judgment can only be acquired by reflection, affection by the discharge of duties, and humanity by the exercise of compassion to every living creature.

Humanity to animals should be particularly inculcated as a part of national education, for it is not at present one of our national virtues. Tenderness for their humble dumb domestics, amongst the lower class, is oftener to be found in a savage than a civilized state. For civilization prevents that intercourse which creates affection in the rude hut, or mud hovel, and leads uncultivated minds who are only depraved by the refinements which prevail in the society, where they are trodden under foot by the rich, to domineer over them to revenge the insults that they are obliged to bear from their superiours.

This habitual cruelty is first caught at school, where it is one of the rare sports of the boys to torment the miserable brutes that fall in their way. The transition, as they grow up, from barbarity to brutes to domestic tyranny over wives, children, and servants, is very easy. Justice, or even benevolence, will not be a powerful spring of action unless it extend to the whole creation; nay, I believe that it may be delivered as an axiom, that those who can see pain, unmoved, will soon learn to inflict it.

The vulgar are swayed by present feelings, and the habits which they have accidentally acquired; but on partial feelings much dependence cannot be placed, though they be just; for, when they are not invigorated by reflection, custom weakens them, till they are scarcely perceptible. The sympathies of our nature are strengthened by pondering cogitations, and deadened by thoughtless use. Macbeth's heart smote him more for one murder, the first, than for a hundred subsequent ones, which were necessary to back it. But, when I used the epithet vulgar, I did not mean to confine my remark to the poor, for partial humanity, founded on present sensations, or whim, is quite as conspicuous, if not more so, amongst the rich.

The lady who sheds tears for the bird starved in a snare, and execrates the devils in the shape of men, who goad to madness the poor ox, or whip the patient ass, tottering under a burden above its strength, will, nevertheless, keep her coachman and horses whole hours waiting for her, when the sharp frost bites, or the rain beats against the well-closed windows which do not admit a breath of air to tell her how roughly the wind blows without. And she who takes her dogs to bed, and nurses them with a parade of sensibility, when sick, will suffer her babes to grow up crooked in a nursery. This illustration of my argument is drawn from a matter of fact. The woman whom I allude to was handsome, reckoned very handsome, by those who do not miss the mind when the face is plump and fair; but her understanding had not been led from female duties by literature,[2] nor her innocence debauched by knowledge. No, she was quite feminine, according to the masculine acceptation of the word; and, so far from loving these spoiled brutes that filled the place which her children ought to have occupied, she only lisped out a pretty mixture of French and English nonsense, to please the men who flocked round her. The wife, mother, and human creature, were all swallowed up by the factitious character which an improper education and the selfish vanity of beauty had produced.

I do not like to make a distinction without a difference, and I own that I have been as much disgusted by the fine lady who took her lap-dog to her bosom instead of her child; as by the ferocity of a man, who, beating his horse, declared, that he knew as well when he did wrong, as a Christian.

This brood of folly shews how mistaken they are who, if they allow women to leave their harams, do not cultivate their understandings, in order to plant virtues in their hearts. For had they sense, they might acquire that domestic taste which would lead them to love with reasonable subordination their whole family, from their husband to the house-dog; nor would they ever insult humanity in the person of the most menial servant by paying more attention to the comfort of a brute, than to that of a fellow-creature.

My observations on national education are obviously hints; but I principally wish to enforce the necessity of educating the sexes together to perfect both, and of making children sleep at home that they may learn to love home; yet to make private support, instead of smothering, public affections, they should be sent to school to mix with a number of equals, for only by the jostlings of equality can we form a just opinion of ourselves.

To render mankind more virtuous, and happier of course, both sexes must act from the same principle; but how can that be expected when only one is allowed to see the reasonableness of it? To render also the social compact truly equitable, and in order to spread those enlightening principles, which alone can meliorate the fate of man, women must be allowed to found their virtue on knowledge, which is scarcely possible unless they be educated by the same

2. Learning.

pursuits as men. For they are now made so inferiour by ignorance and low desires, as not to deserve to be ranked with them; or, by the serpentine wrigglings of cunning they mount the tree of knowledge, and only acquire sufficient to lead men astray.

It is plain from the history of all nations, that women cannot be confined to merely domestic pursuits, for they will not fulfil family duties, unless their minds take a wider range, and whilst they are kept in ignorance they become in the same proportion the slaves of pleasure as they are the slaves of man. Nor can they be shut out if great enterprises, though the narrowness of their minds often make them mar, what they are unable to comprehend.

The libertinism, and even the virtues of superiour men, will always give women, of some description, great power over them; and these weak women, under the influence of childish passions and selfish vanity, will throw a false light over the objects which the very men view with their eyes, who ought to enlighten their judgment. Men of fancy, and those sanguine characters who mostly hold the helm of human affairs, in general, relax in the society of women; and surely I need not cite to the most superficial reader of history the numerous examples of vice and oppression which the private intrigues of female favourites have produced; not to dwell on the mischief that naturally arises from the blundering interposition of well-meaning folly. For in the transactions of business it is much better to have to deal with a knave than a fool, because a knave adheres to some plan; and any plan of reason may be seen through much sooner than a sudden flight of folly. The power which vile and foolish women have had over wise men, who possessed sensibility, is notorious; I shall only mention one instance.

Who ever drew a more exalted female character than Rousseau?[3] though in the lump he constantly endeavoured to degrade the sex. And why was he thus anxious? Truly to justify to himself the affection which weakness and virtue had made him cherish for that fool Theresa. He could not raise her to the common level of her sex; and therefore he laboured to bring woman down to her's. He found her a convenient humble companion, and pride made him determine to find some superiour virtues in the being whom he chose to live with; but did not her conduct during his life, and after his death, clearly shew how grossly he was mistaken who called her a celestial innocent.[4] Nay, in the bitterness of his heart, he himself laments, that

3. A reference to the heroine of Rousseau's novel, *Julie, ou La Nouvelle Héloïse*.
4. Describing in his autobiography his relation with the uneducated Thérèse Le Vasseur, first his mistress, then his wife, Rousseau declared that "My Thérèse's heart was that of an angel. . . . That excellent girl's simplicity of mind equaled her kindness of heart" (*The Confessions*, trans. Christopher Kelly, Vol. 5 of *Collected Writings of Rousseau* [Hanover, N.H., 1995], pp. 297–98).

when his bodily infirmities made him no longer treat her like a woman, she ceased to have an affection for him. And it was very natural that she should, for having so few sentiments in common, when the sexual tie was broken, what was to hold her? To hold her affection whose sensibility was confined to one sex, nay, to one man, it requires sense to turn sensibility into the broad channel of humanity; many women have not mind enough to have an affection for a woman, or a friendship for a man. But the sexual weakness that makes woman depend on man for a subsistence, produces a kind of cattish affection which leads a wife to purr about her husband as she would about any man who fed and caressed her.

Men are, however, often gratified by this kind of fondness, which is confined in a beastly manner to themselves; but should they ever become more virtuous, they will wish to converse at their fire-side with a friend, after they cease to play with a mistress.

Besides, understanding is necessary to give variety and interest to sensual enjoyments, for low, indeed, in the intellectual scale, is the mind that can continue to love when neither virtue nor sense give a human appearance to an animal appetite. But sense will always preponderate; and if women be not, in general, brought more on a level with men, some superiour woman, like the Greek courtezans,[5] will assemble the men of abilities around them, and draw from their families many citizens, who would have stayed at home had their wives had more sense, or the graces which result from the exercise of the understanding and fancy, the legitimate parents of taste. A woman of talents, if she be not absolutely ugly, will always obtain great power, raised by the weakness of her sex; and in proportion as men acquire virtue and delicacy, by the exertion of reason, they will look for both in women, but they can only acquire them in the same way that men do.

In France or Italy, have the women confined themselves to domestic life? though they have not hitherto had a political existence, yet, have they not illicitly had great sway? corrupting themselves and the men with whose passions they played. In short, in whatever light I view the subject, reason and experience convince me that the only method of leading women to fulfil their peculiar duties, is to free them from all restraint by allowing them to participate in the inherent rights of mankind.

Make them free, and they will quickly become wise and virtuous, as men become more so; for the improvement must be mutual, or the injustice which one half of the human race are obliged to submit

5. Often in ancient Greece the courtesans known as the *heterae* were more educated and emancipated than the wives of their male patrons.

to, retorting on their oppressors, the virtue of men will be worm-eaten by the insect whom he keeps under his feet.

Let men take their choice, man and woman were made for each other, though not to become one being; and if they will not improve women, they will deprave them!

I speak of the improvement and emancipation of the whole sex, for I know that the behaviour of a few women, who, by accident, or following a strong bent of nature, have acquired a portion of knowledge superiour to that of the rest of their sex, has often been overbearing; but there have been instances of women who, attaining knowledge, have not discarded modesty, nor have they always pedantically appeared to despise the ignorance which they laboured to disperse in their own minds. The exclamations then which any advice respecting female learning, commonly produces, especially from pretty women, often arise from envy. When they chance to see that even the lustre of their eyes, and the flippant sportiveness of refined coquetry will not always secure them attention, during a whole evening, should a woman of a more cultivated understanding endeavour to give a rational turn to the conversation, the common source of consolation is, that such women seldom get husbands. What arts have I not seen silly women use to interrupt by *flirtation*,[6] a very significant word to describe such a manoeuvre, a rational conversation which made the men forget that they were pretty women.

But, allowing what is very natural to man, that the possession of rare abilities is really calculated to excite over-weening pride, disgusting in both men and women—in what a state of inferiority must the female faculties have rusted when such a small portion of knowledge as those women attained, who have sneeringly been termed learned women, could be singular?—Sufficiently so to puff up the possessor, and excite envy in her contemporaries, and some of the other sex. Nay, has not a little rationality exposed many women to the severest censure? I advert to well known facts, for I have frequently heard women ridiculed, and every little weakness exposed, only because they adopted the advice of some medical men, and deviated from the beaten track in their mode of treating their infants. I have actually heard this barbarous aversion to innovation carried still further, and a sensible woman stigmatized as an unnatural mother, who has thus been wisely solicitous to preserve the health of her children, when in the midst of her care she has lost one by some of the casualties of infancy, which no prudence can ward off. Her acquaintance have observed, that this was the

6. Still a relatively new word in 1792; in his *Dictionary*, Johnson had identified it as women's slang.

consequence of new-fangled notions—the new-fangled notions of ease and cleanliness. And those who pretending to experience, though they have long adhered to prejudices that have, according to the opinion of the most sagacious physicians, thinned the human race, almost rejoiced at the disaster that gave a kind of sanction to prescription.

Indeed, if it were only on this account, the national education of women is of the utmost consequence, for what a number of human sacrifices are made to that moloch[7] prejudice! And in how many ways are children destroyed by the lasciviousness of man? The want of natural affection, in many women, who are drawn from their duty by the admiration of men, and the ignorance of others, render the infancy of man a much more perilous state than that of brutes; yet men are unwilling to place women in situations proper to enable them to acquire sufficient understanding to know how even to nurse their babes.

So forcibly does this truth strike me, that I would rest the whole tendency of my reasoning upon it, for whatever tends to incapacitate the maternal character, takes woman out of her sphere.

But it is vain to expect the present race of weak mothers either to take that reasonable care of a child's body, which is necessary to lay the foundation of a good constitution, supposing that it do not suffer for the sins of its fathers;[8] or, to manage its temper so judiciously that the child will not have, as it grows up, to throw off all that its mother, its first instructor, directly or indirectly taught; and unless the mind have uncommon vigour, womanish follies will stick to the character throughout life. The weakness of the mother will be visited on the children! And whilst women are educated to rely on their husbands for judgment, this must ever be the consequence, for there is no improving an understanding by halves, nor can any being act wisely from imitation, because in every circumstance of life there is a kind of individuality, which requires an exertion of judgment to modify general rules. The being who can think justly in one track, will soon extend its intellectual empire; and she who has sufficient judgment to manage her children, will not submit, right or wrong, to her husband, or patiently to the social laws which make a nonentity of a wife.

In public schools women, to guard against the errors of ignorance, should be taught the elements of anatomy and medicine, not only to enable them to take proper care of their own health, but to make them rational nurses of their infants, parents, and husbands; for the

---

7. The Canaanite idol to whom children were supposedly sacrificed, Moloch signifies any idolatrous object to which great sacrifice is paid.
8. See Exodus 20:5: "I the Lord thy God am a jealous God, visiting the iniquity the fathers upon the children unto the third and fourth generation of them that hate me."

bills of mortality[9] are swelled by the blunders of self-willed old women, who give nostrums of their own without knowing any thing of the human frame. It is likewise proper only in a domestic view, to make women acquainted with the anatomy of the mind, by allowing the sexes to associate together in every pursuit; and by leading them to observe the progress of the human understanding in the improvement of the sciences and arts; never forgetting the science of morality, or the study of the political history of mankind.

A man has been termed a microcosm; and every family might also be called a state. States, it is true, have mostly been governed by arts that disgrace the character of man; and the want of a just constitution, and equal laws, have so perplexed the notions of the worldly wise, that they more than question the reasonableness of contending for the rights of humanity. Thus morality, polluted in the national reservoir, sends off streams of vice to corrupt the constituent parts of the body politic; but should more noble, or rather, more just principles regulate the laws, which ought to be the government of society, and not those who execute them, duty might become the rule of private conduct.

Besides, by the exercise of their bodies and minds women would acquire that mental activity so necessary in the maternal character, united with the fortitude that distinguishes steadiness of conduct from the obstinate perverseness of weakness. For it is dangerous to advise the indolent to be steady, because they instantly become rigorous, and to save themselves trouble, punish with severity faults that the patient fortitude of reason might have prevented.

But fortitude presupposes strength of mind; and is strength of mind to be acquired by indolent acquiescence? by asking advice instead of exerting the judgment? by obeying through fear, instead of practising the forbearance, which we all stand in need of ourselves?—The conclusion which I wish to draw, is obvious; make women rational creatures, and free citizens, and they will quickly become good wives, and mothers; that is—if men do not neglect the duties of husbands and fathers.

Discussing the advantages which a public and private education combined, as I have sketched, might rationally be expected to produce, I have dwelt most on such as are particularly relative to the female world, because I think the female world oppressed; yet the gangrene, which the vices engendered by oppression have produced, is not confined to the morbid part, but pervades society at large: so that when I wish to see my sex become more like moral agents, my heart bounds with the anticipation of the general diffusion of that sublime contentment which only morality can diffuse.

9. Weekly publications of deaths and, later, births in each parish of London and its environs.

Chap. XIII

*Some Instances of the Folly Which the Ignorance of
Women Generates; with Concluding Reflections on the
Moral Improvement That a Revolution in Female
Manners Might Naturally Be Expected to Produce*

There are many follies, in some degree, peculiar to women: sins against reason of commission as well as of omission; but all flowing from ignorance or prejudice, I shall only point out such as appear to be particularly injurious to their moral character. And in animadverting on them, I wish especially to prove, that the weakness of mind and body, which men have endeavoured, impelled by various motives, to perpetuate, prevents their discharging the peculiar duty of their sex: for when weakness of body will not permit them to suckle their children, and weakness of mind makes them spoil their tempers—is woman in a natural state?

SECT. I

One glaring instance of the weakness which proceeds from ignorance, first claims attention, and calls for severe reproof.

In this metropolis a number of lurking leeches infamously gain a subsistence by practising on the credulity of women, pretending to cast nativities,[1] to use the technical phrase; and many females who, proud of their rank and fortune, look down on the vulgar with sovereign contempt, shew by this credulity, that the distinction is arbitrary, and that they have not sufficiently cultivated their minds to rise above vulgar prejudices. Women, because they have not been led to consider the knowledge of their duty as the one thing necessary to know, or, to live in the present moment by the discharge of it, are very anxious to peep into futurity, to learn what they have to expect to render life interesting, and to break the vacuum of ignorance.

I must be allowed to expostulate seriously with the ladies who follow these idle inventions; for ladies, mistresses of families, are not ashamed to drive in their own carriages to the door of the cunning man.[2] And if any of them should peruse this work, I entreat them to answer to their own hearts the following questions, not forgetting that they are in the presence of God.

Do you believe that there is but one God, and that he is powerful, wise, and good?

---

1. Horoscopes.
2. "I once lived in the neighbourhood of one of these men, a *handsome* man, and saw with surprise and indignation, women, whose appearance and attendance bespoke that rank in which females are supposed to receive a superior education, flock to his door" [Wollstonecraft's note]. "Cunning man": fortune-teller.

Do you believe that all things were created by him, and that all beings are dependent on him?

Do you rely on his wisdom, so conspicuous in his works, and in your own frame, and are you convinced that he has ordered all things which do not come under the cognizance of your senses, in the same perfect harmony, to fulfil his designs?

Do you acknowledge that the power of looking into futurity, and seeing things that are not, as if they were, is an attribute of the Creator? And should he, by an impression on the minds of his creatures, think fit to impart to them some event hid in the shades of time yet unborn, to whom would the secret be revealed by immediate inspiration? The opinion of ages will answer this question—to reverend old men, to people distinguished for eminent piety.

The oracles of old were thus delivered by priests dedicated to the service of the God who was supposed to inspire them. The glare of worldly pomp which surrounded these impostors, and the respect paid to them by artful politicians, who knew how to avail themselves of this useful engine to bend the necks of the strong under the dominion of the cunning, spread a sacred mysterious veil of sanctity over their lies and abominations. Impressed by such solemn devotional parade, a Greek, or Roman lady might be excused, if she inquired of the oracle, when she was anxious to pry into futurity, or inquire about some dubious event: and her inquiries, however contrary to reason, could not be reckoned impious.—But, can the professors of Christianity ward off that imputation? Can a Christian suppose that the favourites of the most High, the highly favoured, would be obliged to lurk in disguise, and practise the most dishonest tricks to cheat silly women out of the money—which the poor cry for in vain?

Say not that such questions are an insult to common sense—for it is your own conduct, O ye foolish women! which throws an odium on your sex! And these reflections should make you shudder at your thoughtlessness, and irrational devotion.—For I do not suppose that all of you laid aside your religion, such as it is, when you entered those mysterious dwellings. Yet, as I have throughout supposed myself talking to ignorant women, for ignorant ye are in the most emphatical sense of the word, it would be absurd to reason with you on the egregious folly of desiring to know what the Supreme Wisdom has concealed.

Probably you would not understand me, were I to attempt to shew you that it would be absolutely inconsistent with the grand purpose of life, that of rendering human creatures wise and virtuous: and that, were it sanctioned by God, it would disturb the order established in creation; and if it be not sanctioned by God, do you expect to hear truth? Can events be foretold, events which have not yet assumed a body to become subject to mortal inspection, can they be foreseen by a vicious worldling, who pampers his appetites by preying on the foolish ones?

Perhaps, however, you devoutly believe in the devil, and imagine, to shift the question, that he may assist his votaries; but, if really respecting the power of such a being, an enemy to goodness and to God, can you go to church after having been under such an obligation to him?

From these delusions to those still more fashionable deceptions, practised by the whole tribe of magnetisers,[3] the transition is very natural. With respect to them, it is equally proper to ask women a few questions.

Do you know any thing of the construction of the human frame? If not, it is proper that you should be told what every child ought to know, that when its admirable œconomy has been disturbed by intemperance or indolence, I speak not of violent disorders, but of chronical diseases, it must be brought into a healthy state again, by slow degrees, and if the functions of life have not been materially injured, regimen, another word for temperance, air, exercise, and a few medicines, prescribed by persons who have studied the human body, are the only human means, yet discovered, of recovering that inestimable blessing health, that will bear investigation.

Do you then believe that these magnetisers, who, by hocus pocus tricks, pretend to work a miracle, are delegated by God, or assisted by the solver of all these kind of difficulties—the devil?

Do they, when they put to flight, as it is said, disorders that have baffled the powers of medicine, work in conformity to the light of reason? or, do they effect these wonderful cures by supernatural aid?

By a communication, an adept may answer, with the world of spirits. A noble privilege, it must be allowed. Some of the ancients mention familiar daemons, who guarded them from danger by kindly intimating, we cannot guess in what manner, when any danger was nigh; or, pointed out what they ought to undertake. Yet the men who laid claim to this privilege, out of the order of nature, insisted that it was the reward, or consequence, of superior temperance and piety. But the present workers of wonders are not raised above their fellows by superiour temperance or sanctity. They do not cure for the love of God, but money. These are the priests of quackery, though it is true they have not the convenient expedient of selling masses for souls in purgatory,[4] or churches where they can display crutches, and models of limbs made sound by a touch or a word.

---

3. Practitioners of a fashionable treatment for nervous disorders. The procedure involved the use of magnetic rods as well as hypnotism.
4. In the Roman Catholic church one could purchase a mass to be said to release a deceased person's soul from purgatory.

I am not conversant with the technical terms, or initiated into the arcana, therefore, I may speak improperly; but it is clear that men who will not conform to the law of reason, and earn a subsistence in an honest way, by degrees, are very fortunate in becoming acquainted with such obliging spirits. We cannot, indeed, give them credit for either great sagacity or goodness, else they would have chosen more noble instruments, when they wished to shew themselves the benevolent friends of man.

It is, however, little short of blasphemy to pretend to such powers!

From the whole tenour of the dispensations of Providence, it appears evident to sober reason, that certain vices produce certain effects; and can any one so grossly insult the wisdom of God, as to suppose that a miracle will be allowed to disturb his general laws, to restore to health the intemperate and vicious, merely to enable them to pursue the same course with impunity? Be whole, and sin no more, said Jesus.[5] And, are greater miracles to be performed by those who do not follow his footsteps, who healed the body to reach the mind?

The mentioning of the name of Christ, after such vile impostors, may displease some of my readers—I respect their warmth; but let them not forget that the followers of these delusions bear his name,[6] and profess to be the disciples of him, who said, by their works we should know who were the children of God or the servants of sin. I allow that it is easier to touch the body of a saint, or to be magnetised, than to restrain our appetites or govern our passions; but health of body or mind can only be recovered by these means, or we make the Supreme Judge partial and revengeful.

Is he a man that he should change, or punish out of resentment? He—the common father, wounds but to heal, says reason, and our irregularities producing certain consequences, we are forcibly shewn the nature of vice; that thus learning to know good from evil, by experience, we may hate one and love the other, in proportion to the wisdom which we attain. The poison contains the antidote; and we either reform our evil habits and cease to sin against our own bodies, to use the forcible language of scripture, or a premature death, the punishment of sin, snaps the thread of life.

Here an awful[7] stop is put to our inquiries.—But, why should I conceal my sentiments? Considering the attributes of God, I believe that whatever punishment may follow, will tend, like the anguish of disease, to shew the malignity of vice, for the purpose of reformation. Positive punishment appears so contrary to the nature

5. John 5:14: "Behold, thou art made whole: sin no more, lest a worse thing come unto thee."
6. I.e., call themselves Christians.
7. Awe-inspiring.

of God, discoverable in all his works, and in our own reason, that I could sooner believe that the Deity paid no attention to the conduct of men, than that he punished without the benevolent design of reforming.

To suppose only that an all-wise and powerful Being, as good as he is great, should create a being foreseeing, that after fifty or sixty years of feverish existence, it would be plunged into never ending woe—is blasphemy. On what will the worm feed that is never to die? On folly, on ignorance, say ye—I should blush indignantly at drawing the natural conclusion could I insert it, and wish to withdraw myself from the wing of my God! On such a supposition, I speak with reverence, he would be a consuming fire.[8] We should wish, though vainly, to fly from his presence when fear absorbed love, and darkness involved all his counsels!

I know that many devout people boast of submitting to the Will of God blindly, as to an arbitrary sceptre or rod, on the same principle as the Indians worship the devil. In other words, like people in the common concerns of life, they do homage to power, and cringe under the foot that can crush them. Rational religion, on the contrary, is a submission to the will of a being so perfectly wise, that all he wills must be directed by the proper motive—must be reasonable.

And, if thus we respect God, can we give credit to the mysterious insinuations, which insult his laws? can we believe, though it should stare us in the face, that he would work a miracle to authorize confusion by sanctioning an error? Yet we must either allow these impious conclusions, or treat with contempt every promise to restore health to a diseased body by supernatural means, or to foretell the incidents that can only be foreseen by God.

SECT. II

Another instance of that feminine weakness of character, often produced by a confined education, is a romantic twist of the mind, which has been very properly termed *sentimental*.

Women subjected by ignorance to their sensations, and only taught to look for happiness in love, refine on sensual feelings, and adopt metaphysical notions respecting that passion, which lead them shamefully to neglect the duties of life, and frequently in the midst of these sublime refinements they plump[9] into actual vice.

These are the women who are amused by the reveries of the stupid novelists, who, knowing little of human nature, work up stale tales, and describe meretricious scenes, all retailed in a sentimental jargon, which equally tend to corrupt the taste, and draw the heart

8. Isaiah 66:24: "for their worm shall not die, neither shall their fire be quenched."
9. Plunge.

aside from its daily duties. I do not mention the understanding, because never having been exercised, its slumbering energies rest inactive, like the lurking particles of fire which are supposed universally to pervade matter.[1]

Females, in fact, denied all political privileges, and not allowed, as married women, excepting in criminal cases, a civil existence,[2] have their attention naturally drawn from the interest of the whole community to that of the minute parts, though the private duty of any member of society must be very imperfectly performed when not connected with the general good. The mighty business of female life is to please, and restrained from entering into more important concerns by political and civil oppression, sentiments become events, and reflection deepens what it should, and would have effaced, if the understanding had been allowed to take a wider range.

But, confined to trifling employments, they naturally imbibe opinions which the only kind of reading calculated to interest an innocent frivolous mind, inspires. Unable to grasp any thing great, is it surprising that they find the reading of history a very dry task, and disquisitions addressed to the understanding intolerably tedious, and almost unintelligible? Thus are they necessarily dependent on the novelist for amusement. Yet, when I exclaim against novels, I mean when contrasted with those works which exercise the understanding and regulate the imagination.—For any kind of reading I think better than leaving a blank still a blank, because the mind must receive a degree of enlargement and obtain a little strength by a slight exertion of its thinking powers; besides, even the productions that are only addressed to the imagination, raise the reader a little above the gross gratification of appetites, to which the mind has not given a shade of delicacy.

This observation is the result of experience; for I have known several notable women, and one in particular, who was a very good woman—as good as such a narrow mind would allow her to be, who took care that her daughters (three in number) should never see a novel. As she was a woman of fortune and fashion, they had various masters to attend them, and a sort of menial governess to watch their footsteps. From their masters they learned how tables, chairs, &c. were called in French and Italian; but as the few books thrown in their way were far above their capacities, or devotional, they neither acquired ideas nor sentiments, and passed their time, when not compelled to repeat *words*, in dressing, quarrelling with each other, or conversing with their maids by stealth, till they were brought into company as marriageable.

1. Phlogiston, the substance that, according to a theory that was discredited by the start of the nineteenth century, caused the light and heat occurring during burning.
2. A reference to the doctrine of coverture (see p. 153, n. 6).

Their mother, a widow, was busy in the mean time in keeping up her connections, as she termed a numerous acquaintance, lest her girls should want a proper introduction into the great world. And these young ladies, with minds vulgar in every sense of the word, and spoiled tempers, entered life puffed up with notions of their own consequence, and looking down with contempt on those who could not vie with them in dress and parade.

With respect to love, nature, or their nurses, had taken care to teach them the physical meaning of the word; and, as they had few topics of conversation, and fewer refinements of sentiment, they expressed their gross wishes not in very delicate phrases, when they spoke freely, talking of matrimony.

Could these girls have been injured by the perusal of novels? I almost forgot a shade in the character of one of them; she affected a simplicity bordering on folly, and with a simper would utter the most immodest remarks and questions, the full meaning of which she had learned whilst secluded from the world, and afraid to speak in her mother's presence, who governed with a high hand: they were all educated, as she prided herself, in a most exemplary manner; and read their chapters and psalms before breakfast, never touching a silly novel.

This is only one instance; but I recollect many other women who, not led by degrees to proper studies, and not permitted to choose for themselves, have indeed been overgrown children; or have obtained, by mixing in the world, a little of what is termed common sense: that is, a distinct manner of seeing common occurrences, as they stand detached: but what deserves the name of intellect, the power of gaining general or abstract ideas, or even intermediate ones, was out of the question. Their minds were quiescent, and when they were not roused by sensible objects[3] and employments of that kind, they were low-spirited, would cry, or go to sleep.

When, therefore, I advise my sex not to read such flimsy works, it is to induce them to read something superiour; for I coincide in opinion with a sagacious man, who, having a daughter and niece under his care, pursued a very different plan with each.

The niece, who had considerable abilities, had, before she was left to his guardianship, been indulged in desultory reading. Her he endeavoured to lead, and did lead to history and moral essays; but his daughter, whom a fond weak mother had indulged, and who consequently was averse to every thing like application, he allowed to read novels: and used to justify his conduct by saying, that if she ever attained a relish for reading them, he should have some foundation to work upon; and that erroneous opinions were better than none at all.

3. Material things.

In fact the female mind has been so totally neglected, that knowledge was only to be acquired from this muddy source, till from reading novels some women of superiour talents learned to despise them.

The best method, I believe, that can be adopted to correct a fondness for novels is to ridicule them: not indiscriminately, for then it would have little effect; but, if a judicious person, with some turn for humour, would read several to a young girl, and point out both by tones, and apt comparisons with pathetic incidents and heroic characters in history, how foolishly and ridiculously they caricatured human nature, just opinions might be substituted instead of romantic sentiments.

In one respect, however, the majority of both sexes resemble, and equally shew a want of taste and modesty. Ignorant women, forced to be chaste to preserve their reputation, allow their imagination to revel in the unnatural and meretricious scenes sketched by the novel writers of the day, slighting as insipid the sober dignity and matron graces of history,[4] whilst men carry the same vitiated taste into life, and fly for amusement to the wanton, from the unsophisticated charms of virtue, and the grave respectability of sense.

Besides, the reading of novels makes women, and particularly ladies of fashion, very fond of using strong expressions and superlatives in conversation; and, though the dissipated artificial life which they lead prevents their cherishing any strong legitimate passion, the language of passion in affected tones slips for ever from their glib tongues, and every trifle produces those phosphoric bursts which only mimick in the dark the flame of passion.

SECT. III

Ignorance and the mistaken cunning that nature sharpens in weak heads as a principle of self-preservation, render women very fond of dress, and produce all the vanity which such a fondness may naturally be expected to generate, to the exclusion of emulation and magnanimity.

I agree with Rousseau that the physical part of the art of pleasing consists in ornaments, and for that very reason I should guard girls against the contagious fondness for dress so common to weak women, that they may not rest in the physical part. Yet, weak are the women who imagine that they can long please without the aid of the mind, or, in other words, without the moral art of pleasing. But the moral art, if it be not a profanation to use the word art, when

4. "I am not now alluding to that superiority of mind which leads to the creation of ideal beauty, when he, surveyed with a penetrating eye, appears a tragicomedy, in which little can be seen to satisfy the heart without the help of fancy" [Wollstonecraft's note]. In the first edition of the text it is *life* that is "surveyed with a penetrating eye."

alluding to the grace which is an effect of virtue, and not the motive of action, is never to be found with ignorance; the sportiveness of innocence, so pleasing to refined libertines of both sexes, is widely different in its essence from this superiour gracefulness.

A strong inclination for external ornaments ever appears in barbarous states, only the men not the women adorn themselves; for where women are allowed to be so far on a level with men, society has advanced, at least, one step in civilization.

The attention to dress, therefore, which has been thought a sexual propensity,[5] I think natural to mankind. But I ought to express myself with more precision. When the mind is not sufficiently opened to take pleasure in reflection, the body will be adorned with sedulous care; and ambition will appear in tattooing or painting it.

So far is this first inclination carried, that even the hellish yoke of slavery cannot stifle the savage desire of admiration which the black heroes inherit from both their parents, for all the hardly earned savings of a slave are commonly expended in a little tawdry finery. And I have seldom known a good male or female servant that was not particularly fond of dress. Their clothes were their riches; and, I argue from analogy, that the fondness for dress, so extravagant in females, arises from the same cause—want of cultivation of mind. When men meet they converse about business, politics, or literature; but, says Swift, 'how naturally do women apply their hands to each others lappets and ruffles.'[6] And very natural is it—for they have not any business to interest them, have not a taste for literature, and they find politics dry, because they have not acquired a love for mankind by turning their thoughts to the grand pursuits that exalt the human race, and promote general happiness.

Besides, various are the paths to power and fame which by accident or choice men pursue, and though they jostle against each other, for men of the same profession are seldom friends, yet there is a much greater number of their fellow-creatures with whom they never clash. But women are very differently situated with respect to each other—for they are all rivals.

Before marriage it is their business to please men; and after, with a few exceptions, they follow the same scent with all the persevering pertinacity of instinct. Even virtuous women never forget their sex in company, for they are for ever trying to make themselves *agreeable*. A female beauty, and a male wit, appear to be equally anxious to draw the attention of the company to themselves; and the animosity of contemporary wits is proverbial.

5. I.e., gender-specific tendency.
6. Slightly misquoting Swift's "A Letter to a Young Lady on Her Marriage," in *Miscellanies in Prose and Verse* (London, 1728).

Is it then surprising that when the sole ambition of woman centres in beauty, and interest gives vanity additional force, perpetual rivalships should ensue? They are all running the same race, and would rise above the virtue of mortals, if they did not view each other with a suspicious and even envious eye.

An immoderate fondness for dress, for pleasure, and for sway, are the passions of savages; the passions that occupy those uncivilized beings who have not yet extended the dominion of the mind, or even learned to think with the energy necessary to concatenate that abstract train of thought which produces principles. And that women from their education and the present state of civilized life, are in the same condition, cannot, I think, be controverted. To laugh at them then, or satirize the follies of a being who is never to be allowed to act freely from the light of her own reason, is as absurd as cruel; for, that they who are taught blindly to obey authority, will endeavour cunningly to elude it, is most natural and certain.

Yet let it be proved that they ought to obey man implicitly, and I shall immediately agree that it is woman's duty to cultivate a fondness for dress, in order to please, and a propensity to cunning for her own preservation.

The virtues, however, which are supported by ignorance must ever be wavering—the house built on sand could not endure a storm.[7] It is almost unnecessary to draw the inference.—If women are to be made virtuous by authority, which is a contradiction in terms, let them be immured in seraglios and watched with a jealous eye.—Fear not that the iron will enter into their souls[8]—for the souls that can bear such treatment are made of yielding materials, just animated enough to give life to the body.

> 'Matter too soft a lasting mark to bear,
> 'And best distinguish'd by black, brown, or fair.'[9]

The most cruel wounds will of course soon heal, and they may still people the world, and dress to please man—all the purposes which certain celebrated writers have allowed that they were created to fulfil.

SECT. IV

Women are supposed to possess more sensibility, and even humanity, than men, and their strong attachments and instantaneous

---

7. Matthew 7:26–27: "a foolish man, which built his house upon the sand: And the rain descended, and the floods came, and the winds blew, and beat upon that house; and it fell."
8. An echo of the *Book of Common Prayer*: "the iron entered into his soul" (Morning Prayer, 21st day).
9. Pope, "Of the Characters of Women," lines 3–4.

emotions of compassion are given as proofs; but the clinging affection of ignorance has seldom any thing noble in it, and may mostly be resolved into selfishness, as well as the affection of children and brutes. I have known many weak women whose sensibility was entirely engrossed by their husbands; and as for their humanity, it was very faint indeed, or rather it was only a transient emotion of compassion. Humanity does not consist 'in a squeamish ear,' says an eminent orator. 'It belongs to the mind as well as the nerves.'

But this kind of exclusive affection, though it degrades the individual, should not be brought forward as a proof of the inferiority of the sex, because it is the natural consequence of confined views: for even women of superior sense, having their attention turned to little employments, and private plans, rarely rise to heroism, unless when spurred on by love! and love, as an heroic passion, like genius, appears but once in an age. I therefore agree with the moralist who asserts, 'that women have seldom so much generosity as men;'[1] and that their narrow affections, to which justice and humanity are often sacrificed, render the sex apparently inferior, especially, as they are commonly inspired by men; but I contend that the heart would expand as the understanding gained strength, if women were not depressed from their cradles.

I know that a little sensibility, and great weakness, will produce a strong sexual attachment, and that reason must cement friendship; consequently, I allow that more friendship is to be found in the male than the female world, and that men have a higher sense of justice. The exclusive affections of women seem indeed to resemble Cato's most unjust love for his country.[2] He wished to crush Carthage, not to save Rome, but to promote its vain-glory; and, in general, it is to similar principles that humanity is sacrificed, for genuine duties support each other.

Besides, how can women be just or generous, when they are the slaves of injustice?

SECT. V

As the rearing of children, that is, the laying a foundation of sound health both of body and mind in the rising generation, has justly been insisted on as the peculiar destination of woman, the ignorance that incapacitates them must be contrary to the order of

---

1. Smith, *Theory of Moral Sentiments*, IV, ii, p. 10: "The fair sex, who have commonly much more tenderness than ours, have seldom so much generosity."
2. In *Theory of Moral Sentiments* (VI, ii, 2) Smith also refers to the hatred that Roman senator Marcus Porcius Cato (234–149 B.C.E.) had for the city-state of Carthage: "The sentence with which the elder Cato is said to have concluded every speech . . . , 'It is my opinion likewise that Carthage ought to be destroyed,' was the natural expression of the savage patriotism of a strong but coarse mind" (p. 228).

things. And I contend that their minds can take in much more, and ought to do so, or they will never become sensible mothers. Many men attend to the breeding of horses, and overlook the management of the stable, who would, strange want of sense and feeling! think themselves degraded by paying any attention to the nursery; yet, how many children are absolutely murdered by the ignorance of women! But when they escape, and are destroyed neither by unnatural negligence nor blind fondness, how few are managed properly with respect to the infant mind! So that to break the spirit, allowed to become vicious at home, a child is sent to school; and the methods taken there, which must be taken to keep a number of children in order, scatter the seeds of almost every vice in the soil thus forcibly torn up.

I have sometimes compared the struggles of these poor children, who ought never to have felt restraint, nor would, had they been always held in with an even hand, to the despairing plunges of a spirited filly, which I have seen breaking on a strand: its feet sinking deeper and deeper in the sand every time it endeavoured to throw its rider, till at last it sullenly submitted.

I have always found horses, animals I am attached to, very tractable when treated with humanity and steadiness, so that I doubt whether the violent methods taken to break them, do not essentially injure them; I am, however, certain that a child should never be thus forcibly tamed after it has injudiciously been allowed to run wild; for every violation of justice and reason, in the treatment of children, weakens their reason. And, so early do they catch a character, that the base of the moral character, experience leads me to infer, is fixed before their seventh year, the period during which women are allowed the sole management of children. Afterwards it too often happens that half the business of education is to correct, and very imperfectly is it done, if done hastily, the faults, which they would never have acquired if their mothers had had more understanding.

One striking instance of the folly of women must not be omitted.—The manner in which they treat servants in the presence of children, permitting them to suppose that they ought to wait on them, and bear their humours. A child should always be made to receive assistance from a man or woman as a favour; and, as the first lesson of independence, they should practically be taught, by the example of their mother, not to require that personal attendance, which it is an insult to humanity to require, when in health; and instead of being led to assume airs of consequence, a sense of their own weakness should first make them feel the natural equality of man. Yet, how frequently have I indignantly heard servants imperiously called to put children to bed, and sent away again and again, because master or miss hung about mamma, to stay a little longer.

Thus made slavishly to attend the little idol, all those most disgusting humours were exhibited which characterize a spoiled child.

In short, speaking of the majority of mothers, they leave their children entirely to the care of servants; or, because they are their children, treat them as if they were little demi-gods, though I have always observed, that the women who thus idolize their children, seldom shew common humanity to servants, or feel the least tenderness for any children but their own.

It is, however, these exclusive affections, and an individual manner of seeing things, produced by ignorance, which keep women for ever at a stand, with respect to improvement, and make many of them dedicate their lives to their children only to weaken their bodies and spoil their tempers, frustrating also any plan of education that a more rational father may adopt; for unless a mother concur, the father who restrains will ever be considered as a tyrant.

But, fulfilling the duties of a mother, a woman with a sound constitution, may still keep her person scrupulously neat, and assist to maintain her family, if necessary, or by reading and conversations with both sexes, indiscriminately, improve her mind. For nature has so wisely ordered things, that did women suckle their children, they would preserve their own health, and there would be such an interval between the birth of each child, that we should seldom see a houseful of babes.[3] And did they pursue a plan of conduct, and not waste their time in following the fashionable vagaries of dress, the management of their household and children need not shut them out from literature, or prevent their attaching themselves to a science, with that steady eye which strengthens the mind, or practising one of the fine arts that cultivate the taste.

But, visiting to display finery, card-playing, and balls, not to mention the idle bustle of morning trifling, draw women from their duty to render them insignificant, to render them pleasing, according to the present acceptation of the word, to every man, but their husband. For a round of pleasures in which the affections are not exercised, cannot be said to improve the understanding, though it be erroneously called seeing the world; yet the heart is rendered cold and averse to duty, by such a senseless intercourse, which becomes necessary from habit even when it has ceased to amuse.

But, we shall not see women affectionate till more equality be established in society, till ranks are confounded and women freed, neither shall we see that dignified domestic happiness, the simple grandeur of which cannot be relished by ignorant or vitiated minds; nor will the important task of education ever be properly begun till

---

3. In the eighteenth century it was thought that a woman who was nursing a baby could not become pregnant.

the person of a woman is no longer preferred to her mind. For it would be as wise to expect corn from tares, or figs from thistles, as that a foolish ignorant woman should be a good mother.

SECT. VI

It is not necessary to inform the sagacious reader, now I enter on my concluding reflections, that the discussion of this subject merely consists in opening a few simple principles, and clearing away the rubbish which obscured them. But, as all readers are not sagacious, I must be allowed to add some explanatory remarks to bring the subject home to reason—to that sluggish reason, which supinely takes opinions on trust, and obstinately supports them to spare itself the labour of thinking.

Moralists have unanimously agreed, that unless virtue be nursed by liberty, it will never attain due strength—and what they say of man I extend to mankind, insisting that in all cases morals must be fixed on immutable principles; and, that the being cannot be termed rational or virtuous, who obeys any authority, but that of reason.

To render women truly useful members of society, I argue that they should be led, by having their understandings cultivated on a large scale, to acquire a rational affection for their country, founded on knowledge, because it is obvious that we are little interested about what we do not understand. And to render this general knowledge of due importance, I have endeavoured to shew that private duties are never properly fulfilled unless the understanding enlarges the heart; and that public virtue is only an aggregate of private. But, the distinctions established in society undermine both, by beating out the solid gold of virtue, till it becomes only the tinsel-covering of vice; for whilst wealth renders a man more respectable than virtue, wealth will be sought before virtue; and, whilst women's persons are caressed, when a childish simper shews an absence of mind—the mind will lie fallow. Yet, true voluptuousness must proceed from the mind—for what can equal the sensations produced by mutual affection, supported by mutual respect? What are the cold, or feverish caresses of appetite, but sin embracing death,[4] compared with the modest overflowings of a pure heart and exalted imagination? Yes, let me tell the libertine of fancy when he despises understanding in woman—that the mind, which he disregards, gives life to the enthusiastic affection from which rapture, short-lived as it is, alone can flow! And, that, without virtue, a sexual attachment must expire, like a tallow candle in the socket, creating intolerable disgust. To prove this, I need only observe, that men who have wasted great

4. *Paradise Lost* II.790–98.

part of their lives with women, and with whom they have sought for
pleasure with eager thirst, entertain the meanest opinion of the
sex.—Virtue, true refiner of joy!—if foolish men were to fright thee
from earth, in order to give loose to all their appetites without a
check—some sensual wight of taste would scale the heavens to
invite thee back, to give a zest to pleasure!

That women at present are by ignorance rendered foolish or
vicious, is, I think, not to be disputed; and, that the most salutary
effects tending to improve mankind might be expected from a REVO-
LUTION in female manners, appears, at least, with a face of probability, to rise out of the observation. For as marriage has been termed the
parent of those endearing charities which draw man from the brutal
herd, the corrupting intercourse that wealth, idleness, and folly, produce between the sexes, is more universally injurious to morality than
all the other vices of mankind collectively considered. To adulterous
lust the most sacred duties are sacrificed, because before marriage,
men, by a promiscuous intimacy with women, learned to consider
love as a selfish gratification—learned to separate it not only from
esteem, but from the affection merely built on habit, which mixes a
little humanity with it. Justice and friendship are also set at defiance,
and that purity of taste is vitiated which would naturally lead a man
to relish an artless display of affection rather than affected airs. But
that noble simplicity of affection, which dares to appear unadorned,
has few attractions for the libertine, though it be the charm, which by
cementing the matrimonial tie, secures to the pledges of a warmer
passion the necessary parental attention; for children will never be
properly educated till friendship subsists between parents. Virtue
flies from a house divided against itself [5]—and a whole legion of devils
take up their residence there.

The affection of husbands and wives cannot be pure when they
have so few sentiments in common, and when so little confidence is
established at home, as must be the case when their pursuits are so
different. That intimacy from which tenderness should flow, will
not, cannot subsist between the vicious.

Contending, therefore, that the sexual distinction which men
have so warmly insisted upon, is arbitrary, I have dwelt on an observation, that several sensible men, with whom I have conversed on
the subject, allowed to be well founded; and it is simply this, that the
little chastity to be found amongst men, and consequent disregard
of modesty, tend to degrade both sexes; and further, that the modesty of women, characterized as such, will often be only the artful
veil of wantonness instead of being the natural reflection of purity,
till modesty be universally respected.

5. Matthew 12:25: "every city or house divided against itself shall not stand."

From the tyranny of man, I firmly believe, the greater number of female follies proceed; and the cunning, which I allow makes at present a part of their character, I likewise have repeatedly endeavoured to prove, is produced by oppression.

Were not dissenters,[6] for instance, a class of people, with strict truth, characterized as cunning? And may I not lay some stress on this fact to prove, that when any power but reason curbs the free spirit of man, dissimulation is practised, and the various shifts of art are naturally called forth? Great attention to decorum, which was carried to a degree of scrupulosity, and all that puerile bustle about trifles and consequential solemnity, which Butler's caricature of a dissenter, brings before the imagination, shaped their persons as well as their minds in the mould of prim littleness.[7] I speak collectively, for I know how many ornaments to human nature have been enrolled amongst sectaries; yet, I assert, that the same narrow prejudice for their sect, which women have for their families, prevailed in the dissenting part of the community, however worthy in other respects; and also that the same timid prudence, or headstrong efforts, often disgraced the exertions of both. Oppression thus formed many of the features of their character perfectly to coincide with that of the oppressed half of mankind; or is it not notorious that dissenters were, like women, fond of deliberating together, and asking advice of each other, till by a complication of little contrivances, some little end was brought about? A similar attention to preserve their reputation was conspicuous in the dissenting and female world, and was produced by a similar cause.

Asserting the rights which women in common with men ought to contend for, I have not attempted to extenuate their faults; but to prove them to be the natural consequence of their education and station in society. If so, it is reasonable to suppose that they will change their character, and correct their vices and follies, when they are allowed to be free in a physical, moral, and civil sense.[8]

Let woman share the rights and she will emulate the virtues of man; for she must grow more perfect when emancipated, or justify the authority that chains such a weak being to her duty.—If the latter, it will be expedient to open a fresh trade with Russia for whips;

6. Members of Protestant denominations outside the established (Anglican) church. In 1792 men who were Dissenters were still barred from political and public office in Britain, despite a recent campaign to repeal the Acts of Parliament mandating this discrimination.
7. Likely referring to "An Hypocritical Non-conformist," a character sketch by Samuel Butler, published posthumously in 1759 in his *Genuine Remains in Verse and Prose* (II, pp. 35–51).
8. "I had further enlarged on the advantages which might reasonably be expected to result from an improvement in female manners, towards the general reformation of society; but it appeared to me that such reflections would more properly close the last volume" [Wollstonecraft's note].

a present which a father should always make to his son-in-law on his wedding day, that a husband may keep his whole family in order by the same means;[9] and without any violation of justice reign, wielding this sceptre, sole master of his house, because he is the only being in it who has reason:—the divine, indefeasible earthly sovereignty breathed into man by the Master of the universe. Allowing this position, women have not any inherent rights to claim; and, by the same rule, their duties vanish, for rights and duties are inseparable.

Be just then, O ye men of understanding! and mark not more severely what women do amiss, than the vicious tricks of the horse or the ass for whom ye provide provender—and allow her the privileges of ignorance, to whom ye deny the rights of reason, or ye will be worse than Egyptian task-masters, expecting virtue where nature has not given understanding!

9. Travelers to Russia often noted the submissive nature of Russian wives and Russian husbands' use of whips (said to be given as wedding presents) to secure that submission.

BACKGROUNDS
AND CONTEXTS

Legacies of English Radicalism

The project of envisioning a "revolution in female manners" was bound to lead Wollstonecraft back to the seventeenth century. That century of revolution significantly transformed how individuals in England, or at least property-owning male individuals, understood the authority of government and rights of the governed. The change was brought about by a series of dramatic political crises: the civil war, which erupted in 1642 as consensus about the appropriate forms of Protestant worship collapsed and as Parliament asserted its rights over the prerogatives of the Crown; England's failed experiment with republican government following the execution of King Charles I in 1649; the restoration of hereditary monarchy in 1660; and, finally, in 1688, another revolution that made the monarchs who took the place of the Stuart dynasty accountable to Parliament in ways that Charles and his sons had refused to be. The political pamphlets, treatises, and poems that made sense of this upheaval are an important context for Wollstonecraft's thought, as this section of background reading suggests.

Both her *Vindications* register the influence of, for instance, the writings of John Locke, in which modern concepts of constitutional government, human equality, and human rights, including liberty of conscience, were hammered out in an early, influential form. And the intensity of the second *Vindication*'s engagement with John Milton's *Paradise Lost* is a function not simply of Wollstonecraft's admiration for the poem's scope and daring but also of the political sympathies she shared with the poet, who through the 1640s had defended the English people's right to take up arms against a tyrannical monarch and to choose and change rulers as it saw fit. Dramatizing the consequence of disobedience to rulers—Satan's, Eve's, Adam's—Milton's great poem is intimately linked with those political questions, and Wollstonecraft could not help but be disappointed at how this critic of the divine right of kings appeared nonetheless to have endorsed what she calls the "*divine right* of husbands" (pp. 44–45). And yet, as the philosopher Mary Astell noted already early in the eighteenth century, Milton and Locke, while challenging political hierarchy, had by and large left unquestioned

the gender hierarchy that organized private life. "Not Milton himself," Astell wrote, "would cry up liberty to poor female slaves, or
plead for the lawfulness of resisting a private tyranny." That inconsistency too was a significant aspect of the radical legacy Wollstonecraft inherited.

JOHN MILTON

From Paradise Lost[†]

From *Book 4*

Two of far nobler shape erect and tall,[1]	
Godlike erect with native honor clad	
In naked majesty, seemed lords of all.	290
And worthy seemed for in their looks divine	
The image of their glorious Maker shone:	
Truth, wisdom, sanctitude severe and pure,	
Severe, but in true filial freedom placed,	
Whence true authority in men. Though both	295
Not equal as their sex not equal seemed:	
For contemplation he and valor formed,	
For softness she and sweet attractive grace:	
He for God only, she for God in him.	
His fair large front and eye sublime declared	300
Absolute rule, and hyacinthine locks[2]	
Round from his parted forelock manly hung	
Clust'ring but not beneath his shoulders broad.	
She as a veil down to the slender waist	
Her unadornèd golden tresses wore	305
Dishevelled but in wanton ringlets waved	

---

† *Paradise Lost* was published in ten books in 1667, with a second twelve-book edition,
appearing in 1674 (the basis for the Norton Critical Edition prepared by Gordon Teskey,
the text followed here). At this time, Milton, blind, impoverished, threatened with imprisonment after the Restoration of the monarchy, had survived the wreck of his hopes for his
country's political transformation. The poem reworks the Book of Genesis, justifying "the
ways of God to men" (I.26) while it tells how, as a consequence of Eve's temptation by
Satan, humanity lost Paradise and evil entered our world. For eighteenth-century readers,
the poem's crowning achievement lay in its Christianizing of the epic framework English
literature inherited from classical Greece and Rome and the *Iliad* and *Aeneid* particularly.
Milton does represent a war in heaven, but his epic centers not on the battlefield but on
the domestic arena, as if this might be the sphere of true heroism. All notes are the editor's
unless otherwise noted. All page references to Wollstonecraft are to the present edition.
1. This passage, recalled by Wollstonecraft on p. 22, records Satan's first sight of Adam and
Eve, God's new creation, after his entrance into Eden. On p. 28 Wollstonecraft declares
her affinity with the devil's vantage point in this episode, knowing full well that moralists
such as James Fordyce (whose *Sermons to Young Women* also cites this passage) would
have all women model themselves on Milton's Eve.
2. "Rich, dark hair" [Teskey's note].

As the vine curls her tendrils, which implied
Subjection, but required with gentle sway
And by her yielded, by him best received,
Yielded with coy submission, modest pride,   310
And sweet reluctant amorous delay.

* * *

From *Book 8*

"Let not my words offend Thee, Heav'nly Power,[3]
My Maker, be propitious[4] while I speak.   380
Hast Thou not made me here Thy substitute
And these[5] inferior far beneath me set?
Among unequals what society
Can sort, what harmony or true delight,
Which must be mutual in proportion due   385
Given and received? But in disparity—
The one intense, the other still remiss—
Cannot well suit with either but soon prove
Tedious alike. Of fellowship I speak
Such as I seek, fit to participate   390
All rational delight wherein the brute
Cannot be human consort. They rejoice
Each with their kind, lion with lioness,
So fitly them in pairs thou hast combined.
Much less can bird with beast or fish with fowl   395
So well converse, nor with the ox the ape,
Worse then can Man with beast, and least of all!"

* * *

             Here passion first I felt,[6]   530
Commotion strange! In all enjoyments else
Superior and unmoved, here only weak
Against the charm of beauty's powerful glance.
Or nature failed in me and left some part
Not proof enough such object to sustain   535
Or from my side subducting[7] took perhaps
More than enough, at least on her bestowed

---

3. Describing his first days of life to archangel Raphael, Adam recalls the plea he made to God for companionship. His terms, remembered by Wollstonecraft on p. 23, envision marriage as a relationship not between ruler and ruled but between equals.
4. "Favorable" [Teskey's note].
5. I.e., the animals.
6. In these lines, referenced by Wollstonecraft on p. 64, Adam continues to ponder his union with Eve, the sexual power she exerts, and the conflict between his passion and his reason. A portion of Raphael's response follows, cited by Wollstonecraft on p. 79.
7. "Drawing out, from under" [Teskey's note]. "Or . . . Or": "Following Latin usage, Milton expresses disjunctive propositions not in the form "Either . . . or . . ." but in the form "Or . . . or . . ." I.e., Either Nature left me internally weak in some part (we may guess which), or Nature took more than was necessary out of my side, which made Eve's beauty overwhelming" [Teskey's note].

Too much of ornament, in outward show
Elaborate, of inward less exact.
For well I understand in the prime end   540
Of nature her th' inferior in the mind
And inward faculties which most excel,
In outward also her resembling less
His[8] image who made both and less expressing
The character of that dominion giv'n   545
O'er other creatures. Yet when I approach
Her loveliness so absolute she seems
And in herself complete so well to know
Her own that what she wills to do or say
Seems wisest, virtuousest, discreetest, best.   550
All higher knowledge in her presence falls
Degraded. Wisdom in discourse with her
Loses discount'nanced and like folly shows.
Authority and Reason on her wait
As one intended first, not after made   555
Occasionally. And to consúmmate all,
Greatness of mind and nobleness their seat[9]
Build in her loveliest and create an awe
About her as a guard angelic placed.
To whom the angel with contracted brow: 560
    Accuse not Nature: she hath done her part,
Do thou but thine and be not diffident
Of Wisdom! She[1] deserts thee not if thou
Dismiss not her when most thou need'st her nigh
By áttributing overmuch to things   565
Less excellent as thou thyself perceiv'st.

                              * * *

                         From *Book 10*

                        O why did God,[2]
Creator wise, that peopled highest Heav'n
With spirits masculine, create at last   890
This novelty on earth, this fair defect
Of nature, and not fill the world at once
With men as angels, without feminine,
Or find some other way to generate
Mankind? This mischief had not then befall'n   895
And more that shall befall: innumerable

8. God's
9. "Latin *sedes,* 'dwelling place, throne' " [Teskey's note].
1. "Wisdom" [Teskey's note].
2. Adam's outburst after his recognition that Eve, by persuading him to eat the fruit Satan
   offered, has led him to disobey God and ended their state of innocence. This language of
   woman hating is put under scrutiny several times in Wollstonecraft's text.

Disturbances on earth through female snares
And strait conjunction[1] with this sex. For either
He never shall find out fit mate but such
As some misfortune brings him, or mistake,   900
Or whom he wishes most shall seldom gain
Through her perverseness but shall see her gained
By a far worse or, if she love, withheld
By parents, or his happiest choice too late
Shall meet already linked and wedlock-bound   905
To a fell advérsary, his hate or shame,
Which infinite calamity shall cause
To human life and household peace confound.

* * *

JOHN LOCKE

From The Second Treatise of Civil Government[†]

From *Chapter IV.*

OF SLAVERY.

§ 22. The natural liberty of man is to be free from any superior
power on earth, and not to be under the will or legislative authority of
man, but to have only the law of nature for his rule. The liberty of
man, in society, is to be under no other legislative power, but that
established, by consent, in the commonwealth; nor under the dominion of any will, or restraint of any law, but what that legislative shall
enact, according to the trust put in it. Freedom, then, is not what sir
Robert Filmer tells us, "a liberty for everyone to do what he lists, to
live as he pleases, and not to be tied by any laws:"[1] but freedom of

---

1. "Forced union" [Teskey's note].
† John Locke (1632–1704) published his *Two Treatises* in 1689, the year after England's
Glorious Revolution, but wrote them as early as 1679, when justifying the people's right
to depose a tyrannical ruler was a particularly risky endeavor. In the account of the origins, extent, and aims of government that Locke offered, however, political legitimacy
rests on the consent of the governed, a consent that may always be withdrawn. Because
Locke referred to "natural" liberty and described freedom as inherent to human nature
itself rather than as a privilege attached to a particular social status, the *Second Treatise*
became a key document in the history of human rights—Locke's language is echoed in
Americans' Declaration of Independence and the French Revolutionaries' Declaration of
the Rights of Man and Citizen—as well as the history of constitutional government. The
text here reprints that of the Norton Critical Edition of *The Selected Political Writings of
John Locke*, edited by Paul E. Sigmund. All notes are the editor's.
1. Sir Robert Filmer is Locke's primary antagonist in his *First Treatise of Civil Government*,
which targets Filmer for supporting unchecked royal authority and denying that rulers
were answerable to the ruled. Here Locke quotes the 1679 reprint of Filmer's *Observations upon Aristotle's Politics* (first published 1652).

men under government is, to have a standing rule to live by, common to everyone of that society, and made by the legislative power erected in it; a liberty to follow my own will in all things, where the rule prescribes not; and not to be subject to the inconstant, uncertain, unknown, arbitrary will of another man: as freedom of nature is, to be under no other restraint but the law of nature.

* * *

From *Chapter XV.*

OF PATERNAL, POLITICAL, AND DESPOTICAL POWER,
CONSIDERED TOGETHER.

§ 169. Though I have had occasion to speak of these separately before, yet the great mistakes of late about government having, as I suppose, arisen from confounding these distinct powers one with another, it may not, perhaps, be amiss to consider them here together.[2]

§ 170. First, then, paternal or parental power is nothing but that which parents have over their children, to govern them for the children's good, till they come to the use of reason, or a state of knowledge, wherein they may be supposed capable to understand that rule, whether it be the law of nature, or the municipal law of their country, they are to govern themselves by: capable, I say, to know it, as well as several others, who live as freemen under that law. The affection and tenderness which God hath planted in the breast of parents towards their children, makes it evident, that this is not intended to be a severe arbitrary government, but only for the help, instruction, and preservation of their offspring. But happen it as it will, there is, as I have proved, no reason why it should be thought to extend to life and death, at any time, over their children, more than over any body else; neither can there be any pretence why this parental power should keep the child, when grown to a man, in subjection to the will of his parents, any farther than having received life and education from his parents, obliges him to respect, honour, gratitude, assistance, and support, all his life, to both father and mother. And thus, it is true, the paternal is a natural government, but not at all extending itself to the ends and jurisdictions of that which is political. The power of the father doth not reach at all to the property of the child, which is only in his own disposing.

---

2. Another reference to Filmer, who had proposed that kings inherited their right to rule from Adam and that their absolute power derived from the power that, as Genesis recorded, God granted to Adam as head of a family. Locke's *First Treatise* is devoted in part to disabling the analogies between fathers and kings and between families and states on which Filmer relies.

§ 171. Secondly, political power is that power which every man having in the state of nature, has given up into the hands of the society, and therein to the governors, whom the society hath set over itself, with this express or tacit trust, that it shall be employed for their good, and the preservation of their property: now this power, which every man has in the state of nature, and which he parts with to the society in all such cases where the society can secure him, is to use such means for the preserving of his own property as he thinks good, and nature allows him: and to punish the breach of the law of nature in others, so as (according to the best of his reason) may most conduce to the preservation of himself and the rest of mankind. So that the end and measure of this power, when in every man's hands in the state of nature, being the preservation of all of his society, that is, all mankind in general, it can have no other end or measure, when in the hands of the magistrate, but to preserve the members of that society in their lives, liberties, and possessions; and so cannot be an absolute arbitrary power over their lives and fortunes, which are as much as possible to be preserved; but a power to make laws, and annex such penalties to them, as may tend to the preservation of the whole, by cutting off those parts, and those only, which are so corrupt that they threaten the sound and healthy, without which no severity is lawful. And this power has its original only from compact and agreement, and the mutual consent of those who make up the community.

§ 172. Thirdly, despotical power is an absolute, arbitrary power one man has over another, to take away his life whenever he pleases. This is a power, which neither nature gives, for it has made no such distinction between one man and another, nor compact[3] can convey.

* * *

___

3. Contract.

MARY ASTELL

From Reflections upon Marriage[†]

From *Preface, In Answer to Some Objections*[1]

Far be it from her to stir up sedition of any sort, none can abhor it more; and she heartily wishes that our masters would pay their civil and ecclesiastical governors the same submission, which they themselves exact from their domestic subjects. Nor can she imagine how she any way undermines the masculine empire, or blows the trumpet of rebellion to the moiety of mankind.[2] Is it by exhorting women, not to expect to have their own will in any thing, but to be entirely submissive, when once they have made choice of a lord and master, though he happen not to be so wise, so kind, or even so just a governor as was expected? She did not indeed advise them to think his folly wisdom, nor his brutality that love and worship he promised in his matrimonial oath, for this required a flight of wit and sense much above her poor ability, and proper[3] only to masculine under-standings. However she did not in any manner prompt them to resist, or to abdicate the perjured spouse, though the laws of *God* and the land make special provision for it, in a case wherein, as is to be feared, few men can truly plead not guilty.[4]

'Tis true, through want of learning, and of that superior genius which men as men lay claim to, she was ignorant of the *natural infe-riority* of our sex, which our masters lay down as a self-evident and

---

† Although Mary Astell (1666–1731) was, in the view of several modern readers, England's first feminist, she was also an opponent of revolution, an advocate of absolute monarchy, and a critic of her culture's growing tolerance of religious dissent. Such Tory beliefs—founded on Astell's conviction that social subordination was divinely ordained and that unconditional obedience should be the human lot—complicate any simple understand-ing of what feminism might be. Revisiting the way in which marriage as union between man and woman had traditionally functioned in political thought as a metaphor for polit-ical association, the association between monarch and people included, *Some Reflections upon Marriage* targets the arguments that Astell's radical male contemporaries were mak-ing for liberty and the right to rebel. Astell assails their case by taking up their analogies, highlighting their refusal to include women in their arguments, and showing that there can be no logical foundation for women's exclusion. The byproduct of her pursuit of this argumentative strategy is a devastating, sometimes blackly humorous account of the arbi-trary power husbands were able to exercise over wives. (Astell herself never married.) The excerpts printed here are from the third edition of 1706, which Astell retitled *Reflections upon Marriage*. Astell's spelling, punctuation, and capitalization are modernized. All notes are the editor's.
1. Astell published *Reflections upon Marriage* anonymously, but in this preface, which she added in 1706, she manages, by speaking of herself in the third person, to confirm that she, the author, is a woman.
2. The female half of the population.
3. Belonging.
4. Civil and ecclesiastical law granted Englishwomen the right to petition for legal separa-tion, although not divorce, from husbands whose cruelty extended to physical abuse. "Abdicate": Abandon. "Perjured": Deceitful.

fundamental truth. She saw nothing in the reason of things to make this either a principle or a conclusion, but much to the contrary; it being sedition at least, if not treason, to assert it in this reign.[5] For if by the natural superiority of their sex, they mean that *every* man is by nature superior to *every* woman, which is the obvious meaning, and that which must be stuck to if they would speak sense, it would be a sin in *any* woman to have dominion over *any* man, and the greatest queen ought not to command but to obey her footman, because no municipal laws can supersede or change the law of nature;[6] so that if the dominion of the men be such, the *Salique Law,* as unjust as *Englishmen* have ever thought it, ought to take place over all the Earth, and the most glorious reigns in the *English, Danish, Castilian,* and other annals, were wicked violations of the law of nature![7]

* * *

That the custom of the world has put women, generally speaking, into a state of subjection, is not denied; but the right can no more be proved from the fact, than the predominancy of vice can justify it. A certain great man has endeavoured to prove by reasons not contemptible, that in the original state of things the woman was the superior,[8] and that her subjection to the man is an effect of the Fall, and the punishment of her sin. And that ingenious theorist Mr. *Whiston*[9] asserts, that before the Fall there was a greater equality between the two sexes. However this be, 'tis certainly no arrogance in a woman to conclude, that she was made for the service of *God,* and that this is her end. Because *God* made all things for Himself, and a rational mind is too noble a being to be made for the sake and service of any creature. The service she at any time becomes obliged to pay to a man, is only a business by the by. Just as it may be any man's business and duty to keep hogs; he was not made for this, but if he hires himself out to such an employment, he ought conscientiously to perform it.

* * *

5. In 1702 Queen Anne ascended to the English throne, succeeding her brother-in-law King William.
6. By referring to "the law of nature," Astell takes to its logical endpoint the Lockean position holding that natural law, independent of historical circumstances, should define what was right and just in society and serve as a measuring rod by which actual governments should be judged. She thereby sets a clever trap for her political opponents. Locke's *Two Treatises,* by offering an after-the-fact justification of the Revolution of 1688, had helped bring Queen Anne to the throne.
7. The Salic law, followed in France, by which women were excluded from ever inheriting the throne, was not applied in England, Denmark, or Castile (modern Spain), which had all been reigned over by queens.
8. Possibly the political philosopher Thomas Hobbes, referring to his account of how the sexes may have interacted in the state of nature, before civil society's institution of matrimonial law (*Leviathan* [1651], Chapter xx, "Of Dominion Paternal and Despotical").
9. William Whiston, author of *A New Theory of the Earth, From its Original, to the Consummation of All Things* (1696).

If mankind had never sinned, reason would always have been obeyed, there would have been no struggle for dominion, and brutal power would not have prevailed. But in the lapsed state of mankind, and now that men will not be guided by their reason but by their appetites, and do not what they *ought* but what they *can*, the reason, or that which stands for it, the will and pleasure, of the governor is to be the reason of those who will not be guided by their own, and must take place for order's sake, although it should not be conformable to right reason. Nor can there be any society great or little, from empires down to private families, without a last resort to determine the affairs of that society by an irresistible sentence.[1] Now unless this supremacy be fixed somewhere, there will be a perpetual contention about it, such is the love of dominion; and let the reason of things be what it may, those who have least force, or cunning to supply it,[2] will have the disadvantage. So that since women are acknowledged to have least bodily strength, their being commanded to obey is in pure kindness to them, and for their quiet and security, as well as for the exercise of their virtue. But does it follow that domestic governors have more sense than their subjects, any more than that other governors have? We do not find that any man thinks the worse of his own understanding because another has superior power; or concludes himself less capable of a post of honour and authority, because he is not preferred to it.

* * *

Again, if absolute sovereignty be not necessary in a state, how comes it to be so in a family? or if in a family why not in a state; since no reason can be alleged for the one that will not hold more strongly for the other? If the authority of the husband, so far as it extends, is sacred and inalienable, why not of the prince? The domestic sovereign is without dispute elected,[3] and the stipulations and contract are mutual. Is it not then partial[4] in men to the last degree, to contend for, and practise that arbitrary dominion in their families, which they abhor and exclaim against in the state? For if arbitrary power is evil in itself, and an improper method of governing rational and free agents, it ought not to be practised anywhere. Nor is it less, but rather more mischievous in families than in kingdoms, by how much 100,000 tyrants are worse than one. What though a husband can't deprive a wife of life without being responsible to the law, he may however do what is much more grievous to a generous mind,

---

1. I.e., every society, the society of the family included, must invest power in some authority that will have the final word in arbitrating contentions.
2. Occupy the role of supreme power.
3. Husbands are "elected" in so far as their wives have consented to wed them.
4. Biased.

render life miserable, for which she has no redress, scarce pity which is afforded to every other complainant, it being thought a wife's duty to suffer every thing without complaint. If all *men are born free*, how is it that all women are born slaves? as they must be if the being subjected to the *inconstant, uncertain, unknown, arbitrary will* of men, be the *perfect condition of slavery*? and if the essence of freedom consists, as our masters say it does, in having a *standing rule to live by*?[5] And why is slavery so much condemned and strove against in one case, so highly applauded, and held so necessary and so sacred in another?

* * *

Reflections upon Marriage[6]

For pray, what do men propose to themselves in marriage? What qualifications do they look after in a spouse? What will she bring? is the first enquiry: How many acres? Or how much ready coin? Not that this is altogether an unnecessary question, for marriage without a competency, that is, not only a bare subsistence, but even a handsome and plentiful provision, according to the quality[7] and circumstances of the parties, is no very comfortable condition. They who marry for love, as they call it, find time enough to repent their rash folly, and are not long in being convinced, that whatever fine speeches might be made in the heat of passion, there could be no *real kindness* between those who can agree to make each other miserable. But as an estate is to be considered, so it should not be the *main*, much less the *only* consideration, for happiness does not depend on wealth. *That* may be wanting, and too often is, where *this* abounds. He who marries himself to a fortune only, must expect no other satisfaction than that can bring him, but let him not say that marriage, but that his own covetous or prodigal temper, has made him unhappy. * * *

Few men have so much goodness as to bring themselves to a liking of what they loathed, merely because it is their duty to like; on the contrary, when they marry with an indifferency, to please their friends or increase their fortune, the indifferency proceeds to an aversion, and perhaps even the kindness and complaisance of the poor abused wife shall only serve to increase it. What follows then? There is no content at home, so it is sought elsewhere, and the fortune so unjustly got is as carelessly squandered. The man takes

---

5. Astell's italicized phrases cite John Locke's definitions of slavery and freedom (*Second Treatise*, Chapter iv, paras. 22 and 24).
6. In the passages reprinted here, Astell speculates as to why so many marriages are unhappy.
7. Rank in society. "Competency": sufficient income.

a loose,[8] what should hinder him? He has all in his hands, and custom has almost taken off that small restraint reputation used to lay. The wife finds too late what was the idol the man adored, which her vanity perhaps, or it may be the commands and importunities of relations, would not let her see before; and now he has got *that* into his possession, she must make court to him for a little sorry alimony out of her own estate.[9] If discretion and piety prevail upon her passions she sits down quietly, contented with her lot, seeks no consolation in the multitude of adorers, since he whom only she desired to please, because it was her duty to do so, will take no delight in her wit or beauty. She follows no diversion to allay her grief, uses no cordials to support her spirit, that may sully her virtue or bring a cloud upon her reputation, she makes no appeals to the misjudging crowd, hardly mentions her misfortunes to her most intimate acquaintance, nor lays a load on her husband to ease herself, but would if it were possible conceal his crimes. * * * Nor does she in her retirements reflect so much upon the hand that administers this bitter cup, as consider what is the best use she can make of it. And thus indeed marriage, however unfortunate in other respects, becomes a very great blessing to her. She might have been exposed to all the temptations of a plentiful fortune, have given up herself to sloth and luxury, and gone on at the common rate even of the better sort, in doing no hurt, and as little good. But now her kind husband obliges her to *consider,* and gives opportunity to exercise her virtue; he makes it necessary to withdraw from those gaieties and pleasures of life, which do more mischief under the show of innocence, than they could if they appeared attended with a crime, discomposing and dissolving the mind, and making it incapable of any manner of good, to be sure of anything great and excellent. Silence and solitude, the being forced from the ordinary entertainments of her station, may perhaps seem a desolate condition at first, and we may allow her, poor weak woman! to be somewhat shocked at it, since even a wise and courageous man perhaps would not keep his ground. We would conceal if we could for the honour of the sex, men's being baffled and dispirited by a smaller matter, were not the instances too frequent and too notorious.

But a little time wears off all the uneasiness, and puts her in possession of pleasures, which till now she has unkindly been kept a stranger to. Affliction, the sincerest friend, the frankest monitor, the best instructor, and indeed the only useful school that women are ever put to, rouses her understanding, opens her eyes, fixes her

---

8. Gives himself up to indulgence.
9. The common law of England automatically assigned a woman's property to her husband after their marriage.

attention, and diffuses such a light, such a joy into her mind, as not only informs her better, but entertains her more than ever her *ruel*[1] did though crowded by the men of wit. She now distinguishes between truth and appearances, between solid and apparent good, has found out the instability of all earthly things, and won't anymore be deceived by relying on them, can discern who are the flatterers of her fortune, and who the admirers and encouragers of her virtue, accounting it no little blessing to be rid of those leeches, who only hung upon her for their own advantage. Now sober thoughts succeed to hurry and impertinence, to forms and ceremony, she can secure her time, and knows how to improve it; never truly a happy woman till she came in the eye of the world to be reckoned miserable.

Thus the husband's vices may become an occasion of the wife's virtues.

* * *

But do the women never choose amiss? Are the men only in fault? that is not pretended:[2] for he who will be just must be forced to acknowledge that neither sex are always in the right. A woman indeed can't properly be said to choose; all that is allowed her, is to refuse or accept what is offered. And when we have made such reasonable allowances as are due to the sex, perhaps they may not appear so much in fault as one would at first imagine, and a generous spirit will find more occasion to pity, than to reprove. But sure I transgress—it must not be supposed that the ladies can do amiss! he is but an ill-bred fellow who pretends that they need amendment! They are no doubt on it always in the right, and most of all when they take pity on distressed lovers! whatever they *say* carries an authority that no reason can resist, and all that they *do* must needs be exemplary! This is the modish language, nor is there a man of honour amongst the whole tribe that would not venture his life, nay, and his salvation too in their defence, if any but himself attempts to injure them. But I must ask pardon if I can't come up to these heights, nor flatter them with the having no faults, which is only a malicious way of continuing and increasing their mistakes.

Women, it's true, ought to be treated with civility; for since a little ceremony and outside respect is all their guard, all the privilege that's allowed them, it were barbarous to deprive them of it; and because I would treat them civilly, I would not express my civility at the usual rate. I would not, under pretence of honouring and paying a mighty deference to the ladies, call them fools to their faces; for what are all the fine speeches and submissions that are made, but an

---

1. A lady's morning reception, from the French word for the space in a bedroom between the bedside and the wall.
2. Claimed.

abusing them in a well-bred way? She must be a fool with a witness, who can believe a man, proud and vain as he is, will lay his boasted authority, the dignity and prerogative of his sex, one moment at her feet but[3] in prospect of taking it up again to more advantage; he may call himself her slave a few days, but it is only in order to make her his all the rest of his life.

3. Except.

Education

In her article on the shifting ways in which audiences during the 1790s responded to the *Vindication of the Rights of Woman*, Regina M. Janes observes that initially many of Wollstonecraft's readers appear to have found her argument both familiar and uncontroversial (see the Bibliography). It was only after Wollstonecraft died in 1797 and her husband, William Godwin, published his tactless, tell-all memoir of his late wife in 1798 that the radical proposals the *Vindication* makes for altering the relative positions of the sexes and so altering British society came to overshadow the book's account of the shortcomings in the contemporary practices of female education. Education was indeed a much discussed topic during Wollstonecraft's lifetime, a time often said to have discovered childhood as a meaningful phase of life and marked by its faith in the malleability of the mind. The topic attracted male and female writers across the political spectrum, and books on female education, especially, could sell very well, as Wollstonecraft evidently realized when, in 1787, she elected to begin her career as woman of letters by authoring *Thoughts on the Education of Daughters*. It is unsurprising therefore that readers were halfway inclined to view her second *Vindication* as simply another contribution to an ongoing discussion.

The following selection of texts suggests the diverging ways in which Wollstonecraft's predecessors and contemporaries connected questions about social reform to questions about the formation of the mind. The readings indicate, in particular, how much conflict there was over the place that girls might occupy in the enlightened schemes that, following the example both of John Locke's *Second Treatise* and of his even more influential *Some Thoughts Concerning Education*, envisioned education as a preparation for active citizenship. Writers of improving texts and conduct manuals for girls largely succeeded in arguing that young women required a more serious education than they normally received, if only as a preparation for their roles as wives and mothers. The pressures of the marriage market helped establish some instruction as the norm for middle-class girls. But many issues remained uncertain: for a start, the question of whether (as many authors put it) "the mind had a sex" or whether the apparent difference between the sexes' mental capacities was produced by social institutions rather than being ordained by God or nature.

JOHN LOCKE

From Some Thoughts Concerning Education[†]

§41 We must look upon our Children, when grown up, to be like ourselves, with the same Passions, the same Desires. We would be thought Rational Creatures, and have our Freedom; we love not to be uneasy under constant Rebukes and Brow-beatings; nor can we bear severe Humours and great Distance in those we converse with. Whoever has such treatment when he is a Man, will look out other Company, other Friends, other Conversation, with whom he can be at Ease. * * *

§42 Thus much for the Settling your Authority over your Children in general. Fear and Awe ought to give you the first Power over their Minds, and Love and Friendship in riper Years to hold it: For the Time must come, when they will be past the Rod, and Correction; and then, if the Love of you make them not obedient and dutiful, if the Love of Virtue and Reputation keep them not in Laudable Courses, I ask, what Hold will you have upon them to turn them to it?

* * *

§45 He that has not a Mastery over his Inclinations, he that knows not how to *resist* the Importunity of *present Pleasure or Pain*, for the sake of what Reason tells him is fit to be done, wants the true

---

[†] The impact of Locke's *Some Thoughts Concerning Education*, published in 1693 and reissued throughout the eighteenth century, was tremendous. What seemed novel in Locke's scheme was the liberty it accorded children: Locke insisted that the end point of education was the independence the child would be entitled to claim on attaining the age of reason. That ideal was attractive enough to Wollstonecraft that she cites *Some Thoughts* on p. 163 herein. Locke himself never addressed the socialization of girls except to state in article 6 that "I have said *he* here, because the principal aim of my Discourse, is how a young Gentleman should be brought up from his Infancy, which, in all things, will not so perfectly suit the Education of *Daughters*." Recapitulating Locke's emphasis on self-determination indeed proved tricky for subsequent writers on female education, who often ended up arguing that the woman whose mind had been cultivated would be more capable of self-control than the woman whose upbringing had been neglected and would be readier to reconcile herself to the narrow horizons of life inside the domestic sphere.

The articles excerpted here are from the fifth edition of *Some Thoughts* (1705), the last Locke oversaw. All notes and modernized spellings are the editor's.

Principle of Virtue and Industry, and is in Danger never to be good for anything. This Temper therefore, so contrary to unguided Nature, is to be got betimes; and this Habit, as the true foundation of future Ability and Happiness, is to be wrought into the Mind, as early as may be, even from the first dawnings of any Knowledge, or Apprehension in Children; and so to be confirmed in them, by all the Care and Ways imaginable, by those who have the Over-sight of their Education.

§46 On the other side, if the *Mind* be curbed, and *humbled* too much in Children; if their *Spirits* be abased and *broken* much, by too strict an Hand over them, they lose all their Vigor and Industry, and are in a worse State than the former. For extravagant young Fellows, that have Liveliness and Spirit, come sometimes to be set right, and so make Able and Great Men; but *dejected Minds*, timorous and tame, and *low Spirits*, are hardly ever to be raised, and very seldom attain to any thing. To avoid the Danger that is on either hand, is the great Art; and he that has found a way, how to keep up a Child's Spirit, easy, active and free; and yet at the same time, to restrain him from many things, he has a Mind to, and to draw him to things that are uneasy to him; he, I say, that knows how to reconcile these seeming Contradictions, has, in my Opinion, got the true Secret of Education.

§47 The usual lazy and short way by Chastisement, and the Rod, which is the only Instrument of Government that Tutors generally know, or ever think of, is the most unfit of any to be used in Education; because it tends to both those Mischiefs; which, as we have shown, are the *Scylla* and *Charybdis*, which on the one Hand or the other, ruin all that miscarry.[1]

* * *

§49 This sort of Correction naturally breeds an Aversion to that, which 'tis the Tutor's Business to create a liking to. How obvious is it to observe, that Children come to hate things which were at first acceptable to them, when they find themselves *whipped*, and *chid*, and *teased* about them? And it is not to be wondered at in them, when grown Men would not be able to be reconciled to any thing by such Ways. Who is there that would not be disgusted with any innocent Recreation, in itself indifferent to him, if he should with *Blows*, or ill Language be *haled*[2] to it, when he had no Mind?

---

1. Locke's metaphor alludes to the evil spirits who in classical mythology menaced travelers traversing the Strait of Sicily. Scylla rolled rocks onto passing ships, while Charybdis created a whirlpool able to suck those same ships into the depths of the sea.
2. Hauled.

Or be constantly so treated, for some Circumstance in his Application to it? This is natural to be so. Offensive Circumstances ordinarily infect innocent things which they are joined with: And the very sight of a Cup, wherein any one uses to take nauscous Physick, turns his Stomach, so that nothing will relish well out of it, tho' the Cup be never so clean, and well shaped, and of the richest Materials.[3]

§50 Such a sort of *slavish Discipline* makes a *slavish Temper.* The Child submits and dissembles Obedience, whilst the Fear of the Rod hangs over him; but when that is removed, and by being out of sight, he can promise himself Impunity, he gives the greater Scope to his natural Inclination; which by this way is not at all altered, but, on the contrary, heightened and increased in him, and after such restraint, breaks out usually with the more Violence.

* * *

§108 If * * * they accustom themselves early to silence their Desires, this useful habit will settle in them; and as they come to grow up in Age and Discretion, they may be allowed greater liberty; when Reason comes to speak in them, and not Passion.[4] For whenever Reason would speak, it should be hearkened to. But as they should never be heard, when they speak, for any particular thing they would *have*, unless it be first proposed to them; so they should always be heard, and fairly and kindly answered, when they ask after any thing they would *know*, and desire to be informed about. *Curiosity* should be as carefully *cherished* in Children, as other Appetites suppressed.

However strict an hand is to be kept upon all desires of Fancy, yet there is one case wherein Fancy must be permitted to speak, and be hearkened to also. *Recreation* is as necessary, as Labour, or Food. But because there can be no *Recreation* without Delight, which depends not always on Reason, but oftener on Fancy, it must be permitted Children not only to divert themselves, but to do it after their own fashion; provided it be innocently and without prejudice to their Health: And therefore in this case they should not be denied, if they proposed any particular kind of *Recreation.* Though, I think, in a well-ordered Education, they will seldom be brought to the necessity of asking any such liberty. Care should be taken, that what is of Advantage to them, they should always do with delight; and before

---

3. Locke articulates here the principle that elsewhere he called "the association of ideas" and identified as a chief cause of error in reasoning (*Essay Concerning Human Understanding*, II, xxxiii). Wollstonecraft engages the principle, key to the formation of good habits as well as bad, in Chapter 6 of the *Rights of Woman.* "Physick": medicine.
4. Just before this passage Locke urges his readers to train children in the habit of self-denial by responding in the negative when they ask for things they crave rather than things they need.

they are wearied with one, they should be timely *diverted* to some other useful Employment. But if they are not yet brought to that degree of Perfection, that one way of Improvement can be made a *Recreation* to them, they must be let loose to the childish Play they fancy; which they should be weaned from, by being made Surfeit of it. * * *

This farther Advantage may be made by a free liberty permitted them in their *Recreations*, That it will discover their Natural Tempers, show their Inclinations, and Aptitudes; and thereby direct wise Parents in the choice, both of the Course of Life, and Employment they shall design them for, and of fit Remedies in the meantime to be applied to whatever bent of Nature, they may observe most likely to mislead any of their Children.

MARY ASTELL

From A Serious Proposal to the Ladies[†]
* * *

For since GOD has given Women as well as Men intelligent Souls, why should they be forbidden to improve them? Since he has not denied us the faculty of Thinking, why shou'd we not (at least in gratitude to him) employ our Thoughts on himself their noblest Object, and not unworthily bestow them on Trifles and Gaities and secular Affairs? Being the Soul was created for the contemplation of Truth as well as for the fruition of Good, is it not as cruel and unjust to exclude Women from the knowledge of the one as from the enjoyment of the other? Especially since the Will is blind, and cannot chuse but by the direction of the Understanding; or to speak more properly, since the Soul always *Wills* according as she *Understands*, so that if she Understands amiss, she Wills amiss. And as Exercise enlarges and exalts any Faculty, so thro' want of using it becomes crampt and lessened; if therefore we make little or no use of our Understandings, we shall shortly have none to use; and the more contracted and unemploy'd the deliberating and directive Power is, the more liable is the

---

† The full title of Mary Astell's first book, published in 1694, with a sequel following in 1697, reads *A Serious Proposal to the Ladies, For the Advancement of Their True and Greatest Interest*. Custom confines ladies to trivial pursuits, dressing and dancing, for instance, but your *true* interest, Astell tells her female reader, is instead to "employ your care about that which is really your *self* . . . that particle of Divinity within you." Astell's tract on women's education is famous for its vision of a network of female academies that would provide ladies of quality with an alternative to participation in the marriage market. In these havens (satirized as "Protestant nunneries" by Astell's detractors) Astell hoped that women might find the opportunities for mental improvement all but denied them in the world. The text here is the 1970 Source Book Press reprint of the 1701 edition that put Parts I and II of the *Serious Proposal* back to back: I, pp. 18–20 and II, pp. 129–31. All notes are the editor's.

elective to unworthy and mischievous choices. What is it but the want
of an ingenious Education,[1] that renders the generality of Feminine
Conversations so insipid and foolish and their solitude so insupport-
able? Learning is therefore necessary to render them more agreeable
and useful in company, and to furnish them with becoming entertainments when alone, that so they may not be driven to those miserable
shifts,[2] which too many make use of to put off their Time, that precious Talent that never lies on the hands of a judicious Person. And
since our Happiness in the next World, depends so far on those dispositions which we carry along with us out of this, that without a right
habitude and temper of mind we are not capable of Felicity; and seeing our Beatitude consists in the contemplation of the divine Truth
and Beauty, as well as in the fruition of his Goodness, can Ignorance
be a fit preparative for heaven? Is't likely that she whose Understanding has been busied about nothing but froth and trifles, shou'd be
capable of delighting her self in noble and sublime Truths? Let such
therefore as deny us the improvement of our Intellectuals, either take
up *his* Paradox, who said that *Women have no Souls*, which at a time
when the most contend to have them allow'd to Brutes, wou'd be as
unphilosophical as it is unmannerly, or else let them permit us to cultivate and improve them. There is a sort of Learning indeed which is
worse than the greatest Ignorance: A Woman may study Plays and
Romances all her days, and be a great deal more knowing but never a
jot the wiser. Such a knowledge as this serves only to instruct and put
her forward in the practice of the greatest Follies, yet how can they
justly blame her who forbid, or at least won't afford opportunity of
better? A rational mind *will* be employ'd, it will never be satisfy'd in
doing nothing, and if you neglect to furnish it with good materials, 'tis
like to take up with such as come to hand.

We pretend not that Women shou'd teach in the Church, or usurp
Authority where it is not allow'd them; permit us only to understand
our *own* duty, and not be forc'd to take it upon trust from others; to
be at least so far learned, as to be able to form in our minds a true
Idea of Christianity, it being so very necessary to fence us against the
danger of these *last* and *perilous days*, in which Deceivers a part of
whose Character is to *lead captive silly Women*, need not *creep into
Houses* since they have Authority to proclaim their Errors on the
House top.[3] And let us also acquire a true Practical knowledge, such

---

1. Astell may be referring to an education that is intellectually challenging or, drawing on
another obsolete sense of the word *ingenious*, to one that befits well-born persons
(e.g., the *ladies*—not *women*—of her book's title).
2. Expedients.
3. See 2 Timothy 3:6: "For of this sort are they which creep into houses, and lead captive
silly women laden with sins, led away with divers lusts"; and Luke 12:3: "Therefore what-
soever ye have spoken in darkness shall be heard in the light; and that which ye have spoken in the ear in closets shall be proclaimed upon the housetops."

as will convince us of the absolute necessity of *Holy Living* as well as of *Right Believing*, and that no Heresy is more dangerous than that of an ungodly and wicked Life. And since the *French Tongue* is understood by most Ladies, methinks they may much better improve it by the study of Philosophy (as I hear the *French Ladies* do) *des Cartes, Malebranche*[4] and others, than by reading idle *Novels* and *Romances*. 'Tis strange we shou'd be so forward to imitate their Fashions and Fopperies, and have no regard to what really deserves our Imitation. And why shall it not be thought as genteel to understand *French Philosophy*, as to be accoutred in a *French Mode?* Let therefore the famous Madam *D'acier, Scudery,* &c, and our own imcomparable *Orinda,* excite the Emulation of the English Ladies.[5]

The Ladies, I'm sure, have no reason to dislike this Proposal, but I know not how the Men will resent it to have their enclosure broke down, and Women invited to taste of that Tree of knowledge they have so long unjustly *Monopoliz'd.* But they must excuse me, if I be as partial to my own Sex as they are to theirs, and think Women as capable of Learning as Men are, and that it becomes them as well. For I cannot imagine wherein the hurt lies, if instead of doing mischief to one another, by an uncharitable and vain Conversation, Women be enabled to inform and instruct those of their own Sex at least; the Holy Ghost having left it on record, that *Priscilla* as well as her Husband, catechiz'd the eloquent *Apollos* and the great Apostle found no fault with her.[6] It will therefore be very proper for our

4. Nicolas de Malébranche (1638–1715) was a French theologian who attempted to reconcile Descartes's premises about the structure of thought with Christian teaching, explaining cognition as a function of humans' receptivity to divine ideas. Author of the famous formula "I think, therefore I am," French philosopher and mathematician René Descartes (1596–1650) is often viewed in the history of philosophy as the founder of modern epistemology, advocate of a method in which truth was to be discovered by progressive, rational deduction. Cartesianism was a fashionable topic of conversation in the salons presided over by Frenchwomen in the late seventeenth century. The fact that Descartes was known to have developed many of his ideas in conversation with women, in the letters he exchanged with Princess Elizabeth of Bohemia, for example, likely enhanced the status his philosophy enjoyed in those circles. His account of the relation of mind and body also seemed to give proponents of gender equality a firm philosophical foundation for their argument that the mind had no sex.
5. At a time when learning Greek and Latin was proscribed for girls, even as it was a staple of the education of elite boys, Anne Dacier (1654–1720) was admired for her translations into French of Homer's *Iliad* and *Odyssey*. Another Frenchwoman, Madeleine de Scudéry (1607–1701) was the author of several multivolume romances imagining heroic deeds and gallant love in exotic Mediterranean settings. The Englishwoman Katherine Philips (1631–1664) was the poet known as the "Matchless Orinda"; many of her poems were written in praise of female friendship and Platonic love.
6. Priscilla (or Prisca) is mentioned six times in the New Testament, always in conjunction with her husband, Aquila, a Jew who had been expelled from Rome. Prominent in the early church, they accompanied Paul to Ephesus where they taught Apollos, "an eloquent man, well-versed in the faith." Their house was often used for Christian worship, and Paul always speaks of them with affection.

Ladies to spend part of their time in this Retirement, in adorning their minds with useful Knowledge.

* * *

And indeed as unnecessary as it is thought for Women to have Knowledge, she who is truly good finds very great use of it, not only in the Conduct of her own Soul but in the managment of her Family, in the Conversation of her Neighbours and in all the Concerns of Life.[7] Education of Children is a most necessary Employment, perhaps the chief of those who have any; But it is as Difficult as it is Excellent when well perform'd; and I question not but that the mistakes which are made in it, are a principal Cause of that Folly and Vice, which is so much complain'd of and so little mended. Now this, at least the foundation of it, on which in a great measure the success of all depends, shou'd be laid by the Mother, for Fathers find other Business, they will not be confin'd to such laborious work, they have not such opportunities of observing a Childs Temper, nor are the greatest part of 'em like to do much good, since Precepts contradicted by Example seldom prove effectual. Neither are Strangers so proper for it, because hardly any thing besides Paternal Affection can sufficiently quicken the Care of performing, and sweeten the labour of such a task. But Tenderness alone will never discharge it well, she who wou'd do it to purpose must throughly understand Human nature, know how to manage different Tempers Prudently, be Mistress of her own, and able to bear with all the little humours and follies of Youth, neither Severeity nor Lenity[8] are to be always us'd, it wou'd ruin some to be treated in that manner which is fit for others. As Mildness makes some ungovernable, and as there is a stupor in many from which nothing but Terrors can rouse them, so sharp Reproofs and Solemn Lectures serve to no purpose but to harden others, in faults from which they might be won by an agreeable Address and tender application. GOD himself waits to be gracious and administers his Medicines in the most proper season, and Parents shou'd imitate him in this, for the want of observing it, and of accommodating their Methods to the several Dispositions they have to deal with, is perhaps the reason that many Pious Persons lose the fruit of their Pains and Care.

Nor will Knowledge lie dead upon their hands who have no Children to Instruct; the whole World is a single Ladys Family, her opportunities of doing good are not lessen'd but encreas'd by her being unconfin'd. Particular Obligations do not contract her Mind, but her Beneficence moves in the largest Sphere. And perhaps the Glory of Reforming this Prophane and Profligate Age is reserv'd for

---

7. This excerpt is from Part II, Chapter 3, "Concerning the Improvement of the Understanding."
8. Mildness or gentleness.

you Ladies, and that the natural and unprejudic'd Sentiments of your Minds being handsomly express'd, may carry a more strong conviction than the Elaborate Arguments of the Learned. Such as fence themselves against the Cannon they bring down, may lie open to an Ambuscade[9] from you. And whilst the strong arguings of the Schools like the Wind in the Fable, seems but to harden these Sturdy Sinners, your Persuasions like the Suns mild and powerful rays, may oblige them to cast off that Cloak of Maliciousness in which they are so much intangled. And surely it is worth your while to fit your selves for this: Tis a Godlike thing to relieve even the Temporal wants of our Fellow Creatures, to keep a *Body* from perishing, but it is much more Divine, to *Save a Soul from Death!* * * *

JEAN-JACQUES ROUSSEAU

From Emilius and Sophia; or, A New System of Education[†]

Book v, Sophia
* * *

It is not good for man to be alone; and Emilius is now a man: we have promised him also a companion, who must therefore now be given him. This companion is Sophia. But, in what asylum is she to be found? To discover where she is, it is necessary she should first be known. When we are made acquainted with her character, we shall

9. Ambush. A woman's strong and clear reasoning might be effective against a man who has defended himself by sophistical arguments.
† In his influential 1762 response to Locke's *Some Thoughts Concerning Education*, the philosopher Jean-Jacques Rousseau (1712–1778) aimed to model, through the story of a boy named Émile, an educational program that would allow man's natural goodness to develop, uncorrupted by social influences. Rousseau's principles were adopted enthusiastically by revolutionary politicians in France, who sought to create a political order in which Émile's virtues would be those of the nation, or at least the male nation. Wollstonecraft's first reading of *Émile* was also approving. She declared in a letter dated March 24, 1787, to her sister Everina that she was in love with Rousseau's "paradoxes": "He was a strange inconsistent unhappy clever creature—yet he possessed an uncommon portion of sensibility and penetration" (*Collected Letters*, ed. Janet Todd, pp. 114–15). Wollstonecraft was less charmed, however, by the education Rousseau offered to girls in the work's fifth, concluding book, which registered his belief that girls should be accustomed early to constraint. The excerpt from that book printed here represents Rousseau's response to contemporaries who were calling for girls and boys to be educated alike. His terms make apparent his belief both in women's natural inferiority—their natural artificiality, in fact—and in the menace female sexual power poses to men's self-control and to social order more generally. The text is taken from Volume IV, Book v of William Kenrick's 1762 translation *Emilius and Sophia: or, A New System of Education*, pp. 1–13. All notes are the editor's unless otherwise indicated. Page references to Wollstonecraft refer to the present edition.

be the better able to judge of her habitation; not that when we have found her, our task is at an end. Mr. Locke closes his treatise on education with observing, that, as his young gentleman is fit to be married, it is time to leave him with his mistress. For my own part, as I have not the honour to educate a gentleman, I shall beware of imitating Mr. Locke in this particular.

Sophia should be such a woman, as Emilius is a man; that is, she should possess every thing requisite in the constitution of her species and sex, to fill her place in the physical and moral order of things. To know whether she be so qualified, we shall enter first on an examination into the various instances of conformity and difference between her sex and ours.

In every thing which does not regard the sex, woman is the same as man; she has the same organs, the same necessities, the same faculties: the corporeal machine is constructed in the same manner, its component parts are alike, their operation the same, and the figure similar in both; in whatever light we regard them, they differ from each other only in degree.

On the other hand, in every thing immediately respecting sex, the woman differs entirely from the man; the difficulty of comparing them together, lying in our inability to determine what are those particulars in the constitution of each that immediately relate to the sex. From their comparative anatomy, and even from simple inspection, we perceive some general distinctions between them, that do not appear to relate to sex; and yet there can be no doubt that they do, although we are not capable of tracing their modes of relation. Indeed we know not how far the difference of sex may extend. All that we know, of a certainty, is that whatever is common to both is only characteristic of their species; and that every thing in which they differ, is distinctive of their sex. Under this two-fold consideration, we find so much resemblance and dissimilitude that it appears even miraculous, that nature should form two beings so much alike, and, at the same time, so very different.

This difference and similitude must necessarily have an influence over their moral character: such an influence is, indeed, obvious, and perfectly agreeable to experience; clearly demonstrating the vanity of the disputes that have been held concerning the superiority or equality of the sexes; as if, in answering the different ends for which nature designed them, both were not more perfect than they would be in more nearly resembling each other. In those particulars which are common to both, they are equal; and as to those wherein they differ, no comparison is to be made between them. A perfect man and a complete woman should no more resemble each other in mind than in feature; nor is their perfection reducible to any common standard.

In the union of the sexes, both pursue one common object, but not in the same manner.[1] From their diversity in this particular, arises the first determinate difference between the moral relations of each. The one should be active and strong, the other passive and weak: it is necessary the one should have both the power and the will, and that the other should make little resistance.

This principle being established, it follows that woman is expressly formed to please the man: if the obligation be reciprocal also, and the man ought to please in his turn, it is not so immediately necessary: his great merit lies in his power, and he pleases merely because he is strong. This, I must confess, is not one of the refined maxims of love; it is, however, one of the laws of nature, prior to love itself.

If woman be formed to please and to be subjected to man, it is her place doubtless to render herself agreeable to him, instead of challenging his passion. This violence of his desires depends on her charms; it is by means of these she should urge him to the exertion of those powers which nature hath given him. The most successful method of exciting them is, to render such exertion necessary by her resistance; as in that case, self-love is added to desire, and the one triumphs in the victory which the other obliged him to acquire. Hence arise the various modes of attack and defence between the sexes, the boldness of one sex and the timidity of the other; and, in a word, that bashfulness and modesty with which nature hath armed the weak, in order to subdue the strong.

Can it ever be thought that she[2] hath dictated indifferently the same advances to one as the other, and that the first to form desires should be also the first to display them? What a strange mistake in judgment must be such a conclusion! Their intercourse being productive of consequences so very different to each, can it be natural for both to engage in the mutual conflict with the same readiness and intrepidity? Is it not very evident that, from their unequal waste in the encounter, if reserve did not impose on one the same moderation as nature imposes on the other, the consequence would soon be fatal to both, and that the human race would be brought to destruction by the very means established by nature for its preservation? Considering the influence of women over the passions of men, and how readily they can affect even the remains of an almost exhausted constitution, it is plain that, if there were an unhappy climate on earth, whence philosophy had banished all female reserve, the men, subjected to the tyranny of the women, would be soon sacrificed to

---

1. This paragraph and the two following are quoted in full in the note Wollstonecraft supplies for p. 52. These paragraphs, she claims set out a "philosophy of lasciviousness."
2. Nature.

their charms; particularly in hot countries, where are born more women than men, the latter would all be hurried presently to their graves, without any possibility of helping themselves.

That the females of animals have not the same modesty and reserve, makes nothing against my argument; as their desires are not, like those of women, left without restriction. In the latter, their reserve supplies the place of a physical restraint; while the former have no desires but what arise from physical necessity.[3] This being satisfied, their desire ceases; they no longer repulse the male in appearance,[4] but in reality; acting contrary to the daughter of Augustus, they receive no more passengers on board when the vessel hath compleated its cargo.[5] Even when they are salacious, their time is short and presently over; instinct urges them on, and instinct restrains them. What substitute could be found for this negative instinct, in women, if you deprive them of modesty? To expect that they should have no inclination towards the man, is to expect them to be good for nothing.

The supreme Being intended in every case to do honour to the human species: in leaving the desires of man unlimited, he gave him, at the same time, the law of reason for their regulation, in order that he might be free to command himself: in leaving the passions of woman also unrestrained, he gave her modesty to restrain them. To these he hath further added an actual recompence for the regular use of their respective faculties; to wit, the delight which is taken in modesty, when such is made the standard of our actions. All this appears to me more than equivalent to instinct in brutes.

Whether the female, therefore, of our species, be inclined to gratify the desires of the male or not, she is by nature constantly coy, and betrays a seeming reluctance to yield to his embraces. She does not resist or defend herself, however, always with the same resolution, nor of course with the same success. In order that the assailant should be victorious, it is necessary that the assailed should permit or direct the attack: for of how many artful means is not the latter possessed to compel the former to exert himself? The most free and delightful of all actions admits not of any real violence; both nature and reason are against it; nature, in that she hath provided the

3. I.e., sexual appetite is a matter of biology for female animals and is limited by nature (who has arranged for them to go into heat only at intervals). In women, by contrast, modesty alone puts the brakes on desire.
4. "I have already remarked that shyness and an affected aversion to the males, are common to the females of every species of animals; and that even when they are most disposed to admit their caresses. One must have paid no attention to their actions to doubt of this" [Rousseau's note].
5. Julia, daughter of Augustus, first emperor of Rome, and wife to his lieutenant, Agrippa, was notorious for her sexual promiscuity. Her declaration that she took lovers (received passengers) only when pregnant is reported by Pierre de Bourdeille, Sieur de Brantôme, whose *Vie des dames galantes* (1666) is likely Rousseau's source.

weakest party with sufficient force to make an effectual resistance, when she pleases; and reason, in that real violence on such an occasion, is not only the most brutal of all actions, but the most contrary to its end and design; both because that, by such means, the man declares war against his companion, and thus authorises her to stand up in defence of her person and liberty, even at the hazard of the life of the aggressor; and also because, that the woman is the only proper judge of her own situation, and that a child would have no father, if every man were at liberty to usurp the rights of a husband.

Hence we deduce a third consequence from the different constitutions of the sexes; which is, that the strongest should be master in appearance, and be dependent in fact on the weakest; and that not from any frivolous practice of gallantry, or vanity of protectorship, but from an invariable law of nature, which, furnishing woman with a greater facility to excite desires than she has given man to satisfy them, makes the latter dependent on the good pleasure of the former, and compels him to endeavour to please in his turn, in order to obtain her consent that he should be strongest.[6] On these occasions, the most delightful circumstance a man finds in his victory is, to doubt whether it was the woman's weakness that yielded to his superior strength, or whether her inclinations spoke in his favour: the females are also generally artful enough to leave this matter in doubt. The understanding of women answers, in this respect, perfectly to their constitution: so far from being ashamed of their weakness, they glory in it; their tender muscles make no resistance; they affect to be incapable of lifting the smallest burthens, and would blush to be thought robust and strong. To what purpose is all this? Not merely for the sake of appearing delicate, but through an artful precaution: it is thus they provide an excuse beforehand, and a right to be feeble when they think it expedient.

The progress of our knowledge, increased by our vices, hath made the opinion of the moderns on this head very different from that of the ancients; and we hardly ever hear talk of rapes, as they are become so little necessary, and are no longer credited:[7] whereas they were very common in the earliest ages of the Greeks and Hebrews, because such notions were agreeable to the simplicity of nature, and are such as experienced libertinism only can eradicate. If we have

---

6. Wollstonecraft cites this paragraph on p. 84. Rousseau's speculation that women pretend to be overcome in sexual encounters that they have actually desired might also inspire Wollstonecraft on p. 133, where she expresses outrage over how both Rousseau and John Gregory "desire a wife to leave it in doubt whether sensibility or weakness led her to her husband's arms."

7. "There may happen, however, to be such a disproportion in the strength and age of the parties, as to admit of an actual rape; but as I am here treating of the relative state of the sexes in the common course of nature, I do not suppose any such disproportion" [Rousseau's note].

fewer instances, however, in modern times of such acts of violence, it certainly is not because men are less licentious, but because they have less credulity; such a repulse, as would have intimidated the simple ravisher of former times, would in ours be disregarded with a smile: a resolute silence is now held to be the firmest resistance. There is a law recorded in Deuteronomy, by which a young woman, when debauched, was condemned to suffer with her seducer, in case the crime was committed within the city; but if it happened in the fields or other unfrequented place, the ravisher was punished alone: *for*, says the law, *the damsel cried, and there was none to save her.*[8] This favourable interpretation, doubtless, taught the young women to take care how they were surprised in places that were frequented.

The effect of this change of opinion on manners is very perceptible. Modern gallantry is one of its consequences. The men, finding that their pleasures depended more on the goodwill of the fair sex than they at first imagined, cultivated the art of captivating them by complaisance.

Thus we see how physics insensibly lead us to morals, and in what manner the grosser union of the sexes gave rise, by degrees, to the more refined rules and softer maxims of love. The great influence of the women, therefore, is not owing to the voluntary submission of the men, but to the will of nature: they were possessed of it before they appeared to be so; that very Hercules who violated the fifty daughters of Thestius, was nevertheless compelled to wield the distaff by Omphale; and Sampson himself, strong as he was, was no match for Dalilah.[9] This power of the fair sex cannot be taken from them, even when they abuse it; if ever they could lose their influence, they would undoubtedly have lost it long ago.

There is no parity between man and woman as to the consequences of their sex. The male is such only at certain momentary intervals; the female feels the consequences of her sex all her life, at least during youth; and in order to answer the purposes of it, requires first a suitable constitution. She requires next careful management in her pregnancy, repose in child-bed, ease and a sedentary life during the time of suckling her children, and, to bring them up, such patience, good-humour and affection as nothing can disgust: she serves as the means of their connection with their father; it is she who makes him love them, and gives him the confidence to call them his own. What tenderness and solicitude ought she not to be possessed of, in order to maintain the peace and unity of a whole

8. Deuteronomy 22:22–27.
9. The Book of Judges recounts the story of how the seductive Dalilah had Sampson's hair cut, thus depriving him of his strength. In classical mythology Hercules, feminized in the service of Queen Omphale of Lydia, was reduced to spinning wool for her, having exchanged his club for a distaff.

family! Add to this that her good qualities should not be the effects of virtue, but of taste and inclination, without which the human species would soon be extinct.

The relative duties of the two sexes do not require an equally rigorous observance in both. When women complain, however, of this partiality as unjust, they are in the wrong: this inequality is not of human institution, at least it is not the effect of prejudice, but of reason. It certainly belongs to that party which nature hath more immediately entrusted with the care of children, to be answerable for that charge to the other. Neither of them, indeed, is permitted to violate their mutual engagements; every faithless husband, who deprives his wife of the only compensation for the severer duties of her sex, being guilty of cruelty and injustice. A faithless woman, however, does still more; she dissolves the union of her family, and breaks through all the ties of nature: in giving to a man children which are not of his begetting, she betrays both, and adds perfidy to infidelity. Such an action is naturally productive of the worst of crimes and disorders. If there be a situation in life truly horrid, it is that of an unhappy father, who, placing no confidence in his wife, cannot indulge himself in the most delightful sentiments of the heart; who doubts while he is embracing his child, whether it be not the offspring of another, the pledge of his dishonour, and the usurper of the rights of his real children. What a scene doth a family in such a case present to us! Nothing but a community of secret enemies, whom a guilty woman arms one against the other, by compelling them to pretences of reciprocal affection.

It is not only of consequence, therefore, that a woman should be faithful to her husband, but also that he should think her so. It is requisite for her to be modest, circumspect and reserved; and that she should bear in the sight of others, as well as in her own conscience, the testimony of her virtue. If it be necessary for a father to love his children, it is first necessary for him to esteem their mother. Such are the reasons which place even the preservation of appearances, among the number of female duties, and render their honour and reputation no less indispensible than chastity. From these principles is derived a new motive of obligation and convenience, which prescribes peculiarly to women the most scrupulous circumspection in their manners, conduct and behaviour. To maintain indiscriminately that the two sexes are equal, and that their reciprocal duties and obligations are the same, is to indulge ourselves in idle declamations unworthy of a serious answer.

It is certainly a very superficial manner of reasoning, that of bringing exceptions as proofs to invalidate general laws so well founded. Women, you say, do not always bear children. That is true; their sex is, nevertheless, destined by nature to that end. What! because there are an hundred great cities in the world, where the women, leading a licentious life, have few children, do you pretend that women are naturally barren? What would become of all your populous towns, if the distant countries, where the women live in great chastity and simplicity, did not compensate for the sterility of your town-ladies? A woman who hath borne but four or five children, would, in many provinces, be far from being esteemed a fruitful breeder.[1] In a word, it is to no purpose, that some particular women bear but few children; women in general are not the less formed by nature to become mothers; and it is agreeable to general laws, that nature and manners operate to that end.

But were the intervals between the pregnancy of women so long as is supposed, is it possible for them to change so suddenly their manner of living, without hazard of life or health? Can a woman be one day a nurse, and the next a soldier?[2] * * *

JOHN GREGORY

From A Father's Legacy to His Daughters[†]

From Chapter 2: Conduct and Behaviour

One of the chief beauties in a female character, is that modest reserve, that retiring delicacy, which avoids the public eye, and is disconcerted even at the gaze of admiration.—I do not wish you to be insensible to applause. If you were, you must become, if not worse, at least less amiable women. But you may be dazzled by that admiration, which yet rejoices your hearts.

When a girl ceases to blush, she has lost the most powerful charm

---

1. "Were it not so, the species must necessarily perish; its preservation requiring that every woman, taking one with another, should produce nearly four children: for of all the children that are born, almost the half die before the mothers can have any more: two therefore must remain to represent the father and mother. The propagation of the species in great cities, is far from being in this proportion" [Rousseau's note].
2. Wollstonecraft refers to this question on p. 154.
† A physician, professor at the University of Edinburgh, and participant in the Scottish Enlightenment, John Gregory (1723–1774) did not live to see the success of the advice book that he composed for his daughters: six thousand copies of *A Father's Legacy* were sold between 1774 and 1776, and it remained widely read through the nineteenth century. His text is likely to strike us today as the ancestor of our society's self-help books. An eighteenth-century conduct book like Gregory's described the virtues and skills necessary to middle-class females on the brink of adulthood, educating its female readers in the femininity that was nonetheless, somewhat paradoxically, supposed to come naturally to them. The text reprinted here is that of the second edition (London, 1775), pp. 26–32, 34–36, 49–58. All notes are the editor's. Page references to Wollstonecraft refer to the present edition.

of beauty. That extreme sensibility which it indicates, may be a weakness and incumbrance in our sex, as I have too often felt; but in yours it is peculiarly engaging. Pedants, who think themselves philosophers, ask why a woman should blush when she is conscious of no crime. It is a sufficient answer, that Nature has made you to blush when you are guilty of no fault, and has forced us to love you because you do so.—Blushing is so far from being necessarily an attendant on guilt, that it is the usual companion of innocence.

This modesty, which I think so essential in your sex, will naturally dispose you to be rather silent in company, especially in a large one.—People of sense and discernment will never mistake such silence for dulness. One may take a share in conversation without uttering a syllable. The expression in the countenance shews it, and this never escapes an observing eye.

I should be glad that you had an easy dignity in your behaviour at public places, but not that confident ease, that unabashed countenance, which seems to set the company at defiance. If, while a gentleman is speaking to you, one of superior rank addresses you, do not let your eager attention and visible preference betray the flutter of your heart. Let your pride on this occasion preserve you from that meanness[1] into which your vanity would sink you. Consider that you expose yourselves to the ridicule of the company, and affront one gentleman, only to swell the triumph of another, who perhaps thinks he does you honour in speaking to you.

Converse with men even of the first rank with that dignified modesty which may prevent the approach of the most distant familiarity, and consequently prevent them from feeling themselves your superiors.

Wit is the most dangerous talent you can possess. It must be guarded with great discretion and good nature, otherwise it will create you many enemies. Wit is perfectly consistent with softness and delicacy; yet they are seldom found united. Wit is so flattering to vanity, that they who possess it become intoxicated, and lose all self-command.

Humour is a different quality. It will make your company much solicited; but be cautious how you indulge it.—It is often a great enemy to delicacy, and a still greater one to dignity of character. It may sometimes gain you applause, but will never procure you respect.

Be even cautious in displaying your good sense. It will be thought you assume a superiority over the rest of the company. But if you happen to have any learning, keep it a profound secret, especially

---

1. Pettiness.

from the men, who generally look with a jealous and malignant eye on a woman of great parts, and a cultivated understanding.[2]

* * *

Consider every species of indelicacy in conversation, as shameful in itself, and as highly disgusting to us. All double entendre is of this sort.—The dissoluteness of men's education allows them to be diverted with a kind of wit, which yet they have delicacy enough to be shocked at, when it comes from your mouths, or even when you hear it without pain and contempt.—Virgin purity is of that delicate nature, that it cannot hear certain things without contamination. It is always in your power to avoid these. No man, but a brute or a fool, will insult a woman with conversation which he sees gives her pain; nor will he dare to do it, if she resent the injury with a becoming spirit.—There is a dignity in conscious virtue which is able to awe the most shameless and abandoned of men.

You will be reproached perhaps with prudery. By prudery is usually meant an affectation of delicacy. Now I do not wish you to affect delicacy; I wish you to possess it. At any rate, it is better to run the risk of being thought ridiculous than disgusting.

The men will complain of your reserve. They will assure you that a franker behaviour would make you more amiable. But trust me, they are not sincere when they tell you so.

From *Chapter 3: Amusements*

* * *

An attention to your health is a duty you owe to yourselves and to your friends. Bad health seldom fails to have an influence on the spirits and temper. The finest geniuses, the most delicate minds, have very frequently a correspondent delicacy of bodily constitution, which they are too apt to neglect. Their luxury lies in reading and late hours, equal enemies to health and beauty.

But though good health be one of the greatest blessings of life, never make a boast of it, but enjoy it in grateful silence. We so naturally associate the idea of female softness and delicacy with a correspondent delicacy of constitution, that when a woman speaks of her great strength, her extraordinary appetite, her ability to bear excessive fatigue, we recoil at the description in a way she is little aware of.

* * *

Dress is an important article in female life. The love of dress is natural to you, and therefore it is proper and reasonable. Good sense will regulate your expence in it, and good taste will direct you to dress in such a way as to conceal any blemishes, and set off your beauties, if you have any, to the greatest advantage. But much deli-

---

2. For Wollstonecraft's reaction to this advice see p. 105.

cacy and judgment are required in the application of this rule. A fine woman shews her charms to most advantage, when she seems most to conceal them. The finest bosom in nature is not so fine as what imagination forms. The most perfect elegance of dress appears always the most easy, and the least studied.

Do not confine your attention to dress to your public appearances. Accustom yourselves to an habitual neatness, so that in the most careless undress, in your most unguarded hours, you may have no reason to be ashamed of your appearance.—You will not easily believe how much we consider your dress as expressive of your characters. Vanity, levity, slovenliness, folly, appear through it. An elegant simplicity is an equal proof of taste and delicacy.

In dancing, the principal points you are to attend to are ease and grace. I would have you to dance with spirit; but never allow yourselves to be so far transported with mirth, as to forget the delicacy of your sex.—Many a girl dancing in the gaiety and innocence of her heart, is thought to discover a spirit she little dreams of.[3]

* * *

CATHARINE MACAULAY[†]

From Letters on Education

From *Letter IV.*

Amusement and Instruction of Boys and Girls to Be the Same

* * *

I could say a great deal, Hortensia,[1] on those personal advantages, which the strength of the mother gives to her offspring, and the ill effects which must accrue both to the male and female issue from her feebleness. I could expatiate on the mental advantages which

---

3. For Wollstonecraft's reaction to this counsel, see p. 31.
† From Catharine Macaulay, *Letters on Education. With Observations on Religious and Metaphysical Subjects* (London, 1790), from Letter IV (pp. 48–50), Letter XXI (201–02), and Letter XXIV (218–21). All notes are the editor's unless otherwise noted. Catherine Macaulay (1731–1791) gained international celebrity as a historian and political theorist. She published *Letters on Education* (under the name Catharine Macaulay Graham) at the end of her career, when her reputation had been somewhat tarnished by her second marriage to William Graham, who was, scandalously, her junior by twenty-six years. The *Letters* challenged the conduct book norms for female education in ways that Wollstonecraft found deeply sympathetic when she reviewed the book for the *Analytical Review* in November 1790.
1. In addressing the *Letters on Education* to this fictional correspondent, Macaulay borrows a convention of conduct books for women, which often presented their advice in conversational style and as though it were relayed by mothers or fathers to daughters or by aunts to nieces. The name Hortensia is suggestive: in the history of Rome, Hortensia was known for defending the public spirit of women in a speech that she gave in 42 B.C.E. at the forum, the center of Roman political life where no woman had ever spoken before.

accompany a firm constitution, and on that evenness and complacency of temper, which commonly attends the blessing of health. I
could turn the other side of the argument, and show you, that most
of the caprices, the teasing follies, and often the vices of women,
proceed from weakness, or some other defect in their corporeal
frame; but when I have sifted the subject to the bottom, and taken
every necessary trouble to illustrate and enforce my opinion, I shall,
perhaps, still continue singular in it. My arguments may serve only
to strengthen my ideas, and my sex will continue to lisp with their
tongues, to totter in their walk, and to counterfeit more weakness
and sickness than they really have, in order to attract the notice of
the male; for, says a very elegant author, perfection is not the proper
object of love: we admire excellence, but we are more enclined to
love those we despise.[2]

There is another prejudice, Hortensia, which affects yet more
deeply female happiness, and female importance; a prejudice, which
ought ever to have been confined to the regions of the east, [a] state
of slavery to which female nature in that part of the world has been
ever subjected, and can only suit with the notion of a positive inferiority in the intellectual powers of the female mind. You will soon
perceive, that the prejudice which I mean, is that degrading difference in the culture of the understanding, which has prevailed for
several centuries in all European societies. Our ancestors, on the
first revival of letters, dispensed with an equal hand the advantages
of a classical education to all their offspring; but as pedantry was the
fault of that age, a female student might not at that time be a very
agreeable character. True philosophy in those ages was rarely an
attendant on learning, even in the male sex; but it must be obvious
to all those who are not blinded by the mist of prejudice, that there
is no cultivation which yields so promising a harvest as the cultivation of the understanding; and that a mind, irradiated by the clear
light of wisdom, must be equal to every talk which reason imposes
on it. The social duties in the interesting characters of daughter,
wife, and mother, will be but ill performed by ignorance and levity;
and in the domestic converse of husband and wife; the alternative of
an enlightened, or an unenlightened companion, cannot be indifferent to any man of taste and true knowledge. Be no longer niggards,
then, O ye parents, in bestowing on your offspring, every blessing

2. "See Mr. Burke on the Sublime and Beautiful" [Macaulay's note]. Macaulay quotes
   Edmund Burke's essay on aesthetics, the *Philosophical Enquiry into the Origin of our
   Ideas of the Sublime and the Beautiful*, Part III, section ix. There Burke dissociates the
   beautiful from our ideas of perfection because in the female sex, where beauty is highest,
   beauty "almost always carries with it an idea of weakness and imperfection. Women are
   very sensible of this; for which reason, they learn to lisp, to totter in their walk, to counterfeit weakness, and even sickness."

which nature and fortune renders them capable of enjoying! Confine not the education of your daughters to what is regarded as the ornamental parts of it, nor deny the graces to your sons. Suffer no prejudices to prevail on you to weaken Nature, in order to render her more beautiful; take measures for the virtue and the harmony of your family, by uniting their young minds early in the soft bonds of friendship. Let your children be brought up together; let their sports and studies be the same; let them enjoy, in the constant presence of those who are set over them, all that freedom which innocence renders harmless, and in which Nature rejoices. By the uninterrupted intercourse which you will thus establish, both sexes will find, that friendship may be enjoyed between them without passion. The wisdom of your daughters will preserve them from the bane of coquetry, and even at the age of desire, objects of temptation will lose somewhat of their stimuli, by losing their novelty. Your sons will look for something more solid in women, than a mere outside; and be no longer the dupes to the meanest, the weakest, and the most profligate of the sex. They will become the constant benefactors of that part of their family who stand in need of their assistance; and in regard to all matters of domestic concern, the unjust distinction of primogeniture[3] will be deprived of its sting.

From *Letter XXI*.

Morals Must Be Taught on Immutable Principles
* * *

* * * Know then, good Hortensia, that I have given similar rules for male and female education, on the following grounds of reasoning.

First, That there is but one rule of right for the conduct of all rational beings; consequently that true virtue in one sex must be equally so in the other, whenever a proper opportunity calls for its exertion; and, *vice versa,* what is vice in one sex, cannot have a different property when found in the other.

Secondly, That true wisdom, which is never found at variance with rectitude, is as useful to women as to men; because it is necessary to the highest degree of happiness, which can never exist with ignorance.

Lastly, That as on our first entrance into another world, our state of happiness may possibly depend on the degree of perfection we have attained in this, we cannot justly lessen, in one sex or the other, the means by which perfection, that is another word for wisdom, is acquired.

---

3. The arrangement, dating to the feudal period, whereby eldest sons were the sole heirs to landed property, to the exclusion of their sisters and younger brothers.

It would be paying you a bad compliment, Hortensia, were I to answer all the frivolous objections which prejudice has framed against the giving a learned education to women; for I know of no learning, worth having, that does not tend to free the mind from error, and enlarge our stock of useful knowledge. Thus much it may be proper to observe, that those hours which are spent in studious retirement by learned women, will not in all probability intrude so much on the time for useful avocation, as the wild and spreading dissipation of the present day; that levity and ignorance will always be found in opposition to what is useful and graceful in life; and that the contrary may be expected from a truly enlightened understanding. However, Hortensia, to throw some illustration on what I have advanced on this subject, it may be necessary to shew you, that all those vices and imperfections which have been generally regarded as inseparable from the female character, do not in any manner proceed from sexual causes, but are entirely the effects of situation and education. But these observations must be left to farther discussion.

From *Letter XXIV.*

Flattery—Chastity—Male Rakes

* * *

But the most difficult part of female education, is to give girls such an idea of chastity, as shall arm their reason and their sentiments on the side of this useful virtue. For I believe there are more women of understanding led into acts of imprudence by the ignorance, the prejudices, and the false craft of those by whom they are educated, than from any other cause founded either in nature or in chance. You may train up a docile idiot to any mode of thinking or acting, as may best suit the intended purpose; but a reasoning being will scan over your propositions, and if they find them grounded in falsehood, they will reject them with disdain. When you tell a girl of spirit and reflection that chastity is a sexual virtue, and the want of it a sexual vice, she will be apt to examine into the principles of religion, morals, and the reason of things, in order to satisfy herself on the truth of your proposition. And when, after the strictest enquiries, she finds nothing that will warrant the confining the proposition to a particular sense, she will entertain doubts either of your wisdom or your sincerity; and regarding you either as a deceiver or a fool, she will transfer her confidence to the companion of the easy vacant hour, whose compliance with her opinions can flatter her vanity. Thus left to Nature, with an unfortunate biass on her mind, she will fall a victim to the first plausible being who has formed a design on her person. Rousseau is so sensible of this truth, that he quarrels with human reason, and would put her[4] out of the question in all considerations of duty. But this is being as great a fanatic in morals, as some are in religion; and I should much doubt the reality of that duty which would not stand the test of fair enquiry; beside, as I intend to breed my pupils up to act a rational part in the world, and not to fill up a niche in the seraglio[5] of a sultan, I shall certainly give them leave to use their reason in all matters which concern their duty and happiness, and shall spare no pains in the cultivation of this only sure guide to virtue. I shall inform them of the great utility of chastity and continence; that the one preserves the body in health and vigor, and the other, the purity and independence of the mind, without which it is impossible to possess virtue or happiness. I shall intimate, that the great difference now beheld in the external consequences which follow the deviations from chastity in the two sexes, did in all probability arise from women having been considered as the mere property of the men; and, on this account had no right to dispose of their own persons: that policy adopted this difference, when the plea of property had been given up; and it was still preserved in society from the unruly licentiousness of the men, who finding no obstacles in the delicacy of the other sex, continue to set at defiance both divine and moral law, and by mutual support and general opinion to use their natural freedom with impunity. I shall observe, that this state of things renders the situation of females, in their individual capacity very precarious; for the strength which Nature has given to the passion of love, in order to serve her purposes, has made it the most ungovernal propensity of any which attends us. The snares therefore, that are continually laid for women, by persons who run no risk in compassing their seduction, exposes them to continual danger; whilst the implacability of their own sex, who fear to give up any advantages which a superior prudence, or even its appearances, give them, renders one false step an irretrievable misfortune. That, for these reasons, coquetry in women is as dangerous as it is dishonorable. That a coquet commonly finds her own perdition, in the very flames which she raises to consume others; and that if any thing can excuse the baseness of female seduction, it is the baits which are flung out by women to entangle the affections, and excite the passions of men.

I know not what you may think of my method, Hortensia, which I must acknowledge to carry the stamp of singularity; but for my part, I am sanguine enough to expect to turn out of my hands a careless, modest beauty, grave, manly, noble, full of strength and majesty; and

4. I.e., Reason.
5. Harem.

carrying about her an aegis[6] sufficiently powerful to defend her
against the sharpest arrow that ever was shot from Cupid's bow.
* * *

HANNAH MORE

From Strictures on the Modern System of Female Education[†]

From *Chapter 1. Address to Women of Rank and Fortune, on the Effects of Their Influence in Society*
* * *

At this period, when our country can only hope to stand by opposing a bold and noble *unanimity* to the most tremendous confederacies against religion and order, and governments, which the world
ever saw;[1] what an accession would it bring to the public strength,
could we prevail on beauty, and rank, and talents, and virtue, con-
federating their several powers, to come forward with a patriotism at
once firm and feminine for the general good! I am not sounding an
alarm to female warriors, or exciting female politicians: I hardly
know which of the two is the most disgusting and unnatural character. Propriety is to a woman what the great Roman critic says action
is to an orator; it is the first, the second, the third requisite.[2] A
woman may be knowing, active, witty, and amusing; but without
propriety she cannot be amiable. Propriety is the centre in which all
the lines of duty and of agreeableness meet. It is to character what
proportion is to figure, and grace to attitude. It does not depend on
any one perfection; but it is the result of general excellence. It shows

---

6. Protective armor or shield, associated with Athena, the goddess of wisdom.
† Hannah More (1745–1833) began her career as a playwright but renounced the stage to
  turn her pen to more serious and pious purposes. She was active in the Sunday school
  movement that brought literacy education to the poor in Britain. After 1795 More also
  worked, as the author of dozens of the pamphlets known as the Cheap Repository Tracts,
  to ensure that the texts the poor read were innocent of the seditious "French principles"
  that had fueled the Revolution and inspired calls for parliamentary reform in Britain as
  well. *Strictures,* More's contribution to eighteenth-century debates about the aims and
  limits of education for women, is colored by this same opposition to political radicalism.
  At the same time (as critic Mitzi Myers argued in 1982 in an article reprinted on p. 319
  herein), More also intuited that this moment of crisis in British class relations might represent an opportunity for middle-class women: More's conduct book expands women's
  sphere of influence significantly as it recasts domestic duties both as a kind of national
  service and as professional work. The excerpts printed here are from the first edition of
  Strictures (London, 1799). All notes are the editor's.
1. Britain and France had been at war since 1793, and the British war effort is an important
  context for More's opening chapter of *Strictures.*
2. This description of the art of oratory in fact originated with the Greek statesman Demos-
  thenes (fourth century B.C.E.).

itself by a regular, orderly, undeviating course; and never starts from its sober orbit into any splendid eccentricities; for it would be ashamed of such praise as it might extort by any aberrations from its proper path. It renounces all commendation but what is characteristic; and I would make it the criterion of true taste, right principle, and genuine feeling, in a woman, whether she would be less touched with all the flattery of romantic and exaggerated panegyric, than with that beautiful picture of correct and elegant propriety, which Milton draws of our first mother, when he delineates

> "Those thousand *decencies* which daily flow
> From all her words and actions."[3]

Even the influence of religion is to be exercised with discretion. A female Polemic wanders almost as far from the limits prescribed to her sex, as a female Machiavel or warlike Thalestris.[4] Fierceness and bigotry have made almost as few converts as the sword, and both are peculiarly ungraceful in a female. Even *religious* violence has human tempers of its own to indulge, and is gratifying itself when it would be thought to be "working the righteousness of God." * * *

* * *

From *Chapter 4. Comparison of the Mode of Female Education in the Last Age with the Present*

* * *

But, though a well bred young lady may lawfully learn most of the fashionable arts, yet it does not seem to be the true end of education to make women of fashion *dancers, singers, players, painters, actresses, sculptors, gilders, varnishers, engravers,* and *embroiderers.* Most *men* are commonly destined to some profession, and their minds are consequently turned each to its respective object. Would it not be strange if they were called out to exercise their profession, or to set up their trade, with only a little general knowledge of the trades of all other men, and without any previous definite application to their own peculiar calling? The profession of ladies, to which the bent of *their* instruction should be turned, is that of daughters, wives, mothers, and mistresses of families. They should be therefore trained with a view to these several conditions, and be furnished with a stock of ideas and principles, and qualifications ready to be applied and appropriated, as occasion may demand, to each of these respective situations: for though the arts which merely embellish life must claim admiration; yet when a man of sense comes to marry, it is a companion whom he wants, and not an

---

3. *Paradise Lost* VIII. 601–02, lines in which Adam tries to account for his love for Eve.
4. Thalestris was the queen of the Amazons, the warrior women of Greek mythology. "Machiavel": someone whose talents at manipulation equal those of the Italian political theorist Niccolò Machiavelli.

artist. It is not merely a creature who can paint, and play, and dress, and dance; it is a being who can comfort and counsel him; one who can reason and reflect, and feel, and judge, and discourse, and discriminate; one who can assist him in his affairs, lighten his cares, sooth his sorrows, strengthen his principles, and educate his children.

* * *

That injudicious practice, therefore, cannot be too much discouraged, of endeavouring to create talents which do not exist in nature. *That their daughters shall learn every thing,* is so general a maternal maxim, that even unborn daughters, of whose expected abilities and conjectured faculties, it is presumed, no very accurate judgment can previously be formed, are yet predestined to this universality of accomplishments. This comprehensive maxim, thus almost universally brought into practice, at once weakens the general powers of the mind, by drawing off its strength into too great a variety of directions; and cuts up time into too many portions, by splitting it into such an endless multiplicity of employments. I know that I am treading on tender ground; but I cannot help thinking that the restless pains we take to cram up every little vacuity of life, by crowding one new thing upon another, rather creates a thirst for novelty than knowledge; and is but a well-disguised contrivance to keep us in after-life more effectually from conversing with ourselves. The care taken to prevent *ennui* is but a creditable plan for promoting self-ignorance. We run from one occupation to another (I speak of those arts to which little intellect is applied) with a view to lighten the pressure of time; above all to save us from our own thoughts; whereas, were we thrown a little more on our own hands, we might at last be driven, by way of something to do, to try to get acquainted with our own hearts; and though our being less absorbed by this busy trifling and frivolous hurry, might render us somewhat more sensible of the tædium of life, might not this very sensation tend to quicken our pursuit of a better? For an awful[5] thought here suggests itself. If life be so long that we are driven to set at work every engine to pass away the tediousness of time; how shall we do to get rid of the tediousness of eternity? an eternity in which not one of these acquisitions will be of the least use. Let not then the soul be starved by feeding it on these husks, for it can be no more nourished by them than the body can be fed with ideas and principles.

* * *

Let me be allowed to repeat, that I mean not with preposterous praise to descant on the ignorance or the prejudices of past times, nor absurdly to regret that vulgar system of education which rounded the little circle of female acquirements within the limits of the sampler and the receipt book. Yet if a preference almost exclusive

5. Awe-inspiring.

was then given to what was merely useful, a preference almost exclusive also is now assigned to what is merely ornamental. And it must be owned, that if the life of a young lady, formerly, too much resembled the life of a confectioner, it now too much resembles that of an actress; the morning is all rehearsal, and the evening is all performance: and those who are trained in this regular routine, who are instructed in order to be exhibited, soon learn to feel a sort of impatience in those societies in which their kind of talents are not likely to be brought into play: the talk of an auditor becomes dull to her, who has been used to be a performer.

* * *

From *Chapter 6. Filial Obedience Not the Character of the Age*

Among the real improvements of modern times, and they are not a few, it is to be feared that the growth of filial obedience cannot be included. Who can forbear observing and regretting in a variety of instances, that not only sons but daughters have adopted something of that spirit of independence, and disdain of control, which characterise the times? And is it not obvious that domestic manners are not slightly tinctured with the hue of public principles? The *rights of man* have been discussed, till we are somewhat wearied with the discussion. To these have been opposed with more presumption than prudence *the rights of woman*.[6] It follows according to the natural progression of human things, that the next stage of that irradiation which our enlighteners are pouring in upon us as will produce grave descants on the *rights of children*.

This revolutionary spirit in families suggests the remark that among the faults with which it has been too much the fashion of recent times to load the memory of the incomparable Milton, one of the charges brought against his private character (for with his political character we have here nothing to do) has been, that he was so severe a father as to have compelled his daughters, after he was blind, to read aloud to him for his sole pleasure Greek and Latin authors of which they did not understand a word. But this is in fact nothing more than an instance of the strict domestic regulations of the age in which Milton lived; and should not be brought forward as a proof of the severity of his individual temper. Nor indeed in any case should it ever be considered as an hardship for an affectionate child to amuse an afflicted parent, though it should be attended with a heavier sacrifice of her own pleasure than in the present instance.

* * *

6. Referring to Thomas Paine's defense of the Revolution in France, *Rights of Man* (1791–92), and to Wollstonecraft.

Wollstonecraft's Revolutionary Moment

One reason Wollstonecraft was able to look beyond conventional notions of sexual difference and to imagine that there might be other, as yet unrealized, ways of being female may be that she, like many contemporaries, had the sense that she was living at a moment of unprecedented human possibility. In July 1789 British readers learned that the common people had attacked the Bastille, royal power's imposing symbol in Paris, and liberated its political prisoners. A month later came word that the deputies who formed the new National Assembly of France had proclaimed the Declaration of the Rights of Man and Citizen. That act at one blow abolished the feudal system that had prevailed in France for a thousand years. The declaration set out in its stead a vision of government as existing to guarantee individual rights and the rule of law. It seemed a moment for new beginnings, in Britain as well as France. At the start of the 1790s, that impression inspired the new efforts that were made toward the reform of the British Parliament, the abolition of the slave trade, and the repeal of the long-standing laws that had rendered religious Dissenters second-class citizens.

Certainly, the Revolution was a turning point for Wollstonecraft herself. As Barbara Taylor observes in *Mary Wollstonecraft and the Feminist Imagination* (see Bibliography), Wollstonecraft had been a "lady-author" for some time; but in 1791, in the course of defending the Revolution against the criticisms of the politician Edmund Burke, she became something much rarer: a woman philosopher. Through her reading of Burke's *Reflections on the Revolution in France* and through her attention, especially, to the gendered terms in which this spokesman for the old aristocratic order depicted the Revolution, Wollstonecraft also discovered the topics—for instance, the cooperative relations between systems of class and sex subordination—that would engage her for the remainder of her career.

Wollstonecraft's *Vindication of the Rights of Men* was, in fact, one of scores of responses to Burke's *Reflections,* a book that in its turn reacted against another, a sermon by Richard Price that greeted the

Revolution as harbinger of humanity's increased "ardour for liberty." The texts assembled in this section, written by Price, Burke, and Wollstonecraft, highlight the pamphlet war that Price detonated with this *Discourse on the Love of Our Country*. British writers debated French politics so energetically—and in ways that encouraged a mass audience to feel as if they too had a say in political matters—because that upheaval across the Channel challenged the authority of the British state. It made it necessary to justify, if possible, the inherited privileges enjoyed in Britain by a narrow oligarchy of propertied gentlemen. It made people wonder whether all forms of monarchy (even the constitutional monarchy Britain had acquired through its Glorious Revolution of 1688) were usurpations of the sovereignty of the people.

An excerpt from Wollstonecraft's *Historical and Moral View of the Origin and Progress of the French Revolution* winds up this section. A retrospect on the events of 1789 and an attempt to infer their lessons, it is written at a moment when the Revolution had taken a tragic turn but when, in Wollstonecraft's view, the ideals of its early phase still remained salvageable.

RICHARD PRICE

From A Discourse on the Love of Our Country[†]

We are met to thank God for that event in this country to which the name of THE REVOLUTION has been given; and which, for more than a century, it has been usual for the friends of freedom, and more especially Protestant Dissenters, under the title of the REVOLUTION SOCIETY, to celebrate with expressions of joy and exultation. * * * By a bloodless victory, the fetters which despotism had been long preparing for us were broken; the rights of the people were asserted, a tyrant expelled, and a Sovereign of our own choice appointed in his room. Security was given to our property, and our consciences

---

[†] Richard Price (1723–1791) was a prominent Unitarian clergyman as well as a mathematician, philosopher, and political theorist who published on topics ranging from American independence to Britain's national debt to the theory of probability. He delivered this sermon, as readers who read it in published form learned on the title page, "On Nov. 4, 1789, at the Meeting-House in the Old Jewry, to the Society for Commemorating the Revolution in Great Britain." The London Revolution Society had been founded a year earlier to mark the centenary of the Glorious Revolution of 1688, the revolution that had deposed King James II and produced the Declaration of Right, established a limited monarchy, and guaranteed civil rights for men of property. The text printed here follows that of the first edition, which Wollstonecraft reviewed for the *Analytical Review* in December 1789 (*Works*, ed. Janet Todd and Marilyn Butler, VII, pp. 185–87). All notes are the editor's.

were emancipated. The bounds of free enquiry were enlarged; the volume in which are the words of eternal life, was laid more open to our examination; and that *aera* of light and liberty was introduced among us, by which we have been made an example to other kingdoms, and became the instructors of the world. Had it not been for this deliverance, the probability is, that, instead of being thus distinguished, we should now have been a base people, groaning under the infamy and misery of popery and slavery. Let us, therefore, offer thanksgivings to God, the author of all our blessings. * * * It is well known that King James was not far from gaining his purpose; and that probably he would have succeeded, had he been less in a hurry. But he was a fool as well as a bigot. He wanted courage as well as prudence; and, therefore, fled, and left us to settle quietly for ourselves that constitution of government which is now our boast. We have particular reason, as Protestant Dissenters, to rejoice on this occasion. It was at this time we were rescued from persecution, and obtained the liberty of worshipping God in the manner we think most acceptable to him. It was then our meeting houses were opened, our worship was taken under the protection of the law, and the principles of toleration gained a triumph. We have, therefore, on this occasion, peculiar reasons for thanksgiving.—But let us remember that we ought not to satisfy ourselves with thanksgivings. Our gratitude, if genuine, will be accompanied with endeavours to give stability to the deliverance our country has obtained, and to extend and improve the happiness with which the Revolution has blest us.—Let us, in particular, take care not to forget the principles of the Revolution. This Society has, very properly, in its Reports, held out these principles, as an instruction to the public. I will only take notice of the three following:

First: The right to liberty of conscience in religious matters.

Secondly: The right to resist power when abused. And,

Thirdly: The right to chuse our own governors; to cashier them for misconduct; and to frame a government for ourselves.

* * *

I would farther direct you to remember, that though the Revolution was a great work, it was by no means a perfect work; and that all was not then gained which was necessary to put the kingdom in the secure and complete possession of the blessings of liberty.—In particular, you should recollect, that the toleration then obtained was imperfect. It included only those who could declare their faith in the doctrinal articles of the church of England. It has, indeed, been since extended, but not sufficiently; for there still exist penal laws on account of religious opinions, which (were they carried into execution) would shut up many of our places of worship, and silence and imprison some of our ablest and best men.—The TEST LAWS are also still in force; and deprive of eligibility to civil and military offices, all who cannot conform to the established worship. It is with great pleasure I find that the body of Protestant Dissenters, though defeated in two late attempts to deliver their country from this disgrace to it, have determined to persevere. Should they at last succeed, they will have the satisfaction, not only of removing from themselves a proscription they do not deserve, but of contributing to lessen the number of public iniquities. For I cannot call by a gentler name, laws which convert an ordinance appointed by our Saviour to commemorate his death, into an instrument of oppressive policy,[1] and a qualification of rakes and atheists for civil posts.—I have said, *should* they succeed—but perhaps I ought not to suggest a doubt about their success. And, indeed, when I consider that in Scotland the established church is defended by no such test—that in Ireland it has been abolished—that in a great neighbouring country it has been declared to be an indefeasible right of all citizens to be equally eligible to public offices—that in the same kingdom a professed Dissenter from the established church holds the first office in the state—that in the Emperor's dominions *Jews* have been lately admitted to the enjoyment of equal privileges with other citizens—and that in this very country, a Dissenter, though excluded from the power of *executing* the laws, yet is allowed to be employed in *making* them.—When, I say, I consider such facts as these, I am disposed to think it impossible that the enemies of the repeal of the Test Laws should not soon become ashamed, and give up their opposition.

But the most important instance of the imperfect state in which the Revolution left our constitution, is the *inequality of our representation*. I think, indeed, this defect in our constitution so gross and so palpable, as to make it excellent chiefly in form and theory. You should remember that a representation in the legislature of a kingdom is the *basis* of constitutional liberty in it, and of all legitimate government; and that without it a government is nothing but an usurpation. When the representation is fair and equal, and at the same time vested with such powers as our House of Commons possesses, a kingdom may be said to govern itself, and consequently to possess true liberty. When the representation is partial, a kingdom possesses liberty only partially; and if extremely partial, it only gives a *semblance* of liberty; but if not only extremely partial, but corruptly chosen, and under corrupt influence after being chosen, it becomes a *nuisance*, and produces the worst of all forms of government—a

---

1. The Test and Corporation Acts of 1661 and 1673 continued in 1789 to bar Protestant men outside the fold of the established (Anglican) church from the universities, Parliament, and the professions, making them second-class citizens. Without betraying their religious convictions, Dissenters could not pass the "test" of taking the sacrament according to Anglican rites.

government by corruption, a government carried on and supported by spreading venality and profligacy through a kingdom. May heaven preserve this kingdom from a calamity so dreadful! It is the point of depravity to which abuses under such a government as ours naturally tend, and the last stage of national unhappiness. We are, at present, I hope, at a great distance from it. But it cannot be pretended that there are no advances towards it, or that there is no reason for apprehension and alarm.

* * *

What an eventful period is this! I am thankful that I have lived to it; and I could almost say, *Lord, now lettest thou thy servant depart in peace, for mine eyes have seen thy salvation.*[1] I have lived to see a diffusion of knowledge, which has undermined superstition and error—I have lived to see the rights of men better understood than ever; and nations panting for liberty, which seemed to have lost the idea of it.—I have lived to see THIRTY MILLIONS of people, indignant and resolute, spurning at slavery, and demanding liberty with an irresistible voice; their king led in triumph, and an arbitrary monarch surrendering himself to his subjects.—After sharing in the benefits of one Revolution, I have been spared to be a witness to two other Revolutions, both glorious.[3] And now, methinks, I see the ardour for liberty catching and spreading; a general amendment beginning in human affairs; the dominion of kings changed for the dominion of laws, and the dominion of priests giving way to the dominion of reason and conscience.

Be encouraged, all ye friends of freedom, and writers in its defence! The times are auspicious. Your labours have not been in vain. Behold kingdoms, admonished by you, starting from sleep, breaking their fetters, and claiming justice from their oppressors! Behold, the light you have struck out, after setting *America* free, reflected to *France,* and there kindled into a blaze that lays despotism in ashes, and warms and illuminates *Europe*!

Tremble all ye oppressors of the world! Take warning all ye supporters of slavish governments, and slavish hierarchies! Call no more (absurdly and wickedly) REFORMATION, innovation. You cannot now hold the world in darkness. Struggle no longer against increasing light and liberality. Restore to mankind their rights; and consent to the correction of abuses, before they and you are destroyed together.

2. Luke 2:29–30.
3. I.e., the American Revolution and the French.

EDMUND BURKE

From Reflections on the Revolution in France[†]

* * *

History will record, that on the morning of the 6th of October 1789,[1] the king and queen of France, after a day of confusion, alarm, dismay, and slaughter, lay down, under the pledged security of public faith, to indulge nature in a few hours of respite, and troubled melancholy repose. From this sleep the queen was first startled by the voice of the centinel at her door, who cried out to her, to save herself by flight—that this was the last proof of fidelity he could give—that they were upon him, and he was dead. Instantly he was cut down. A band of cruel ruffians and assassins, reeking with his blood, rushed into the chamber of the queen, and pierced with an hundred strokes of bayonets and poniards the bed, from whence this persecuted woman had but just time to fly almost naked, and through ways unknown to the murderers had escaped to seek refuge at the feet of a king and husband, not secure of his own life for a moment.

This king, to say no more of him, and this queen, and their infant children (who once would have been the pride and hope of a great and generous people) were then forced to abandon the sanctuary of the most splendid palace in the world, which they left swimming in blood, polluted by massacre, and strewed with scattered limbs and mutilated carcases. Thence they were conducted into the capital of their kingdom. Two had been selected from the unprovoked, unresisted, promiscuous slaughter, which was made of the gentlemen of birth and family who composed the king's body guard. These two gentlemen, with all the parade of an execution of justice, were

---

† The political theorist and parliamentarian Edmund Burke (1729–1797) began writing the *Reflections* immediately after encountering Price's *Discourse* in January 1790 and published it in November the same year. He packaged his response to Price as a letter (as the subtitle puts it) "Intended to Have Been Sent to a Gentleman in Paris." (A Frenchman named Chames-Jean-François de Pont who knew of Burke's support for American independence had indeed written to Burke soliciting his opinion of France's revolution, apparently expecting that Burke would champion this liberal cause as well.) Burke offers in this work an interpretation of Britain's prior history of revolution very different from that adhered to by Price's London Revolution Society as well as a contrasting understanding of the interactions between the French king and people during 1789. This excerpt is from the first, best-selling edition of the *Reflections*. The selection begins with Burke's take on a key event in those interactions. All notes are the editor's unless otherwise indicated.

1. On October 5 an armed crowd of seven thousand marched from Paris, where there was a dire food shortage, to the court at Versailles, seeking in part to force the king to institute the measures that might save the city from famine. Burke here portrays the aftermath of that march, when, following the killing of members of their guard, the royal family was brought back to Paris and installed in the palace of the Tuileries.

cruelly and publickly dragged to the block, and beheaded in the great court of the palace. Their heads were stuck upon spears, and led the procession; whilst the royal captives who followed in the train were slowly moved along, amidst the horrid yells, and shrilling screams, and frantic dances, and infamous contumelies, and all the unutterable abominations of the furies of hell, in the abused shape of the vilest of women.[2] After they had been made to taste, drop by drop, more than the bitterness of death, in the slow torture of a journey of twelve miles, protracted to six hours, they were, under a guard, composed of those very soldiers who had thus conducted them through this famous triumph, lodged in one of the old palaces of Paris, now converted into a Bastile for kings.

Is this a triumph to be consecrated at altars? to be commemorated with grateful thanksgiving? to be offered to the divine humanity with fervent prayer and enthusiastick ejaculation?—These Theban and Thracian Orgies, acted in France, and applauded only in the Old Jewry,[3] I assure you, kindle prophetic enthusiasm in the minds but of very few people in this kingdom; although a saint and apostle, who may have revelations of his own, and who has so completely vanquished all the mean superstitions of the heart, may incline to think it pious and decorous to compare it with the entrance into the world of the Prince of Peace, proclaimed in an holy temple by a venerable sage, and not long before not worse announced by the voice of angels to the quiet innocence of shepherds.[4]

At first I was at a loss to account for this fit of unguarded transport. I knew, indeed, that the sufferings of monarchs make a delicious repast to some sort of palates. There were reflexions which might serve to keep this appetite within some bounds of temperance. But when I took one circumstance into my consideration, I was obliged to confess, that much allowance ought to be made for the Society, and that the temptation was too strong for common discretion; I mean, the circumstance of the Io Pæan[5] of the triumph, the animating cry which called "for *all* the BISHOPS to be hanged

---

2. Women played a lead role in the October march from Paris to Versailles. Commenting flintily in her *Vindication of the Rights of Men* on Burke's choice of words in this passage Wollstonecraft wrote, "Probably you mean women who gained a livelihood by selling vegetables or fish, who never had had any advantages of education" (pp. 67–68).
3. The name given to the chapel where Price had addressed the London Revolution Society. "Theban and Thracian orgies": The rites belonging to the ancient Greek cults of Dionysus and Artemis, respectively.
4. In a preface published alongside the fourth edition of his *Discourse*, Price insisted that his reference to "a king led in triumph" designated the journey Louis XVI had taken to Paris after the fall of the Bastille in July 1789, when the French king showed himself to his people as "the restorer of their liberty." Burke was deliberately misconstruing him, Price stated, in assuming that the passage in which he quoted the gospel of Luke had been his response to the riot and slaughter that occurred at Versailles on October 6.
5. Hymn of praise.

on "the lamp-posts,"[6] might well have brought forth a burst of enthusiasm on the foreseen consequences of this happy day. I allow to so much enthusiasm some little deviation from prudence. I allow this prophet to break forth into hymns of joy and thanksgiving on an event which appears like the precursor of the Millenium, and the projected fifth monarchy, in the destruction of all church establishments.[7] There was, however (as in all human affairs there is) in the midst of this joy something to exercise the patience of these worthy gentlemen, and to try the long-suffering of their faith. The actual murder of the king and queen, and their child, was wanting to the other auspicious circumstances of this *"beautiful day."* The actual murder of the bishops, though called for by so many holy ejaculations, was also wanting. A groupe of regicide and sacrilegious slaughter, was indeed boldly sketched, but it was only sketched. It unhappily was left unfinished, in this great history-piece of the massacre of innocents. What hardy pencil of a great master, from the school of the rights of men, will finish it, is to be seen hereafter. The age has not yet the compleat benefit of that diffusion of knowledge that has undermined superstition and error; and the king of France wants another object or two, to consign to oblivion, in consideration of all the good which is to arise from his own sufferings, and the patriotic crimes of an enlightened age.[8]

Although this work of our new light and knowledge, did not go to the length, that in all probability it was intended it should be carried; yet I must think, that such treatment of any human creatures must be shocking to any but those who are made for accomplishing Revolutions. But I cannot stop here. Influenced by the inborn feelings of my nature, and not being illuminated by a single ray of this new-sprung modern light, I confess to you, Sir, that the exalted rank of the persons suffering, and particularly the sex, the beauty, and the amiable qualities of the descendant of so many kings and emperors, with the tender age of royal infants, insensible only through infancy and innocence of the cruel outrages to which their parents were exposed, instead of being a subject of exultation, adds not a little to any sensibility on that most melancholy occasion.

I hear that the august person,[9] who was the principal object of our preacher's triumph, though he supported himself, felt much on that

6. *"Tous les Eveques à la lanterne"* [Burke's note].
7. Prophecies in the Books of Daniel and Revelation foretold that the fifth monarchy—usually assumed to refer to the rule of the papacy—would end human history and usher in the apocalypse. Burke likely intends his readers to recall the Puritan sect who called themselves the fifth-monarchy men and who were associated with the other English revolution of the seventeenth century—not the Glorious Revolution of 1688 that the London Revolution Society honored but the one with the regicide of Charles I at its center.
8. Omitted here is a long footnote in which Burke quotes an eye-witness report on the captive king's entrance into Paris.
9. I. e., King Louis XVI.

shameful occasion. As a man, it became him to feel for his wife and his children, and the faithful guards of his person, that were massacred in cold blood about him; as a prince, it became him to feel for the strange and frightful transformation of his civilized subjects, and to be more grieved for them, than solicitous for himself. It derogates little from his fortitude, while it adds infinitely to the honour of his humanity. I am very sorry to say it, very sorry indeed, that such personages are in a situation in which it is not unbecoming to praise the virtues of the great.

I hear, and I rejoice to hear, that the great lady, the other object of the triumph, has borne that day (one is interested that beings made for suffering should suffer well) and that she bears all the succeeding days, that she bears the imprisonment of her husband, and her own captivity, and the exile of her friends, and the insulting adulation of addresses, and the whole weight of her accumulated wrongs, with a serene patience, in a manner suited to her rank and race, and becoming the offspring of a sovereign distinguished for her piety and her courage;[1] that like her she has lofty sentiments; that she feels with the dignity of a Roman matron; that in the last extremity she will save herself from the last disgrace, and that if she must fall, she will fall by no ignoble hand.[2]

It is now sixteen or seventeen years since I saw the queen of France, then the dauphiness, at Versailles; and surely never lighted on this orb, which she hardly seemed to touch, a more delightful vision. I saw her just above the horizon, decorating and cheering the elevated sphere she just began to move in,—glittering like the morning-star, full of life, and splendor, and joy. Oh! what a revolution! and what an heart must I have, to contemplate without emotion that elevation and that fall! Little did I dream that, when she added titles of veneration to those of enthusiastic, distant, respectful love, that she should ever be obliged to carry the sharp antidote against disgrace concealed in that bosom; little did I dream that I should have lived to see such disasters fallen upon her in a nation of gallant men, in a nation of men of honour and of cavaliers. I thought ten thousand swords must have leaped from their scabbards to avenge even a look that threatened her with insult.—But the age of chivalry is gone.—That of sophisters,[3] œconomists, and calculators, has succeeded; and the glory of Europe is extinguished for ever. Never, never more, shall we behold that generous loyalty to rank and sex, that proud submission, that dignified obedience, that subordination of the heart, which kept alive, even in servitude itself, the

1. Marie Antoinette was the daughter of Maria Theresa, empress of Austria.
2. Like the women of classical Rome when they endured defeat, Marie Antoinette, Burke suggests, will kill herself to preserve her chastity rather than suffer the disgrace of rape.
3. Those who reason with clever and fallacious arguments.

spirit of an exalted freedom. The unbought grace of life, the cheap defence of nations, the nurse of manly sentiment and heroic enterprize is gone! It is gone, that sensibility of principle, that chastity of honour, which felt a stain like a wound, which inspired courage whilst it mitigated ferocity, which ennobled whatever it touched, and under which vice itself lost half its evil, by losing all its grossness.

This mixed system of opinion and sentiment had its origin in the antient chivalry; and the principle, though varied in its appearance by the varying state of human affairs, subsisted and influenced through a long succession of generations, even to the time we live in. If it should ever be totally extinguished, the loss I fear will be great. It is this which has given its character to modern Europe. It is this which has distinguished it under all its forms of government, and distinguished it to its advantage, from the states of Asia, and possibly from those states which flourished in the most brilliant periods of the antique world. It was this, which, without confounding ranks, had produced a noble equality, and handed it down through all the gradations of social life. It was this opinion which mitigated kings into companions, and raised private men to be fellows with kings. Without force, or opposition, it subdued the fierceness of pride and power; it obliged sovereigns to submit to the soft collar of social esteem, compelled stern authority to submit to elegance, and gave a domination vanquisher of laws, to be subdued by manners.

But now all is to be changed. All the pleasing illusions, which made power gentle, and obedience liberal, which harmonized the different shades of life, and which, by a bland assimilation, incorporated into politics the sentiments which beautify and soften private society, are to be dissolved by this new conquering empire of light and reason. All the decent drapery of life is to be rudely torn off. All the superadded ideas, furnished from the wardrobe of a moral imagination, which the heart owns, and the understanding ratifies, as necessary to cover the defects of our naked shivering nature, and to raise it to dignity in our own estimation, are to be exploded as a ridiculous, absurd, and antiquated fashion.

On this scheme of things, a king is but a man; a queen is but a woman; a woman is but an animal; and an animal not of the highest order. All homage paid to the sex in general as such, and without distinct views, is to be regarded as romance and folly. Regicide, and parricide, and sacrilege, are but fictions of superstition, corrupting jurisprudence by destroying its simplicity. The murder of a king, or a queen, or a bishop, or a father, are only common homicide; and if the people are by any chance, or in any way gainers by it, a sort of homicide much the most pardonable, and into which we ought not to make too severe a scrutiny.

On the scheme of this barbarous philosophy, which is the off-spring of cold hearts and muddy understandings, and which is as void of solid wisdom, as it is destitute of all taste and elegance, laws are to be supported only by their own terrors, and by the concern, which each individual may find in them, from his own private speculations, or can spare to them from his own private interests. In the groves of *their* academy, at the end of every visto, you see nothing but the gallows. Nothing is left which engages the affections on the part of the commonwealth. On the principles of this mechanic philosophy, our institutions can never be embodied, if I may use the expression, in persons; so as to create in us love, veneration, admiration, or attachment. But that sort of reason which banishes the affections is incapable of filling their place. These public affections, combined with manners, are required sometimes as supplements, sometimes as correctives, always as aids to law. The precept given by a wise man, as well as a great critic, for the construction of poems, is equally true as to states. *Non satis est pulchra esse poemata, dulcia sunto.*[4] There ought to be a system of manners in every nation which a well-formed mind could be disposed to relish. To make us love our country, our country ought to be lovely.

* * *

MARY WOLLSTONECRAFT

From A Vindication of the Rights of Men[†]

Sir,

It is not necessary, with courtly insincerity, to apologise to you for thus introducing on your precious time, not to profess that I think it an honour to discuss an important subject with a man whose literary abilities have raised him to notice in the state. I have not yet learned to twist my periods, nor, in the equivocal idiom of politeness, to disguise my sentiments, and imply what I should be afraid to utter: if,

---

4. From the Latin poet Horace's *Art of Poetry:* "It is not enough for poems to be fine; they must charm."

† Wollstonecraft's response to Burke's *Reflections* was one of the first salvos in the pamphlet war. *A Vindication of the Rights of Men*, framed as her letter to Burke, was written in a white heat of indignation and published early in December 1790. That first edition was anonymous, but the second was not. The revelation that Burke's antagonist was female startled reviewers who took it for granted that the political treatise was the most masculine of genres: "The rights of man asserted by a fair lady!" quipped the sardonic critic for the *Gentleman's Magazine:* "The age of chivalry cannot be over, or the sexes have changed their ground." The three excerpts printed here are taken from Wollstonecraft's second, revised edition. All notes are the editor's unless otherwise indicated. All page references to Wollstonecraft's *Vindication of the Rights of Woman* are to the present edition.

therefore, in the course of this epistle, I chance to express contempt, and even indignation, with some emphasis, I beseech you to believe that it is not a flight of fancy; for truth, in morals, has ever appeared to me the essence of the sublime; and, in taste, simplicity the only criterion of the beautiful.[1] But I war not with an individual when I contend for the *rights of men* and the liberty of reason. You see I do not condescend to cull my words to avoid the invidious phrase, nor shall I be prevented from giving a manly definition of it, by the flimsy ridicule which a lively fancy has interwoven with the present acceptation of the term. Reverencing the rights of humanity, I shall dare to assert them; not intimidated by the horse laugh that you have raised, or waiting till time has wiped away the compassionate tears which you have elaborately laboured to excite.

From the many just sentiments interspersed through the letter before me, and from the whole tendency of it, I should believe you to be a good, though a vain man, if some circumstances in your conduct did not render the inflexibility of your integrity doubtful; and for this vanity a knowledge of human nature enables me to discover such extenuating circumstances, in the very texture of your mind, that I am ready to call it amiable, and separate the public from the private character.

* * *

Quitting now the flowers of rhetoric, let us, Sir, reason together; and, believe me, I should not have meddled with these troubled waters, in order to point out your inconsistencies, if your wit had not burnished up some rusty, baneful opinions, and swelled the shallow current of ridicule till it resembled the flow of reason, and presumed to be the test of truth.

I shall not attempt to follow you through "horse-way and footpath;"[2] but, attacking the foundation of your opinions, I shall leave the superstructure to find a centre of gravity on which it may lean till some strong blast puffs it into air; or your teeming fancy, which the ripening judgment of sixty years has not tamed, produces another Chinese erection, to stare, at every turn, the plain country people in the face, who bluntly call such an airy edifice—a folly.[3]

The birthright of man, to give you, Sir, a short definition of this disputed right, is such a degree of liberty, civil and religious, as is compatible with the liberty of every other individual with whom he is united in a social compact, and the continued existence of that compact.

1. Throughout this *Vindication* Wollstonecraft's strategy is to resurrect ideas informing Burke's early publication on aesthetic theory, the *Philosophical Enquiry into the Origin of our Ideas of the Sublime and the Beautiful* (from 1757), and use them to trip up the author of *Reflections on the Revolution*.
2. *King Lear* IV.i.56.
3. Pagodas were fashionable ornaments in later eighteenth-century landscape gardening.

Liberty, in this simple, unsophisticated sense, I acknowledge, is a fair idea that has never yet received a form in the various governments that have been established on our beauteous globe; the demon of property has ever been at hand to encroach on the sacred rights of men, and to fence round with awful pomp laws that war with justice. But that it results from the eternal foundation of right—from immutable truth—who will presume to deny, that pretends to rationality—if reason has led them to build their morality[4] and religion on an everlasting foundation—the attributes of God?

I glow with indignation when I attempt, methodically, to unravel your slavish paradoxes, in which I can find no fixed first principle to refute; I shall not, therefore, condescend to shew where you affirm in one page what you deny in another; and how frequently you draw conclusions without any previous premises:—it would be something like cowardice to fight with a man who had never exercised the weapons with which his opponent chose to combat, and irksome to refute sentence after sentence in which the latent spirit of tyranny appeared.

I perceive, from the whole tenor of your Reflections, that you have a mortal antipathy to reason; but, if there is any thing like argument, or first principles, in your wild declamation, behold the result:—that we are to reverence the rust of antiquity, and term the unnatural customs, which ignorance and mistaken self-interest have consolidated, the sage fruit of experience: nay, that, if we do discover some errors, our *feelings* should lead us to excuse, with blind love, or unprincipled filial affection, the venerable vestiges of ancient days. These are gothic[5] notions of beauty—the ivy is beautiful, but, when it insidiously destroys the trunk from which it receives support, who would not grub it up?

Further, that we ought cautiously to remain for ever in frozen inactivity, because a thaw, whilst it nourishes the soil, spreads a temporary inundation; and the fear of risking any personal present convenience should prevent a struggle for the most estimable advantages. This is sound reasoning, I grant, in the mouth of the rich and short-sighted.

* * *

There appears to be such a mixture of real sensibility and fondly cherished romance in your composition, that the present crisis carries you out of yourself; and since you could not be one of the grand movers, the next *best* thing that dazzled your imagination was to be a

---

4. "As religion is included in my idea of morality, I should not have mentioned the term without specifying all the simple ideas which that comprehensive word generalizes; but as the charge of atheism has been very freely banded about in the letter I am considering, I wish to guard against misrepresentation" [Wollstonecraft's note].
5. Barbarous.

conspicuous opposer. Full of yourself, you make as much noise to convince the world that you despise the revolution, as Rousseau did to persuade his contemporaries to let him live in obscurity.

Reading your Reflections warily over, it has continually and forcibly struck me, that had you been a Frenchman, you would have been, in spite of your respect for rank and antiquity, a violent revolutionist; and deceived, as you now probably are, by the passions that cloud your reason, have termed your romantic enthusiasm an enlightened love of your country, a benevolent respect for the rights of men. Your imagination would have taken fire, and have found arguments, full as ingenious as those you now offer, to prove that the constitution, of which so few pillars remained, that constitution which time had almost obliterated, was not a model sufficiently noble to deserve close adherence. And, for the English constitution, you might not have had such a profound veneration as you have lately acquired; nay, it is not impossible that you might have entertained the same opinion of the English Parliament, that you professed to have during the American war.

Another observation which, by frequently occurring, has almost grown into a conviction, is simply this, that had the English in general reprobated the French revolution, you would have stood forth alone, and been the avowed Goliah of liberty.[6] But, not liking to see so many brothers near the throne of fame, you have turned the current of your passions, and consequently of your reasoning, another way. Had Dr. Price's sermon not lighted some sparks very like envy in your bosom, I shrewdly suspect that he would have been treated with more candour; nor is it charitable to suppose that any thing but personal pique and hurt vanity could have dictated such bitter sarcasms and reiterated expressions of contempt as occur in your Reflections.

But without fixed principles even goodness of heart is no security from inconsistency, and mild affectionate sensibility only renders a man more ingeniously cruel, when the pangs of hurt vanity are mistaken for virtuous indignation, and the gall of bitterness for the milk of Christian charity.

Where is the dignity, the infallibility of sensibility, in the fair ladies, whom, if the voice of rumour is to be credited, the captive negroes curse in all the agony of bodily pain, for the unheard of tortures they invent? It is probable that some of them, after the sight of a flagellation, compose their ruffled spirits and exercise their tender feelings by the perusal of the last imported novel.—How true these tears are to nature, I leave you to determine. But these ladies may have read your Enquiry concerning the origin of our ideas of the

6. 1 Samuel 17:4–54.

Sublime and Beautiful, and, convinced by your arguments, may have laboured to be pretty, by counterfeiting weakness.

You may have convinced them that *littleness* and *weakness* are the very essence of beauty; and that the Supreme Being, in giving women beauty in the most supereminent degree, seemed to command them, by the powerful voice of Nature, not to cultivate the moral virtues that might chance to excite respect, and interfere with the pleasing sensations they were created to inspire. Thus confining truth, fortitude, and humanity, within the rigid pale of manly morals, they might justly argue, that to be loved, woman's high end and great distinction! they should 'learn to lisp, to totter in their walk, and nick-name God's creatures.'[7] Never, they might repeat after you, was any man, much less a woman, rendered amiable by the force of those exalted qualities, fortitude, justice, wisdom, and truth; and thus forewarned of the sacrifice they must make to those austere, unnatural virtues, they would be authorized to turn all their attention to their persons, systematically neglecting morals to secure beauty.—Some rational old woman indeed might chance to stumble at this doctrine, and hint, that in avoiding atheism you had not steered clear of the mussulman's creed;[8] but you could readily exculpate yourself by turning the charge on Nature, who made our idea of beauty independent of reason. Nor would it be necessary for you to recollect, that if virtue has any other foundation than worldly utility, you have clearly proved that one half of the human species, at least, have not souls; and that Nature, by making women *little, smooth, delicate, fair* creatures,[9] never designed that they should exercise their reason to acquire the virtues that produce opposite, if not contradictory, feelings. The affection they excite, to be uniform and perfect, should not be tinctured with the respect which moral virtues inspire, lest pain should be blended with pleasure, and admiration disturb the soft intimacy of love. This laxity of morals in the female world is certainly more captivating to a libertine imagination than the cold arguments of reason, that give no sex to virtue. If beautiful

<hr/>

7. Wollstonecraft remembers and blends Hamlet's misogynistic account of women (*Hamlet* III.i.144–45) and the passage from Burke's *Philosophical Enquiry into the . . . Sublime and the Beautiful* (III, ix) in which Burke asserts that the idea of beauty, rather than being associated with perfection, involves "an idea of weakness and imperfection." He continues, "Women are very sensible of this, for which reason, they learn to lisp, to totter in their walk, to counterfeit weakness, and even sickness." The next sentence of the *Philosophical Enquiry* suggests the aesthetic principles that will in 1790 underpin Burke's portrait of Marie Antoinette in the *Reflections*: "Beauty in distress is much the most affecting power." (All quotations are from the critical edition of the *Philosophical Enquiry* prepared by James T. Boulton [Notre Dame and London, 1968], p. 110.) For additional reactions to this section of the *Philosophical Enquiry*, see Wollstonecraft's *Vindication of the Rights of Woman*, p. 13 and Macaulay's *Letters on Education*, p. 240 herein.
8. The belief, wrongly ascribed to followers of Islam, that women had no souls.
9. All these are attributes that Burke's *Philosophical Enquiry* associates with the beautiful rather than the sublime (see Part III, section xiii ["Beautiful objects small"]; xiv ["Smoothness"]; xvi ["Delicacy"]; and xvii ["Beauty in colour"]).

weakness be interwoven in a woman's frame, if the chief business of her life be (as you insinuate) to inspire love, and Nature has made an eternal distinction between the qualities that dignify a rational being and this animal perfection, her duty and happiness in this life must clash with any preparation for a more exalted state. So that Plato and Milton were grossly mistaken in asserting that human love led to heavenly, and was only an exaltation of the same affection; for the love of the Deity,[1] which is mixed with the most profound reverence, must be love of perfection, and not compassion for weakness.

To say the truth, I not only tremble for the souls of women, but for the good natured man, whom every one loves. The *amiable* weakness of his mind is a strong argument against its immateriality, and seems to prove that beauty relaxes the *solids* of the soul as well as the body.

It follows then immediately, from your own reasoning, that respect and love are antagonist principles;[2] and that, if we really wish to render men more virtuous, we must endeavour to banish all enervating modifications of beauty from civil society. We must, to carry your argument a little further, return to the Spartan regulations, and settle the virtues of men on the stern foundation of mortification and self-denial; for any attempt to civilize the heart, to make it humane by implanting reasonable principles, is a mere philosophic dream. If refinement inevitably lessens respect for virtue, by rendering beauty, the grand tempter, more seductive; if these relaxing feelings are incompatible with the nervous exertions of morality, the sun of Europe is not set; it begins to dawn, when cold metaphysicians try to make the head give laws to the heart.

But should experience prove that there is a beauty in virtue, a charm in order, which necessarily implies exertion, a depraved sensual taste may give way to a more manly one—and *melting* feelings to rational satisfactions. Both may be equally natural to man; the test is their moral difference, and that point reason alone can decide.

Such a glorious change can only be produced by liberty. * * *

* * *

But, among all your plausible arguments, and witty illustrations, your contempt for the poor always appears conspicuous, and rouses my indignation. The following paragraph in particular struck me, as breathing the most tyrannic spirit, and displaying the most factitious

---

1. Plato, *Symposium* 210a–11c; *Paradise Lost* VIII.589–92. Cf. *Vindication of the Rights of Woman*, p. 79.
2. Cf. Burke's *Philosophical Enquiry*, Part III, section xiii: "There is a wide difference between admiration and love. The sublime, which is the cause of the former, always dwells on great objects, and terrible; the latter on small ones, and pleasing; we submit to what we admire, but we love what submits to us; in the one case we are forced, in the other we are flattered into compliance" (p. 113).

feelings. 'Good order is the foundation of all good things. To be enabled to acquire, the people, without being servile, must be tractable and obedient. The magistrate must have his reverence, the laws their authority. The body of the people must not find the principles of natural subordination by art rooted out of their minds. They *must* respect that property of which they *cannot* partake. *They must labour to obtain what by labour can be obtained; and when they find, as they commonly do, the success disproportioned to the endeavour, they must be taught their consolation in the final proportions of eternal justice.* Of this consolation, whoever deprives them, deadens their industry, and strikes at the root of all acquisition as of all conservation. He that does this, is the cruel oppressor, the merciless enemy, of the poor and wretched; at the same time that, by his wicked speculations, he exposes the fruits of successful industry, and the accumulations of fortune, (ah! there's the rub)[3] to the plunder of the negligent, the disappointed, and the unprosperous.[4]

This is contemptible hard-hearted sophistry, in the specious form of humility, and submission to the will of Heaven.—It is, Sir, *possible* to render the poor happier in this world, without depriving them of the consolation which you gratuitously grant them in the next. They have a right to more comfort than they at present enjoy; and more comfort might be afforded them, without encroaching on the pleasures of the rich: not now awaiting to enquire whether the rich have any right to exclusive pleasures. What do I say?—encroaching! No; if an intercourse were established between them, it would impart the only true pleasure that can be snatched in this land of shadows, this hard school of moral discipline.

I know, indeed, that there is often something disgusting in the distresses of poverty, at which the imagination revolts, and starts back to exercise itself in the more attractive Arcadia of fiction.[5] The rich man builds a house, art and taste give it the highest finish. His gardens are planted, and the trees grow to recreate the fancy of the planter, though the temperature of the climate may rather force him to avoid the dangerous damps they exhale, than seek the umbrageous retreat. Every thing on the estate is cherished but man;—yet, to contribute to the happiness of man, is the most sublime of all enjoyments. But if, instead of sweeping pleasure-grounds, obelisks, temples, and elegant cottages, as *objects* for the eye, the heart was allowed to beat true to nature, decent farms would be scattered over the estate, and plenty smile around. Instead of the poor being subject to the griping hand of an avaricious steward, they would be

---

3. Echoing *Hamlet* III.i.167. "The rub": the flaw in the reasoning.
4. "Page 351" [Wollstonecraft's note].
5. Mythical land of pastoral simplicity, whose happy inhabitants were imagined as living in the manner of the golden age.

watched over with fatherly solicitude, by the man whose duty and pleasure it was to guard their happiness, and shield from rapacity the beings who, by the sweat of their brow, exalted him above his fellows.

* * *

MARY WOLLSTONECRAFT

From An Historical and Moral View of the Origin and Progress of the French Revolution[†]
* * *

But the irresistible energy of the moral and political sentiments of half a century, at last kindled into a blaze the illuminating rays of truth, which, throwing new light on the mental powers of man, and giving a fresh spring to his reasoning faculties, completely undermined the strong holds of priestcraft and hypocrisy.

At this glorious era, the toleration of religious opinions in America, which the spirit of the times, when that continent was peopled with persecuted europeans, produced, aided, not a little, to diffuse these rational sentiments, and exhibited the phenomenon of a government established on the basis of reason and equality. The eyes of all Europe were watchfully fixed on the practical success of this experiment in political science; and whilst the crowns of the old world were drawing into their focus the hard-earned recompence of the toil and care of the simple citizens, who lived detached from courts, deprived of the comforts of life, the just reward of industry, or, palsied by oppression, pined in dirt and idleness; the anglo-americans appeared to be another race of beings, men formed to enjoy the advantages of society, and not merely to benefit those who governed; the use to which they had been appropriated in almost every state;

---

† The title page of Wollstonecraft's *Historical and Moral View* has the notation "Volume the First," but in fact no additional volumes followed the first one, published in late 1794. Wollstonecraft, resident in France (and pregnant) while composing the book, experienced firsthand the bloody turn the Revolution took after the executions of Louis XVI and Marie Antoinette, the outbreak of war between France and Britain, and the ascendancy of Robespierre's Committee of Public Safety. A sense of danger and loss inflects the *Historical and Moral View*, which nonetheless limits itself to the prehistory and early, less-troubled phase of the Revolution, aiming to demonstrate "that the Revolution was neither produced by the abilities or intrigues of a few individuals; nor was the effect of sudden and short-lived enthusiasm; but the natural consequence of intellectual improvement." These excerpts are taken from the facsimile reprint of the second, 1795 edition of the *Historical and Moral View* (Delmar, N.Y., 1975). All notes are the editor's unless otherwise noted. The first selection here is from Book I's account of how the revolution in America prepared the ground for that in France. In the second passage Wollstonecraft interrupts her chronicle of the events of July 1789: this portrait of the French queen gives Wollstonecraft a way to unlock the corruption of the monarchical system.

considered only as the ballast which keeps the vessel steady, necessary, yet despised. So conspicuous in fact was the difference, that,
when frenchmen became the auxiliaries of those brave people,[1] during their noble struggle against the tyrannical and inhuman ambition of the british court, it imparted to them that stimulus, which
alone was wanting to give wings to freedom, who, hovering over
France, led her indignant votaries to wreak their vengeance on the
tottering fabric of a government, the foundation of which had been
laid by benighted ignorance, and it's walls cemented by the calami-
ties of millions that mock calculation—and, in it's ruins a system
was entombed, the most baneful to human happiness and virtue.

America fortunately found herself in a situation very different
from all the rest of the world; for she had it in her power to lay the
first stones of her government, when reason was venturing to can-
vass prejudice. Availing herself of the degree of civilization of the
world, she has not retained those customs, which were only the
expedients of barbarism; or thought that constitutions formed by
chance, and continually patched up, were superiour to the plans of
reason, at liberty to profit by experience.

When society was first regulated, the laws could not be adjusted
so as to take in the future conduct of it's members, because the faculties of man are unfolded and perfected by the improvements made
by society: consequently the regulations established as circumstances required were very imperfect. What then is to hinder man,
at each epoch of civilization, from making a stand, and new model-
ling the materials, that have been hastily thrown into a rude mass,
which time alone has consolidated and rendered venerable?

When society was first subjugated to laws, probably by the ambition of some, and the desire of safety in all, it was natural for men to
be selfish, because they were ignorant how intimately their own
comfort was connected with that of others; and it was also very natural, that humanity, rather the effect of feeling than of reason,
should have a very limited range. But, when men once see, clear as
the light of heaven,—and I hail the glorious day from afar!—that on
the general happiness depends their own, reason will give strength
to the fluttering wings of passion, and men will *"do unto others, what
they wish they should do unto them."*[2]

What has hitherto been the political perfection of the world? In
the two most celebrated nations it has only been a polish of manners, an extension of that family love, which is rather the effect of
sympathy and selfish passions, than reasonable humanity. And in

1. In 1778 France entered the War of Independence as the Americans' ally.
2. Luke 6:31.

what has ended their so much extolled patriotism? In vain glory and barbarity—every page of history proclaims. And why has the enthusiasm for virtue thus passed away like the dew of the morning, dazzling the eyes of it's admirers? Why?—because it was factitious virtue.

During the period they had to combat against oppression, and rear an infant state, what instances of heroism do not the annals of Greece and Rome display! But it was merely the blaze of passion, "live smoke;" for after vanquishing their enemies, and making the most astonishing sacrifices to the glory of their country, they became civil tyrants, and preyed on the very society, for whose welfare it was easier to die, than to practise the sober duties of life, which insinuate through it the contentment that is rather felt than seen. Like the parents who forget all the dictates of justice and humanity, to aggrandize the very children whom they keep in a state of dependence, these heroes loved their country, because it was their country, ever showing by their conduct, that it was only a part of a narrow love of themselves.

It is time, that a more enlightened moral love of mankind should supplant, or rather support physical affections. It is time, that the youth approaching manhood should be led by principles, and not hurried along by sensations—and then we may expect, that the heroes of the present generation, still having their monsters to cope with, will labour to establish such rational laws throughout the world, that men will not rest in the dead letter, or become artificial beings as they become civilized.

We must get entirely clear of all the notions drawn from the wild traditions of original sin: the eating of the apple, the theft of Prometheus, the opening of Pandora's box, and the other fables, too tedious to enumerate, on which priests have erected their tremendous structures of imposition, to persuade us, that we are naturally inclined to evil: we shall then leave room for the expansion of the human heart, and, I trust, find, that men will insensibly render each other happier as they grow wiser. It is indeed the necessity of stifling many of it's most spontaneous desires, to obtain the factitious virtues of society, that makes man vicious, by depriving him of that dignity of character, which rests only on truth. For it is not paradoxical to assert, that the social virtues are nipt in the bud by the very laws of society. One principal of action is sufficient—Respect thyself—whether it be termed fear of God—religion; love of justice—morality; or, self-love—the desire of happiness. Yet, how can a man respect himself; and if not, how believe in the existence of virtue; when he is practising the daily shifts, which do not come under the cognisance of the law, in order to obtain a respectable situation in life? It seems, in fact, to be the business of a civilized man, to harden his heart, that on it he may sharpen the wit; which, assuming the appellation of sagacity, or cunning, in different characters, is only a proof, that the head is clear, because the heart is cold.

Besides, one great cause of misery in the present imperfect state of society is, that the imagination, continually tantalized, becomes the inflated wen of the mind, draining off the nourishment from the vital parts. Nor would it, I think, be stretching the inference too far, to insist, that men become vicious in the same proportion as they are obliged, by the defects of society, to submit to a kind of self-denial, which ignorance, not morals, prescribes.

But these evils are passing away; a new spirit has gone forth, to organise the body-politic; and where is the criterion to be found, to estimate the means, by which the influence of this spirit can be confined, now enthroned in the hearts of half the inhabitants of the globe? Reason has, at last, shown her captivating face, beaming with benevolence; and it will be impossible for the dark hand of despotism again to obscure it's radiance, or the lurking dagger of subordinate tyrants to reach her bosom. The image of God implanted in our nature is now more rapidly expanding; and as it opens, liberty with maternal wing seems to be soaring to regions far above vulgar annoyance, promising to shelter all mankind.

* * *

The courtly, dignified politeness of the queen, with all those complacent graces which dance round flattered beauty, whose every charm is drawn forth by the consciousness of pleasing, promised all that a sanguine fancy had pourtrayed of future happiness and peace.[3] From her fascinating smiles, indeed, was caught the careless hope, that, expanding the heart, makes the animal spirits vibrate, in every nerve, with pleasure:—yet, she smiled but to deceive; or, if she felt some touches of sympathy, it was only the unison of the moment.

It is certain, that education, and the atmosphere of manner in which a character is formed, change the natural laws of humanity; otherwise it would be unaccountable, how the human heart can be so dead to the tender emotions of benevolence, which most forcibly teach us, that real or lasting felicity flows only from a love of virtue, and the practice of sincerity.

3. Marie Antoinette (1755–1793), daughter of Maria Theresa, the empress of Austria, was married off at age fourteen to the heir to the French throne so as to cement the two nations' alliance. The French never ceased to suspect that her true loyalties lay with Austria rather than with France and, in particular, with her brother the Holy Roman emperor Joseph II. The Abbé de Vermond, the tutor who prepared Marie Antoinette for her royal role, accompanied her from Vienna to Versailles to ease her transition to French court life.

The unfortunate queen of France, beside the advantages of birth and station, possessed a very fine person; and her lovely face, sparkling with vivacity, hid the want of intelligence. Her complexion was dazzlingly clear; and, when she was pleased, her manners were bewitching; for she happily mingled the most insinuating voluptuous softness and affability, with an air of grandeur, bordering on pride, that rendered the contrast more striking. Independence also, of whatever kind, always gives a degree of dignity to the mien; so that monarchs and nobles, with most ignoble souls, from believing themselves superiour to others, have actually acquired a look of superiority.

But her opening faculties were poisoned in the bud; for before she came to Paris, she had already been prepared, by a corrupt, supple abbé, for the part she was to play; and, young as she was, became so firmly attached to the aggrandizement of her house, that, though plunged deep in pleasure, she never omitted sending immense sums to her brother, on every occasion. The person of the king, in itself very disgusting, was rendered more so by gluttony, and a total disregard of delicacy, and even decency in his apartments: and, when jealous of the queen, for whom he had a kind of devouring passion, he treated her with great brutality, till she acquired sufficient finesse to subjugate him. Is it then surprizing, that a very desirable woman, with a sanguine constitution, should shrink abhorrent from his embraces; or that an empty mind should be employed only to vary the pleasures, which emasculated her circean[4] court? And, added to this, the histories of the Julias and Messalinas of antiquity,[5] convincingly prove, that there is no end to the vagaries of the imagination, when power is unlimited, and reputation set at defiance.

Lost then in the most luxurious pleasures, or managing court intrigues, the queen became a profound dissembler; and her heart hardened by sensual enjoyments to such a degree, that when her family and favourites stood on the brink of ruin, her little portion of mind was employed only to preserve herself from danger. As a proof of the justness of this assertion, it is only necessary to observe, that, in the general wreck, not a scrap of her writing has been found to criminate her; neither has she suffered a word to escape her to exasperate the people, even when burning with rage, and contempt. The effect that adversity may have on her choked understanding time will show;[6] but during her prosperity, the moments of languor, that glide into the interstices of enjoyment, were passed in the most

4. Wollstonecraft compares the queen to Circe, the nymph in Homer's *Odyssey* whose witch-craft transformed men into beasts.
5. In the history of ancient Rome, Julia, daughter of Emperor Augustus and wife of Agrippa, and Messalina, wife of Emperor Claudius, were notorious for their promiscuity.
6. "This was written some months before the death of the queen" [Wollstonecraft's note].

childish manner; without the appearance of any vigour of mind, to palliate the wanderings of the imagination.—Still she was a woman of uncommon address; and though her conversation was insipid, her compliments were so artfully adapted to flatter the person she wished to please or dupe, and so eloquent is the beauty of a queen, in the eyes even of superiour men, that she seldom failed to carry her point when she endeavoured to gain an ascendancy over the mind of an individual. Over that of the king she acquired unbounded sway, when, managing the disgust she had for his person, she made him pay a kingly price for her favours. A court is the best school in the world for actors; it was very natural then for her to become a complete actress, and an adept in all the arts of coquetry that debauch the mind, whilst they render the person alluring.

* * *

The Wollstonecraft Controversy

As the texts in this section—from the raucous reception history of the *Vindication of the Rights of Woman*—suggest, there was a "Wollstonecraft controversy" in Britain during the 1790s as well as a revolution controversy. The one was inextricable from the other. The majority of reviewers welcomed the *Vindication of the Rights of Woman* when it first appeared: William Enfield, whose discussion of the book is excerpted here, is representative in treating its arguments respectfully, even as he downplays some of their more radical aspects (the call for women's participation in the political process, for instance). However, as the news from France got grimmer and as the anger intensifying in Britain over an unreformed electoral system made it seem as though revolution were possible there as well, the world-transformative tenor of Wollstonecraft's proposals got harder to ignore and harder to discuss dispassionately. Her egalitarianism came to seem irredeemably tainted by its association with French paradigms.

Sadly, the year after Wollstonecraft's death in 1797, her opponents received a boost from an unlikely quarter: her widower. In 1798 William Godwin published his *Memoirs of the Author of the Vindication of the Rights of Woman*. As the selections of that biography reprinted here suggest, he committed himself in composing it to a program of utter candor, and the details about Wollstonecraft's sexual history he furnished—the revelation, for instance, that she had been an unwed mother and that she had attempted suicide when abandoned by her lover, Gilbert Imlay—were seized on both greedily and disapprovingly. Those who had gone on record with their admiration for Wollstonecraft had to worry now about how their approval might be construed—a worry audible in some of the readings that follow. Conservatives who had mistrusted the *Vindication* all along felt vindicated. *This* was what the rights for which Wollstonecraft had advocated boiled down to, cackled the *Anti-Jacobin Review* in its review of Godwin, "the right of women to indulge their inclinations with every man they like"; it turned out that Wollstonecraft's program was not even novel, this reviewer continued, but instead "as old as prostitution." *The Rights of Woman* never ceased to be read, even as conservatism became entrenched in British society, but henceforth the book tended to be overshadowed by its author's life—a situation that prevailed well into the twentieth century. And henceforth an almost ritualistic disavowal of Wollstonecraft's example appears to have been expected of female authors in particular, as a gesture to placate the forces of morality.

ANONYMOUS

From Review of *A Vindication of the Rights of Woman*[†]

One of the strictest proofs in mathematical demonstrations, is the reducing the question to an absurdity; by allowing, for instance, that the proposition is not true, and then showing that this would lead to the most obvious inconsistencies. Miss Wollstonecraft has converted this method of proceeding with the same success: reasoning on the boasted principles of the Rights of Man, she finds they lead very clearly to the object of her work, a Vindication of the Rights of Woman; and, by the absurdity of many of her conclusions, shows, while we admit the reasoning, that the premises must be, in some respects, fallacious.

> 'Dismissing then those pretty feminine phrases, which the men condescendingly use to soften our slavish dependence, and despising that weak elegancy of mind, exquisite sensibility, and sweet docility of manners, supposed to be the sexual characteristics of the weaker vessel, I wish to shew that elegance is inferior to virtue, that the first object of laudable ambition is to obtain a character as a human being, regardless of the distinction of sex; and that secondary views should be brought to this simple touchstone.'[1]

This is the outline of her plan; but before she proceeds to show that this change would be suitable, useful, advantageous, it will be first necessary to prove that there is no sexual distinction of character; that the female mind is equally fitted for the more arduous mental operations; that women are equally able to pursue the toilsome

---

[†] Published in two parts in the *Critical Review* n.s. 7, vol. 4 (1792): 389–98; vol. 5 (1792): 132–41. This selection, from the most negative of the reviews the *Rights of Woman* received when it was first published, reprints pp. 389–93 of the first installment. All notes are the editor's unless otherwise indicated. All page references to Wollstonecraft are to the present edition.

1. The quotation from Wollstonecraft is from p. 12.

road of minute, laborious, investigation; that their judgments are equally sound, their resolution equally strong. After this is done, the benefit derived must be considered; and, when all are strong, to whom must the weaker operations belong? The female Plato will find it unsuitable to 'the dignity of her virtue' to dress the child, and descend to the disgusting offices of a nurse: the new Archimedes will measure the shirts by means of the altitude taken by a quadrant; and the young lady, instead of studying the softer and more amiable arts of pleasing, must contend with her lover for superiority of mind, for greater dignity of virtue; and before she condescends to become his wife, must prove herself his equal or superior.—It may be fancy, prejudice, or obstinacy, we contend not for a name, but we are infinitely better pleased with the present system; and, in truth, dear young lady, for by the appellation sometimes prefixed to your name we must suppose you to be young, endeavour to attain 'the weak elegancy of mind,' the 'sweet docility of manners,' 'the exquisite sensibility,' the former ornaments of your sex; we are certain you will be more pleasing, and we dare pronounce that you will be infinitely happier. Mental superiority is not an object worth contending for, if happiness be the aim. But, as this is the first female combatant in the new field of the Rights of Woman, if we smile only, we shall be accused of wishing to decline the contest; if we content ourselves with paying a compliment to her talents, it will be styled inconsistent with 'true dignity,' and as showing that we want to continue the 'slavish dependence.'—We must contend then with this new Atalanta;[2] and who knows whether, in this modern instance, we may not gain two victories by the contest? There is more than one batchelor in our corps; and, if we should *succeed*, miss Wollstonecraft may take her choice.

* * *

The pathetic address ad hominem,[3] on the injustice and cruelty of subjugating women, is interesting and well expressed. It is true, that women cannot 'by *force* be confined to domestic concerns:' it is equally true, that 'they will neglect private duties, to disturb, by cunning tricks, the orderly plans of reason;' and sometimes, we may add, even for worse purposes. We agree too, that no coercion should be established 'in society, and *the common law of gravity prevailing, the sexes will fall into their proper place:*' nor shall we object to another passage, that 'if women are not permitted to enjoy *legitimate rights,*

2. In the Greek myth she promised to marry the man who could defeat her in a race; the penalty for losing to her was death.
3. "As we write this article professedly for the service of the lady, we ought to apologise for the Latin word. It may be englished '*personal* address;'—but 'hominem' is a word, in this instance, peculiarly happy, for it means man or woman—either exclusively man, or those *manly females* who endeavour to imitate men" [Anonymous's note].

they will render both men and themselves vicious to obtain *illicit privileges.*[4] But to be serious.

We should despise ourselves, if we were capable to garble sentences, in order to make them bear a different or a double meaning. The meaning of miss Wollstonecraft must be obvious, and we have only marked the equivocal nature of her language by Italics. If the whole was not as defective in reasoning as in propriety, we should not for a moment have indulged a smile. The object of this dedication, and indeed of her whole work, is to show that women should participate in the advantages of education and knowledge, that they may be more suitable companions for their husbands, better tutors in the earlier periods of their children's lives, and more useful active citizens. When she steps from the stilts of patriotism, and omits the last object, she reasons with accuracy and propriety; not always indeed in a regular method, or by a well compacted chain of argument, but sometimes with a force carrying conviction. When we proceed to examine the subject more closely, and enquire into the degree of education and mental improvement necessary, we suspect that we must greatly differ. Are the mental powers to be regulated only, and generally informed, or are the sciences to be regularly taught? If a young woman be led to examine a subject coolly, to compare different arguments, to estimate the different degrees of evidence which each subject admits of, and to trace with some attention the evolutions of the human mind: above all, if she indulges a habit of reflection, and is neither afraid nor ashamed to look at her own errors, and investigate their source, she will be a more pleasing companion, a better wife and mother, a more useful member of society. All this a frequent reflection, and the conversation of a sensible man, will teach better than books, if we except those general essays, which, while they improve the mental faculties, add to the stock of ideas; and those works, which instruct the mind by the experience of former ages, or trace its exertions in different circumstances; we allude to history and travels, for we, *at present,* exclude the more elegant works of entertainment.

* * *

4. The quotation from Wollstonecraft is from p. 8 herein.

WILLIAM ENFIELD

From Review of *A Vindication of the Rights of Woman*†

Philosophy, which, for so many ages, has amused the indolent recluse with subtle and fruitless speculations, has, at length, stepped forth into the public walks of men, and offers them her friendly aid in correcting those errors which have hitherto retarded their progress toward perfection, and in establishing those principles and rules of action, by which they may be gradually conducted to the summit of human felicity. Inveloped as mankind at present are with the mists of prejudice, and encumbered on every side with institutions and customs, which prevent the free expansion of their intellectual and moral powers, it is the interest of private individuals, and the duty of those who are entrusted with the care of the public welfare, wherever, or in whatever character, this divine Instructress appears, to give her an honourable reception, and an attentive hearing. Among the most enlightened people of antiquity, Wisdom, as well as Beauty, was deified under a female form; and in modern language it is still usual to give Philosophy and Wisdom a female personification. What is this but a tacit concession in favour of the female part of the species, that they are no less capable of instructing than of pleasing?—and how jealous forever WE may be of our *right* to the proud pre-eminence which we have assumed, the women of the present age are daily giving us indubitable proofs that mind is of no sex, and that, with the fostering aid of education, the world, as well as the nursery, may be benefited by their instructions.

In the class of philosophers, the *author* of this treatise—whom we will not offend by styling, authoress—has a right to a distinguished place. The important business, here undertaken, is to correct errors, hitherto universally embraced, concerning the female character; and to raise woman, from a state of degradation and vassalage, to her proper place in the scale of existence; where, with the dignity of independence, she may discharge the duties and enjoy the happiness of a rational Being. The fundamental principle, on which the whole argument of this work is founded, is that, except in affairs of love, sexual distinctions ought to be disregarded, and women be considered in the light of rational creatures; who, in common with

† Published in *Monthly Review* n.s. 8 (June 1792): 198–209. The selections reprinted here are from pp. 198–99 and 208–09, omitting a middle section devoted to long quotations and summaries of the work. The review, published anonymously, has been ascribed to William Enfield (1741–1797), a Dissenting minister and author of books on education. All the notes are the editor's.

men, are placed in this world to unfold their faculties, and whose first object of ambition ought to be to obtain a character as a human Being. It is acknowledged that more attention has lately been paid to the education of women than formerly: but it is at the same time maintained, that the method, in which they are commonly educated, only tends to enfeeble both the body and the mind, and to render them insignificant objects of desire. In order to correct this error, which is considered by Miss Wollstonecraft as a gross violation of justice against one half of the species, and as prolific in mischief to the whole; and after some general observations on the rights and duties of human beings, and on the causes of the present imperfect state of human society; the prevailing opinion of a sexual character is discussed, and its influence on female education and manners is, with equal solidity of reasoning, and strength of colouring, represented at large. * * *

* * *

* * * It will be easily perceived that the author is possessed of great energy of intellect, vigour of fancy, and command of language; and that the performance suggests many reflections, which well deserve the attention of the public, and which, pursued under the direction of good sense and sage experience, may greatly contribute to the improvement of the condition and character of the female world. We do not, however, so zealously adopt Miss W.'s plan for a REVOLUTION in female education and manners, as not to perceive that several of her opinions are fanciful, and some of her projects romantic. We do not see, that the condition or the character of women would be improved, by assuming an active part in civil government. It does not appear to us to be necessary, in order to enlighten the understandings of women, that we should prohibit the employment of their fingers in those useful and elegant labours of the needle, for which, from the days of Penelope,[1] they have obtained so much deserved applause. Certain associations, now too firmly established to be easily broken, forbid us to think that women are degraded by the trivial attention which the men are inclined to pay them; or that it would be any increase of the pleasures of society, if, 'except where love animates the behaviour, the distinction of sex were to be confounded.'[2] This distinction, we apprehend, will never be overlooked, till the time arrives, "when we shall neither marry nor be given in marriage, but be as the angels of God in heaven."[3] Notwithstanding all this, however, we entirely agree with the fair

1. A reference to the faithful wife in Homer's *Odyssey* and her skill in weaving, a skill that buys Penelope time when she is being pressured to renounce hope of Odysseus's return and to remarry.
2. The quotation from Wollstonecraft is from p. 62 herein.
3. Matthew 22:30.

writer, that both the condition and the character of women are capable of great improvement; and that, by means of a more rational plan of female education, in which a judicious attention should be paid to the cultivation of their understanding and taste, as well as of their dispositions and manners, women might be rendered at once more agreeable, more respectable, and more happy in every station of life. Both men and women should certainly in the first place, regard themselves, and should be treated by each other, as human beings. It might, perhaps, in some measure, contribute to this end, if, beside the sexual appellations of man and woman, we had some general term to denote the species, like Ανθρωπος and *Homo* in the Greek and Roman languages. The want of such a general term is a material defect in our language.

What practical measures may be reasonably adopted, in order to produce the improvement so strongly recommended in this work, we expect to be more distinctly informed in the second part; in which we are promised a more minute consideration of the laws relative to women, and of their particular duties.

ANNA LAETITIA BARBAULD

The Rights of Woman[†]

Yes, injured Woman! rise, assert thy right!
Woman! too long degraded, scorned opprest;
O born to rule in partial[1] Law's despite,
Resume thy native empire o'er the breast!

Go forth arrayed in panoply[2] divine;   5
That angel pureness which admits no stain;
Go, bid proud Man his boasted rule resign,
And kiss the golden sceptre of thy reign.

[†] When, in 1792, Wollstonecraft cited her writings—admiringly in the fifth chapter of the *Vindication of the Rights of Woman*, with irritation in the fourth—the poet and essayist Anna Laetitia Barbauld (1743–1825) was a central figure in radical intellectual culture. This poem, which likely records Barbauld's reaction to her appearance in Wollstonecraft's book, may have been written in 1792 but was published much later, in a posthumous selection of Barbauld's works that appeared in 1825. Although "The Rights of Woman" has been read as recommending to women exactly the cultural segregation between the political sphere of rights and the private sphere of love that Wollstonecraft rejected, it is notable that Barbauld was politically active through the 1790s, publishing poems and pamphlets in support of the abolition of the slave trade and the rights of Dissenting Protestants. All the notes are the editor's.
1. Biased.
2. Suit of armor.

Go, gird thyself with grace; collect thy store
Of bright artillery glancing from afar;   10
Soft melting tones thy thundering cannon's roar,
Blushes and fears thy magazine[3] of war.

Thy rights are empire: urge no meaner claim,—
Felt, not defined, and if debated, lost;
Like sacred mysteries, which withheld from fame,   15
Shunning discussion, are revered the most.

Try all that wit and art suggest to bend
Of thy imperial foe the stubborn knee;
Make treacherous Man thy subject, not thy friend;
Thou mayst command, but never canst be free.   20

Awe the licentious, and restrain the rude;
Soften the sullen, clear the cloudy brow:
Be, more than princes' gifts, thy favours sued;—
She hazards all, who will the least allow.

But hope not, courted idol of mankind,   25
On this proud eminence secure to stay;
Subduing and subdued, thou soon shalt find
Thy coldness soften, and thy pride give way.

Then, then, abandon each ambitious thought,
Conquest or rule thy heart shall feebly move,   30
In Nature's school, by her soft maxims taught,
That separate rights are lost in mutual love.

THOMAS TAYLOR

From A Vindication of the Rights of Brutes[†]

Advertisement

The particular design of the following sheets, is to evince by demon-
strative arguments, the perfect equality of what is called the irrational species, to the human; but it has likewise a more general

---

3. Storehouse of arms.
† Thomas Taylor (1758–1835) rose from humble beginnings (his father was a maker of
corsets) to become a philosopher and acclaimed translator of Neo-Platonist philosophy.
These excerpts from his anonymously published *Vindication* are from his prefatory Adver-
tisement and a part of Chapter 6, "On the Importance of Understanding the Language of
Brutes, and Restoring Them to Their Natural Equality with Mankind." Though the *Oxford
Dictionary of National Biography* reports that Taylor's contemporaries noticed his fondness
for cats, the text's support for animal rights is certainly insincere, a contrivance that
advances Taylor's satiric ends. The text here is that of the modern reprint of the 1792 London edition, with introduction by Louise Schutz Boas (Gainesville: Scholars' Facsimiles and
Reprints, 1966), pp. iii–vii and 80–84. All notes are the editor's unless otherwise indicated.

design; and this is no other, than to establish the equality of all things, as to their intrinsic dignity and worth. Indeed, after those wonderful productions of Mr. PAINE[1] and Mrs. WOOLSTONCRAFT, such a theory as the present, seems to be necessary, in order to give perfection to our researches into the rights of things; and in such an age of discovery and independence as the present, the author flatters himself, that his theory will be warmly patronized by all the lovers of novelty, and friends of opposition, who are happily, at this period, so numerous both in France and England, and who are likely to receive an unbounded increase.

The author indeed, is well aware, that even in these luminous days, there are still many who will be so far from admitting the equality of brutes to men, that they will not even allow the equality of mankind to each other. Perhaps too, they will endeavour to support their opinion from the authority of Aristotle in his politics, where he endeavours to prove, that some men are naturally born slaves, and others free; and that the slavish part of mankind ought to be governed by the independent, in the same manner as the soul governs the body, that is, like a despot or a tyrant. "For (says he) those who are born with strong bodily and weak mental powers, are born to serve; and on the contrary, whenever the mind predominates over the body, it confers natural freedom on its possessor."[2] But this is a conclusion which will surely be ridiculed by every genuine modern, as it wholly proceeds on a supposition, that mind and body are two distinct things, and that the former is more excellent than the latter; though almost every one is now convinced, that soul and body are only nominally distinguished from each other, and are essentially the same.

In short, such is the prevalence of truth, and such the futility of Aristotle, that his distinction between master and servant is continually losing ground; so that all subordination seems to be dying away, and an approximation to equality taking place among the different orders of mankind. The truth of this observation is particularly evident in female servants, whose independent spirit, which is mistaken by some for boldness and impudence, is become the subject of general surprize; and who so happily rival their mistresses in dress, that excepting a little awkwardness in their carriage, and roughness in their hands, occasioned by untwisting the wide-bespattering radii of the mop, and strenuously grasping the scrubbing-brush, there is no difference between my lady and her house-maid. We may therefore

1. Thomas Paine (1737–1809) wrote the most widely read defense of the French Revolution. Framed as a response to Burke's *Reflections on the Revolution in France,* the first part of Paine's *Rights of Man* is estimated to have sold an astonishing two hundred thousand copies in the year after its publication in 1791.
2. See *Politics* I, v. Aristotle's treatise was written c. 335–23 B.C.E.

reasonably hope, that this amazing rage for liberty will continually increase; that mankind will shortly abolish all government as an intolerable yoke; and that they will as universally join in *vindicating the rights of brutes*, as in asserting the prerogatives of man.

* * *

From *Chapter 6*
* * *

And here I cannot refrain from mentioning a most singular advantage, which would arise from an association with dogs, when their language is perfectly understood by us; the advantage I allude to, respects a thing of no less importance than the instruction of youth in one of the most interesting particulars belonging to juvenile tuition. Every one knows how universally prevalent the practice of self-pollution is become amongst children; and how dreadful its consequences are in debilitating the constitution, and corrupting the morals of the unhappy youths who are the votaries of this detestable vice. Now that extraordinary genius, Mrs. Wollstonecraft, proposes the following remedy for this pernicious practice, in that great work of hers, called, *Elements of Morality for Children:*[3]—"I am thoroughly persuaded," says she, "that the most efficacious method to root out this dreadful evil, which poisons the source of human happiness, would be to speak to children of the organs of generation as freely as we speak of the other parts of the body, and explain to them the noble use, which they were designed for, and how they may be injured." She adds, "I have conversed with the most sensible school-masters on this subject, and they have confirmed me in my opinion." This plan is beyond all doubt a most striking proof of her uncommon capacity, and the truth of her grand theory, *the equality of the female nature with the male;* for whoever considers this affair with the attention it deserves, must be convinced, that if children were but told how the genital parts may be injured, and how they are to be employed in a natural way, they would not have the least curiosity to make any experiments, which might tend to frustrate the benevolent intention of nature.

But however great and original this thought may be, yet it would certainly be very much improved, by committing the instruction of youth in this particular to dogs; for these sagacious animals, all of whom appear to be Cynic philosophers,[4] would not only be very well calculated to explain the noble use for which the parts were

---

3. "Page 14 of the Introductory Address." [Taylor's note]. The quotation is from Wollstonecraft's introduction to Christian Gotthilf Salzmann's *Elements of Morality, for the Use of Children,* which she translated in 1790.
4. There was in fact a school of "cynic" (originally stoic) philosophers in ancient Athens; our word *cynic* comes from the Greek word for "dog."

designed, but would be very willing, at any time, and in any place, to give them specimens of the operation of the parts in the natural way. Not to mention, that they would likewise teach them how to get above those foolish habits, decency and shame, which false opinion first introduced [to mankind].

* * *

MARY HAYS

From Letters and Essays, Moral and Miscellaneous†

[*Essay 3, "On the Influence of Authority and Custom on the Female Mind and Manners"*]

Of all bondage, mental bondage is surely the most fatal; the absurd despotism which has hitherto, with more than gothic barbarity, enslaved the female mind, the enervating and degrading system of manners by which the understandings of women have been chained down to frivolity and trifles, have increased the general tide of effeminacy and corruption. To conform to the perpetual fluctuation of fashion (and few have the courage to dare the "slow and moving finger of scorn,"[1] which is pointed at every external singularity) requires almost their whole time and attention, and leaves little leisure for intellectual improvement.

* * *

A few distinguished individuals, feeling the powers of their own minds (for what can curb the celestial energy of genius?) are endeavouring to dispel the magical illusions of custom, and restore degraded woman to the glory of rationality, and to a fitness for immortality. The rights of woman, and the name of Woollstonecraft, will go down to posterity with reverence, when the pointless sarcasms of witlings[2] are forgotten. I am aware that some men of real good sense and candor, have supposed that the idea of there being no sexual character, is carried in this most admirable work a little too far. Let them reflect for a moment on the extremes which the opposite opinion has produced; and say from whence arises the

---

† In 1793, when she published her collection, Mary Hays (1759–1843) was beginning her career as a woman of letters, assisted by the rather stern advice she received from an older friend, Mary Wollstonecraft. The essay reprinted here anticipates Hays's full-length discussion of the subjection of women, *Appeal to the Men of Great Britain in Behalf of Women* (1798). There is a modern facsimile reprint of *Letters and Essays* in the Garland Series *The Feminist Controversy in England*, ed. Gina Luria (New York, 1974), which is the basis for the text here, which reprints pp. 19–22 and 28–29. All notes are the editor's.
1. *Othello* IV.ii.56–57.
2. Those who fancy themselves witty.

most formidable danger? Is there any cause to apprehend that we may subject our feelings too much to the guidance of reason? Or that we shall conduct the business of our families with too much order and equity: to the wise and good only, I now appeal! would you not dare to give up any of the allurements of the mistress (if indeed any need be given up worth the preserving) to the refined pleasure of living with a rational and equal companion? In such an intercourse, when enlivened by love, if happiness resides on earth, surely it is to be found! where the advantages are reciprocal, for each reflects back with interest, the light they receive. Similarity of mind and principle is the only true basis of harmony. Great superiority of either side causes a narrow jealousy, or a painful constraint; there is nothing so irksome as to converse with people who cannot understand you.

* * *

But the vindicator of female rights is thought by some sagacious married men to be incompetent to form any just opinion of the cares and duties of a conjugal state, from never having entered the matrimonial lists, because perhaps she has not met with the man who knows how properly to value her, or having met, may, alas! have lost. Wonderful free-masonry this! and ridiculous as wonderful. To be sure those who are eagerly engaged in play, with all their self-interest up in arms, are much better judges of the game than the cool impartial looker on; and a West-India Planter must understand the justice of the Slave-Trade far better than an English House of Commons, to say nothing of the very superior and extraordinary political wisdom necessarily belonging to the office of Prime Minister, of which the profane vulgar can form no idea! What nonsense this! Does it need a serious refutation? From such notions (most devoutly I repeat a part of the liturgy) good Lord deliver us.

* * *

WILLIAM GODWIN

From Memoirs of the Author of A Vindication of the Rights of Woman[†]

Never did any author enter into a cause, with a more ardent desire to be found, not a flourishing and empty declaimer, but an effectual champion. She considered herself as standing forth in defence of one half of the human species, labouring under a yoke which,

† In 1791 Wollstonecraft first met the political radical and philosopher William Godwin, at the house of her publisher, Joseph Johnson. Thomas Paine, author of *Rights of Man,* was

through all the records of time, had degraded them from the station of rational beings, and almost sunk them to the level of the brutes. She saw indeed, that they were often attempted to be held in silken fetters, and bribed into the love of slavery; but the disguise and the treachery served only the more fully to confirm her opposition. She regarded her sex, in the language of Calista, as

"In every state of life the slaves of men:"[1]

the rich as alternately under the despotism of a father, a brother, and a husband; and the middling and the poorer classes shut out from the acquisition of bread with independence, when they are not shut out from the very means of an industrious subsistence. Such were the views she entertained of the subject; and such the feelings with which she warmed her mind.

The work is certainly a very bold and original production. The strength and firmness with which the author repels the opinion of Rousseau, Dr. Gregory, and Dr. James Fordyce, respecting the condition of women, cannot but make a strong impression upon every ingenuous[2] reader. The public at large formed very different opinions respecting the character of the performance. Many of the sentiments are undoubtedly of a rather masculine description. The spirited and decisive way in which the author explodes the system of gallantry, and the species of homage with which the sex is usually treated, shocked the majority. Novelty produced a sentiment in their mind, which they mistook for a sense of injustice. The pretty, soft creatures that are so often to be found in the female sex, and that class of men who believe they could not exist without such pretty, soft creatures to resort to, were in arms against the author of so heretical and blasphemous a doctrine. There are also, it must be confessed, occasional passages of a stern and rugged feature, incompatible with the true stamina of the writer's character. But, if they did not belong to her fixed and permanent character, they belonged to her character *pro tempore*[3]; and what she thought, she scorned to qualify.

also present, and in recalling the occasion Godwin admits to being more eager to make *his* acquaintance, but his and Mary's next meeting, in 1796, left each with a better impression of the other. In the first of these excerpts, from Chapter 6 of the *Memoirs*, Godwin recounts Wollstonecraft's writing of the *Rights of Woman*. In the second and third excerpts, both from Chapter 9, Godwin traces, with the frankness that scandalized readers in 1798, the history of his connection with Wollstonecraft. (Later readers, such as Virginia Woolf, were not scandalized but took inspiration from the ways in which Godwin and Wollstonecraft collaborated on a brave experiment in the reinvention of domesticity.) Less than two years after their second meeting, ten days after giving birth to their daughter, Mary, Wollstonecraft died, on September 10, 1797. The text here is that of the first edition of the *Memoirs* (London, 1798), pp. 78–84, 153–57, and 165–69. All notes are the editor's.
1. From Nicholas Rowe's tragedy *The Fair Penitent* (1703) 3.1.40–41. Calista is the name of Rowe's suffering heroine.
2. Frank, open, or candid.
3. For the time being; temporarily.

Yet, along with this rigid, and somewhat amazonian temper, which characterised some parts of the book, it is impossible not to remark a luxuriance of imagination, and a trembling delicacy of sentiment, which would have done honour to a poet, bursting with all the visions of an Armida and Dido.[4]

The contradiction, to the public apprehension, was equally great, as to the person of the author, as it was when they considered the temper of the book. In the champion of her sex, who was described as endeavouring to invest them with all the rights of man, those whom curiosity prompted to seek the occasion of beholding her, expected to find a sturdy, muscular, raw-boned virago; and they were not a little surprised, when, instead of all this, they found a woman, lovely in her person, and, in the best and most engaging sense, feminine in her manners.

The Vindication of the Rights of Woman is undoubtedly a very unequal performance, and eminently deficient in method and arrangement. When tried by the hoary and long-established laws of literary composition, it can scarcely maintain its claim to be placed in the first class of human productions. But when we consider the importance of its doctrines, and the eminence of genius it displays, it seems not very improbable that it will be read as long as the English language endures. The publication of this book forms an epocha[5] in the subject to which it belongs; and Mary Wollstonecraft will perhaps hereafter be found to have performed more substantial service for the cause of her sex, than all the other writers, male or female, that ever felt themselves animated in the behalf of oppressed and injured beauty.

The censure of the liberal critic as to the defects of this performance, will be changed into astonishment, when I tell him, that a work of this inestimable moment, was begun, carried on, and finished in the state in which it now appears, in a period of no more than six weeks.

* * *

When we met again, we met with new pleasure, and, I may add, with a more decisive preference for each other. It was however three weeks longer, before the sentiment which trembled upon the tongue, burst from the lips of either. There was, as I have already said, no period of throes and resolute explanation attendant on the tale. It was friendship melting into love. Previously to our mutual

---

4. In Virgil's epic, the *Aeneid* (c. 29–19 B.C.E.), Dido is the queen of Carthage who commits suicide when Aeneas abandons her in order to heed the call of duty and continue his voyage to Italy. In Torquato Tasso's epic poem *Jerusalem Delivered* (1581) Armida is the seductress who lures Christian knights into an enchanted garden where they lose all desire to return to battle.
5. A common variant usage of the period for "epoch," or a point in time defined by a particular event or moment in the history of anything.

declaration, each felt half-assured, yet each felt a certain trembling anxiety to have assurance complete.

Mary rested her head upon the shoulder of her lover, hoping to find a heart with which she might safely treasure her world of affection; fearing to commit a mistake, yet, in spite of her melancholy experience, fraught with that generous confidence, which, in a great soul, is never extinguished. I had never loved till now; or, at least, had never nourished a passion to the same growth, or met with an object so consummately worthy.

We did not marry. It is difficult to recommend any thing to indiscriminate adoption, contrary to the established rules and prejudices of mankind; but certainly nothing can be so ridiculous upon the face of it, or so contrary to the genuine march of sentiment, as to require the overflowing of the soul to wait upon a ceremony, and that which, wherever delicacy and imagination exist, is of all things most sacredly private, to blow a trumpet before it, and to record the moment when it has arrived at its climax.

There were however other reasons why we did not immediately marry. Mary felt an entire conviction of the propriety of her conduct. It would be absurd to suppose that, with a heart withered by desertion, she was not right to give way to the emotions of kindness which our intimacy produced, and to seek for that support in friendship and affection, which could alone give pleasure to her heart, and peace to her meditations. It was only about six months since she had resolutely banished every thought of Mr. Imlay;[6] but it was at least eighteen that he ought to have been banished, had it not been for her scrupulous pertinacity in determining to leave no measure untried to regain him. Add to this, that the laws of etiquette ordinarily laid down in these cases, are essentially absurd, and that the sentiments of the heart cannot submit to be directed by the rule and the square. But Mary had an extreme aversion to be made the topic of vulgar discussion; and, if there be any weakness in this, the dreadful trials through which she had recently passed, may well plead in its excuse. She felt that she had been too much, and too rudely spoken of, in the former instance; and she could not resolve to do any thing that should immediately revive that painful topic.

For myself, it is certain that I had for many years regarded marriage with so well-grounded an apprehension, that, notwithstanding the partiality for Mary that had taken possession of my soul, I should have felt it very difficult, at least in the present stage of our intercourse, to have resolved on such a measure. Thus, partly from similar, and partly from different motives, we felt alike in this, as we

6. Gilbert Imlay (1754–1828), the American entrepreneur and former soldier whom Wollstonecraft met in Paris in 1793 and who was the father of her first child, Fanny. Imlay's infidelities twice drove Wollstonecraft to attempt suicide.

did perhaps in every other circumstance that related to our intercourse.

I have nothing further that I find it necessary to record, till the
commencement of April 1797. We then judged it proper to declare
our marriage, which had taken place a little before. The principal
motive for complying with this ceremony, was the circumstance of
Mary's being in a state of pregnancy. She was unwilling, and perhaps
with reason, to incur that exclusion from the society of many valuable and excellent individuals, which custom awards in cases of this
sort. * * *

* * *

I think I may venture to say, that no two persons ever found in
each other's society, a satisfaction more pure and refined. What it
was in itself, can now only be known, in its full extent, to the sur-
vivor. But, I believe, the serenity of her countenance, the increasing
sweetness of her manners, and that consciousness of enjoyment that
seemed ambitious that every one she saw should be happy as well as
herself, were matters of general observation to all her acquaintance.
She had always possessed, in an unparalleled degree, the art of com-
municating happiness, and she was now in the constant and unlimited exercise of it. She seemed to have attained that situation, which
her disposition and character imperiously demanded, but which she
had never before attained; and her understanding and her heart felt
the benefit of it.

While we lived as near neighbours only, and before our last
removal, her mind had attained considerable tranquillity, and was
visited but seldom with those emotions of anguish, which had been
but too familiar to her. But the improvement in this respect, which
accrued upon our removal and establishment, was extremely obvious. She was a worshipper of domestic life. She loved to observe the
growth of affection between me and her daughter, then three years
of age, as well as my anxiety respecting the child not yet born. Pregnancy itself, unequal as the decree of nature seems to be in this
respect, is the source of a thousand endearments. No one knew better than Mary how to extract sentiments of exquisite delight, from
trifles, which a suspicious and formal wisdom would scarcely deign
to remark. A little ride into the country with myself and the child,
has sometimes produced a sort of opening of the heart, a general
expression of confidence and affectionate soul, a sort of infantine,
yet dignified endearment, which those who have felt may understand, but which I should in vain attempt to pourtray.

In addition to our domestic pleasures; I was fortunate enough
to introduce her to some of my acquaintance of both sexes, to
whom she attached herself with all the ardour of approbation and
friendship.

Ours was not an idle happiness, a paradise of selfish and transitory pleasures. It is perhaps scarcely necessary to mention, that, influenced by the ideas I had long entertained upon the subject of cohabitation, I engaged an apartment, about twenty doors from our house in the Polygon, Somers Town, which I designed for the purpose of my study and literary occupations. Trifles however will be interesting to some readers, when they relate to the last period of the life of such a person as Mary. I will add therefore, that we were both of us of opinion, that it was possible for two persons to be too uniformly in each other's society. Influenced by that opinion, it was my practice to repair to the apartment I have mentioned as soon as I rose, and frequently not to make any appearance in the Polygon, till the hour of dinner. We agreed in condemning the notion, prevalent in many situations in life, that a man and his wife cannot visit in mixed society, but in company with each other; and we rather sought occasions of deviating from, than of complying with, this rule. By these means, though, for the most part, we spent the latter half of each day in one another's society, yet we were in no danger of satiety. We seemed to combine, in a considerable degree, the novelty and lively sensation of a visit, with the more delicious and heart-felt pleasures of domestic life.

* * *

RICHARD POLWHELE

From The Unsex'd Females[†]

* * *

Survey with me, what ne'er our fathers saw,
A female band despising NATURE's law,[1]
As "proud defiance"[2] flashes from their arms,
And vengeance smothers all their softer charms.
I shudder at the new unpictur'd scene,   15
Where unsex'd woman vaunts the imperious mien;
Where girls, affecting to dismiss the heart,
Invoke the Proteus of petrific art;
With equal ease, in body or in mind,
To Gallic[3] freaks or Gallic faith resign'd,   20
The crane-like neck, as Fashion bids, lay bare,
Or frizzle, bold in front, their borrow'd hair;
Scarce by a gossamery film carest,
Sport, in full view, the meretricious breast;
Loose the chaste cincture,[4] where the graces shone,   25
And languish'd all the Loves, the ambrosial zone;
As lordly domes inspire dramatic rage,
Court prurient Fancy to the private stage;
With bliss botanic[5] as their bosoms heave,
Still pluck forbidden fruit, with mother Eve,   30

---

† Richard Polwhele (1760–1838) was an Anglican minister; the author of numerous religious tracts, political satires, and topographical and historical works; and a contributor to
   the *Anti-Jacobin Review*—the journal that was established in 1798 for the express purpose of discrediting the radical political cause by editors who were also members of the
   British government. In *The Unsex'd Females* (1798), Polwhele responds to Wollstonecraft
   and to William Godwin's account of her in both verse and prose. (The bulk of his book is,
   in fact, taken up by the lengthy footnotes, reprinted here only in part, in which Polwhele
   annotates his own lines.) The "female band" (line 12) whom the poem assails is headed
   up by Wollstonecraft. Polwhele also addresses, as lines 91 to 106 (not included here)
   indicate, the women writers Anna Laetitia Barbauld, Mary Robinson, Charlotte Smith,
   Helen Maria Williams, Ann Yearsley, Mary Hays, and the artists Angelica Kauffmann and
   Emma Crewe. They collectively are faulted for violating gender distinctions—that is, for
   "unsexing" themselves by emulating Wollstonecraft in her rejection of soft charms and
   feminine allure. The excerpt here consists of lines 11 to 90, from Polwhele's first edition.
   All notes are the editor's unless otherwise indicated.
1. "Nature is the grand basis of all laws human and divine: and the woman, who has no
   regard to nature, either in the decoration of her person, or the culture of her mind, will
   soon 'walk after the flesh, in the lust of uncleanness, and despise government'" [Pol-
   whele's note]. Polwhele quotes 2 Peter 2:10.
2.   "'A troop came next, who crowns and armour, wore,
        And proud defiance in their looks they bore.'
        [Alexander] Pope [*The Temple of Fame*]
   The Amazonian band—the female Quixotes of the new philosophy, are, here, too justly
   characterised * * * " [Polwhele's note].
3. French customs, thought, or language.
4. Loose the girdle, or wide belt surrounding the waist and upper torso.
5. "Botany has lately become a fashionable amusement with the ladies. But how the study of
   the sexual system of plants can accord with female modesty, I am not able to comprehend.

For puberty in sighing florets pant,
Or point the prostitution of a plant;
Dissect[6] its organ of unhallow'd lust,
And fondly gaze the titillating dust;
With liberty's sublimer views expand,   35
And o'er the wreck of kingdoms[7] sternly stand;
And, frantic midst the democratic storm,
Pursue, Philosophy! thy phantom-form.
    Far other is the female shape and mind,
By modest luxury heighten'd and refin'd;   40
Those limbs, that figure, tho' by Fashion grac'd,
By Beauty polish'd, and adorn'd by Taste;
That soul, whose harmony perennial flows,
In Music trembles, and in Color glows;
Which bids sweet Poesy reclaim the praise   45
With faery light to gild fastidious days,
From sullen clouds relieve domestic care,
And melt in smiles the withering frown of war.
Ah! once the female Muse, to NATURE true,
The unvalued store from FANCY, FEELING drew;   50
Won, from the grasp of woe, the roseate hours,
Cheer'd life's dim vale, and strew'd the grave with flowers.
    But lo! where, pale amidst the wild, she draws
Each precept cold from sceptic Reason's vase;
Pours with rash arm the turbid stream along,   55
And in the foaming torrent whelms the throng.
    Alas! her pride sophistic flings a gloom,
To chase, sweet Innocence! thy vernal bloom,
Of each light joy to damp the genial glow,
And with new terrors clothe the groupe of woe,   60
Quench the pure daystar in oblivion deep,
And, Death! restore thy "long, unbroken sleep."

---

* * * I had, at first written:

More eager for illicit knowledge pant,
With lustful boys anatomize a plant;
The virtues of its dust prolific speak,
Or point its pistill with unblushing cheek.

I have, several times, seen boys and girls botanizing together" [Polwhele's note].
6. "Miss Wollstonecraft does not blush to say, in an introduction to a book designed for the use of young ladies, that, 'in order to lay the axe at the root of corruption, it would be proper to familiarize the sexes to an unreserved discussion of those topics, which are generally avoided in conversation from a principle of false delicacy; and that it would be right to speak of the organs of generation as freely as we mention our eyes or our hands.' To such language our botanizing girls are doubtless familiarized: and, they are in a fair way of becoming worthy disciples of Miss W. If they do not take heed to their ways, they will soon exchange the blush of modesty for the bronze of impudence" [Polwhele's note]. Polwhele quotes Wollstonecraft's "Introductory Address to Parents" in her translation of Christian Gotthilf Salzmann's *Elements of Morality, for the Use of Children.*
7. "The female advocates of Democracy in this country, though they have had no opportunity of imitating the French ladies, in their atrocious acts of cruelty; have yet assumed a stern serenity in the contemplation of those savage excesses * * * " [Polwhele's note].

See Wollstonecraft, whom no decorum checks,
Arise, the intrepid champion of her sex;
O'er humbled man assert the sovereign claim,   65
And slight the timid blush[8] of virgin fame.
    "Go, go," she cries, "ye tribes of melting maids,
Go, screen your softness in sequester'd shades;
With plaintive whispers woo the unconscious grove,
And feebly perish, as depis'd ye love.   70
What tho' the fine Romances of Rousseau
Bid the frame flutter, and the bosom glow;
Tho' the rapt Bard, your empire fond to own,
Fall prostrate and adore your living throne,
The living throne his hands presum'd to rear,   75
Its seat a simper, and its base a tear;[9]
Soon shall the sex disdain the illusive sway,
And wield the sceptre in yon blaze of day;
Ere long, each little artifice discard,
No more by weakness[1] winning fond regard;   80
Nor eyes, that sparkle from their blushes, roll,
Nor catch the languors of the sick'ning soul,
Nor the quick flutter, nor the coy reserve,
But nobly boast the firm gymnastic nerve;[2]
Nor more affect with Delicacy's fan   85
To hide the emotion from congenial man;
To the bold heights where glory beams, aspire,
Blend mental energy with Passion's fire,
Surpass their rivals in the powers of mind
And vindicate *the Rights of womankind*."[3]   90

* * *

8. "That Miss Wollstonecraft was a sworn enemy to blushes, I need not remark. But many of my readers, perhaps, will be astonished to hear, that at several of our boarding-schools for young ladies, a blush incurs a penalty" [Polwhele's note].
9. "According to Rousseau, the empire of women is the empire of softness—of address: their commands, are caresses; their menaces, are tears" [Polwhele's note].
1. "'Like monarchs, we have been flattered into imbecillity, by those who wish to take advantage of our weakness;' says Mary Hays [*Essays and Letters*, p. 92.] But, whether flattered or not, women were always weak: and female weakness hath accomplished, what the force of arms could not effect" [Polwhele's note].
2. "Miss Wollstonecraft seriously laments the neglect of all muscular exercises, at our female Boarding-schools" [Polwhele's note].
3. At this point Polwhele introduces his roll call of women writers whose revolutionary sympathies and licentiousness make them unsexed and objectionable. Then to close (lines 175–206), he wheels on stage a group of writers whose femininity he approves, prominent among them "Miss Hannah More," a character, he states, "in all points, diametrically opposite to Miss Wollstonecraft."

MARY HAYS

From Memoirs of Mary Wollstonecraft[†]

The intrepid spirit, daring flights, lofty pretentions, and disdain of
sanctioned opinions, which characterize the productions of the vindicator of the Rights of Woman, have combined to excite an extraordinary degree of attention; which some events, of a peculiar nature,
in her personal history have had a tendency to increase. By the distinction which the reputation of superior talents confers, their possessors are exalted to a dangerous pre-eminence: attention is roused,
curiosity excited, their claims are subjected to a scrutiny, in which
all the nobler and all the baser passions become equally interested.
While, on one side, by the partiality of affection and the blind enthusiasm of implicit admiration, their excellencies are made the theme
of exaggerated panegyric: on the other, those errors or frailties to
which they are liable, in common with their species, or those excesses that more peculiarly belong to ardent characters, are invidi-
ously sought after, propagated with malignity, amplified by envy,
distorted by prejudice, and received with triumph by the vulgar of
every rank, by the interested, the ignorant, and the malicious. Persons of the finest and most exquisite genius have probably the greatest sensibility, consequently the strongest passions, by the fervor of
which they are too often betrayed into error. Vigorous minds are
with difficulty restrained within the trammels of authority; a spirit of
enterprise, a passion for experiment, a liberal curiosity, urges them
to quit beaten paths, to explore untried ways, to burst the fetters of
prescription, and to acquire wisdom by an individual experience.

The preceding reflections are not unappropriate to the subject of
the present narrative, in whose character strong light and shade
appear to have been blended. If, by her quick feelings, prompt judgments, and rapid decisions, she was sometimes betrayed into false
conclusions, her errors were expiated by sufferings, that, while they
disarm severity, awaken sympathy and seize irresistibly upon the
heart. Let it not be forgotten, that if the excess of certain virtues
encroach on the limits of vice, yet faults of this description have a
generous source. Those whom a calmer temperament conduct in an
even path, deviating neither to the right nor to the left, will find their

---

† Mary Hays followed William Godwin's *Memoirs* with her own narrative of Wollstonecraft's
life, published in *The Annual Necrology for 1797–8* (London, 1800). Reprinted here are
pp. 411–12 and 422–23. All notes are the editor's. Hays's defensive tone perhaps suggests
why, when in 1803 she published the six-volume compilation *Female Biography, or Memoirs of Illustrious and Celebrated Women of All Ages and Countries,* she left Wollstonecraft
out of it. For more on Hays, see dagger note on p. 281 herein.

reward in the safety of their course. But it is to speculative and enterprising spirits, whom stronger powers and more impetuous passions impel forward, regardless of established usages, that all great changes and improvements in society have owed their origin. If, intoxicated by contemplating the grand projects in their imagination, they deviate into extravagance, and lose sight of the nature of man, their theories remain to be corrected by experience, while, in the gratitude of posterity, the contemporary cry of interest will be absorbed and forgotten.

To advance on the scale of reason half the species, is no ignoble ambition. The efforts of the extraordinary woman whose life we are about to review, were directed to the emancipation of her own sex, whom she considered as sunk in a state of degradation, glorying in their weakness; voluntarily surrendering the privilege of rational agents, and contending, in her own emphatic language, "for the sentiment that brutalized them."

*   *   *

A just confidence in her own talents, increased probably by the success of this publication [*A Vindication of the Rights of Men*] now induced [Wollstonecraft] to essay her strength on a subject that affected her still more; a subject which she had keenly felt, on which she had deeply meditated, which her sex, her situation, all the circumstances of her life, irresistibly led her to consider,—*A Vindication of the Rights of Woman.*—There are few situations in which a woman of cultivated understanding has not occasion to observe and deplore, the systematic vassalage, the peculiar disadvantages, civil and social, to which she is subjected, even in the most polished societies, on the account of her sex. It might be difficult to convince such a woman, conscious of superiority to the majority of men with whom she converses, that nature has placed between them, in what respects intellectual attainments, an insuperable barrier: she would be tempted to remind such partial reasoners of the reply given to the philosopher who disputed the existence of motion, when his adversary gravely rose up and walked before him.

It is little wonderful that the magnanimous advocate of freedom, and the opponent of Burke, should throw down the gauntlet, challenge her arrogant oppressors, and, hurried away by a noble enthusiasm, deny the existence of a sexual character.

In the cause of half the human race she stood forth, deprecating and exposing, in a tone of impassioned eloquence, the various means and arts by which woman had been forcibly subjugated, flattered into imbecility, and invariably held in bondage. Dissecting the opinions, and commenting upon the precepts of those writers who, having expressly considered the condition of the female sex, had suggested means for its improvement, she endeavours, with force

and acuteness, to convict them of narrow views, voluptuous prejudices, contradictory principles, and selfish, though impolitic ends. It
is but justice to add, that the principles of this celebrated work are to
be found in Catharine Macauley's [sic] *Treatise on Education*.[1] It
may also be here observed, that in the intellectual advancement of
women, and their consequent privileges in society, is to be traced the
progress of civilization, or knowledge gradually superseding the
dominion of *brute-force*.

A production thus bold and spirited, excited attention and pro-
voked discussion; prejudices were shocked, vanity wounded, interest
alarmed, and indolence roused: yet, amidst the virulence of opposition, the clamours of ignorance, the cavils of superstition, and the
misrepresentation of wilful perversion, seeds were scattered that
promised, when the ferment had subsided, a rich and abundant harvest. The high masculine tone, sometimes degenerating into coarse-
ness, that characterizes this performance, is in a variety of parts
softened and blended with a tenderness of sentiment, an exquisite
delicacy of feeling, that touches the heart, and takes captive the
imagination. As a composition it discovers considerable power and
energy of thought; but in perspicuity and arrangement it must be
confessed to be defective: its style, though frequently rich and glowing, is sometimes inflated, and generally incorrect. It is to be regret-
ted, that the author's intention of revising and remedying these
defects in a future edition, was protracted, and ultimately defeated.
Its faults are perhaps to be attributed to the rapidity with which it
was composed and committed to the press; being, we are informed,
begun and completed within a period of six weeks. It would be
unnecessary to comment on the imprudence and impolicy mani-
fested (whatever be the talents of the writer) by such precipitation. A
second part was promised to the public, for which but scanty materials were found, after her decease, among the papers of the author.

* * *

1. See the selection in this volume from Catharine Macaulay's *Letters on Education*, p. 239.

MARIA EDGEWORTH

From Belinda†

From *Chapter 17.* *"Rights of Woman"*

* * *

There was a kind of drollery about Mrs. Freke, which, with some people, made the odd things she said pass for wit. Humour she really possessed; and when she chose it, she could be diverting to those who like buffoonery in women. She had set her heart upon winning Belinda over to her party. She began by flattery of her beauty; but as she saw that this had no effect, she next tried what could be done by insinuating that she had a high opinion of her understanding, by talking to her as an esprit fort.[1]

"For my part," said she, "I own I should like a strong devil better than a weak angel."

"You forget," said Belinda, "that it is not Milton, but Satan, who says,

"Fallen spirit, to be weak is to be miserable."[2]

"You read, I see!—I did not know you were a reading girl.—So did I once! but I never read now. Books only spoil the originality of genius. Very well for those who can't think for themselves—But when one has made up one's opinions, there is no use in reading."

"But to *make* them up," replied Belinda, "may it not be useful?"

"Of no use upon earth to minds of a certain class.—You, who can think for yourself, should never read."

"But I read that I may think for myself."

"Only ruin your understanding, trust me. Books are full of trash—nonsense—Conversation is worth all the books in the world."

"And is there never any nonsense in conversation?"

"What have you here?" continued Mrs. Freke, who did not choose to attend to this question; exclaiming as she reviewed each of the books on the table in their turns, in the summary language of presumptuous ignorance. "'Smith's Theory of Moral Sentiments'—Milk and water! 'Moore's Travels'—Hasty pudding! 'La Bruyere'—Nettle

---

† The Anglo-Irish novelist and educational theorist Maria Edgeworth published, as Wollstonecraft did, with the liberal publisher Joseph Johnson, but in the climate of suspicion women writers had to negotiate after 1798 Edgeworth needed to ward off the suggestion that she and Wollstonecraft might have anything else in common. The satire contained in this chapter from Edgeworth's 1801 novel of education may be seen as her preemptive move to disarm critics on the lookout for symptoms of feminism. The novel's cast of characters includes a certain Harriet Freke, a caricatured Wollstonecraft who tries in Chapter 17 to persuade the heroine, Belinda Stanhope, to renounce her rational if placid domestic happiness with the Percival family and join her own flashier social circle. All notes are the editor's.
1. Freethinker.
2 *Paradise Lost* I.157.

porridge! This is what you were at when I came in, was it not?" said she, taking up a book in which she saw Belinda's mark, "'Essay on the Inconsistency of Human Wishes.'³ Poor thing! who bored you with this task?"

"Mr. Percival recommended it to me, as one of the best essays in the English language."

"The devil! They seem to have put you in a course of the bitters— a course of the woods might do your business better. Do you ever hunt?—Let me take you out with me some morning—You'd be quite an angel on horseback."

* * *

She thought, that if Belinda's opinion of the understanding of *these Percivals* could be lowered, she should rise in her opinion: accordingly, she determined to draw Mr. Percival into an argument.

"I've been talking treason, I believe, to Miss Portman," cried she, "for I've been opposing some of your opinions, Mr. Percival."

"If you opposed them all, madam," said Mr. Percival, "I should not think it treason."

"Vastly polite!—But I think all our politeness hypocrisy. What d'ye say to that?"

"You know that best, madam!"

"Then I'll go a step farther; for I'm determined you shall contradict me.—I think all virtue is hypocrisy."

"I need not contradict you, madam," said Mr. Percival, "for the terms which you make use of contradict themselves."

"It is my system," pursued Mrs. Freke, "that shame is always the cause of the vices of women."

"It is sometimes the effect," said Mr. Percival; "and, as cause and effect are reciprocal, perhaps you may, in some instances, be right."

"O! I hate qualifying arguers—Plump assertion or plump denial for me—You shan't get off so—I say, shame is the cause of all women's vices."

"False shame, I suppose you mean?" said Mr. Percival.

"Mere play upon words!—All shame is false shame—We should be a great deal better without it. What say you, Miss Portman?— Silent—hey?—Silence that speaks!"

"Miss Portman's blushes," said Mr. Vincent, "speak *for* her."

"*Against* her,"—said Mrs. Freke—"Women blush because they understand."

---

3. Belinda's improving reading includes: Adam Smith's 1759 *Theory of Moral Sentiments*, the travelogs of the physician John Moore (1729–1802), and the French author Jean de la Bruyère's *Characters, or the Manners of the Age* (1699). The "Essay on the Inconsistency of Human Wishes" may be Anna Laetitia Barbauld's widely praised "Against Inconsistency in our Expectations" (1773).

"And you would have them understand without blushing?" said Mr. Percival. "So would I; for nothing can be more different than innocence and ignorance. Female delicacy—" "This is just the way you men spoil women," cried Mrs. Freke, "by talking to them of the *delicacy of their sex,* and such stuff. This *delicacy* enslaves the pretty delicate dears."

"No; it enslaves us," said Mr. Vincent.

"I hate slavery! Vive la liberté!" cried Mrs. Freke—"I'm a champion for the Rights of Women."

"I am an advocate for their happiness," said Mr. Percival, "and for their delicacy, as I think it conduces to their happiness."

"I'm an enemy to their delicacy, as I am sure it conduces to their misery."

"You speak from experience?" said Mr. Percival.

"No, from observation.—Your most delicate women are always the greatest hypocrites; and, in my opinion, no hypocrite can or ought to be happy."

"But you have not proved the hypocrisy," said Belinda. "Delicacy is not, I hope, an indisputable proof of it?—If you mean *false* delicacy—"

"To cut the matter short at once," cried Mrs. Freke, "why, when a woman likes a man, does not she go and tell him so honestly?"

Belinda, surprised by this question from a woman, was too much abashed instantly to answer.

"Because she's a hypocrite. That is and must be the answer."

"No," said Mr. Percival, "because, if she be a woman of sense, she knows that by such a step she would disgust the object of her affection."

"Cunning!—cunning!—cunning!—the arms of the weakest."

"Prudence!—prudence!—prudence!—the arms of the strongest. Taking the best means to secure our own happiness without injuring that of others, is the best proof of sense and strength of mind, whether in man or woman. Fortunately for society, the same conduct in ladies which best secures their happiness most increases ours."

Mrs. Freke beat the devil's tattoo[4] for some moments, and then exclaimed—"You may say what you will, but the present system of society is radically wrong:—whatever is, is wrong."[5]

"How would you improve the state of society?" asked Mr. Percival calmly.

"I'm not tinker general to the world," said she.

"I am glad of it," said Mr. Percival; "for I have heard that tinkers often spoil more than they mend."

4. Drummed her fingers on a tabletop.
5. Playing on Alexander Pope's "Whatever IS, is RIGHT" in *Essay on Man* I, l. 294.

"But if you want to know," said Mrs. Freke, "what I would do to improve the world, I'll tell you: I'd have your sex taught to say, Horns! horns! I defy you."

"This would doubtless be a great improvement," said Mr. Percival; "but you would not overturn society to attain it? would you? Should we find things much improved by tearing away what has been called the decent drapery of life?"[6]

"Drapery, if you ask me my opinion," cried Mrs. Freke, "drapery, whether wet or dry, is the most confoundedly indecent thing in the world."

"That depends on *public* opinion, I allow," said Mr. Percival. "The Lacedæmonian ladies,[7] who were veiled only by public opinion, were better covered from profane eyes, than some English ladies are in wet drapery."

"I know nothing of the Lacedæmonian ladies, I took my leave of them when I was a schoolboy—girl—I should say."

* * *

BENJAMIN SILLIMAN

From The Letters of Shahcoolen[†]

[*Second Letter*]

False philosophy, striving to impress upon mankind the conviction, that it soars above common pleasures, and common ideas, has ever affected to despise and to degrade that sex, which the great Brumma has given us to alleviate, by their delightful tenderness, all the pains, and to animate all the joys of this life. Knowing, as thou dost, my warm partiality for this lovliest, best part of creation, thou canst not be

---

6. Citing Edmund Burke's description of the consequences of the French Revolution's overthrow of the age of chivalry: "All the decent drapery of life is to be rudely torn off." See *Reflections on the Revolution in France*, on p. 257 herein.
7. The young women of ancient Sparta, who dispensed with clothing when they trained as athletes.
† Americans might have been expected to lend a sympathetic ear to Wollstonecraft's critique of the corrupting effects of unnatural social distinctions. But Americans also enrolled themselves enthusiastically in Richard Polwhele's smear campaign against "unsexed females." *The Letters of Shahcoolen*, published serially in Noah Webster's *New York Commercial Advertiser* in 1801 when the author Benjamin Silliman (1779–1864), a future Yale professor, was twenty-two, numbers among the many American publications that identified Wollstonecraft as an adherent of a "new philosophy" aiming to bring down the family, state, and church. Silliman presents the *Letters* as the epistles that a certain Shahcoolen, a Hindu philosopher visiting Philadelphia, sends back home to India, a vantage-point that permits him greater latitude in commenting on contemporary mores. There is a facsimile edition of the Boston 1802 reprint of the *Letters* (Gainseville: Scholars' Facsimiles and Reprints, 1962), the basis for the text here. All notes are the editor's unless otherwise indicated.

surprised, that in all the countries through which I have passed, their happiness has been among the earliest subjects of my investigation.

Know then, that a total renovation of the female character, and a destination in society, totally new, is one grand object contemplated by that new philosophy, of which, in my last epistle, I gave some small account.

Mary Woolstonecraft, [sic] a female philosopher of the *new school*, has written, within these few years past, a book, which she named "A *vindication of the Rights of Woman;*" composed, for the express purpose of rousing her sex from their inglorious repose, and of stimulating them to a vigorous exertion of their native *energies*.

She discards all that sexual tenderness, delicacy and modesty, which constitute the female loveliness; boldly pronounces them equal to the rougher sex in every thing but bodily strength; and even imputes their deficiency, in this particular, principally to a falsely refined education. She asserts that a husband is a *paltry* bauble, compared with *the attainments of reason*; that the female should be subject, or superior to the male, just in proportion to those attainments; and that the want of them constitutes the only obligation for the submission of the wife to the husband. This female philosopher indignantly rejects the idea of a sex in the soul, pronouncing the sensibility, timidity and tenderness of women, to be merely artificial refinements of character, introduced and fostered by men, to render sensual pleasure more voluptuous. She indeed professes a high regard for chastity; but unfortunately the practice of her life was at war with her precepts. She admitted one *sentimental lover* after another, to the full fruition of her charms, and proved the *attainments of reason*, to be, in her view, sources of pleasure, far inferior, in value, to the pleasures of sense.

In short, polluted as she was by the *last crime of woman*, MARY stepped forth as the champion and reformer of her sex; she wished to strip them of every thing feminine, and to assimilate them, as fast as possible, to the masculine character.

O, my dear El Hassan, how opposite her views to every thing, which *we* deem lovely in the sex! O, lovely ALAGRA, the brightest gem that sparkles on the beauteous plains of AGIMERE, how would thy virgin soul shrink back at the contemplation of a female soul *unsexed* a man in female form!

A complete exhibition of the regenerating system of this female lunatic, would fatigue thy patience, and occupy too large a portion of these epistles.

So singular, however, is her system and so directly opposed to the received opinions of mankind, that I cannot refrain from tracing an imperfect outline. Not satisfied with masculine ideas, and masculine habits, Mary Wollstonecraft wished, as the consummation of female independence, to introduce the sex into the Camp, the Rostrum and the Cabinet; and although she does not recommend a total dereliction of *the household good*, still she would not cramp the female energies by an occupation so much beneath their dignity, except so far, as stern necessity commands.

She seriously advocates the right of female representation—for in this country, and in some parts of Europe, the right of representation, which in an epistle from England, I have already explained, is fully established.[1]

Suppose, my dear friend, that a band of female representatives, beautiful as the thirty RAGINIS,[2] who, crowned with flowery wreaths, dance to the muse of NARED, among the spicy groves of MALDOOVAN, should mix with a Legislative band; would not the cares of Legislation be excluded by the witchcraft of love! The charms of the fair Orator would plead more powerfully than her tongue, and gallantry would induce compliance, where reason would have simulated to strenuous opposition.

In the Cabinet, their sway would be still more complete. Smiles, tears and sighs would decide the fate of nations; and beauty would direct the march of armies on the frontiers, and the course of navies upon the ocean.

It is true that in *defensive* war *only*, Miss Woolstonecraft [sic] indulges the idea, which even *she* allows to be an enthusiastic one, of seeing the exploits of ancient heroines renewed, and the deadly weapon directed by the hand of Beauty.

This idea of hers is undoubtedly a most ingenious one. At the sight of a band of heroines, beautiful as the morning, marching forward to the combat, what warrior's sword would not drop from his hand?—what soldier would not surrender himself a prisoner!

Had the God RAMA, when he led forth his army of APES, and spread destruction among his enemies, only exchanged his apes for beautiful virgins, his victory would have been less bloody, and his conquest more complete.

As a necessary preparative for the support of bodily fatigue, the female philosopher recommends an early initation of females into the athletic sports, and gymastic exercises of boys and young men.

She would have them run, leap, box, wrestle, fence and fight, that the united exertion of bodily and mental energy may produce, by mysterious cooperation, that amazing force of character, of which she supposes her sex to be capable.

1. Technically speaking, women had the right to vote in America until they were constitutionally forbidden it in the Fourteenth Amendment, which mentioned only "male citizens." Their right to do so had been a state matter—and in some states they had voted—until after the Civil War.
2. "Female Passions" [Silliman's note].

She even recommends that these sports should be mutually shared between girls and boys, that the distinction of sex may remain concealed, until the physical progress of the body, calling into operation the latent passions, shall discover the wonderful secret.

This strange philosopher, my dear El Hassan, has detained me, by the novelty of her doctrines, longer than I intended. Perhaps in some future communication, I may notice some of her remaining tenets; and I intend particularly to delineate the practical influence, which they have already acquired over the female sex in this country.

Keep this philosophy a profound secret from the fair daughters of Hindustan, for, thou canst not divine what influence its novelty, and the idea of independence on man may have over the heart even of the modest, unassuming Hindu.

WILLIAM THOMPSON

From Appeal of One Half the Human Race, Women, against the Pretensions of the Other Half, Men[†]

From *Introductory Letter to Mrs. Wheeler*

Honored with your acquaintance, ambitious of your friendship, I have endeavoured to arrange the expression of those feelings, sentiments, and reasonings, which have emanated from your mind. In the following pages you will find discussed on paper, what you have so often discussed in conversation—a branch of that high and important subject of morals and legislation, the condition of women, of one half the human race, in what is called civilised society. Though not to me is that "diviner inspiration given,"[1] which can clothe with the grace and eloquence of your unpremeditated effusions the calm stream of argument; though, not having been in the situation you have been, to suffer from the inequalities of sexual

† In nineteenth-century Britain it was often the socialists who kept the arguments of the *Vindication of the Rights of Woman* in circulation, as the career of William Thompson (1775–1833) illustrates. Born into the Anglo-Irish gentry, Thompson was a supporter of the nascent British trade union movement and in his best known book, *An Inquiry into the Principles of the Distribution of the Wealth* (1824), critiqued the prevailing ideology of free markets and free competition and set out an alternative vision of a network of cooperative communities. Thompson's worry over how the workers' movement, like the Utilitarians who had been his intellectual mentors, tended to sideline women's labors and suffering, helped inspire the *Appeal,* which he published in London in 1825. Another inspiration, as his Introductory Letter confirms, was Thompson's conversations with the Anglo-Irish woman of letters and pioneering socialist feminist Anna Doyle Wheeler (1785–1848?). All notes are the editor's.
1. Thomas Gray, "Stanzas to Mr. Bentley" (1751–53).

laws, I cannot join with a sensibility equal to yours, in your lofty indignation and contempt of the puerilities and hypocrisy with which men seek to cover or to palliate their life-consuming and mind- and joy-eradicating oppressions, tempered always however with benevolence even to the foolish oppressors themselves; though I do not *feel* like you—thanks to the chance of having been born a man—looking lonely on the moral desolation around; though I am free from personal interest in the consideration of this question; yet can I not be inaccessible to the plain facts and reason of the case. Though long accustomed to reflect on this subject, to you am I indebted for those bolder and more comprehensive views which perhaps can only be elicited by concentration of the mind on one darling though terrific theme. To separate your thoughts from mine were now to me impossible, so amalgamated are they with my own: to the public this is indifferent; but to me how flattering, could I hope that any suggestions of mine had so amalgamated themselves in your mind!

The days of dedication and patronage are gone by. It is *not* with the view of obtaining the support of your name or your influence to the cause of truth and humanity that these lines are addressed to you. Truth must stand on its own foundation. The smiles of wealth, of power, or of beauty, are extraneous considerations, and should not be put into the scale to supply the want of argument. Whatever bias of judgement is given to the solicitations of either of these, is so much given to passion or sinister interest, to the prejudice of truth. She is strong, immortal: fear not; she must ultimately, on even ground, prevail.

I address you then simply to perform towards you a debt of justice; to show myself possessed of that sincerity which I profess to admire. I love not literary any more than any other species of piracy: I wish to give everything to its right owner. Anxious that you should take up the cause of your proscribed sex, and state to the world in writing, in your own name, what you have so often and so well stated in conversation, and under feigned names in such of the periodical publications of the day as would tolerate such a theme, I long hesitated to arrange our common ideas, even upon a branch of the subject like the present. Anxious that the hand of a woman should have the honor of raising from the dust that neglected banner which a woman's hand nearly thirty years ago unfolded boldly, in face of the prejudices of thousands of years, and for which a woman's heart bled, and her life was all but the sacrifice—I hesitated to write. Were courage the quality wanting, you would have shown, what every day's experience proves, that women have more fortitude in endurance than men. Were comprehensiveness of mind, above the narrow views which too often marred Mary Wolstonecroft's pages and narrowed their usefulness, the quality wanting,—above the timidity and impotence of conclusion accompanying the gentle eloquence of Mary Hays, addressed, about the same time that Mary Wolstonecroft wrote, in the shape of an *"Appeal"* to the then closed ears of unreasoning men;[2] yours was the eye which no prejudice obscured, open to the rays of truth from whatever quarter they might emanate. But leisure and resolution to undertake the drudgery of the task were wanting. A few only therefore of the following pages are the exclusive produce of your mind and pen, and written with your own hand. The remainder are our joint property, I being your interpreter and the scribe of your sentiments.

* * *

You look forward, as I do, to a state of society very different from that which now exists, in which the effort of all is to out wit, supplant, and snatch from each other; where interest is systematically opposed to duty; where the so-called system of morals is little more than a mass of hypocrisy preached by knaves, unpractised by them, to keep their slaves, male as well as female, in blind uninquiring obedience; and where the whole motley fabric is kept together by fear and blood. You look forward to a better aspect of society, where the principle of benevolence shall supersede that of fear; where restless and anxious individual competition shall give place to mutual co-operation and joint possession; where individuals in large numbers, male and female, forming voluntary associations, shall become a mutual guarantee to each other for the supply of all useful wants, and form an unsalaried and uninsolvent insurance company against all insurable casualties; where perfect freedom of opinion and perfect equality will reign amongst the co-operators; and where the children of all will be equally educated and provided for by the whole, even these children longer the slaves of individual caprice.[3]

In truth, under the present arrangements of society, the principle of individual competition remaining, as it is, the master-key and moving principle of the whole social organization, *individual* wealth the great object sought after by all, and the quantum of happiness of each individual (other things being equal) depending on the quantum of wealth, the means of happiness, possessed by each; it seems impossible—even were all unequal legal and unequal moral restraints removed, and were no secret current of force or influence exerted to baffle new regulations of equal justice—that women should attain to equal happiness with men. Two circumstances—

2. A reference to Mary Hays's *Appeal to the Men of Great Britain in Behalf of Women* (1798).
3. Thompson would later describe the workings of such voluntary associations in detail in his *Practical Directions for the Speedy and Economical Establishment of Communities* (1830).

permanent inferiority of strength, and occasional loss of time in gestation and rearing infants—must eternally render the average exertions of women in the race of the competition for wealth less successful than those of men. The pleasant compensation that men now affect to give for these two natural sources of inferior accumulation of wealth on the part of women (aggravated a thousand degrees by their exclusions from knowledge and almost all means of useful exertions, the very lowest only excepted), is the existing system of marriage; under which, for the mere faculty of eating, breathing and living, in whatever degree of comfort husbands may think fit, women are reduced to domestic slavery, without will of their own, or power of locomotion, otherwise than as permitted by their respective masters.

While these two natural impediments in the way of the production or accumulation of wealth, and of course of the independence and equal enjoyments of women, exist—and exist they must—it should seem that the present arrangements of society, founded on individual competition, and of course allowing of no real compensation for these impediments, are absolutely irreconcilable with the equality, in point of the command of enjoyments, of women with men. Were all partial restraints, were unequal laws and unequal morals removed, were all the means and careers of all species of knowledge and exertion equally open to both sexes; still the barriers of physical organization must, under the system of individual competition, keep depressed the average station of women beneath that of men. Though in point of knowledge, talent, and virtue, they might become their equals; in point of independence *arising from wealth* they must, under the present principle of social arrangements, remain inferior.

No doubt, so much the more dastardly appears the baseness of man, that not satisfied with these indisputable advantages of organization in the pursuit of happiness on his own theatre of free competition, he paralyses to impotence even those means which Nature has given his feebler competitor, nor ceases his oppression till he has made her his slave. The more physical advantages Nature has given man, the *less* excusable is he in superadding factitious advantages, by the abuse of strength, to those which are natural and unavoidable. Were he generous, were he just, knew he how to promote his own happiness, he would be anxious to afford *compensations* for these physical inconveniences, instead of aggravating them; that he might raise woman to a perfect equality in all things with himself, and enjoy the highest pleasures of which his nature is susceptible— those of freedom, of voluntary association amongst perfect equals. Perhaps out of the system of "Association" or "Mutual Co-operation" such happiness is not to be expected.

But I hear you indignantly reject the boon of equality with such creatures as men now are. With you I would equally elevate both sexes. Really enlightened women, disdaining equally the submissive tricks of the slave and the caprices of the despot, breathing freely only in the air of the esteem of equals, and of mutual, *unbought, uncommanded,* affection, would find it difficult to meet with associates worthy of them in men as now formed, full of ignorance and vanity, priding themselves on a *sexual* superiority, entirely independent of any merit, any superior qualities, or pretensions to them, claiming respect from the strength of their arm and the lordly faculty of producing beards attached by nature to their chins! No: unworthy of, as incapable of appreciating, the delight of the society of such women, are the great majority of the existing race of men. The pleasures of mere animal appetite, the pleasures of commanding (the prettier and more helpless the slave, the greater these pleasures of the brute), are the only pleasures which the majority of men seek for from women, are the only pleasures which their education and the hypocritical system of morals with which they have been necessarily imbued, permit them to expect. To wish for the fragrance of the rose, we must have an organization capable of receiving pleasure from it, and must be persuaded that such lovely flowers as roses exist. To wish for the enjoyment of the higher pleasures of sympathy and communication of knowledge between the sexes, heightened by that mutual grace and glow, that decorum and mutual respect, to which the feeling of perfect, unrestrained equality in the intercourse gives birth, a man must have heard of such pleasures, must be able to conceive them, and must have an organization from nature or education, or both, capable of receiving delight from them when presented to him. To enjoy these pleasures, to which their other pleasures, a few excepted, are but the play of children or brutes, the bulk of men want a sixth sense; they want the capacity of feeling them, and of believing that such things are in nature to be found. A mole cannot enjoy the "beauties and glories" (as a Professor terms them) of the visible world; nor can brute men enjoy the intellectual and sympathetic pleasures of equal intercourse with women, such as some are, such as all might be. Real and comprehensive knowledge, physical and moral, equally and impartially given by education and by all other means to both sexes, is the key to such higher enjoyments.

Even under the present arrangements of society, founded as they all are on the basis of individual competition, nothing could be more easy than to put the *rights* of women, political and civil, on a perfect equality with those of men. It is only to abolish all prohibitory and exclusive laws,—statute or what are called "common,"—the remnants of the barbarous customs of our ignorant ancestors; particularly the horrible and odious inequality and indissolubility of that disgrace of civilization, the present marriage code. Women then might exert in a free career with men their faculties of mind and body, to whatever degree developed, in pursuit of happiness by means of exertion, as men do. But this would not raise women to an equality of happiness with men: their rights might be equal, but not their happiness, because unequal powers under free competition must produce unequal effects.

In truth, the system of the most enlightened of the school of those reformers called political economists, is still founded on exclusions. Its basis is too narrow for human happiness. A more comprehensive system, founded on equal benevolence, on the true developement of the principle of Utility, is wanting. Let the *competitive* political economists be satisfied with the praise of causing the removal of some of the rubbish of ignorant restrictions, under the name of laws, impeding the developement of human exertion in the production of wealth. To build up a new fabric of social happiness, comprehending equally the interests of all existing human beings, has never been contemplated by them, and is altogether beyond the scope of their little theories; aiming at the utmost at increasing the number of what they style the happy middling orders, but leaving the great bulk of human beings to eternal ignorance and toil, requited by the mere means of prolonging from day to day an unhealthy and precarious existence. To a new science, the *social science*, or the science of promoting human happiness, that of political economy, or the mere science of producing wealth by individual competition, must give way.

* * *

CRITICISM

CRITICISM

ELISSA S. GURALNICK

Radical Politics in Mary Wollstonecraft's
A *Vindication of the Rights of Woman*†

Since its publication in 1792, A *Vindication of the Rights of Woman* has been treated almost exclusively as a feminist manifesto, a simple defense of women's rights. Although critics have generally allowed that the *Rights of Woman* enlarges upon the political tenets expounded in the *Rights of Men,* little attention has been paid to the relationship between the two documents. It has been as if the warning implied in the March 1792 issue of the *Analytical Review* has been carefully and universally heeded: "It might be supposed that Miss W. had taken advantage of the popular topic of the 'Rights of Man' in calling her work 'A Vindication of the Rights of Woman,' had she not already published a work, one of the first answers that appeared to Mr. Burke, under the title of, 'A Vindication of the Rights of Men.' But in reality the present work is an elaborate *treatise of female education.*"[1] As the *Analytical* reviewer seems to have wished, A *Vindication of the Rights of Woman* has never been thoroughly examined as a political tract, a radical critique of society from broad egalitarian premises.

Yet the *Rights of Woman* is a radical political tract, even before it is a radical feminist tract. In fact, the feminism that animates the *Rights of Woman* is merely a special instance of the political radicalism that animates the *Rights of Men.* To ignore this fact is to misconstrue much of the basic character of A *Vindication of the Rights of Woman.* It is to fail, as Wollstonecraft's critics have usually done, to understand the propriety of the work's apparent digressions into such tenuously related material as the tyrannical abuse of power by kings and the effeteness of their courts, or the detrimental effects upon society of the existence of a standing army and navy, or the mistakes of educators who would lead boys too early into an understanding of the vices of the world. And it is to underestimate as well the full extent of the social reform that Wollstonecraft envisions as necessary to ameliorate the condition of women in her society. A *Vindication of the Rights of Woman* cannot be properly interpreted except as a statement of political radicalism—more bold, more uncompromising, and more intelligently argued than the earlier *Vindication of the Rights of Men.*

† From *Studies in Burke and His Time* 18 (1977): 155–66. Reprinted with permission of Texas Tech University Press.
1. *Analytical Review* 12 (1792): 248–49.

Indeed, for all its spirit, the *Rights of Men* is not an impressive political document. It was conceived far too exclusively as a vituperative attack on the person and politics of Edmund Burke.[2] As the great British spokesman for conservative public polity, and as an apparent deserter from the cause of freedom he had espoused in approving the American Revolution, Burke was a natural butt for Wollstonecraft, committed as she was to egalitarian principles. But in his *Reflections on the Revolution in France*, Burke had offended Wollstonecraft on more than philosophical grounds. With an injustice that she could not allow to go unnoticed, Burke had maligned the Reverend Richard Price—dissenting minister, political radical, and friend to Wollstonecraft from her days as schoolmistress in Newington Green. Price's sermon, *A Discourse on the Love of Our Country*, had served as the immediate provocation for the *Reflections*, and Burke had not concealed his scorn for the style or opinions of the eminent dissenter.[3] Wollstonecraft, only weeks after the publication of the *Reflections*, responded in kind, heaping on her opponent a wrath and a contempt she made no effort to disguise. Unabashedly, she characterized Burke as an unprincipled charlatan, given to wit above judgment, eloquence above honest simplicity, and opportunism above integrity.

In place of Burke's argument in defense of his political conservatism—an argument that Wollstonecraft thought to proceed from a spurious reliance upon supposed common sense[4]—Wollstonecraft offered an argument from reason. Reason tempered by passion, she contended, not only rejects Burke's appeal to tradition and the wisdom of antiquity, but also urges a spirit of revisionism founded on several clear truths: namely, that freedom is the birthright of all men; that the progress of virtue in civilization depends upon the equality of all men; that prescription and property are destructive of that equality and consequently injurious to the progress of virtue; that blind submission to authority is debasing to the men who kneel

2. A perceptive analysis of style and rhetoric in the *Rights of Men* appears in James T. Boulton, *The Language of Politics in the Age of Wilkes and Burke* (London: Routledge and Kegan Paul, 1963), pp. 167–76. Boulton shows that Wollstonecraft's criticism of Burke—whose style she finds too much marked by passion and imagination and too little controlled by reason—is equally applicable to her own prose style in this emotional pamphlet. Boulton concludes that Wollstonecraft conveys the impression of being "a writer whose views were strongly felt and vigorously communicated; many of the strictures she directs at the *Reflections* are valid and telling; but the chief weakness is Wollstonecraft's inability to embody at all times in her prose those qualities of intellectual honesty and emotional discipline which she claimed were of prime importance to a political philosopher. She condemns Burke and, by the same token, is herself condemned" (pp. 175–76).
3. Edmund Burke, *Reflections on the Revolution in France*, in *Works*, 6 vols. (London: Bohn, 1854), 2: 285 ff.
4. For Wollstonecraft's discussion of Burke's premises, see *A Vindication of the Rights of Men* (1790), ed. Eleanor Louise Nicholes (Gainesville: Scholars' Facsimiles and Reprints, 1960), p. 68.

and ruinous to the men before whom the knee is bent. Elaboration of these truths vies with castigation of Burke as the principal focus of the *Rights of Men*; and the disorganization that follows from Wollstonecraft's divided purpose is compounded by the technique of free association that permits topic to succeed topic haphazardly throughout the text. In its incoherent organization, as in its rational and egalitarian premises, the *Rights of Men* looks ahead to its far more famous successor, *A Vindication of the Rights of Woman*.

The *Rights of Men* looks ahead, too, in the character of the figurative language that emerges from close reading of the text. Although Wollstonecraft was not a dedicated or inventive user of metaphor or simile in her prose, she does appear to be struggling in the *Rights of Men* to discover a particular figure—one fit to describe the condition of men (and women) who have been made deficient in their humanity by reason either of undue wealth and power or of staggering poverty and abjectness. From the first pages of her answer to Burke, Wollstonecraft shows herself to be at once interested in this problem of dehumanization and incapable of describing it fully. She is not content to say of the rich, who "pamper their appetites, and supinely exist without exercising mind or body," merely that "they have ceased to be men." Groping after an expression harsh enough to describe their debasement, she calls them "artificial monster[s]," the deformed products of "hereditary property—hereditary honours." A vivid metaphor, but not, it seems, a satisfactory one; for it is never used again. Sixteen pages later, the rich are spoken of together with the uneducated lower classes, both emerging in description as vulgar "creatures of habit and impulse." The metaphor is ugly, particularly in its application to the poor, whom Wollstonecraft pitied; thus it, too, is abandoned. As the text proceeds, Wollstonecraft argues that sophistication, libertinism, servility, and depraved sensuality are unmanly; but she finds no comprehensive figure by which to represent that unmanliness.[5]

Not, at least, quite yet. But a figure is in the making—one that is at once startling and obvious, simple and extraordinary. That which is unmanly is, of course, womanly; and the realization that woman can be used as a general figure for the social and even political debasement of all mankind emerges sporadically but surely as the *Rights of Men* proceeds. As early as the third paragraph of the text, the possibility shyly obtrudes itself with Wollstonecraft's likening of a wit to a "celebrated beauty, [anxious] to raise admiration on every occasion, and excite emotion, instead of the calm reciprocation of mutual esteem and unimpassioned respect." Later, "luxury and effeminacy" are identified as the curses of the aristocracy, and "profligates

5. Ibid., pp. 10–11, 12, 28, 42, 47, 50, 116.

of rank" are said to be "emasculated by hereditary effeminacy." As Wollstonecraft's attention turns to and from the special problem of woman's place in society—as woman becomes characterized as a flattered doll, vain, inconsiderate, intentionally weak and delicate, and designedly lacking in the "manly morals" of "truth, fortitude, and humanity"—the metaphor urges itself more strongly upon Wollstonecraft and reader alike. Although not so insistent or complex in this text as in the *Vindication of the Rights of Woman*, the figure does reach a kind of climax in the *Rights of Men* when Wollstonecraft attacks the quality of Burke's patriotism and piety: "You love the church, your country, and its laws, you repeatedly tell us, because they deserve to be loved; but from you this is not a panegyric: weakness and indulgence are the only incitements to love and confidence that you can discern, and it cannot be denied that the tender mother you venerate deserves, on this score, all your affection."[6] Here in her description of the church as a weak, imprudent mother is the germ, already beginning to grow, of the figure which will animate and complicate the *Vindication of the Rights of Woman*, helping to make this later text altogether as radical in its politics as in its sociology.

For if the *Rights of Woman* is a political treatise, it is so primarily by virtue of the fact that Wollstonecraft consciously describes political as well as social realities in England through and by means of the social condition of the country's women. In his biography of Mary Wollstonecraft, Ralph Wardle notes that the central thesis of the *Rights of Woman* is "that women as well as men are entitled by birthright to liberty and equality, and that if their rights are withheld, they will deter the progress of civilization." Truly Mary enjoyed at least one flash of genius, and that came when she recognized "the similarity between the plight of oppressed womankind and that of oppressed mankind, and concluded that the solutions were identical."[7] The flash of genius Wardle identifies is genius indeed, but not accurately described; for the similarity he notes is more complex than he allows. Oppressed womankind serves in the *Rights of Woman* not merely as a figure for oppressed and impoverished mankind, but as a figure for all men, high as well as low, who are implicated in social and political contracts which condone inequality of rank, wealth, and privilege.

Indeed, it is significant that in the *Rights of Woman* Wollstonecraft more often likens women to the rich and powerful than to the poor and weak, as would seem most natural. Women are oppressed, it is true; but their oppression is, ironically, the consequence of their

---

6. Ibid. pp. 4, 51, 97, 47–48, 52, 111–15, 112, 124.
7. *Mary Wollstonecraft: A Critical Biography* (Lawrence: University of Kansas Press, 1951), p. 157.

privileged status as pampered creatures of whom no mental competence or moral intelligence is expected. As Wollstonecraft argues in
the course of her exposition, "birth, riches, and every extrinsic advantage that exalt a man above his fellows, without any mental exertion,
sink him in reality below them. In proportion to his weakness, he is
played upon by designing men, till the bloated monster has lost all
traces of humanity."[8] Speaking primarily of middle-class women, but
warning that "the whole female sex are, till their character is formed,
in the same condition as the rich," Wollstonecraft argues that women
are born to indulgence, and powerful in the very weakness that is the
beauty and cunning by which they lord it over the men who imprison
them. Thus, women can be seen to "act as men are observed to act
when they have been exalted by the same means." They are, in short,
"either abject slaves or capricious tyrants"[9]—different sides of the
same devalued coin.

So it is that Wollstonecraft can argue that women enjoy "illegitimate power" and receive "regal homage." They are like Turkish
bashaws, like despots, like kings, like Roman emperors, like "viceregents allowed to reign over a small domain"—and, conversely, all
such tyrants are like women. When Wollstonecraft opines that

> it is impossible for any man, when the most favourable circum-
> stances concur, to acquire sufficient knowledge and strength of
> mind to discharge the duties of a king, entrusted with uncon-
> trouled power; how then must they be violated when his very
> elevation is an insuperable bar to the attainment of either wis-
> dom or virtue; when all the feelings of a man are stifled by flat-
> tery, and reflection shut out by pleasure! Surely it is madness to
> make the fate of thousands depend on the caprice of a weak fel-
> low creature, whose very station sinks him *necessarily* below the
> meanest of his subjects![1]

we can only understand that the regal character has been feminized
in its degradation. Such is the inevitable conclusion to be drawn
from the metaphoric pattern of the text.

That Wollstonecraft herself has drawn this very conclusion is evident from her discussion of the military. Soldiers, kings, and women,
she contends somewhat disjointedly, are linked by similar, vicious
characteristics. Soldiers, after all, by reason of their participation in
a rigid military hierarchy, are types of the enslaved monarch: "Every
corps is a chain of despots, who, submitting and tyrannizing without

---

8. *A Vindication of the Rights of Woman, with Strictures on Political and Moral Subjects*
(London, 1792), p. 91. [In the present edition the quotation is found on p. 49. All subsequent quotations from the *Rights of Woman* will be cited by two page numbers—the first
a reference to the 1792 edition, the second a reference to this Norton Critical Edition—
Editor.]
9. Wollstonecraft, *Rights of Woman*, pp. 122/62, 92/49.
1. Ibid., pp. 38/24, 80/43, 115/59, 85/46, 119/60, 89/48, 98/52, 24–25/19.

exercising their reason, become dead weights of vice and folly on the community." And every individual within every corps is characterized by womanly indolence, polished manners, and love of ornamental dress. Officers, especially, are "particularly attentive to their persons, fond of dancing, crowded rooms, adventures, and ridicule. Like the *fair* sex, the business of their lives is gallantry.—They were taught to please, and they only live to please." Lest we miss the point, Wollstonecraft concludes a long quotation from Rousseau—actually an extended comparison of the respective intellectual provinces of men and women—with the single comment. "I hope my readers still remember the comparison, which I have brought forward, between women and officers." Officers, we are made to realize, have been emasculated, womanized, by their exalted position within the body politic; and war has become "rather the school of *finesse* and effeminacy, than of fortitude."[2]

Emasculated, too, are the rich; for "wealth and female softness equally tend to debase mankind." Thus, the society of the great, like the society of women, is insipid. "Women, in general, as well as the rich of both sexes, have acquired all the follies and vices of civilization, and missed the useful fruit"; for both "neglect the duties of humanity"—women, by failing to cultivate their bodies and intellects for the benefit of their families; the rich, by failing to develop their physical and mental powers, in accordance with the laws of nature, for their own benefit and that of the state. Once again, Wollstonecraft drives home her point with a slyly framed quotation:

> When do we hear of women who, starting out of obscurity, boldly claim respect on account of their great abilities or daring virtues? Where are they to be found?—'To be observed, to be attended to, to be taken notice of with sympathy, complacency, and approbation, are all the advantages which they seek.'— True! my male readers will probably exclaim; but let them, before they draw any conclusion, recollect that this was not written originally as descriptive of women, but of the rich. In Dr. Smith's Theory of Moral Sentiments, I have found a general character of people of rank and fortune, that, in my opinion, might with the greatest propriety be applied to the female sex. I refer the sagacious reader to the whole comparison.[3]

The effeminate rich, like the effeminate military, enjoy social and political status at the expense of their own masculinity.

So natural is it for Wollstonecraft to argue that women enjoy the degradation of the exalted, that she rarely likens them to the truly abject. Occasionally, they are compared to the "mass of mankind"—

2. Ibid., pp. 27/20, 43/26–27, 79/43, 132/154.
3. Ibid., pp. 108/56, 107/56, 129/65, 138/69, 122–123/62.

"obsequious slaves, who patiently allow themselves to be penned up"; occasionally, their condition is likened to that of the poor. And in one outstanding instance, the wife who patiently drudges for her husband is said to be "like a blind horse in a mill." But characteristically, woman is described as a privileged slave, an underling comfortable in a debasement of which she herself approves. Thus, she is very much like a courtier who grovels before the king and, as a reward for his congeniality, enjoys himself a certain amount of groveling from others:

> From whence arises the easy fallacious behavior of a courtier? From his situation, undoubtedly: for standing in need of dependents, he is obliged to learn the art of denying without giving offence, and, of evasively feeding hope with the chameleon's food: thus does politeness sport with truth, and eating away the sincerity and humanity natural to man, produce the fine gentleman.
>
> Women in the same way acquire, from a supposed necessity, an equally artificial mode of behaviour.[4]

Woman is that saddest of spectacles—a human being of possible merit, defrauded of her potential and trivialized. And in so far as men are like her in their positions within the body politic, they too are defrauded and trivialized.

It is for this reason, no doubt, that Wollstonecraft so closely associates the betterment of woman's plight with the rise of the classless society.[5] Effeminacy—with all its implications of weakness, vanity, and amorality—must be banished from the state, and from all social and political institutions within the state, even as it is banished from individuals. The *Vindication of the Rights of Woman* cannot be a feminist document without also being a radical political tract, if only because Wollstonecraft perceives the private and public problems of her country to be inextricably related. "A man has been termed a microcosm; and every family might also be called a state," she asserts. "Public virtue is only an aggregate of private."[6] So long, then, as private virtue permits the indulgence and the debasement of woman, the state and all the individuals in it will suffer from a similar degradation.

It can thus be argued that Wollstonecraft does not digress from her subject when she turns her attention to what appear to be tangential matters. Although her text could be organized more coherently and the connections among her points stated more clearly, she does not willfully wander from her just domain. The conduct of

4. Ibid., pp. 109/56, 134/67, 144/72, 298–299/139.
5. See, for instance, ibid., pp. 38/24 and 74/41.
6. Ibid., pp. 411/187, 445/201.

parents toward children, of teachers toward pupils, of bishops toward country vicars, of military officers toward underlings, of monarchs toward subjects—these are all, after their fashion, types of the conduct of husbands toward wives; and as such, all bear examination and criticism. Even such "episodical observations" as those in which Wollstonecraft mourns the demise of the British hero or decries the vicious self-interest of the British statesman have their relevance. Such disgraces are intimately related to the paucity of virtue in British society, and virtue is condemned to moulder so long as woman is abused and happy in her abuse. As Wollstonecraft notes in her introduction to the *Rights of Woman,* "weak, artificial beings, raised above the common wants and affections of their race, in a premature unnatural manner, undermine the very foundation of virtue, and spread corruption through the whole mass of society!"[7] Women—especially those who are or who aspire to be ladies—are preeminently such beings; and the evidence of the corruption to which they contribute is as much Wollstonecraft's subject as the defense of their misappropriated rights.

Ultimately, it is the premise of Wollstonecraft's feminism that the establishment of women's rights must be allied to a complete transformation of society and the body politic. If the *Rights of Woman* seems less radical than such a premise would suggest, that is only because Wollstonecraft has had the tact merely to hint at the character society will assume when its transformation is complete. Reason, of course, will prevail; and a total leveling of distinctions among men (and women) will have been accomplished. More than any other end, Wollstonecraft desires the establishment of unexceptioned equality among all rational beings. She will allow a superior place in the order of things only to God, who merits homage by virtue of his wisdom and justice, not by virtue of his power. Even God himself cannot be a tyrant in Wollstonecraft's perfect society: he must be rational and virtuous, so that his character may serve as a foundation for human morality. Men, meanwhile, must regulate their behavior "according to . . . common laws," recognizing a lesson in the fact that "the eccentric orbit of the comet never influences astronomical calculations respecting the invariable order established in the motion of the principal bodies of the solar system." Eccentricity—even the eccentricity of the hero or the genius—is, for Wollstonecraft, unnecessary and perhaps detrimental to the common good.

> It is not for the benefit of society that a few brilliant men should be brought forward at the expence of the multitude. It is true, that great men seem to start up, as great revolutions occur, at proper intervals, to restore order, and to blow aside the clouds

7. Ibid., pp. 327–329/151–52, 5/11.

that thicken over the face of truth; but let more reason and virtue prevail in society, and these strong winds would not be necessary.

The welfare of society is not built on extraordinary exertions; and were it more reasonably organized, there would be still less need of great abilities, or heroic virtues.[8]

Three years later, in writing her history of the French Revolution, Wollstonecraft would return to this point, blaming the failure of the century's great social movement on those luminaries whose "patriotism expir[ed] with their popularity":

It will be only necessary to keep in mind the conduct of all the leading men, who have been active in the revolution, to perceive, that the disasters of the nation have arisen from the same miserable source of vanity, and the wretched struggles of selfishness; when the crisis required, that all enlightened patriots should have united and formed a band, to have consolidated the great work; the commencement of which they had accelerated. In proportion as these desertions have taken place, the best abilities which the country contained have disappeared. And thus it has happened, that ignorance and audacity have triumphed, merely because there were not found those brilliant talents, which, pursuing the straight forward line of political economy, arrest, as it were, the suffrage of every well disposed citizen.—Such talents existed in France: and had they combined, and directed their views by a pure love of their country, to one point; all the disasters, which in overwhelming the empire have destroyed the repose of Europe, would not have occurred to disgrace the cause of freedom.[9]

If talent is to be an object of Wollstonecraft's respect, it must be employed for society's benefit by individuals indifferent to their own personal stake in the success they might achieve through largely individual endeavor. Talent, in other words—like wisdom, reason, and virtue—must be respected as an abstraction; and its possessors must be content to work for the common good without distinguishing themselves from the common man.[1]

8. Ibid., pp. 307/142, 372–373/171, 136/68.
9. *An Historical and Moral View of the Origin and Progress of the French Revolution* (London, 1794), pp. 301–2.
1. Early in the *French Revolution* (p. 7), Wollstonecraft announces the strength of her commitment to total equality among men by charging government with the responsibility of leveling natural inequalities: "Nature having made men unequal, by giving stronger bodily and mental powers to one than to another, the end of government ought to be, to destroy this inequality by protecting the weak." Essentially, she wishes to maintain the advantages which accrue to society from men of superior intelligence and training, while diminishing the disadvantages which arise from the social and political privilege usually accorded them.

How the perfect society of patriotic equals is to be established Wollstonecraft does not say, although there is evidence in the *Rights of Woman* that she believed its eventual establishment to be simply in the nature of things. "Every thing around us," she argues at one point, "is in a progressive state":[2] everything that survives the difficulties of existence develops from a weak and vulnerable infancy to a strong and dignified maturity. Society is no exception. In its infancy, it suffers the domination of an aristocracy that soon gives way, under the pressures of "clashing interests," to a monarchy and hierarchy; later, as civilization enlightens the multitude, the monarchy finds itself forced to maintain its unjustified power by means of a deception and a corruption which at once poison the populace and point out their own antidote—"the perfection of man in the establishment of true civilization."[3] Such, Wollstonecraft would later argue, was the experience of the French, whose

> revolution was neither produced by the abilities or intrigues of a few individuals; nor was the effect of sudden and short-lived enthusiasm; but the natural consequence of intellectual improvement, gradually proceeding to perfection in the advancement of communities, from a state of barbarism to that of polished society, till now arrived at the point when sincerity of principles seems to be hastening the overthrow of the tremendous empire of superstition and hypocrisy, erected upon the ruins of gothic brutality and ignorance.[4]

Nature, Wollstonecraft seems to assert, will provide for our own best interests in her own good time; we need only assist her by recognizing the character of those interests and working patiently on their behalf.

It is perhaps for this reason that Wollstonecraft poses so few practical solutions to the problems she identifies in the *Rights of Woman*. No measures she might suggest could possibly rival the wisdom of those measures that will naturally arise in the course of civilization's gradual development. Wollstonecraft need not attempt to incite revolution or even reform. She need only assist the slow, unalterable movement of progress by clarifying the character of those social problems which will demand solution in future years and by adumbrating the probable shape those solutions will take.[5] If, then, the *Rights of Woman* appears somewhat timid in the few proposals for

2. *Rights of Woman*, p. 242/115.
3. Ibid., pp. 29–31/21.
4. *French Revolution*, pp. vii–viii.
5. Indeed, the example of the French Revolution would later evoke in Wollstonecraft a firm commitment to gradualism. In her history of the Revolution, Wollstonecraft would argue that only an excessive degeneracy and tyranny of the aristocracy can justify a people's "having recourse to coercion, to repel coercion." For if the progress of reason is likely to bring about a melioration of conditions in government, "it then seems injudicious for statesmen to force the adoption of any opinion, by aiming at the speedy destruction of obstinate prejudices; because these premature reforms, instead of promoting, destroy the

reform that it offers, that appearance is largely misleading. As Wollstonecraft explains in the first chapter of her text, "Rousseau exerts himself to prove that all *was* right originally: a crowd of authors that all *is* now right: and I, that all will *be* right."[6] For Wollstonecraft, "all will *be* right" only when the whole of society has undergone a radical reordering. In the promise of that reordering lies the exteme political radicalism that is at once the premise and the sine qua non of *A Vindication of the Rights of Woman*.

MITZI MYERS

Reform or Ruin: "A Revolution in Female Manners"[†]

Charting domestic reformation in 1798, the *Annual Register* maintained that the French Revolution had "illustrated the connection between good morals and the order and peace of society more than all the eloquence of the pulpit, and the disquisitions of moral philosophers had done for many centuries." An early adherent of the view that the English grew Victorian as the French turned republican, this journalist sketches a cultural turnabout from the alarmingly prevalent "levity and licentiousness of French manners" in the upper ranks and the fashionable circles who mimicked them to reverence for religion, marriage, and domesticity as the guarantors of social cohesion.[1] The *Register* thus summarizes the interconnected topics of the escalating reform or ruin polemic which is a distinctive strand in the decade's ideological warfare, motifs milked for all they were worth not only by reactionaries, but also by reformers of every persuasion, from radicals to Evangelicals.[2]

---

comfort of those unfortunate beings, who are under their dominion, affording at the same time to despotism the strongest arguments to urge opposition to the theory of reason" (*French Revolution*, pp. 69–70).
6. *Rights of Woman*, p. 22/17.
† From *Studies in Eighteenth-Century Culture* 11 (1982): 199–216. Reprinted by permission.
1. *The Annual Register; or, a View of the History, Politics, and Literature, for the Year 1798*, 2nd ed. (London: W. Otridge, 1806), p. 229. For evidence that French noblewomen self-consciously adopted domesticity as a similar response to revolutionary upheaval, see Margaret H. Darrow, "French Noblewomen and the New Domesticity, 1750–1850," *Feminist Studies*, 5, no. 1 (Spring 1979), 41–65. Darrow argues for "an explicit, causal relationship between political developments and familial change," p. 57. Even before the war, middle-class English travelers were prone to contrasting Parisian ladies "enslaved by fashion" with their own enlightened domesticity; for a typical example, see *The Works of Anna Laetitia Barbauld*, ed. Lucy Aiken (London: Longman, 1825), II, 103.
2. See Richard A. Soloway, "Reform or Ruin: English Moral Thought during the First French Republic," *Review of Politics*, 25, no. 1 (Jan. 1963), 110–28; and *Prelates and People: Ecclesiastical Social Thought in England, 1783–1852* (London: Routledge and Kegan Paul, 1969), pp. 26–45, for an overview of the motif epitomized in John Bowdler's title of 1797—*Reform or Ruin: Take Your Choice!*

320   MITZI MYERS

Among these interlocking themes, woman's role is stellar. Long-term cultural and economic shifts—expanding female education, the increasing impact of middle-class ethics and affluence, the rise of Evangelicalism—united with the explosive hopes and fears kindled by the French Revolution to make woman's influence and activities a matter of grave concern. In the new climate of moral seriousness engendered by the complex (and complexly used) example of dissolute France, the female population was recognized as vital to the nation's well-being. If the decay of states resulted from a general depravity of manners, woman provided a focal point for moral regeneration. Indeed, of all the dangers menacing England, none, claimed that busy pamphleteer John Bowles, was so destructive to the "social machine" as female modesty sacrificed to Gallicized aristocratic fashion, "a much more formidable enemy than Buonoparte himself." Bowles's obsession with feminine manners stems from the (supposedly) "obvious and indissoluble connection, which Providence has been pleased to establish between female chastity and the welfare and safety of civil society," a link endlessly rehearsed from the *Anti-Jacobin* and the *British Critic* to scores of novels.[3] Women moralists too called for "a revolution in female manners," for a reconstituted domestic ideal, as a key means of preserving and purifying the country, but, converting problem into opportunity, they maneuvered the issue with an adroit and ambitious mastery which far outstrips the simplistic hysteria of such male reactionaries as Bowles.[4] This essay explores representative female writers' exploitation of moral reform as a woman's issue, challenging the stereotypical opposition of the ideologies of domesticity and feminism and suggesting some ways of reading, some revisionist strategies for decoding the period's mentorial advice.

"Changes of Times, and Fashions, still demand / New Lessons to instruct the Female Band," remarked one mid-century conduct book writer.[5] No period more aptly illustrates his observation than the revolutionary decades, which witnessed an energetic proliferation of both radical and conservative directives to women. The conventional interpretation of the new lessons for females in that time of convulsive change has recently been reiterated by Lawrence Stone,

3. John Bowles, *Remarks on Modern Female Manners, as Distinguished by Indifference to Character, and Indecency of Dress* (London: F. and C. Rivington, 1802), p. 12; *A View of the Moral State of Society, at the Close of the Eighteenth Century, Much Enlarged, and Continued to the Commencement of the Year 1804, with a Preface Addressed Particularly to the Higher Orders* (London: F. and C. Rivington, 1804), p. 37.
4. Mary Wollstonecraft, *A Vindication of the Rights of Woman, with Strictures on Political and Moral Subjects*, p. 49 (and also p. 202) [Myers cited the 1975 Norton Critical Editon, ed. Carol H. Poston. Page references to the present edition are being supplied for this volume—Editor.]
5. Thomas Marriott, *Female Conduct: Being an Essay on the Art of Pleasing. To be practised by the Fair Sex, before, and after Marriage. A Poem, in Two Books* (London: W. Owen, 1759), p. 79.

whose formulation follows closely that of Maurice Quinlan forty years since. Quinlan's pioneering inquiry into how Victorianism antedated Victoria locates the nineties as a "turning point in English social history," the era when a conservative corpus of manners was fathered by reaction to the revolution and mothered by educators like Hannah More who lauded a newly created standard of womanly excellence, the "model female." Quinlan reads the *Rights of Woman* as sui generis, a radical call for female self-assertion which leagued all other preceptors against the rebel Wollstonecraft. Stressing the importance of extreme femininity and urging women to be a species apart, they called upon their audience "to accept [woman's] subordinate position and to stake all upon the bargaining power of . . . sexual attraction. It was to be," says Quinlan, seriously misrepresenting their stance, females' "one forte, guarded by rules of decorum and made mysterious by the disguise of frailty."[6]

The Family, Sex and Marriage, Stone's massive study of English domestic history, similarly confers a symbolic value on More's popularity. Stone draws a sharp dichotomy between woman's status in the eighteenth-century ambience of "affective individualism" ("relative" equality, companionate marriage, sexual permissiveness) and her devaluation and subordinance in the Evangelically fueled resurgence of patriarchalism which he finds characteristic of the nineteenth. The remarkable success of More's fictionalized conduct book *Coelebs in Search of a Wife* (1808)—it sold eleven editions in nine months, thirty before More's death[7]—Stone believes, "marks the end of an era in husband-wife relations: the Amelia Rattles were out, the Lucilla Stanleys were in." (Since More's anti-heroine Amelia is "boisterous," a "hoyden," "a mass of accomplishments . . . without one particle of mind, one ray of common sense, or one shade of delicacy," any student of eighteenth-century feminine exemplars must wonder when she was ever in.)[8] *Coelebs*, says Stone, "celebrates the ideal woman . . . devoted in domestic duties, religious, modest in dress, silent unless spoken to, deferential to men, and devoted to good works." The brand "new ideal of womanhood" iconized in More's Lucilla "involved total abnegation, making the wife a slave to convention, propriety, and her husband." For Stone, late-eighteenth-century feminism thus "died a swift and natural

6. Maurice J. Quinlan, *Victorian Prelude: A History of English Manners, 1700–1830* (1941; rpt. Hamden, Conn.: Archon Books, 1965), pp. 69, 143.
7. M. G. Jones, *Hannah More* (1952; rpt. New York: Greenwood Press, 1968), p. 193. Henry Thompson, *The Life of Hannah More: with Notices of her Sisters* (London: T. Cadell, 1838), p. 2, notes that *Coelebs* was even translated into Icelandic.
8. Lawrence Stone, *The Family, Sex and Marriage in England, 1500–1800* (New York: Harper and Row, 1977), p. 668; Hannah More, *Coelebs in Search of a Wife, comprehending Observations on Domestic Habits and Manners, Religion and Morals*, in *The Complete Works of Hannah More* (New York: J. C. Derby, 1856), II, 356–57.

322 MITZI MYERS

death, not to be revived again until the twentieth century."⁹ More recently and more demeaningly yet, Lynne Agress's *The Feminine Irony* indicts en masse late eighteenth- and early nineteenth-century women writers as "devil's disciples" for perpetuating a "passive, inferior, feminine stereotype" rather than protesting the second-class standing they inherited from an imperfectly illumined Enlightenment.¹ Again, More is the premier villain; Wollstonecraft, the lonely exception.

Modern scholarship, then, myopically reproduces the anti-Jacobin opposition of More and Wollstonecraft, the contrast between the bishop and the hyena in petticoats epitomized in Walpole's letters or Richard Polwhele's *The Unsex'd Females*.² Rightly emphasizing the ferment over womanhood seething in the nineties, Quinlan and Stone reincarnate as new what were old standards, familiar favorites in the conduct book repertoire of femininity, while failing to consider the positive redirections factored into the ostensible traditionalism of reformers like More. Conversely, overaccenting Wollstonecraft's iconoclasm obscures the degree to which her demands are typical of a wide spectrum of women writers. In the nineties, in fact, female educators of every stripe—from radicals like Catharine Macaulay Graham, Wollstonecraft, Mary Hays, and Anne Frances Randall (who was probably Mary Robinson), to moderates like Clara Reeve, Maria Edgeworth, Anna Laetitia Barbauld, Priscilla Wakefield, and Mary Ann Radcliffe, to religionists like Sarah Trimmer, More, and Jane West—vigorously attacked the deficiencies of fashionable training and values. In their different ways, they seek to endow woman's role with more competence, dignity, and consequence. Downgrading the ornamental and pleasing to magnify the useful and moral, they dwell on the disjunction between functional education for ethical living and the current "phrenzy of accomplishments" geared merely to seduce success in a disadvantageous marriage market.³ Female instructors in general were increasingly prodding their auditors to take responsibility for realizing their own potential, to become self-improved, albeit modest, mistresses of their own—and the nation's—destiny. Such women, gently or stringently reformist

9. Stone, pp. 668, 342. In view of Stone's presentation of More as the arch-propagandist of repression, it is surprising to find her described elsewhere in the text (p. 352) as a "feminist educational reformer."
1. Lynne Agress, *The Feminine Irony: Women on Women in Early-Nineteenth-Century English Literature* (Rutherford, N.J.: Fairleigh Dickinson University Press, 1978), pp. 172, 16.
2. *Horace Walpole's Correspondence*, ed. W. S. Lewis, Robert A. Smith, and Charles H. Bennett, XXXI (New Haven: Yale University Press, 1961), 397; Richard Polwhele, *The Unsex'd Females: A Poem* (1798; rpt. New York: Garland, 1974), pp. 35–36 n. [For a selection from Polwhele's poem, see p. 288 herein—*Editor*.]
3. Hannah More, *Strictures on the Modern System of Female Education, with a View of the Principles and Conduct prevalent among Women of Rank and Fortune* (1799; rpt. New York: Garland Publishing Co., 1974), I, 62.

in orientation, had female co-workers, discreet rebels among the horde of novelists overtly preoccupied with propriety, and notable male contemporaries like the Evangelical Thomas Gisborne as well as numerous nineteenth-century successors.

Situating these variant models of female reform within a theoretical context based on current work in social anthropology offers a more sensitive and nuanced approach than clichés of bifurcation reducing most women to passive victims, to mindless mouthpieces of patriarchal attitudes. Edwin and Shirley Ardener's analysis of dominant and muted groups draws attention to the subtleties and ambiguities of belief systems generated by the culturally inarticulate.[4] Subordinate groups like women must shape their world views *through* the dominant models, transforming their own perceptions and needs as best they can in terms of received frameworks. If women's alternative or counterpart models are not acceptably encoded in the prevailing male idiom, female concerns will not receive a proper hearing. Women's ways of ordering, of making significant their situation, must thus be carefully disinterred from the dominant structures which muffle them. Even though female models of reality and desire mostly follow the ground rules, their unique deviations from the norms make a woman's world of difference. Women's interpretations of their roles are not fully coincident with men's. If writers enjoin the primacy of familial duties, as do both More and Wollstonecraft, they may yet invest women's roles with powerful, even subversive meanings quite different from conventional ascriptions of weakness and public insignificance. Since female models characteristically operate in terms of strategically redefining and rescripting traditional markers, the linguistic surface of such sexual pronouncements must be carefully scrutinized for imperfect integrations, submerged conflicts, covert messages—for all the meanings which hover interstitially.

Not only do the texts of prescriptive works demand solicitous sifting, but their contexts, their membership in wider ideological movements, also require investigation. In an important essay focusing modern reexamination of Evangelicalism, for instance, Gerald Newman persuasively questions the orthodoxy of such polemicists as More, concluding that they did "much more indeed to subvert the established order than to uphold it" and that the neopuritans "should be regarded as moral and social revolutionaries."[5] Masters and mistresses of propaganda specializing in fifth column tactics, they obeyed the injunction to be "wise as serpents, and harmless as

4. Shirley Ardener, ed., *Perceiving Women* (London: Malaby Press, 1975), pp. vii–xxiii.
5. Gerald Newman, "Anti-French Propaganda and British Liberal Nationalism in the Early Nineteenth Century: Suggestions toward a General Interpretation," *Victorian Studies*, 18, no. 4 (June 1975), 401.

doves," infiltrating and undermining the traditional order from within through their genius for organization and for manipulation of public opinion. The revised view of Evangelicalism as a militant vanguard of emergent middle-class consciousness convincingly demonstrates how diverse anti-French political strategies (whether anti-old or anti-new regimes) mutated into a much broader social and moral critique of aristocratic mores and modes, paving the way for progressive nineteenth-century liberalism. To downplay political hostilities and connect middle-class groups seldom considered together is to illuminate the pervasiveness and the ideological significance of reformist ethics as an agent of the class redistribution of moral authority necessary for fundamental social change.[6]

Although Newman cites "the puritanical strictures on upper-class habits laid down equally by Mary Wollstonecraft and Hannah More," he does not pursue his insight to probe the intersection of moral reform, class tension, and gender consciousness.[7] Yet, despite the fulminations Wollstonecraft occasioned (and these derived even more from her checkered life than from her work), what most strikingly emerges from close interrogation of competing radical and Evangelical domestic ideologies is the similar psychological and emotional dynamic, the unexpected congruence of the ideals and programs expressed in such politically polar works as Wollstonecraft's *Rights of Woman* (1792) and More's *Strictures on the Modern System*

6. Matthew 10:16; see Newman, "Anti-French Propaganda," pp. 385–418; Ford K. Brown, *Fathers of the Victorians: The Age of Wilberforce* (Cambridge: Cambridge University Press, 1961); Bernard Semmel, *The Methodist Revolution* (New York: Basic Books, 1973); Michael Hennell, "A Little-Known Social Revolution," *Church Quarterly Review*, 143 (Jan.–March 1947), 189–207; V. Kiernan, "Evangelicalism and the French Revolution," *Past and Present*, no. 1 (Feb. 1952), pp. 44–56; G. F. A. Best, "The Evangelicals and the Established Church in the Early Nineteenth Century," *Journal of Theological Studies*, n.s. 10, pt. 1 (April 1959), 63–78; and "Evangelicalism and the Victorians," in *The Victorian Crisis of Faith: Six Lectures*, ed. Anthony Symondson (London: SPCK, 1970), pp. 37–56; Ernest Marshall Howse, *Saints in Politics: The "Clapham Sect" and the Growth of Freedom* (London: George Allen and Unwin, 1953); Charles I. Foster, *An Errand of Mercy: The Evangelical United Front, 1790–1837* (Chapel Hill: University of North Carolina Press, 1960); Kathleen Heasman, *Evangelicals in Action: An Appraisal of their Social Work in the Victorian Era* (London: Geoffrey Bles, 1962); Ian Bradley, *The Call to Seriousness: The Evangelical Impact on the Victorians* (London: Jonathon Cape, 1976); Standish Meacham, "The Evangelical Inheritance," *The Journal of British Studies*, 3, no. 1 (Nov. 1963), 88–104; Harold Perkin, *The Origins of Modern English Society, 1780–1880* (London: Routledge and Kegan Paul, 1969), esp. pp. 280–90; Muriel Jaeger, *Before Victoria* (London: Chatto and Windus, 1956), pp. 31–52; David Spring, "The Clapham Sect: Some Social and Political Aspects," *Victorian Studies*, 5, no. 1 (Sept. 1961), 35–48; "Aristocracy, Social Structure, and Religion in the Early Victorian Period," *Victorian Studies*, 6, no. 3 (March 1963), 263–80; and "Some Reflections on Social History in the Nineteenth Century," *Victorian Studies*, 4, no. 1 (Sept. 1960), 55–64; Asa Briggs, "Middle-Class Consciousness in English Politics, 1780–1846," *Past and Present*, no. 9 (April 1956), pp. 65–74. Brown's assessment differs from others cited, but his analysis of Evangelical strategy is to the point. Stone and Randolph Trumbach, *The Rise of the Egalitarian Family: Aristocratic Kinship and Domestic Relations in Eighteenth-Century England* (New York: Academic Press, 1978), argue that the eighteenth-century English aristocracy was already beginning to embrace the domestic ideal, but upper-class laxity and levity remained an article of faith in middle-class reformist rhetoric.
7. Newman, "Anti-French Propaganda," p. 402, n. 28.

of Female Education (1799), *Coelebs's* thematic precursor. (The same might be said for the works of the radical Mary Hays and the orthodox Jane West.) "It is amazing," observed their contemporary Mary Berry, studying More and Wollstonecraft in tandem, how much the two "agree on all the great points of female education. H. More will, I dare say, be very angry when she hears this."[8] No doubt, for More emphatically refused to read Wollstonecraft and thought her a dangerous malcontent.[9] Nevertheless, the parallels between the two texts extend far beyond their mutual insistence on the radical renovation of female education and manners as prerequisites to a moral restructuring of society.

Wollstonecraft's enlightened womanhood and More's doctrines of Evangelical femininity, her authoritative codification of woman's sphere, responsibilities, and powers, demonstrate alike the extent to which reformist educators had assimilated and were purveying the ascendant bourgeois ethic sanctifying useful industry and family, an ideology which was at that historical juncture for the most part progressive, criticizing, not celebrating the status quo.[1] But at the same time—and this is a crucial point—female moral reformers were recasting that ethic in women's terms for women's benefit, suiting to their own needs the general middle-class protest against aristocratic license and inutility and inflecting bourgeois modes to fit the feminine sphere of endeavor. Moral reform, radically or Evangelically permuted, offered such activist ideologues a body of legitimating imperatives and a vocabulary for venting female dissatisfaction and rendering telling critiques of a society governed by worldly libertine males, as well as for formulating counterpart models based on middle-class female values and priorities. For them, to reform is to reform. Applying the corrective insights stimulated by woman's unsettled status in a transitional era, they ask what constitutes the good society and how women can further it. Significantly, their social strictures both partake of and subtly subvert certain constituents of the bourgeois nexus. Proponents of the humanizing values associated with home, they do not endorse domesticity as decorative gloss or quiescent retreat. Rather, they interpret domestic culture as proffering active roles, constructive channels through

8. *Extracts of the Journals and Correspondence of Miss Berry from the Year 1783 to 1852*, ed. Lady Theresa Lewis (London: Longmans, Green, 1865), II, 91.

9. *Memoirs of the Life and Correspondence of Mrs. Hannah More*, ed. William Roberts (London: R. B. Seeley and W. Burnside, 1834), II, 371.

1. For progressive bourgeois ideology, see Isaac Kramnick, "Religion and Radicalism: English Political Theory in the Age of Revolution," *Political Theory: An International Journal of Political Philosophy*, 5, no. 4 (Nov. 1977), 505–34; and "Children's Literature and Bourgeois Ideology: Observations on Culture and Industrial Capitalism in the Later Eighteenth Century," in *Culture and Politics from Puritanism to the Enlightenment*, ed. Perez Zagorin (Berkeley: University of California Press, 1980), pp. 203–40. I am grateful to Professor Kramnick for allowing me to read the latter in manuscript.

which women can aid in revitalizing the world to conform to the values of home, not the materialistic marketplace. Defining domesticity in terms of social responsibility, they negotiate available ideologies into habitability.

Combatants for the allegiance of their increasingly leisured, marginally educated countrywomen, Wollstonecraft and More both strive to replace the regnant ideal of pliant, unproductive urbanity with socially functional middle-class models. Had More looked into Wollstonecraft, she would have discovered an analysis of contemporary female frivolity, incompetence, and maldirected energies, of "weak and wretched" women, commensurate with her own, as well as a similar idealistic myth of what properly fortified female minds might accomplish: a more respectable and powerful status underscoring women's need for purposeful, nationally significant work (whether charitable or paid) and endowing them with weighty authority as mothers and educators, a reordering of the state through the wise nurture of children, a reining in of male behavior and attitudes to a chaste and modest single standard.[2] The "ideal of passive womanhood" frequently attributed to the Evangelicals is very much a misnomer.[3] For at the heart of both More's and Wollstonecraft's works lies a pattern of female domestic heroism, an image of activity, strength, fortitude, and ethical maturity, of self-denial, purity, and truth. It is God, however differently envisioned, who empowers what are essentially revivified spiritual ideals. If life is probationary, an education for immortality, then woman is not mere flesh for male consumption, not a being delimited by sexual attraction (as Quinlan would have it), but a creature of rationally educable mind and aspiring soul, a potent spiritual agent whose most exigent duties are personal improvement and social regeneration.

Both women thus challenge popular conduct book recommendations for feminine training and behavior—hide your wit, your learning, your health—and define themselves in opposition to the usual arts of flattery, dissimulation, and manipulative pleasing, signal women's restiveness in their elegant niche and implicitly querying Stone's optimistic conclusions about eighteenth-century female status. Indicting what they call the Mohammedan view of woman as docile matter catering to masculine appetite (perhaps best exemplified in Rousseau's Sophia), they claim homage not to charm and modish graces, but to mind and moral excellence. They deplore a female education fixated on the body and senses, for moral reform entails mental enlargment, a puritan work ethic of the mind. Finding

2. The quoted phrase is from *Rights of Woman*, p. 9.
3. By, for example, David Monaghan, "*Mansfield Park* and Evangelicalism: A Reassessment," *Nineteenth-Century Fiction*, 33, no. 2 (Sept. 1978), 230.

women's brains and morality in a state of ill repair, both prescribe a regimen of rigorous ethical and intellectual cultivation to exercise the faculties of readers starved on elegant abstracts, vitiated by "stupid novelists" and artificial male gallantry. They go in for "dry tough reading" and bracing character formation.[4] If they appropriate bourgeois stress on motherhood, they infuse the evolving ideal with spiritual and mental backbone and public import, each writer transforming the parable of the talents into an exemplum of maternal heroism and power.[5] If they push the middle-class virtues of accountability, diligence, discipline, and order, they also deride social emulation and self-indulgence to preach a genuine upward mobility—that of the soul. More does not hew to the orthodoxly genteel line on woman's role any more than does Wollstonecraft, nor is her "new ideal" wholly retrograde. She inculcates not passive submission, but reasoned acquiescence to established custom, and that only up to a point. As with Wollstonecraft, and with comparable important consequences, her ultimate frame of reference is non-secular. Evangelical spiritual egalitarianism, like feminism, offers a path to autonomy and transcendence of sex. It is no accident that both like to cite that fruitfully ambiguous verse "be not conformed to this world."[6]

Each preceptor in her own way is a reformer who works to extend female agency through the moral revision of conventions. Wollstonecraft's radicalism, for example, is firmly embedded within the bourgeois paradigm. Modifying middle-class domesticity to fit her own purposes, she creates an alternative, potentially revolutionary female ideology within a scaffolding of cultural givens. Like such other mentors as Jane West, she makes an initial point of addressing not ladies, but "those in the middle class, because they appear to be in the most natural state." For men at least, the necessity of exertion ensured the "notorious" consequence that "the middle class contains most virtue and abilities." But its women "ape the fashions of the nobility," fall prey to "factitious manners" imported from aristocratic France, and, exasperatingly, all yearn to be "ladies. Which is simply to have nothing to do." In fact, she concludes, her own "observation with respect to the middle rank, the one in which talents thrive best, extends not to women." Since static women will halt all progress, the

---

4. *Rights of Woman*, p. 192; *Strictures*, I, 165.
5. Matthew 25:14–28; see *Rights of Woman*, p. 55; *Strictures*, I, 52–53; for the evolution of analogous patterns of moral motherhood in America, see Linda K. Kerber, "Daughters of Columbia: Educating Women for the Republic, 1787–1805," in *The Hofstadter Aegis: A Memorial*, ed. Stanley Elkins and Eric McKitrick (New York: Alfred A. Knopf, 1974), pp. 36–59; and Ruth H. Bloch, "American Feminine Ideals in Transition: The Rise of the Moral Mother, 1785–1815," *Feminist Studies*, 4, no. 2 (June 1978), 101–26.
6. ". . . but be ye transformed by the renewing of your mind," Romans 12:2; for examples, see More, "An Estimate of the Religion of the Fashionable World," *Works*, I, 297; *Strictures*, II, 194, 239; *Collected Letters of Mary Wollstonecraft*, ed. Ralph M. Wardle (Ithaca and London: Cornell University Press, 1979), p. 118.

Rights of Woman is designed to remedy this unhealthy enervation by guiding them back to nature, reason, and virtue, to the "severe duties" and "domestic pleasures" of Wollstonecraft's desideratum: "more observant daughters, more affectionate sisters, more faithful wives, more reasonable mothers—in a word, better citizens." She tirelessly contrasts duty and diversion, the life style of enlightened domesticity and elite gallantry. Women are to shun the stigmata of the frivolous great world—dress, pleasure, and sway—relishing instead the "minutiae of domestic taste," the "simple grandeur" of "dignified domestic happiness."[7] Pointedly reversing aristocratic attributes— sensuality, indolence, luxury, privilege—the new woman's world projected by middle-class radicalism exalts modesty for both sexes, serviceable work, education, and, above all, mothering.

Wollstonecraft asserts (if sometimes without elaboration) many claims integral to modern feminism, suing for coeducation, economic independence, legal equality, and freer access to jobs and professions, yet, despite her often inflammatory rhetoric, the core of her manifesto remains middle-class motherhood, a feminist, republicanized adaptation of the female role normative in late eighteenth-century bourgeois notions of the family. Nature enlists women to fulfill "peculiar duties": "the rearing of children, that is, laying a foundation of sound health both of body and mind in the rising generation, has justly been insisted on as the peculiar destination of woman." In accordance with this female destiny, women are naturally "susceptible of the attached affections." Indeed, though Wollstonecraft derides sexual virtues and sentimental propaganda casting all women in one languid mold, she also affirms, taking for granted the female's primary responsibility for child care, that "whatever tends to incapacitate the maternal character, takes woman out of her sphere." No more than More (or, for that matter, Mill) does she aspire to pluck most women out of their families or dissever them from their relative duties.[8]

On the contrary, Wollstonecraft aggrandizes, heroizes the maternal mission, elevating woman's status by making her familial roles the linchpin of a new society. Although she does not suggest that woman's only possible place is the home, motherhood provides a pervasive rationale for better education, as well as for civil existence and work. The more enlightened understanding women acquire, the more they will take to those offices nature annexes to their gender. As "active citizen,' the average woman will advance the common welfare by managing her family, educating her children, and assisting her neighbors, also standing ready for work outside the home to

7. *Rights of Woman*, pp. 11, 62, 80, 61, 156, 82, 13, 158, 175, 200.
8. *Rights of Woman*, pp. 174, 198, 175, 186, 60.

facilitate family maintenance if necessary. In thus carrying out her communal obligations, she eludes the spirit of degrading dependence and self-respectingly earns her keep, while also developing her own autonomous moral character. Like Mill, Wollstonecraft has recently been faulted as a feminist theorist for failing to challenge the nuclear family as an institution or to question its constraints on female life. Her acceptance of natural sex roles, of rationalized marriage and motherhood as public service in the national interest, it is argued, limits her application of egalitarian principles to women. But for Wollstonecraft, nature and reason validate the bourgeois family as a key corrective to the sins of an oppressive, class-bound establishment. Only through training generations of reform-oriented citizens can the "pestiferous purple" of rank and riches ultimately be exorcized. Her vision of radical progress, of "public freedom and universal happiness," depends on the private virtue nourished by chaste fathers and "patriot" mothers. Marriage civilizes man, families school humanitarian republicans, and domestic affections cement the general good.[9] Her radical politics operates through the militant moral posture inherent in middle-class ideology.

Intent on reinventing bourgeois domestic conventions in women's favor, Wollstonecraft elides any possible antagonism between their "first duty . . . to themselves as rational creatures" and their next "as citizens, . . . that, which includes so many, of a mother." The text cancels conflict between individual autonomy and corporate duty in declaring, for instance, that "the being who discharges the duties of its station is independent." Such configurations illuminate Wollstonecraft's argumentative and emotional logic, revealing how her expressivism was tempered by and shaped through current models of public belief. Critic of sexual stereotyping though she was, Wollstonecraft's feminism is very much conditioned by and justified in terms of revisionist bourgeois ideology, that idyll of a harmonious and socially productive domesticity which haunted her imagination and punctuates her text. On the one hand, even the eighteenth-century's

---

9. See *Rights of Woman*, pp. 160, 178, 7, 155, 20, 8, 6, 202, 166, 153. The importance and comforts of being a mother are also thematically stressed in Wollstonecraft's unfinished last novel, written after she herself had become one. See, for example, the strong statement on p. 154, *Mary, A Fiction and The Wrongs of Woman*, ed. Gary Kelly (London: Oxford University Press, 1976). For critiques of Wollstonecraft's values, see Virginia Sapiro, "Feminist Studies and the Discipline: A Study of Mary Wollstonecraft," *The University of Michigan Papers in Women's Studies*, 1, no. 1 (Feb. 1974), 178–200; and Nancy M. Theriot, "Mary Wollstonecraft and Margaret Fuller: A Theoretical Comparison," *International Journal of Women's Studies*, 2, no 6. (Nov–Dec. 1979), 560–74. For similar criticism of Mill, see Susan Moller Okin, *Women in Western Political Thought* (Princeton: Princeton University Press, 1979), pp. 226, 30. Elissa S. Guralnick, "Radical Politics in Mary Wollstonecraft's *A Vindication of the Rights of Woman*," *Studies in Burke and His Time*, 18 (Autumn 1977), 155–66, stresses Wollstonecraft's radicalism, but also observes that the text offers no practical political program. [Guralnick's essay is reprinted on p. 309 herein—*Editor*.]

foremost female radical equates private need and public contribution, demands no rights without concomitant duties. Her translation
of feminism into the language of social purification and spiritual
endeavor demonstrates the female strategy of self-assertion through
virtue, of being good as potential power. "I will be *good*, that I may
deserve to be happy," she was to write in the greatest psychic crisis of
her life.[1] On the other hand, Wollstonecraft's tailoring of her con-
ceptual framework shows how female marginality clarifies moral
insight, evolving dynamic models of resistance within a dominant
superstructure.

If Wollstonecraft's new society predicates the ultimate deletion of
the great as a class (servants and the poor perdure—their lot is com-
miserated with but not resolved), More embarks on a reclamation
project. A firm believer in the efficacy of example to chasten or corrupt, she shepherded the *ton* toward social helpfulness and the
"almost sacred joys of *home*." "Reformation must begin with the
GREAT," she intones, or the reformer merely throws "odours into
the stream while the springs are poisoned." Lamenting that the
"middle orders have caught the contagion" of fashionable emulation
and that "this revolution of [their] manners" has almost rendered
obsolete the adage "'most worth and virtue are to be found in the
middle station,'" she scolded women of rank and fortune into trading their lazy Frenchified habits for the strenuous exertion of feminine influence in her *Strictures*, while establishing a voguish pattern
of bourgeois domestic culture in *Coelebs*. Like Wollstonecraft, she
posits a reform or ruin dichotomy, attesting women's potency to
undermine or save their country. They bear, in More's view, special
civil and social responsibilities. Yoking gender and regeneration, she
proclaims that educated women's moral force, by example and
exhortation (she herself was a formidable model), can resurrect society on a Christian basis. *Strictures*, for instance, opens with an invigorating evocation of female power, urging women to its "most
appropriate" exercise: "to raise the depressed tone of public morals."
Trafficking in mere manners is a "low mark, a prize not worthy of
their high and holy calling."[2] Her terminology of moral reform insists
on female agency; her works comprise a practical, comprehensive
program for converting the standard *topos* of feminine influence
from pacifying sham to redemptive fact. Not only must patricians
embrace middle-class and Christian values, but men, forsaking aristocratic male honor, must also accede to the feminization of their

---

1. *Rights of Woman*, p. 153; *Collected Letters*, p. 233. For an idyllic bourgeois vignette, see
   Rights of Woman, p. 151.
2. "Sensibility: An Epistle to the Honourable Mrs. Boscawen," *Works*, I, 35 (cf. *Strictures*, II,
   161); "Thoughts on the Importance of the Manners of the Great to General Society,"
   Works, I, 274; *Strictures*, I, 62–63, 4–5.

ethos in the name of Jesus.[3] More's conflation of Christian and feminine virtues to female advantage cuts two ways, enduing women with quiet strength and courage and weaning men from their lax codes to that of the domestic milieu. She adjures females to self-discipline, but the worldly latitude forbidden them is not allowed to men either and what is good for women is also salutary for men.

More's subsumption of the feminine in the Christian is the root of her pious, public-spirited tour de force. Supplely preserving conventional appearances, she gives them a new direction, not only investing woman's traditional province with national relevance but also expanding her sphere. In line with general Evangelical professionalization, she ennobles woman's work into a vocation: "the profession of ladies . . . is that of daughters, wives, mothers, and mistresses of families." But women are not, cloistered, to renounce the outside world. Rather, following More's incessant emphasis on active virtue, they are to broaden their nurturing and reformative functions: the "superintendance of the poor" is "their immediate office"; "*charity is the calling of a lady; the care of the poor is her profession.*"[4] More inoculates everyday routine with aggressive virtue: women must not only discountenance vice, for example, but debar the guilty rake from society. One historian of feminism remarks that, "without in the least intending" it, devout women like More and Sarah Trimmer who mapped out new female fields were really fomenting mid-Victorian feminist revolt.[5] She had in mind More's manifold philanthropical contributions, both personal and authorial—what might be labeled social feminism—but in fact the drift of More's explicitly conservative message is toward a liberating reworking of feminine ideology. She avers not only women's capability to define their own sphere—an issue of autonomy however bounded that sphere—but also their fitness for ethical stewardship. A partisan of her sex amply possessing Evangelic tactical shrewdness, More was a female crusader infinitely more successful than Wollstonecraft or any other competitor. She furbishes her goals in palatable form and hones those ideals paid cultural lip service to achieve her own ends, playing within the rules of the game while taking on the substantive reorganization of the dominant male culture's beliefs and values. Underneath its discreet surface, a More text is alive with submerged power, not that derived of dominance but a positive power of ability, competence, energy—a negative power of refusal, the right, indeed duty, to say no

3. For examples of strictures on male honor and of the conflation of Christian and feminine virtues, see "Fashionable World," *Works*, I, 284, 288–89; and "Preface to the Tragedies," *Works*, I, 504–5.
4. For Evangelical professionalization, see Bradley, pp. 156–78; *Strictures*, I, 97, 98, 117; *Coelebs, Works*, II, 372.
5. Ray Strachey, *"The Cause": A Short History of the Women's Movement in Great Britain* (1928; rpt. Port Washington, New York: Kennikat Press, 1969). p. 13.

to custom, on Christian grounds of course. (A complete analysis of the complex rhetorical counterpoint through which she manages to convey female power while upholding sexual complementarity and deftly sidestepping impropriety would require a separate essay.) Rhythmically alternating the systole of ingratiating genuflection and the diastole of combative assertion, it is also predictably rife with latent contradictions and undrawn conclusions.

Yet More clearly offered much to her readers—a diet of "wholesome occupation, vigorous exertion, and systematic employment" seasoned by "rational and domestic enjoyments."[6] The comment of a young American attuned to nuance is instructive: "what an important sphere a woman fills! how thoroughly she ought to be qualified for it—but I think hers the more honourable employment than a man's for all men feel so grand and boast so much—and make such a pother about their being lords of the world below . . . oh every man of sense must humbly bow before woman. She bears the sway, not man as he presumptuously supposes."[7] Outlining the advantages of separate spheres, of women's role as "lawful possessors of a lesser domestic territory," More persuasively infuses their domestic vocation with social and political resonance. Nor is the Evangelical view of marriage she presents a regression to patriarchy. If she likes to talk of mutual dependence, she is a firm advocate of companionate marriage. Her heroine Lucilla Stanley may be too good for modern tastes, but she is indisputably a woman of character, a wife to be consulted, not dictated to. Participating in "all the dignity of equality," she is "not only the associate, but the inspirer of [Coelebs's] virtues"—his "coadjutress," "directress," and "presiding genius."[8] More's stress on philanthropy also spoke to female needs, as Wilberforce's reflection on the improved status of unmarried women indicates: "formerly there seemed to be nothing useful in which they could naturally be busy, but now they may always find an object in attending the poor." His diagnosis is echoed more ambivalently by that astute observer Lucy Aiken (Mrs. Barbauld's niece), who traced the overexuberances of the charitable "rage" to More, but knew "no one circumstance by which the manners, studies, and occupations of Englishwomen have been so extensively modified, or so strikingly contradistinguished from those of a former generation." They were, she thought in 1842, a hardier, more active lot.[9]

6. *Strictures*, II, 126, 201.
7. Mehitable May Dawes (Goddard), diary entry for June 12, 1815, quoted in Nancy F. Cott, *The Bonds of Womanhood: "Woman's Sphere" in New England, 1780–1835* (New Haven and London: Yale University Press, 1977), p. 99.
8. *Strictures*, II, 22; *Coelebs, Works*, II, 306, 372.
9. Wilberforce is quoted in Jaeger, p. 29; *Memoirs, Miscellanies and Letters of the Late Lucy Aikin: Including Those Addressed to the Rev. Dr. Channing from 1826 to 1842*, ed. Philip Hemery Le Breton (London: Longman, Green, Longman, Roberts, and Green, 1864), pp. 421–22, 435. According to Mrs. Barbauld, philanthrophy was a full-blown fad by 1813;

Female activity and usefulness are indeed More's forte. Accepting constraints, she construes them as moral heroism, delivering the expected, but on her own terms: let girls "not be instructed to practise gentleness merely on the low ground of its being decorous and feminine and pleasing, and calculated to attract human favour," as the male conduct book writers she sardonically paraphrases counsel, but "on the high principle of obedience to Christ . . . a perfect pattern of imitation." The "divine Alchymy" of vital religion dilates female prerogative, licenses therapeutic moral imperialism, for in religion women are men's full equals, in truth their superiors and guides. Christianity generously reimburses women for earthly handicaps (a topic on which More can be tart) and opens a lawful avenue to achievement. More's Christian heroism is daily, domestic, full of small private amendments with public reverberations—requisite for men but peculiarly suited to the women whose ascriptive meekness and charity Christianity so strikingly ranks above society's rougher male standards.[1] In her pre-Evangelical days, More had likened women to fine porcelain vases on high shelves, but in 1799 pleaded for "a patriotism at once firm and feminine for the general good," for the "young Christian militant" who could "awaken the drowsy spirit of religious principle." When, in an England trembling before "the most tremendous confederacies against religion and order, and governments, which the world ever saw," More pronounced religious rebirth the one thing needful, it is not surprising that she tapped a receptive female constituency eager to believe that on their influence depended "the very existence" of civilization, that the "dignity of the work" to which they were summoned was "no less than that of preserving the ark of the Lord." Doing the good work of moral reform, they enrolled as Providence's agents.[2]

Moral reform, then, was the complex issue of the day, and it was preeminently a female issue, witnessing the dialectic through which women, enmeshed in ideologies, use cultural definitions to try to shape their own lives, partly complying with and partly taking charge of their destinies. However amenable to variant subplots, it both testifies to female agency and ratifies woman's socially functional

see her *Works*, II, 107–8. For recent documentation of the rage, see. F. K. Prochaska, "Women in English Philanthropy 1790–1830," *International Review of Social History*, 19, pt. 3 (1974), 426–45; and Barbara Corrado Pope, "Angels in the Devil's Workshop: Leisured and Charitable Women in Nineteenth-Century England and France," *Becoming Visible: Women in European History*, ed. Renate Bridenthal and Claudia Koonz (Boston: Houghton Mifflin, 1977), pp. 296–324.

1. *Strictures*, I, 143, 138; II, 30–41, 93. Wilberforce's view of women parallels More's in his very popular *A Practical View of the Prevailing Religious System of Professed Christians, in the Higher and Middle Classes in this Country, Contrasted with Real Christianity*; 6th ed. (London: T. Cadell and W. Davies, 1798), pp. 445–47.

2. "Essays on Various Subjects, Principally Designed for Young Ladies," *Works*, I, 550 (More did not, perhaps significantly, include this 1777 work in her 1830 edition.); *Strictures*, I, 4–6, 83, 54; II, 97.

centrality. Though their remedies differ in many details, Wollstonecraft and More each diagnose England's moral—and almost mortal— illness in analogous terms. Perceiving a society infected with fashionable corruption, both preach a militantly moral middle-class reform grounded in women's potentiality. Delineating a female vision of the world, they put familial experience first. It is certainly true that conservatives identified feminists and male radicals who dared to reassess family structure and the relationship between the sexes as a threat. Terrified of collapse on the home front, they shored up domestic verities to strengthen the nation for its external battles. As the *Annual Register* spelled out, "The grand spring and cement of society is, the divine principle of love, branching forth from conjugal into parental, fraternal, and filial affection, an attachment to kindred, neighbours, countrymen."[3] Because domesticity and patriotism were thus inextricably joined, women, sex, and the family were thematic obsessions of anti-Jacobin polemic. The foundations of national morality were laid in private families: the home was fount of civic virtue, custodian of social stability, bulwark against political subversion. But radicals like Wollstonecraft (and Hays) were equally anxious for a renovated domestic ideal: marriage, says Wollstonecraft, is the "cement of society," the "foundation of almost every social virtue." For each side, then, woman's role as "chaste wife, and serious mother" is pivotal.[4]

Both More and Wollstonecraft also avow the wider warrant of female example to effect national change and spur women to "labour by reforming themselves to reform the world."[5] Anti-sensuality, prochastity, both orchestrate modesty, self-control, and purity as human values rather than primarily feminine ones. Women were no longer to be merely the customary refiners of manners and the victims of those duplicitous manners, not the votaries of love, but the reformers of male and female morals alike and the beneficiaries of those reformed morals. Seeking to remodel traditional sexual codes and ethical systems to satisfy the needs of the time, radicals and Evangelicals alike were assailing the double standard of aristocratic French gallantry and immorality, espousing moral reform for all classes and sexes. Such alternative (but not mutually exclusive) domestic ideologies as More's model of Evangelical femininity and Wollstonecraft's rational womanhood are parallel, even symbiotic, female responses to political upheaval, attempts to take advantage of national unease to repattern domestic life through new schematic images of social order. Both were part of the larger and eventually successful bourgeois campaign to rehabilitate a degenerate culture

3. *The Annual Register . . . for . . . 1798*, pp. 229–30.
4. *Rights of Woman*, pp. 174, 76, 31.
5. *Rights of Woman*, p. 49.

through propaganda for enlightened domesticity and societal reform. If the demands of such radicals as Wollstonecraft for equal political rights were premature, their demands for forceful female social leverage and for freedom from sexual exploitation were not. From the positive perspective of moral reform, the doctrines of femininity are more profitably viewed not as the unequivocal opposite of feminism in the nineties, but rather as a perhaps necessary precondition to, a stage of preparation for, nineteenth-century feminism.

CORA KAPLAN

From Wild Nights: Pleasure/Sexuality/Feminism[†]

The Rights of Woman and Feminine Sexuality: Mary Wollstonecraft

The reputation of Mary Wollstonecraft's *A Vindication of the Rights of Woman* (1792), the founding text of Anglo–American feminism, generally precedes and in part constructs our reading of it. We are likely to look for, and privilege, its demands for educational, legal and political equality; these are, after all, the demands that link Wollstonecaft's feminism to our own. If we give ourselves up to *A Vindication*'s eloquent but somewhat rambling prose, we will also discover *passim* an unforgettable early account of the making of a lady, an acute, detailed analysis of the social construction of femininity, which appropriates the developmental psychology of enlightenment and romantic thought. It is certainly possible to engage with *A Vindication* so far and no farther, to let most of its troubling historical meanings and contradictions drop away, so that we may take away from it an unproblematic feminist inheritance. How much use can we make of this legacy without a sense of the history that produced it? Read *A Vindication* for its historical meanings and another text emerges, one that is arguably as interested in developing a class sexuality for a radical, reformed bourgeoisie as in producing an analysis of women's subordination and a manifesto of her rights.

This part of Wollstonecraft's project deserves our attention too, for only by understanding why Wollstonecraft wanted women to become full, independent members of the middle class, can we make

---

† Cora Kaplan. "Wild Nights: Pleasure/Sexuality/Feminism." In *Sea Changes. Essays on Culture and Feminism* (London: Verso, 1986), pp. 34–50. First published 1983. Reprinted by permission.

sense of the negative and prescriptive assault on female sexuality that is the *leitmotif* of *A Vindication* where it is not the overt subject of the text.

It is usual to see the French Revolution as the intellectual and political backdrop to *A Vindication*; it would be more useful to see it as the most important condition of its production. As Margaret Walters has pointed out, *A Vindication* sums up and rearticulates a century of feminist ideas,[1] but its immediate stake was in the political advance of a revolutionary vanguard—the middle-class itself, as Wollstonecraft and others imagined it. Every opinion in the text is written in the glare of this politically charged and convulsive moment, and the area of Wollstonecraft's thought most altered and illuminated by that glare is sexuality. In her two attempts at fiction, *Mary, a Fiction* and *Maria or The Wrongs of Woman*, one produced a few years before *A Vindication* and the other incomplete at her death in 1797, women's feelings and desires, as well as the importance of expressing them, are valorized. But in *A Vindication* Wollstonecraft turned against feeling, which is seen as reactionary and regressive, almost counter-revolutionary. Sexuality and pleasure are narcotic inducements to a life of lubricious slavery. Reason is the only human attribute appropriate to the revolutionary character, and women are impeded by their early and corrupt initiation in the sensual, from using theirs.

Why is *A Vindication* so suffused with the sexual, and so severe about it? This is the question that I will explore at some length below. Wollstonecraft's feminism and her positions on sexuality were, at this point in her life, directly bound up with her radical politics—they can only be understood through each other. In untangling the knotted meanings of the sexual in our own history, our own politics, it is useful to understand the different but recurring anxieties it has stirred for other feminisms, other times.

A Vindication of the Rights of Woman offers the reader a puritan sexual ethic with such passionate conviction that self-denial seems a libidinized activity. And so it was, in the sense that a reform of sexual behaviour was Wollstonecraft's precondition for radical change in the condition of women; permitting the development of their reason and independence. The democratic imperatives—equality and liberty for all classes of persons—have been, for so long now, the well worn staples of liberal and left rhetoric that it is hard to remember that they were being invoked in new ways and with unprecedented exuberance in the 1790s. When we try to puzzle out the meanings of

1. Margaret Walters, 'The Rights and Wrongs of Women: Mary Wollstonecraft, Harriet Martineau, Simone de Beauvoir', in Juliet Mitchell and Ann Oakley eds., *The Rights and Wrongs of Women*, Harmondsworth, 1979, pp. 304–378.

A *Vindication* it is the negative construction of the sexual in the midst of a positive and progressive construction of the social and political we must question. In that contradiction—if indeed it is a contradiction—our present conflict over sexual politics is still partly embedded.

Written in six weeks at the height of British left optimism about events in France, *A Vindication* came out early in 1792, the same year as the second part of Tom Paine's *Rights of Man*, a year before William Godwin's *Political Justice*. Each was, equally, a response to the political moment. All three were crucial statements about the social and political possibilities of a transformed Britain. An almost millenarial fervour moved British radicals in these years. Their political and philosophical ideas were being put into practice only a few hundred miles away; there were signs of reasoned and purposeful unrest at home among ordinary working people. The end of aristocratic privilege and autocratic rule in France was to be taken as a sign of universal change. The downfall of the Bastille, Thomas Paine exulted, included the idea of the downfall of despotism.

A Vindication engages with radical romantic politics at a moment when the practical realization of such a politics seemed as near as France itself. Wollstonecraft had already written one short pamphlet, *A Vindication of the Rights of Men* (1790), in support of the revolution, and was still to write a long piece on its behalf.[2] In *A Vindication of the Rights of Woman*, her most important work, she took advantage of an open moment of political debate to intervene on behalf of women from inside the British left intelligentsia. Its message is urgent precisely because social and political reform seemed not just possible, but inevitable. The status of women as moral and political beings had become one fairly muted instance of the unresolved contradictions within the republican and democratic tendencies of the time. The overlapping tendencies of enlightenment and romantic thought emphasized the natural virtue rather than innate depravity of human beings, their equality before God, and the evils brought about by unequal laws and hereditary privilege. Arguments initially directed at a corrupt ruling class on behalf of a virtuous bourgeoisie inevitably opened up questions of intra-class power relations. With *A Vindication* Wollstonecraft challenged her own political camp, insisting that women's rights be put higher on the radical agenda. Addressed to Talleyrand, taking issue with Rousseau, speaking the political jargon of her English contemporaries, *A Vindication* invited the enlightenment heritage, the dead and the living, to extend the new humanism to the other half of the race. With a

---

2. Mary Wollstonecraft, *Historical and Moral View of the Origin and Progress of the French Revolution*, 1794.

338 CORA KAPLAN

thriving revolution under way, the political and intellectual credit of republican sympathisers was as high as their morale. It seemed like the right moment to ask them to pay their debt to women.

The opening pages of *A Vindication* share the aggressive, confident mood and tone that had developed under the threat and promise of the revolutionary moment. Ridiculing the 'turgid bombast' and 'flowery diction' of aristocratic discourse, Wollstonecraft offers the reader instead, 'sincerity' and 'unaffected' prose, the style and standards of the class of men and women to whom she was speaking—'I pay particular attention to those in the middle class, because they appear to be in the most natural [i.e. least corrupted] state.' Her unapologetic class bias was shared with her radical contemporaries—it is hardly surprising that idealized humanity as it appears in her text is a rational, plain speaking, bourgeois man. Denying any innate inequality between the sexes except physical strength, she promises to 'first consider women in the grand light of human creatures, who, in common with men, are placed on this earth to unfold their faculties', and addresses her sisters boldly as 'rational creatures' whose 'first object of laudable ambition' should be 'to obtain a character as a human being, regardless of the distinctions of sex. . . .'[3]

How to attain this character? In Paine's *Rights of Man* the reader was told that inequality and oppression were the effects of culture rather than nature. The text itself is a politicizing event, first constructing and then working on an uncorrupted rational subject. Paine hoped, and his enemies feared, that some sort of direct political action to unseat despotic power would follow from a sympathetic reading of his pamphlet. The message and intention of *A Vindication* are very different. Nowhere does Wollstonecraft pose women, in their present 'degraded' condition, as either vanguard or revolutionary mass. Like the corrupt aristocracy, to whom they are frequently compared, they are, instead, a *lumpen* group who must undergo strenuous re-education in order that they might renounce the sensual, rid themselves of 'soft phrases, susceptibility of heart, delicacy of sentiment, and refinement of taste' . . . 'libertine notions of beauty' and the single-minded 'desire of establishing themselves—the only way women can rise in the world—by marriage.'[4] Before the middle-class woman can join the middle-class man in advocating and advancing human progress she must be persuaded to become 'more masculine and respectable', by giving up her role both as 'insignificant objects of desire' and as desiring subject.[5]

3. Wollstonecraft, *A Vindication*, ed. Carol H. Poston (New York: W. W. Norton, 1975), pp. 11–12. [Page references are for this Norton Critical Edition.—*Editor*]
4. Ibid., p. 13.
5. Ibid., p. 13.

Even in its own day *A Vindication* must have been a short, sharp shock for women readers. Men might be able to mobilize reason and passion, in them equitably combined, to change the world immediately; women, crippled and stunted by an education for dependence, must liberate themselves from a slavish addiction to the sensual before their 'understandings' could liberate anyone else. At later moments of political crisis feminists could, and would, portray women as vanguard figures, subordinated members of the propertied class who understood more about oppression, as a result, than their bourgeois male comrades. Not here. Read intertextually, heard against the polyphonic lyricism of Paine, Godwin and the dozens of ephemeral pamphleteers who were celebrating the fact and prospect of the revolution, *A Vindication* was a sobering read. Wollstonecraft sets out on an heroic mission to rescue women from a fate worse than death, which was, as she saw it, the malicious and simultaneous inscription of their sexuality and inferiority as innate, natural difference. This was how her political mentor and gender adversary Rousseau had placed them, too weak by nature to reach or be reached by sweet reason. Rousseau's influence was great, not least on Wollstonecraft herself. She accepts Rousseau's ascription of female inferiority and locates it even more firmly than he does in an excess of sensibility. Since lust and narcissism were evil they must belong to social relations rather than human nature; this was Rousseau's own position in relation to men. Accordingly, female sexuality insofar as it is vicious is inscribed in *A Vindication* as the effect of culture on an essentially ungendered nature. By tampering with the site of degrading sexuality without challenging the moralising description of sexuality itself, Wollstonecraft sets up heartbreaking conditions for women's liberation—a little death, the death of desire, the death of female pleasure.

Even if *A Vindication* is preoccupied with the sexual as the site and source of women's oppression, why is woman's love of pleasure so deeply stigmatized as the sign of her degradation? In refusing to interpret women's unbounded desire as a natural mark of sexual difference or the appropriate preoccupation of her mediated place in the social, Wollstonecraft is resisting a whole range of bourgeois positions around gender sexuality, positions rapidly hardening into the forms of bourgeois morality that would dominate nineteenth century ruling class gender relations. Her debate with Rousseau is central, because, like her, Rousseau wished to harness his gender ideologies to radical social and political theories. Rousseau's *Emile* is the place where he spells out the theoretical and socially expedient premises that excluded women from equal participation in the enlightenment projects for human liberation and individual transcendence. Arguing for the sexual assymetry of natural endowment,

Rousseau insisted that women's 'first propensities' revealed an excess of sensibility, easily 'corrupted or perverted by too much indulgence.' In civil society women's amoral weakness must not be given its natural scope lest it lead, as it inevitably must, to adultery and its criminal consequence, the foisting of illegitimate heirs on bourgeois husbands. The remedy is borrowed back from the techniques of aristocratic despotism, elsewhere in Rousseau so violently condemned: women '. . . must be subject all their lives, to the most constant and severe restraint, which is that of decorum; it is therefore, necessary to accustom them early to such confinement that it may not afterwards cost them too dear. . . . We should teach them above all things to lay a due restraint on themselves.'[6]

Acknowledging, with crocodile tears, the artificiality of the social, while insisting on its necessity, Rousseau invokes a traditionally unregenerate Eve partnered to an Adam who has been given back his pre-lapsarian status. 'The life of a modest woman is reduced, by our absurd institutions, to a perpetual conflict with herself: but it is just that this sex should partake of the sufferings which arise from those evils it hath caused us.'[7] *Emile* lays out, in fascinating detail, the radical project for the education and adult gender relations of an enlightened bourgeoisie, a project that depended for its success on the location of affection and sexuality in the family, as well as the construction of the bourgeois individual as the agent of free will. The struggle between reason and passion has an internal and external expression in Rousseau, and the triumph of reason is ensured by the social nature of passion. Since male desire needs an object, and women are that infinitely provocative object, the social subordination of women to the will of men ensures the containment of passion. In this way Rousseau links the potential and freedom of the new middle class to the simultaneous suppression and exploitation of women's nature.

Rousseau plays on the already constructed sexual categorization of women into two groups—the virtuous and depraved. By insisting that these divisions are social rather than natural constructs— women are not depraved by nature—Rousseau can argue for social and civil restraints on women. Michel Foucault points out that the process of constructing women first and foremost as a sexual subject was in itself a class bound project: '. . . it was in the "bourgeois" or aristocratic family that the sexuality of children and adolescents

---

6. Jean-Jacques Rousseau, *Emile*, Barbara Foxley, tr., London, 1974, p. 332. Passages from *Emile* can all be found in Book V of this edition. However I have cited Rousseau as quoted by Wollstonecraft who comments on large chunks of Book V in *A Vindication*. [Wollstonecraft's source was the anonymous translation by William Kenrick (publ. 1762–63), excerpted herein, pp. 229–36.—*Editor*]
7. Ibid., pp. 332–3.

was first problematized. . . . the first figure to be invested by the deployment of sexuality, one of the first to be "sexualized" was the "idle" woman. She inhabited the outer edge of the "world", in which she always had to appear as value, and of the family, where she was assigned a new identity charged with conjugal and parental obligation.'[8]

Mary Wollstonecraft stood waist-deep in these already established and emergent sexual ideologies. At the time she was writing *A Vindication* she was neither willing nor able to mount a wholesale critique either of bourgeois sexual mores or the wider areas of gender relations. Her life was shortly to go through some very rapid changes, which would, ironically, mark her as one of the 'degraded' women so remorselessly pilloried in her text. A year and a half after her essay was published she was living with a young American, Gilbert Imlay, in France; two years later she was an unmarried mother. *A Vindication* is a watershed in her life and thought, but this crisis is marked in a curiously wilful way. The text expresses a violent antagonism to the sexual; it exaggerates the importance of the sensual in the everyday life of women, and betrays the most profound anxiety about the rupturing force of female sexuality. Both *Emile* and *A Vindication* share a deep ambivalence about sexuality. Images of dirt, disease, decay and anarchic power run as a symbolic under-text in both works, too frequently located in women's sexual being rather than in any heterosexual practice. This distaste is pervasively articulated in *A Vindication*, adumbrated on the first page with an arresting description of French gender relations as 'the very essence of sensuality' dominated by 'a kind of sentimental lust' which is set against the ideal of 'personal reserve, and sacred respect for cleanliness and delicacy in domestic life. . . .'[9] The images of sexuality throughout are so gripping and compulsive that it is hard to tear oneself away to the less vivid analysis that insists, with commendable vigour, that these filthy habits are a social construction, foisted on each generation of women by male-dominated and male-orientated society.

The place of female sexuality in *A Vindication* is over-determined by political as well as social history. Like many of the progressive voices of the late eighteenth century, Wollstonecraft had built her dreams of a new society on the foundation of Rousseau's *Social Contract* and *Essay on Inequality*. Rousseau's writings, insofar as they spoke about human beings rather than men, offered cold reason warmed with feeling in a mixture that was very attractive to the excitable radical temperaments of Wollstonecraft's generation.

8. Michel Foucault, *The History of Sexuality: Volume 1: An Introduction*, London, 1979, p. 121.
9. Wollstonecraft, *A Vindication*, pp. 5–6.

Rousseau, Paine wrote in 1791, expressed 'a loveliness of sentiment in favor of liberty, that excites respect and elevates the human faculties'—a judgement widely shared. How unlovely then, for Wollstonecraft to consider that in *Emile* Rousseau deliberately withholds from women because of the 'difference of sex' all that is promised to men. Rousseau's general prejudices and recommendations for women—functional, domestic education, nun-like socialization, restricted activity and virtual incarceration in the home—colluded with the gender bias and advice of more reactionary bourgeois authors, as well as society at large. The sense in which Rousseau's prescriptions were becoming the dominant view can be heard in the different imaginary readers addressed by the texts. In the section on women *Emile* slips in and out of a defensive posture, arguing, if only tactically, with an anonymous feminist opponent for the imposition of a stricter regime on women. Wollstonecraft too is on the defensive but her composite reader-antagonist was a society that believed in and followed Rousseau's novel advice to the letter. *Emile* offered its ideas as a reform of and reaction to liberal ideas on female education and behaviour. Thirty years on, *A Vindication* suggested that female sexual morality had become laxer, operating under just such a regime of restraint and coercion as Rousseau had laid out.

The project of *Emile* was to outline the social and sexual relations of an idealized bourgeois society by giving an account of the education and courtship of its youth. *A Vindication* appropriates part of this project, the elaborate set of distinctions between the manners and morals of the aristocracy and those of the new middle class. The anti-aristocratic critique is foregrounded and set in focus by the French Revolution: its early progress exposed the corruption of the ruling classes to a very wide and receptive audience. When Wollstonecraft suggests that vain, idle and sensuous middle-class women are to be compared with the whole of the hereditary aristocracy who live only for pleasure she strikes at two popular targets. When she identifies the aestheticized and artificial language of the ruling class—'a deluge of false sentiments and overstretched feelings', 'dropping glibly from the tongue' as the language of novels and letters, she implies that it is also the language of women, or of the society adultress. At one level she is simply producing a gendered and eroticized version of Paine's famous attack on Burke's prose style and sentiments, in *Rights of Man, part 1*. At another, the massing of these metaphors of debased and disgusting female sexuality, even when they are ostensibly directed at the behaviour of a discredited class has the effect of doubling the sexual reference. Paine's comment—'He pities the plumage and forgets the dying bird'—already carries sexual and gendered meanings. Because a naturally whorish and disrupting female sexuality was so profoundly a part of traditional symbol and reference, used to tarnish whatever object it was applied to, it became extremely difficult for Wollstonecraft to keep her use of such images tied to a social and environmental analysis. She herself is affected by the traditional association.

In *A Vindication* women's excessive interest in themselves as objects and subjects of desire is theorized as an effect of the ideological inscription of male desire on female subjects who, as a result, bear a doubled libidinal burden. But the language of that sober analysis is more innovatory, less secure, and less connotative than the metaphorical matrix used to point and illustrate it. As a consequence, there is a constant slippage back into a more naturalized and reactionary view of women, and a collapse of the two parts of the metaphors into each other. Thus, Wollstonecraft tries to argue *against* restraint and dependence by comparing the situation of women to slaves and lap-dogs—'. . . for servitude not only debases the individual, but its effects seem to be transmitted to posterity. Considering the length of time that women have been dependent, is it surprising that some of them hug their chains, and fawn like the spaniel.'[1]

But it is the metonymic association of 'slave,' 'women,' 'spaniel' that tends to linger, rather than the intended metaphoric distance, the likeness and unlikeness between them.

The same effect occurs when Wollstonecraft borrows a chunk of contemporary radical analysis of the mob to support her position that women need the same freedom and liberal education as men. In enlightenment theory a libidinal economy is brought to bear on subordinated groups: mass social violence is seen as the direct result of severe repression, which does not allow for the development of self-control or self governance. The mob's motive may be a quasi-rational vengeance against oppressors, but the trigger of that violence is the uncontrolled and irrational effect of sudden de-repression. Sexual symbolism is already prefigured in this analysis, so that when Wollstonecraft draws on it as a metaphor for women's uncontrolled sexual behaviour she reinforces the identification of loose women and mob violence. 'The bent bow recoils with violence, when the hand is suddenly relaxed that forcibly held it'—the sexual metaphor here, as elsewhere, is top-heavy, tumbling, out of control, like the imaginary force of female sexuality itself. Here, and at many other points in the text, *A Vindication* enhances rather than reduces the power of female sexuality, constructing it, unintentionally, as an

1. Ibid., p. 88.

intimate and immediate threat to social stability, nearer than the already uncomfortably near Parisian mob. It is no wonder that many nineteenth-century feminists, for whom the mob and the French Revolution were still potent symbols of disorder, found the book, for all its overt sexual puritanism, disturbing and dangerous.

The blurring of sexual and political metaphor so that sexuality is effectively smeared all over the social relations under discussion emphasises Wollstonecraft's deliberate privileging of sensibility and pleasure as the ideological weapons of patriarchy. Picking up on the negative vibes about female sexuality in *Emile*, she beats Rousseau with his own stick (as it seems) by making the sensual both viler and more pervasive in women's lives as a result of his philosophy of education put into practice. Wollstonecraft too wishes bourgeois women to be modest and respectable, honest wives and good mothers, though she wishes them to be other things as well. Yet only by imagining them *all*, or almost all, crippled and twisted into sexual monsters by society as it is can she hope to persuade her readers to abandon a gender specific and deforming education for femininity.

Yet the most incisive and innovative elements of *A Vindication* are deeply bound into its analysis of the construction of gender in childhood. The book gives us a complex and detailed account of the social and psychic processes by which gender ideologies become internalized adult subjectivity. This account is spread across the two-hundred-odd pages of the book and is extraordinary both as observation and as theory. Here is the childhood of little girls brought up, *à la* Rousseau, to be women only:

> 'Every thing they see or hear serves to fix impressions, call forth emotions, and associate ideas, that give a sexual character to the mind. False notions of beauty and delicacy stop the growth of their limbs and produce a sickly soreness, rather than delicacy of organs . . . This cruel association of ideas, which every thing conspires to twist into all their habits of thinking, or, to speak with more precision, of feeling, receives new force when they begin to act a little for themselves; for they then perceive that it is only through their address to excite emotions in men that pleasure and power are to be obtained.'[2]

It is exaggerated; it is even fantasy up to a point. Yet reading this passage, I was both shaken by its eloquence and pricked by its accuracy.

Only an unusual 'native vigour' of mind can overturn such a vicious social construction, for: 'So ductile is the understanding, and yet so stubborn, that the associations which depend on adventitious

2. Ibid., p. 124.

circumstances, during the period that the body takes to arrive at maturity, can seldom be disentangled by reason. One idea calls up another, its old associate, and memory faithful to first impressions . . . retraces them with mechanical exactness.'[3]

Here, in part, is the romantic theory of the unconscious, its operations laid bare to draw a particularly bleak conclusion about the fate of women.

The need to exaggerate the effects of a gender biased rearing and education led Wollstonecraft to overemphasize the importance of sexuality in women's lives. *A Vindication* is hardly a realistic reconstruction of the day to day activities and preoccupations of bourgeois women, the author herself not excepted. Rather it is an abstract formulation of the sort of social and psychic tendencies that a one-sided reactionary socialization could produce. It is unfortunate that Wollstonecraft chose to fight Rousseau in his own terms, accepting his paradigm of a debased, eroticized femininity as fact rather than ideological fiction. Woman's reason may be the psychic heroine of *A Vindication*, but its gothic villain, a polymorphous perverse sexuality, creeping out of every paragraph and worming its way into every warm corner of the text, seems in the end to win out. It is again too easy to forget that this suffusing desire is a permanent male conspiracy to keep women panting and dependent as well as house-bound and pregnant. What the argument moves towards, but never quite arrives at, is the conclusion that it is male desire that must be controlled and contained if women are to be free and rational. This conclusion cannot be reached because an idealized bourgeois male is the standard towards which women are groping, as well as the reason they are on their knees. Male desire may be destructive to women, but it remains a part of positive male identity. A wider education and eros-blunting forays into the public world of work and politics keeps the rational in control of the sensual in men, and is the recommended remedy for women too. Wollstonecraft thought gender difference socially constructed but she found practically nothing to like in socially constructed femininity. With masculinity it was quite different—'masculine' women are fine as long as they don't hunt and kill. Yet there could be nothing good about feminized men, since the definitions of the feminine available in *A Vindication* are shot through with dehumanizing and immoral sensuality. It's not surprising that women together—girls in boarding schools and women in the home—can only get up to unsavory personal familiarities, 'nasty, or immodest habits.' This description backs up an argument, possibly forceful in its own time, for mixed education and a

3. Ibid., p. 123–24.

freer association of adult men and women; it rounds off the denigra-
tion of women's world in *A Vindication*.

Ironically, it is the revolutionary moment, with its euphoric faith
in total social transformation that permits Wollstonecraft to obliter-
ate women and femininity in their unreformed state. Although
A Vindication outlines a liberal and unsegregated programme for
female education and a wider scope for women's newly developed
reason in the public and private world, it has nothing complimentary
to say about women as they are. Their overheated sensibility is never
seen as potentially creative. One can see how the moral analysis and
the social description in *A Vindication* could be appropriated for a
more conservative social theory, which might advocate a degree of
exercise for women's adolescent bodies and minds, but would confine them to a desexualized domestic sphere as wives and mothers.

The novels of Jane Austen, Wollstonecraft's contemporary, are the
most obvious immediate example of a conservative recuperation of
Wollstonecraft. *Northanger Abbey* paraphrases Wollstonecraft on
the dangers to the young female reader of the gothic and sentimental novel, and *Mansfield Park* reads in many places like a fictional
reworking of *A Vindication*. Possibly influence, partly mere conver-
gence, the voices of the two women whose politics were deeply
opposed, echo each other. It is Wollstonecraft who writes that 'while
women live, as it were by their personal charms, how can we expect
them to discharge those ennobling duties which equally require
exertion and self-denial', but it might as easily be Austen on Mary
Crawford. In the same sentence, and in much the same terms, Wollstonecraft denounces hereditary aristocracy. The appropriation of
much of Wollstonecraft's writing for conservative social and political
ideologies went unacknowledged because of her outcast social status and her revolutionary sympathies.

Nevertheless, mid-century women writers and feminists, looking
for ways to legitimize their feminism and their sexuality, as well as
their desire to write them both out together, found small comfort in
A Vindication, where the creative and the affective self are split up
and separated. In fiction and poetry, that discursive space open to
women but sheltered from the harshest judgements of Victorian
morality, late romantic women writers, as sick of Wollstonecraft's
regime, if they knew it, as she had been sick of Rousseau's, tenta-
tively began to construct the idea of a libidinized female imagination
and, through it, women's right to reason and desire. Authority for
such an unmediated and eroticized relation to art and life had to be
sought in and stolen from male romantic manifestos. Nothing suggests more unequivocally how deep the effects of separate gender
sexualities went, than a quick look at the 1802 introduction to *Lyrical Ballads* after a long look at *A Vindication*. The bourgeois poet

was the romantic radical incarnated. Here is Wordsworth, like Mary Wollstonecraft a supporter of the revolution, telling the reader, as she never could, that the poet is a man 'endued with more lively sensibility, more enthusiasm and tenderness' than other men, 'a man pleased with his own passions and volitions, and who rejoices more than other men in the spirit of life that is in him.'[4] The appropriate, democratic subjects for his art were 'moral sentiments and animal sensations' as they existed in everyday life.[5]

We must remember to read *A Vindication* as its author has instructed us, as a discourse addressed mainly to women of the middle class. Most deeply class-bound is its emphasis on sexuality in its ideological expression, as a mental formation, as the source of woman's oppression. The enchilding of women—their relegation to the home, to domestic tasks and concerns, while men's productive labour was located elsewhere—was a developing phenomenon of middle-class life in the eighteenth century. The separation of home and work in an industrial culture affected the working class too, but it was not the men only who worked outside the home: nor was the sexual division of labour along these lines a working-class ideal until well on in the nineteenth century. The romantic conception of childhood, already naturalized in *A Vindication*, had no place in working-class life. Nor did female narcissism and a passion for clothes have the same meanings for, or about, working-class women, who, as Wollstonecraft observes in *Maria*, were worked too hard at 'severe manual labour' to have much time or thought for such things. The ideal of education, opening up wider fields for the exercise of the mind, was part of a bourgeois agenda for social improvement that would 'lift' the poor as well as women. Sequential pregnancies, exhausting child care in the grimmest conditions, the double yoke of waged and unpaid domestic labour, none of these are cited in *A Vindication* as the cause of women's degradation. *Maria* includes an honorable if genteel attempt to describe the realities of life for working class women. *A Vindication* is more class bound and more obsessive; a brief, though not unsympathetic passage on the horrors of prostitution, and a few references to the dirty backstairs habits that female servants pass on to ladies is the selective and sexualized attention that working class women get in *A Vindication*.

Most of Wollstonecraft's difficulties are with the obviously binding power of the binary categories of class sexuality. Rather than challenge them, she shifts her abstract women around inside them or tries to reverse their symbolism. The middle-class married adultress

---

4. William Wordsworth and Samuel Taylor Coleridge, *Lyrical Ballads*, London, 1976, pp. 255–56.
5. Ibid., p. 261.

is magically transformed by liberty and education into the modest
rational wife. If women in public and in promiscuous gatherings,
whether schoolroom or workplace, were considered sexually endangered, Wollstonecraft would eroticize the safe home and the all-girls
establishment, so that these harems and not the outside world are
the places where modesty is at risk. It doesn't work, but it's a good try.
It doesn't work because Wollstonecraft herself wishes to construct
class differentiation through existing sexual categories. The negative
effects of the text fell on the middle-class women which it is so eager
to construct and instruct.

In *Sex, Politics and Society, The regulation of sexuality since 1800*,
Jeffrey Weeks, summarizing and extending Foucault, reminds us
that: '. . . the sexual apparatus and the nuclear family were produced
by the bourgeoisie as an aspect of its own self-affirmation, not as a
means of controlling the working class: . . . there are class sexualities (and different gender sexualities) not a single uniform sexuality.
Sexuality is not a given that has to be controlled. It is an historical
construct that has historical conditions of existence.'[6]

If we apply these comments, we can see that the negative gender
sexuality Wollstonecraft constructs was one of several competing
gender sexualities of the late eighteenth century. As Margaret Walters indicates, contemporary femininity grips Wollstonecraft even as
she argues against it: a sexually purified femininity was equally a
precondition for any optimistic, liberal re-ordering of intra-class
gender relations, or female aspiration. But Walters is wrong in seeing this struggle as one between feminism and femininity. There is
no feminism that can stand wholly outside femininity as it is posed
in a given historical moment. All feminisms give some ideological
hostage to femininities and are constructed through the gender
sexuality of their day as well as standing in opposition to them. Wollstonecraft saw her middle class, for a few years at least, as a potentially revolutionary force. The men and women in it would exercise
their understandings on behalf of all mankind. It was important to
her that the whole of this class had access to reason, and that
women's liberation was posed within a framework that was mini-
mally acceptable to popular prejudices. That is why, perhaps, she
finds herself promising the reader that the freedom of women was
the key to their chastity. Within the enlightenment and romantic
problematics, reason was always the responsible eldest son and
sensibility—emotion, imagination, sensuality—the irresponsible rake,
catalyst of change. Class differentiation through the redefinition of
sexual mores was a process so deeply entrenched, in Wollstonecraft's

6. Jeffrey Weeks, *Sex, Politics and Society: The Regulation of Sexuality since 1800* (London:
Longman, 1980), p. 10.

time, that the moral positions around sexual behaviour seemed almost untouchable. Feminists of her generation did not dare to challenge them head on, although Wollstonecraft was beginning to work over this dangerous terrain, in her life and in her fiction at the time of her death. The combination of equal rights and self-abnegating sexuality in *A Vindication* has had special attractions for feminists who led very public lives, and found it terrifying and tactically difficult to challenge too many prejudices at once. As a liveable formula for independent female subjectivity though, it never had much going for it— not because an immanent and irrepressible sexuality broke through levels of female self-denial, but rather because the anti-erotic ethic itself foregrounded and constructed a sexualized subject.

As long as the double standard survives gender sexualities will be torn by these contradictions. When Wollstonecraft's ideas for mixed education and wider public participation for women began to be put into practice, women started to query and resist the gender ideologies in which they had been raised. With some help from a popularized psychoanalytic theory, pleasure and sexuality were written into a reworked version of female romantic individualism. Both individualism and these new gender sexualities are, quite properly, heavily contested areas within feminism. Wollstonecraft's project, with its contradictory implications, suggests some of the problems involved in the moralization of sexuality on behalf of any political programme, even a feminist one.

* * *

MARY POOVEY

[*A Vindication of the Rights of Woman* and Female Sexuality]†

* * *

In October 1791 Mary Wollstonecraft informed her new friend, William Roscoe, that she had begun sitting for the portrait he had commissioned. "I do not imagine that it will be a very striking likeness," she apologized playfully; "but, if you do not find me in it, I will send you a more faithful sketch—a book that I am now writing, in which *I* myself . . . shall certainly appear, head and heart."[1] The

† From Mary Poovey, *The Proper Lady and the Woman Writer*, pp. 69–81. Copyright © 1984 by The University of Chicago. All rights reserved. Reprinted by permission.
1. *Collected Letters of Mary Wollstonecraft*, ed. Ralph M. Wardle (Ithaca and London: Cornell University Press, 1979), pp. 202–3, 6 October 1791.

"sketch" was *A Vindication of the Rights of Woman* (1792), and, as this letter suggests, Wollstonecraft's second political tract proves that during the preceding year she had progressed considerably in her ability to understand not only political issues but also her own place within them. In discovering that her most natural allies in the debate conducted in *The Rights of Men* were women (and not, as that work suggested, either liberal bourgeois males or the poor), Wollstonecraft was more nearly able to come to terms with the emotionalism that disrupted that argument; in learning to harness her emotion and by recognizing its fellow in the emotionalism of other women, she seems to have begun to perceive that the problem that had always undermined her self-confidence was collective rather than personal.

The first of Wollstonecraft's breakthroughs in *The Rights of Woman* was the insight that individual responses are, first and foremost, responses to situations and that, in a telling way, what made the middle-class woman into a Proper Lady was her "situation." Women, like the rich, are "swallowed up . . . *localized* . . . by the rank they are placed in, by *courtesy*."

> Women, commonly called Ladies, are not to be contradicted in company, are not allowed to exert any manual strength; and from them the negative virtues only are expected, when any virtues are expected, patience, docility, good-humour, and flexibility; virtues incompatible with any vigorous exertion of intellect.[2]

"Rest on yourself," Wollstonecraft replied to the request for advice from the young author Mary Hays, for special danger awaits the woman writer who, accustomed to "courtesy," can be placated by meaningless praise. "An author, especially a woman, should be cautious lest she too hastily swallows the crude praises which partial friend and polite acquaintance bestow thoughtlessly when the supplicating eye looks for them" (*MWL*, p. 219; 12 November 1792).

Wollstonecraft's second important realization in *The Rights of Woman* was that the attitudes and expectations that perpetuate female weakness are institutionalized by the very texts that purport to be "authorities" and even by the values encoded in language. Women respond to local situations as Proper Ladies because from their childhood on they are instructed to conceive of themselves according to masculine assumptions of what "feminine" behavior is. Thus one major cause of the "barren blooming" that Wollstonecraft discerns in women is "a false system of education, gathered from the books written on this subject by men who, considering females

2. *The Rights of Woman*, p. 63 [All subsequent references will appear parenthetically in the text and refer to this Norton Critical Edition.—*Editor*]

rather as women than human creatures, have been more anxious to make them alluring mistresses than affectionate wives and rational mothers" (p. 10). By teaching women to understand themselves solely by men's judgments, to submit to the restraint of propriety, and to pursue their educations only with regard to man's happiness, these male "authorities"—and the women who echo them—have deprived women of the opportunity for self-exertion and, therefore, of the possibility for self-improvement.

The ideal paradigm of maturation that Wollstonecraft introduced in *The Rights of Men* obviously demands an educational program diametrically opposed to this feminine cultivation of "negative virtues." Her assumption here, which anchors the paradigm, is that all human beings are equal in their fundamental capacity to reason; discriminatory education should thus be eliminated because it is detrimental to the improvement of humanity as a whole. Women, as women, have been denied the "rights of man"; they have lost their legitimate position within the collective noun through an education that has denied them maturity.[3] In order to combat this assumption of essential difference and to break down the behavior that institutionalizes it, Wollstonecraft asserts that women, as a social group, have much in common with other, largely male groups. Her basic strategy is to emphasize the similarities between female behavior and that of other groups: the wealthy (pp. 196, 200), soldiers (p. 26), wits (p. 61), and Dissenters (p. 203). Arguing "from analogy," she then asserts that it is reasonable and morally requisite to teach women to recognize their essential affinities with men. Only then will women perceive the crucial relationship between their private actions and the welfare of society at large (p. 193). Only when women are considered—and consider themselves—human beings rather than sexual objects, only when their education develops rather than suppresses their reason, only when they are granted the legal equality they by nature deserve, will they be able to contribute to the overall improvement of humanity. Wollstonecraft insists that her argument is not based on special interest; because she is intent on effacing all sexual discrimination, she declares herself "disinterested" and claims to speak with the neutral voice of the species, "the firm tone of humanity" (p. 5).

Perceiving her own voice as the generalized, ideal voice of collective humanity relieves Wollstonecraft of much of the insecurity that marked *The Rights of Men*. She claims that her admonitions now have the widest possible base; they transcend the charge of egotism

3. For a discussion of this aspect of *The Rights of Woman*, see Janet M. Todd, "The Language of Sex in *A Vindication of the Rights of Woman*," *Mary Wollstonecraft Newsletter* 1, no. 2 (April 1973): 10–17.

or self-interest, and they derive their authority from the instances of reason that, as she continues to argue, are everywhere evident. This position gives Wollstonecraft the confidence to embark on the course of direct confrontation she advocated but did not pursue in *The Rights of Men*. In *The Rights of Woman* she is finally able to identify and aggressively challenge the "authorities" she holds most responsible for female education: Rousseau, and conduct-book writers like Drs. Gregory and Fordyce.

The root of the wrongs of women, according to Wollstonecraft, is the general acceptance of the idea that women are *essentially* sexual beings—or, as Rousseau phrases it, "a male is only a male now and again, the female is always a female . . . ; everything reminds her of her sex."[4] Wollstonecraft's response to this sexual characterization of women is simply to reverse the charge: not *women*, she argues, but *men* are dominated by their sexual desires; *men's* insatiable appetites are the root of both economic inequality and social injustice. Arguments about women's "natural" inferiority, then, are only men's rationalizations for the superior social position they have unjustifiably seized, and their talk of "natural" female wantonness is merely a cover for the sexual appetite that men both fear and relish in themselves. Rousseau is the "sensualist" Wollstonecraft attacks most sytematically for indulging in "voluptuous reveries": "Rousseau declares that a woman should never, for a moment, feel herself independent, that she should be governed by fear to exercise her natural cunning, and made a coquetish slave in order to render her a more alluring object of desire, a *sweeter* companion to man, whenever he chooses to relax himself" (p. 28). Thus Rousseau's "discovery" of the "natural law" governing women, she charges, is simply a creation of his own repressed desire:

> Rousseau respected—almost adored virtue—and yet he allowed himself to love with sensual fondness. His imagination constantly prepared inflammable fewel for his inflammable senses; but, in order to reconcile his respect for self-denial, fortitude, and those heroic virtues, which a mind like his could not coolly admire, he labours to invert the law of nature, and broaches a doctrine pregnant with mischief and derogatory to the character of supreme wisdom. [P. 46]

Rousseau, as a "voluptuous tyrant," simultaneously rationalizes his own sensuality and gratifies it, and, at the same time, he punishes the being who tempts him to this self-indulgence by making her responsible for sexual control. Here Wollstonecraft is very close to

4. Rousseau, *Émile*, trans. Barbara Foxley (New York: Dutton/Everyman, 1974), p. 324.

perceiving how a set of beliefs can be generated from or adopted because of local needs and psychological imperatives. Moreover, she intuits the dynamics of repression and compensation at work in this production: as forbidden longings are censured, sexual desire erupts in another, more permissible form:

> All Rousseau's errors in reasoning arose from sensibility. . . . When he should have reasoned he became impassioned, and reflection inflamed his imagination instead of enlightening his understanding. Even his virtues also led him further astray; for, born with a warm constitution and lively fancy, nature carried him toward the other sex with such eager fondness, that he soon became lascivious. Had he given way to these desires, the fire would have extinguished itself in a natural manner; but virtue, and a romantic kind of delicacy, made him practise self-denial; yet, when fear, delicacy, or virtue, restrained him, he debauched his imagination, and reflecting on the sensations to which fancy gave force, he traced them in the most glowing colours, and sunk them deep into his soul. [Pp. 97]

The imagination, far from being the moral faculty philosophers like Adam Smith described, becomes the agent of vicarious gratification; and when the imagination becomes "debauched" in the name of virtuous self-denial, the artist seduces his reader as he indulges himself: "And thus making us feel whilst dreaming that we reason, erroneous conclusions are left in the mind" (p. 97).

Although Wollstonecraft's most direct attack centers on Rousseau and the conduct-book writers, in footnotes and asides she challenges a much more intimidating cultural "authority"—John Milton.[5] Wollstonecraft knows that Milton's portrayal of Eve's "sweet attractive grace, and docile blind obedience" (p. 22) stands behind Rousseau's Sophie. Milton, she implies, is as much a "sensualist" as Rousseau. He acknowledged that Eve is formed precisely in the image of Adam's innermost desires, made "thy likeness, thy fit help, thy other self, / Thy wish, exactly to thy heart's desires" (*Paradise Lost* 8. 450–51). Wollstonecraft therefore asserts that Eve, as sensuality incarnate, with her "wanton ringlets" and "coy submission" (*PL* 4. 306, 310), her "glowing cheek" and "tresses discompos'd" (*PL* 5.10), stands as commentary not on woman but on the men from whose imagination she sprang—from Milton's Adam and, before him, from Milton himself. With anger restrained only by her veneration for Milton,

---

5. For a discussion of the role Milton plays in the writings of other nineteenth- and twentieth-century women, see Sandra M. Gilbert and Susan Gubar, *The Madwoman in the Attic: The Woman Writer and the Nineteenth-Century Literary Imagination* (New Haven: Yale University Press, 1979), pp. 187–212.

Wollstonecraft cites the words the poet placed in Eve's mouth as
evidence against him:

> To whom thus Eve with *perfect beauty* adorn'd.
> My Author and Disposer, what thou bidst
> *Unargued* I obey; So God ordains;
> God is *thy law, thou mine*: to know no more
> Is Woman's *happiest* knowledge and her *praise*.
> [*PL* 4. 634–38; Wollstonecraft's italics]

It is significant that Wollstonecraft cannot attack Milton directly. Of
all the cultural "authorities" she engages, Milton is clearly the most
imposing, not only because of his preeminence in the English literary, political, and religious traditions but because of the special veneration accorded to Milton by Johnson's London circle. The fact
that she can record her outrage against Milton only by allusions and
by italicizing words in a quoted text (as in the passage just quoted)
suggests the extent to which she is still reluctant to take her aggres-
sion to its logical extreme.

From the disguised but ever-present force of male desire, Wollstonecraft charges, all the evils that oppress women follow. Kept in a
prolonged mental childhood to enhance the "innocence" men find
so appealing, women are denied access to the personal experience
necessary to the formation of a strong "human character" (p. 48).
She clearly sees the paradox inherent in this deprivation: denied all
challenging encounters and education, women are actually trapped
within experience—the narrow domain of their own personal, *sensual* experience. Consequently incapable of "generalizing ideas, of
drawing comprehensive conclusions from individual observations"
(p. 58), women become obsessed with immediate impressions and
gratifications. Because men indulge *their* sensual desires, women,
trying to please, become slaves to their own senses and thus hostage
to every transient emotion. Far from being the beneficiaries of "sensibility," women are actually the victims of feeling:

> Their senses are inflamed, and their understandings neglected,
> consequently they become the prey of their senses, delicately
> termed sensibility, and are blown about by every momentary gust
> of feeling. . . . Ever restless and anxious, their over exercised
> sensibility not only renders them uncomfortable themselves, but
> troublesome, to use a soft phrase, to others. All their thoughts
> turn on things calculated to excite emotion; and feeling, when
> they should reason, their conduct is unstable, and their opinions
> are wavering. . . . By fits and starts they are warm in many pur-
> suits; yet this warmth, never concentrated into perseverance,
> soon exhausts itself. . . . Miserable indeed, must be that being
> whose cultivation of mind has only tended to inflame its pas-
> sions! [Pp. 65–66].

Wollstonecraft cannot deny that women are, for the most part, satisfied with the sensual gratification of male attention. And, because they are, they participate in men's voluptuous designs. By internalizing "false notions of beauty and delicacy" (p. 124), they cultivate that "sexual character" of the mind that actually strengthens their chains. Women embrace their inessentialness; thoughts of men continually occupy their minds; they seek out lovers whose ingratiating manners flatter their self-images; they are content to derive their identities from their relationships to men—as "daughters, wives, and mothers" (p. 29). No wonder, Wollstonecraft laments, that men accuse women of intellectual superficiality and sensual self-indulgence. Indeed, Pope's maxim that "ev'ry Woman is at heart a Rake" is not only a man's wish-fulfilling projection but a self-fulfilling prophecy as well (p. 125). If women do not always rest content within this masculine fantasy of power and self-indulgence, their violations are at best indirect and surreptitious. Cunning is the resort of the powerless who would not lose the illusion of power, and tyranny over her helpless servants and children serves to vent an oppressed woman's wrath.

So intent is Wollstonecraft to reject the prevalent stereotype of women as *all* sexuality that she comes close to arguing that women have *no* innate sexual desires at all. Repeatedly she implies that female sexuality is only a learned response to *male* sexuality, a strategy unconsciously adopted in order to win the emotional acceptance that women really want. "Men are certainly more under the influence of their appetites than women," she flatly states (p. 145). What seems like sexual desire in women is actually either "sympathy" or disguised vanity:

> The sexual attention of man particularly acts on female sensibility, and this sympathy has been exercised from their youth up. A husband cannot long pay those attentions with the passion necessary to excite lively emotions, and the heart, accustomed to lively emotions, turns to a new lover, or pines in secret, the prey of virtue or prudence. I mean when the heart has really been rendered susceptible, and the taste formed; for I am apt to conclude, from what I have seen in fashionable life, that vanity is oftener fostered than sensibility by the mode of education, and the intercourse between the sexes, which I have reprobated; and that coquetry more frequently proceeds from vanity than from that inconstancy, which overstrained sensibility naturally produces. [Pp. 69–70]

Promiscuity and repression surely exist; yet Wollstonecraft is at pains to argue that such responses to sexual agitation are rare and, if the euphemism "*over-strained* sensibility" is significant, unnatural. It should not surprise us that Wollstonecraft goes on to describe an ideal marriage as one without passion ("a master and mistress of a

family ought not to continue to love each other with passion"
[p. 34]), and she asserts with apparent assurance that women will
easily be able to transform sexual desire into the more "serious" and
"austere" emotions of friendship (p. 138).

Yet the closer we read Wollstonecraft's *Vindication*, the clearer it
becomes that her defensive denial of female sexuality in herself and
in women in general is just that—a *defense* against what she feared:
desire doomed to repeated frustration. Contrary to her assertions,
Wollstonecraft's deepest fear centers not on the voraciousness of
male sexual desire but on what she fears is its brevity. Thus, while she
can insist that "in the exercise of their maternal feelings providence
has furnished women with a natural substitute for love," this substitute turns out to be necessary because, inevitably, the "lover [will
become] only a friend" (p. 161). The devoted mother she describes
proves to be a "neglected wife," driven to seek from her children the
gratification that her "unhappy marriage" no longer provides. And the
heroism of the self-sacrificing widow, which she celebrates, turns out
to be barren and decidedly equivocal: "Raised to heroism by misfortunes, she represses the first faint dawning of a natural inclination,
before it ripens into love, and in the bloom of life forgets her sex. . . .
Her children have her love, and her brightest hopes are beyond the
grave, where her imagination often strays" (p. 55).

Such repression is necessary, Wollstonecraft implies, because, far
from being the learned response she asserts it is (and wishes it
were), female sexuality is actually as demanding as male sexuality;
perhaps it is even more urgent. In two remarkable passages Wollstonecraft betrays the fact that she shares the moralists' anxiety
about female appetite. The first passage begins with an indictment
of indecorous eating habits. Men are the worst offenders on this
score, but, she acknowledges, "some women, particularly French
women, have also lost a sense of decency in this respect; for they will
talk very calmly of an indigestion. It were to be wished that idleness
was not allowed to generate, on the rank soil of wealth, those
swarms of summer insects that feed on putrefaction, we should not
then be disgusted by the sight of such brutal excesses" (p. 145).
While Wollstonecraft's scorn for the idle rich accounts for part of
her venom here, her subsequent association of the "refinement of
eating" with "refinements of love" more fully explains her vitriolic
language. She goes on to describe female voluptuaries as "the slaves
of casual lust . . . who are, literally speaking, standing dishes to
which every glutton may have access" (p. 146). Clearly her disgust
embraces both sexes here, for she is indicting sexual desire itself:
"The depravity of the appetite which brings the sexes together," she
argues, or "sensual gust," is dignified only when "the feelings of a
parent mingl[e] with an instinct merely animal" (p. 146).

In a second telling passage, however, Wollstonecraft implies that female sexuality might even be more voracious—and hence more blameworthy—than male desire. In a final attempt to denigrate the appetite she feels increasingly unable to deny, Wollstonecraft argues that platonic "feeling" provides a gratification that is superior to sexual pleasure. "What are the cold, or feverish caresses of appetite," she asks, "but sin embracing death, compared with the modest over-flowings of a pure heart and exalted imagination?" (p. 201). The personification here is Wollstonecraft's final embedded allusion to *Paradise Lost*. The scene to which it refers, in book 2, culminates in Milton's first image of female procreation. Death is the son of Sin by Satan; the incestuous coupling of Sin and Death produces innumerable Hell Hounds, which prey upon their mother in a hideous cycle of painful procreation: "These yelling Monsters," Sin laments,

> hourly conceiv'd
> And hourly born, with sorrow infinite
> To me, for when they list into the womb
> That bred them they return, and howl and gnaw
> My Bowels, thir repast.
> [*PL* 2. 796–800]

However, in her allusion to this Miltonic image, Wollstonecraft makes one significant alteration. In *Paradise Lost* the ghastly cycle of birth and death is the result of a rape, which Sin graphically describes to Satan:

> I fled, and cri'd out *Death*;
> Hell trembl'd at the hideous Name, and sigh'd
> From all her Caves, and back resounded *Death*.
> I fled, but he pursu'd (though more, it seems,
> Inflam'd with lust than rage) and swifter far,
> Mee overtook his mother all dismay'd,
> And in embraces forcible and foul
> Ingend'ring with me, of that rape begot
> These yelling Monsters.
> [*PL* 2. 787–95]

Wollstonecraft's Sin, however, seems much more obliging; indeed, syntactically, *she* is the aggressor: "sin embracing death." Almost parenthetically, and almost certainly unconsciously, Wollstonecraft betrays her fear that female desire might in fact court man's lascivious and degrading attentions, that the subordinate position women have been given might even be deserved. Until women can transcend their fleshly desires and fleshly forms, they will be hostage to the body—a body that in giving birth originates death, that in demanding physical satisfaction makes itself vulnerable to frustration and pain.

The suspicion Wollstonecraft reveals here that female appetite
might be the precipitating cause of women's cultural objectification
also helps account for her vehement disgust with female physicality.
Abhorring those "nasty, or immodest habits" that girls in boarding
school acquire, she goes on to attack, in surprisingly vitriolic language, the "gross degree of familiarity" that "sisters, female intimates,
or ladies and their waiting-women" exhibit toward one another
(p. 135). She cautions all girls to wash and dress alone, lest they take
up "some still more nasty customs, which men never fall into.
Secrets are told—where silence ought to reign; and that regard to
cleanliness . . . is violated in a beastly manner" (pp. 135–36). It is
difficult to know exactly what Wollstonecraft is referring to here; her
insistent delicacy may result from some personal memory or a general revulsion from eighteenth-century girls' boarding-school conditions.[6] But, whatever the original offense, it is clear that her disgust
involves female bodies and female desires—and all the ramifications
of sexuality that she does not want to think about here.

For most late eighteenth-century writers, such an attack on female
sexuality would have centered, at some point, on the imagination, for
that faculty was generally understood to be the "*source* of sexual feeling."[7] Certainly Wollstonecraft's ambivalence about imagination in
The Rights of Men leads us to expect this. But here she is careful to
distinguish between imagination, which directs an individual's desire
toward spiritual gratification, and "appetite," which fixes his or her
attention on sensual objects. Essentially, Wollstonecraft is desexual-
izing imagination so that she can explain how a substitute gratification can satisfy sexual desire. Echoing eighteenth-century moralists,
she characterizes imagination in sexual terms (it is a "vigorous" principle, "panting after" its object in "eager pursuit"); but its ultimate
function is to "absorb every meaner affection and desire" as it leads
the individual toward the happiness that is profoundly "not material"
(pp. 79–80). That Wollstonecraft continues to use sexual imagery to
describe this substitute happiness suggests, however, that she is at
least dimly aware that religious consolation *is* a substitute gratification. "True voluptuousness must proceed from the mind" (p. 201),
she argues, but intellectual "voluptuousness" is an image that proclaims the primacy of the senses. Wollstonecraft intends to strip the
maturation process completely of its sexual character; but if she succeeds in making the sexes equal, she fails to eliminate the sexual
component that is the source of her ongoing anxiety.

---

6. Nina Auerbach also discusses Wollstonecraft's anxiety about the "subtle sexual contagion"
   of women's schools. See her *Communities of Women: An Idea in Fiction* (Cambridge,
   Mass.: Harvard University Press, 1978), pp. 14–15.
7. See Patricia Meyer Spacks, "Ev'ry Woman is at Heart a Rake," *Eighteenth-Century
   Studies* 8, no. 1 (Fall 1974): 38.

In her attempt to shore up her character, to control the emotional energy that threatened to explode her political argument in *The Rights of Men*, Wollstonecraft has turned her argument outward. The result is a more perceptive analysis both of ideology and of her own position within it. But while her basic assumption—that women are primarily reasoning rather than sexual beings—enabled her to create a self-image sufficiently strong to attack prejudices and practices that traditionally had wholly silenced women's voices in political discussions, her inability to acknowledge or fully assimilate the profoundly unreasonable longings of her own emotional or physical being caused her to weaken the argument she had so effectively begun. For Wollstonecraft does not extend to women the same insight she used in exploding Rousseau's euphemisms and evasions; that is, she does not develop the idea that either women's characteristically volatile sensibility or her own scheme for emotional gratification might be a sublimation of sexual energy. In order to sidestep the investigation of sexuality that this insight would necessitate—and the admission of "weakness" it would entail—Wollstonecraft repeatedly turns her argument away from every potentially dangerous acknowledgment that women have sexual or physical needs.

We can see one consequence of this evasion in her own use of euphemisms and circuitous phrasing. Whenever Wollstonecraft approaches a subject that arouses her own volatile emotions, her language becomes both obscure and abstract; she shuns concrete nouns as if they were bodies she is trying to cover over. In fact, she will fully indulge her feeling only when its object is physically absent or unidentified. Even then she uses artificial and abstract rhetoric to generalize her emotion and to idealize the provocative situation. Her celebration of modesty is a particularly clear example of the results her abstractions could produce:

> Modesty! Sacred offspring of sensibility and reason!—true delicacy of mind!—may I unblamed presume to investigate thy nature, and trace to its covert the mild charm, that mellowing each harsh feature of a character, renders what would otherwise only inspire cold admiration—lovely!—Thou that smoothest the wrinkles of wisdom, and softenest the tone of the sublimest virtues till they all melt into humanity;—thou that spreadest the ethereal cloud that, surrounding love, heightens every beauty, it half shades, breathing those coy sweets that steal into the heart, and charm the senses—modulate for me the language of persuasive reason, till I rouse my sex from the flowery bed, on which they supinely sleep life away! [Pp. 128–29]

Wollstonecraft's celebration of "mellowing," "smoothing," "melting," and "shading" suggests the extent to which she is attempting to dematerialize her subject. Perhaps an even more revealing text is the one in which she defines "human rapture." Here the emotion is twice removed from its physical object and it is described in poetic clichés notable primarily for their imprecision and immateriality. The "rapture," predictably, is not for the physical person but only for "whatever had touched the person"—the glove or slipper, for example—of "an absent or lost friend":

> A shadowy phantom glides before us, obscuring every other object; yet when the soft cloud is grasped, the form melts into common air, leaving a solitary void, or sweet perfume, stolen from the violet, that memory long holds dear. [P. 132]

Although Wollstonecraft repeatedly professes to admire clarity, this image not only describes obscurity but is itself purposefully vague. Only in such a "fairy ground" of spiritual relationships and in such abstract and impersonal language can she allow herself to imagine intense feeling, for in this immaterial context desire can be neither sexual nor literal nor demanding of satisfaction.

An even more severe consequence of Wollstonecraft's refusal to acknowledge female sexuality is her reluctance to consider women as a group capable of achieving solidarity or taking the initiative for social reform. Because she considers the root of culture's values to be *men's* sexual desire, she continues to portray social reform strictly in terms of individual men's acts of self-denial and self-control. Certainly her understanding of the determinate relationship between the individual and institutional or historical forces is more sophisticated in *The Rights of Woman* than in *The Rights of Men*. In it she explicitly acknowledges, for example, the limited efficacy of individual effort (especially in education; see pp. 24, 166) and the necessity for societywide changes in legal, political, and employment policies (see pp. 154, 155, 156). But when she calls for change, her summons always encourages an alteration in *individual,* particularly *male,* attitudes. "Let men become more chaste and modest" (p. 14), let the nobility "prefer" the practice of reason (p. 24), let "mankind become more reasonable" (p. 60); only then can social change begin. The terms used may pass as generic nouns and pronouns, but they most frequently designate males. Wollstonecraft is generally *not* challenging women to *act.* When she calls for a "revolution in female manners" (p. 49), for example, she is not advocating a feminist uprising to overthrow manners but rather a general acquiescence in the gradual turning that the word "revolution" was commonly taken to mean in the eighteenth century. Women are simply to wait for this revolution to *be* effected, for their dignity to *be* restored, for their reformation to *be* made necessary. The task is primarily men's, and it involves not confrontation but self-control. Wollstonecraft defers her discussion of legal inequality to the promised second volume (which she never wrote) because, in her scheme, social legislation is less effective than individual self-control. And in *The Rights of Woman*, Wollstonecraft emphasizes independence rather than equality both because she conceives of society as a collection of individual attitudes rather than legal contracts and because she imagines relationships to be fundamentally antagonistic rather than cooperative. The major antagonism, however, is not against an external force but against one's own self—against fear and, especially, against desire. This idea, of course, is actually only a generalization of the behavior traditionally advocated for women; it is the Protestant ethic stripped of its component of personal assertion and material reward.

It is partly because Wollstonecraft so thoroughly distrusts her own sexuality that she rejects a female speaking voice in *The Rights of Woman*. While occasionally she speaks self consciously as a woman ("in the name of my sex" [p. 158]), more frequently she distinguishes between herself and "them" ("I plead for my sex—not for myself" [p. 5]); "I do not wish them [women] to have power over men; but over themselves" [p. 67]). At least once she speaks "as man with man," but even then she aspires not to a masculine voice but to a voice totally unconscious of sexuality. Here she is adopting Rousseau's definition of men and simply bringing the definition of women in line with the implicit asexual ideal. "Men are not always men in the company of women, nor would women always remember that they are women, if they were allowed to acquire more understanding" (p. 131, n. 1). Occasionally she addresses women, but both her formal, self-consciously rhetorical address and her condescension distance her from her natural allies: "Hapless woman! what can be expected from thee . . . ?" (p. 103); "O ye foolish women! . . . ignorant ye are in the most emphatical sense of the word" (p. 189). Wollstonecraft clearly wants most of all to distinguish herself from all sexual categories so as to attain a neutral voice. She speaks comfortably "as a philosopher" and "as a moralist" (p. 38), but in her most cherished self-image she speaks to her "dear contemporaries" as "a fellow creature," using the "firm tone of humanity" (pp. 92, 158, 5). She even dramatizes herself as achieving a stance of almost Miltonic "disinterestedness":

> Let me now as from an eminence survey the world stripped of all its false delusive charms. The clear atmosphere enables me to see each object in its true point of view, while my heart is still. I am calm as the prospect in a morning when the mists, slowly dispersing, silently unveil the beauties of nature, refreshed by rest. [P. 117]

Despite the natural tropes, this description actually characterizes the speaker; *she* is as "calm as the prospect" cleansed of mists, and *hers* are the "unveil[ed] . . . beauties." In this ideal, disembodied state, Wollstonecraft transcends her femaleness—and with it, presumably, the agitations that make her female heart, now still, cry out.

From her evasions and her aspirations, it seems clear that the price Wollstonecraft felt her new profession exacted was her female sexuality. This was a price she thought she was more than willing to pay; for if the ideal writer has no sex, he or she is therefore free from both the body's limitations and its demands. Adopting this characterization of the writer could theoretically protect Wollstonecraft from the painful vacillations of feeling she had alternately repressed and indulged during her youth. At the same time, this persona allowed her a certain amount of social self-confidence, especially in Joseph Johnson's circle, where feminine graces seemed to be irrelevant and such women as Anna Barbauld were acknowledged as intellectual equals by being criticized as such. But it also, of course, blinded Wollstonecraft to crucial emotional and physical needs— needs that were increasingly demanding attention. That she could mistake her growing passion for Henry Fuseli for a purely "rational desire"—even to the point of proposing, to his wife, that she, Wollstonecraft, should join the Fuseli household—attests to the extent of her self-deception and to the power of the desire she tried to philosophize away. Although it made her famous, *The Rights of Woman* did not provide Wollstonecraft with the "stability of character" to which she aspired. Late in 1792, after Fuseli had rejected her advances, she found herself again painfully self-divided, her "heart" once more at war with her beloved reason. "I am a strange compound of weakness and resolution!" she wrote to Joseph Johnson.

> There is certainly a great defect in my mind—my wayward heart creates its own misery—Why I am made thus I cannot tell; and, till I can form some idea of the whole of my existence, I must be content to weep and dance like a child—long for a toy, and be tired of it as soon as I get it. [*MWL*, p. 221; c. late 1792]

Whether or not Wollstonecraft was correct in deducing a fundamentally nonsexual human essence is, of course, beside the point, for the tensions in her argument demonstrate that, even in her own terms, she had not resolved the complexities of the issue, either theoretically or practically. Clearly, simply to recognize the structure of sexual oppression and inequality, as Mary Wollstonecraft did, was not sufficient to achieve genuine freedom. Remaining a prisoner of the category she most vehemently tried to reject, she allowed what looked like an externalization of rage to return remorselessly to herself. The frustrations behind the contradictions evident in *The Vindication of the Rights of*

Woman, her strongest polemic, would be dispelled only when she found a way to allow the writer and the woman to speak with one voice.

CLAUDIA L. JOHNSON

From The Distinction of the Sexes[†]

* * *

Wollstonecraft has been seen as advocating masculinity in women; but the *Rights of Woman* is more striking for relentlessly savaging the femininity of men. This feature of her work alerts us to the tension between the feminist and republican strands of her political writing, for vindicating women's rights becomes linked for Wollstonecraft to the championing of male strength. As a liberal feminist, Wollstonecraft argues that sexual difference is not politically significant—that rights are to be enjoyed by "human creatures" irrespective of sex—even as the Commonwealth tradition she inherits constantly invites her to denounce the social arrangements Burke favors on the grounds that they are "effeminate"—craven, frivolous, enervated, irrational, voluptuous, given to frippery. On the one hand, accordingly, we find Wollstonecraft arguing that gender, far from being a political problem, takes care of itself without state interference: "Let there be then no coercion *established* in society, and the common law of gravity prevailing, the sexes will fall into their proper places" (VRW 8 emphasis MW's).[1] On the other hand, gender both *within* masculinity as well as *between* the sexes is evidently so much of a problem that the nation is in danger because males have surrendered their manhood—indeed some, "thanks to early debauchery," are "scarcely men in their outward form" (VRW 25)—and as a result men must be cajoled back into manliness, and gender yanked back into alignment with its ostensibly "natural" function.

Wollstonecraft, then, does not so much recommend the eradication of sexual difference as she does complain that manners judged acceptable in this "present corrupt state of society" (VRW 25) *already* confound sexual difference in pernicious ways. The *Rights of Woman* protests the masculinization of sensitivity Burke had celebrated. Sentimental men, in prizing and appropriating affective qualities

---

† From Claudia L. Johnson, "The Distinction of the Sexes: The *Vindications,*" Chapter 1 of *Equivocal Beings: Politics, Gender, and Sentimentality in the 1790s* (Chicago: University of Chicago Press, 1995) p. 29–40. Copyright © 1995 by The University of Chicago. All rights reserved. Reprinted by permission.

1. [All quotations from the *Rights of Woman* are from Carol H. Poston's 1987 Norton Critical Edition, abbreviated VRW. Page references to the present edition are being supplied for this volume.—*Editor*]

once assigned to women, either relegate women to a disfiguring, hyperfeminized position of bad excess or leave them to take on a tattered ill-fitting mantle of rational masculinity that has become available to them only because it has lost its wonted cultural prestige. Wollstonecraft is infinitely more disturbed by the permeability of the lines of sexual differentiation from the male side than outraged by insurmountable division between men and women: "From every quarter have I heard exclamations against masculine women," she observes, "but where are they to be found?" (VRW 11). Wollstonecraft finds none. But what really worries her is that under the sentimental dispensation she cannot find masculine men either. It is bad enough that women, she reiterates, have been brought up to be weak, idle, spoiled, dependent, and self-indulgent. But when *men* typify women's worst faults, we cannot wonder to find mankind enthralled by tyrants: "Educated in slavish dependence, and enervated by luxury and sloth," she writes, teasing the unwary into assuming that she is talking about women, "where shall we find men who will stand forth to assert the rights of man;—or claim the privilege of moral beings?" (VRW 49) If Wollstonecraft could find them, she wouldn't have to vindicate either the rights of women or the rights of men. Attributing women's love of pleasure not to inherent frivolity but to poor education, she observes that although a whole class of men are just as vain and hedonistic as women are, no one has ever argued that frivolity is the essence of *their* sex, or that subjection is proper for *them* since they clearly enjoy it so much. "It would be just as rational," she writes, "to declare that the courtiers in France, when a destructive system of despotism had formed their character, were not men, because liberty, virtue, and humanity, were sacrificed to pleasure and vanity" (VRW 65).

But this is what Wollstonecraft does argue, for she consistently presumes that manliness and liberty are virtually synonymous. Women and men both are kept in subjection by effeminacy. Real men, unlike courtly fops, would tolerate neither the indignity of absolute monarchy nor the frivolity of prettified chivalric codes. The strategy of the *Rights of Woman* is to rouse men to claim the liberties of their sex, and to convince them to invite women to share those liberties, for manly men, she hopes—vainly, as her fiction and her biography attest—would scorn to have women on other terms. Accordingly, ridicule and cajolery are her principal rhetorical tools. In *Rights of Men*, Wollstonecraft attempted to sting Burke's pride by suggesting that it would be unmanly of her to bring the force of reason to bear against his pretty flights of fancy—"It would be something like cowardice to fight with a man who had never exercised the weapons with which his opponent chose to combat."[2] Similarly, here she consistently uses

2. Mary Wollstonecraft, *A Vindication of the Rights of Men*. 2nd Edition (London, 1790) p. 9. All subsequent references are to VRM and appear in the text.

THE DISTINCTION OF THE SEXES

shame ("I presume that *rational* men will excuse me for endeavouring to persuade them to be more masculine and respectable" (VRW 13), and flattery ("When will a great man arise with sufficient strength of mind to puff away the fumes which pride and sensuality have thus spread over the subject?" [VRW 29] to stir men to manliness.[3]

Thus, even where *Rights of Woman* censures the comportment of women, the shame falls upon men and the culture they have created to cater to their finicky sensibilities, not women's. Although Wollstonecraft always insists that women's vices result from the education they have received at the hands of libertine males, her descriptions of female comportment at first seem as though they would not be out of place in virulently misogynist literature: a "pitiful cunning," she complains, "disgracefully characterizes the female mind" (VRW 173), "[g]entleness, docility, and a spaniel-like affection" are women's "cardinal virtues" (VRW 37); a fine lady she knows "takes her dogs to bed, and nurses them with a parade of sensibility, when sick" but allows "her babes to grow up crooked in a nursery" (VRW 182); at the other end of the spectrum, girls in "nurseries and boarding schools" acquire from servants "very nasty tricks" (VRW 135) that Wollstonecraft shrinks from specifying. Notably absent from such characterizations of modern womanhood is any effort to elicit the charms of sympathy; if anything, her descriptions are relentlessly degraded. Unlike the women who populate sentimental fiction by men and unlike Burke's own Marie-Antoinette, the women described in *Rights of Woman* are never "interesting" victims languishing in chains that somehow never seem to cramp their minds, sour their dispositions, or detract from the comeliness of their persons.

Wollstonecraft's decision to present women's faults as revolting rather than endearing proceeds not from a basic hostility to women, but rather from a critical determination to detach female weakness from male sentimentality, which not only enjoys such abjection, but also elevates this enjoyment to a political virtue. It is typically assumed that Wollstonecraft's object here and throughout *Rights of Woman* is Rousseau, and it is true that the relish for the hypersexualization of women in *Emile* is often singled out for scorn.[4] But Rousseau's very obviousness as a target has diverted our attention from

3. Gary Kelly argues along similar lines in "Mary Wollstonecraft as *Vir Bonus*," *English Studies in Canada* 5 (1979), pp. 275-91, much of which is absorbed into *Revolutionary Feminism*, chap. 5.
4. Wollstonecraft clearly did feel compelled by Rousseau's fantasy of life before and without gender in *The Second Discourse*. For a discussion of Rousseau's notoriously inconsistent thoughts on gender difference and social contract theory, see Thomas Laqueur, *Making Sex: Body and Gender from the Greeks to Freud* (Cambridge, Mass.: Harvard University Press, 1990), pp. 196–204; and Carole Pateman, *The Sexual Contract* (Stanford: Stanford University Press, 1988).

Wollstonecraft's other and more local aims. There is something in Wollstonecraft's discussion of Rousseau reminiscent of the already conventionalized criticism Samuel Johnson leveled at that other great republican Wollstonecraft reprimands, John Milton: "[T]hey who most loudly clamour for liberty do not most liberally grant it . . . He thought woman made only for obedience, and man only for rebellion."[5] To Johnson, of course, the republican male's tendency to be a leveler abroad and a tyrant at home pointed to damning hypocrisy. But to a fellow traveler like Wollstonecraft, Rousseau's commitment to a voluptuous "male aristocracy" (VRW 93) in the private sphere seems so maddeningly inconsistent with the "manly" inservility she is glad to admire elsewhere in his work that he stands as an object lesson in the danger of trying to abolish the tyranny of rank without sweeping away the tyranny of sex along with it. Accordingly, Rousseau is an ally scolded for his short sightedness, while Burke remains the larger ideological foe, the one who specifically celebrates the interrelationship of both "aristocracies" of rank and sex. Rousseau might have surrendered to a sensuality that was unworthy of him, but it was Burke who had approvingly theorized such sensuality politically by arguing in the *Enquiry* that "beauty in distress is much the most affecting beauty," and that "we submit to what we admire, but we love what submits to us; in one case we are forced, in the other we are flattered into compliance."[6] And although the love of woman is specular, courtly, and theatrical in Burke, and domesticated and privatized in Rousseau, Wollstonecraft recognizes no difference in the political consequences of the gallantry they each recommend. To her, sentimental effusions about female charms are strategically mystified lust, and as such they are denounced in *Rights of Men* as the fantasy of a "debauched" (VRM 121) and "libertine" (VRM 114) imagination; and in *Rights of Woman* as the "voluptuous reveries" of "overweening sensibility" (VRW 28). Only by emphasizing the disgusting rather than alluring consequences of female education can she expose the unworthy depravity of male sensibilities—whether monarchical or republican—habituated to eroticizing them. Wollstonecraft's feminist critique thus crosses political boundaries, scandalously transforming Burke and Rousseau into allies; and to be sure, she could not fail to have hoped that Talleyrand-Périgord and all friends of the French Republic would be

---

5. *Lives of the English Poets,* ed. G. Birkbeck Hill (Oxford University Press: Oxford, 1905), vol. 1, p. 157. Johnson is mentioned with great respect throughout the *Rights of Woman.*
6. Burke, *A Philosophical Enquiry into the Origin of Our Ideas of the Sublime and the Beautiful,* ed. J. T. Boulton (Notre Dame, Ind.: University of Notre Dame Press, 1968, c. 1958), pp. 110, 113.

ashamed to discover that they cherished notions that put them on Burke's side.

Wollstonecraft does not stop with the assertion that women's wrongs are corrupting rather than endearing. In a move that would make *Rights of Woman* unintelligible if read without attention to its republican provenance, she further asserts that women's weaknesses render them imperious rather than docile. Like *Rights of Men*, *Rights of Woman* insists upon the mutually degrading tendencies of relations based on subordination. Accordingly it elaborates the paradox that women's subjection makes them despotic. Men ought to resent in women the same power they resent in kings; and they ought to reclaim the power they were weak enough to surrender when they enthroned women and monarchs alike. Although she laments that women whose commendable aim is to be respected rather than to be loved are likely to be "hunted out of society as masculine" (VRW 38), she herself deploys a counterargument at least as vicious as the one she protests here. Some women *ought* to be hunted out of society as masculine, but they are the ones we think of as quintessentially feminine: women "have been drawn out of their sphere by false refinement, and not by an endeavour to acquire masculine qualities" (VRW 24). Wollstonecraft develops this argument indirectly, through a series of loaded analogies, sex-coded in at once obvious and confounding ways. Women, for example, are like "soldiers" and "military men" in that stunting education has made them idle and frivolous; possessing only "superficial knowledge," and capable only of the "minor virtues" of "punctilious politeness," both soldiers and women are "attentive to their persons, fond of dancing, crowded rooms, adventures, and ridicule" and live only "to please" (VRW 26–27). Or, women are like kings, for the "passions of men have . . . placed women on thrones" (VRW 60). And elsewhere, women are like those other, notoriously despotic and misogynist titleholders: women get power by "playing on the *weakness* of men; and they may well glory in their illicit sway, for like Turkish bashaws, they have more real power than their masters" (VRW 43).

Wollstonecraft expects readers to be appalled to discover, first, that the very women whom men as diverse as Burke and Rousseau endeavor for everybody's good to protect by keeping in their place already occupy customarily masculine positions; and, second and conversely, that those positions themselves are feminine and hence unworthy of esteem. True, such satirically freighted analogies are by no means the only kinds that Wollstonecraft employs. She also describes women as slaves, dolls, pets, or beasts of burden who smile beneath the lash because they dare not snarl. Still, these subtler parallels are pervasive, peculiar, and rarely discussed. Designed to make us ask how the strong (men) have become irresponsibly weak, and the weak (women) illegitimately strong, they remind us that the sentimental theory Wollstonecraft takes on is intrinsically political, purporting in part to explain how authority is diffused among strong and weak, governors and governed. The unmanly reversal she deplores is the very one Burke cherishes as the chief virtue of the "mixed system of opinion and sentiment" he calls "chivalry." The sentiment of chivalry, Burke explains, "mitigated kings into companions, and raised private men to be fellows with kings. Without force, or opposition, it subdued the fierceness of pride and power; it obliged sovereigns to submit to the soft collar of social esteem, and compelled stern authority to submit to elegance, and gave a domination vanquisher of laws, to be subdued by manners".[7]

To Burke, the apparent reversals effected through chivalric sentimentalism are commendable because they disembrute power, in monarchs and in males. By passing off the weak as the strong and the strong as the weak, chivalry represses resentment from below and paranoid despotism from above. Thus are kings made mild, even if (as in France) their sovereignty is structurally absolute: under chivalry they too appear *subdued, obliged, compelled,* to *submit* to a system of manners that takes them down and brings "private men" up. Thus too are women adored rather than raped by men who take self-approving pleasure in seeing themselves as women's servants rather than their masters. Without such sentiments, which make "power gentle, and obedience liberal," the only hierarchies are powerful men over weak men, and men over women and other animals. On such a scheme, "a king is but a man; a queen is but a woman; a woman is but an animal; and an animal not of the highest order" (RRF 128). Burke grants that the sentiments he recommends may be "pleasing illusions" which cannot stand up to the "new conquering empire of light and reason" (RRF 128) associated with enlightenment *philosophes*. But the aggressively phallic imagery implicit in the "new conquering empire of light and reason," like that more graphically invoked with "cruel ruffians and assassins" stabbing the queen's bed "with an hundred strokes of bayonets and poignards" while she flies "almost naked" to "seek refuge at the feet of a king and husband, not secure of his own life for a moment" (RRF 121–22), suggests that there are kinds of masculinity best repudiated. Imbued with emotions beautified by the chivalric state, men should feel like women, Burke implies, although the miracle of chivalry is that such feeling is now constructed as manly, since to reason is to side with vulgar

7. [Edmund Burke, *Reflections on the Revolution in France* in *The Writings and Speeches of Edmund Burke*, ed. L. G. Mitchell (Oxford: Clarendon Press, 1989), p. 127. All subsequent references are to RRF, and appear parenthetically in the text.—*Editor*].

"sophisters, oeconomists, and calculators" entirely "destitute of all taste and elegance" (RRF 128) who would not balk at stripping queens and kingdoms alike of beautiful, civilizing garments.

But Wollstonecraft refuses the chivalric bait which lured an entire generation into thinking that the Revolution must be opposed at least in part because it licensed cruelty to women.[8] When Burke asserts that under the revolutionary dispensation a queen is only a woman, and a woman is only an animal, she airily returns in *Rights of Man*, "All true, Sir; if she is not more attentive to the duties of humanity than queens and fashionable ladies in general are". Her strategy in *Rights of Woman* is likewise to discredit chivalric sentimentality for conducing to an intolerable equivocality of gender and power. She exposes it as a ruse, in effect as a sort of drag show whereby queens perversely become tyrants, kings become queens, and men conceal the grossness of their power beneath the skirts of the beautiful for as long as woman's garb is not a liability—much like the men at Versailles who dressed in women's clothing to get past palace guards who, as Wollstonecraft remarks, were "unwilling, or ashamed, to fire on women."[9] Wollstonecraft accounts for this hoax by explaining that as the people of a state become more enlightened, rulers are obliged "to gloss over their oppression with a shew of right" and "make covert corruption hold fast the power which was formerly snatched by open force" (VRW 21). The diffusion of courtly manners accomplishes this covert operation, for through the mediation of manners compliancy to social rules is secured invisibly within the subject him- or herself, thus obviating the need for the sovereign to enforce authority through overtly disciplinary acts. This is why Wollstonecraft uses metaphors of infection when she talks about the ideological work of chivalric manners. Using the rather turgid phrase "pestiferous purple" (VRW 21), Wollstonecraft links the color of regal "drapery" in which Burke invests the state with the color of putrefaction that takes the subject over from the inside, consuming his power without his knowing it. Accordingly, a king "first becomes a luxurious monster, or a fastidious sensualist, and then makes the contagion which his unnatural state spread, the instrument of tyranny" (VRW 21).

Wollstonecraft develops her analysis of the beautification of the state and the consequent diffusion of unwholesome polymorphousness when explaining how Louis XIV "spread factitious manners, and

---

8. For an illuminating discussion of this aspect of reactionary British culture, see Linda Colley, *Britons: Forging the Nation 1707–1837* (New Haven and London: Yale University Press, 1992), pp. 250–62.
9. Wollstonecraft, *An Historical and Moral View of the Origin and Progress of the French Revolution* (London, 1790), p. 427.

caught, in a specious way, the whole nation in his toils" (VRW 61). For most English readers, Burke excepted, Louis XIV stands for the detested institution of absolute monarchy, and she could count on the reading public to disapprove of the "artful chain of despotism" (VRW 61) he forged to accommodate subjects to his tyranny. As Kay once again has shown, Wollstonecraft relishes the chance to bring Adam Smith's political analysis into conjunction with her feminist critique. For how did the sun king impress his subjects with his princely puissance? *Not*, Wollstonecraft, quoting Smith, explains, by the "scrupulous and inflexible justice of all his undertakings"; *not* by "the dangers and difficulties with which they were attended"; *not* by "his extensive knowledge, by his exquisite judgement, or by his heroic valour"; but rather by a parade of "frivolous accomplishments" that any garden variety female could rival: by the "gracefulness of his shape, and the majestic beauty of his person"; by the "sound of his voice"; by his "step" and deportment" (VRW 64).[1] For Wollstonecraft, there is a connection between the regal deployment of extravagant effeminacy in men, along with its overvaluation of women ("women . . . obtained in his reign that prince-like distinction so fatal to reason and virtue" [VRW 61]) and men's loss of political liberty. Once men take women as their models, they will no longer value, much less be able to exert, that manly spirit of liberty she wishes them to reclaim.

In some ways, then, Wollstonecraft's critique of courtly sentiments as it relates to king and subjects on one hand, and men and women on the other, is simple and stable: kings extend and conceal their authority by feminizing their subjects, just as men extend and conceal their dominion over women by encouraging them to cultivate qualities that depotentiate them: "[W]hy do not [women] discover, when 'in the noon of beauty's power,' that they are treated like queens only to be deluded by hollow respect, till they are led to resign, or not assume, their natural prerogatives? Confined then in cages like the feathered race, they have nothing to do but to plume themselves, and stalk with mock majesty from perch to perch" (VRW 60). Far from disembruting the powerful, male sentimentality artfully embrutes the powerless by proffering the illusion of power. "I do not wish [women] to have power over men," Wollstonecraft insists, "but over themselves" (VRW 67), and it is not outside, but inside chivalry that women are denied this power, and are treated like animals, not of the highest order. And if woman are, as it seems, "like the brutes . . . principally created for the use of man," then men ought to "let them

1. Carol Kay's discussions of Wollstonecraft's uses of Smith have been foundational for me. See "Canon, Ideology, and Gender: Mary Wollstonecraft's Critique of Adam Smith," *New Political Science* 15 (1986), pp. 63–76; and "On the Verge of Politics: Border Tactics for Eighteenth-Century Studies," *boundary* 2 12 (1984), pp. 197–215.

patiently bite the bridle, and not mock them with empty praise" (VRW 39). The *Rights of Woman* concludes with a sarcastic plea either to desist with such cant at last or to turn to Russia, where absolute power wears its true face, for the plain truth: grant women the rights to "emulate the virtues of man," or "open a fresh trade with Russia for whips: a present which a father should always make to his son-in-law on his wedding day, that a husband may . . . without any violation of justice reign, wielding this sceptre, sole master of his house" (VRW 203–04). In state and parlor, then, sentimentality is to be rejected because it obfuscates brutalizing power relationships, justifying them by claiming them to be the reverse of what they are, and relegating criticism to the realm of the coldhearted.

But Wollstonecraft's analysis is more complex and asymmetrical than this. For a democrat and a feminist, to compare women to emperors, despots, and kings is to risk countervailing and perhaps self-defeating implications. On one hand, Wollstonecraft classifies women as the principal, deluded victims of a sentimental ideology that degrades women as it pretends to exalt them; on the other hand, she classifies women in an empowered position as monarchical perpetrators of a sentimental ideology emasculating to all subjects, and accordingly as the terrible reactionaries who would rather not "resign the privileges of rank and sex" (VRW 158). Granted, these contradictions are what Wollstonecraft faults sentimental discourse for trafficking in. She ridicules its "heterogeneous associations" (VRW 38) and its "unintelligible paradoxes" (VRW 95) with a vigor that probably owes much to her admiration for Samuel Johnson, whom many progressive women writers—such as Macaulay and Hays—regarded with great respect. But Wollstonecraft appears to produce converse mutations of these paradoxes. Though she occasionally states that woman is presently "either a slave or a despot" (VRW 59), she treats woman as though she were both at the same time:

> Women as well as despots have now perhaps more power than they would have if the world . . . were governed by laws deduced from the exercice of reason (VRW 43–44).

and

> The *divine right* of husbands, like the divine right of kings, may, it is to be hoped, in this enlightened age, be contested without danger (VRW 44–45, emphasis MW's).

Or

> [T]he regal homage which [women] receive is so intoxicating, that till the manners of the times are changed, and formed on more reasonable principles, it may be impossible to convince

> them that the illegitimate power, which they obtain, by degrad-
> ing themselves is a curse (VRW 24)

and

> Let not men then in the pride of power, use the same argu-
> ments that tyrannic kings and venal ministers have used, and
> fallaciously assert that woman ought to be subjected because
> she has always been so. (VRW 49)

If women are victims of male despotism, Wollstonecraft's severity
with women seems misplaced. But if they have and misuse power,
then it is not clear why she regards renewed trade in horsewhips
from Russia for the correction of unruly wives as such a bad idea.
Can't Wollstonecraft make up her mind?

Once again, Wollstonecraft is tilting with Burke when she says that
"a king is always a king—and a woman is always a woman: his authority and her sex, ever stand between them and rational converse"
(VRW 61); or that your average fine lady "is not a more irrational
monster than some of the Roman emperors, who were depraved by
lawless power" (VRW 48). For him, as we have seen, womanhood is
figured at first as a delightful and then as a helplessly distressed
queen. But Wollstonecraft reverses woman's sex, presenting her as
another kind of "equivocal being," a tyrannical female-king, thus
turning Burkean sentimentalism inside out. The comparisons make
sense because for her a king, despite his authority, is always an impotent and vulnerable figure. Presenting the monarch as vulnerable to
the machinations of crafty ministers is, of course, nothing new in the
history of British political discourse. But in figuring the king as a
woman, Wollstonecraft advances the political and sexual fronts of
her argument in polyvalent ways: "Women," she writes, "have been
duped by their lovers, as princes by their ministers, whilst dreaming
that they reigned over them" (VRW 27). "Some allowance," she continues later, "should be made for a sex, who, like kings, always see
things through a false medium" (VRW 46). Like a pampered,
benighted woman, then, a king is finally no more than "a weak fellow
creature, whose very station sinks him *necessarily* below the meanest
of his subjects!" since even under "the most favourable circumstances" what she terms "the feelings of a man" will be "stifled by flattery, and reflection shut out by pleasure!" (VRW 19).

The linkage of womanhood to kingship has implications that, as
should be clear by now, move in both directions, *e*masculating in
one and *im*masculating in the other. It diminishes the capacity of
the king, but it intensifies that of a woman, suggesting that even if
she is impotent, she is by no means innocuous. In saying as much,
Wollstonecraft is in my opinion actually bringing to the surface a
possibility about the monstrousness of woman's illegitimate power

suppressed but still visible in Burke. Manifestly, he defends the old regime because it mollifies power, making a safe place for otherwise helpless women. But not all women are so needful. Unlike Ronald Paulson, who has contended that Burke represents the revolution itself as female, I find that Burke's text in many respects minimizes women's role in the uprising, most famously in the sections where the revolutionaries are described as would-be gang-rapists. In this respect the *Reflections* differs markedly from Paine's *Rights of Man* (1791–92) and Wollstonecraft's own *Historical and Moral View of the Origin and Progress of the French Revolution* (1794), which both cover the same material.[2] Those sections of the *Reflections* that describe the storming of the palace at Versailles and the forced procession of the king and queen to Paris contain Burke's most powerful and memorable prose. Yet one can easily read them and never realize that the uncivilized mob he denounces consisted largely of women. The presence of women as an insurrectionary force is made known only now and then through an occasional, luridly monstrous detail, as if they just happened by. Comparing the rebels to cannibals and Indians is one of Burke's favorite figures. The march to Paris, for example, resembled "a procession of American savages, entering into Onondaga, after some of their murders called victories, and leading into hovels hung round with scalps, their captives, overpowered with the scoffs and buffets of women as ferocious as themselves" (RRF 117). Women appear later when Burke describes this march in more detail, compounding savagery by hellishness, as the king and queen "were slowly moved along, amidst the horrid yells, and shrilling screams, and frantic dances, and infamous contumelies, and all the unutterable abominations of the furies of hell, in the abused shape of the vilest of women" (RRF 122).

But isolating these passages gives them a prominence they lack in context. What is most striking about the long paragraph from which they come is that it is packed entirely with passive constructions— e.g., the royal captives "were conducted"; two of their bodyguards "had been selected"; they "were cruelly and publickly dragged to the block"; their heads "were stuck upon spears." These constructions highlight the persecution of the captives, but they also obscure the identity, and with that the sex, of the persecutors. But, while Burke surely could assume that his readers knew about the *poissardes*, his own prose does nothing to highlight their identity as women, let

2. Ronald Paulson, *Representations of Revolution* (1798–1820) (New Haven: Yale University Press, 1983), pp. 72–73. Although I am much indebted to Paulson's study, I have trouble reconciling the claim that the revolution is female to the claim that the revolution is an oedipal challenge to the power of the king, a view underlying much of his discussion. Also see Neil Hertz, "Medusa's Head: Male Hysteria under Political Pressure," *Representations* 4 (1983), pp. 27–54, which has influenced me a good deal.

alone their monstrosity as virile women. Far from it. Once women
appear, it is amidst such a busy-ness of carnage that the fact receives
no particular emphasis. And finally, of course, what exactly is an
"abused shape of the vilest of women"? Is Burke gothically fantasiz-
ing creatures from hell assuming the shape of women? Is he saying
that such females, as "mere" working-class jades and prostitutes, are
"unsexed females" and thus not really women at all? Is he alluding
with unnecessary and puzzling indirection to the common practice of
men assuming women's dress to engage in politically subversive activities?[3] Whatever the case, Burke never unequivocally foregrounds
women as the agents of rebellion, for doing so would deprive his theory of sentimental chivalry of one of its rationales: it would not fit his
design to represent that libidinous "band of ruffians" assaulting the
queen's bed as mostly or partly women, who when stripped of sentimental ideology about their amiable delicacy are far from being weak
animals subject to the brutal lust of stronger men.[4]

For Wollstonecraft, by contrast, the sex of the crowd poses no
problem. Because it is her purpose to explode rather than shore up
notions about female delicacy that sustain sentimental masculinity,
it costs her nothing as a feminist or as a republican, crestfallen at
the turn of events in post-Revolutionary France, to observe in *An
Historical and Moral View* that the mob "consisted mostly of market
women, and the lowest refuse of the streets who had thrown off the
virtues of one sex without having power to assume more than the
vices of the other."[5] Of course, women of every class, like "slaves
and mobs" in general, behave riotously "when once they [break]

3. Natalie Z. Davis has explained that it was commonly the practice from the seventeenth
century onward in France as well as England for men engaging in political protest to dress
in women's clothing, both as a means of concealment and as a carnivalesque assumption
of the energy and irresponsibility of unruly women. See *Society and Culture in Early Modern France* (Stanford: Stanford University Press, 1975), pp. 147–50. Addressing the sexual identity of the marchers more directly than Burke, Wollstonecraft observes that men
dressed as women were among the crowd.
4. For a contrasting argument, insisting on the femaleness of the crowd, see Linda M. G.
Zerilli, "Text/Woman as Spectacle: Edmund Burke's 'French Revolution,'" *The Eighteenth
Century: Theory and Interpretation* 33 (1992), pp. 47–52, which opposes the Queen's
comforting beauty to the unnerving sublimity of revolutionary women.
5. Wollstonecraft, *Historical and Moral View*, p. 426. In other respects, however, Wollstonecraft's account is clearly indebted to Burke. Wollstonecraft too indulges in gothic
depictions of savagery in the political spheres, only the villains in her version, not surprisingly, are the palace guards committed to suppressing the revolution: They "promised, as
they drained the cup in her [the Queen's] honour, not to sheath their swords, till France
was compelled to obedience, and the national assembly dispersed. With savage ferocity
they danced to the sound of music attuned to slaughter, whilst plans of death and devas-
tation gave zest to the orgies, that worked up their animal spirits to the highest pitch" (pp.
160–61). Still, it is worth noting that Wollstonecraft's representation of the culpable
excess of female insurgents in part appears to legitimate the brutal crackdown on
women's political clubs after the execution of Marie-Antoinette. See Lynn Hunt, "The
Bad Mother," in *The Family Romance of the French Revolution* (Berkeley: University of
California Press, 1992), pp. 89–123; Dominique Godineau, *Les femmes tricoteuses* (Paris:
Alinea, 1989), pp. 268–70; and Dorinda Outram, *The Body and the French Revolution*
(New Haven and London: Yale University Press, 1989).

loose from authority" (VRW 88), for "if women are not permitted to enjoy legitimate rights, they will render both men and themselves vicious, to obtain illicit privileges" (VRW 8). The context of bad female power helps untangle Wollstonecraft's conceits about female kings. Until women are accorded the capacity of responsible self-command—i.e., "the power to assume more than the vices" of men—they will be immasculated, but not worthily masculine. Irresponsible and undemocratic power relations corrupt in both directions, degrading rulers and ruled alike. Men of England and France ought to extend political rights to women, then, not so much because women deserve a fair chance as because unless men do, their own liberty will be insecure. Godwin's obliviousness to this emphasis is exceedingly painful. Summarizing Wollstonecraft's achievement in *Rights of Woman*, he gives her pride of place among writers animated "in the behalf of oppressed and injured beauty," as if Wollstonecraft had been motivated by gallantry, as if women deserved rights on the grounds of their beauty alone. In the second edition of the *Memoirs*, Godwin evidently thought twice about his misplaced chivalry and omitted his allusion to the injured fair ones, emending the passage to read "animated by the contemplation of their oppressed and injured state."[6]

BARBARA TAYLOR

The Religious Foundations of Mary Wollstonecraft's Feminism[†]

> Gracious Creator of the whole human race! hast thou created such a being as woman, who can trace Thy wisdom in Thy works, and feel that Thou alone art by Thy nature exalted above her, for no better purpose . . . [than] to submit to man, her equal—a being who, like her, was sent into the world to acquire virtue? Can she consent to be occupied merely to please him—merely to adorn the earth—when her soul is capable of rising to Thee?   (VRW 5:136)[1]

Admirers of Mary Wollstonecraft are often reluctant to see her as a religious thinker. This should not surprise us. The reiterated

---

6. William Godwin, *Memoirs of the Author of 'The Rights of Woman,'* ed. Richard Holmes (Harmondsworth: Penguin, 1987), p. 232.
† Barbara Taylor, "The Religious Foundations of Mary Wollstonecraft's Feminism," in *The Cambridge Companion to Mary Wollstonecraft*, ed. Claudia L. Johnson (Cambridge: Cambridge University Press, 2003), pp. 99–118. Copyright © Cambridge University Press 2002. Reprinted with the permission of Cambridge University Press.
1. Taylor cites Mary Wollstonecraft, *A Vindication of the Rights of Woman* in *Works of Mary Wollstonecraft*, ed. Marilyn Butler and Janet Todd (London: Pickering and Chatto: New York: New York University Press, 1989), 5: 136, p. 49 in this Norton Critical Edition.

"appeals to God and virtue," in A *Vindication of the Rights of Woman*
are "a dead letter to feminists now," a leading feminist critic tells us,
and if by dead letter is meant a failed communication, then it is certainly true that of all aspects of Wollstonecraft's thought it is her
religious faith that has failed to speak to modern interpreters.[2] Most
studies do no more than gesture toward it, and then usually dismiss
it as ideological baggage foisted on her by her times, with no positive
implications for her views on women. A *Vindication of the Rights of
Woman* is generally located in a tradition of Enlightenment humanism that is assumed to have been at least indifferent to religion, if
not actively hostile to it.

So it is startling, on looking closely at the *Rights of Woman*, to find
that it contains at least fifty discussions of religious themes, ranging
from brief statements on one or other doctrinal point to extended
analyses of women's place within a divinely-ordered moral universe.
Nor are these discussions in any sense peripheral to the main message of the text. If Wollstonecraft's faith becomes a dead letter to us,
then so does much of her feminism, so closely are they harnessed
together. The famous call for a "revolution of female manners" in the
Rights of Woman on close inspection proves to be first and foremost a
summons to women to a right relationship with their Maker. "In
treating . . . of the manners of women, let us, disregarding sensual
arguments, trace what we should endeavor to make them in order to
cooperate . . . with the Supreme Being" (VRW 23):

> . . . for . . . if they be really capable of acting like rational crea-
> tures, let them not be treated like slaves; or, like the brutes who
> are dependent on the reason of man, when they associate with
> him; but cultivate their minds, give them the salutary sublime
> curb of principle, and let them attain conscious dignity by feel-
> ing themselves only dependent on God.   (VRW 40)

It is through the exercise of "a rational will that only bows to God"
that women may achieve that self-respect on which inner freedom is
founded. "These may be Utopian dreams," Wollstonecraft writes,
but "thanks to that Being who impressed them on my soul, and gave
me sufficient strength of mind to dare to exert my own reason, till,
becoming dependent only on Him for the support of my virtue, I
view, with indignation, the mistaken notions that enslave my sex"
(VRW 40). It was thanks to God, in other words, that Mary
Wollstonecraft became a feminist.

Wollstonecraft's family were inactive members of the Church
of England, and according to her husband and biographer, William

---

2. Ann Snitow, "A Gender Diary", *Feminism and History*, ed. Joan Wallach Scott, (Oxford
University Press, 1996), 529.

Godwin, she "received few lessons of religion in her youth."[3] Nonetheless, for the first twenty-eight years of her life she was a regular churchgoer and her first published work, *Thoughts on the Education of Daughters* (1787), was steeped in orthodox attitudes, advocating "fixed principles of religion" and warning of the dangers of rationalist speculation and deism. For women in particular, the young Wollstonecraft argued, clear-cut religious views were essential: "for a little refinement only leads a woman into the wilds of romance, if she is not religious; nay more, there is no true sentiment without it, nor perhaps any other effectual check to the passions".[4] In the same year that *Thoughts* was published, however, Wollstonecraft stopped attending church, and by the time she produced her last published book, *A Short Residence in Sweden*, she had performed an apparent volte face, writing approvingly of freethinkers who "deny the divinity of Jesus Christ, and . . . question the necessity or utility of the christian system".[5] The abandonment of christian orthodoxy, however, only served to underline her commitment to what had become a highly personal faith. "Her religion," as Godwin wrote in his *Memoirs* of her shortly after her death, "was almost entirely of her own creation. But she was not on that account less attached to it, or the less scrupulous in discharging what she considered as its duties" (Memoirs, 215).[6]

At the time Godwin met Wollstonecraft she had not been a churchgoer for over four years. Nonetheless, on that occasion they managed to have a row about religion in which, as Godwin recalled, "her opinions approached much nearer to the received one, than mine" (Memoirs, 236). When they met again, in 1796, Godwin was an atheist. This meeting was much more successful than the first: they became friends, then lovers, then husband and wife—and meanwhile went on disagreeing about religion. "How can you blame me for taking refuge in the idea of a God, when I despair of finding sincerity here on earth?" Wollstonecraft demanded at one low point two months before her death.[7] At any rate, little as he would have wanted it, it was Godwin who had the last word, since after his wife's

3. William Godwin, *Memoirs of the Author of a Vindication of the Rights of Woman*; first published 1798 (Harmondsworth: Penguin, 1987), 215.
4. *Thoughts on the Education of Daughters* in *Works of Mary Wollstonecraft*, ed. Marilyn Butler and Janet Todd (London: Pickering and Chatto; New York: New York University Press, 1984), 4:33.
5. *Letters Written During a Short Residence in Sweden, Norway and Denmark*, in *Works*, 6:276.
6. This emphasis on Wollstonecraft's piety in *Memoirs* does not seem to have registered with many readers, including one who claimed that Godwin's book gave "a striking view of a Woman of fine talents . . . sinking a victim to the strength of her Passions & feelings because destitute of the support of Religious principles" (James Woodrow, quoted in Gary Kelly, *Women, Writing and Revolution, 1790–1827* [Oxford: Clarendon Press, 1993], 27.)
7. Letter to William Godwin, 4 July 1797. Letters, 404.

premature death it was left to him to produce an account of her religious beliefs in his *Memoirs*.

Wollstonecraft's religion, Godwin wrote, was "in reality, little allied to any system of forms" and "was founded rather in taste, than in the niceties of polemical discussion":

> Her mind constitutionally attached itself to the sublime and the amiable. She found an inexpressible delight in the beauties of nature, and in the splendid reveries of the imagination. But nature itself, she thought, would be no better than a vast blank, if the mind of the observer did not supply it with an animating soul. When she walked amidst the wonders of nature, she was accustomed to converse with her God. To her mind he was pictured as not less amiable, generous and kind, than great, wise and exalted.   (Memoirs, 215)

This representation of Wollstonecraft's deity as a wishful mental projection owes too much to Godwin's own religious skepticism to be wholly reliable.[8] Her friend Mary Hays's alternative depiction of Wollstonecraft's God as "a being higher, more perfect, than visible nature" whom she "adored . . . amidst the beauties of Nature, or . . . in the still hour of recollection," better captures Wollstonecraft's *credo*.[9] Both Godwin and Hays rightly stress the central role of passion and imagination in Wollstonecraft's theology. Both also—much less plausibly—represent her as indifferent to theological controversy. Her "faith relied not upon critical evidence or laborious investigation," Hays claimed,[1] which in Godwin's version became a depressingly condescending portrait of his wife's mind in action. "She adopted one opinion," Godwin wrote, "and rejected another, spontaneously, by a sort of tact, and the force of a cultivated imagination; and yet, though perhaps, in the strict sense of the term, she reasoned little, it is surprising what a degree of soundness is to be found in her determinations" (Memoirs, 272–3).

"She reasoned little . . .": and this of the woman who translated and reviewed theological works in three languages, was conversant with major theological debates of her period, and who consistently argued that true religion was not a mere matter of enthusiastic sentiment but rather "a governing principle of conduct, drawn from self-knowledge, and rational opinion respecting the attributes of

---

8. A note found in Godwin's papers after his death, written sometime in 1787, contained the following: "Religion is among the most beautiful and most natural of all things; that religion which 'sees God in clouds and hears Him in the wind', which endows every object of sense with a living soul, which finds in the system of nature whatever is holy, mysterious, and venerable, and inspires the bosom with sentiments of awe and veneration" (quoted in Charles Kegan Paul, *William Godwin: His Friends and Contemporaries* [1876], 1:28). The similarity to the views he attributed to Wollstonecraft is obvious.
9. Mary Hays, "Memoirs of Mary Wollstonecraft," *Annual Necrology*, 1797/8 (1800), 416.
1. *Ibid.*, 416.

God" (VRW 121). This refusal to take Wollstonecraft seriously as a religious thinker was symptomatic of the anxieties aroused in Godwin by his wife's intellectual status. But it was also indicative of an important shift of opinion in the eighteenth century, as religious belief became increasingly aligned with the feminine and both came under the rule of sentiment, what Godwin described as the "empire of feeling." In the second edition of his *Memoirs* Godwin revised his account of Wollstonecraft's "intellectual character" so as to make some of these connections more explicit. The difference between the sexes, he argued there, corresponds to the psychological opposition between reason and emotion—and he and Wollstonecraft exemplified this divide, he being dominated by "habits of deduction" while she enjoyed an "intuitive sense of the pleasures of the imagination" which eventually aroused his own emotions as well: "Her taste awakened mine; her sensibility determined me to a careful development of my feelings" (Memoirs, 276–7). So while the Philosopher could not follow his wife into her religious beliefs, he nonetheless became a convert to the deep sense of personal truth reflected in them, the "fearless and unstudied veracity" of Wollstonecraft's womanly heart.

This portrait of the woman of sensibility (at one point Godwin called Wollstonecraft a "female Werther") tells us less about Wollstonecraft than it does about prevailing sexual mores—and Godwin's haphazard attempts to keep his wife's stormy history within the boundaries of them. This is not to deny that Wollstonecraft enjoyed donning the cloak of female Wertherism at times. But the idea of a uniquely feminine emotionality was anathema to her, a central target of her feminism. Religious sentimentality of the kind typically associated with women she particularly disdained. Drawing a line between this sort of "irrational enthusiasm" and the deep emotions of the true believer was not easy, however, and Wollstonecraft worked hard at clarifying the distinction. Her ambiguous attitude toward sensibility (which has so received much attention from recent commentators) is best understood in this context, as part of her wider endeavor to define an authentic religious subjectivity. What shape does a woman's inner life take when it is lived in a right relationship with her Maker?

For a feminist, this question inevitably raised issues of power and entitlement. The centrality of religion to Wollstonecraft's worldview is evident in virtually every aspect of her thought, from her uncompromising egalitarianism to her hostility toward British commercialism—modern mammon, as she saw it—to her ardent faith in an imminent age of universal freedom and happiness. The utopian optimism coloring her politics was basically Christian in origin, although marked by other influences too, most notably Rousseauism. Elsewhere I have

traced in detail the religious roots of her radical *credo*, in its many
diverse manifestations.[2] In this essay I concentrate specifically on her
feminist ideals, as enunciated in *A Vindication of the Rights of Woman*
(1792) and prefigured in her first novel, *Mary, A Fiction* (1788). His-
torians seeking to identify the origins of modern Western feminism
have generally located them in secular developments: the rise of liberal political ideals, the reformist intellectual programme inaugurated
by Enlightenment, the expressive opportunities opened to women by
the eighteenth-century expansion of print culture. These, *inter alia*,
are important factors. But for proto-feminist lines of argument with
the longest pedigree and greatest ideological clout, we must look first
to religion, or rather to that body of Christian doctrine which, at its
most consistent, had strongly positive implications for women's private and public status. Pushed to the limit of their revisionary potential, teachings pertaining to the equality of souls and human likeness
to God offered female believers a vision of sacralized selfhood sharply
at odds with worldly subordination. Gender distinctions and their
social consequences were both thrown into question. "Human nature
itself, which is complete in both sexes, has been made in the image of
God," Saint Augustine had written, and thus in the spirit "there is no
sex,"[3] or as Simone de Beauvoir put it with characteristic trenchancy
centuries later, "religion. . . . cancels the advantage of the penis".[4]
Attacking misogynist representations of women as weakly infantile,
Wollstonecraft repeatedly accused their inventors of purveying the
Muslim viewpoint that women "have not souls" (VRW 10)[5] (a popular
misreading of Islamic doctrine at the time). As children of God, we
are all equal in His sight, Wollstonecraft reminded readers of the
Rights of Woman; thus "[i]t be not philosophical to speak of sex when
the soul is mentioned" (VRW 38).

The appeal of this stance to pro-woman thinkers long antedated
Wollstonecraft, and has long survived her. Feminism, it is worth
recalling, has for most of its history been deeply embedded in religious belief. Eighteenth- and nineteenth-century western feminists
were nearly all active Christians, and even the more secularized varieties of feminism that emerged in western societies in the 1970s still
carried powerful undercurrents of religious belief. Obviously, the

2. Barbara Taylor, *Mary Wollstonecraft and the Feminist Imagination* (Cambridge University
Press, 2002).
3. Quoted in Genevieve Lloyd, *The Man of Reason: Male and Female in Western Philosophy*
(London: Methuen, 1984), 30–1.
4. Simone de Beauvoir, *The Second Sex*, 1949 (English ed., Harmondsworth: Penguin,
1972), 633. De Beauvoir's discussion of the egalitarian implications of Christianity for
women is in many respects very reminiscent of Wollstonecraft's, although her perspective
is that of an analytical unbeliever: "A sincere faith is a great help to the little girl in avoiding an inferiority complex: she is neither male nor female, but God's creature" (633).
5. *A Vindication of the Rights of Men* in *Works*, 5:45. Subsequent references are to this edition, abbreviated VRM. In this volume, see p. 258.—*Editor*.]

religions which have engaged feminists internationally over the centuries have been so varied that any attempt to offer a general account of them would be foolhardy. But given the centrality of Wollstonecraft to the self-image of western feminism, understanding her theology may give us more than local insights into the religious impulse as it has operated across the feminist tradition.

In Wollstonecraft's Protestant England, the spiritual equality of women had long been an important minority theme. Puritan sects in particular, with their fierce emphasis on the democracy of God's grace, had provided generations of female believers with a language of spiritual self-assertion; and even the Church of England had harbored godly feminists. "Whatever . . . Reasons Men may have for despising Women, and keeping them in Ignorance and Slavery, it can't be from their having learnt to do so in Holy Scripture," the High Anglican Mary Astell claimed in 1700, adding stoutly that "the Bible is for, and not against us . . ."[6] Calls to a higher life—whether it meant an intensification of female piety in the home or even, as in the case of seventeenth- and eighteenth-century women preachers, leaving their households to spread God's Word—was a route to enhanced self-esteem and moral status, and sometimes to the potential subversion of Female Duty. "I chose to obey God rather than man," one female preacher wrote on abandoning her husband in order to serve her Maker,[7] and the appeal of such forms of religious obedience to many insubordinate female spirits is easily imagined.

The religious revival which swept Britain from the 1730s on carried such aspirations in its wake, although with mixed results. The decline of the militant spirit which had fostered the revival, combined with stricter policing of sexual divisions within its ranks, led to women's claims often being pushed to the margins of the movement or outside evangelicalism entirely. By the 1780s, at the point when Wollstonecraft began pronouncing on such matters, St. Paul's strictures against the ministry of women had become a staple of popular sermonizing. The eruption of female voices that occurred during the early stages of the French Revolution intensified repressive criticism. "The influence of religion is to be exercised with discretion [by women]," the leading Evangelical tractarian Hannah More (one of Wollstonecraft's fiercest detractors) warned in 1799, since "a female Polemic wanders almost as far from the limits prescribed to her sex, as a female Machiavel."[8]

6. Mary Astell, "Some Reflections Upon Marriage," first published in 1700; 1706 edn. reprinted in Bridget Hill, *The First English Feminist* (Aldershot: Gower Publishing, 1986), 84. [see also p. 214 herein.—*Editor*]
7. A Methodist woman preacher quoted in L. F. Church, *More About the Early Methodist People* (London, 1949), 168.
8. Hannah More, *Strictures on the Modern System of Female Education* (London, 1799), 1:7. [see p. 245 herein.—*Editor*]

These fluctuations in the fortunes of female believers were accompanied by changing perceptions of the significance of gender in the Christian self. The soul may be sexless, but its earthly vehicles patently are not: a fact assigned increasing significance over the course of the eighteenth century. From the mid-century on preachers of all stripes could be heard arguing that female religious feeling was intrinsically more powerful than that of men, a view reinforced by the idealization of pity as the primary Christian sentiment. The cult of feminine sensibility, evident in both fiction and moral literature, derived largely from this source. Womankind, the Newcastle vicar John Brown explained in a sermon delivered in 1765, has a greater "sensibility of pain" than men, and thus a greater capacity to emphathize with the sufferings of others, while at the same time taking its "highest Delight . . . in a grateful Subordination to its Protector."[9] These emotional predispositions, combined with the "calmer" lives women lead, mean that while "in man, Religion is generally the Effect of Reason" in women "it may almost be called the Effect of Nature" (13). Such innate piety, Brown concluded (on a note heard with increasing frequency over succeeding decades) gave women a uniquely authoritative role in moral life, since

> a Mind thus gentle and thus adorned exalts subordination itself
> into the Power of Superiority and Command . . . the Influence
> and irresistible Force of Virtue.   (15)

Women may be men's inferiors in social and political life, but in matters of the spirit they are preeminent. This line of argument clearly had attractions as a defense against women's secular claims. But it could also pose serious hazards for sexual conservatives, particularly in its more militant formulations. Wollstonecraft's first novel, *Mary, A Fiction* exemplified these dangers. *Mary*, published in 1788, features a heroine of such radiant piety that she outshines the feebler moral lights of all around her. Even as a child, Mary's emotional life is dominated by "devotional sentiments" (M 1:11);[1] as a young adult, which is where the novel finds her, she is, if anything, even more saintly, with a mind focused always on God and a heart so attuned to the needs and sufferings of her fellow man that for her no "sensual gratification" can compare to the joy of feeling her "eyes moistened after having comforted the unfortunate" (M 1:59). This compassionate sensibility benefits everyone around her (although they remain disappointingly ungrateful) while at the same time bestowing an "enthusiastic greatness" on Mary's soul. She "glanced from earth to heaven," Wollstonecraft tells us, and "caught the light

9. John Brown, DD, *On the Female Character and Education* (London, 1765), 12, 10.
1. *Mary, A Fiction* in *Works*, 1:11. [All subsequent references are to this edition, hereafter abbreviated M.—*Editor*]

of truth" which, like her author, she was then ever eager to shed on others—"her tongue was ever the faithful interpreter of her heart" (M 1:59). And why should Mary keep silent, when heart and soul have so much to say? Christian militancy irresistibly posed the question, and even women ostensibly opposed to all that Wollstonecraft stood for, often found themselves responding to the call in unconventional ways. Hannah More may have held female polemicists to be ungodly, but this didn't prevent her from publishing tens of thousands of pious works exhorting women to use their superior moral influence against Satan, the slave trade, and French "democratical" politics. Soon (although not in Wollstonecraft's lifetime) many women Evangelicals began explicitly linking doctrines of female moral leadership to demands for practical improvements in women's own political and legal status.

Being a proper Christian woman, then, was a paradoxical affair, bestowing important ethical prerogatives to be exercised only under conditions of psychological and practical submission. In Book v of *Emile*, his famous statement on women's nature and entitlements, Rousseau had argued that a woman should always defer to the religious views of her father or husband,[2] and most women probably agreed—"conforming", as Wollstonecraft put it, "as a dependent creature should, to the ceremonies of the Church which she was brought up in, piously believing that wiser heads than her own have settled that business . . ." (VRW 53–54). Certainly mainstream moralists were as likely to denounce women with independent religious views as they were to condemn the godless. The immensely influential handbook of advice to young women written by Dr. John Gregory (and criticized by Wollstonecraft in the *Rights of Woman*) specifically counseled them against all religious study while at the same time emphasizing that "even those men who are themselves unbelievers dislike infidelity in *you*." Lack of piety in women, Gregory noted, was taken as "proof of that hard and masculine spirit, which of all your faults, *we* [men] dislike the most" while its presence was men's best security for "that female virtue in which *they* are most interested," i.e., chastity.[3] James Fordyce similarly condemned any sign of intellectual independence in women while at the same time recommending public devotions as a way of displaying female face and form to most pleasing effect.[4] "Why are women to be thus bred up with a desire of conquest?" was Wollstonecraft's irritable response to all this: "Do religion and virtue offer no stronger motives, no brighter reward?" (VRW 101).

2. Jean-Jacques Rousseau, *Emile, or On Education*, 1765 (English edn. London: Penguin, 1991), 377–8.
3. Dr. John Gregory, *A Father's Legacy to His Daughters* (London, 1823), 159–60.
4. James Fordyce, *Sermons to Young Women*, 1765 (London, 1766), 2:163.

Women conduct-book writers by contrast tended to emphasize
women's intellectual relationship to God, urging close study of the
Bible and familiarity with major theological works. Women writers
published biblical commentary, entered into public debate with
male theologians, and wrote essays in which Female Duty was
spelled out with fierce moral stringency. The brand of female devotion promoted by these women was based on mind as well as heart,
and in this they were clearly spiritual sisters to the heroine of Wollstonecraft's *Mary, A Fiction*, and also to the redoubtable Mrs. Mason
of Wollstonecraft's *Original Stories From Real Life*, written for children. Mrs. Mason, a Christian propagandist with a formidable sense
of her own self-worth, tells her little pupils that they must learn not
only to love God but also to mimic Him. "[T]o attain any thing
great," she informs them, "a model must be held up to our understanding, and engage our affections" in such a way that we learn "to
copy his attributes" and "imitate Him." "We are his children when
we try to resemble Him . . . convinced that truth and goodness must
constitute the very essence of the soul . . .".[5] The tone is conven-
tionally didactic, but to urge a little girl to find "dignity and happiness" from mimicking God when the most to which she was
generally meant to aspire was (in the words of the *Rights of Woman*)
"to model her soul to suit the frailities of her [husband]" (VRW 36)
was not just pious conventionalism. This affirmation of women's
capacity to apprehend and identify with the divine, expressed in
nearly all female writings of the period, was so fundamental to
women's sense of ethical worth, and so far-reaching in its egalitarian
implications, that it can properly be described as one of the founding impulses of feminism.

The young Mary of Wollstonecraft's first novel is clearly indebted
to these protofeminist elements of English Protestantism while at
the same time rejecting evangelical extremism and Establishment
reaction. "The cant of weak enthusiasts have made the consolations
of Religion . . . appear . . . ridiculous," Wollstonecraft wrote to her
sister in 1784,[6] and by the time she wrote *Mary, A Fiction* this view
was hardening into a wholesale condemnation of all varieties of
Christian "fanaticism." The fictional Mary begins her career as a
professing Anglican with an evangelical tinge. But as the novel
progresses she becomes increasingly unorthodox. Like her author,
she feels closest to God not in church but in the contemplation of
His works, particularly "the grand or solemn features of Nature" in
which her sensitive heart delights. She does not scorn Scripture, but
nor does she unthinkingly accept it, for "her mind was not like a mir-

---

5. *Original Stories from Real Life* in *Works*, 4:423, 431.
6. Letter to Everina Wollstonecraft, January 1784, *Letters*, 87.

ror" merely reflecting what was before it, but an instrument of rational criticism. Traveling in Portugal, she enters a Catholic church in the company of some "deistical" Englishmen, and then:

> Mary thought of both the subjects, the Romish tenets, and the deistical doubts; and though not a sceptic, thought it right to examine the evidence on which her faith was built. She read Butler's Analogy, and some other authors: and these researches made her a christian from conviction, and she learned charity, particularly with respect to sectaries; saw that apparently good and solid arguments might take their rise from different points of view; and she rejoiced to find that those she should not concur with had some reason on their side.   (M 1:29)

Mary, in other words, is well on her way to becoming a typical Enlightenment intellectual, eschewing blind faith and evangelical purism in favor of "rational religious impulses" and liberal toleration. The trajectory roughly followed Wollstonecraft's own. Four years before the publication of *Mary* she had moved with her sisters to Newington Green, north of London, to run a girls' school there. Newington Green had long been a hotbed of religious and political radicalism; its presiding spirit at the time of Wollstonecraft's arrival was Richard Price, minister to the local community of Rational Dissenters (or Unitarians, as they became known). Price and his fellow Unitarian, the Birmingham scientist and preacher Joseph Priestley, were leading figures in the English radical intelligentsia, and while Wollstonecraft never became a Unitarian she attended Price's chapel, studied his sermons, and came to deeply admire his personal and political integrity. Price was "one of the best of men," she wrote shortly after his death, in the *Rights of Woman* (VRW 19).

Rational Dissent was a variety of Protestant Nonconformity forged by and for the *avant-garde* educated middle class. The most cerebral of the Nonconformist sects, Rational Dissent offered its adherents a bracing brew of Lockean psychology, Newtonian cosmology, rationalist morality and reform politics. Its creed was antitrinitarian (the divinity of Christ was denied) and its deity was a benign Supreme Being with a judicious regard for all His creatures and no taste for hellfire. Calvinism, with its savagely anti-humanist ethos, was repudiated in favor of a vision of mankind as essentially good and inherently perfectible. "We must get entirely clear of all the notions . . . of original sin . . . to leave room for the expansion of the human heart," as Wollstonecraft wrote in 1794.[7]

In common with all Nonconformists, Rational Dissenters were subject to the Test Acts—discriminatory laws barring them from

---

7. *An Historical and Moral View of the French Revolution* in *Works*, 6:21–2 [see p. 267 in this Norton Critical Edition—*Editor*].

holding office under the Crown or in municipal corporations, and from taking degrees at Oxford and Cambridge. The struggle to repeal the Acts, which lasted many decades, was at its height when Wollstonecraft was attending Price's chapel, and the political stridency with which it infused the Unitarians' rhetoric clearly struck a chord in their young fellow-traveler. The analogy between the oppression of women and the penalties suffered by Dissenters was readily drawn, and Wollstonecraft herself drew it in the *Rights of Woman* (where she also claimed however that both Dissenters and women were psychologically deformed by their secondary status). But more important for her feminism was Unitarianism's emphasis on private reasoned judgment as the foundation of true religion: a principle to which the circumstances of both Dissenters and women gave real political bite. The fictive Mary's cool weighing of doctrinal choices, and her insistence that all religious beliefs (including those of "sectaries," i.e. Dissenters) be respected, reflected this viewpoint—its radicalism much heightened in this instance by the sex of its proponent. By 1790, in her *A Vindication of the Rights of Men*, Wollstonecraft was prepared to be more explicit. "I look into my own mind," she wrote,

> my heart is human, beats quick with human sympathies—and I FEAR God. . . . I fear that sublime power, whose motive for creating me must have been wise and good; and I submit to the moral laws which my reason deduces from this view of my dependence on him. It is not his power that I fear—it is not to an arbitrary will, but to unerring *reason* I submit.   [VRM 5:34]

"[T]o act according to the dictates of reason," she wrote further on, "is to conform to the law of God" [VRM 5:51].

This appeal to the inner authority of the individual believer was at the heart of all varieties of Enlightened theism. "*Intra te quaere Deum*," as Basil Willey has noted, was the motto of the age:

> look for God within thyself. And what exactly would you find when you looked within? Not the questionable shapes revealed by psycho-analysis, but something much more reassuring: the laws of God and Nature inscribed upon the heart . . .[8]

The will of God, as Rousseau put it in his immensely influential credo of the Vicar of Savoyard, is "written by nature with ineffaceable characters in the depths of my heart. I have only to consult myself . . ."[9] Wollstonecraft's fictive Mary, contemplating scenes of public devotion, observes that true religion "does not consist in ceremonies" but in doing good and loving God. She, like her author,

8. Basil Willey, *The Eighteenth Century Background* (London: Chatto and Windus, 1946), 7.
9. Rousseau, *Emile*, 286.

experiences her deepest religious emotions during moments of
solitary contemplation, when the absence of all loved ones makes
her particularly "sensible of the presence of her Almighty Friend"
(M 1:27).

Rational Dissent did not go so far as this in rejecting religious
observance, but its political case for toleration was founded on the
same reverence for personal conviction. "Every man ought to be left
to follow his conscience because then only he acts virtuously," Price
argued.[1] No earthly power has any rights over our private judgments,
and no restriction on conscience is ever legitimate. "Liberty," Price
wrote in his 1758 *Review of the Principal Questions and Difficulties
in Morals* (with which Wollstonecraft was clearly familiar) "is the
power of acting and determining: And it is self-evident, that where
such a power is wanting, there can be no moral capacities."[2] Liberty
and reason, Price went on, "constitute the capacity of virtue"; or as
Wollstonecraft put it: "the conduct of an accountable being must be
regulated by the operations of its own reason; or on what foundation
rests the throne of God? . . . Liberty is the mother of virtue" (VRW
40). Only those free to think and act for themselves will take their
place by God's throne. Rousseau's ideal woman may have expected
men to legislate for her in religious matters, or Milton's Eve may
have willingly deferred to male spiritual authority—"God is thy law,
thou mine: to know no more/Is women's happiest knowledge and her
praise" Eve warbles away to Adam in *Paradise Lost*—but against
these models of feminine self-abnegation Wollstonecraft invoked
the protestant imperative for direct dealing with one's Maker. If no
priest may stand between creature and Creator, why should a mere
man stand between a woman and her God?

> For if it be allowed that women were destined by Providence to
> acquire human virtues, and, by the exercise of their under-
> standings, that stability of character which is the firmest
> ground to rest our future hopes upon, they must be permitted
> to turn to the foundation of light, and not forced to shape their
> course by the twinkling of a mere satellite.   (VRW 23)

Only a soul "perfected by the exercise of its own reason" is
"stamped with the heavenly image," but "man ever placed between
[woman] and reason, she is always represented as only created to see
through a gross medium" and so is estranged from her own moral
potential. This alienation from grace is the nadir of female oppression, since it denies to women that inner mirroring of God's virtues
which leads to ethical fulfilment. Universal reason is God's gift to

1. Richard Price, *Review of The Principal Questions and Difficulties in Morals*, 1756
   (Oxford: Clarendon Press, 1974), 180.
2. Ibid., 181.

all, the manifestation of His presence within, but men's jealous claims to reason's prerogatives would damn women to spiritual ignorance, and thus flout God's purpose. For if the Father of All Creation smiles equally on all His offspring, who are men to raise themselves to a higher position in His sight? "Let us then, as children of the same parent . . . reason together, and learn to submit to the authority of Reason . . ." Wollstonecraft urges her readers. For "they alone are subject to blind authority who have no reliance on their own strength. They are free—who will be free!" (VRW 108).

Seen in this light, women's emancipation is not only a *desideratum* for this life, but the chief prerequisite for women's eternal salvation. This emphasis in the *Rights of Woman* on secular gains as a means to spiritual goals is possibly one of the most difficult to appreciate today, yet Wollstonecraft's text is suffused with it. The line of argument is clear. If the human soul were not immortal—if our brief existence invariably terminated at death—then female oppression, however censurable in itself, would be only one more of those infinite woes which make up our lot in this vale of tears. Social revolution throws into relief the injustice of women's subordinate status and offers opportunities for change; but it is the prospect of life beyond all such mortal contrivances which makes women's sufferings as a sex wholly reprehensible—for in enslaving women on earth men have also been denying them heaven. Rational Dissent held mortal existence to be a probationary state, a trial period, from which the souls of the virtuous alone would emerge into eternal bliss. Wollstonecraft consistently endorsed this view, and then pointed out its implications. For if women are disallowed the conditions necessary for the acquisition of virtue, then "how [they] are to exist in that state where there is neither to be marrying nor giving in marriage, we are not told":

> For though moralists have agreed that the tenor of life seems to prove that *man* is prepared . . . for a future state, they constantly concur in advising *woman* only to provide for the present. Gentleness, docility, and a spaniel-like affection are, on this ground, consistently recommended as the cardinal virtues of the sex; and disregarding the arbitrary economy of nature, one writer has declared that it is masculine for a woman to be melancholy. She was created to be the toy of man, his rattle, and it must jingle in his ears whenever, dismissing reason, he chooses to be amused.   (VRW 37).

But "if morality has an eternal foundation" then "whoever sacrifices virtue, strictly so called, to present convenience . . . lives only for the passing day" at the expense of futurity. To propitiate men, women neglect absolute morality in favor of the relative merits—chastity, humility, diffidence—assigned to their sex, and the result is their spiritual nullification. "I wish to sum up what I have said in a few words," Wollstonecraft wrote in conclusion to the third chapter of the *Rights of Woman*, in what could well serve as a *coda* to the entire text: "for I here throw down my gauntlet, and deny the existence of sexual virtues. . . . For man and woman, truth must be the same" (VRW 55).

Here indeed is the puritan voice, stiff with ethical rigor. Moral absolutism of this kind has always had strong appeal for feminists, wary of the laid-back pragmatism of elite sophisticates, and hostile to the traditionalist morality of Burkean conservatives. It is all very well, as Wollstonecraft told Burke, for those in power to pretend to moral instincts which are somehow, mysteriously, always in accord with the *status quo*; for the disenfranchised, however, the assertion of ethical imperatives that transcend and potentially subvert the moral commonsense of an age is a powerful weapon against established authority. "It is time to separate unchangeable morals from local manners" she insisted in the *Rights of Woman* (49), to bring all humanity under God's law. But as far as women are concerned,

> the fanciful female character, so prettily drawn by poets and novelists, demanding the sacrifice of truth and sincerity; virtue [to them] becomes a relative idea, having no other foundation than utility; and of that utility men pretend arbitrarily to judge, shaping it to their own convenience.   (VRW 55)

Where there is no absolute standard of right, power maintains its own codes of expedience. Men, like all despots, seek grounds for their rule in precept and custom, so that the ruled appear duty-bound to obey. Wollstonecraft's refutation of this authoritarianism further revealed her debt to Rational Dissent, and in particular to its anti-voluntarist view of the respective obligations of God and mankind. Anti-voluntarist theology, at its simplest, holds that the power of God is constrained by His goodness; or as Price put it, in his *Review of Morals*, God's "sovereign authority" derives "not merely from his almighty power" but from the "infinite excellencies of his nature as the foundation of reason and wisdom".[3] Worship, in other words, is not blind submission to an omnipotent force, for (in Wollstonecraft's words) "what good effect can the latter mode of worship have on the moral conduct of a rational being?" (VRW 50). Conservatives like Edmund Burke might hold that unthinking deference was authority's due, but for Wollstonecraft, as she told Burke in the *Rights of Men*, true worship was never servile but a rational reverence

3. Ibid., 113.

for those divine perfections that human virtues mimic. It is not to arbitrary might but to Virtue itself to which she submits:

> Submit—yes; I disregard the charge of arrogance, to the law that regulates his just resolves; and the happiness I pant after must be the same in kind, and produced by the same exertions as his—though unfeigned humility overwhelms every idea that would presume to compare the goodness which the most exalted being could acquire, with the grand source of life and bliss.   (VRM 5:34)

We love God because He deserves our love, not because He commands it; and the fruit of this worship is that "enlightened self-love" which is every believer's entitlement.

This emphasis on *esteem* as the key element in religious devotion had important consequences beyond the theological. For if it is not power but virtue that elicits respect in the divine sphere, why should this not be true of intimate human relationships as well? "It were to be wished," Wollstonecraft writes, "that women would cherish an affection for their husbands, founded on the same principle that devotion [to God] ought to rest upon"—which sounds shockingly retrograde until one realizes her precise meaning: that husbands, like deities, should be loved inasmuch—and only inasmuch—as they possess virtues entitling them to wifely respect. "No other firm base is there under heaven—for let [women] beware of the fallacious light of sentiment; too often used as a softer phrase for sensuality" (VRW 51). It is not power, romance, or—most emphatically—sexual desire which should tie women to their menfolk, but only shared love of the Good.

Wollstonecraft's astringent attitude to heterosexual love has attracted criticism from some modern feminists, repelled by what they regard as her chilly prudishness. Perusing the *Rights of Woman*, the grounds for this criticism would seem incontestable. "The depravity of the appetite which brings the sexes together," Wollstonecraft writes, is deplorable—inside marriage as well as out. "Nature must ever be the standard of taste—the gauge of appetite—yet how grossly is nature insulted by the voluptuary" (VRW 146) which is redeemable only, and barely, by the natural requirements of reproduction. "The feelings of a parent mingling with an instinct merely animal, give it dignity" by mixing "a little mind and affection with a sensual gust" (VRW 146); but once children have arrived the duties of parenthood are incompatible with further erotic indulgence.

> In order to fulfil the duties of life, and to be able to pursue with vigour the various employments which form the moral character, a master and mistress of a family ought not to continue to love each other with passion. I mean to say that they

ought not to indulge those emotions which disturb the order
of society, and engross the thoughts that should otherwise
be employed. . . . I will go still further, and advance, without
dreaming of a paradox, that an unhappy marriage is often
advantageous to a family, and that the neglected wife is, in general, the best mother. . . .   (VRW 34)

Even for an age of intensifying sexual restrictions, this was pretty
repressive stuff. And it is views like these, unsurprisingly, that have
led scholars like Mary Poovey and Cora Kaplan to brand Wollstonecraft a sexual puritan. The *Rights of Woman*, Kaplan has elo-
quently and influentially argued, "expresses a violent antagonism to
the sexual, it exaggerates the importance of the sensual in the everyday life of women and betrays the most profound anxiety about the
rupturing force of female sexuality."[4] Mary Poovey, in her major
study of Wollstonecraft's relationship to eighteenth-century sexual
ideology, develops a similar argument, pointing out that Wollstonecraft's sexual outlook was heavily inflected by the repressive
codes of propriety characteristic of the new middle class.[5] In one
sense this is clearly right. Both in spirit and content, much of Wollstonecraft's anti-erotic rhetoric can easily be recognized as part of
that bourgeois project—so characteristic of the eighteenth-century
middle class – to enhance middle-rank standing by contrasting its
sober-minded decency to the moral laxity of the idle rich. The image
of the eroticized woman to be found throughout Wollstonecraft's
writings is thus both polemical and class specific: a caricature of
aristocratic womanhood common to virtually all middle-class morality literature. "Love, in their bosoms, taking place of every nobler
passion," Wollstonecraft writes of "women of fashion," "their sole
ambition is to be fair, to raise emotion instead of inspiring respect;
and this ignoble desire, like the servility in absolute monarchies,
destroys all strength of character" (VRW 40).

There is far more to be said on this question of class bias in Wollstonecraft's sexual thinking than I have space for here. But the
emphasis given to it by Kaplan, Poovey, and likeminded commentators has been at the expense of a larger historical point. Evaluating
Wollstonecraft's erotic ideals in isolation from her wider philosophic
commitments, particularly her religious convictions, obscures their
psycho-ethical content and reduces their revisionary force. Like all
eighteenth-century moralists, Wollstonecraft's ideas about sexual
love were not freestanding but embedded in a universalist ethical

4. Cora Kaplan, "Wild Nights: Pleasure/Sexuality/Feminism," *Sea Changes: Culture and Feminism* (London: Verso, 1986), 41. [see p. 335 herein.—*Editor*]
5. Mary Poovey, *The Proper Lady and the Woman Writer: Ideology as Style in the Works of Mary Wollstonecraft, Mary Shelley, and Jane Austen* (University of Chicago Press, 1984). [see pp. 349–63 herein.—*Editor*]

creed, which in her case meant in her idiosyncratic brand of enlightened Christianity. Erotic attachments were not (or at least not only)
the stuff of private passion and politicking, as they are for modern
feminists, but modes of psycho-ethical relating—to oneself as well
as to others – with transcendent significance. For Wollstonecraft, in
other words, love was a sacred affair.

Reflecting on what has been said thus far about the pivotal part
played by religion in Wollstonecraft's feminism, it is not difficult to
see why this was so. Striving to free women not just from male
power but from the inner corruption induced by oppression, the
aspect of female love that concerned Wollstonecraft the most was its
impact on women's moral destiny and ethical self-image: matters
for which, in the 1790s, religion still provided the most compelling
paradigm. For Wollstonecraft, what was at stake in heterosexual love
was not just what a woman was permitted to *feel*, but who she was
able to *be*: what kind of feminine self is inscribed in the erotic bond,
and how does this love bear on the infinitely higher attachments of
which every soul is capable? The answer the *Rights of Woman gives*
is unequivocal: "[I]f [women] be moral beings, let them have a
chance to become intelligent; and let love to man be only a part of
that glowing flame of universal love, which, after encircling humanity, mounts in graceful incense to God" (VRW 72).

For Wollstonecraft, loving God is the basis of a rightly ordered
moral personality. Unlike the Rational Dissenters of her circle who,
anxious to avoid "enthusiasm," generally confined their devotional
sentiments to the judiciously appreciative, for Wollstonecraft to know
God is to adore Him—and this not only because His perfections
inspire adoration but because the epistemic impulse toward Him is
essentially erotic in character. The love Wollstonecraft had for her
Maker, according to Mary Hays, was a "delicious sentiment," a "sublime enthusiasm" fueled by a "fervent imagination, shaping itself to
ideal excellence, and panting after good unalloyed."[6] It was this passionate idealizing attachment that, for Wollstonecraft, was the emotional basis of ethical self-identity. "The mind of man is formed to
admire perfection," she wrote to her sister Everina in 1784, "and perhaps our longing after it and the pleasure we take in observing
a shadow of it is a *faint line* of that Image that was first stamped on the
soul."[7] This amatory yearning after the Good is love's fullest expression, since "He who formed the human soul, only can fill it, and the
chief happiness of an immortal being must arise from the same source
as its existence".[8] Yet this pious ardor, while infinitely superior to

6. Hays, "Wollstonecraft," 416.
7. Letter to Everina Wollstonecraft, January 1784, Letters, 87.
8. Wollstonecraft, "The Cave of Fancy," in *Works*, 1:206.

human love, should not—as in so many brands of Christian theology—be treated as the antithesis of earthly love, but rather as its product and proper fulfillment. Love of others, including physical love, is the emotional ground from which transcendent love arises.

> Earthly love leads to heavenly, and prepares us for a more exalted state; if it does not change its nature, and destroy itself, by trampling on the virtue, that constitutes its essence, and allies us to the Deity.[9]

This theme—human love as the progenitor of divine love—first appeared in Wollstonecraft's writings in the late 1780s, and persisted, with some modifications, until her death.[1] An unpublished allegory drafted in 1787, *The Cave of Fancy*, rehearsed the argument which was then more fully dramatized a year later in *Mary, A Fiction*. Caught up in an adulterous passion for a dying romantic genius, the fictive Mary defends her feelings by insisting (quoting Milton) that "earthly love is the scale by which to heavenly we may ascend"; on the death of her lover she turns her heart wholly toward her Maker with the consoling reflection that true happiness is to be had only in His presence (M 1:46, chapters 25–31). Eros may begin its upward flight with the human affections, but its ultimate route must be heavenward.

Scattered references throughout her writings signal Wollstonecraft's awareness of the platonic roots of this ideal. If women are merely to be loved for their "animal perfection," she rebuked Burke in 1790, then "Plato and Milton were grossly mistaken in asserting that human love led to heavenly"; but if one accepts the platonic view that love of the divine is "only an exaltation of [earthly] affection" then women too must be loved for their rational virtues rather than their physical attributes (VRM 5:46). The feminist twist was new, but the general argument had its source in what James Turner has described as the "Christianisation of the Platonic Eros" to be found in Augustine and many varieties of post-Augustinian theology, leading up to Milton.[2] "Thy affections are the steps; thy will the way;" Augustine had written, "by loving thou mountest, by neglect thou descendest."[3] Desires that ascend toward God are to be radically distinguished from those that descend toward earthly things, yet both are designated as eros—the love which links humanity to

9. Ibid.
1. For a fuller account of the evolution of this idea over the course of Wollstonecraft's intellectual career, see my *Wollstonecraft and the Feminist Imagination*.
2. James G. Turner, *One Flesh: Paradisial Marriage and Sexual Relations in the Age of Milton* (Oxford: Clarendon Press, 1987), 32.
3. Quoted in Turner, *One Flesh*, 32. For an influential discussion of the relationship between divine and earthly love in Christian theology, see Anders Nygren, *Agape and Eros* (London, SPCK, 1982), and for the significance of Christian Platonism in the formation of eighteenth-century British moral philosophy see John K. Sheriff, *The Good-Natured Man: the Evolution of a Moral Ideal, 1660–1880* (Tuscaloosa: University of Alabama Press, 1982).

the divine. Those moralists who would disdain earthly affections, Christian platonists therefore argued, are in fact apostates, denying their connection to God. "They . . . who complain of the delusions of passion," Wollstonecraft wrote, "do not recollect that they are exclaiming against a strong proof of the immortality of the soul" (VRW 80).

The most immediate sources for this platonic element in Wollstonecraft's thought were obviously Milton, whom she quoted endlessly and whose ambiguous views on women she worried at throughout the *Rights of Woman*, but also, and even more equivocally, Rousseau, for whom Plato's had been the "true philosophy of lovers"[4] and whose platonic-romantic heroine, the saintly Julie of his 1761 novel *La Nouvelle Héloïse*, set a fashion for ideal love across late 18th century Europe. Wollstonecraft's quarrel with Rousseau's depiction of women in *Emile*—an argument framing much of the *Rights of Woman*—is sometimes assumed to imply her wholesale repudiation of his ideas. In fact the sharpness of her critique is not the anger of an entrenched opponent but that of a disappointed disciple, lambasting her favourite mentor for substituting prejudice for truth. Rousseau's views on women, as Wollstonecraft pointed out, were in fact notoriously contradictory. While the female protagonist of *Emile*, Sophie, is a patriarch's dream of feminine decorum and submission, Julie of *La Nouvelle Héloïse* is very much the Wollstonecraftian woman: strong-willed, morally authoritative, and engaged in a "perfect union of souls" with her lover, St. Preux, that ultimately draws them both closer to God.[5] Julie's shadow falls long over Wollstonecraft's divinized love philosophy. "An imagination of this vigorous cast," Wollstonecraft writes of Rousseau's novel, " . . . can depict love with celestial charms, and dote on the grand ideal object—it can imagine a degree of mutual affection that shall refine the soul, and not expire when it has served as a 'scale to heavenly', and, like devotion, make it absorb every meaner affection and desire . . . " (VRW 79–80).

In the *Rights of Woman*, Wollstonecraft holds up Julie as an example of a "modest" woman, meaning one who, while in this case not technically chaste (Julie and St. Preux make love twice) is pure in heart and mind (VRW 134). Modesty in women—a topic to which Wollstonecraft devotes an entire chapter—is not, contrary to conventional opinion, a narrowly feminine virtue but rather the moral condition proper to all of God's human creation (VRW 134). The modest woman, like the modest man, is dignified, reserved, self-

---

4. Jean-Jacques Rousseau, *La Nouvelle Héloïse*, 1761; translated as *Eloisa, or a Series of Original Letters* (London, 1767), 2:14.
5. Ibid., 34.

respecting, and sexually continent—the last, however, not for reasons of "worldly prudence" or public reputation but because she knows her body is a "Temple of the living God" (VRW 137). In addition to this, the modest woman is also—as Wollstonecraft carefully demonstrates over the course of the *Rights of Woman*—a natural feminist: resolute of mind, fiercely independent (even in relation to male relatives), and possessed of "the dignity of a rational will that only bows to God" (VRW 39). As an ideal of emancipated womanhood, this may seem a long way from recent feminist ambitions. But if we bypass it in favor of a more familiar, secularized version of Wollstonecraft's project, we lose both the historic woman and her principal mission: to liberate women from masculine tyranny not in order that they should become free-floating agents, stripped of all obligatory ties, but in order to bind them more closely to their God.

Mary Wollstonecraft:
A Chronology

1759 April 27. Born in the Spitalfields district of London, second child and first daughter of Edward John Wollstonecraft and Elizabeth Dickson.

1763–68 The Wollstonecraft family moves to Epping, Barking, Essex, and Beverly, Yorkshire where the father tries, in each place unsuccessfully, to establish himself as a gentleman farmer.

1774 Family returns to Hoxton, a suburb of London, Mr. Wollstonecraft having failed at farming.

1775 Wollstonecraft meets Fanny Blood, the woman who, Godwin said, became "the ruling passion of her mind."

1776 Family moves to Langharne, Wales.

1777 Family returns to the London suburb of Walworth, where Mary and Fanny live near each other.

1778 Mary Wollstonecraft takes employment as a companion to Mrs. Dawson of Bath; during her tenure also visits in Southampton and Windsor.

1780 Wollstonecraft returns home to nurse her dying mother.

1782 Mrs. Wollstonecraft dies; Mary's sister, Eliza, marries Meredith Bishop; Mr. Wollstonecraft remarries a woman known only as "Lydia" and returns to Wales; and Mary goes to live with Fanny and her family, where her needlework helps to maintain the struggling Blood family.

1783 Birth of Eliza and Meredith Bishop's daughter.

1784 Wollstonecraft, having been summoned by Mr. Bishop, goes to attend her sister Eliza who has suffered a postpartum breakdown. Mary secretly removes Eliza to Hackney, then Islington, convinced that her sister's breakdown resulted from cruel usage by her husband. A legal separation is obtained for the Bishops, but the mother does not have custody of her child, who dies before age one year.

Mary and Eliza Wollstonecraft and Fanny Blood open a school in Islington, moving it later to Newington Green where they are joined by Everina, the third Wollstonecraft sister. Newington Green offers Wollstonecraft the friendship of Reverend Richard Price, famous liberal of the period.

1785   Fanny Blood goes to Lisbon to marry Hugh Skeys. Soon pregnant, she sends for Wollstonecraft to be with her at the birth of her child, and, at Mary's arrival, Fanny is already in premature labor. She dies in her friend's arms on November 29, the baby dying soon after.

1786   After her return from Portugal Wollstonecraft finds the school in financial trouble and closes it.

Writes *Thoughts on the Education of Daughters*, her first book.

Takes job as governess to elder daughters of Viscount Kingsborough of Mitchelstown, County Cork, Ireland, residing briefly, before her removal to Ireland, at Eton, where she observes at firsthand one of the oldest and most famous public (what would be called in America "private") preparatory schools.

1787   Goes with Kingsboroughs to Dublin, thence to Bristol, where she is dismissed from their employ by Lady Kingsborough.

Returns to London, determined to make her living by her pen, to be (as she announces to her sister Everina) "the first of a new genus."

1788   Joseph Johnson, her publisher and friend, releases her first novel *Mary, a Fiction* and her children's book, *Original Stories from Real Life*, as well as her translation from the French of Jacques Necker's *Of the Importance of Religious Opinions*.

Begins writing for the *Analytical Review*, a monthly just established by Joseph Johnson and Thomas Christie.

1789   Johnson publishes her anthology *The Female Reader*, under the pen name "Mr. Creswick." She becomes romantically involved with the artist Henry Fuseli.

1790   Johnson publishes her translation from the German of Christian Salzmann's *Elements of Morality, for the Use of Children*; publishes (anonymously) *A Vindication of the Rights of Men*, the first published response to Edmund Burke's *Reflections on the Revolution in France*.

1791   Second edition of *A Vindication of the Rights of Men* appears, this time with the author's name.

Wollstonecraft moves to new quarters in Store Street.
Begins work on *A Vindication of the Rights of Woman*.

1792   Publication of *A Vindication of the Rights of Woman* in
            January; a second, revised and corrected edition appears
            later the same year.
            Involvement with Fuseli ends; leaves for Paris alone in
            December.

1793   Meets Gilbert Imlay, American explorer, author, and
            entrepreneur.
            Moves from Paris to the outlying suburb of Neuilly for
            safety in the revolution-torn country.
            In September, moves back to Paris, is registered as Gil-
            bert Imlay's wife at the American embassy for the
            protection which American citizenship would afford her.

1794   Joins Imlay in Le Havre in February.
            May 14. Fanny Imlay born.
            Imlay returns to Paris, soon followed by Wollstonecraft
            and Fanny; then he returns to London and the mother
            and her baby stay on in Paris alone.
            Publication of her *Historical and Moral View of the Ori-
            gin and Progress of the French Revolution*.

1795   Wollstonecraft and Fanny follow Imlay to London. Tries
            to commit suicide but the attempt is discovered by Imlay.
            In June, leaves as Imlay's business envoy on a trip to
            the Scandinavian countries, accompanied by Fanny and
            Marguerite, the child's nurse.
            In October, discovering that Imlay is living with an
            actress, attempts suicide a second time by jumping off
            Putney Bridge.

1796   Publication of *Letters Written during a Short Residence
            in Sweden, Norway, and Denmark*.
            Meets William Godwin for the second time; Wollstone-
            craft and Godwin become lovers.

1797   March 29. Mary Wollstonecraft and William Godwin
            married at Old St. Pancras Church; the couple entertain
            guests jointly at No. 29, the Polygon, but work in sepa-
            rate quarters during the day.
            August 30. Mary Wollstonecraft Godwin born.
            September 10. Mary Wollstonecraft dies of septicaemia
            and is buried five days later in churchyard of Old
            St. Pancras Church.

1798   Publication by William Godwin of *Posthumous Works of
            the Author of A Vindication of the Rights of Woman*, along
            with his *Memoirs of the Author of* A Vindication of the
            Rights of Woman.

1851   Percy Florence Shelley moves the remains of Wollstone-
              craft and Godwin to Bournemouth to rest beside their
              daughter (and his mother) Mary Wollstonecraft Godwin
              Shelley.

Selected Bibliography

• indicates works included or excerpted in this Norton Critical Edition.

Selected Editions of Wollstonecraft's Works

The Works of Mary Wollstonecraft. 7 vols. Ed. Janet Todd and Marilyn Butler. London: Pickering and Chatto; New York: New York University Press, 1989.

The Female Reader; or Miscellaneous Pieces, in Prose and Verse; Selected from the Best Writers, and Disposed under Proper Heads; for the Improvement of Young Women. London, 1789. Rept. with introduction by Moira Ferguson. Delmar, NY: Scholars' Facsimiles and Reprints, 1980.

• *An Historical and Moral View of the Origin and Progress of the French Revolution and the Effect It Has Produced in Europe.* London, 1794. Rept. with introduction by Janet Todd. Delmar, NY: Scholars' Facsimiles and Reprints, 1975.

Mary: A Fiction. Ed. Gary Kelly. London: Oxford University Press, 1976.

Original Stories from Real Life, with Conversations, Calculated to Regulate the Affections, and Form the Mind to Truth and Goodness. London, 1788. Rept. Washington, DC: Woodstock Books, 2001.

A Short Residence in Sweden, Norway and Denmark. Ed. Richard Holmes. London: Penguin, 1987.

Thoughts on the Education of Daughters, with Reflections on Female Conduct, in the More Important Duties of Life. London, 1787. Rept. with introduction by Gina Luria. New York: Garland, 1974.

The Vindications. Ed. D. L. Macdonald and Kathleen Scherf. Peterborough, Ontario, Canada: Broadview Press, 1997.

Posthumous Works of the Author of A Vindication of the Rights of Woman. Ed. William Godwin. London, 1798. Rept. with introduction by Gina Luria. New York: Garland, 1974.

The Wrongs of Woman, or, Maria. Ed. Gary Kelly. London: Oxford University Press, 1976.

The Collected Letters of Mary Wollstonecraft. Ed. Ralph M. Wardle. Ithaca, NY: Cornell University Press, 1979.

The Collected Letters of Mary Wollstonecraft. Ed. Janet Todd. New York: Columbia University Press, 2003.

Biographies

Flexner, Eleanor. *Mary Wollstonecraft.* New York: Coward, McCann and Geoghegan, 1972.

Franklin, Caroline. *Mary Wollstonecraft: A Literary Life.* Basingstoke, Hampshire, UK: Palgrave, 2004.

George, Margaret. *One Woman's "Situation": A Study of Mary Wollstonecraft.* Urbana: University of Illinois Press, 1970.

• Godwin, William. *Memoirs of the Author of* A Vindication of the Rights of Woman. Ed. Pamela Clemit and Gina Luria Walker. Peterborough, Ont., Canada: Broadview Press, 2001.

• Hays, Mary. "Memoirs of Mary Wollstonecraft." In *Annual Necrology, 1797–8.* London: 1800, 411–60.

St. Clair, William. *The Godwins and the Shelleys: A Biography of a Family.* New York: Norton, 1989.

Sunstein, Emily. *A Different Face: The Life of Mary Wollstonecraft.* Boston and Toronto: Little, Brown, 1975.

Todd, Janet. *Mary Wollstonecraft: A Revolutionary Life.* London: Weidenfeld and Nicholson, 2000.

Tomalin, Claire. *The Life and Death of Mary Wollstonecraft*. London: Weidenfeld and Nicholson, 1974. Rev. ed., Harmondsworth, UK: Penguin, 1992.

Wardle, Ralph M., *Mary Wollstonecraft: A Critical Biography*. Lawrence: University of Kansas Press, 1951.

Criticism

ANTHOLOGIES

Falco, Maria J., ed. *Feminist Interpretations of Mary Wollstonecraft*. University Park: Pennsylvania State University Press, 1996.

• Johnson, Claudia L., ed. *The Cambridge Companion to Mary Wollstonecraft*. Cambridge: Cambridge University Press, 2002.

Jump, Harriet Devine, ed. *Mary Wollstonecraft and the Critics, 1788–2001*. 2 vols. London and New York: Routledge, 2003.

Todd, Janet, and Marie Mulvey-Roberts, eds. *Mary Wollstonecraft: A Bicentennial*. Special issue of *Women's Writing* 4, no. 2 (1997).

Yeo, Eileen James, ed. *Mary Wollstonecraft and 200 Years of Feminism*. London and New York: River Orams Press, 1997.

ARTICLES AND BOOKS ABOUT WOLLSTONECRAFT AND HER AGE

Badowska, Ewa. "The Anorexic Body of Liberal Feminism: Mary Wollstonecraft's *A Vindication of the Rights of Woman*." *Tulsa Studies in Women's Literature* 17 (1998): 283–303.

Barker-Benfield, G. J. "Mary Wollstonecraft: Eighteenth-Century Commonwealth Woman." *Journal of the History of Ideas* 50 (1989): 95–115.

Bewell, Alan. "'Jacobin Plants': Botany as Social Theory in the 1790s." *The Wordsworth Circle* 20 (1989): 132–39.

Binhammer, Katherine. "Thinking Gender with Sexuality in 1790s' Feminist Thought." *Feminist Studies* 28 (2002): 667–90.

Cole, Lucinda. "(Anti)Feminist Sympathies: The Politics of Relationship in Smith, Wollstonecraft, and More." *English Literary History* 58 (1991): 107–40.

Conger, Syndy McMillen. *Mary Wollstonecraft and the Language of Sensibility*. Rutherford, N.J.: Fairleigh Dickinson University Press; London: Associated University Presses, 1994.

Davidson, Jenny. "Revolutions in Female Manners." In *Hypocrisy and the Politics of Politeness: Manners and Morals from Locke to Austen*. Cambridge: Cambridge University Press, 2004, 76–107.

Eberle, Roxanne. *Chastity and Transgression in Women's Writing, 1792–1897: Interrupting the Harlot's Progress*. Basingstoke, Hampshire, UK: Palgrave, 2002.

Ferguson, Frances. "Wollstonecraft Our Contemporary." *Gender and Theory: Dialogues in Feminist Criticism*. Ed. Linda Kauffman. Oxford: Blackwell, 1989, 51–62.

Ferguson, Moira. "Mary Wollstonecraft and the Problematic of Slavery." *Feminist Review* 42 (1992): 82–102.

Furniss, Tom. "Nasty Tricks and Tropes: Sexuality and Language in Mary Wollstonecraft's *Rights of Woman*." *Studies in Romanticism* 32 (1993): 177–209.

Goldman, Emma. "Mary Wollstonecraft: Her Tragic Life and Her Passionate Struggle for Freedom." *Feminist Studies* 17 (1981): 114–21.

Gubar, Susan. "Feminist Misogyny: Mary Wollstonecraft and the Paradox of 'It takes one to Know One.'" *Feminist Studies* 20 (1994): 453–73.

Guest, Harriet. "The Dream of a Common Language: Hannah More and Mary Wollstonecraft." *Textual Practice* 9 (1995): 303–23.

• Guralnick, Elissa. "Radical Politics in Mary Wollstonecraft's *A Vindication of the Rights of Woman*." *Studies in Burke and His Time* 18 (1977): 155–66.

Janes, R. M. "On the Reception of Mary Wollstonecraft's *A Vindication of the Rights of Woman*." *Journal of the History of Ideas* 39 (1978): 293–302.

• Johnson, Claudia L. *Equivocal Beings: Politics, Gender, and Sentimentality in the 1790s, Wollstonecraft, Radcliffe, Burney, Austen*. Chicago: University of Chicago Press, 1995.

Jones, Vivien. "Advice and Enlightenment: Mary Wollstonecraft and Sex Education." In *Women, Gender and Enlightenment*. Ed. Sarah Knott and Barbara Taylor. Basingstoke, Hampshire, UK: Palgrave Macmillan, 2005, 140–55.

Jump, Harriet Devine. "No Equal Mind: Mary Wollstonecraft and the Young Romantics." *Charles Lamb Bulletin* n.s. 79 (1992): 225–38.

• Kaplan, Cora. *Sea Changes: Culture and Feminism*. London: Verso, 1986.

Kay, Carol. "Canon, Ideology, and Gender: Mary Wollstonecraft's Critique of Adam Smith." *New Political Science* 15 (1986): 63–76.

Kelly, Gary. *Revolutionary Feminism: The Mind and the Career of Mary Wollstonecraft.* London: Macmillan; New York: St. Martin's, 1992.

Korsmeyer, Carolyn W. "Reason and Morals in the Early Feminist Movement: Mary Wollstonecraft." In *Women and Philosophy: Toward a Theory of Liberation.* Ed. Carol C. Gould and Marx W. Wartofsky. New York: Putnam, 1976, 97–111.

Landes, Joan B. *Women and the Public Sphere in the Age of the French Revolution.* Ithaca, N.Y.: Cornell University Press, 1988.

Moore, Jane. "Promises, Promises: the Fictional Philosophy in Mary Wollstonecraft's *Vindication of the Rights of Woman.*" In *The Feminist Reader: Essays in Gender and the Politics of Literary Criticism.* Ed. Catherine Belsey and Jane Moore. New York: Basil Blackwell, 1989, 155–74.

• Myers, Mitzi. "Reform or Ruin: 'A Revolution in Female Manners'." *Studies in Eighteenth-Century Culture* 11 (1982): 199–216.

Paulson, Ronald. *Representations of Revolution (1789–1820).* New Haven, Conn., and London: Yale University Press, 1983.

• Poovey, Mary. *The Proper Lady and the Woman Writer: Ideology as Style in the Works of Mary Wollstonecraft, Mary Shelley, and Jane Austen.* Chicago: University of Chicago Press, 1984.

Reiss, Timothy. "Revolution in Bounds: Wollstonecraft, Women, and Reason." *Gender and Theory: Dialogues in Feminist Criticism.* Ed. Linda Kauffman. Oxford: Blackwell, 1989, 11–50.

Sapiro, Virginia. *A Vindication of Political Virtue: The Political Theory of Mary Wollstonecraft.* Chicago: University of Chicago Press, 1992.

Shanley, Mary Lyndon. "Mary Wollstonecraft on Sensibility, Women's Rights, and Patriarchal Power." In *Women Writers and the Early Modern British Political Tradition.* Ed. Hilda L. Smith. Cambridge: Cambridge University Press, 1998, 148–67.

Sutherland, Kathryn. "Writings on Education and Conduct: Arguments for Female Improvement." In *Women and Literature in Britain, 1700–1800.* Ed. Vivien Jones. Cambridge: Cambridge University Press, 2000, 25–45.

Tauchert, Ashley. *Mary Wollstonecraft and the Accent of the Feminine.* Basingstoke, Hampshire, UK: Palgrave Macmillan, 2002.

Taylor, Barbara. *Mary Wollstonecraft and the Feminist Imagination.* Cambridge: Cambridge University Press, 2002.

Wang, Orrin N. C. "The Other Reasons: Female Alterity and Enlightenment Discourse in Mary Wollstonecraft's *A Vindication of the Rights of Woman.*" *Yale Journal of Criticism* 5 (1991): 129–49.

Wingrove, Elizabeth. "Getting Intimate with Wollstonecraft in the Republic of Letters." *Political Theory* 33 (2005): 344–69.

Woolf, Virginia. "Mary Wollstonecraft." *The Nation and Athenaeum* 46 (5 October 1929): 13–15. Rept. as "Four Figures." *The Common Reader.* 2d ser. London: Hogarth Press, 1932, 140–72.